Knowledge

Knowledge

Readings in Contemporary Epistemology

Edited by

Sven Bernecker
and
Fred Dretske

OXFORD
UNIVERSITY PRESS

OXFORD
UNIVERSITY PRESS

Great Clarendon Street, Oxford OX2 6DP

Oxford University Press is a department of the University of Oxford.
It furthers the University's objective of excellence in research, scholarship,
and education by publishing worldwide in

Oxford New York

Auckland Bangkok Buenos Aires Cape Town Chennai
Dar es Salaam Delhi Hong Kong Istanbul Karachi Kolkata
Kuala Lumpur Madrid Melbourne Mexico City Mumbai Nairobi
São Paulo Shanghai Taipei Tokyo Toronto

Oxford is a registered trade mark of Oxford University Press
in the UK and in certain other countries

Published in the United States
by Oxford University Press Inc., New York

Introduction and selection © Oxford University Press, 2000

First published 2000
Reprinted 2002, 2004

British Library Cataloguing in Publication Data

Data available

Library of Congress Cataloging in Publication Data

Data available

ISBN 0–19–875261–X

10 9 8 7 6 5 4

Typeset in Adobe Minion
by RefineCatch Limited, Bungay, Suffolk
Printed in Great Britain by
Ashford Colour Press
Gosport, Hants

Preface

We assembled this reader with two goals in mind. First of all, we wanted to provide a pedagogical tool for those teaching contemporary epistemology to both lower and upper level undergraduates. We have each taught courses in epistemology, and we have each been frustrated by the lack of an introductory reader that contains seminal papers on a wide variety of epistemological topics. There are several good collections of recent writings in the theory of knowledge, but most of them focus on just a few issues of the field. Our goal was to provide a full review to date of contemporary epistemology, including frequently neglected topics such as dominant responses to skepticism, introspection, memory, and testimony. In choosing selections we have also sought expression of opposing views hoping that this will help kindle the dialogue so essential to real learning.

Our second goal was to provide a helpful resource manual for those working in epistemology. In making relatively inaccessible essays available, this volume will be useful for anyone working in the field of epistemology.

It is customary to remark that, due to space limitations, many fine papers had to be left out. Often this disclaimer is made merely to be polite, but not in this case. The literature in epistemology has mushroomed in the past four decades, and there is simply no way to include all of the worthy material. One can also envision additional sections that might be added to a volume of this nature. Candidate topics include: feminist, social, evolutionary, and virtue epistemology, transcendental arguments and verificationism, inferential knowledge, the realism/anti-realism debate, epistemic logic, skepticism regarding other minds, rule following skepticism, belief revision, and the ethics of belief.

We have written a brief synoptic introduction to each of the parts. Moreover, we have tried, by appending suggestions for further reading at the end of each introduction, to suggest ways the interested reader may delve more deeply into the issues and pursue issues not directly discussed here as well.

We thank Peter Godfrey-Smith and Peter Graham for helpful suggestions for improvements. Finally we wish to thank Peter Momtchiloff of Oxford University Press for his enthusiasm and professional advice.

Munich
Durham
1999

Sven Bernecker
Fred Dretske

Contents

Part I

Justified True Belief

Introduction

WHEN Edmund Gettier published his brief paper 'Is Justified True Belief Knowledge' (Chapter 2) in 1963, it was thought by many epistemologists that he had destroyed a long-standing tradition regarding the correct analysis of knowledge. The traditional view which can, for example, be traced back to Plato's *Theaetetus* (*c*.400 BC) and Kant's *Critique of Pure Reason* (1781) claims that what distinguishes knowledge from mere true belief and lucky guessing is that it is based on some form of justification, evidence, or supporting reasons. Thus, knowledge is said to be justified true belief. Gettier showed that there are cases of justified true belief that are not cases of knowledge, and hence that the traditional analysis of knowledge is wrong. Whatever the reality of the tradition, no epistemologist since Gettier has seriously and successfully defended the traditional view. Gettier changed the course of contemporary epistemology.

The traditional analysis of knowledge applies primarily to propositional knowledge (also referred to as 'knowing that' or 'factual knowledge'). Propositional knowledge takes the form 'S knows that P' where P stands for a declarative sentence expressing some proposition. Apart from propositional knowledge philosophers recognize two main kinds of knowledge, namely practical knowledge (or 'knowing how') and knowledge of people, places and things (or 'knowledge by acquaintance'). Within propositional knowledge one can distinguish between inferential (or demonstrative) and non-inferential (or direct, basic, immediate) knowledge. Inferential knowledge is the product of suitable deductive or inductive inferences from other propositions that serve as evidence or justification. Gettier and the literature that Gettier's paper spawned focuses on inferential propositional knowledge. It is this notion of knowledge that is fundamental to human cognition and required both for theoretical speculation and practical judgement.

According to the traditional analysis, propositional knowledge has three individually necessary and jointly sufficient conditions: justification, truth, and belief. The truth condition requires that any known proposition be true. A person cannot know that Clyde is rich unless, in fact, Clyde is rich. The belief condition claims that knowing that Clyde is rich implies believing he is rich. A person need not be absolutely certain that something is true in order to know that it is. The belief condition only requires some kind of acceptance in the interest of obtaining truth. A. J. Ayer (Chapter 1), in articulating the traditional analysis, describes it as 'being sure'. Finally, the justification condition requires that a known proposition be evidentially supported. The justification condition is there in order to prevent lucky guesses from counting as knowledge if the guesser is sufficiently confident to believe his own guess. Epistemic justification for a belief is justification for the belief's truth, not its usefulness or its social respectability. According to the tradition, a belief can be justified in a way sufficient for knowledge even if the justification is not conclusive—even if it is the sort of justification one can have for a false proposition (though, of course, one could not know a false proposition to be true by having such a justification for it). Thus the necessity for an independent truth condition. In constructing his counterexamples, Gettier indicates that he is assuming that the justification needed for knowledge is a justification of this 'weak' sort, the kind one can have for a false proposition.

To show that the traditional analysis of knowledge is inadequate, Gettier develops two cases in which a person has justified true belief but lacks knowledge. They have a common pattern: A person, S, justifiably believes P (which happens to be false) and bases his belief in Q (which happens to be true) on P. Since P logically implies Q, and S knows it does, S has excellent reasons (viz., P) for believing Q. But, Gettier claims, S does not know that Q. His examples bear out this judgement. In each case, despite the fact that S has a justified true belief in Q, S does not know Q. Knowledge cannot be identified with justified true belief.

The response to Gettier's paper was overwhelming. Some suggested that Gettier's counterexamples were defective or overlooked some obvious point about justification (Feldman, Chapter 3, discusses one such possibility); others accepted the counterexamples and amended the traditional analysis by proposing additional conditions on knowledge designed to block Gettier-type cases (e.g., Goldman, Chapter 4, Lehrer and Paxson, Chapter 5); still others, instead of adding conditions, suggested changes in how existing conditions (e.g., justification) were to be understood (Dretske, Chapter 6; Lehrer and Paxson, Chapter 5, can also be understood as a version of this strategy).

Goldman proposes a causal supplement to the tripartite definition of empirical knowledge. To know that P, the belief that P must be caused by the fact that P. (Goldman actually proposes something a little more complex, but this is good enough for now.) To know that P, it is not enough to be justified in truly believing it; you must, in addition, be causally related to the facts that make your belief true. Many philosophers are attracted to a causal analysis of this sort because it deals effectively with Gettier's examples (not to mention according with intuitive judgements about perception and memory). At least Goldman's theory deals effectively with the examples Gettier actually used (whether it deals with others is questionable). To see how this fourth clause helps with Gettier cases, note that in each of Gettier's examples an appropriate causal relation is absent. In his second example, for instance, what causes Smith to believe that Jones owns a Ford or Brown is in Barcelona are not the facts that make his belief true (viz., that Brown is in Barcelona) but something else—the facts that cause him to believe—falsely—that Jones owns a Ford. So Goldman's condition is not satisfied. The facts that make his belief true (viz., that Brown is in Barcelona) are not the facts that cause him to believe. That is why, despite having a justified true belief, the believer lacks knowledge.

Causal theories of knowledge have difficulties accounting for mathematical knowledge, a priori knowledge, and empirical knowledge of existential or universal generalizations. Can the 'fact' that triangles—*all* of them—have three sides really cause one to believe they have three sides? Causal theories also have difficulties with ordinary matter-of-fact knowledge, the sort of knowledge for which the theory is specifically designed. Some of these problems are discussed in the selections from Lehrer and Paxson (Chapter 5) and Dretske (Chapter 6).

A causal theory of knowledge responds to the Gettier challenge by proposing an added condition on knowledge. Lehrer and Paxson also adopt this strategy by insisting that the kind of justification required (in the third condition) for knowledge be *undefeated* (fourth condition) justification. Dretske, on the other hand, keeps the original three conditions and merely reinterprets the justification required for knowledge in a special way—as *conclusive* justification. Lehrer and Paxson can also be read as doing the same thing—not as adding a fourth condition, but merely reinterpreting what kind of justification (i.e., undefeated) is required by the third condition.

The basic idea behind the defeasibility account of knowledge proposed by Lehrer and Paxson is that sometimes justified true belief is not knowledge because the justification is incomplete in certain crucial respects. Not all of the important evidence has been taken into consideration. There are some facts which, if the person were to know them, would seriously weaken her justification for believing. Consider Gettier's first example. Smith thinks that the man who will get the job has ten coins in his pocket (this is true) because he justifiably thinks that Jones will get the job (false) and justifiably thinks that Jones has ten coins in his pocket (true). If he learned that Jones was not going to get the job, though, this would defeat his justification for thinking that the man who will get the job has ten coins in his pocket. So Smith, though he has a justification for truly thinking what he does, does not have an *undefeated* justification. There are truths which, if Smith learned them, would undermine his justification for thinking that the man who will get the job has ten coins in his pocket. Requiring undefeated justification for knowledge avoids Gettier's examples.

Lehrer and Paxson show that this crude version of the defeasibility analysis is too strong since there will always be some unpossessed evidence that is negatively relevant to the justification in question. According to them the difference between defeating and non-defeating evidence has to do with whether the person is justified in believing the evidence to be false. Knowledge is justified true belief which is undefeated by a proposition which the believer has a justification for believing false.

This definition seems to imply that no false belief can ever be indefeasibly justified since there are always some truths whose addition would destroy the justification. If this is so, then undefeated justification turns out to be a form of conclusive justification—something one cannot have for false beliefs. If this is so, then defeasibility theories of knowledge would be rejecting a key assumption of traditional analyses, the assumption (that Gettier uses in constructing his counterexamples) that the kind of justification required for knowledge is a kind that can be had for false beliefs.

Dretske exploits this possibility in 'Conclusive Reasons' (Chapter 6). He proposes to understand the kind of justification required of knowledge as conclusive justification—evidence or reasons one cannot have for something false. This effect is achieved by defining a conclusive reason for P as some condition or fact, R, that would not be the case unless P were true. To know that P one must have evidence one would not have unless what one believes was true (one need not know that one's evidence is conclusive). Since Gettier's examples can only be constructed by using inconclusive justifications (for the false propositions that are used as reasons for accepting a true proposition), this has the effect of avoiding Gettier-like counterexamples. Since, according to this definition of knowledge, Smith does not know that Jones is the man who will get the job (Gettier's first example) nor that Jones owns a Ford (second example) these propositions cannot be used, as Gettier uses them, to support knowledge of the propositions they imply.

Further reading

Almeder, R., 'The Invalidity of Gettier-Type Counterexamples', *Philosophia. Philosophical Quarterly of Israel* 13 (1983), pp. 67–74.

Boardman, W., 'Conclusive Reasons and Scepticism', *The Australasian Journal of Philosophy* 56 (1978), pp 32–40.

Chisholm, R. M., *The Foundations of Knowing*, Brighton, Harvester Press, 1982, Ch. 3.

Dretske, F., Enc, B., 'Causal Theories of Knowledge', *Midwest Studies in Philosophy 9. Causation and Causal Theories* (1984), pp 517–28.

Harman, G., *Thought*, Princeton, Princeton University Press, 1973, Ch. 7–9.

Kaplan, M., 'It's Not What You Know That Counts', *The Journal of Philosophy* 82 (1985), pp. 350–63.

Klein, P. D., 'A Proposed Definition of Propositional Knowledge', *The Journal of Philosophy* 68 (1971), pp. 471–82.

Klein, P. D., 'Knowledge, Causality, and Defeasibility', *The Journal of Philosophy* 73 (1976), pp. 792–812.

Lehrer, K., *Knowledge*, Oxford, Clarendon Press, 1974, Ch. 1, 9.

Moser, P. K., *Knowledge and Evidence*, Cambridge, Cambridge University Press, 1989.

Pappas, G. S. and Swain, M., eds., *Essays on Knowledge and Justification*, Ithaca, Cornell University Press, 1978.

Roth, M. D. and Galis, L., eds., *Knowing*, New York, Random House, 1970.

Shope, R. K., *The Analysis of Knowing*, Princeton, Princeton University Press, 1983.

Slaght, R., 'Is Justified True Belief Knowledge? A Selective Critical Survey of Recent Work', *Philosophy Research Archives* 3 (1977), pp. 1–135.

Sturgeon, S., 'The Gettier Problem', *Analysis* 53 (1993), pp. 156–64.

Swain, M., *Reasons and Knowledge*, Ithaca, Cornell University Press, 1981.

Thalberg, I., 'In Defense of Justified True Belief', *The Journal of Philosophy* 66 (1969), pp. 794–803.

The Gettier Problem

Chapter 1
Knowing as having the right to be sure

A. J. Ayer

THE mistaken doctrine that knowing is an infallible state of mind may have contributed to the view, which is sometimes held, that the only statements that it is possible to know are those that are themselves in some way infallible. The ground for this opinion is that if one knows something to be true one cannot be mistaken. As we remarked when contrasting knowledge with belief, it is inconsistent to say 'I know but I may be wrong'. But the reason why this is inconsistent is that saying 'I know' offers a guarantee which saying 'I may be wrong' withdraws. It does not follow that for a fact to be known it must be such that no one could be mistaken about it or such that it could not have been otherwise. It is doubtful if there are any facts about which no one could be mistaken, and while there are facts which could not be otherwise, they are not the only ones that can be known. But how can this second point be reconciled with the fact that what is known must be true? The answer is that the statement that what is known must be true is ambiguous. It may mean that it is necessary that if something is known it is true; or it may mean that if something is known, then it is a necessary truth. The first of these propositions is correct; it restates the linguistic fact that what is not true cannot properly be said to be known. But the second is in general false. It would follow from the first only if all truths were necessary, which is not the case. To put it another way, there is a necessary transition from being known to being true; but that is not to say that what is true, and known to be true, is necessary or certain in itself.

If we are not to be bound by ordinary usage, it is still open to us to make it a rule that only what is certain can be known. That is, we could decide, at least for the

A. J. Ayer, 'Knowing as Having the Right to be Sure' in *The Problem of Knowledge* (London, Macmillan, 1956) pp. 22–4, 28–34, 41–4, reprinted by permission of Macmillan.

purposes of philosophical discourse, not to use the word 'know' except with the implication that what was known was necessarily true, or, perhaps, certain in some other sense. The consequence would be that we could still speak of knowing the truth of a priori statements, such as those of logic and pure mathematics; and if there were any empirical statements, such as those describing the content of one's present experience, that were certain in themselves, they too might be included: but most of what we now correctly claim to know would not be knowable, in this allegedly strict sense. This proposal is feasible, but it does not appear to have anything much to recommend it. It is not as if a statement by being necessary became incapable of being doubted. Every schoolboy knows that it is possible to be unsure about a mathematical truth. Whether there are any empirical statements which are in any important sense indubitable is, as we shall see, a matter of dispute: if there are any they belong to a very narrow class. It is, indeed, important philosophically to distinguish between necessary and empirical statements, and in dealing with empirical statements to distinguish between different types and degrees of evidence. But there are better ways of bringing out these distinctions than by tampering with the meaning, or the application, of the verb 'to know.'

[...]

The answers which we have found for the questions we have so far been discussing have not yet put us in a position to give a complete account of what it is to know that something is the case. The first requirement is that what is known should be true, but this is not sufficient; not even if we add to it the further condition that one must be completely sure of what one knows. For it is possible to be completely sure of something which is in fact true, but yet not to know it. The circumstances may be such that one is not entitled to be sure. For instance, a superstitious person who had inadvertently walked under a ladder might be convinced as a result that he was about to suffer some misfortune; and he might in fact be right. But it would not be correct to say that he knew that this was going to be so. He arrived at his belief by a process of reasoning which would not be generally reliable; so, although his prediction came true, it was not a case of knowledge. Again, if someone were fully persuaded of a mathematical proposition by a proof which could be shown to be invalid, he would not, without further evidence, be said to know the proposition, even though it was true. But while it is not hard to find examples of true and fully confident beliefs which in some ways fail to meet the standards required for knowledge, it is not at all easy to determine exactly what these standards are.

One way of trying to discover them would be to consider what would count as satisfactory answers to the question How do you know? Thus people may be credited with knowing truths of mathematics or logic if they are able to give a valid proof of them, or even if, without themselves being able to set out such a proof, they have obtained this information from someone who can. Claims to know empirical statements may be upheld by a reference perception, or to memory, or to testimony, or to historical records, or to scientific laws. But such backing is not always strong enough for knowledge. Whether it is so or not depends upon the circumstances of the particular case. If I were asked how I knew that a physical object of a certain sort was in such and such a place, it would, in general, be a sufficient answer for me to say that I could see it; but if my eyesight were bad and the light were dim, this answer might not be sufficient. Even though I was right, it might still be said that I did not really know that the object was there. If I have a poor memory and the event which I claim to remember is remote, my memory of it may still not amount to knowledge, even though in this instance it does not fail me. If a witness is unreliable, his unsupported evidence may not enable us to know that what he says is true, even in a case where we completely trust him and he is not in fact deceiving us. In a given instance it is possible to decide whether the backing is strong enough to justify a claim to knowledge. But to say in general how strong it has to be would require our drawing up a list of the conditions under which perception, or memory, or testimony, or other forms of evidence are reliable. And this would be a very complicated matter, if indeed it could be done at all.

Moreover, we cannot assume that, even in particular instances, an answer to the question 'How do you know?' will always be forthcoming. There may very well be cases in which one knows that something is so without its being possible to say how one knows it. I am not so much thinking now of claims to know facts of immediate experience, statements like 'I know that I feel pain,' which raise problems of their own into which we shall enter later on. In cases of this sort it may be argued that the question how one knows does not arise. But even when it clearly does arise, it may not find an answer. Suppose that someone were consistently successful in predicting events of a certain kind, events, let us say, which are not ordinarily thought to be predictable, like the results of a lottery. If his run of successes were sufficiently impressive, we might very well come to say that he knew which number would win, even though he did not reach this conclusion by any rational method, or indeed by any method at all. We might say that he knew it by intuition, but this would be to assert no more than that he did know it but that we could not say how. In the same way, if someone were consistently successful in reading the minds of others without having any of the usual sort of evidence, we might say that he knew these things telepathically. But in default of any further explanation this would come down to saying merely that he did know them, but not by any ordinary means. Words like 'intuition' and 'telepathy' are brought in just to disguise the fact that no explanation has been found.

But if we allow this sort of knowledge to be even theoretically possible, what becomes of the distinction between knowledge and true belief? How does our man who knows what the results of the lottery will be differ from one who only makes a series of lucky guesses? The answer is that, so far as the man himself is concerned, there need not be any difference. His procedure and his state of mind, when he is said to know what will happen, may be exactly the same as when it is said that he is only guessing. The difference is that to say that he knows is to concede to him the right to be sure, while to say that he is only guessing is to withhold it. Whether we make this concession will depend upon the view which we take of his performance. Normally we do not say that people know things unless they have followed one of the accredited routes to knowledge. If someone reaches a true conclusion without appearing to have any adequate basis for it, we are likely to say that he does not really know it. But if he were repeatedly successful in a given domain, we might very well come to say that he knew the facts in question, even though we could not explain how he knew them. We should grant him the right to be sure, simply on the basis of his success. This is, indeed, a point on which people's views might be expected to differ. Not everyone would regard a successful run of predictions, however long sustained, as being by itself a sufficient backing for a claim to knowledge. And here there can be no question of proving that this attitude is mistaken. Where there are recognized criteria for deciding when one has the right to be sure, anyone who insists that their being satisfied is still not enough for knowledge may be accused, for what the charge is worth, of misusing the verb 'to know.' But it is possible to find, or at any rate to devise, examples which are not covered in this respect by any established rule of usage. Whether they are to count as instances of knowledge is then a question which we are left free to decide.

It does not, however, matter very greatly which decision we take. The main problem is to state and assess the grounds on which these claims to knowledge are made, to settle, as it were, the candidate's marks. It is a relatively unimportant question what titles we then bestow upon them. So long as we agree about the marking, it is of no great consequence where we draw the line between pass and failure, or between the different levels of distinction. If we choose to set a very high standard, we may find ourselves committed to saying that some of what ordinarily passes for knowledge ought rather to be described as probable opinion. And some critics will then take us to task for flouting ordinary usage. But the question is purely one of terminology. It is to be decided, if at all, on grounds of practical convenience.

One must not confuse this case, where the markings are agreed upon, and what is in dispute is only the bestowal of honours, with the case where it is the markings themselves that are put in question. For this second case is philosophically important, in a way in which the other is not. The sceptic who asserts that we do not know all that we think we know, or even perhaps that we do not strictly know anything at all, is not suggesting that we are mistaken when we conclude that the recognized criteria for knowing have been satisfied. Nor is he primarily concerned with getting us to revise our usage of the verb 'to know,' any more than one who challenges our standards of value is trying to make us revise our usage of the word 'good.' The disagreement is about the application of the word, rather than its meaning. What the sceptic contends is that our markings are too high; that the grounds on which we are normally ready to concede the right to be sure are worth less than we think; he may even go so far as to say that they are not worth anything at all. The attack is directed, not against the way in which we apply our standards of proof, but against these standards themselves. It has, as we shall see, to be taken seriously because of the arguments by which it is supported.

I conclude then that the necessary and sufficient conditions for knowing that something is the case are first that what one is said to know be true, secondly that one be sure of it, and thirdly that one should have the right to be sure. This right may be earned in various ways; but even if one could give a complete description of them it would be a mistake to try to build it into the definition of knowledge, just as it would be a mistake to try to incorporate our actual standards of goodness into a definition of good. And this being so, it turns out that the questions which philosophers raise about the possibility of knowledge are not all to be settled by discovering what knowledge is.

[...]

The quest for certainty has played a considerable part in the history of philosophy: it has been assumed that without a basis of certainty all our claims to knowledge must be suspect. Unless some things are certain, it is held, nothing can be even probable. Unfortunately it has not been made clear exactly what is being sought. Sometimes the word 'certain' is used as a synonym for 'necessary' or for 'a priori.' It is said, for example, that no empirical statements are certain, and what is meant by this is that they are not necessary in the way that a priori statements are, that they can all be denied without self-contradiction. Accordingly, some philosophers take a priori statements as their ideal. They wish, like Leibniz, to put all true statements on a level with those of formal logic or pure mathematics; or, like the existentialists, they attach a tragic significance to the fact that this cannot be done. But it is perverse to see tragedy in what could not conceivably be otherwise; and the fact that all empirical statements are contingent, that even when true they can be denied without self-contradiction, is itself a matter of necessity. If empirical statements had the formal validity which makes the truths of logic unassailable they could not do the work that we expect of them; they would not be descriptive of anything that happens. In demanding for empirical statements the safeguard of logical necessity, these philosophers have failed to see that they would thereby rob them of their factual content.

Neither is this the only way in which their ideal of a priori statements fails them. Such statements are, indeed, unassailable, in the sense that, if they are true, there are no circumstances in which they could have been false. One may conceive of a world in which they had no useful application, but their being useless would not render them invalid: even if the physical processes of addition or subtraction could for some reason not be carried out, the laws of arithmetic would still hold good. But from the fact that a priori statements, if they are true, are unassailable in this sense, it does not follow that they are immune from doubt. For, as we have already remarked, it is possible to make mistakes in mathematics or in logic. It is possible to believe an a priori statement to be true when it is not. And we have seen that it is vain to look for an infallible state of intuition, which would provide a logical guarantee that no mistake was being made. Here too, it may be objected that the only reason that we have for concluding that any given a priori statement is false is that it contradicts some other which is true. That we can discover our errors shows that we have the power to correct them. The fact that we sometimes find ourselves to be mistaken in accepting an a priori statement, so far from lending favour to the suggestion that all those that we accept are false, is incompatible with it. But this still leaves it open for us to be at fault in any particular case. There is no special set of a priori statements of which it can be said that just these are beyond the reach of doubt. In very many instances the doubt would not, indeed, be serious. If the validity of some logical principle is put in question, one may be able to find a way of proving or disproving it. If it be suggested that the proof itself is suspect, one may obtain reassurance by going over it again. When one has gone over it again and satisfied oneself that there is nothing wrong with it, then to insist that it may still not be valid, that the conclusion may not really have been proved, is merely to pay lip service to human fallibility. The doubt is maintained indefinitely, because nothing is going to count as its being resolved. And just for this reason it is not serious. But to say that it is not serious is not logically to exclude it. There can be doubt so long as there is the possibility of error. And there must be the possibility of error with respect to any statement, whether empirical or a priori, which is such that from the fact that someone takes it to be so it does not follow logically that it is so. We have established this point in our discussion of knowledge, and we have seen that it is not vitiated by the fact that in the case of a priori statements there may be no other ground for accepting them than that one sees them to be true.

Philosophers have looked to a priori statements for security because they have assumed that inasmuch as these statements may themselves be certain, in the sense of being necessary, they can be certainly known. As we have seen, it may even be maintained that only what is certainly true can be certainly known. But this, it must again be remarked, is a confusion. A priori statements can, indeed, be known, not because they are necessary but because they are true and because we may be entitled to feel no doubt about their truth. And the reason why we are entitled to feel no doubt about their truth may be that we can prove them, or even just that we can see them to be valid; in either case there is an appeal to intuition, since we have at some point to claim to be able to see the validity of a proof. If the validity of every proof had to be proved in its turn, we should fall into an infinite regress. But to allow that there are times when we may justifiably claim the right to be sure of the truth of an a priori statement is not to allow that our intuitions are infallible. One is conceded the right to be sure when one is judged to have taken every reasonable step towards making sure: but this is still logically consistent with one's being in error. The discovery of the error refutes the claim to knowledge; but it does not prove that the claim was not, in the circumstances, legitimately made. The claim to know an a priori statement is satisfied only if the statement is true; but it is legitimate if it has the appropriate backing, which may, in certain cases, consist in nothing more than the statement's appearing to be self-evident. Even so, it may fail: but if such claims were legitimate only when there was no logical possibility of error, they could not properly be made at all.

Thus, if the quest for certainty is simply a quest for knowledge, if saying that a statement is known for certain amounts to no more than saying that it is known, it may find its object in a priori statements, though not indeed in them uniquely. If, on the other hand, it is a search for conditions which exclude not merely the fact, but even the possibility, of error, then knowledge of a priori statements does not satisfy it. In neither case is the fact that these a priori statements may themselves be certain, in the sense of being necessary, relevant to the issue. Or rather, as we have seen, it is relevant only if we arbitrarily decide to make it so.

Chapter 2

Is justified true belief knowledge?

Edmund L. Gettier

VARIOUS attempts have been made in recent years to state necessary and sufficient conditions for someone's knowing a given proposition. The attempts have often been such that they can be stated in a form similar to the following:[1]

   (a) S knows that P   *IFF*   (i) P is true,
                                    (ii) S believes that P, and
                                      (iii) S is justified in believing that P.

For example, Chisholm has held that the following gives the necessary and sufficient conditions for knowledge:[2]

   (b) S knows that P   *IFF*   (i) S accepts P,
                                    (ii) S has adequate evidence for P, and
                                    (iii) P is true.

Ayer has stated the necessary and sufficient conditions for knowledge as follows:[3]

   (c) S knows that P   *IFF*   (i) P is true,
                                      (ii) S is sure that P is true, and
                                    (iii) S has the right to be sure that P is true.

I shall argue that (a) is false in that the conditions stated therein do not constitute a *sufficient* condition for the truth of the proposition that S knows that P. The same argument will show that (b) and (c) fail if 'has adequate evidence for' or 'has the right to be sure that' is substituted for 'is justified in believing that' throughout.

I shall begin by noting two points. First, in that sense of 'justified' in which S's being justified in believing P is a necessary condition of S's knowing that P, it is possible for a person to be justified in believing a proposition that is in fact false. Secondly, for any proposition P, if S is justified in believing P, and P entails Q, and S deduces Q from P and accepts Q as a result of this deduction, then S is justified in believing Q. Keeping these two points in mind, I shall now present two cases in which the conditions stated in (a) are true for some proposition, though it is at the same time false that the person in question knows that proposition.

Edmund L. Gettier, 'Is Justified True Belief Knowledge?' in *Analysis* 23, (1963) pp. 121–3 (Oxford, Blackwell Publishers, 1963), reprinted by permission of Analysis Committee, Queen's College, Cambridge.

1. Plato seems to be considering some such definition at *Theaetetus* 201, and perhaps accepting one at *Meno* 98.
2. Roderick M. Chisholm, *Perceiving: a Philosophical Study*, Cornell University Press (Ithaca, New York, 1957), p. 16.
3. A. J. Ayer, *The Problem of Knowledge*, Macmillan (London, 1956), p. 34. [In this volume, p. 10]

Case I:

Suppose that Smith and Jones have applied for a certain job. And suppose that Smith has strong evidence for the following conjunctive proposition:

(d) Jones is the man who will get the job, and Jones has ten coins in his pocket.

Smith's evidence for (d) might be that the president of the company assured him that Jones would in the end be selected, and that he, Smith, had counted the coins in Jones's pocket ten minutes ago. Proposition (d) entails:

(e) The man who will get the job has ten coins in his pocket.

Let us suppose that Smith sees the entailment from (d) to (e), and accepts (e) on the grounds of (d), for which he has strong evidence. In this case, Smith is clearly justified in believing that (e) is true.

But imagine, further, that unknown to Smith, he himself, not Jones, will get the job. And, also, unknown to Smith, he himself has ten coins in his pocket. Proposition (e) is then true, though proposition (d), from which Smith inferred (e), is false. In our example, then, all of the following are true: (*i*) (e) is true, (*ii*) Smith believes that (e) is true, and (*iii*) Smith is justified in believing that (e) is true. But it is equally clear that Smith does not *know* that (e) is true; for (e) is true in virtue of the number of coins in Smith's pocket, while Smith does not know how many coins are in Smith's pocket, and bases his belief in (e) on a count of the coins in Jones's pocket, whom he falsely believes to be the the man who will get the job.

Case 2:

Let us suppose that Smith has strong evidence for the following proposition:

(f) Jones owns a Ford.

Smith's evidence might be that Jones has at all times in the past within Smith's memory owned a car, and always a Ford, and that Jones has just offered Smith a ride while driving a Ford. Let us imagine, now, that Smith has another friend, Brown, of whose whereabouts he is totally ignorant. Smith selects three place-names quite at random, and constructs the following three propositions:

(g) Either Jones owns a Ford, or Brown is in Boston;
(h) Either Jones owns a Ford, or Brown is in Barcelona;
(i) Either Jones owns a Ford, or Brown is in Brest-Litovsk.

Each of these propositions is entailed by (f). Imagine that Smith realizes the entailment of each of these propositions he has constructed by (f), and proceeds to accept (g), (h), and (i) on the basis of (f). Smith has correctly inferred (g), (h), and (i) from a proposition for which he has strong evidence. Smith is therefore completely justified in believing each of these three propositions. Smith, of course, has no idea where Brown is.

But imagine now that two further conditions hold. First, Jones does *not* own a Ford, but is at present driving a rented car. And secondly, by the sheerest coincidence, and entirely unknown to Smith, the place mentioned in proposition (h) happens really to be the place where Brown is. If these two conditions hold then Smith does *not* know that (h) is true, even though (*i*) (h) *is* true, (*ii*) Smith does believe that (h) is true, and (*iii*) Smith is justified in believing that (h) is true.

These two examples show that definition (a) does not state a *sufficient* condition for someone's knowing a given proposition. The same cases, with appropriate changes, will suffice to show that neither definition (b) nor definition (c) do so either.

Can we ever know that which is out side ourselves? Case one – if there were no Jones, would Smith know the truth?

Chapter 3

An alleged defect in Gettier counter-examples

Richard Feldman

A NUMBER of philosophers have contended that Gettier counter-examples to the justified true belief analysis of knowledge all rely on a certain false principle. For example, in their recent paper, 'Knowledge Without Paradox'[1] Robert G. Meyers and Kenneth Stern argue that '(c)ounter-examples of the Gettier sort all turn on the principle that someone can be justified in accepting a certain proposition h on evidence p even though p is false.'[2] They contend that this principle is false, and hence that the counter-examples fail. Their view is that one proposition, p, can justify another, h, only if p is true. With this in mind, they accept the justified true belief analysis.

D. M. Armstrong defends a similar view in *Belief, Truth and Knowledge*.[3] He writes:

> This simple consideration seems to make redundant the ingenious arguments of . . . Gettier's . . . article. . . . Gettier produces counter-examples to the thesis that justified true belief is knowledge by producing true beliefs based on justifiable believed grounds. . . . but where these grounds are in fact *false*. But because possession of such grounds could not constitute possession of *knowledge*. I should have thought it obvious that they are too weak to serve as suitable grounds.[4]

Thus he concludes that Gettier's examples are defective because they rely on the false principle that false propositions can justify one's belief in other propositions. Armstrong's view seems to be that one proposition, p, can justify another, h, only if p is known to be true (unlike Meyers and Stern who demand only that p in fact be true).[5]

I think, though, that there are examples very much like Gettier's that do not rely on this allegedly false principle. To see this, let us first consider one example in the form in which Meyers and Stern discuss it, and then consider a slight modification of it.

Richard Feldman, 'An Alleged Defect in Gettier Counter-Examples' in *The Australasian Journal of Philosophy* 52 (1974) pp. 68–9, reprinted by permission of the author.

1. Robert G. Myers and Kenneth Stern, 'Knowledge Without Paradox,' *The Journal of Philosophy* 70, no. 6 (March 22, 1973): 147–60.
2. Ibid., p. 147.
3. D. M. Armstrong, *Belief, Truth and Knowledge* (Cambridge, Eng., 1973).
4. Ibid., p. 152.
5. Armstrong ultimately goes on to defend a rather different analysis.

Suppose Mr. Nogot tells Smith that he owns a Ford and even shows him a certificate to that effect. Suppose, further, that up till now Nogot has always been reliable and honest in his dealings with Smith. Let us call the conjunction of all this evidence m. Smith is thus justified in believing that Mr. Nogot who is in his office owns a Ford (r) and, consequently, is justified in believing that someone in his office owns a Ford (h).[6]

As it turns out, though, m and h are true but r is false. So, the Gettier example runs. Smith has a justified true belief in h, but he clearly does not know h.

What is supposed to justify h in this example is r. But since r is false, the example runs afoul of the disputed principle. Since r is false, it justifies nothing. Hence, if the principle is false, the counter-example fails.

We can alter the example slightly, however, so that what justifies h for Smith is true and he knows that it is. Suppose he deduces from m its existential generalization:

(n) There is someone in the office who told Smith that he owns a Ford and even showed him a certificate to that effect, and who up till now has always been reliable and honest in his dealings with Smith.

(n), we should note, is true and Smith knows that it is, since he has correctly deduced it from m, which he knows to be true. On the basis of n Smith believes h—someone in the office owns a Ford. Just as the Nogot evidence, m, justified r—Nogot owns a Ford—in the original example, n justifies h in this example. Thus Smith has a justified true belief in h, knows his evidence to be true, but still does not know h.

I conclude that even if a proposition can be justified for a person only if his evidence is true, or only if he knows it to be true, there are still counter-examples to the justified true belief analysis of knowledge of the Gettier sort. In the above example, Smith reasoned from the proposition m, which he knew to be true, to the proposition n, which he also knew, to the truth h; yet he still did not know h. So some examples, similar to Gettier's, do not 'turn on the principle that someone can be justified in accepting a certain proposition . . . even though (his evidence) . . . is false.'[7]

6. Meyers and Stern, 151.
7. Ibid., p. 147.

Responses to Gettier

Chapter 4

A causal theory of knowing*

Alvin I. Goldman

Sᴉɴᴄᴇ Edmund L. Gettier reminded us recently of a certain important inadequacy of the traditional analysis of 'S knows that p,' several attempts have been made to correct that analysis.[1] In this paper I shall offer still another analysis (or a sketch of an analysis) of 'S knows that p,' one which will avert Gettier's problem. My concern will be with knowledge of empirical propositions only, since I think that the traditional analysis is adequate for knowledge of nonempirical truths.

Consider an abbreviated version of Gettier's second counterexample to the traditional analysis. Smith believes

(q) Jones owns a Ford

and has very strong evidence for it. Smith's evidence might be that Jones has owned a Ford for many years and that Jones has just offered Smith a ride while driving a Ford. Smith has another friend, Brown, of whose whereabouts he is totally ignorant. Choosing a town quite at random, however, Smith constructs the proposition

(p) Either Jones owns a Ford or Brown is in Barcelona.

Seeing that q entails p, Smith infers that p is true. Since he has adequate evidence for q, he also has adequate evidence for p. But now suppose that Jones does *not* own a Ford (he was driving a rented car when he offered Smith a ride), but, quite by

Alvin I. Goldman, 'A Causal Theory of Knowing' in *The Journal of Philosophy* 64 (1967), pp. 357–72 reprinted by permission of Columbia University, New York.

* I wish to thank members of the University of Michigan Philosophy Department, several of whom made helpful comments on earlier versions of this paper.

1. 'Is True Justified Belief Knowledge?' *Analysis* 23 (1963): [Ch. 2 in this volume] 121–3. I say 'reminded' because essentially the same point was made by Russell in 1912. Cf. *The Problems of Philosophy* (Oxford, 1912), ch. 13, pp. 132 ff. New analyses have been proposed by Michael Clark, 'Knowledge and Grounds: A Comment on Mr. Gettier's Paper,' *Analysis* 24 (1963): 46–8; Ernest Sosa, 'The Analysis of "Knowledge that p",' *Analysis* 25 (1964): 1–3; and Keith Lehrer, 'Knowledge, Truth, and Evidence,' *Analysis* 25 (1965): 168–75.

coincidence, Brown happens to be in Barcelona. This means that p is true, that Smith believes p, and that Smith has adequate evidence for p. But Smith does not know p.

A variety of hypotheses might be made to account for Smith's not knowing p. Michael Clark, for example, points to the fact that q is false, and suggests this as the reason why Smith cannot be said to know p. Generalizing from this case, Clark argues that, for S to know a proposition, each of S's grounds for it must be *true*, as well as his grounds for his grounds, etc.[2] I shall make another hypothesis to account for the fact that Smith cannot be said to know p, and I shall generalize this into a new analysis of 'S knows that p.'

Notice that what *makes p* true is the fact that Brown is in Barcelona, but that this fact has nothing to do with Smith's believing p. That is, there is no *causal* connection between the fact that Brown is in Barcelona and Smith's believing p. If Smith had come to believe p by reading a letter from Brown postmarked in Barcelona, then we might say that Smith knew p. Alternatively, if Jones did own a Ford, and his owning the Ford was manifested by his offer of a ride to Smith, and this in turn resulted in Smith's believing p, then we would say that Smith knew p. Thus, one thing that seems to be missing in this example is a causal connection between the fact that makes p true [or simply: the fact that p] and Smith's belief of p. The requirement of such a causal connection is what I wish to add to the traditional analysis.

To see that this requirement is satisfied in all cases of (empirical) knowledge, we must examine a variety of such causal connections. Clearly, only a sketch of the important kinds of cases is possible here.

Perhaps the simplest case of a causal chain connecting some fact p with someone's belief of p is that of *perception*. I wish to espouse a version of the causal theory of perception, in essence that defended by H. P. Grice.[3] Suppose that S sees that there is a vase in front of him. How is this to be analyzed? I shall not attempt a complete analysis of this, but a necessary condition of S's seeing that there is a vase in front of him is that there be a certain kind of causal connection between the presence of the vase and S's believing that a vase is present. I shall not attempt to describe this causal process in detail. Indeed, to a large extent, a description of this process must be regarded as a problem for the special sciences, not for philosophy. But a certain causal process—viz., that which standardly takes place when we say that so-and-so *sees* such-and-such—must occur. That our ordinary concept of sight (i.e., knowledge acquired by sight) includes a causal requirement is shown by the fact that if the relevant causal process is absent we would withhold the assertion that so-and-so *saw* such-and-such. Suppose that, although a vase is directly in front of S, a laser photograph[4] is interposed between it and S, thereby blocking it from S's view. The photograph, however, is one of a vase (a different vase), and when it is

2. *Op cit.* Criticisms of Clark's analysis will be discussed below.

3. 'The Causal Theory of Perception,' *Proceedings of the Aristotelian Society*, Supp. vol. 35 (1961) [Ch. 30 in this volume].

4. If a laser photograph (hologram) is illuminated by light waves, especially waves from a laser, the effect of the hologram on the viewer is exactly as if the object were being seen. It preserves three-dimensionality completely, and even gives appropriate parallax effects as the viewer moves relative to it. Cf. E. N. Leith and J. Upatnieks, 'Photography by Laser,' *Scientific American*, 212, 6 (June 1965): 24.

illuminated by light waves from a laser, it looks to S exactly like a real vase. When the photograph is illuminated, S forms the belief that there is a vase in front of him. Here we would deny that S *sees* that there is a vase in front of him, for his view of the real vase is completely blocked, so that it has no causal role in the formation of his belief. Of course, S might *know* that there was a vase in front of him even if the photograph is blocking his view. Someone else, in a position to see the vase, might tell S that there is a vase in front of him. Here the presence of the vase might be a causal ancestor of S's belief, but the causal process would not be a (purely) *perceptual* one. S could not be said to *see* that there is a vase in front of him. For this to be true, there must be a causal process, but one of a very special sort, connecting the presence of the vase with S's belief.

I shall here assume that perceptual knowledge of facts is noninferential. This is merely a simplifying procedure, and not essential to my account. Certainly a percipient does not *infer* facts about physical objects from the state of his brain or from the stimulation of his sense organs. He need not know about these goings-on at all. But some epistemologists maintain that we directly perceive only sense data and that we infer physical-object facts from them. This view could be accommodated within my analysis. I could say that physical-object facts cause sense data, that people directly perceive sense data, and that they infer the physical-object facts from the sense data. This kind of process would be fully accredited by my analysis, which will allow for knowledge based on inference. But for purposes of exposition it will be convenient to regard perceptual knowledge of external facts as independent of any inference.

Here the question arises about the scope of perceptual knowledge. By perception I can know noninferentially that there is a vase in front of me. But can I know noninferentially that the painting I am viewing is a Picasso? It is unnecessary to settle such issues here. Whether the knowledge of such facts is to be classed as inferential or noninferential, my analysis can account for it. So the scope of non-inferential knowledge may be left indeterminate.

I turn next to memory, i.e., knowledge that is based, in part, on memory. Remembering, like perceiving, must be regarded as a causal process. S remembers *p* at time *t* only if S's believing *p* at an earlier time is a cause of his believing *p* at *t*. Of course, not every causal connection between an earlier belief and a later one is a case of remembering. As in the case of perception, however, I shall not try to describe this process in detail. This is a job mainly for the scientist. Instead, the kind of causal process in question is to be identified simply by example, by 'pointing' to paradigm cases of remembering. Whenever causal processes are of that kind— whatever that kind is, precisely—they are cases of remembering.[5]

A causal connection between earlier belief (or knowledge) of *p* and later belief (knowledge) of *p* is certainly a necessary ingredient in memory.[6] To remember a

---

5. For further defense of this kind of procedure, with attention to perception, cf. Grice, *op. cit.* [Ch. 30 in this volume].

6. Causal connections can hold between states of affairs, such as believings, as well as between events. If a given event or state, in conjunction with other events or states, 'leads to' or 'results in' another event or state (or the same state obtaining at a later time), it will be called a 'cause' of the latter. I shall also speak of 'facts' being causes.

fact is not simply to believe it at t_0 and also to believe it at t_1. Nor does someone's knowing a fact at t_0 and his knowing it at t_1 entail that he remembers it at t_1. He may have perceived the fact at t_0, forgotten it, and then relearned it at t_1 by someone's telling it to him. Nor does the inclusion of a memory 'impression'—a feeling of remembering—ensure that one really remembers. Suppose S perceives p at t_0, but forgets it at t_1. At t_2 he begins to believe p again because someone tells him p, but at t_2 he has no memory impression of p. At t_3 we artificially stimulate in S a memory impression of p. It does not follow that S remembers p at t_3. The description of the case suggests that his believing p at t_0 has no causal effect whatever on his believing p at t_3; and if we accepted this fact, we would deny that he remembers p at t_3.

Knowledge can be acquired by a combination of perception and memory. At t_1, the fact p causes S to believe p, by perception. S's believing p at t_0 results, via memory, in S's believing p at t_1. Thus, the fact p is a cause of S's believing p at t_1, and S can be said to know p at t_1. But not all knowledge results from perception and memory alone. In particular, much knowledge is based on *inference*.

As I shall use the term 'inference', to say that S knows by 'inference' does not entail that S went through an explicit, conscious process of reasoning. It is not necessary that he have 'talked to himself,' saying something like 'Since such-and-such is true, p must also be true'. My belief that there is a fire in the neighborhood is based on, or inferred from, my belief that I hear a fire engine. But I have not gone through a process of explicit reasoning, saying 'There's a fire engine; therefore there must be a fire.' Perhaps the word 'inference' is ordinarily used only where explicit reasoning occurs; if so, my use of the term will be somewhat broader than its ordinary use.

Suppose S perceives that there is solidified lava in various parts of the countryside. On the basis of this belief, plus various 'background' beliefs about the production of lava, S concludes that a nearby mountain erupted many centuries ago. Let us assume that this is a highly warranted inductive inference, one which gives S adequate evidence for believing that the mountain did erupt many centuries ago. Assuming this proposition is true, does S know it? This depends on the nature of the causal process that induced his belief. If there is a continuous causal chain of the sort he envisages connecting the fact that the mountain erupted with his belief of this fact, then S knows it. If there is no such causal chain, however, S does not know that proposition.

Suppose that the mountain erupts, leaving lava around the countryside. The lava remains there until S perceives it and infers that the mountain erupted. Then S does know that the mountain erupted. But now suppose that, after the mountain has erupted, a man somehow removes all the lava. A century later, a different man (not knowing of the real volcano) decides to make it look as if there had been a volcano, and therefore puts lava in appropriate places. Still later, S comes across this lava and concludes that the mountain erupted centuries ago. In this case, S cannot be said to know the proposition. This is because the fact that the mountain did erupt is not a cause of S believing that it erupted. A necessary condition of S's knowing p is that his believing p be connected with p by a causal chain.

In the first case, where S knows p, the causal connection may be diagrammed as in Figure 1. (p) is the fact that the mountain erupted at such-and-such a time. (q) is the fact that lava is (now) present around the countryside. 'B' stands for a belief, the expression in parentheses indicating the proposition believed, and the subscript designating the believer. (r) is a 'background' proposition, describing the ways in which lava is produced and how it solidifies. Solid arrows in the diagram represent causal connections; dotted arrows represent inferences. Notice that, in Figure 1, there is not only an arrow connecting (q) with S's belief of (q), but also an arrow connecting (p) with (q). In the suggested variant of the lava case, the latter arrow would be missing, showing that there is no continuous causal chain connecting (p) with S's belief of (p). Therefore, in that variant case, S could not be said to know (p).

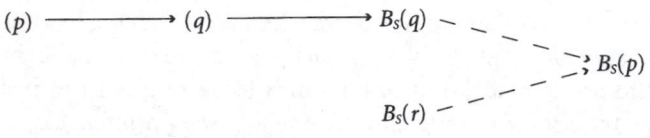

Figure 1

I have said that p is causally connected to S's belief of p, in the case diagrammed in Figure 1. This raises the question, however, of whether the inferential part of the chain is itself a causal chain. In other words, is S's belief of q a cause of his believing p? This is a question to which I shall not try to give a definitive answer here. I am inclined to say that inference *is* a causal process, that is, that when someone *bases* his belief of one proposition on his belief of a set of other propositions, then his belief of the latter propositions can be considered a cause of his belief of the former proposition. But I do not wish to rest my thesis on this claim. All I do claim is that, if a chain of inferences is 'added' to a causal chain, then the entire chain is causal. In terms of our diagram, a chain consisting of solid arrows plus dotted arrows is to be considered a causal chain, though I shall not take a position on the question of whether the dotted arrows represent causal connections. Thus, in Figure 1, p is a cause of S's belief of p, whether or not we regard S's belief of q a cause of his belief of p.[7]

Consider next a case of knowledge based on 'testimony.' This too can be analyzed causally. p causes a person T to believe p, by perception. T's belief of p gives rise to (causes) his asserting p. T's asserting p causes S, by auditory perception, to believe that T is asserting p. S infers that T believes p, and from this, in turn, he infers that p is a fact. There is a continuous causal chain from p to S's believing p, and thus, assuming that each of S's inferences is warranted, S can be said to know p.

This causal chain is represented in Figure 2. 'A' refers to an act of asserting a

---

7. A fact can be a cause of a belief even if it does not *initiate* the belief. Suppose I believe that there is a lake in a certain locale, this belief having started in a manner quite unconnected with the existence of the lake. Continuing to have the belief, I go to the locale and perceive the lake. At this juncture, the existence of the lake becomes a cause of my believing that there is a lake there. This is analogous to a table top that is supported by four legs. When a fifth leg is inserted flush beneath the table top, it too becomes a cause of the table top's not falling. It has a causal role in the support of the table top even though, before it was inserted, the table top was adequately supported.

proposition, the expression in parentheses indicating the proposition asserted and the subscript designating the agent. (q), (r), (u), and (v) are background propositions. (q) and (r), for example, pertain to T's sincerity; they help S conclude, from the fact that T asserted p, that T really believes p.

$$B_S(r) \qquad\qquad B_S(v)$$

$$(p) \longrightarrow B_T(p) \longrightarrow A_T(p) \longrightarrow B_S(A_T(p)) \quad\dashrightarrow\quad B_S(B_T(p)) \quad\dashrightarrow\quad B_S(p)$$

$$B_S(q) \qquad\qquad B_S(u)$$

Figure 2

In this case, as in the lava case, S knows p because he has correctly reconstructed the causal chain leading from p to the evidence for p that S perceives, in this case, T's asserting (p). This correct reconstruction is shown in the diagram by S's inference 'mirroring' the rest of the causal chain. Such a correct reconstruction is a necessary condition of knowledge based on inference. To see this, consider the following example. A newspaper reporter observes p and reports it to his newspaper. When printed, however, the story contains a typographical error so that it asserts not-p. When reading the paper, however, S fails to see the word 'not', and takes the paper to have asserted p. Trusting the newspaper, he infers that p is true. Here we have a continuous causal chain leading from p to S's believing p; yet S does not know p. S thinks that p resulted in a report to the newspaper about p and that this report resulted in its printing the statement p. Thus, his reconstruction of the causal chain is mistaken. But, if he is to know p, his reconstruction must contain no mistakes. Though he need not reconstruct *every* detail of the causal chain, he must reconstruct all the important links.[8] An additional requirement for knowledge based on inference is that the knower's inferences be warranted. That is, the propositions on which he bases his belief of p must genuinely confirm p very highly, whether deductively or inductively. Reconstructing a causal chain merely by lucky guesses does not yield knowledge.

With the help of our diagrams, we can contrast the traditional analysis of knowing with Clark's analysis (*op. cit.*) and contrast each of these with my own analysis. The traditional analysis makes reference to just three features of the diagrams. First, it requires that p be true; i.e., that (p) appear in the diagram. Secondly, it requires that S believe p; i.e., that S's belief of p appear in the diagram. Thirdly, it requires that S's inferences, if any, be warranted; i.e., that the sets of beliefs that are at the tails of dotted arrows must jointly highly confirm the belief at the head of these arrows. Clark proposes a further requirement for knowledge. He requires that *each* of the beliefs in S's chain of inference be *true*. In other words, whereas the traditional analysis requires a fact to correspond to S's belief of p, Clark requires that a

8. Clearly we cannot require someone to reconstruct every detail, since this would involve knowledge of minute physical phenomena, for example, of which ordinary people are unaware. On the other hand, it is difficult to give criteria to identify which details, in general, are 'important.' This will vary substantially from case to case.

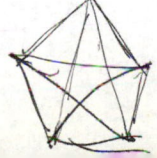

fact correspond to *each* of S's beliefs on which he based his belief of p. Thus, corresponding to each belief on the right side of the diagram there must be a fact on the left side. (My diagrams omit facts corresponding to the 'background' beliefs.)

As Clark's analysis stands, it seems to omit an element of the diagrams that my analysis requires, viz., the arrows indicating causal connections. Now Clark might reformulate his analysis so as to make implicit reference to these causal connections. If he required that the knower's beliefs include *causal beliefs* (of the relevant sort), then his requirement that these beliefs be true would amount to the requirement that there *be* causal chains of the sort I require. This interpretation of Clark's analysis would make it almost equivalent to mine, and would enable him to avoid some objections that have been raised against him. But he has not explicitly formulated his analysis this way, and it therefore remains deficient in this respect.

Before turning to the problems facing Clark's analysis, more must be said about my own analysis. So far, my examples may have suggested that, if S knows p, the fact that p is a cause of his belief of p. This would clearly be wrong, however. Let us grant that I can know facts about the future. Then, if we required that the known fact cause the knower's belief, we would have to countenance 'backward' causation. My analysis, however, does not face this dilemma. The analysis requires that there be a causal *connection* between p and S's belief, not necessarily that p be a *cause* of S's belief. p and S's belief of p can also be causally connected in a way that yields knowledge if both p and S's belief of p have a *common* cause. This can be illustrated as follows.

T intends to go downtown on Monday. On Sunday, T tells S of his intention. Hearing T say he will go downtown, S infers that T really does intend to go downtown. And from this S concludes that T will go downtown on Monday. Now suppose that T fulfills his intention by going downtown on Monday. Can S be said to know that he would go downtown? If we ever can be said to have knowledge of the future, this is a reasonable candidate for it. So let us say S did know that proposition. How can my analysis account for S's knowledge? T's going downtown on Monday clearly cannot be a cause of S's believing, on Sunday, that he would go downtown. But there is a fact that is the common cause of T's going downtown and of S's belief that he would go downtown, viz., T's intending (on Sunday) to go downtown. This intention resulted in his going downtown and also resulted in S's believing that he would go downtown. This causal connection between S's belief and the fact believed allows us to say that S *knew* that T would go downtown.

The example is diagrammed in Figure 3. (p) = T's going downtown on Monday. (q) = T's intending (on Sunday) to go downtown on Monday. (r) = T's telling S (on Sunday) that he will go downtown on Monday. (u) and (v) are relevant background propositions pertaining to T's honesty, resoluteness, etc. The diagram reveals that q is a cause both of p and of S's belief of p. Cases of this kind I shall call *Pattern 2* cases of knowledge. Figures 1 and 2 exemplify *Pattern 1* cases of knowledge.

Notice that the causal connection between q and p is an essential part of S's knowing p. Suppose, for example, that T's intending (on Sunday) to go downtown

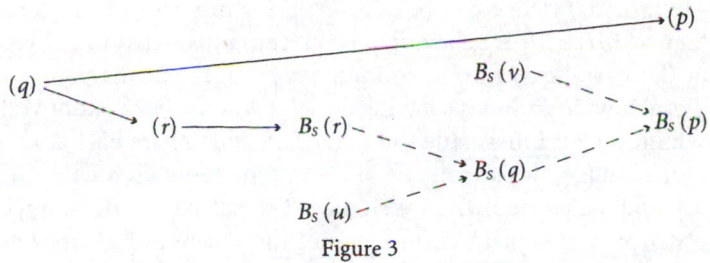

Figure 3

does not result in, or cause, T's going downtown on Monday. Suppose that T, after telling S that he would go downtown, changes his mind. Nevertheless, on Monday he is kidnapped and forced, at the point of a gun, to go downtown. Here both q and p actually occur, but they are not causally related. The diagram in Figure 3 would have to be amended by deleting the arrow connecting (q) with (p). But if the rest of the facts of the original case remain the same, S could not be said to know p. It would be false to say that S knew, on Sunday, that T would go downtown on Monday.

Pattern 2 cases of knowledge are not restricted to knowledge of the future. I know that smoke was coming out of my chimney last night. I know this because I remember perceiving a fire in my fireplace last night, and I infer that the fire caused smoke to rise out of the chimney. This case exemplifies Pattern 2. The smoke's rising out of the chimney is not a causal factor of my belief. But the fact that there was a fire in the fireplace was a cause both of my belief that smoke was coming out of the chimney and of the fact that smoke was coming out of the chimney. If we supplement this case slightly, we can make my knowledge exemplify *both* Pattern 1 and Pattern 2. Suppose that a friend tells me today that he perceived smoke coming out of my chimney last night and I base my continued belief of this fact on his testimony. Then the fact was a cause of my current belief of it, as well as an *effect* of another fact that caused my belief. In general, numerous and diverse kinds of causal connections can obtain between a given fact and a given person's belief of that fact.

Let us now examine some objections to Clark's analysis and see how the analysis presented here fares against them. John Turk Saunders and Narayan Champawat have raised the following counter example to Clark's analysis:[9]

Suppose that Smith believes

(p) Jones owns a Ford

because his friend Brown whom he knows to be generally reliable and honest yesterday told Smith that Jones had always owned a Ford. Brown's information was correct, but today Jones sells his Ford and replaces it with a Volkswagen. An hour later Jones is pleased to find that he is the proud owner of two cars: he has been lucky enough to win a Ford in a raffle. Smith's belief in p is not only justified and true, but is fully grounded, e.g., we suppose that each link in the . . . chain of Smith's grounds is true.

Clearly Smith does not know p; yet he seems to satisfy Clark's analysis of knowing.

9. 'Mr. Clark's Definition of "Knowledge",' *Analysis* 25 (1964): 8–9.

Smith's lack of knowledge can be accounted for in terms of my analysis. Smith does not know p because his believing p is not causally related to p, Jones's owning a Ford *now*. This can be seen by examining Figure 4. In the diagram, (p) = Jones's owning a Ford now; (q) = Jones's having always owned a Ford (until yesterday); (r) = Jones's winning a Ford in a raffle today. (t), (u), and (v) are background propositions. (v), for example, deals with the likelihood of someone's continuing to own the same car today that he owned yesterday. The subscript 'B' designates Brown, and the subscript 'S' designates Smith. Notice the absence of an arrow connecting (p) with (q). The absence of this arrow represents the absence of a causal relation between (q) and (p). Jones's owning a Ford in the past (until yesterday) is not a cause of his owning one now. Had he continued owning the same Ford today that he owned yesterday, there would be a causal connection between q and p and, therefore, a causal connection between p and Smith's believing p. This causal connection would exemplify Pattern 2. But, as it happened, it is purely a coincidence that Jones owns a Ford today as well as yesterday. Thus, Smith's belief of p is not connected with p by Pattern 2, nor is there any Pattern 1 connection between them. Hence, Smith does not know p.

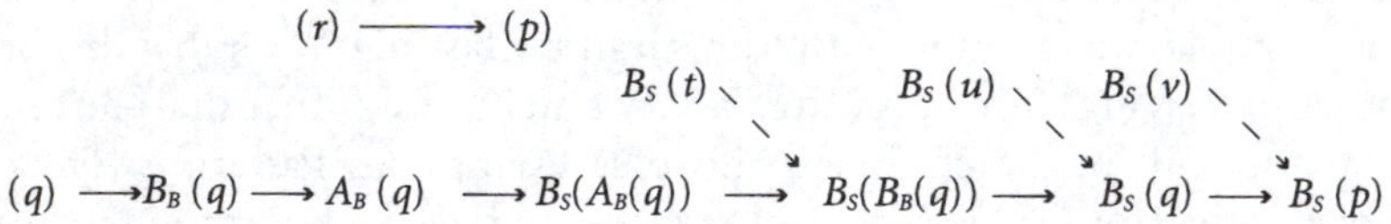

$$(r) \longrightarrow (p)$$

$$(q) \longrightarrow B_B(q) \longrightarrow A_B(q) \longrightarrow B_S(A_B(q)) \longrightarrow B_S(B_B(q)) \longrightarrow B_S(q) \longrightarrow B_S(p)$$

with $B_S(t)$, $B_S(u)$, $B_S(v)$ as background terms feeding into the chain.

Figure 4

If we supplement Clark's analysis as suggested above, it can be saved from this counterexample. Though Saunders and Champawat fail to mention this explicitly, presumably it is one of Smith's beliefs that Jones's owning a Ford yesterday would *result* in Jones's owning a Ford now. This was undoubtedly one of his grounds for believing that Jones owns a Ford now. (A complete diagram of S's beliefs relevant to p would include this belief.) Since this belief is false, however, Clark's analysis would yield the correct consequence that Smith does not know p. Unfortunately, Clark himself seems not to have noticed this point, since Saunders and Champawat's putative counterexample has been allowed to stand.

Another sort of counterexample to Clark's analysis has been given by Saunders and Champawat and also by Keith Lehrer. This is a counterexample from which his analysis cannot escape. I shall give Lehrer's example (*op. cit.*) of this sort of difficulty. Suppose Smith bases his belief of

(p) Someone in his office owns a Ford

on his belief of four propositions

(q) Jones owns a Ford
(r) Jones works in his office
(s) Brown owns a Ford
(t) Brown works in his office

In fact, Smith knows q, r, and t, but he does not know s because s is false. Since s is false, not *all* of Smith's grounds for *p* are true, and, therefore, on Clark's analysis, Smith does not know *p*. Yet clearly Smith does know *p*. Thus, Clark's analysis is *too strong*.

Having seen the importance of a causal chain for knowing, it is fairly obvious how to amend Clark's requirements without making them too weak. We need not require, as Clark does, that *all* of S's grounds be true. What is required is that enough of them be true to ensure the existence of at least *one* causal connection between *p* and S's belief of *p*. In Lehrer's example, Smith thinks that there are two ways in which he knows *p*: via his knowledge of the conjunction of *q* and *r*, and via his knowledge of the conjunction of *s* and *t*. He does not know *p* via the conjunction of *s* and *t*, since *s* is false. But there is a causal connection, via *q* and *r*, between *p* and Smith's belief of *p*. And this connection is enough.

Another sort of case in which one of S's grounds for *p* may be false without preventing him from knowing *p* is where the false proposition is a dispensable background assumption. Suppose S bases his belief of *p* on seventeen background assumptions, but only sixteen of these are true. If these sixteen are strong enough to confirm *p*, then the seventeenth is dispensable. S can be said to know *p* though one of his grounds is false.

Our discussion of Lehrer's example calls attention to the necessity of a further clarification of the notion of a 'causal chain.' I said earlier that causal chains with admixtures of inferences are causal chains. Now I wish to add that causal chains with admixtures of logical connections are causal chains. Unless we allow this interpretation, it is hard to see how facts like 'Someone in the office owns a Ford' or 'All men are mortal' could be *causally* connected with beliefs thereof.

The following principle will be useful: *If x is logically related to y and if y is a cause of z, then x is a cause of z.* Thus, suppose that *q* causes S's belief of *q* and that *r* causes S's belief of *r*. Next suppose that S infers *q* & *r* from his belief of *q* and of *r*. Then the facts *q* and *r* are causes of S's believing *q* & *r*. But the fact *q* & *r* is logically related to the fact *q* and to the fact *r*. Therefore, using the principle enunciated above, the fact *q* & *r* is a cause of S's believing *q* & *r*.

In Lehrer's case another logical connection is involved: a connection between an existential fact and an instance thereof. Lehrer's case is diagrammed in Figure 5. In addition to the usual conventions, logical relationships are represented by double solid lines. As the diagram shows, the fact *p*—someone in Smith's office owning a Ford—is logically related to the fact *q* & *r*—Jones's owning a Ford and Jones's working in Smith's office. The fact *q* & *r* is, in turn, logically related to the fact *q* and to the fact *r*. *q* causes S's belief of *q* and, by inference, his belief of *q* & *r* and of *p*.

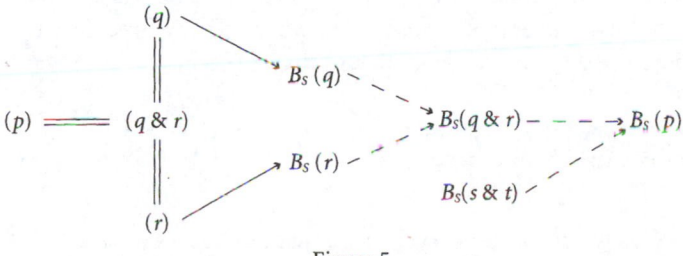

Figure 5

Similarly, *r* is a cause of *S*'s belief of *p*. Hence, by the above principle, *p* is a cause of *S*'s belief of *p*. Since Smith's inferences are warranted, even setting aside his belief of *s* & *t*, he knows *p*.

In a similar way, universal facts may be causes of beliefs thereof. The fact that all men are mortal is logically related to its instances: John's being mortal, George's being mortal, Oscar's being mortal, etc. Now suppose that *S* perceives George, John, Oscar, etc. to be mortal (by seeing them die). He infers from these facts that all men are mortal, an inference which, I assume, is warranted. Since each of the facts, John is mortal, George is mortal, Oscar is mortal, etc., is a cause of *S*'s believing that fact, each is also a cause of *S*'s believing that all men are mortal. Moreover, since the universal fact that all men are mortal is logically related to each of these particular facts, this universal fact is a cause of *S*'s belief of it. Hence, *S* can be said to know that all men are mortal. In analogous fashions, S can know various other logically compound propositions.

We can now formulate the analysis of knowing as follows:

S knows that p if and only if *the fact p is causally connected in an 'appropriate' way with S's believing p.*

'Appropriate', knowledge-producing causal processes include the following:

(1) perception
(2) memory
(3) a causal chain, exemplifying either Pattern 1 or 2, which is correctly reconstructed by inferences, each of which is warranted (background propositions help warrant an inference only if they are true)[10]
(4) combinations of (1), (2), and (3)

We have seen that this analysis is *stronger* than the traditional analysis in certain respects: the causal requirement and the correct-reconstruction requirement are absent from the older analysis. These additional requirements enable my analysis to circumvent Gettier's counterexamples to the traditional one. But my analysis is *weaker* than the traditional analysis in another respect. In at least one popular interpretation of the traditional analysis, a knower must be able to justify or give evidence for any proposition he knows. For *S* to know *p* at *t*, *S* must be able, at *t*, to *state* his justification for believing *p*, or his grounds for *p*. My analysis makes no such requirement, and the absence of this requirement enables me to account for cases of knowledge that would wrongly be excluded by the traditional analysis.

I know now, for example, that Abraham Lincoln was born in 1809.[11] I originally came to know this fact, let us suppose, by reading an encyclopedia article. I believed that this encyclopedia was trustworthy and that its saying Lincoln was born in 1809

10. Perhaps background propositions that help warrant *S*'s inference must be *known* by *S*, as well as true. This requirement could be added without making our analysis of '*S* knows that *p*' circular. For these propositions would not include *p*. In other words, the analysis of knowledge could be regarded as recursive.

11. This kind of case is drawn from an unpublished manuscript of Gilbert Harman.

must have resulted from the fact that Lincoln was indeed born in 1809. Thus, my original knowledge of this fact was founded on a warranted inference. But now I no longer remember this inference. I remember that Lincoln was born in 1809, but not that this is stated in a certain encyclopedia. I no longer have any pertinent beliefs that highly confirm the proposition that Lincoln was born in 1809. Nevertheless, I know this proposition now. My original knowledge of it was preserved until now by the causal process of memory.

Defenders of the traditional analysis would doubtlessly deny that I really do know Lincoln's birth year. This denial, however, stems from a desire to protect their analysis. It seems clear that many things we know were originally learned in a way that we no longer remember. The range of our knowledge would be drastically reduced if these items were denied the status of knowledge.

Other species of knowledge without explicit evidence could also be admitted by my analysis. Notice that I have not closed the list of 'appropriate' causal processes. Leaving the list open is desirable, because there may be some presently controversial causal processes that we may later deem 'appropriate' and, therefore, knowledge-producing. Many people now doubt the legitimacy of claims to extrasensory perception. But if conclusive evidence were to establish the existence of causal processes connecting physical facts with certain persons' beliefs without the help of standard perceptual processes, we might decide to call such beliefs items of knowledge. This would be another species of knowledge in which the knower might be unable to justify or defend his belief. My analysis allows for the possibility of such knowledge, though it doesn't commit one to it.

Special comments are in order about knowledge of our own mental states. This is a very difficult and controversial topic, so I hesitate to discuss it, but something must be said about it. Probably there are some mental states that are clearly distinct from the subject's belief that he is in such a state. If so, then there is presumably a causal process connecting the existence of such states with the subject's belief thereof. We may add this kind of process to the list of 'appropriate' causal processes. The more difficult cases are those in which the state is hardly distinguishable from the subject's believing that he is in that state. My being in pain and my believing that I am in pain are hardly distinct states of affairs. If there is no distinction here between the believing and the believed, how can there be a causal connection between them? For the purposes of the present analysis, we may regard identity as a 'limiting' or 'degenerate' case of a causal connection, just as zero may be regarded as a 'limiting' or 'degenerate' case of a number. It is not surprising that knowledge of one's own mental state should turn out to be a limiting or degenerate case of knowledge. Philosophers have long recognized its peculiar status. While some philosophers have regarded it as a paradigm case of knowledge, others have claimed that we have no 'knowledge' of our mental states at all. A theory of knowledge that makes knowledge of one's own mental states rather different from garden-variety species of knowledge is, in so far forth, acceptable and even welcome.

In conclusion, let me answer some possible objections to my analysis. It might be doubted whether a causal analysis adequately provides the meaning of the word 'knows' or of the sentence (-schema) 'S knows p.' But I am not interested in giving the *meaning* of 'S knows *p*'; only its *truth conditions*. I claim to have given one correct set of truth conditions for 'S knows *p*.' Truth conditions of a sentence do not always provide its meaning. Consider, for example, the following truth-conditions statement: 'The sentence "Team *T* wins the baseball game" is true if and only if team *T* has more runs at the end of the game than the opposing team.' This statement fails to provide the meaning of the sentence 'Team *T* wins the baseball game'; for it fails to indicate an essential part of the meaning of that sentence, viz., that to win a game is to achieve the presumed goal of playing it. Someone might fully understand the truth conditions given above and yet fail to understand the meaning of the sentence because he has no understanding of the notion of 'winning' in general.

Truth conditions should not be confused with verification conditions. My analysis of 'S knows *p*' does not purport to give procedures for *finding out* whether a person (including oneself) knows a given proposition. No doubt, we sometimes do know that people know certain propositions, for we sometimes know that their beliefs are causally connected (in appropriate ways) with the facts believed. On the other hand, it may often be difficult or even impossible to find out whether this condition holds for a given proposition and a given person. For example, it may be difficult for me to find out whether I really do remember a certain fact that I seem to remember. The difficulties that exist for *finding out* whether someone knows a given proposition do not constitute difficulties for my analysis, however.

In the same vein it should be noted that I have made no attempt to answer skeptical problems. My analysis gives no answer to the skeptic who asks that I start from the content of my own experience and then prove that I know there is a material world, a past, etc. I do not take this to be one of the jobs of giving truth conditions for 'S knows that *p*.'

The analysis presented here flies in the face of a well-established tradition in epistemology, the view that epistemological questions are questions of logic or justification, not causal or genetic questions. This traditional view, however, must not go unquestioned. Indeed, I think my analysis shows that the question of whether someone knows a certain proposition is, in part, a causal question, although, of course, the question of what the correct analysis is of 'S knows that *p*' is not a causal question.

Chapter 5

Knowledge: undefeated justified true belief

Keith Lehrer and Thomas D. Paxson, Jr.

IF a man knows that a statement is true even though there is no other statement that justifies his belief, then his knowledge is basic. Basic knowledge is completely justified true belief. On the other hand, if a man knows that a statement is true because there is some other statement that justifies his belief, then his knowledge is nonbasic. Nonbasic knowledge requires something in addition to completely justified true belief; for, though a statement completely justifies a man in his belief, there may be some true statement that *defeats* his justification. So, we must add the condition that his justification is not defeated. Nonbasic knowledge is undefeated justified true belief. These analyses will be elaborated below and subsequently defended against various alternative analyses.[1]

I

We propose the following analysis of basic knowledge: S has basic knowledge that h if and only if (i) h is true, (ii) S believes that h, (iii) S is completely justified in believing that h, and (iv) the satisfaction of condition (iii) does not depend on any evidence p justifying S in believing that h. The third condition is used in such a way that it entails neither the second condition nor the first. A person can be completely justified in believing that h, even though, irrationally, he does not; and a person can be completely justified in believing that h, even though, unfortunately, he is mistaken.[2] Furthermore, the third condition does not entail that there is any statement

Keith Lehrer, Thomas D. Paxson, Jr., 'Knowledge: Undefeated Justified True Belief' in *The Journal of Philosophy* 66 (1969) pp. 225–37, reprinted with permission of Columbia University, New York.

1. This analysis of knowledge is a modification of an earlier analysis proposed by Keith Lehrer, 'Knowledge, Truth, and Evidence,' *Analysis* 35.5, 107 (April 1965): 168–75. It is intended to cope with objections to that article raised by Gilbert H. Harman in 'Lehrer on Knowledge,' *Journal of Philosophy*, 63, 9 (April 28, 1966): 241–7, and by Alvin Goldman, Brian Skyrms, and others. Criticisms of various alternative analyses of knowledge are given in Lehrer's earlier article, and the reader is referred to that article; such discussion will not be repeated here. The distinction between basic and nonbasic knowledge that is elaborated here was suggested by Arthur Danto in 'Freedom and Forebearance,' in *Freedom and Determinism* (New York: Random House, 1965), pp. 45–63.

2. Harman's criticism of Lehrer's earlier article rested on his interpreting Lehrer as saying that a person can be completely justified in believing something only if he does believe it. This interpretation leads to problems and is repudiated here.

or belief that justifies *S* in believing that *h*. The analysis, then, is in keeping with the characterization of basic knowledge given above. In basic knowledge, *S* is completely justified in believing that *h* even if it is not the case that there is any statement or belief that justifies his believing that *h*.

There are cases in which a person has some, perhaps mysterious, way of being right about matters of a certain sort with such consistency that philosophers and others have said that the person knows whereof he speaks. Consider, for example, the crystal-ball-gazing gypsy who is almost always right in his predictions of specific events. Peter Unger suggests a special case of this.[3] His gypsy is always right, but has no evidence to this effect and, in fact, believes that he is usually wrong. With respect to each specific prediction, however, the gypsy impulsively believes it to be true (as indeed it is). Whether or not the predictive beliefs of the ordinary gypsy and Unger's gypsy are cases of knowledge depends, we contend, on whether they are cases of basic knowledge. This in turn depends on whether the gypsies are completely justified in their beliefs. It is plausible to suggest that these are cases of knowledge, but this is only because it is also plausible to think that the gypsies in question have some way of being right that completely justifies their prognostications. We neither affirm nor deny that these are cases of knowledge, but maintain that, if they are cases of knowledge, then they are cases of *basic* knowledge.

It is consistent with our analysis of knowledge to admit that a man knows something even though no statement constitutes evidence that completely justifies his believing it. Philosophers have suggested that certain memory and perceptual beliefs are completely justified in the absence of such evidential statements. We choose to remain agnostic with respect to any claim of this sort, but such proposals are not excluded by our analysis.

II

Not all knowledge that *p* is basic knowledge that *p*, because sometimes justifying evidence is essential. Consider the following analysis of nonbasic knowledge: (i) *h* is true, (ii) *S* believes that *h*, and (iii*) *p* completely justifies *S* in believing that *h*. In this analysis, *p* is that (statement) which makes *S* completely justified in believing that *h*. Note that (iii*), like (iii), does not entail (ii) or (i).

This analysis of nonbasic knowledge is, of course, defective. As Edmund Gettier has shown, there are examples in which some false statement *p* entails and hence completely justifies *S* in believing that *h*, and such that, though *S* correctly believes that *h*, his being correct is mostly a matter of luck.[4] Consequently, *S* lacks knowledge, contrary to the above analysis. Other examples illustrate that the false statement which creates the difficulty need not *entail h*. Consider, for example, the case

---

3. 'Experience and Factual Knowledge,' *Journal of Philosophy*, 64, 5 (March 16, 1967): 152–73, esp. pp. 165–7; see also his 'An Analysis of Factual Knowledge,' *ibid.*, 65, 6 (March 21, 1968): 157–70, esp. pp. 163–4.
4. 'Is Justified True Belief Knowledge?' *Analysis* 33.6, 96 (June 1963): 121–3 [Ch. 2 in this volume].

of the pyromaniac described by Skyrms.[5] The pyromaniac has found that Sure-Fire matches have always ignited when struck. On the basis of this evidence, the pyromaniac is completely justified in believing that the match he now holds will ignite upon his striking it. However, unbeknownst to the pyromaniac, this match happens to contain impurities that raise its combustion temperature above that which can be produced by the friction. Imagine that a burst of Q-radiation ignites the match just as he strikes it. His belief that the match will ignite upon his striking it is true and completely justified by the evidence. But this is not a case of knowledge, because it is not the striking that will cause the match to ignite.

Roderick Chisholm has pointed out that justifications are defeasible.[6] In the examples referred to above, there is some true statement that would defeat any justification of S for believing that h. In the case of the pyromaniac, his justification is defeated by the true statement that striking the match will not cause it to ignite. This defeats his justification for believing that the match will ignite upon his striking it.

Thus we propose the following analysis of nonbasic knowledge: S has nonbasic knowledge that h if and only if (i) h is true, (ii) S believes that h, and (iii) there is some statement p that completely justifies S in believing that h and no other statement defeats this justification. The question we must now answer is—what does it mean to say that a statement defeats a justification? Adopting a suggestion of Chisholm's, we might try the following: when p completely justifies S in believing that h this justification is defeated by q if and only if (i) q is true, and (ii) the conjunction of p and q does not completely justify S in believing that h.[7] This definition is strong enough to rule out the example of the pyromaniac as a case of knowledge. The statement that the striking of a match will *not* cause it to ignite, which is true, is such that when it is conjoined to any statement that completely justifies the pyromaniac in believing that the match will ignite, the resultant conjunction will fail to so justify him in that belief. Given this definition of defeasibility, the analysis of nonbasic knowledge would require that a man who has nonbasic knowledge that h must have some justification for his belief that is not defeated by any true statement.

However, this requirement is somewhat unrealistic. To see that the definition of defeasibility under consideration makes the analysis of nonbasic knowledge excessively restrictive, we need only notice that there can be true statements that are misleading. Suppose I see a man walk into the library and remove a book from the library by concealing it beneath his coat. Since I am sure the man is Tom Grabit, whom I have often seen before when he attended my classes, I report that I know that Tom Grabit has removed the book. However, suppose further that Mrs. Grabit,

5. 'The Explication of "X knows that p",' *Journal of Philosophy*, 64, 12 (June 22, 1967): 373–89.

6. *Theory of Knowledge* (Englewood Cliffs, N.J.: Prentice-Hall, 1966), p. 48.

7. Chisholm, 'The Ethics of Requirement,' *American Philosophical Quarterly*, 1, 2 (April 1964): 147–53. This definition of defeasibility would make our analysis of nonbasic knowledge very similar to one Harman derives from Lehrer's analysis and also one proposed by Marshall Swain in 'The Analysis of Non-Basic Knowledge' (unpublished).

the mother of Tom, has averred that on the day in question Tom was not in the library, indeed, was thousands of miles away, and that Tom's identical twin brother, John Grabit, was in the library. Imagine, moreover, that I am entirely ignorant of the fact that Mrs. Grabit has said these things. The statement that she has said these things would defeat any justification I have for believing that Tom Grabit removed the book, according to our present definition of defeasibility. Thus, I could not be said to have nonbasic knowledge that Tom Grabit removed the book.

The preceding might seem acceptable until we finish the story by adding that Mrs. Grabit is a compulsive and pathological liar, that John Grabit is a fiction of her demented mind, and that Tom Grabit took the book as I believed. Once this is added, it should be apparent that I did know that Tom Grabit removed the book, and, since the knowledge must be nonbasic, I must have nonbasic knowledge of that fact. Consequently, the definition of defeasibility must be amended. The fact that Mrs. Grabit said what she did should not be allowed to defeat any justification I have for believing that Tom Grabit removed the book, because I neither entertained any beliefs concerning Mrs. Grabit nor would I have been justified in doing so. More specifically, my justification does not depend on my being completely justified in believing that Mrs. Grabit did *not* say the things in question.

To understand how the definition of defeasibility must be amended to deal with the preceding example, let us consider an example from the literature in which a justification deserves to be defeated. Suppose that I have excellent evidence that completely justifies my believing that a student in my class, Mr. Nogot, owns a Ford, the evidence consisting in my having seen him driving it, hearing him say he owns it, and so forth. Since Mr. Nogot is a student in my class who owns a Ford, someone in my class owns a Ford, and, consequently, I am completely justified in believing that someone in my class owns a Ford. Imagine that, contrary to the evidence, Mr. Nogot does not own a Ford, that I have been deceived, but that unknown to me Mr. Havit, who is also in my class, does own a Ford. Though I have a completely justified true belief, I do not know that someone in my class owns a Ford. The reason is that my sole justification for believing that someone in my class does own a Ford is and should be defeated by the true statement that Mr. Nogot does not own a Ford.

In the case of Tom Grabit, the true statement that Mrs. Grabit said Tom was not in the library and so forth, should not be allowed to defeat my justification for believing that Tom removed the book, whereas in the case of Mr. Nogot, the true statement that Mr. Nogot does not own a Ford, should defeat my justification for believing that someone in my class owns a Ford. Why should one true statement but not the other be allowed to defeat my justification? The answer is that in one case my justification depends on my being completely justified in believing the true statement to be false while in the other it does not. My justification for believing that Tom removed the book does not depend on my being completely justified in believing it to be false that Mrs. Grabit said Tom was not in the library and so forth. But my justification for believing that someone in my class owns a Ford does depend on my being completely justified in believing it to be false that Mr. Nogot does not own a Ford. Thus, a defeating statement must be one which, though true, is such that the subject is completely justified in believing it to be false.[8]

The following definition of defeasibility incorporates this proposal: when p completely justifies S in believing that h, this justification is defeated by q if and only if (i) q is true, (ii) S is completely justified in believing q to be false, and (iii) the conjunction of p and q does not completely justify S in believing that h.

This definition of defeasibility, though basically correct, requires one last modification to meet a technical problem. Suppose that there is some statement h of which S has nonbasic knowledge. Let us again consider the example in which I know that Tom Grabit removed the book. Now imagine that there is some true statement which is completely irrelevant to this knowledge and which I happen to be completely justified in believing to be false, for example, the statement that I was born in St. Paul. Since I am completely justified in believing it to be false that I was born in St. Paul, I am also completely justified in believing to be false the conjunctive statement that I was born in St. Paul and that q, whatever q is, because I am completely justified in believing any conjunction to be false if I am completely justified in believing a conjunct of it to be false. Therefore, I am completely justified in believing to be false the conjunctive statement that I was born in St. Paul and Mrs. Grabit said that Tom Grabit was not in the library and so forth. Moreover, this conjunctive statement is true, and is such that, when it is conjoined in turn to any evidential statement that justifies me in believing that Tom Grabit removed the book, the resultant extended conjunction will not completely justify me in believing that Tom Grabit removed the book. Hence, any such justification will be defeated.[9] Once again, it turns out that I do not have nonbasic knowledge of the fact that Tom is the culprit.

In a logical nut, the problem is that the current definition of defeasibility reduces to the preceding one. Suppose there is a true statement q such that, for any p that completely justifies S in believing h, the conjunction of p and q does not completely justify me in believing that h. Moreover, suppose that I am not completely justified in believing q to be false, so that, given our current definition of defeasibility, q does not count as defeating. Nevertheless, if there is any true statement r, irrelevant to both p and q, which I am completely justified in believing to be false, then we can indirectly use q to defeat my justification for believing h. For I shall be completely justified in believing the conjunction of r and q to be false, though in fact it is true, because I am completely justified in believing r to be false. If the conjunction of q and p does not completely justify me in believing that h, then, given the irrelevance of r, neither would the conjunction of r, q and p justify me in believing that h. Hence, my justifications for believing h would be defeated by the conjunction r and

---

8. In Skyrms' example of the pyromaniac cited earlier, the defeating statement is not one which the pyromaniac need believe; Skyrms suggests that the pyromaniac neither believes nor disbelieves that striking the match will cause it to ignite. Nevertheless, the pyromaniac would be completely justified in believing that striking the Sure-Fire match will cause it to ignite. Hence the statement that striking the match will *not* cause it to light is defeating.

9. A similar objection to Lehrer's earlier analysis is raised by Harman, p. 243.

q on the current definition of defeasibility as surely as they were by *q* alone on the preceding definition.

The defect is not difficult to repair. Though *S* is completely justified in believing the conjunction of *r* and *q* to be false, one consequence of the conjunction, *q*, undermines my justification but is not something I am completely justified in believing to be false, while another consequence, *r*, is one that I am completely justified in believing to be false but is irrelevant to my justification. To return to our example, I am completely justified in believing to be false the conjunctive statement that I was born in St. Paul and that Mrs. Grabit said that Tom was not in the library and so forth. One consequence of this conjunction, that Mrs. Grabit said that Tom was not in the library and so forth, undermines my justification but is not something I am completely justified in believing to be false, while the other consequence, that I was born in St. Paul, is something I am completely justified in believing to be false but is irrelevant to my justification. The needed restriction is that those consequences of a defeating statement which undermine a justification must themselves be statements that the subject is completely justified in believing to be false.

We propose the following definition of defeasibility: if *p* completely justifies *S* in believing that *h*, then this justification is defeated by *q* if and only if (i) *q* is true, (ii) the conjunction of *p* and *q* does not completely justify *S* in believing that *h*, (iii) *S* is completely justified in believing *q* to be false, and (iv) if *c* is a logical consequence of *q* such that the conjunction of *c* and *p* does not completely justify *S* in believing that *h*, then *S* is completely justified in believing *c* to be false.

With this definition of defeasibility, we complete our analysis of nonbasic knowledge. We have defined nonbasic knowledge as true belief for which some statement provides a complete and undefeated justification. We previously defined basic knowledge as true belief for which there was complete justification that did not depend on any justifying statement. We define as knowledge anything that is either basic or nonbasic knowledge. Thus, *S* knows that *h* if and only if *S* has either basic or nonbasic knowledge that *h*. Having completed our analysis, we shall compare it with other goods in the epistemic marketplace to demonstrate the superiority of our ware.

III

The analysis offered above resembles two recent analyses formulated by Brian Skyrms and R. M. Chisholm. Both philosophers distinguish between basic and nonbasic knowledge, and both analyze knowledge in terms of justification. Moreover, these analyses are sufficiently restrictive so as to avoid yielding the result that a person has nonbasic knowledge when his justification is defeated by some false statement. However, we shall argue that both of these analyses are excessively restrictive and consequently lead to skeptical conclusions that are unwarranted.

Skyrms says that a man has nonbasic knowledge that *p* if and only if he has either derivative or nonderivative knowledge that *p*. He analyzes the latter two kinds of knowledge as follows:

Derivative Knowledge: X has derivative knowledge that p if and only if there is a statement 'e' such that:

(i) X knows that e

(ii) X knows that 'e' entails 'p'

(iii) X believes that p, on the basis of the knowledge referred to in (i) and (ii)

Nonderivative Knowledge: X has nonderivative knowledge that p if and only if there is a statement 'e' such that:

(i) X knows that e

(ii) X knows that 'e' is good evidence for 'p'

(iii) X believes that p on the basis of the knowledge referred to in (i) and (ii)

(iv) 'p' is true

(v) There is no statement 'q' (other than 'p') such that:

    (a) X knows that 'e' is good evidence of 'q'

    (b) X knows that 'q' entails 'p'

    (c) X believes that 'p' on the basis of the knowledge referred to in (a) and (b)

    (*op cit.*, 381)

Later in his paper, Skyrms points out a defect in his analysis of nonderivative knowledge, namely, that the words, 'There is a statement 'e' such that . . .' must be replaced by some such expression as 'There is some statement 'e' consisting of the total evidence of X relevant to p such that . . .' or else the analysis will lead to trouble (387).

We shall now show why this analysis is unsatisfactory. According to Skyrms, a man who knows that a disjunction is true without knowing any specific disjunct to be true, has nonderivative knowledge of the disjunction (380). Indeed, his analysis of nonderivative knowledge is simply a generalization of his analysis of knowledge with respect to such disjunctions. But his analysis is overrestrictive in the case of our knowledge of disjunctions. Suppose I know that a business acquaintance of mine, Mr. Romeo, arrived in Rochester from Atlanta on either one of two flights, either AA 107 or AA 204. My evidence is that these are the only two flights into Rochester from Atlanta, that Mr. Romeo telephoned earlier from Atlanta to say he would be arriving on one of these two flights, that he is now in Rochester, and that no other flight to Rochester or nearby would enable Mr. Romeo to be in Rochester at the present time. On the basis of this evidence, I may on Skyrms' analysis be said to have nonderivative knowledge that Mr. Romeo arrived on either AA 107 or AA 204. So far so good.

However, suppose that we add to my evidence that, when I meet Mr. Romeo at the airport shortly after the arrival of AA 204 (the later flight), he tells me that he just arrived on AA 204. By Skyms' analysis I now *lack* nonderivative knowledge that Mr. Romeo arrived on either AA 107 or AA 204. The reason is that condition (v) of his analysis of nonderivative knowledge is no longer satisfied with respect to that disjunction. I now have good evidence that Mr. Romeo arrived on AA 204, and I believe that disjunction on the basis of my knowledge that this evidence is good evidence for the statement 'Mr. Romeo arrived on AA 204' and this statement entails 'Mr. Romeo arrived on either AA 107 or AA 204.' Thus, there is a statement q that satisfies condition (a), (b), and (c) under (v) where 'p' is the disjunction.

The consequence that I now lack nonderivative knowledge that Mr. Romeo arrived on either AA 107 or AA 204 would not be fatal if it could be argued that I have derivative knowledge of that disjunction because I know that Mr. Romeo arrived on AA 204. But there is an unmentioned twist of romance in our tale. In fact, Mr. Romeo arrived on the earlier flight, AA 107, and, having entertained his secret love, deceitfully told me he arrived on the later flight. Thus, I do not know that Mr. Romeo arrived on AA 204, because he did not so arrive. By Skyrms' analyses, I have neither derivative nor nonderivative knowledge that Mr. Romeo arrived on either AA 107 or AA 204, and, therefore, I lack nonbasic knowledge of that disjunction. So, as Skyrms would have it, I do not know that Mr. Romeo arrived on either of those flights. However, although there is much of interest that I do not know in this case, I surely do know, on the basis of my original evidence which I may yet brandish with epistemic righteousness, that Mr. Romeo must have arrived on either AA 107 or AA 204. He did so arrive, and my evidence completely justifies me in believing that he did, regardless of the fact that Mr. Romeo spoke with a crooked tongue. Since I do have knowledge of the disjunction, Skyrms' analyses must be rejected.

Chisholm's analysis of knowledge is very similar to ours except for the condition intended to deal with situations in which, though a man has completely justified true belief, his justification is undermined by some false statement. In the sort of cases we have been considering, Chisholm's analysis requires, among other conditions, that if a person knows that h, then there is a proposition p such that p justifies h but p does not justify any false statement.[10] However, it seems reasonable to suppose that every statement, whatever epistemic virtues it might have, completely justifies at least one false statement. This supposition is supported by the fact that justification in Chisholm's system need not be deductive justification. Any nondeductive justification may fail to be truth-preserving; that is, the conclusion may be false though the premise be true. Thus, though our analysis is in a number of ways indebted to Chisholm's proposals, the foregoing argument is our reason for concluding that Chisholm's analysis would lead to some form of skepticism, that is, to the conclusion that people do not know some things they would generally and reasonably be said to know.

IV

Having indicated our reasons for rejecting those analyses which are most similar to our own, we shall now turn to some analyses that differ from ours in more fundamental ways. Peter Unger has analyzed knowledge as follows: For any sentential value of p, (at a time t) a man knows that p if and only if (at t) it is not at all accidental that the man is right about its being the case that p.[11] Unger nowhere rules out the possibility that there are some cases in which it is not at all accidental

10. Chisholm; see footnote at end of chap. 1, *Theory of Knowledge*, p. 23.
11. 'An Analysis of Factual Knowledge,' p. 158.

that a man is right simply because he has justification for believing what he does. So it could be that any case that satisfies our conditions for knowledge would satisfy his as well. But there are cases that satisfy his analysis though they fail to satisfy ours.

Let us consider an example. A hologram, or laser photograph, when illuminated by laser light looks three-dimensional even with respect to parallax effects when the viewer shifts his position. Imagine that holography has been so perfected that a laser-illuminated hologram of an object can, under certain observational conditions, be indistinguishable from the real thing.[12] More particularly, suppose that a man, Mr. Promoter, seeking to demonstrate the remarkable properties of laser photography, constructs a boxlike device which contains a vase, a laser photograph of the vase, and a laser source by which the photograph may be illuminated. The device is so constructed that Mr. Promoter by turning a knob may show a viewer the vase or the illuminated laser photograph of the vase, and the visual experience of the viewer when he sees the vase will be indistinguishable from his visual experience when confronted with the photograph. Of course, the very purpose of constructing the device is to arrange things so that people will be completely deceived by the photograph. Now suppose I walk up to the viewer, innocent as the fool who stones the water to destroy his twin, and peer in at the illuminated photograph. Blissfully ignorant of the technical finesse being used to dupe me, I take what I see to be a vase. I believe that the box contains a vase. I am right, there is a vase in the box, and it is not at all accidental that I am right. For Mr. Promoter has constructed the device in such a way that, though I do not see the vase, I will believe quite correctly that there is one there. On Unger's analysis, I know that there is a vase in the box when I see the illuminated laser photograph.

However, it is perfectly apparent that I know nothing of the sort. Any justification I have for believing that there is a vase in the box is defeated by the fact that I do not see a vase in the box but merely a photograph of one. On our analysis it would follow that I do *not* know there is a vase in the box, and that result is the correct one.

Unger might object that it is to some extent accidental that I am right in thinking there is a vase in the box, because I might have had the same visual experiences even if there had been no vase in the box. Hence his analysis yields the same result as ours in this case. But this objection, if taken seriously, would lead us to reject Unger as a skeptic. To see why, imagine that, contrary to the preceding example, Mr. Promoter turns off his device for the day, leaving the knob set so that when I enter the room the vase is before my eyes. I could reach out and touch it if I wished, but good manners restrain me. Nevertheless, there is nothing between me and the vase; I see it and know that it is before my eyes in just the way that I see and know that countless other objects sit untouched before me. However, the statement—I might have had the same visual experience even if there had been no vase in the box—is true in this case as in the former one where I was deceived by the photograph. If this

12. Cf. Alvin Goldman, 'A Causal Theory of Knowing,' *Journal of Philosophy*, 64, 12 (June 22, 1967): 357–72; p. 359 [in this volume p. 19n].

truth shows that my being right in the former case was to some extent accidental, then it would also show that my being right in the present case was to some extent accidental. Therefore, either Unger must agree that the truth of this statement fails to show that my being right in the former case was accidental, in which case his analysis would yield the result that I know when in fact I am ignorant; or he must maintain that its truth shows that my being right in the present case was accidental, in which case his analysis yields the result that I am ignorant when in fact I know. Thus, his analysis is unsatisfactory.

Finally, we wish to consider another kind of theory suggested by Alvin Goldman. His analysis is as follows: S knows that p if and only if the fact that p is causally connected in an 'appropriate' way with S's believing that p (*op cit.*, 369 [in this volume p. 28]). We wish to assert, in opposition to Goldman, that the causal etiology of belief may be utterly irrelevant to the question of what a man knows. Consider yet a third round between Mr. Promoter and me. This time I imagine that I enter as in the first example, where the photograph is illuminated, and become completely and thoroughly convinced that there is a vase in the box. Now imagine that Mr. Promoter, amused with his easy success, tells me that I am quite right in thinking there is a vase in the box, but he then goes on to show me how the device is constructed, removing parts and lecturing about lasers from smirk-twisted lips. With respect to the etiology of my belief that there was a vase in the box, it is possible that my belief was fixed from the time I first looked at the photograph and, moreover, was so firmly and unequivocally fixed that the subsequent revelations neither altered nor reinforced it. This belief is to be *causally explained* by my mistakenly believing that I was seeing a vase when I first entered the room and by the facts about the illuminated laser photograph that caused that erroneous belief. There is no 'appropriate' causal connection between the fact that there is a vase in the box and my belief that p; so, according to Goldman's analysis, I did not know that there was a vase in the box.

There is something to recommend this result. When I first looked into the device, I did not see the vase, and, consequently, I did not *then* know that there was a vase in the box then. However, after Mr. Promoter's revelations, when I do really see the vase, I do then know that there is a vase in the box. This is not due to any change in the causal etiology of my belief that there is a vase in the box. So, according to Goldman, I still do not know. But Goldman is wrong. I do subsequently know that there is a vase in the box, not because of any change in the causal etiology of the belief, but because I then have some justification for the belief that I formerly lacked. The justification consists of what I learned from Mr. Promoter's demonstration about the box and its contents. In short, there is no reason to suppose that all new evidence that a man could appeal to in order to justify a belief changes the causal etiology of that belief. And such evidence may make the difference between true belief and knowledge.

V

We have contended that our analysis of knowledge in terms of undefeated justified true belief has various advantages over competing analyses. Unlike some of our competitors, we do not presuppose any one theory of justification rather than another. Since current theories of justification are highly controversial, we have employed a notion of justification that is consistent with diverse theories on this subject. By so doing, we hope to have presented a satisfactory analysis of knowledge without waiting for the development of an equally satisfactory theory of justification.

Moreover, the problems that confront a theory of justification can be formulated in terms of the locutions we have introduced in our analysis. For example, Chisholm has maintained that some statements are self-justifying, and, in our terminology this amounts to answering affirmatively the question whether it is ever the case that some statement h completely justifies a person in believing that h.[13] Some philosophers have affirmed that all justification must be either inductive or deductive; others have denied this and affirmed that there are other forms of justification as well. In our terminology, this question may be formulated as the question whether, when a statement p completely justifies a person in believing h, the justified statement must be deduced or induced from the justifying statement or whether there are other alternatives. Finally, philosophers have disagreed about the kind of statement that may justify a man in believing something: whether those statements must be known, or whether they need not be, whether they must include all of a man's evidence, or whether they might exclude some of his evidence, and so forth. We have avoided dogmatically assuming one or the other of these alternatives.

Nevertheless, it may be found that only one theory of justification is suitable to supplement our analysis. Our claim is that, on any satisfactory theory of justification, some knowledge must be undefeated completely justified true belief, and the rest is basic.

13. R. M. Chisholm and others, *Philosophy* (Englewood Cliffs, N.J.: Prentice-Hall, 1964), pp. 263–77.

Chapter 6

Conclusive reasons*

Fred Dretske

CONCLUSIVE reasons have a modal as well as an epistemic character. In having conclusive reasons to believe that P is the case one's epistemic credentials are such as to eliminate the possibility of mistake. This, at least, is how I propose to understand them for the remainder of this paper. Letting the symbol '$\diamondsuit$' represent the appropriate modality (a yet to be clarified sense of *possibility*), I shall say, then, that R is a conclusive reason for P if and only if, given R, $\sim \diamondsuit \sim P$ (or, alternatively, $\sim \diamondsuit (R . \sim P)$). This interpretation allows us to say of any subject, S, who believes that P and who has conclusive reasons for believing that P, that, given these reasons, he *could not be wrong* about P or, given these reasons, *it is false that he might be mistaken* about P.

Suppose, then, that

(1) S knows that P and he knows this on the basis (simply) of R entails
(2) R would not be the case unless P were the case.[1]

The latter formula expresses a connection between R and P which is strong enough, I submit, to permit us to say that if (2) is true, then R is a conclusive reason for P. For if (2) is true, we are entitled, not only to deny that, given R, not-P *is* the case, but also that, given R, not-*P might* be the case. That is to say, (2) eliminates R and not-P as a possible (joint) state of affairs and, when we are *given* R, it eliminates not-P as a possible state of affairs. This is so because (2) entails the falsity of,

(3) Although R is the case P might not be the case.

If we express (3) as 'Given R, $\diamondsuit \sim P$', then (2) entails that it is false that, given R, $\diamondsuit \sim P$ which is equivalent to, given R, $\sim \diamondsuit \sim P$; and this is precisely the required feature of conclusive reasons given above. Hence, when (2) is true, R is a conclusive reason for P.

What follows is an amplification of the above sketch—hence, an argument for the view that in those cases where knowledge that P rests on evidence, grounds, or

Fred Dretske, 'Conclusive Reasons' in *The Australasian Journal of Philosophy* 49 (1971) pp. 1–22, reprinted by permission of the author.

* An early version of this paper was read to the Philosophy Department at The University or Illinois, Chicago Circle. More recently it was read at The University of North Carolina's Colloquium in Philosophy with Professor Robert Sleigh commenting.

1. I shall be using 'R' and 'P' to replace a variety of related grammatical units. Depending on the sentential context, they sometimes serve as noun phrases, sometimes as full indicative sentences, sometimes for appropriate transformations of the indicative.

reasons, when the question 'How does S know?' can sensibly be asked and answered, the evidence, grounds, or reasons must be conclusive. Anything short of conclusive reasons, though it may provide one with justified true beliefs, fails to give the kind of support requisite to knowledge. I shall also urge that the possession of conclusive reasons to believe, properly qualified, is also a sufficient condition for knowledge.

1. Knowing P on the basis of R: the connection between (1) and (2).

Suppose S, in order to assure himself that his child's temperature is normal (no fever), places a thermometer in the child's mouth, extracts it after several minutes, and observes a reading of 98.6°F. In remarking to the doctor that his child's temperature is normal S is asked how he knows. S responds, naturally enough, by saying, 'I just took his temperature'. Let us assume, then, that we have an instantiation of (1):

> (1a) S knows that his child's temperature is normal and he knows this on the basis of the (normal) reading on the thermometer (which he has just placed in the child's mouth, etc.).

Can one consistently affirm (1a) and deny the corresponding instantiation of (2)?

> (2a) The thermometer would not have read 98.6° unless the child's temperature was normal.

If it is not already obvious that one cannot consistently affirm (1a) and deny (2a), I think it can be made obvious by considering the kind of thing which would show (2a) to be false. For example, if Charles, familiar with the particular thermometer in question, should say, 'Oh, I know that thermometer; it is fairly accurate for temperatures below 98° but it sticks at 98.6 for almost any higher temperature,' we have been given solid grounds for rejecting (2a). Simultaneously, however, we have been given solid grounds for rejecting (1a). If it is *that* kind of thermometer, then if S's only basis for thinking his child's temperature normal is a 98.6 reading on it, then he does not *know* that his child's temperature is normal. It *might* be normal, of course, but if S knows that it is, he must have more to go on than the reading on this (defective) thermometer.

Other attempts to show (2a) false have the same effect; they immediately undermine R (the reading on the thermometer) as an adequate basis for someone's knowing that the child's temperature is normal (P). For in rejecting (2a) we reject the thermometer as a reliable device for discovering whether a person's temperature is normal, and knowledge is not acquired by relying on what is unreliable in precisely those respects in which we rely on it.

We frequently purport to know things on the basis of testimony. James has a large stamp collection and, after giving a detailed description of it, invites S to his home to see it. S declines, but he later refers to James' stamp collection in conversation. It is easy enough to imagine circumstances in which it would be natural for someone to ask S how he knew, what reasons he had for thinking, that James had such a collection. And it is just as easy to imagine S, in response to such a query, referring to his conversation with James. Let us assume, then, that

> (1b) S knows that James has a stamp collection and he knows this on the basis of James' description (and invitation)

is true. I am not now concerned to argue that one can know something of this sort in this way; the question is, rather, whether (2b) must be true *if* (1b) is true.

> (2b) James would not have said he had a stamp collection, described it in such detail, and issued an invitation unless he had a stamp collection.

If James is the sort of fellow about which (2b) cannot be truly asserted, then he is not the sort of fellow who can be trusted on such matters as this. If James is the sort of fellow who sometimes says such things as a joke, who would (or might) concoct such elaborate stories for his own amusement (or whatever), who would (or might) whimsically issue an invitation of this sort under totally false pretexts, then, despite the fact that he is (by hypothesis) telling the truth on this occasion, his testimony is hardly the sort on which one can rest a claim to know. In denying (2b) one is conceding that James would, or might, have said what he did without possessing a stamp collection, and in the light of this concession one cannot go on to insist that, nonetheless, S *knows* he has a stamp collection on the basis, simply, of what James said.

In a recent article Gilbert Harman contrasts two cases, *the lottery case* and *the testimony case*.[2] Although S, say, has only one among thousands of tickets in a lottery and, hence, has an extremely slender chance of winning, we naturally reject the idea that S could know that he was going to lose on the basis of a correct probability estimate (well over 99.9%) of his losing. Even if S correctly predicts that he is going to lose, we would deny that he knew he was going to lose if the *only* basis he had for this belief was the fact that his chances of winning were so slight.[3] Harman compares this case with the situation in which we often seem prepared to say that S knows that P when he is told that P is the case by some other person (testimony case). Although probability estimates are not altogether appropriate here, we do know that people sometimes lie, sometimes they are honestly mistaken, and so on. There always seems to be a chance that what a person tells us is not the case however sincere or credible he may appear, and the order of magnitude of this chance seems to be comparable to the chance we might win in some appropriate lottery situation. Why, then, are we prepared to say that we know in the one case but

---

2. 'Knowledge, Inference, and Explanation', in *American Philosophical Quarterly*, July, 1968.

3. Of course S may have said 'I know I am going to lose' and he may say now, after he has lost, 'I knew I was going to lose', but these expressions are normally accepted without epistemological quibbling because they are taken as little more than expressions of resignation or despair. With this use of the verb 'to know', one can know one is going to lose and *still* spend a dollar for a ticket and a chance at the prize—a fact about human beings which is puzzling if they believe they know (in any epistemologically relevant sense) that they are going to lose.

not in the other? Harman has some revealing remarks to make about these cases, but I mention them only to bring out their relevance to the present discussion. For I think this contrast strengthens the view that (2) is normally accepted as a necessary consequence of (1), that when we are unwilling to endorse the corresponding instantiation of (2) we are unwilling to talk of anyone knowing that P is the case on the basis of the evidence expressed by R. In many testimony situations we are, I believe, willing to affirm (2): the person would not have said it unless it was so. In the lottery case, however, the connection between R and P expressed by this subjunctive conditional fails to be realized, and it fails no matter how great the probabilities become. Adjusting the wording of (2) to suit the example in question[4] we have

(2c) If S were going to win the lottery, his chances of winning would not be 1/m (m being the number of tickets sold).

Whatever (finite) value we give to 'm', we know this is false since someone whose chances of winning are 1/m *will* win, and since there is nothing special about S which would require him to have a better chance of winning than anyone else in order to win, we reject (2c) as false. Hence, we reject the idea that S can know he is going to lose on the basis of the fact that his chances of losing are $(m - 1)/m$.

Alvin Goldman, in developing a causal account of knowledge, constructs a situation in which S is said to know that a nearby mountain (I will call it M) erupted many years ago. He knows this on the basis of the presence of solidified lava throughout the countryside surrounding the mountain.[5] According to Goldman, a necessary condition for S's knowing that M erupted many years ago on the basis of the present existence and distribution of the lava is that there be a causal connection between the eruption of the mountain and the present existence and distribution of the lava. I do not wish to dispute this claim at the moment since the view I am advancing is even stronger: *viz.* that a necessary condition for S to know that M erupted on this basis is that

(2d) The lava would not be here, and distributed in this manner, unless M erupted

is true. (2d) is a stronger claim than that the eruption of M is causally connected

---

4. The wording of (2) will sometimes have to be adjusted to suit the particular instantiation in question. The chief factors determining this adjustment are the relative temporal locations of R, P, and the time of utterance and also the causal connections, if any, which are believed to hold between R and P. The particular wording I have given (2) is most appropriate when P is some state of affairs antecedent to (or contemporaneous with) both R and the time of utterance. This, of course, is the result of the fact that (2) is most often used when P is some state of affairs causally responsible for the present condition R. When P is a future state we might express (2) as: R would not be the case unless P were going to happen. For example, he would not have registered unless he were going to vote. I do not wish to preclude the possibility of knowing that something *will* occur on the basis of present evidence by restricting the wording of (2). The difficulty, of course, is that when P is some future state, the subjunctive relating it to R generally becomes somewhat questionable. We prefer to say, in our more cautious moods, that if he were not *planning* to vote, he would not have registered (acknowledging, thereby, the fact that contingencies may interfere with the execution of his plans). But in the same cautious moods we prefer to say, not that we know he is going to vote (because he registered), but that we know he plans or intends to vote.

5. 'A Causal Theory of Knowing', *Journal of Philosophy*, June 22, 1967, p. 361 [in this volume p. 21].

with the present existence and distribution of the lava. (2d) requires, in addition, that M's eruption be necessary for the present state of affairs. To illustrate, consider the following embellishment on Goldman's example. Not far from M is another mountain, N. The geology of the area is such that at the point in time at which M erupted something, so to speak, was bound to give; if M had not erupted, N would have. Furthermore, the location of N is such that if it, rather than M, had erupted, the present distribution of lava would have been, in all respects relevant to S's taking it as a reason for believing M erupted, the same. In such circumstances Goldman's necessary condition is satisfied, but mine is not. (2d) is false; it is false that the lava would not be here, and distributed in this fashion, unless M had erupted. For if, contrary to hypothesis, M had not erupted, N would have; leaving the very same (relevant) traces.

In such circumstances I do not think we could say that S knew that M erupted on the basis of the present existence and distribution of lava. For, by hypothesis, *this* state of affairs would have obtained whether M erupted or not and, hence, there is nothing about this state of affairs which favours one hypothesis (M erupted) over a competing hypothesis (N erupted). S is still correct in supposing that M did erupt, still correct in supposing that it was M's eruption which is causally responsible for the present existence and distribution of lava, but he does not know it was M that erupted—not unless he has some additional grounds which preclude N. If he has such additional grounds, call them Q, then we can say that he knows that M erupted and he knows this on the basis of R *and* Q. In this case, however, the corresponding instantiation of (2) is also satisfied: R *and* Q would not be the case unless M erupted. As things stand, the most that S could know, on the basis simply of the present existence and distribution of lava, is that *either M or N erupted.* (2) permits us to say this much, and no more, about what can be known on the basis of lava flow.

The case becomes even clearer if we exploit another of Harman's examples.[6] Harold has a ticket in a lottery. The odds against his winning are 10,000 to 1. The prize, call it an X, is something that Harold does not now have nor could he reasonably expect to obtain one by means other than winning the lottery. Enter a philanthropic gentleman, Rockaford, who decides to give Harold an X if (as seems likely) he should fail to win one in the lottery. Things go as one would expect; Harold holds a losing ticket. Rockaford keeps his word and gives Harold an X. S, familiar with the above circumstances but unaware of whether Harold won or lost in the lottery, finds Harold with his newly acquired X. S infers that Harold received his X from Rockaford. He concludes this because he knows that the only other way Harold might have acquired an X is by winning the lottery and the odds against that happening are enormous. The following conditions are satisfied: (a) Harold received his X from Rockaford; (b) S believes that Harold received his X from Rockaford; (c) S is warranted in believing this since the chances of his having received it in any other way are negligible; (d) Rockaford's generous gift of an X to Harold is the (causal?) explanation of Harold's present possession of an X; and,

6. In 'Knowledge, Inference, and Explanation', pp. 168–9. I have adapted the example somewhat.

finally (e) S correctly reconstructs (to use Goldman's language) the causal chain of events which brought about Harold's possession of an X. Yet, why does it seem clear (at least to myself—and apparently to Harman) and S does *not* know that Rockaford gave Harold his X. Because

(2e) Harold would not have an X unless Rockaford gave him one is plainly false.[7] If Rockaford had not given him an X, it would have been because Harold already possessed one as a winner in the lottery. Hence, Harold would possess an X even if Rockaford had not given him one. It is not true that R would not be the case *unless* P; hence, not true that S knows that P on the basis of R.[8]

(2), therefore, expresses something stronger than a causal relationship between R and P. It should be pointed out, however, that it expresses something which is, in certain important respects, weaker than a universal association between states or conditions similar to R and states or conditions similar to P. When 'R' and 'P' are expressions which stand for particular conditions or states of affairs, as will often be the case when we know one thing on the basis of something else, (2) expresses a connection between more *determinate* states of affairs than those described by talking about states similar to R and P. If someone remarks, mid-way through a poker hand, that if his neighbour had not folded (dropped from the game) he (the speaker) would have been dealt a royal flush, he is obviously not maintaining that *whenever* his neighbour remains in the game, he (the speaker) is rewarded with a royal flush. Rather, he is talking about *this* hand (already holding four cards to the royal flush), *this particular* distribution of cards in the remainder of the deck, *this particular* seating arrangement, and so on. He is not saying that his neighbour's remaining in the game is, quite generally, sufficient for his receipt of a royal flush. Rather, he is saying that *in the particular circumstances which in fact prevailed on this occasion*, circumstances which include such things as card distribution, arrangement of players, etc., an occurrence of the first sort (neighbour remains in game) will invariably be followed by one of the second sort (his receipt of a royal flush). One cannot falsify his claim by showing that he would not have received a royal flush, despite his neighbour's remaining in the game, if the card distribution in the deck had been different from what it in fact was. For his claim was a claim about the inevitable sequence of events *with that distribution of cards.*

Statements such as (2), then, even when R and P are expressions for particular states of affairs, express a general uniformity, but this general uniformity is not that whenever a state similar to R is the case, then a state similar to P will also be (or

---

7. There is a way of reading (2e) which makes it sound true—*viz.* if we illicitly smuggle in the fact that Harold *has lost* the lottery. That is, (2e') 'Harold, having lost the lottery, would not have an X unless Rockaford had given him one', is true. But this version of (2) makes R, the reason S has for believing Rockaford gave him an X, not only Harold's possession of an X but also *his having lost the lottery*. This, by hypothesis, is not part of S's reason; hence, not properly included in (2e). (2e) must be read in something like the following fashion: Harold would not have an X, whatever the outcome of the lottery, unless Rockaford had given him one. With this reading it is clearly false.

8. It is difficult to say whether this is a counter-example to Goldman's analysis. I think it satisfies all the conditions he catalogues as sufficient for knowledge, but this depends on how strictly Goldman intends the condition that S must be warranted in inferring that P is the case from R.

have been) the case. The uniformity in question concerns the relationship between states similar to R and P *under a fixed set of circumstances*. Whenever (a state such as) R *in circumstances* C then (a state such as) P where the circumstances C are defined in terms of those circumstances which actually prevail on the occasion of R and P. But does C include *all* the circumstances that prevail on the occasion in question or only *some* of these? Clearly not all the circumstances since this would trivialize every subjunctive conditional of this sort. Even if we restrict C to only those circumstances logically independent of R and P we still obtain a trivialization. For, to use Goldman's mountain example (as embellished), C would still include the fact that N did not erupt (since this is logically independent of both R and P), and this is obviously one of the circumstances *not* held fixed when we say that the lava would not be here unless M erupted. For in asserting his subjunctive we mean to be asserting something which would be *false* in the situation described (N would have erupted if M had not) whereas if we hold this circumstance (N did not erupt) fixed, the uniformity between the presence of lava and M's eruption would *hold*.

I think that our examples, not to mention an extensive literature on the subject,[9] point the way to a proper interpretation of C. The circumstances which are assumed constant, which are tacitly held fixed, in conditionals such as (2), are those circumstances prevailing on the occasion in question (the occasion on and between which the particular states R and P obtain) which are logically and causally independent of the state of affairs expressed by P.[10] When we have a statement in the subjunctive which (unlike (2)) is counterfactual (the antecedent gives expression to a state of affairs which does or did not obtain), then C includes those circumstances prevailing on the occasion which are logically and causally independent of the state of affairs (or lack of such state) expressed by the *antecedent* of the conditional. In our poker game, for example, we can say that S's statement (I would have got a royal flush if my neighbour had stayed in the game) *fixes* that set of circumstances which are logically and causally independent of his neighbour's staying in the game (i.e. the antecedent since the statement is counterfactual). Hence, if there is another

9. I am not proposing a solution to the problem to which Nelson Goodman (*Fact, Fiction and Forecast*, Chapter 1), Roderick Chisholm ('The Contrary-to-Fact Conditional,' *Mind* 55, 1946) and others addressed themselves in trying to specify the 'relevant conditions' associated with counter-factuals. I shall use the notion of 'causality' in my treatment, a device which both Goodman and Chisholm would regard as question-begging. I am not, however, attempting to offer an extensional-ist analysis of the subjunctive conditional; I am merely trying to get clear in what way such conditionals are stronger than the statement of a causal relationship between R and P and yet (in one sense) weaker than a statement of the universal association between states similar to R and P.

10. This characterization of the circumstances 'C' has interesting and, I believe, significant repercus-sions for subjunctives having the form of (2) in which R expresses some present (or past) state of affairs and P expresses some future state of affairs. Although I lack the space to discuss the point here, I believe an important asymmetry is generated by a shift in the relative temporal locations of R and P. I also believe, however, that this asymmetry is faithfully reflected in the difference between knowing what will happen on the basis of present data and knowing what *did* happen on the basis of present data. In other words, I feel that an asymmetry in (2), arising from a shift in the relative temporal locations of R and P, helps one to understand the difference we all feel between knowing, on the one hand, what did happen or is happening, and, on the other hand, what will happen.

player in the game (whose presence or absence affects the cards dealt to S) who would have dropped if S's neighbour had not dropped, then this person's remaining in the game is *not* held fixed, not included in C, because it is causally connected to the state of affairs expressed by the antecedent in S's statement. Therefore, we can show S's statement to be false if we can show that such a circumstance prevailed, and it is along these lines that one would surely argue in attempting to show S that he was wrong, wrong in saying that he would have received a royal flush if his neighbour had stayed in the game.

On the other hand, one cannot show that S's statement is false by showing that, were the cards differently arranged in the remainder of the deck, he would not have received his royal flush; for the arrangement of cards in the remainder of the deck (unlike the presence or absence of our other player) is (presumably) independent of S's neighbour's departure from the game. Hence, it is one of the conditions held fixed, included in C, by S's statement, and we are not allowed to consider alterations in it in assessing the general implication of S's statement.

Or consider our original thermometer example. Recall, the statement in question was: 'The thermometer would not have read 98.6° unless the child's temperature was normal.' Suppose someone responds, 'Oh, it would have (or might have) if the thermometer was broken.' It is important to understand that one can grant the truth of this response without abandoning the original assertion; for the original assertion had, as its general implication, *not* a statement expressing a uniform relationship between states of affairs similar to the child's temperature (normal body temperature) and states of affairs similar to the thermometer reading (a reading of 98.6), but, rather, a uniformity between such states *under a fixed set of circumstances*. And, if I am right, this fixed set of circumstances includes *the actual state of the thermometer* (defective or accurate); it is one of those circumstances prevailing on the occasion in question which is causally and logically independent of the child's temperature. Hence, this circumstance cannot be allowed to vary as it is in the above response by the words 'if the thermometer was broken'. To determine the truth of the original assertion we must suppose that the thermometer is accurate (or defective) *whatever the actual condition is*. If, therefore, the thermometer was not broken or otherwise defective on that occasion, then the suggestion that it would (or might) have read the same despite a feverish child if it were broken or defective is, although quite true, irrelevant to the truth of the statement: 'It would not have read 98.6 unless the child's temperature was normal.'

One final important feature of (2). I have said that, generally speaking, the placeholders 'R' and 'P' represent expressions designating *specific* states of affairs or conditions. When this is so, (2) still has a general implication, but the general implication, expressing a uniform relationship between states of affairs similar to R and P, *has its scope restricted* to situations in which the circumstances C (as specified above) obtain. Since we are talking about specific states of affairs in most instantiations of (2), it becomes extremely important to observe the sorts of referring expressions embodied within both 'R' and 'P'. For example, when I say, 'John would not have said it was raining unless it was raining' I am talking about *John* and about a *particular utterance* of his. *Someone else* might have said this without its being true; John may have said *something else* without its being true. Nonetheless, *John* would not have said *it was raining* unless it was. An incurable liar about most things, John has a pathological devotion to accuracy on matters concerning the weather. In such a case, although John is, admittedly, a most unreliable informant on most matters, we can say that he would not have said it was raining unless it was so. This is only to say that the referring expressions to be found in 'R' and 'P' *help to define the scope* of the implied generalization. Recall, the implied generalization was about states of affairs *similar* to (the particular states) R and P. Similar in what respect? The sort of referring expressions to be found within 'R' and 'P' help us to answer this question. In the case of John above, the general implication involved, not *a person's saying something* (under circumstances C), not *John's saying something* (under circumstances C), but John's saying something about the weather (under circumstances C).

2. The possibility of mistake: the connection between (2) and (3).

Taking a cue from the fact that (2) expresses some form of necessary relationship between R and P, I have (in my opening remarks) expressed (2) as: Given R, $\sim \diamond \sim$ P (or, alternatively, $\sim \diamond(R \, . \sim P))$. I think the full justification for expressing (2) in this fashion lies in the fact that (2) and (3) are contradictories, and since (3) may be rendered as:

(3) Given R, $\diamond \sim$ P (or, alternatively, $\diamond(R \, . \sim P)$)

(2) may be represented as 'Given R, $\sim \diamond \sim$ P'.

To see that this is so, it should be noticed that in denying the connection between R and P expressed by (2) we do not commit ourselves to anything as strong as:

(4) R would be the case even though not-P were the case.

(4) is the *contrary* of (2), not its contradictory, since both (2) and (4) may turn out false.[11] For example, suppose S asserts,

(2g) I would have won the lottery if I had bought two tickets (instead of only one).

We may deny the truth of this contention without committing ourselves to the truth of

(4g) You would have lost even if you had bought two tickets.

All that is intended in denying (2g) is that the purchase of two tickets is connected with winning in the alleged manner, that the purchase of two tickets would have assured him of winning. Its failing to be connected in the manner alleged is,

11. A point which Goodman acknowledges in a footnote: 'Literally a semifactual and the corresponding counterfactual are not contradictories but contraries, and both may be false.' *Fact, Fiction and Forecast*, p. 32, note 2.

however quite consistent with *his winning* with two tickets. What we commit ourselves to in denying (2g) is:

(3g) You *might* have lost even with two tickets.

(3g) asserts what (2g) denies; *viz.* that even with two tickets it is *still* a matter of chance, the possibility of losing is *not* eliminated by holding two tickets instead of one.

As a matter of common practice, of course, we often employ something similar to (4) in denying (2). This is understandable enough since the truth of (4) does entail the falsity of (2). The point I am driving at, however, is that we need not affirm anything as strong as (4) in denying (2); all we are required to affirm is that R and not-P *might* both be the case or that, even though R is given, P *might not* be the case. That is to say, the proper expression for the negation of (2) is (3); and if we understand (3) as affirming 'Given R, $\diamond \sim$ P' (alternatively $\diamond$(R . $\sim$ P)), then we are justified in representing (2) as 'Given R , $\sim \diamond \sim$ P' (alternatively, $\sim\diamond$(R . $\sim$ P)). If someone says, 'James would not have come without an invitation', we can deny this without supposing that James would have come without an invitation. For suppose we know that if James had not received an invitation, he would have flipped a coin to decide whether to go or not. In such a case, it is not true that he would not have come without an invitation, but neither is it true that he would have come without an invitation. The fact is that *he might have come* (depending on the outcome of the toss) without an invitation.

Before proceeding there is an important ambiguity which must be eliminated. There is a use of the word 'might' (and related modal terms) which gives expression to the speaker's epistemic state in relation to some situation. It is a use of the word 'might' which is naturally followed by a parenthetical 'for all I know'. For example, in saying, 'He might win the election' the speaker is most naturally understood as expressing the fact that he does not know whether he will win the election or not, that he has no (or there are no) very convincing grounds for supposing he will lose. This use of the word can properly be deployed even when the state of affairs in question is *physically* or *logically* impossible. S, for instance, may concede the premises of our valid argument but, nonetheless, ignorant of its validity, insist that the conclusion might (for all he knows) be false even though the premises are true.

Contrasted with this epistemic use of the modal terms is what we might call an *objective* sense of these terms, a sense of the term 'could' (for example) in which if R entails P then, independent of what S knows about the logical relationship between R and P, it is false to say that R and not-P, could (or might) both be the case. Moreover, if we accept the results of modern physics, then in this objective sense of the term S's statement that there are objects which *can* travel faster than the speed of light is false, and it is false even though, *for all he knows*, there are objects which can. In this objective sense one is making a remark about the various possibilities for the occurrence, or joint occurrence, of events or the co-existence of states of affairs, and in this sense ignorance of what is the case is no guarantee that one's statements about what *might* or *could* be the case are true. The possibilities must actually be as one alleges. When S (knowing that James had an invitation to come) asserts that James, being the sort of fellow he is, might (even) have come without an invitation, he is making a remark *about James* and what James is inclined to do or capable of doing. He is obviously not registering some fact about his ignorance of whether or not James possesses an invitation.

The modal term appearing in (3) is meant to he understood in the objective sense. (3) is meant to be a statement about the possibilities for the joint realization of two states of affairs (R and not-P) independent of what the speaker happens to know about the actual realization of P (R being given). Drawing from our discussion in the preceding section, we can say that if (2) is true, if R would not be the case unless P were the case, then *in these circumstances* (specified earlier) P is a state of affairs which is necessary to the realization of R. Hence, in these circumstances it is false to say that R and not-P might both be the case or that, given R, not-P might be the case, and it is false whether or not anyone appreciates the fact that it is false.

We have here a more or less *particularized* impossibility; (3), as well as (2), is tied to the circumstances, C, specified earlier. Nothing else but (a state such as) P could have brought about (a state such as) R *in these circumstances*. Often, of course, our statements about what could be the case, about what is possible, are broader in scope. They do not restrict themselves to the particular set of circumstances prevailing on some specific occasion. They are statements to the effect that, whatever the circumstances on this occasion happened to be, there are (nonetheless) circumstances in which a state relevantly similar to R is, or might easily be, brought about without a state relevantly similar to P. S may admit, for example, that the thermometer would not have read 98.6 unless the child's temperature was normal— hence, concede that it would be false to say that in these circumstances (given the thermometer reading) the child might (nonetheless) have a fever. Yet, he may go on to insist that one *can* get a normal reading on a thermometer with a feverish child. One can do so when one has a defective thermometer, when the child is sucking an ice cube, and so on. That is, one *can* have R without P in *other* circumstances. These 'general' possibilities are, however, quite consistent with the 'particularized' impossibilities expressed by (3). Most genuine impossibilities can be made possible by enlarging the frame of reference, by relaxing the conditions tacitly taken as fixed in the original statement of impossibility. I can't swim the English Channel; this despite the fact that I could *if* I had trained since a boy, been endowed with the requisite endurance, etc.

If I may summarize the argument up to this point in preparation for the following section: (1) entails (2), if S knows that P, and he knows this on the basis (simply) of R, then R would not be the case unless P were the case. Furthermore, (2) gives expression to a connection between R and P which permits us to say that when R is given, in the kind of circumstances which actually prevailed on the occasion in question, the possibility of not-P is eliminated. The sense of the word 'possible' that is operative here is, I submit, the *same* sense of this word that is operating in our strongest statements about what is physically possible; the difference between the possibility expressed in (3) and other, apparently stronger, statements of what is possible and impossible is simply a shift in the set of circumstances which is taken as fixed. The impossibility expressed by (3) is an impossibility relative to those circumstances, C, held fixed in (2), and it is this fact which makes (3) the contradictory of (2) and, hence, which makes its negation a logical consequence of (1).

3. Conclusive reasons

Let us call R a conclusive reason for P if and only if R would not be the case unless P were the case.[12] This makes logically conclusive reasons (LCR) a subclass of conclusive reasons. Conclusive reasons depend, simply, on the truth of (2); logically conclusive reasons require that the truth of (2) be demonstrable on purely logical and definitional grounds. When the conditional is true, but not logically true, we can speak of the conclusive reasons as being *empirically conclusive* (ECR).

Of course, R may *be* a conclusive reason for believing P without anyone believing P, much less having R as their reason for believing. I shall say, therefore, that S *has conclusive reason*, R, for believing P if and only if:

(A) R is a conclusive reason for P (i.e. (2) is true),
(B) S believes, without doubt, reservation, or question, that P is the case and he believes this on the basis of R,
(C) (i) S knows that R is the case or
     (ii) R is some experiential state of S (about which it may not make sense to suppose that S *knows* that R is the case; at least it no longer makes much sense to ask *how* he knows).

With only minor embellishments, to be mentioned in a moment, I believe that S's having conclusive reasons for believing P is *both* a necessary and a sufficient condition for his knowing that P is the case. The appearance of the word 'know' in this characterization (in (Ci)) does not render it circular as a characterization of knowledge since it can be eliminated by a recursive application of the three conditions until (Cii) is reached.

If S has conclusive reasons for believing P, then it is *false* to say that, given these grounds for belief, and the circumstances in which these grounds served as the basis for his belief, *S might be mistaken about P*. Having conclusive reasons, as I have just defined it, not only implies that P is the case, it not only implies that S believes that P is the case, but it also implies that, in the circumstances in which he came to believe that P, his basis for believing that P was sufficiently secure to eliminate the possibility of his being mistaken about P. This goes a long way toward capturing everything that philosophers have traditionally required of knowledge. Indeed, in certain respects it goes beyond it in requiring a stronger connection between one's reasons or grounds and what one believes (on the basis of these reasons or grounds) than has normally been demanded by those wishing to preserve our

---

12. Recall footnote 4 concerning the particular wording of (2); I intend those remarks to apply to this definition or 'conclusive reasons'.

ordinary knowledge claims from sceptical criticism.[13] Since, however, I have already argued for the necessity of (A), for R's being a conclusive reason for P, I shall concentrate on the question of whether or not S's having a conclusive reason for believing P is sufficient for his knowing that P.

Several preliminary points must be mentioned briefly. It may be thought that in arguing for the impossibility of mistake as a necessary condition for knowing that P I have been wasting my time. It may be thought that if S knows that P, then P *cannot* be false since S's knowing that P entails P; hence, S *cannot* be mistaken in believing that P. In answer to this objection it should be pointed out that the impossibility of mistake which I have been talking about is an impossibility which arises in virtue of a *special connection* between S's reasons, R, and what he consequently believes, P. It is not the trivial impossibility of being wrong about something which (by hypothesis) you know. When philosophers concern themselves with the possibility of mistake in putative cases of knowledge, they are not concerned with the possibility of mistake which is trivially avoidable by saying that *if* you do know that P, then you cannot be mistaken about P. They are concerned, rather, with that possibility as it exists in relation to one's evidence or grounds for believing P, and *that* is the possibility with which (2) is concerned.

The point may be put in another way. Both

I. R would not be the case unless P were the case
    R is the case

and

2. R ⊃ P (when it is *not* true that R would not be the case unless P)
    R

constitute conclusive grounds, logically conclusive grounds, for believing P. Neither set of premises would be true unless P were true, and this fact is in both

13. It is this stronger connection which blocks the sort of counterexample which can be generated to justified-true-belief analyses of knowledge. Gettier's (and Lehrer's) examples, for instance, are directed at those analyses which construe knowledge in terms of a *degree* of justification which is compatible with being justified in believing something false (both Gettier and Lehrer mention this feature at the beginning of their discussion). The counter-examples are then constructed by allowing S to believe that P (which is false) *with the appropriate degree of justification* letting P entail Q (which is true), and letting S believe that Q on the basis of its logical relationship to P. We have, then, a case where S truly believes that Q *with the appropriate degree of justification* (this degree of justification is allegedly preserved through the entailment between P and Q), but a case where S does *not know* that Q (since his means of arriving at it were so clearly defective). On the present analysis, of course, the required connection between S's evidence and P is strong enough to *preclude* P's being false. One cannot have *conclusive* reasons for believing something which is false. Hence, this sort of counter-example cannot be generated. Part of the motivation for the present analysis is the conviction (supported by Gettier-like examples) that knowledge, if it embodies an evidential relation at all, must embody a strong enough one to eliminate the *possibility* of mistake. See Edmund Gettier's 'Is Justified True Belief Knowledge?' *Analysis*, 23.6, June 1963 [Ch. 2 in this volume] and Keith Lehrer, 'Knowledge, Truth and Evidence', *Analysis*, 25.5, April 1965. I should also mention here that these same sorts of considerations seemed to move Brian Skyrms toward a similar analysis; see especially pp. 385–6 in his 'The Explication of "X Knows That P"', *The Journal of Philosophy*, June 22, 1967.

cases demonstrable on purely logical and definitional grounds. But the significant difference between I and 2 is that in I, but *not* in 2, the second premise *alone* turns out to be a *conclusive* reason (ECR). If we were searching for conclusive reasons to believe P, then in the second case we would require as our reasons *both premises*, and this would require that we knew that both premises were true (see clause (C) in having conclusive reasons). In case I, however, the second premise alone is a conclusive reason and, hence, to have conclusive reasons it is required *only that we know that R is the case*. We need not (as in case 2) know that the first premise is true. All that is required in case I for R alone to be a conclusive reason is that the first premise be true; there is nothing that requires S to know that the first premise is true in order to have R as his conclusive reason for believing P. For if the first premise is true (regardless of whether S knows it is true or not) then (3) is false; hence, possibility of S's being mistaken about P has been successfully avoided—and it has been successfully avoided *whether or not S knows it has been avoided*.

In speaking of conclusive reasons I do not wish to suggest that in having R as a conclusive reason S must be in a position to *give* R as his reason. R may simply be a certain experience which S has undergone and, having undergone this experience, come to the belief that P was the case on the basis of (as a result of) this experience. He may find it difficult, or impossible, to give verbal expression to R. He may have forgotten it. Or it may consist in something's looking a particular way to him which he finds difficult to describe. Still, if the way the thing looks to S is such that it would not look that way unless it had the property Q, then its looking that way to S is a conclusive reason for S's believing that it has the property Q; and if S believes that it is Q *on this basis*, then he has, in the way the thing looks to him, a conclusive reason for believing it Q.

Also, there are a number of things which people commonly profess to know (Sacramento is the capital of California, the earth is roughly spherical) for which there is no definite piece of evidence, no single state of affairs or easily specifiable set of such states, which even approximates a conclusive reason. In such cases, although we can cite no single piece of data which is clinching and, hence, are at a loss for conclusive reasons when asked to give reasons (or when asked 'How do you know?') we, nonetheless, often enough have conclusive reasons in a vast spectrum of experiences which are too diverse to admit of convenient citation. Countless experiences converge, so to speak, on the truth of a given proposition, and this variety of experience may be such that although one *may* have had any *one* of these experiences without the proposition in question being true, one *would not* have had *all* of them unless what one consequently believes was true. The fallibility of source A and the fallibility of source B does not automatically entail that when A and B *agree* about P's being the case, that, nonetheless, P might still be false. For it may be that A and B *would not* both have indicated that P was the case unless P was the case although neither A nor B, taken by themselves, provide conclusive reasons for P. For example, although any single newspaper account may be in error on a particular point, several independent versions (wire services, of course, tend to eliminate this independence) may be enough to say that we know that something is so *on the basis of the newspaper accounts.* All of them would not have been in such close agreement unless their account was substantially correct.[14]

Finally, I do not wish to suggest by my use of the word 'reason' that when S has conclusive reasons for believing P, S has *reasoned* his way to the conclusion that P is the case from premises involving R or that S has consciously used R as a reason in arriving at the belief that P. I am inclined to think (but I shall not now argue it) that when one knows that P, on whatever basis this might be, little or no reasoning is involved. I would prefer to describe it as follows: sometimes a person's conviction that P is the case can be traced to a state of affairs (or cluster of situations) which satisfies the three conditions defining the possession of conclusive reasons. When it can be so traced, then he knows; when it cannot be so traced, then we say he does not know although he may be right about P's being the case. Of course, his belief may be *traceable* to such a source without our being able to trace it. In such a case we are mistaken in saying that he does not know.

Turning now to the question of whether having conclusive reasons to believe, as defined by (A)–(C), constitutes a sufficient condition for knowledge, I shall mention and briefly respond to what I consider to be the most serious objections to this proposal.

There is, first, a tendency to conflate knowing that P with knowing that one knows that P. If this is done then conditions (A)–(C) will immediately appear insufficient since they do not describe S as knowing or having any basis for believing that R, his basis for believing P, constitutes an adequate basis, much less a conclusive basis, for believing P. Even if one does not go this far there is still a tendency to say that if S knows that P, then S must at least *believe* that he knows that P is the case. If one adopts this view then, once again, conditions (A)–(C) appear inadequate since they do not describe (nor do they entail) that S believes he knows that P is the case. I see no reason, however, to accept either of these claims. We naturally expect of one who knows that P that he believe that he knows, just as we expect of someone who is riding a bicycle that he believe he is riding one, but in neither case is the belief a *necessary* accompaniment. The confusion is partially fostered, I believe, by a failure to distinguish between what is implied in knowing that P, and what is implied (in some sense) by someone's *saying* he knows that P. Consider, however, cases in which we freely ascribe knowledge to agents in which it seems quite implausible to assign the level of conceptual sophistication requisite to their believing something about knowledge, believing something about their epistemic relation to the state of affairs in question. A dog may know that his master is in the room, and I (at least) want to say that he can know this in a straightforward sense without (necessarily) possessing the conceptual understanding which seems to be

14. The fact that as newspapers sometimes print things which are false does not mean that we cannot know that something is true on the basis of a single newspaper account. The relevant question to ask (as in the case of a person's testimony—see section 1) is not whether *newspapers* sometimes print false stories, not even whether *this newspaper* sometimes prints false stories, but whether *this newspaper* would have printed *this story* if it were not true. The *Midville Weekly Gazette*'s story about dope addiction on the campus may not correspond with the facts, but would *The Times* have printed this story about the President's visit to Moscow if it were not true?

required to say of him that he believes he knows this, believes that he has good reasons, or believes *anything* about his epistemic relation to the fact that his master is in the room.[15] Yet, it seems perfectly natural to say of a dog that it knows (sometimes) when his master is in the room. And this is not, let me add, simply a matter of the dog's being right about something. For if we knew that the dog thought his master was in the room on the basis, say, of certain sounds and smells (sounds and smells that were, generally speaking, a reliable sign of his master) when these sounds and smells were totally unrelated to his master's presence in the room *on this occasion*, we would not say the dog knew even if he happened to be right about his master's being in the room. Imagine a blind dog's being 'taken in' by a thief in his master's clothing while the master lies unconscious in the corner. The dog, taken in as he is by the thief, certainly thinks his master is in the room, and he is right (although, of course, he is wrong about this man's being his master). But just as clearly the dog does not know that his master is in the room. We require conclusive reasons even in the case of animals. Would the dog have smelled what he did, and heard what he did, if his master was not in the room? If he *would have*, or *might have*, then he doesn't know.[16]

Furthermore, consider a sceptic who talked himself into believing that his grounds for believing in an external world were not sufficiently good to truly say he *knew* there was an external world and, hence, no longer believed, positively disbelieved, that he knew there was an external world. I think that as long as he continued to believe (without doubt, reservation or question) that there was an external world, and continued to believe it on the same basis as we do, he would

---

15. This seems to be the essence of Arthur Danto's argument (against Hintikka) that 'S knows that P' does not entail 'S knows that S knows that P' in 'On Knowing that We Know', *Epistemology: New Essays in the Theory of Knowledge*, Avrum Stroll (ed.), 1967, pp. 49–51.

16. Robert Sleigh has suggested an interesting modification of this case—one that would appear to cause difficulty. Suppose that the dog *is* taken in by the thief but, in addition, circumstances are such that the thief *would not* be in the room *unless* the dog's master was also there. It may be a bit difficult to imagine circumstances of this sort, but other examples (not involving animals as the knowers) can easily be manufactured (Chisholm's example of a man mistaking a sheep dog for a sheep in a field works nicely when the further condition is added that the dog would not be there unless there were some sheep in the field). With such a modification it would seem that the dog has conclusive reasons for believing his master present since it would not have heard and smelled what it did unless its master was present. But does the dog know that its master is present? I think it natural to read this situation in such a way that the dog believes that its master is in the room *because* it mistakenly believes that this man (the thief) is his master. If read in this way, of course, there is no difficulty since the dog's basis for believing that his master is present is obviously defective—it is not true, nor does the dog know, that this man is his master. If, however, we read this case in such a way that the dog simply takes the sounds and smells as a sign of his master's presence (without misidentifying anyone) then the dog *does* have conclusive reasons (he would not have smelled and heard what he did unless his master was present) but I should want to say that in this case *he knows* that his master is present. I do not think that this is an excessively strained interpretation. It seems to me quite similar to situations in which we know that something is so on the basis of some indicator or sign (e.g. an instrument reading) but are ignorant as to the mechanism *in virtue of which* that indicator or sign is a reliable (conclusive) index or what we purport to know.

know there was an external world (assuming here that *we* know it) *whatever* he happened to believe about what he knew.[17]

The remarks I have just made about believing that one knows apply, *a fortiori*, to knowing that one knows. One qualifies for knowledge when one has conclusive reasons for believing; one need not, in addition, know that one has conclusive grounds. To know that one has conclusive reasons, empirically conclusive reasons, means that one knows that (A) is true and this, in turn, means that one has logically conclusive reasons (see case I above). Knowing that one knows is a form of inoculation against sceptical challenges to the quality of ones empirically conclusive reasons; one *knows* that R would not be the case unless P were the case. Lacking such inoculation, however, one still knows. One is simply less prepared to defend (justify) the *claim* to knowledge; but inability to justify the truth of what one claims, is seldom, if ever, a refutation of the truth of what one claims, and this applies to knowledge claims as well as any other.

There is a certain type of counter-example which exploits this confusion, and I would like to mention it at this point to further clarify the intent of conditions (A)–(C). Suppose S, for a perfectly silly reason, or by sheer accident, comes to the true belief that (a state such as) R is a conclusive reason for believing that (a state such as) P is or was the case. Happening upon a state such as R in the appropriate circumstances, then, he believes that P is the case on the basis of R. Doesn't he now have *conclusive reasons* for believing P? But isn't it equally obvious that he does *not* know that P is the case? Yes and no. Yes, he does have conclusive reasons (as I have defined this). No, it is not obvious that he does not know that P is the case. I believe that this objection trades on the very confusion we have just discussed; that is, it mistakenly supposes that if S does not know that R is conclusive for P (has no legitimate basis for believing this), then S does not know that P is the case (has no legitimate basis for believing this). Or, what I think amounts to the very same thing, it fallaciously concludes that S (given his basis for belief) might be wrong about P from the fact that S (given his basis for belief) might be wrong about R's being conclusive for P. Or, to put it in still another way, it incorrectly supposes that if it is, either wholly or in part, accidental that S is right about R's being conclusive for P, then it is also, either wholly or in part, accidental that he is right about P's being the case. Such inferences are fallacious and, I believe, they are fallacious in the same way as the following two examples: (a) Concluding that it was sheer luck (chance), a mere accident, that declarer made his bid of seven spades because it was sheer luck (chance), a mere accident, that he was dealt thirteen spades; (b) Concluding that the window was broken accidentally because the man who threw the brick through it came by the belief that bricks break windows in an accidental (silly, unreasonable, or what have you) way.

---

17. Examples such as this, along with other more systematic considerations, convince me that not only should we not require that S believe he has conclusive reasons in order to know, but also that we should not require that he not believe he does not have conclusive reasons. If a person's believing that he knows is compatible with his not knowing, why shouldn't a person's believing that he does not know be compatible with his knowing?

Sometimes the stage is set for a non-accident in a purely accidental way. In the above case it *is* accidental that S knows that P on the basis of R, but this does not make it accidental that he is right about P—for he believes P on the basis of R and R simply would not be the case unless P were the case. Given R, it is not at all accidental that he is right about P. What *is* accidental is that he was correct in believing that R was a conclusive reason for P, but all this shows is that he does not know that R is conclusive for P, does not know that he knows that P. And with this much I am in full agreement.[18]

Sceptical arguments have traditionally relied on the fact that S, in purporting to know that P on the basis of R, was conspicuously unable to justify the quality of his reasons, was hopelessly incapable of providing satisfactory documentation for the truth of (A). The conclusion fallaciously drawn from this was that S did not know that P was true (simply) on the basis of R. Clearly, however, all that follows from the fact that S has little or no grounds for thinking (A) true is that he lacks satisfactory grounds for thinking he knows that P is true. It does not follow that he does not know that P is true. Knowing that P is the case on the basis of R involves knowing that R is the case (and believing P on that basis) *when (A) is true.* It is the truth of (A), not the fact that one knows it true, which makes R conclusive for P.

There is another respect in which traditional sceptical arguments have been on the mark. One way of expressing my argument is to say that the familiar and (to some) extremely annoying challenge, 'Couldn't it be an illusion (fake, imitation, etc.)?' or 'Isn't it possible that you are dreaming (hallucinating, etc.)?' is, in a certain important respect, quite proper and appropriate *even when there is no special reason to think you are dreaming, hallucinating, confronting a fake, etc.* For our knowledge claims do entail that the evidence or grounds one has for believing *would not* have been available if what one consequently believes (and claims to know) were false; hence, they do entail that, given one's evidence or grounds, *it is false that one might be mistaken* about what one purports to know. (1) does entail the falsity of (3); hence, (1) can be shown to be false not only by showing that S *is* dreaming or hallucinating or whatever, but also by showing that he might be, that his experience or information on which he bases his belief that P can be had in such circumstances as these without P being the case. It is not in the propriety or relevance of these challenges that scepticism has gone awry. On the contrary, the persistent and continuing appeal of scepticism lies in a failure to come to grips with this challenge, in a refusal to acknowledge its legitimacy and, hence, *answer it.* It simply will not do to insist that in concerning himself with the possibility of mistake a sceptic is setting artificially high standards for knowledge and, therefore, may be ignored when considering ordinary knowledge claims. (1) does imply that (3) is false, and it seems

18. In speaking of 'accidentality' in this connection I have in mind Peter Unger's analysis of knowledge in terms of its not being at all accidental that the person is right (see his 'An Analysis of Factual Knowledge', *Journal of Philosophy*, March 21, 1968). That is, I want to claim that any S satisfying conditions (A)–(C) is a person of whom it is true to say that it is not at all accidental that he is right about P's being the case, although it may be accidental that this is no accident (it may be accidental that he *has* conclusive reasons, that he has reasons in virtue of which it is not at all accidental that he is right about P).

to me quite a legitimate line of argument for the sceptic to insist that if (3) is true, if you might be dreaming or whatever, then (1) is false—you do not know, on the basis of your present visual, auditory, etc. experiences, what you purport to know.

I think there are several confusions to be found in traditional scepticism, but one of them is not that of insisting that to know that P on the basis of R, R must *somehow* preclude the possibility of not-P. The confusions lie elsewhere. If one interprets the 'might' (or 'could') of (3) too narrowly (as simply 'logically possible') then, of course, (3) will, in almost all interesting cases, turn out true and (therefore) (1) false. Even if one liberalizes the interpretation of (3), and thinks of it as representing some form of physical impossibility as I have, there is still the tendency to think of this physical impossibility in its most general sense, as the impossibility of violating some natural law which holds *in all circumstances* and not, as I have argued, the impossibility of having R with not-P in the particular circumstances which in fact prevail on the occasion in question. The most subtle confusion, however, is the one mentioned in the preceding paragraphs—the fallacy of supposing that in knowing that P we must somehow be able to justify the fact that we know that P. Doubtless we should have some justification for (1) if we assert it, but our lack of such a justification reflects, *not on the truth* of what we have said, but *on the propriety of our saying it*. What would show that we did not know that P on the basis of R is the truth of (3), not our incapacity to show it false (by showing (2) true for instance). For if (2) is true, then, in answer to the sceptic's question, 'Couldn't you be hallucinating?' or 'Might it not be a fake or imitation of some sort?' the correct response, whether or not we *know* it correct, whether or not we can *show* it correct is 'No!'

Still, even if one should accept the arguments up to this point, there are genuine difficulties with taking as a sufficient condition for knowledge, the possession of conclusive reasons to believe. I shall not try to absorb these difficulties in this paper; I have tried to do so with respect to a more restricted set of cases (visual perception) in another place.[19] Whether these complications can be handled in the much more general type of situation I have been discussing I leave open—only suggesting the lines along which I think they can be satisfactorily handled. The two examples I present do not affect my argument that the possession of conclusive reasons is a *necessary* condition for knowledge.

S, upon inspecting an immersed chemical indicator, declares that the solution in which it is immersed is a base. He believes (correctly) that the indicator is the sort which turns from yellow to blue only when immersed in a base. The indicator is Thymol Blue and would not have turned from yellow to blue (in these conditions) unless the solution were a base. The following three conditions are satisfied:

(A') The indicator's change in colour (yellow to blue) is a conclusive reason for believing that the solution is a base.

(B') S believes that the solution is a base and he believes this on the basis of the indicator's change in colour.

(C') S knows that the indicator changed from yellow to blue (he saw it change— saw *that* it changed).

19. *Seeing and Knowing* (Chicago; 1969), Chapter 3.

I have said that these three conditions were sufficient for knowledge. Does S know that the solution is a base? Before answering this question the reader should be informed that there is another chemical indicator, Bromophenal Blue, which also turns from yellow to blue but *only when* immersed in an *acid*. S, however, is quite unaware of the existence of other such indicators. He merely assumes that *a* yellow indicator turning blue is a positive test for a base. S's ignorance on this point does not alter the fact that the above three conditions are satisfied. Yet, despite the satisfaction of these conditions, I find it (in some cases) most implausible to say he knows that the solution is a base. Whether he knows or not depends in a crucial way on our understanding of condition (B') above. The indicator's change in colour, although it is a conclusive reason, has its conclusiveness, so to speak, restricted in scope to the range of cases in which Thymol Blue is the indicator (or, if this laboratory only uses Thymol Blue, in which the indicator is *from* this laboratory or of the sort used in this laboratory). What is a conclusive reason for believing the solution to be a base is that a *Thymol Blue* indicator (or an indicator from this laboratory) changed from yellow to blue when immersed in it, *not* simply that an (unspecified) chemical indicator changed from yellow to blue. The fact that *this* indicator *happens to be* Thymol Blue is what accounts for the truth of (A') above. Since, however, it is a Thymol Blue indicator's (or some other appropriately specified indicator's) colour transformation which is conclusive, we must (see condition (B')) require that S's basis for believing the solution a base be that a *Thymol Blue indicator* (or *such-and-such indicator*) changed from yellow to blue. He need not, once again, know that a Thymol Blue's colour transformation (or such-and-such indicator's transformation) *is conclusive*, but he must be exploiting those things about the indicator's transformation *in virtue of which it is conclusive.* In some cases an A's being B is a conclusive reason for believing P only in virtue of the fact that it is, in particular, an A (or, say, something which is Q) which is B; in such cases we must understand condition (B) as requiring that S's basis for believing P include, not only the fact that this (something or other) is B, but also that this something or other is, in particular, *an A* (or something which is Q). And this requires of us in addition that we understand condition (C) above in such a way that S not only know that R is the case, know (let us say) that A is B, but also know that it is, in particular, *an A* which is B.[20]

20. This type of restriction is required for the sort of example discussed in my article 'Reasons and Consequences', *Analysis*, April, 1968. In this article I argued that one could know that *the* A is B (e.g. the widow was limping) while having little, if any, justification for believing that it was, in particular, a widow who was limping (hence, one could know that the widow was limping *without* knowing that *it was a widow* who was limping). Since, however, the statement 'The widow is limping' implies 'There is (or it is) a widow who is limping', I took this as showing that S can know that P, know that P entails Q, and yet not know that Q. On the present analysis of conclusive reasons, of course, P is a conclusive reason for Q (since P entails Q) and anyone who believed Q on the basis of P should (on this analysis) know that Q. The restriction being discussed in the text blocks this result by requiring S to know those things in particular about P which makes it conclusive for Q. In this example S must know that *it is a widow* who is limping since it is this aspect of his conclusive reason (the widow is limping) in virtue of which it functions as a conclusive reason for believing that there is a widow who is limping. I am indebted to Bruce Freed for clarification on this point.

One further example to illustrate a distinct, but closely related, difficulty. Suppose K is behaving in such a way that it is true to say that he would not be behaving in that way unless he was nervous. Suppose S purports to know that K is nervous and when asked how he knows this, replies by saying, 'From the way he is behaving.' Once again, our three conditions are satisfied, or can easily be assumed to be satisfied. Yet, if we suppose that the distinctive thing about K's behaviour is that he is doing B_1 *while* performing B_2, then if S is relying on B_1 (or B_2) alone, we should not say that he knows that K is nervous. It is quite true that the basis for S's belief (that K is nervous) is K's behaviour, and in this (relatively unspecified) sense we might say that S is relying on the significant aspects of the situation, but the fact is that the crucial aspects (those aspects which make K's behaviour conclusive) are more specific than those on which S is relying in purporting to know. We must insist, therefore, that S's basis for believing P be *as specific* in regard to the relevant aspects of R as is necessary to capture the distinctive (i.e. conclusive, those figuring essentially in the satisfaction of (2)) features of the situation.

I think both of the above qualifications can be summarized by saying that when one has conclusive reasons, then this is sufficient for knowing that P is the case when those reasons are *properly specific*, both with regard to *what it is* that displays the particular features on which one relies *and* on the particular features themselves. A complete statement of these restrictions is, however, far beyond the scope of this paper. Suffice it to say that the possession of conclusive reasons for believing is a necessary condition for knowledge and, properly qualified along the lines suggested here, also (I think) sufficient.

Part II

Externalism and Internalism

Introduction

THE distinction between externalism and internalism is the most widely used distinction in contemporary epistemology, one that has been applied both to accounts of justification and to accounts of knowledge. In its broadest formulation, internalism about epistemic *justification* is the view that all of the factors required for a belief to be justified must be cognitively accessible to—already known or experienced by—the subject and thus internal to her mind. Externalism about justification is the view that some of the justifying factors may be external to the subject's cognitive perspective. Some of the facts that make a true belief into knowledge may be unknown—indeed, unknowable—to the knower. Internalism about *knowledge* maintains that for a justified true belief to be knowledge the subject must know or at least justifiably believe that her belief is justified. According to externalism about knowledge, for a subject to have knowledge the justification condition must hold (in one form or another), but it is not necessary that she know or justifiably believe that it holds. She can know without having any reason to think she knows. While parallel internalist and externalist views cannot both hold for justification alone or for knowledge alone, internalism about justification and externalism about knowledge are compatible.

The most prominent recent externalist theories have been versions of *reliabilism*. While externalism is only a negative thesis consisting in the denial that justification and knowledge are completely internal, reliabilism is a positive thesis maintaining that what qualifies a belief as knowledge or as justified is its reliable linkage to the facts that make the belief true. What makes this view externalist is the absence of any requirement that the knower have any sort of cognitive access to, any appreciation of, the relation of reliability that makes her true belief knowledge. Advocates of reliabilism about knowledge—Armstrong, Chapter 7, Goldman, Chapter 8, and Dretske, Chapter 9—argue that the only condition (besides truth and belief) that needs be met for a belief that P to count as knowledge is that it stands in some externalist relationship to the facts that make the belief true. The externalist (or naturalistic) relationship, which is commonly expressed by means of subjunctive conditionals, ensures that if P were not true, the subject would not believe that P. In a slightly different formulation, a subject knows that P if she believes that P, P is true, and she would not believe that P unless P was true. The idea is that to know that P the belief must not be accidentally true. It must 'track', 'hook up with', or 'indicate' the facts that make the belief true. The theory is externalist, because it makes knowledge depend on factors that are not necessarily accessible to the knower.

Armstrong (Chapter 7), an early defender of a reliability theory of knowledge, describes the relation that must exist between a knower's beliefs about the world and the world itself as the relation that exists between a properly functioning thermometer and the temperature it registers. If S is to know that P, then S's belief that P must indicate that P in the way a reliable thermometer indicates that it is 40° C. If this relation holds between S's beliefs and the world, then S knows about the world whether or not he knows (or is justified in believing) that he is a properly functioning instrument—whether or not he knows he knows. It is important to remember that Armstrong proposes this theory as a theory of non-inferential knowledge. It is, basically, a theory about how the knower must be related to the facts if she is to perceive (i.e., see, hear, smell)—and, hence, know—that P.

According to Goldman (Chapter 8), a subject knows that P if she can distinguish or discriminate the truth of P from possible alternatives, i.e., states of affairs in which P is false. As a comparison to Armstrong, one might note that this is exactly what a good thermometer does—discriminate the actual temperature from other possible temperatures. It is not enough, for example, to truly believe of the woman in front of you that she is Judy to know it. If you cannot distinguish her from Trudy (her twin sister) then, despite the truth of your belief, and despite the justification for it (she looks exactly like Judy), knowledge is absent. If knowledge required the discrimination of *all* possible alternatives, though, there would be little or no knowledge (must you be able to distinguish Judy from cleverly disguised imposters?). In order to avoid this sceptical outcome, Goldman restricts the scope of possible alternatives that a knower has to be able to discriminate to *relevant* ones only. Several possible views are discussed about what might be deemed 'relevant'. Though Goldman favours one option (according to which an alternative is relevant if it produces the same or a similar perceptual experience than P), he does not endorse any. He remains neutral about the range of alternatives (to P) one must be able to discriminate from P in order to know that P. This issue remains a continuing problem for reliability theories of knowledge (cf. Chapters 24–26).

Dretske (Chapter 9) articulates a reliability theory of knowledge in terms of information. Knowledge, he says, is information-caused belief. The notion of information underlying this conception is adapted from the mathematical theory of communication, but it is, basically, the same sort of reliability relationship that Armstrong and Goldman (and Dretske in Chapter 6) are talking about. Thermometers, for example, carry information about the temperature when they are working properly. According to Dretske, for a belief to carry the information that P, it not only has to be caused by a reliable process which just happens to carry the information that P. The very properties of the process that are responsible for its carrying the information that P also have to be responsible for reliably causing the belief that P. In other words, the knower must be able to discriminate between the information generating properties of the source of her belief and other irrelevant properties, so that she would not have formed her belief in the absence of these information-relevant properties. Once again, the theory is externalist because a person, in order to know that P, need not know (or be justified in believing) that the signals she is receiving, those that cause her to believe that P, carry the information that P. In order to receive (and be caused to believe by) information, you need not have information that you are getting information.

As we have seen above, the basic idea of internalism is that what determines whether a belief is justified for a person or qualifies as knowledge are internal factors or states to which the person has cognitive or epistemic access. Thus, a person can, in principle, determine, by reflection alone, whether her belief is justified. On externalist views, by contrast, knowledge-producing properties of a belief—being produced by a reliable belief-producing mechanism, for example—are not something to which a person need (though she might) have epistemic access. The chief motive for internalism is epistemic *deontologism*, i.e., the view that being justified in holding a belief is having fulfilled one's epistemic duties and obligations in forming that belief. The epistemic duties arise from the goal of believing what is true and not believing what is false. The deontological notion of justification is normative; justification is not something that happens to a person; it is something one achieves by one's own efforts. If, therefore, justification is a function of meeting obligations, the factors that determine whether a belief is justified must be internal to the subject's mind. Deontology implies internalism.

Chisholm (Chapter 10) begins by cautioning against internalists and externalists talking past one another. Some externalists, he suggests, are not really interested in analysing the traditional notions of knowledge and justification, the ideas that Plato, for example, was concerned with. If this is true, of course, then there really is no disagreement; internalists are talking about one thing, externalists about something else. Chisholm goes on to argue that externalist theories of justification are either empty (by which he means they equate justified belief with true belief and fail, therefore, to tell us what justification is) or they use elements that are not external in character (e.g., something's being *evident* to the believer).

While Chisholm combines internalism with foundationalism (cf. Chisholm Chapter 18), BonJour (Chapter 11) and Lehrer (Chapter 12) combine internalism with coherentism. Coherentism and foundationalism are the two dominant theories regarding the epistemic relation in which beliefs stand to each other.

Foundationalism divides our beliefs into two classes: those which need support from others and those which can support others and do not stand in need of justification. We thus acquire the picture of our beliefs forming a pyramid with non-basic beliefs being supported by reasoning that traces back ultimately to the basic beliefs. The basic beliefs are immediately justified, i.e., their justification does not depend on any further justified belief (cf. Part 2I). *Coherentism*, on the other hand, denies that there is a class of beliefs which justify other beliefs without standing in need of justification themselves. According to coherence theories, individual beliefs are justified by the entire system of beliefs in which they cohere. The fundamental idea is that the items in coherent systems of beliefs must mutually support each other. All justification is inferential. A belief is unjustified if the coherence of the set would be increased by abandoning the belief. And if the set of beliefs is more coherent with this belief as a member rather than with any alternative, the belief is justified. This notion of justification is relative to individual believers.

In a selection from his influential book, *The Structure of Empirical Knowledge*, BonJour (Chapter 11) develops a coherence theory of knowledge and justification. A coherence theory of justification claims that a belief can only be justified 'from within', from the relations of mutual support (logical, probabilistic, explanatory) that it bears to other beliefs. Its aim, therefore, is thoroughly internalistic. A coherentist justification— consisting, as it does, in the relations of beliefs to one another— is completely accessible to the believer himself. In developing this theory, BonJour rejects a linear model of justification in which beliefs are ordered in some hierarchy in which lower level beliefs support higher level beliefs: A justifying B, B justifying C, and so on. According to this picture, the regress problem (what justifies the A we use in our justification of B?) is unavoidable and leads, in the end, to foundationalism, an externalistic theory according to which some beliefs are not justified by other beliefs but, rather, by their external relation to the facts.

One of the problems BonJour explicitly faces is the threat that coherence theories of justification relapse into externalism by equating justification of a belief that P with overall coherence of the person's total belief system (of which the belief that P is a member) and people simply do not have 'access' to such global features of their system of beliefs (hence, they cannot *tell*, from the inside, as it were, whether their beliefs are justified).

Lehrer (Chapter 12) also defends a coherence theory of knowledge and justification (for a fuller treatment of his theory of knowledge as undefeated justified true belief, cf. Chapter 5). Contrary to externalism (for example, Dretske Chapter 9) it is not, Lehrer claims, the acquisition of information that is important to human knowledge, but the certification of that information as trustworthy, and *certification* is an internalist notion. He distinguishes between subjective (personal) and objective (verific) justification, the latter being the kind of subjective justification one has when false propositions are eliminated from one's background belief system. Knowledge requires complete justification, both personal and verific (i.e., objective) justification. In order to know one must not only get information, one must be justified in thinking one is getting it. Though he is a well-known coherence theorist, the theory Lehrer presents here is, in fact, a hybrid theory. It combines external factors (to know you must actually be getting information; you must actually be verifically justified), factors which the believer may have no cognitive access to, with internal factors (you must be subjectively justified in thinking you are trustworthy).

A general problem with coherentism is the so-called *isolation objection*. The objection states that coherence may be a necessary but not a sufficient condition for justification because, by itself, it does not allow the distinction of truth from illusory but consistent theories. Fairytales, dreams and hallucinations may sometimes be coherent. A completely internal and subjective notion of justification, such as consistency, cannot bridge the gap between mere true belief which might be no more than a lucky guess and knowledge which must be grounded in some connection between internal subjective conditions and empirical data.

BonJour's (Chapter 14), Chisholm's (Chapter 10), and Foley's (Chapter 13) essays present a thoroughgoing critique of externalism in general and reliabilism in particular. Foley challenges the *necessity* of the reliabilist justification condition by constructing cases where this condition is not satisfied, but where the believer seems intuitively to be justi-fied. If two people are subjectively indistinguishable, if they have all the same beliefs and experiences, then if one is rational (justified) in believing P, so is the other. Yet, we can imagine these two persons embedded in much different worlds—the second, but not the first, in a world (a 'demon' world) in which most of his beliefs are false. So, Foley con-cludes, rationality or justification cannot be a matter, as the externalist insists, of the external relations that exist between the believer and his world. Since we do not regard the fact that we have been deceived (or will be deceived, or would be deceived) as precluding rationality, rationality has nothing to do with the reliability of our beliefs.

Chisholm and Foley go on to argue that reliabilist accounts of knowledge are also unsatisfactory. A reliabililty theory of knowledge has no way to specify the (reliable) process which is supposed to confer knowledge. Either the process is specified so narrowly (*this* kind of process, the one that produced *this* true belief) that every process turns out to be reliable or demon-world counterexamples are easily multiplied. The problem of providing an account of process-types that are reliable is called the *problem of generality*.

According to BonJour (Chapter 14), externalism is a foundationalist theory designed to avoid the infinite regress problem: if every justified belief could be justified only by inferring it from some further justified belief, there would have to be an infinite regress of justifications. Externalism provides a solution to the regress problem for, on this view, the justification of a belief depends on the obtaining of an appropriate relation between the believer and the world and need not involve any further beliefs so that no further regress of justification is generated. BonJour's critique of externalism is an indirect argument for coherentism, i.e., the view according to which all beliefs are known or justified in virtue of their relations to other beliefs, specifically, in virtue of belonging to a coherent system of beliefs (cf. BonJour's Chapter 11).

BonJour's objection to externalism rests on the internalist intuition that epistemic justification requires that the acceptance of the belief in question be rational, which in turn requires that the believer be aware of a reason for thinking that the belief is true. He challenges the *sufficiency* of the externalist justification condition by constructing cases where this condition is satisfied, but where the believer seems intuitively not to be justified. BonJour's examples involve people who possess reliable clairvoyant powers, but who have no reason to think that they have such cognitive powers and perhaps even good reasons to the contrary. On the basis of these powers, they each come to believe that the president is in New York, which, in fact, he is. The claim is that these people are not justified in accepting the belief that the president is in New York, despite the fact that the reliabilist condition is satisfied.

In response to BonJour's challenge Bach (Chapter 15) bites the bullet and insists that BonJour's clairvoyants are in fact justified in believing that the president is in New York. Bach distinguishes between a person being justified in holding a belief and the belief itself being justified. On Bach's view, BonJour's clairvoyants lack the former, but not the latter kind of justification. They have perfectly good reasons for knowing that the president is in New York, but they lack reasons for claiming that they know this. Bach argues that since justified beliefs commonly result from default reasoning, the internalist demand that in addition to the belief being justified, a person needs to be justified in holding the belief is psychologically unrealistic and epistemologically inadequate.

Another more conciliatory response to BonJour's challenge is to maintain that a justified belief resulting from a reliable belief-forming process must not be undermined by any other evidence the subject possesses. This negative coherence condition ensures that for a belief to become knowledge it must not be incoherent with the background information the subject possesses. This is roughly Alston's strategy in 'An Internalist Externalism' (Chapter 16). As the title suggests, Alston attempts to bridge externalism and internalism. The account is externalist in that he holds that a person is justified in believing a proposition only if she believes it on the basis of reliable grounds. The account is internalist because Alston insists that these grounds must be accessible to the believer.

Four general lines of argument are commonly advanced in favour of externalism.

(1) Some pursue the externalist programme because they think it important to ascribe knowledge to higher animals, small children, unsophisticated adults, and certain artificial cognitive devices. Such ascriptions seem incompatible with internalism, since the beliefs and inferences required by internalism about justification are too complicated to be plausibly ascribed to such subjects. (2) Others pursue externalism because they think it is a good way to naturalize epistemology (cf. Quine Chapter 20). It promises to be a way of eliminating normative language in epistemology—the language of rationality, justification, and so on—and substitute natural relations (causal, informational, etc.) between animal and environment in our understanding of such knowledge-yielding processes as perception and memory. (3) Others embrace externalism because internalism has conspicuously failed to provide defensible, non-sceptical solutions to the classical problems of epistemology while externalism makes these problems easily solvable. Internalists, of course, think the externalist solution is much *too* easy. (4) Still others pursue externalism because it yields answers to questions that otherwise remain puzzling. Why, for instance, can one know that P without knowing (or being justified in believing) that one knows it? Because, the externalist replies, knowledge has little or nothing to do with subjective justification; it is a matter of standing in the right relations to the facts. Needless to say, there is an internalist reply for each of these four arguments in favor of externalism.

It is unlikely that there will be a conclusive argument in favour of either internalism or externalism. Both approaches can cite powerful intuitions for their support. Internalists stress the epistemically responsible character of our true beliefs while externalists stress their non-accidental character. Each approach has its strength in a different field. Internalism tends to be most successful with regard to inferential and theoretical beliefs. Externalism, on the other hand, is particularly convincing in cases of non-inferential and perceptual beliefs.

Further reading

Alston, W. P., *Epistemic Justification*, Ithaca, Cornell University Press, 1989, Parts 1–3.

Annis, D. B., 'A Contextualist Theory of Epistemic Justification', *American Philosophical Quarterly* 15 (1978), pp. 213–9.

Audi, R., *The Structure of Justification*, Cambridge, Cambridge University Press, 1993, Parts 1–2.

Bender, J. W., ed., *The Current State of the Coherence Theory. Critical Essays on the Epistemic Theories of Keith Lehrer and Lawrence BonJour with Replies*, Dordrecht, Reidel, 1989.

Blanchard, B., *The Nature of Thought*, 2 Vol., London, Allen & Unwin, 1939.

Chisholm, R. M., *Theory of Knowledge*, 3rd edition, Englewood Cliffs/NJ, Prentice-Hall, 1989.

Craig, F., *Knowledge and the State of Nature*, Oxford, Clarendon, 1990, Ch. 3–8.

Dretske, F. I., *Knowledge and the Flow of Information*, Cambridge/MA, MIT Press, Part 2.

Foley, R., *The Theory of Epistemic Rationality*, Cambridge/MA, Harvard University Press, 1987.

Fumerton, R., *Metaepistemology and Skepticism*, Lanham/MD, Rowman & Littlefield, 1995, Ch. 3.

Goldman, A. I., *Epistemology and Cognition*, Cambridge/MA, Harvard University Press, 1986, Chs. 3–5.

Goldman, A. I., 'Strong and Weak Justification', *Philosophical Perspectives 2: Epistemology*, 1988, pp. 51–69.

Haack, S., *Evidence and Inquiry*, Oxford, Basil Blackwell, 1993.

Kim, K., 'Internalism and Externalism in Epistemology', *American Philosophical Quarterly* 30 (1993), pp. 303–16.

Lehrer, K., *Theory of Knowledge*, Boulder, Westview Press, 1990, Ch. 5–7.

Lycan, W., *Judgment and Justification*, Cambridge, Cambridge University Press, 1988, Ch. 5.

The Monist 68, No. 1–2 (1985), special issue on 'Knowledge, Justification, and Reliability'.

Moser, P. K., *Empirical Justification*, Dordrecht, Reidel, 1985.

Philosophia. Philosophical Quarterly of Israel 19, No. 4 (1989), special issue on A. I. Goldman's *Epistemology and Cognition*.

Plantinga, A., *Warrant. The Current Debate*, New York, Oxford University Press, 1993.

Pollock, J. L., *Contemporary Theories of Knowledge*, Savage, Rowman & Littlefield, 1986, Ch. 2–4.

Sosa, E., *Knowledge in Perspective*, Cambridge, Cambridge University Press, 1991, Chs. 8–10.

Synthese 74 (1988), special issue on 'Internalism'.

Taylor, K. A., 'Belief, Information and Semantic Content: A Naturalist's Lament', *Synthese* 71 (1987), pp. 97–124.

Van Cleve, J., 'Foundationalism, Epistemic Principles, and the Cartesian Circle', *The Philosophical Review* 88 (1979), pp. 55–91.

In addition consult the 'Further reading' section at the end of Part III.

Externalism

Chapter 7

The thermometer-model of knowledge

David M. Armstrong

I<small>N</small> this chapter a theory of non-inferential knowledge will be developed. [...]

1. What are the paradigms of non-inferential knowledge?

It would be extremely convenient if, in the course of discussion of non-inferential knowledge, one could point to uncontroversial examples of such knowledge. The examples could then be used in testing whether particular philosophical accounts of non-inferential knowledge are correct or not.

In the case of knowledge *simpliciter*, such uncontroversial cases are available. I *know* that the earth is round. I *know* that there is a piece of paper in front of me now. If a philosophical theory of the nature of knowledge yields the consequence that I do *not* know these things, then this is a conclusive (I do not say logically conclusive) reason for rejecting the theory.

Unfortunately, however, in the case of the more technical notion of *non-inferential* knowledge, no such uncontroversial examples are available. It has taken an abstract argument even to show that there must be such knowledge, and it is hard to give cases that are clearly beyond controversy. At the same time, it is unsatisfactory if no examples are used, or at least borne in mind. I shall therefore put forward a view of where non-inferential knowledge is to be found. At the same

David M. Armstrong, 'The Thermometer-Model of Knowledge' in *Belief, Truth and Knowledge* (Cambridge, Cambridge University Press, 1973), pp. 162–75, 178–83, reprinted by permission of Cambridge University Press.

time, however, the actual *analysis* of non-inferential knowledge, which will be our subsequent business, will not depend upon the identification of cases of non-inferential knowledge to be suggested in this section.

I suggest that at least one place where non-inferential knowledge is to be found is in *the simpler judgements of perception*. I do not say that this is the only place where non-inferential knowledge is found. (The simpler judgements of introspection would be one further *locus* of such knowledge.) Nor is it the case that all our simpler judgements of perception are instances of non-inferential knowledge. First, such judgements can be false. Second, even where they are true, it is possible for them to fall short of being knowledge. Third, even where they are knowledge, it is possible for them to be inferential knowledge. All that is asserted is that instances of non-inferential knowledge are common among the simpler judgements of perception.

What is meant by 'the simpler judgements of perception'? I have in mind such judgements as 'There is a noise within earshot', 'It is getting hotter', 'There is something red and round over there', 'There is something pressing on my body' and so on. Very often, I suggest, such judgements are instances of non-inferential knowledge.

It may help to illuminate this suggestion if I contrast it with two other views of where non-inferential knowledge is to be found which have some currency in modern philosophy. The two views are, respectively, more pessimistic and more optimistic than the moderate view advocated here.

According to the 'pessimistic' view of non-inferential knowledge, it is not possible, as our moderate view assumes, to have non-inferential knowledge of states of affairs in the physical world. Non-inferential knowledge of sensory matters, the pessimists hold, is confined to knowledge of the perceiver's own sensory states. All that we can possibly know non-inferentially about sensory matters is such things as 'It sounds to me as if there is a noise within earshot', 'It feels to me as if it is getting hotter', 'It looks to me as if there is something red and round over there', 'It feels to me as if there is something pressing on my body', where these statements are taken simply to express judgements about the perceiver's current sensory state.

Historically, this 'pessimistic' view is linked with the idea that non-inferential knowledge must be logically indubitable. It is, however, logically independent of this idea. The 'pessimistic' view is even more closely bound up with the Representative theory of perception, according to which all our knowledge of the physical environment is an inference, however unselfconscious, from the *data* of the perceiver's own sensory states. It is because I see no reason to accept the Representative theory (for reasons which do not concern us here) that I see no reason to accept the 'pessimistic' view that non-inferential knowledge is confined to the subject's own sensory states.

Notice, however, that the 'moderate' view need in no way reject the positive contentions of the 'pessimistic' view. A moderate can perfectly well admit that there can be, and regularly is, non-inferential knowledge of our own sensory states, and mental states generally.

The 'optimist' about non-inferential knowledge will again be perfectly prepared to accept the positive contentions of the 'pessimist' and the 'moderate'. But he thinks that the sphere of non-inferential knowledge is wider still. He thinks that we know non-inferentially things of a much more complex sort than those admitted by the 'pessimist' and the 'moderate'. Suppose that I am looking at a dog just in front of me, that the light is good, and that I am in my right mind. Unless other conditions are quite extraordinary, I will *know* that there is a dog in front of me. But the 'optimist' about non-inferential knowledge will claim further that this is *non-inferential* knowledge.

The strength of the 'optimistic' view lies in our ordinary speech and thought. It seems extraordinary, when there is a dog slap in front of our eyes, to say we *infer* that there is a dog there. Surely we *contrast* cases like that of the dog with cases where it is a matter of inferring?

On the other hand, if we consider the actual process by which we come to know that there is a dog before our eyes, it becomes more plausible to say that the knowledge involves inference. We come to know that there is a dog there as a result of light-waves reaching our eyes, and the information which can be conveyed by the light-waves is limited. A material thing having a similar physical constitution to the portion of the surface of the dog which is in our field of view, but which did not resemble a dog in any other way (a 'surface-simulacrum'), would have the same effect on the eyes and mind as the dog. It is tempting, and I think correct, to conclude that the presence of a *whole* dog is inferred from more elementary information.

One thing which gives trouble here is the temptation to make inferring a far more explicit, hesitating and self-conscious affair than it always is. When we start thinking about the psychological process of inferring, it is natural to concentrate upon such cases. For, by hypothesis, these are the cases where we take special notice of the inferring. But it is wrong to restrict inferring to such cases. [...]

Notice that this dispute between 'pessimistic', 'moderate', and 'optimistic' views of where non-inferential knowledge is to be found is an *empirical* dispute. There is certainly no *a priori* objection to the idea that we could have non-inferential knowledge that there is a dog before us. It is simply that, from what we know of perception, it seems (to me, at any rate) an unlikely hypothesis. The question in what areas non-inferential knowledge is found seems to be a *psychological* question, a question about the cognitive structure and powers of the human mind. In espousing the 'moderate' view I am opting for a psychological theory which seems to me to be plausible.

[...]

2. The 'thermometer' view of non-inferential knowledge

Suppose that 'p' is true, and A believes that p, but his belief is not supported by any reasons. 'P' might be the proposition that there is a sound in A's environment. (The previous section indicates why this example is chosen.) What makes such a belief a case of knowledge? My suggestion is that there must be a *law-like connection* between the state of affairs Bap and the state of affairs that makes 'p' true such that, given Bap, it must be the case that p.

The quickest way to grasp the suggestion is to use a model. Let us compare non-inferential beliefs to the temperature-readings given by a thermometer. In some cases, the thermometer-reading will fail to correspond to the temperature of the environment. Such a reading may be compared to non-inferential false belief. In other cases, the reading will correspond to the actual temperature. Such a reading is like non-inferential true belief. The second case, where reading and actual environmental temperature coincide, is then sub-divided into two sorts of case. First, suppose that the thermometer is a bad one, but that, on a certain occasion, the thermometer-reading coincides with the actual temperature. [...] Such a reading is to be compared with non-inferential true belief which falls short of knowledge. Suppose finally that the thermometer is a good one, so that a reading of 'T°' on the thermometer ensures that the environmental temperature is T°. Such a reading is to be compared with non-inferential *knowledge*. When a true belief unsupported by reasons stands to the situation truly believed to exist as a thermometer-reading in a good thermometer stands to the actual temperature, then we have non-inferential knowledge.

I think the picture given by the thermometer-model is intuitively clear. The problem is to give a formal account of the situation.

Here is one immediate difficulty. Laws of nature are connections between things (in the widest sense of 'things') of certain *sorts*. But the suggested connection between belief-state and situation which makes the belief true is a connection between particular states of affairs: between singulars.

The reply to this is that the belief-state is an *instance* of a certain sort of thing: a person believing a certain sort of proposition. Equally, the situation is an instance of a certain sort of thing: say, a certain sort of sound within earshot of the believer. So we can say that a law-like connection holds between the two singulars in virtue of the fact that the two are of certain sorts, and things of these sorts are connected by a law.

Here, however, we must be careful. What is the law that is involved? Take the example of knowing non-inferentially that there is a sound in one's environment. A believes that there is a sound in his environment now, and indeed there is. Do we want to say that A *knows* there is a sound in his environment only if the whole situation is covered by the following law-like generalization: 'If anybody believes that there is a sound in his environment, then there is indeed a sound in his environment'? Of course not. The proposed generalization is clearly false, because people have sometimes believed that there was a sound in their environment when there was none. Yet we are not led by this to say that nobody ever *knows* that such sounds are occurring.

The model of the thermometer gives us further assistance here. For a thermometer to be reliable on a certain occasion in registering a certain temperature as T° we do not demand that there be a true law-like generalization: 'If any thermometer registers "T°", then the temperature is T°.' In the first place, we recognize that there can be good and bad thermometers. In the second place, we do not even demand that a good thermometer provide a reliable reading under every condition. We recognize that there may be special environmental conditions under which even a 'good' thermometer is unreliable.

What do we demand? Let us investigate a far less stringent condition. Suppose, on a certain occasion, a thermometer is reliably registering 'T°'. There must be some property of the instrument and/or its circumstances such that, if anything has this property, and registers 'T°', it must be the case, as a matter of natural law, that the temperature *is* T°. We might find it extremely hard to specify this property (set of properties). The specification might have to be given in the form of a blank cheque to be filled in only after extensive investigation. But it may be relatively easy to recognize that a certain thermometer is operating reliably, and so that such specification is possible. [. . .]

Let us now try applying this to the case of non-inferential knowledge. A's non-inferential belief that p is non-inferential *knowledge* if, and only if:

(i) p is the case
(ii) There is some specification of A such that, if any person is so specified, then, if they further believe that p, then p is the case.

Putting the suggestion in a more formal way (though it will soon be seen that the formula is ill-formed as it stands, and requires amendment):

A's non-inferential belief that p is a case of non-inferential *knowledge* if, and only if:

(i) p
(ii) ($\exists$ H)[Ha & there is a law-like connection in nature (x) if Hx, then (if Bxp, then p)].

It is important to remember that in condition (ii) Bxp and p are here to be taken as states of affairs rather than propositions. We might have written ^{s}Bxp and ^{s}p.[1]

---

1. [From pp. 5–6: A note on symbolism. At a number of points, formulae familiar from 'epistemic logic' will be employed. Thus, 'A believes that p' will sometimes be written 'Bap' and 'A knows that p' will be written 'Kap'. Very often, however, when I use such expressions as 'Bap' and 'Kap' reference will not be being made to some proposition but to some state of affairs or situation: A's believeing or knowing that p. Thus, in the course of the argument it may be said that 'Baq is the cause of Bap'. This will mean that A's believing that q brings it about that A believes that p. Max Deutscher has suggested that on such occasions it might be better to write "^{s}Baq is the cause of ^{s}Bap' to indicate that it is situations, not propositions, that are in question. I will occasionally adopt his suggestion. But since I think that the context normally makes it clear how the formulae are to be taken, aesthetic reasons plead in favour of omitting such superscripts wherever possible.]

Notice also that H is being used as a 'predicate variable' in the predicate position. Many would object to this practice, but it is by far the most convenient way of saying what I want to say.

It may seem strange that there can be a law-like connection holding between a state of affairs of a certain sort, on the one hand, and a further law-like connection, on the other. But in fact this is a commonplace in nature, as the thermometer case shows. *If* the thermometer is properly constructed, *then*, as a result of this, *if* the thermometer registers 'T°', *then* the temperature is T°. The same thing may therefore hold in the case of beliefs.

What are law-like connections of nature? I should like to avoid committing myself on this issue beyond what is absolutely necessary. The essential points seem to be these.

First, they are the sort of connections which can in principle be investigated by scientific method: by observation and, in particular, by experiment. In the case of a thermometer the investigation would not be difficult, in the case of beliefs it could be very difficult indeed, but there is no difference in principle between the cases. Were the particular thermometer-reading and the actual temperature at that time connected in a law-like way? We experiment with the thermometer, or a sufficiently similar one, and so draw a conclusion about the original situation. It is far harder to experiment with the beliefs of human beings, and so there may be much more guesswork in the assertion that a similar connection exists. But I take this to be a mere practical difficulty. (It does have the consequence, which seems to be perfectly acceptable, that it will often be difficult to determine when we do, and when we do not, *know.*)

Second, the law-like generalizations which record the existence of such connections yield counterfactual or, more generally, subjunctive conditionals. If the temperature of the environment on that occasion had not been T°, then the reading on the thermometer would not have been 'T°'. If p had not been the case, then it would not have been the case that A believed that p.

Third, the connection between belief and state of affairs is a connection which holds independently of us who may record its existence. It is an ontological connection. It is not, however, a *causal* connection. The state of affairs Bap does not bring the state of affairs that makes 'p' true into existence. [. . .] It is frequently the case that this state of affairs brings the state of affairs Bap into existence. But even that does not occur in all cases.

This, I hope, is as far as it is necessary to commit ourselves on the nature of the general connections involved. Some philosophers, in the spirit of Hume, maintain that a satisfactory account of law-like connection can be given without assuming the existence of anything except regularities of various sorts among otherwise unconnected phenomena. Other philosophers argue that some far stronger necessity in the nature of things is required. But this whole great dispute is an ontological problem which will receive no attention here. It may he hoped that, whatever answers are given to the problem, an account of non-inferential knowledge in terms of law-like connection will be unaffected. For in our account the notion of law-like connection is taken as a largely unanalysed primitive.

So much by way of explaining our formula. Unfortunately, it is not in its final form. A series of objections require discussion and some of these require that the formula be modified.

One modification is urgently required. As the formula has just been presented it is certainly ill-formed. p is a place-holder or dummy for a particular state of affairs. How then is it possible to bring p within the scope of a universal quantifier? How can we talk of states of affairs of the *sort* p?

But at this point we remember that the *proposition* p asserts a particular matter of fact ('It is hot here now'). All such propositions must involve (a) reference to some individual and (b) predicating some property of that individual. Putting it another way, such propositions must have the form Fa, or, as it will be more convenient to write because the letters 'F' and 'a' have already been given another use in this book, the form Jc. It is not just that there must exist a proposition with the form Jc that is logically equivalent to p. The structure of Ideas in the belief-state must actually have the form Jc. And once this point is appreciated, we can say that the second condition asserts a general connection between (a) beliefs that have the form Jc and (b) the actual obtaining of what is believed.

Our formula can now be rewritten. A's non-inferential belief that c is a J is a case of non-inferential *knowledge* if, and only if:

(i) Jc
(ii) ($\exists$ H)[Ha & there is a law-like connection in nature (x)(y) {if Hx, then (if BxJy, then Jy)}].

x ranges over beings capable of cognition. Since this account of non-inferential knowledge is restricted to beliefs about 'particular matters of fact', [. . .] y can range over particulars which figure in such beliefs. Suppose that what is believed is the proposition that it is hot here now. 'J' might then be 'hot in the immediate environment of the believer'. A believes it is hot here now, that is, he believes it is hot in his immediate environment. Further, A's current condition and situation is such that if *any* person who is in that condition and situation believes that it is hot in his immediate environment then, indeed, that immediate environment is hot.

[. . .]

3. Deutscher's objection

We must now take notice of an objection, due to Max Deutscher (private communication), which will force us to place a restriction on H, that is, the specification of A's condition and circumstances within which a belief of that sort is reliable.

We noticed briefly that the situation of c's being J is, very often, the thing which brings BaJc into existence. For instance, the sound in my environment is the thing which brings it about that I come to believe that there is a sound in my environment. (Just as the environmental temperature T° brings it about that the thermometer registers 'T°'.) At the same time, however, not every case where the situation of c's being J brings about the situation BaJc is a case where KaJc. We have already seen this in our brief discussion of Causal analyses of non-inferential knowledge. To re-describe the case mentioned there. A is suffering from auditory hallucinations, which he takes to be genuine. Like an object which is liable to explode under the impact of almost any slight shock, he is in such a state that almost any sensory stimulus will make him believe (normally falsely) that there is a sound in his environment. From time to time, however, the stimulus that makes him believe that there is a sound in his environment *is in fact a sound*. He has a 'veridical hallucination'! Here c's being J was causally responsible for BaJc, but we should want to deny that the belief was a case of knowledge.

At first sight, this 'veridical hallucination' case may seem to pose no problems for our formula. What we speak of as a cause is seldom a *necessary* condition of its effect. In the case under discussion, the sound is certainly not a necessary condition for producing the belief that there is a sound in the environment. Only if c's being J were a *necessary* causal condition of BaJc, which would make BaJc sufficient for c's being J (although coming after that state of affairs in time), would it seem that the conditions laid down in our formula for knowledge were met.

But, and this is Deutscher's point, we have forgotten about conditions H. Our formula set no limits on H. Condition (ii) of our formula, it will be remembered, was:

$$(\exists H)[Ha \text{ \& there is a law-like connection in nature } (x)(y)$$
$$\{if Hx, then (if BxJy, then Jy)\}].$$

H can be any general property, non-relational and/or relational, that the believer A has, however complex this property may be. Now suppose that in the 'veridical hallucination' situation we go on specifying certain of A's properties in indefinitely greater and greater detail. Will we not inevitably arrive at a complex property H that A has, such that, given a believer who had just that complex property *and* believed that there was a sound in his environment, then there *must* (nomically must) have been a sound there? In a situation so closely specified, the *only* thing which could cause the belief that there is a sound in the environment *is* such a sound. For the detailed description of A and his environment, if it is *sufficiently* detailed, will be such as to rule out any other cause. (Whatever operates, leaves signs of its operations about. Absence of these signs means that thing is not operating. These are not necessary truths. But we believe them to be true!) So even in the 'veridical hallucination' case, it seems, the law-like condition 'if Hx, then (if BxJy, then Jy)' will be satisfied, provided H is specified in sufficient detail. And there is no bar in the formula to specifying H in indefinite detail. Which yields us a result we cannot accept, that the 'veridical hallucination' case is a case of knowledge.

It seems that some restricting condition must be placed upon H in order to rule out such a counter-case.

In order to solve the problem, let us go back to our ever-useful model of the thermometer. Let us first construct the thermometer-equivalent of the 'veridical hallucination' case. It is possible to conceive of a thoroughly unsatisfactory thermometer which is acted upon by an environment at T°, and that this environmental temperature, by some strange fluke, happens on a particular occasion to make the thermometer register 'T°'. Yet if we were to specify the thermometer's constitution *and environment* on that occasion in sufficient detail, it would (almost certainly) be empirically impossible that the thermometer *as so specified* should have registered 'T°' except through the action of an environment at T°.

Now have we got a thermometer which is *reliable* (in respect of registering 'T°') in these highly specific conditions? We would resist this conclusion. Why? The answer, I think, is that thermometers are built to *use*, and a thermometer of that sort would be no use, even if we knew and could identify the conditions in which its reading of 'T°' had to be correct. For the conditions would be so highly idiosyncratic that in all probability they would never occur more than once. Rather, what is wanted is a thermometer which will register correctly *in a variety of conditions*. But in order to ensure this, the conditions in which it gives a correct reading must not be specified too closely. Indeed, the more unspecified these are, then, all other things being equal, the more useful the thermometer will be. These conditions are the thermometer-equivalent of condition H in our formula.

The same sort of considerations apply in the case of non-inferential knowledge. There is a sense in which knowledge is a pragmatic concept. Why are we interested in the distinction between knowledge and mere true belief? Because the man who has *mere* true belief is unreliable. He was right this time, but if the same sort of situation crops up again he is likely to get it wrong. (The point made by the luckless Meno, but brushed aside by Socrates.) But if it is empirically impossible or even very unlikely that the situation will crop up again, then the distinction loses almost all its *point*.

So I think it is fair to put the following restriction upon H. H must not be so specified that the situation becomes unique, or for all practical purposes unique. H must be such that the situation has some real probability or at least possibility of being repeated. And, all other things being equal, the less specific H is the greater the 'value' of A's knowledge, because this increases the probability of repetition.

It is clear that this restriction on H is not a very precise one. (Notice the ambiguity in the formulations of the previous paragraph.) It may therefore leave us with borderline cases which are awkward to adjudicate upon. But it does seem an intelligible and real restriction, it is not a relative one, and it is one which flows naturally out of the 'pragmatic' nature of the concept of knowledge. [. . .]

But although the scope of H is thus restricted so that it cannot be too specific, it is important to notice that there is one *restriction* on H's scope that must not be demanded. H must not be restricted to the *non-relational* properties of the believer A. That this restriction is too severe is most simply seen in terms of the analogy of the thermometer. It is not a conclusive objection to a thermometer that it is only reliable in a certain sort of environment. In the same way, reliability of belief, but only within a certain sort of environment, would seem to be sufficient for the believer to earn the accolade of knowledge if that sort of environment is part of his boundary-conditions.

The fact that H's scope can extend to *relational* properties of A has an important consequence. It was argued in Part I of this book that *belief* was a state (and in the case of general beliefs a dispositional state) of the believer. States are (a sub-class of) non-relational properties of the object which is in that state. But it now seems that non-inferential knowledge, at least, is not, or at any rate need not be, a state. A belief-state which is not knowledge might be knowledge, if the circumstances had been more favourable, without necessitating any difference in the believer's mind. So, although any particular belief-state is or is not knowledge (or is a border-line case), there is *this* element of 'relativity' in the notion of knowledge.

Before concluding this section, I shall make one note on the model of the thermometer. This model has proved so useful in explicating my view, which might even be called the 'thermometer' account of non-inferential knowledge, that it is important to notice that one characteristic of a good thermometer plays no part in the account. Registration of temperature and actual temperature reflect each other. Given that a reliable thermometer is registering 'T°', then the environmental temperature is T°. It is this feature which has been important for us. But, equally, given that the environmental temperature is T°, then the good thermometer will register 'T°'. Now this second feature is not necessary for non-inferential knowledge. Given that a person knows that c is J non-inferentially, then his belief is a reliable one, in the way which we have spelt out. He is in some condition and/or circumstances H which must not be too narrowly specified, such that if a person is in H, and believes something of that sort, then, as a matter of law-like connection, that thing believed is the case. But it does not follow that if a person is in circumstances/condition H, and c is J, then that person believes that c is J. Such a person may have no opinion at all on the matter. He may fail to register 'Jc'. In this respect, then, the reliable thermometer is too strong a model for non inferential knowledge.

In order to remove this defect from the thermometer-model it would be necessary to have a thermometer which, although reliable when it *was* operating, might give a non-reading from which nothing in general could be deduced about the temperature. A reliable watch exhibits this feature when it is not wound up, except that its hands do still register a time. (It is also worth noticing that in the case of a properly set, wound-up reliable watch the time of day is not the *cause* of the watch registering the time of day correctly. In this, it is unlike the reliable thermometer. Yet, like the reliable thermometer, a reliable watch is a useful model for non-inferential knowledge.)

[...]

4. Further objections

But our troubles are not over. The two objections now to be considered are naturally connected and may be considered together.

The first problem was pointed out by Christopher Murphy, then an undergraduate at Sydney University. The trouble lies in the latter portion of the second condition:

> (ii) ... there is a law-like connection in nature (x)(y)
> {if Hx, then (if BxJy, then Jy)}.

By the logical operation of exportation, presumably valid in this context, this is equivalent to:

$$\ldots (x)(y)\{if\ (Hx\ \&\ BxJy),\ then\ Jy\}.$$

Now suppose that there is, as there might be, a law-like connection between situations of the sort H and situations of the sort J. Suppose in particular:

$$(x)(if\ Hx,\ then\ (\exists y)Jy).$$

A simple example falling under this formula would be one where H is a physiological condition of a certain quickly fatal sort, J is death, and x is the very same person as y. If any person is in physiological condition H, then that person dies shortly. Suppose now that this person *irrationally* acquires a (true) belief that he will die shortly. On our formula, his belief would have to be accounted knowledge.

A similar difficulty has been pointed out by Ken Waller (private communication). To produce Waller's case, we set up a law-like connection between belief-states and situations of the sort J. Suppose, for instance, that there is a chemical which must be present in a man's brain if he is to have *any* belief. If he believes anything, then the belief-chemical must be present in his brain. But now suppose that he somehow acquires the belief that a certain chemical is present in his brain. It happens to be the belief-chemical. Given our formula, this belief *must* be knowledge. But it seems obvious that it might in fact be a case of mere true belief.

What seems to be required in order to exclude Murphy's and Waller's cases is that, in our formula, the conditions H and the particular nature of the belief held should all be *nomically* relevant to the situations of the sort J. In Murphy's case, if we consider simply the belief, there is no law-like connection between it and situations of the sort J. In Waller's case, if we consider simply the particular content of the belief, there is no law-like connection between beliefs with this sort of content and situations of the sort J. Where two particulars are connected in a law-like way, they are connected *qua* particulars *of a certain sort* and not in virtue of other characteristics they may happen to have. Murphy and Waller have simply constructed cases where the particulars involved are not connected *qua* believers (Murphy) or *qua* believers of a certain sort of proposition (Waller), although in fact the beliefs are true. So we meet Murphy's and Waller's objection simply by stipulating that nothing but *nomically relevant characterizations* appear in our formula.

The principle seems easy enough, but the formal statement of this new restriction is rather complex. It might be thought that we could exclude Murphy's case by modifying condition (ii), the relevant portion of which at present reads:

$$\ldots (x)(y)\{if\ Hx,\ then\ (if\ BxJy,\ then\ Jy)\}$$

simply by adding, within the scope of the quantifiers:

$$\sim(if\ Hx,\ then\ Jy).$$

This, however, would be too strong. It can be the case that (if Hx, then Jy), and yet it still be possible to credit the believer with knowledge that c is J. If there is *a law-like connection between the belief and the condition H*, then, even if H by itself ensures J, we still have a case of knowledge. The belief will ensure Ha, which will ensure Jc, and so, by transitivity, the belief will ensure Jc. The addition should therefore instead take the form:

$$\text{if (if Hx, then Jy), then (if BxJy, then Hx).}$$

In Waller's sort of case, H together with x's holding a belief ensures a situation of the sort J. This suggests adding to condition (ii), within the scope of the quantifiers, the following condition:

$$\sim(P)(\text{if BxP, then Jy})$$

where 'P' ranges over all propositions. Once again, however, this condition would be too restricting. It would make it impossible for somebody to *know* that he had the belief-chemical in his brain. What we should say, rather, is that *if* H together with any belief whatsoever ensures a situation of the sort J, then the actual belief held must ensure H. (The belief automatically ensures that *some* belief is held, so the latter condition need not be explicitly mentioned.) So the condition will become:

$$\text{if (P)(if BxP, then Jy), then (if BxJy, then Hx).}$$

In this way, I think, we can exclude all but nomically relevant characteristics from our formula. But since, as we have just seen, formal statement is both complex and tricky, I will for the future simply allow the condition of nomic relevance to appear as an unformalized restriction on our formula.

5. Self-fulfilling beliefs

But the last paragraph of the previous section brings up a point which will force a final modification in our formula.

A's believing that c is J is a certain sort of state: a state of A's mind. Like all states, it endows the object that is in that state with certain causal powers. Now suppose that A has a belief that c is J for which he has no reasons, but which, in the circumstances A is in, brings it about that c is J. The analogy in the case of the thermometer would be an instrument that, by registering 'T°', brought it about that the temperature of the environment *was* T°. Of course, we should not call it a thermometer.

Such cases are not merely conceivable, they are empirically possible and sometimes occur. Consider the case of a sick man who, for no reason at all, believes that he will recover. Is it not possible, in view of what we know about the effect of psychological states upon bodily conditions, that that belief should be the cause of his recovery? (Without it, he would have died.) Again, consider the case of a child who takes it into his head, for no reason at all, that he will receive a certain toy for Christmas. His kind-hearted parents, who had not intended to give him this toy, learn of his belief and proceed to make it true.

Now in both cases of self-fulfilling beliefs it seems that, in the situation the believer is in, the belief ensures its own truth. In A's situation, if BaJc, then Jc. Furthermore, the conditions, H, under which this sequence occurs, might well, on occasion, be sufficiently general to permit the real possibility of other believers with beliefs of the same sort to be in the situation H. So the suggested conditions for non-inferential knowledge might well obtain. But would we ever be prepared to speak of *knowledge* here?

The situation is a peculiar one, and my intuitions, and I would suppose other people's, are not completely clear on the matter. But it seems, on the whole, that we ought not to speak of knowledge here. The essential point of a 'faculty of knowledge', is that it should, in respect of what is known, be passive to the world. If the 'reflection' is achieved by our mind moulding the world, we are not knowing but creating. (Although there may be a model here for God's knowledge of his creation.)

How, then, should we amend our account of non-inferential knowledge to exclude such cases? It could be done by simply adding a third clause to our formula:

$$\text{(iii) it is not the case that Bap is the cause of p.}$$

If, however, we consider the second condition:

$$\text{(ii) } (\exists\, H)\ [Ha\ \&\ \text{there is a law-like connection in nature}$$
$$(x)(y)\{\text{if Hx, then (if BxJy, then Jy)}\}]$$

then we have already introduced one modification as a restriction upon the scope of H in this formula (there must be a real possibility of the repetition of conditions H), and another as a restriction to nomically relevant properties in the formula as a whole. We might therefore introduce this new restriction as a comment upon the relation between BxJy and Jy.

We must first introduce and define the notion of a (natural) *sign*. Black clouds, for instance, are a sign of rain. We may distinguish between sign as token and sign as type. The following definition of a sign-token is then attractive. It is a particular of a certain sort, such that if the particular comes under the cognizance of a suitably knowledgeable person as a particular of that sort, that person can make a more or less reliable (inductive) inference to the existence of some further particular state of affairs. (The inference might be that the very same particular was of some further sort.)

But this definition, although on the right track, is a trifle too wide. Suppose that a certain sort of wound ensures death. A suitably trained person might infer from the fact that A had that sort of wound that A would die. The wound answers to our definition of a sign. But we should be reluctant to say the wound was a sign of ensuing death. Compare this with a special pallor which the wounded man might exhibit from which death could also be inferred. We would be happy to say that the *pallor* was a sign that death approached.

What is the difference between the wound and the pallor? I think that we say that the wound is not a sign of death because it is, *qua* wound, the *cause* of death. An effect can be a sign of its cause. A corpse may be a sign of foul play. But a cause is not a sign of its effect. (Black clouds are a cause of rain, but not in virtue of their blackness.) But, I think, with this restriction, our original definition of 'sign' can stand.

Returning now to our definition of non-inferential knowledge, we need not now stipulate, as an independent condition, that it be not the case that BaJc bring it about that c is J. Instead we can stipulate that the relation in our second condition between BxJy and Jy, be that of sign to thing signified.

Our definition now becomes:

A's non-inferential belief that c is J is a case of non-inferential *knowledge* if, and only if:

(i) Jc

(ii) $(\exists H)[Ha$ & there is a law-like connection in nature $(x)(y)$ {if Hx, then (if $BxJy$, then Jy)}].

The following restrictions are placed on (ii)

(a) H must be such that there is a real possibility of the situation covered by the law-like connection recurring.

(b) The properties mentioned are nomically relevant to the law-like connection.

(c) The relation of BxJy to Jy is that of *completely reliable sign* to thing signified.

It will be pointed out in the next chapter that, given that A believes that c is J, condition (i) – that c is in fact J – is redundant. But otherwise our definition of non-inferential knowledge in terms of non-inferential belief is now fully before us.

The formulation of restriction (c) to condition (ii) in terms of the notion of a reliable sign helps to bring out a very important point about our account of non-inferential knowledge. The knower himself will not have evidence for what he knows. That is the meaning of 'non-inferential'. But his own belief-state, together with the circumstances he is in, could function for somebody *else* (God perhaps) as completely reliable evidence, in particular as a completely reliable sign, of the truth of the thing he believes. The subject's belief is not based on reasons, but it might be said to be reasonable (justifiable), because it is a sign, a completely reliable sign, that the situation believed to exist does in fact exist.

Chapter 8

Discrimination and perceptual knowledge*

Alvin I. Goldman

THIS paper presents a partial analysis of perceptual knowledge, an analysis that will, I hope, lay a foundation for a general theory of knowing. Like an earlier theory I proposed,[1] the envisaged theory would seek to explicate the concept of knowledge by reference to the causal processes that produce (or sustain) belief. Unlike the earlier theory, however, it would abandon the requirement that a knower's belief that p be causally connected with the fact, or state of affairs, that p.

What kinds of causal processes or mechanisms must he responsible for a belief if that belief is to count as knowledge? They must be mechanisms that are, in an appropriate sense, 'reliable.' Roughly, a cognitive mechanism or process is reliable if it not only produces true beliefs in actual situations, but would produce true beliefs, or at least inhibit false beliefs, in relevant counterfactual situations. The theory of knowledge I envisage, then, would contain an important counterfactual component.

To be reliable, a cognitive mechanism must enable a person to *discriminate* or *differentiate* between incompatible states of affairs. It must operate in such a way that incompatible states of the world would generate different cognitive responses. Perceptual mechanisms illustrate this clearly. A perceptual mechanism is reliable to the extent that contrary features of the environment (e.g., an object's being red, versus its being yellow) would produce contrary perceptual states of the organism, which would, in turn, produce suitably different beliefs about the environment. Another belief-governing mechanism is a reasoning mechanism, which, given a set of antecedent beliefs, generates or inhibits various new beliefs. A reasoning mechanism is reliable to the extent that its functional procedures would generate new true beliefs from antecedent true beliefs.

My emphasis on discrimination accords with a sense of the verb 'know' that has been neglected by philosophers. The O.E.D. lists one (early) sense of 'know' as '*to distinguish* (one thing) *from* (another)', as in 'I know a hawk from a handsaw' (*Hamlet*) and 'We'll teach him to know Turtles from Jayes' (*Merry Wives of Windsor*).

Alvin I. Goldman, 'Discrimination and Perceptual Knowledge', in *The Journal of Philosophy*, 73 (1976), pp. 771–91, reprinted by permission of Columbia University, New York.

* An early version of this paper was read at the 1972 Chapel Hill Colloquium. Later versions were read at the 1973 University of Cincinnati Colloquium, and at a number of other philosophy departments. For comments and criticism, I am especially indebted to Holly Goldman, Bruce Aune, Jaegwon Kim, Louis Loeb, and Kendall Walton.

1. 'A Causal Theory of Knowing,' *Journal of Philosophy*, 64, 12 (June 22, 1967): 357–72; reprinted in M. Roth and L. Galis, eds., *Knowing* (New York: Random House, 1970). [Ch. 4 in this volume]

Although it no longer has great currency, this sense still survives in such expressions as 'I don't know him from Adam,' 'He doesn't know right from left,' and other phrases that readily come to mind. I suspect that this construction is historically important and can be used to shed light on constructions in which 'know' takes propositional objects. I suggest that a person is said to know that p just in case he *distinguishes* or *discriminates* the truth of p from relevant alternatives.

A knowledge attribution imputes to someone the discrimination of a given state of affairs from possible alternatives, but not necessarily all logically possible alternatives. In forming beliefs about the world, we do not normally consider all logical possibilities. And in deciding whether someone knows that p (its truth being assumed), we do not ordinarily require him to discriminate from all logically possible alternatives. Which alternatives are, or ought to be considered, is a question I shall not fully resolve in this paper, but some new perspectives will be examined. I take up this topic in section I.

I

Consider the following example. Henry is driving in the countryside with his son. For the boy's edification Henry identifies various objects on the landscape as they come into view. 'That's a cow,' says Henry, 'That's a tractor,' 'That's a silo,' 'That's a barn,' etc. Henry has no doubt about the identity of these objects; in particular, he has no doubt that the last-mentioned object is a barn, which indeed it is. Each of the identified objects has features characteristic of its type. Moreover, each object is fully in view, Henry has excellent eyesight, and he has enough time to look at them reasonably carefully, since there is little traffic to distract him.

Given this information, would we say that Henry *knows* that the object is a barn? Most of us would have little hesitation in saying this, so long as we were not in a certain philosophical frame of mind. Contrast our inclination here with the inclination we would have if we were given some additional information. Suppose we are told that, unknown to Henry, the district he has just entered is full of papier-mâché facsimiles of barns. These facsimiles look from the road exactly like barns, but are really just façades, without back walls or interiors, quite incapable of being used as barns. They are so cleverly constructed that travelers invariably mistake them for barns. Having just entered the district, Henry has not encountered any facsimiles; the object he sees is a genuine barn. But if the object on that site were a facsimile, Henry would mistake it for a barn. Given this new information, we would be strongly inclined to withdraw the claim that Henry *knows* the object is a barn. How is this change in our assessment to be explained?[2]

Note first that traditional justified-true-belief account of knowledge is of no help in explaining this change. In both cases Henry truly believes (indeed, is certain) that the object is a barn. Moreover, Henry's 'justification' or 'evidence' for the

---

2. [Addendum added in 1992] The barn facsimile example was originally suggested to me as a puzzle by Carl Ginet. Gail Stine (1976) also uses the example, which she would have heard when I read a version of this paper at Wayne State University in about 1974.

proposition that the object is a barn is the same in both cases. Thus, Henry should either know in both cases or not know in both cases. The presence of facsimiles in the district should make no difference to whether or not he knows.

My old causal analysis cannot handle the problem either. Henry's belief that the object is a barn is caused by the presence of the barn; indeed, the causal process is a perceptual one. Nonetheless, we are not prepared to say, in the second version, that Henry knows.

One analysis of propositional knowledge that might handle the problem is Peter Unger's non-accidentality analysis.[3] According to this theory, S knows that p if and only if it is not at all accidental that S is right about its being the case that p. In the initial description of the example, this requirement appears to be satisfied; so we say that Henry knows. When informed about the facsimiles, however, we see that it is accidental that Henry is right about its being a barn. So we withdraw our knowledge attribution. The 'non-accidentality' analysis is not very satisfying, however, for the notion of 'non-accidentality' itself needs explication. Pending explication, it isn't clear whether it correctly handles all cases.

Another approach to knowledge that might handle our problem is the 'indefeasibility' approach.[4] On this view, S knows that p only if S's true belief is justified *and* this justification is not defeated. In an unrestricted form, an indefeasibility theory would say that S's justification j for believing that p is defeated if and only if there is some true proposition q such that the conjunction of q and j does not justify S in believing that p. In slightly different terms, S's justification j is defeated just in case p would no longer be evident for S if q were evident for S. This would handle the barn example, presumably, because the true proposition that there are barn facsimiles in the district is such that, if it were evident for Henry, then it would no longer be evident for him that the object he sees is a barn.

The trouble with the indefeasibility approach is that it is too strong, at least in its unrestricted form. On the foregoing account of 'defeat' as Gilbert Harman shows,[5] it will (almost) always be possible to find a true proposition that defeats S's justification. Hence, S will never (or seldom) know. What is needed is an appropriate restriction on the notion of 'defeat' but I am not aware of an appropriate restriction that has been formulated thus far.

The approach to the problem I shall recommend is slightly different. Admittedly, this approach will raise problems analogous to those of the indefeasibility theory, problems which will not be fully resolved here. Nevertheless, I believe this approach is fundamentally on the right track.

What, then, is my proposed treatment of the barn example? A person knows that p, I suggest, only if the actual state of affairs in which p is true is *distinguishable* or

3. 'An Analysis of Factual Knowledge,' *Journal of Philosophy*, 65, 6 (Mar. 21, 1968): 157–70; reprinted in Roth and Galis, *op. cit.*

4. See, for example, Keith Lehrer and Thomas Paxson, Jr., 'Knowledge: Undefeated Justified True Belief,' *Journal of Philosophy*, 66, 8 (Apr. 24, 1969): 225–37 [Ch. 5 in this volume], and Peter D. Klein, 'A Proposed Definition of Propositional Knowledge,' *Journal of Philosophy*, 68 (Aug. 19, 1971): 471–82

5. *Thought* (Princeton, N.J.: University Press, 1973), p. 152.

discriminable by him from a relevant possible state of affairs in which *p* is false. If there is a relevant possible state of affairs in which *p* is false and which is indistinguishable by him from the actual state of affairs, then he fails to know that *p*. In the original description of the barn case there is no hint of any relevant possible state of affairs in which the object in question is not a barn but is indistinguishable (by Henry) from the actual state of affairs. Hence, we are initially inclined to say that Henry knows. The information about the facsimiles, however, introduces such a relevant state of affairs. Given that the district Henry has entered is full of barn facsimiles, there is a relevant alternative hypothesis about the object, viz., that it is a facsimile. Since, by assumption, a state of affairs in which such a hypothesis holds is indistinguishable by Henry from the actual state of affairs (from his vantage point on the road), this hypothesis is not 'ruled out' or 'precluded' by the factors that prompt Henry's belief. So, once apprised of the facsimiles in the district, we are inclined to deny that Henry knows.

Let us be clear about the bearing of the facsimiles on the case. The presence of the facsimiles does not 'create' the possibility that the object Henry sees is a facsimile. Even if there were no facsimiles in the district, it would be possible that the object on that site is a facsimile. What the presence of the facsimile does is make this possibility *relevant*, or it makes us *consider* it relevant.

The qualifier 'relevant' plays an important role in my view. If knowledge required the elimination of all logically possible alternatives, there would be no knowledge (at least of contingent truths). If only *relevant* alternatives need to be precluded, however, the scope of knowledge could be substantial. This depends, of course, on which alternatives are relevant.

The issue at hand is directly pertinent to the dispute—at least one dispute—between skeptics and their opponents. In challenging a claim to knowledge (or certainty), a typical move of the skeptic is to adduce an unusual alternative hypothesis that the putative knower is unable to preclude: an alternative compatible with his 'data.' In the skeptical stage of his argument, Descartes says that he is unable to preclude the hypothesis that, instead of being seated by the fire, he is asleep in his bed and dreaming, or the hypothesis that an evil and powerful demon is making it appear to him that he is seated by the fire. Similarly, Bertrand Russell points out that, given any claim about the past, we can adduce the 'skeptical hyothesis' that the world sprang into being five minutes ago, exactly as it then was, with a population that 'remembered' a wholly unreal past.[6]

One reply open to the skeptic's opponent is that these skeptical hypotheses, are just 'idle' hypotheses, and that a person can know a proposition even if there are 'idle' alternatives he cannot preclude. The problem, of course, is to specify when an alternative is 'idle' and when it is 'serious' ('relevant'). Consider Henry once again. Should we say that the possibility of a facsimile before him is a serious or relevant possibility if there are no facsimiles in Henry's district, but only in Sweden? Or if a single facsimile once existed in Sweden, but none exist now?

There are two views one might take on this general problem. The first view is that

6. *The Analysis of Mind* (London: Allen & Unwin, 1921), pp. 159–60.

there is a 'correct' answer, in any given situation, as to which alternatives are relevant. Given a complete specification of Henry's situation, a unique set of alternatives is determined: either a set to which the facsimile alternative belongs or one to which it doesn't belong. According to this view, the semantic content of 'know' contains (implicit) rules that map any putative knower's circumstances into a set of relevant alternatives. An analysis of 'know' is incomplete unless it specifies these rules. The correct specification will favor either the skeptic or the skeptic's opponent.

The second view denies that a putative knower's circumstances uniquely determine a set of relevant alternatives. At any rate, it denies that the semantic content of 'know' contains rules that map a set of circumstances into a single set of relevant alternatives. According to this second view, the verb 'know' is simply not so semantically determinate.

The second view need not deny that there are *regularities* governing the alternative hypotheses a speaker (i.e., an attributer or denier of knowledge) thinks of, and deems relevant. But these regularities are not part of the semantic content of 'know'. The putative knower's circumstances do not *mandate* a unique selection of alternatives; but psychological regularities govern which set of alternatives are in fact selected. In terms of these regularities (together with the semantic content of 'know'), we can explain the observed use of the term.

It is clear that some of these regularities pertain to the (description of the) putative knower's circumstances. One regularity might be that the more *likely* it is, given the circumstances, that a particular alternative would obtain (rather than the actual state of affairs), the more probable it is that a speaker will regard this alternative as relevant. Or, the more *similar* the situation in which the alternative obtains to the actual situation, the more probable it is that a speaker will regard this alternative as relevant. It is not only the circumstances of the putative knower's situation, however, that influence the choice of alternatives. The speaker's own linguistic and psychological context are also important. If the speaker is in a class where Descartes's evil demon has just been discussed, or Russell's five-minute-old-world hypothesis, he may think of alternatives he would not otherwise think of and will perhaps treat them seriously. This sort of regularity is entirely ignored by the first view.

What I am calling the 'second' view might have two variants. The first variant can be imbedded in Robert Stalnaker's framework for pragmatics.[7] In this framework, a proposition is a function from possible words into truth values; the determinants of a proposition are a sentence and a (linguistic) context. An important contextual element is what the utterer of a sentence presupposes, or takes for granted. According to the first variant of the second view, a sentence of the form S knows that p does not determine a unique proposition. Rather, a proposition is determined by such a sentence together with the speaker's presuppositions concerning the relevant alternatives.[8] Skeptics and nonskeptics might make different

7. 'Pragmatics' in Donald Davidson and Harman, eds., *Semantics of Natural Language* (Boston: Reidel, 1972).

8. Something like this is suggested by Fred Dretske, in 'Epistemic Operators,' *Journal of Philosophy*, 67 (1970): 1007–1023, p. 1022. [Addendum added in 1992] I should emphasize that Dretske himself uses the phrase 'relevant alternatives', probably its first occurrence in the literature.

presuppositions (both presuppositions being 'legitimate'), and, if so, they are simply asserting or denying different propositions.

One trouble with this variant is its apparent implication that, if a speaker utters a knowledge sentence without presupposing a fully determinate set of alternatives, he does not assert or deny any proposition. That seems too strong. A second variant of the second view, then, is that sentences of the form 'S knows that p' express vague or indeterminate propositions (if they express 'propositions' at all), which can, but need not, be made more determinate by full specification of the alternatives. A person who *assents* to a knowledge sentence says that S discriminates the truth of p from relevant alternatives; but he may not have a distinct set of alternatives in mind. (Similarly, according to Paul Ziff, a person who says something is 'good' says that it answers to *certain* interests;[9] but he may not have a distinct set of interests in mind.) Someone who *denies* a knowledge sentence more commonly has one or more alternatives in mind as relevant, because his denial may stem from a particular alternative S cannot rule out. But even the denier of a knowledge sentence need not have a full set of relevant alternatives in mind.

I am attracted by the second view under discussion, especially its second variant. In the remainder of the paper, however, I shall be officially neutral. In other words, I shall not try to settle the question of whether the semantic content of 'know' contains rules that map the putative knower's situation into a unique set of relevant alternatives. I leave open the question of whether there is a 'correct' set of relevant alternatives, and if so, what it is. To this extent, I also leave open the question of whether skeptics or their opponents are 'right.' In defending my analysis of 'perceptually knows', however, I shall have to discuss particular examples. In treating these examples I shall assume some (psychological) regularities concerning the selection of alternatives. Among these regularities is the fact that speakers do not *ordinarily* think of 'radical' alternatives, but are caused to think of such alternatives, and take them seriously, if the putative knower's circumstances call attention to them. Since I assume that radical or unusual alternatives are not *ordinarily* entertained or taken seriously, I may appear to side with the opponents of skepticism. My official analysis, however, is neutral on the issue of skepticism.

II

I turn now to the analysis of 'perceptually knows'. Suppose that Sam spots Judy on the street and correctly identifies her as Judy, i.e., believes she is Judy. Suppose further that Judy has an identical twin, Trudy, and the possibility of the person's being Trudy (rather than Judy) is a relevant alternative. Under what circumstances would we say that Sam *knows* it is Judy?

If Sam regularly identifies Judy as Judy and Trudy as Trudy, he apparently has some (visual) way of discriminating between them (though he may not know how

---

9. That 'good' means *answers to certain interests* is claimed by Ziff in *Semantic Analysis* (Ithaca, N.Y.: Cornell, 1960), ch. 6.

he does it, i.e., what cues he uses). If he does have a way of discriminating between them, which he uses on the occasion in question, we would say that he *knows* it is Judy. But if Sam frequently mistakes Judy for Trudy, and Trudy for Judy, he presumably does not have a way of discriminating between them. For example, he may not have sufficiently distinct (visual) memory 'schemata' of Judy and Trudy. So that, on a particular occasion, sensory stimulation from either Judy *or* Trudy would elicit a Judy-identification from him. If he happens to be right that it is Judy, this is just accidental. He doesn't *know* it is Judy.

The crucial question in assessing a knowledge attribution, then, appears to be the truth value of a counterfactual (or set of counterfactuals). Where Sam correctly identifies Judy as Judy, the crucial counterfactual is: 'If the person before Sam were Trudy (rather than Judy), Sam would believe her to be Judy.') If this counterfactual is true, Sam doesn't know it is Judy. If this counterfactual is false (and all other counterfactuals involving relevant alternatives are also false), then Sam may know it is Judy.

This suggests the following analysis of (noninferential) perceptual knowledge.

S (noninferentially) *perceptually knows that p* if and only if

(1) *S* (noninferentially) perceptually believes that *p*,
(2) *p* is true, and
(3) there is no relevant contrary *q* of *p* such that, if *q* were true (rather than *p*), then *S* would (still) believe that *p*.

Restricting attention to relevant possibilities, these conditions assert in effect that the only situation in which *S* would believe that *p* is a situation in which *p* is true. In other words, *S*'s believing that *p* is sufficient for the truth of *p*. This is essentially the analysis of noninferential knowledge proposed by D. M. Armstrong in *A Materialist Theory of the Mind* (though without any restriction to 'relevant' alternatives), and refined and expanded in *Belief, Truth, and Knowledge.*[10]

This analysis is too restrictive. Suppose Oscar is standing in an open field containing Dack the dachshund. Oscar sees Dack and (noninferentially) forms a belief in (P):

(P) The object over there is a dog.

Now suppose that (Q):

(Q) The object over there is a wolf

is a relevant alternative to (P) (because wolves are frequenters of this field). Further suppose that Oscar has a tendency to mistake wolves for dogs (he confuses them with malamutes, or German shepherds). Then if the object Oscar saw were Wiley the wolf, rather than Dack the dachshund, Oscar would (still) believe (P). This means that Oscar fails to satisfy the proposed analysis with respect to (P), since (3) is violated. But surely it is wrong to deny—for the indicated reasons—that Oscar *knows* (P) to be true. The mere fact that he would erroneously take a wolf to be a dog hardly shows that he doesn't know a *dachshund* to be a dog! Similarly, if someone looks at a huge redwood and correctly believes it to be a tree, he is not

10. *A Materialist Theory of the Mind* (New York: Humanities, 1968), pp. 189 ff., and *Belief, Truth and Knowledge* (New York: Cambridge, 1973), chs. 12 [Ch. 7 in this volume] and 13.

disqualified from knowing it to be a tree merely because there is a very small plant he would wrongly believe to be a tree, i.e., a bonsai tree.

The moral can be formulated as follows. If Oscar believes that a dog is present because of a certain way he is 'appeared to,' then this true belief fails to be knowledge if there is an alternative situation in which a non-dog produces the same belief by means of the same, or a very similar, appearance. But the wolf situation is not such an alternative: although it would produce in him the same belief, it would not be by means of the same (or a similar) appearance. An alternative that disqualifies a true perceptual belief from being perceptual knowledge must be a 'perceptual equivalent' of the actual state of affairs.[11] A *perceptual equivalent* of an actual state of affairs is a possible state of affairs that would produce the same, or a sufficiently similar, perceptual experience.

The relation of perceptual equivalence must obviously be relativized to *persons* (or organisms). The presence of Judy and the presence of Trudy might be perceptual equivalents for Sam, but not for the twins' own mother (to whom the twins look quite different). Similarly, perceptual equivalence must be relativized to *times*, since perceptual discriminative capacities can be refined or enhanced with training or experience, and can deteriorate with age or disease.

How shall we specify alternative states of affairs that are candidates for being perceptual equivalents? First, we should specify the *object* involved. (I assume for simplicity that only one object is in question.) As the Judy-Trudy case shows, the object in the alternative state of affairs need not be identical with the actual object. Sometimes, indeed, we may wish to allow non-actual possible objects. Otherwise our framework will be unable in principle to accommodate some of the skeptic's favorite alternatives, e.g., those involving demons. If the reader's ontological sensibility is offended by talk of possible objects, I invite him to replace such talk with any preferred substitute.

Some alternative states of affairs involve the same object but different properties. Where the actual state of affairs involves a certain ball painted blue, an alternative might be chosen involving the same ball painted green. Thus, specification of an alternative requires not only an object, but properties of the object (at the time in question). These should include not only the property in the belief under scrutiny, or one of its contraries, but other properties as well, since the property in the belief (or one of its contraries) might not be sufficiently determinate to indicate what the resultant percept would be like. For full generality, let us choose a *maximal set of* (nonrelational) *properties*. This is a set that would exhaustively characterize an object (at a single time) in some possible world.[12]

11. My notion of a perceptual equivalent corresponds to Jaakko Hintikka's notion of a 'perceptual alternative.' See 'On the Logic of Perception,' in N. S. Care and R. H. Grimm, eds., *Perception and Personal Identity* (Cleveland, Ohio: Case Western Reserve, 1969).

12. I have in mind here purely qualitative properties. Properties like *being identical with Judy* would be given by the selected object. If the set of qualitative properties (at a given time) implied which object it was that had these properties, then specification of the object would be redundant, and we could represent states of affairs by ordered pairs of maximal sets of (qualitative) properties and DOE relations. Since this is problematic, however, I include specification of the object as well as the set of (qualitative) properties.

An object plus a maximal set of (nonrelational) properties still does not fully specify a perceptual alternative. Also needed are relations between the object and the perceiver, plus conditions of the environment. One relation that can affect the resultant percept is *distance*. Another relational factor is *relative orientation*, both of object vis-à-vis perceiver and perceiver vis-à-vis object. The nature of the percept depends, for example, on which side of the object faces the perceiver, and on how the perceiver's bodily organs are oriented, or situated, vis-à-vis the object. Thirdly, the percept is affected by the current state of the *environment*, e.g., the illumination, the presence or absence of intervening objects, and the direction and velocity of the wind.

To cover all such elements, I introduce the notion of a *distance-orientation-environment* relation, for short, a *DOE relation*. Each such relation is a conjunction of relations or properties concerning distance, orientation, and environmental conditions. One DOE relation is expressed by the predicate 'x is 20 feet from y, the front side of y is facing x, the eyes of x are open and focused in y's direction, no opaque object is interposed between x and y, and y is in moonlight'.

Since the health of sensory organs can affect percepts, it might be argued that this should be included in these relations, thereby opening the condition of these organs to counterfactualization. For simplicity I neglect this complication. This does not mean that I don't regard the condition of sensory organs as open to counterfactualization. I merely omit explicit incorporation of this factor into our exposition.

We can now give more precision to our treatment of perceptual equivalents. Perceptual states of affairs will be specified by ordered triples, each consisting of (1) an object, (2) a maximal set of non-relational properties, and (3) a DOE relation. If S perceives object b at t and if b has all the properties in a maximal set J and bears DOE relation R to S at t, then the actual state of affairs pertaining to this perceptual episode is represented by the ordered triple $\langle b, J, R \rangle$. An alternative state of affairs is represented by an ordered triple $\langle c, K, R^* \rangle$, which may (but need not) differ from $\langle b, J, R \rangle$ with respect to one or more of its elements.

Under what conditions is an alternative $\langle c, K, R^* \rangle$ a perceptual equivalent of $\langle b, J, R \rangle$ for person S at time t? I said that a perceptual equivalent is a state of affairs that would produce 'the same, or a very similar' perceptual experience. That is not very committal. Must a perceptual equivalent produce exactly the same percept? Given our intended use of perceptual equivalence in the analysis of perceptual knowledge, the answer is clearly No. Suppose that a Trudy-produced percept would be qualitatively distinct from Sam's Judy-produced percept, but similar enough for Sam to mistake Trudy for Judy. This is sufficient grounds for saying that Sam fails to have knowledge. Qualitative identity of percepts, then, is too strong a requirement for perceptual equivalence.

How should the requirement be weakened? We must not weaken it too much, for the wolf alternative might then be a perceptual equivalent of the dachshund state of affairs. This would have the unwanted consequence that Oscar doesn't know Dack to be a dog.

The solution I propose is this. If the percept produced by the alternative state of affairs would not differ from the actual percept in any respect that is causally relevant to S's belief, this alternative situation is a perceptual equivalent for S of the actual situation. Suppose that a Trudy-produced percept would differ from Sam's Judy-produced percept to the extent of having a different eyebrow configuration. (A difference in shape between Judy's and Trudy's eyebrows does not ensure that Sam's percepts would 'register' this difference. I assume, however, that the eyebrow difference would be registered in Sam's percepts.) But suppose that Sam's visual 'concept' of Judy does not include a feature that reflects this contrast. His Judy-concept includes an 'eyebrow feature' in the sense that the absence of eyebrows would inhibit a Judy-classification. It does not include a more determinate eyebrow feature, though: Sam hasn't learned to associate Judy with distinctively shaped eyebrows. Hence, the distinctive 'eyebrow shape' of his actual (Judy-produced) percept is not one of the percept-features that is causally responsible for his believing Judy to be present. Assuming that a Trudy-produced percept would not differ from his actual percept in any *other* causally relevant way, the hypothetical Trudy-situation is a perceptual equivalent of the actual Judy-situation.

Consider now the dachshund-wolf case. The hypothetical percept produced by a wolf would differ from Oscar's actual percept of the dachshund in respects that *are* causally relevant to Oscar's judgment that a dog is present. Let me elaborate. There are various kinds of objects, rather different in shape, size, color, and texture, that would be classified by Oscar as a dog. He has a number of visual 'schemata,' we might say, each with a distinctive set of features, such that any percept that 'matches' or 'fits' one of these schemata would elicit a 'dog' classification. (I think of a schema not as a 'template,' but as a set of more-or-less abstract—though iconic—features.[13]) Now, although a dachshund and a wolf would each produce a dog-belief in Oscar, the percepts produced by these respective stimuli would differ in respects that are causally relevant to Oscar's forming a dog-belief. Since Oscar's dachshund-schema includes such features as having an elongated, sausagelike shape, a smallish size, and droopy ears, these features of the percept are all causally relevant, when a dachshund is present, to Oscar's believing that a dog is present. Since a hypothetical wolf-produced percept would differ in these respects from Oscar's dachshund-produced percept, the hypothetical wolf state of affairs is not a perceptual equivalent of the dachshund state of affairs for Oscar.

The foregoing approach requires us to relativize perceptual equivalence once again, this time to the belief in question, or the property believed to be exemplified. The Trudy situation is a perceptual equivalent for Sam of the Judy situation *relative to the property of being* (identical with) *Judy*. The wolf situation is not a perceptual equivalent for Oscar of the dachshund situation *relative to the property of being a dog*.

I now propose the following definition of perceptual equivalence

If object b has the maximal set of properties J and is in DOE relation R to S at t, if S has some percept P at t that is perceptually caused by b's having J and being in R to S at t and if P noninferentially causes S to believe (or sustains S in believing) of object b that it has property F, then

13. For a discussion of iconic schemata, see Michael I. Posnar, *Cognition: An Introduction* (Glenview, Ill.: Scott, Foresman, 1973), ch. 3.

⟨c,K,R*⟩ is a perceptual equivalent of ⟨b,J,R,⟩ for S at t relative to property F if and only if

(1) if at t object c had K and were in R* to S, then this would perceptually cause S to have some percept P* at t,

(2) P* would cause S noninferentially to believe (or sustain S in believing) of object c that it has F, and

(3) P* would not differ from P in any respect that is causally relevant to S's F-belief.

Since I shall analyze the *de re, relational, or transparent* sense of 'perceptually knows', I shall want to employ, in my analysis, the *de re* sense of 'believe'. This is why such phrases as 'believe ... of object b' occur in the definition of perceptual equivalence. For present purposes, I take for granted the notion of (perceptual) *de re* belief. I assume, however, that the object *of which* a person perceptually believes a property to hold is the object he perceives, i.e., the object that 'perceptually causes' the percept that elicits the belief. The notion of *perceptual causation* is another notion I take for granted. A person's percept is obviously caused by many objects (or events), not all of which the person is said to perceive. One problem for the theory of perception is to explicate the notion of perceptual causation, that is, to explain which of the causes of a percept a person is said to perceive. I set this problem aside here.[14] A third notion I take for granted is the notion of a (noninferential) *perceptual belief,* or perceptual 'taking.' Not all beliefs that are noninferentially caused by a percept can be considered perceptual 'takings'; 'indirectly' caused beliefs would not be so considered. But I make no attempt to delineate the requisite causal relation. Several other comments on the definition of perceptual equivalence are in order. Notice that the definition is silent on whether J or K contains property, F, i.e., whether F is exemplified in either the actual or the alternative states of affairs. The relativization to F (in the definiendum) implies that an F-belief is produced in both situations, not that F is exemplified (in either or both situations). In applying the definition to cases of putative knowledge, we shall focus on cases where F belongs to J (so S's belief is true in the actual situation) but does not belong to K (so S's belief is false in the counterfactual situation). But the definition of perceptual equivalence is silent on these matters.

Though the definition does not say so, I assume it is possible for object c to have all properties in K, and possible for c to be in R* to S while having all properties in K. I do not want condition 1 to be vacuously true, simply by having an impossible antecedent.

It might seem as if the antecedent of (1) should include a further conjunct, expressing the supposition that object b is absent. This might seem necessary to handle cases in which, if c were in R* to S, but b remained in its actual relation R to S, then b would 'block' S's access to c. (For example, b might be an orange balloon floating over the horizon, and c might be the moon.) This can be handled by the definition as it stands, by construing R*, where necessary, as including the absence of object b from the perceptual scene. (One cannot *in general* hypothesize that b is absent, for we want to allow object c to be identical with b.)

The definition implies that there is no temporal gap between each object's having

14. I take this problem up in 'Perceptual Objects,' forthcoming in *Synthese.*

its indicated properties and DOE relation and the occurrence of the corresponding percept. This simplification is introduced because no general requirement can be laid down about how long it takes for the stimulus energy to reach the perceiver. The intervals in the actual and alternative states may differ because the stimuli might be at different distances from the perceiver.

III

It is time to turn to the analysis of perceptual knowledge, for which the definition of perceptual equivalence paves the way. I restrict my attention to perceptual knowledge of the possession, by physical objects, of nonrelational properties. I also restrict the analysis to *noninferential* perceptual knowledge. This frees me from the complex issues introduced by inference, which require separate treatment.

It may be contended that all perceptual judgment is based on inference and, hence, that the proposed restriction reduces the scope of the analysis to nil. Two replies are in order. First, although cognitive psychology establishes that percepts are affected by cognitive factors, such as 'expectancies', it is by no means evident that these causal processes should be construed as inferences. Second, even if we were to grant that there is in fact no noninferential perceptual belief, it would still be of epistemological importance to determine whether noninferential perceptual knowledge of the physical world is conceptually possible. This could be explored by considering merely possible cases of noninferential perceptual belief, and seeing whether, under suitable conditions, such belief would count as knowledge.

With these points in mind, we may propose the following (tentative) analysis:

At t S noninferentially perceptually knows of object b that it has property F if and only if
 (1) for some maximal set of nonrelational properties *J* and some DOE relation *R*, object *b* has (all the members of) *J* at *t* and is in *R* to *S* at *t*
 (2) *F* belongs to *J*,
 (3) (A) *b*'s having *J* and being in *R* to *S* at *t* perceptually causes *S* at *t* to have some percept *P*,[15]

15. Should (3A) be construed as implying that *every* property in *J* is a (perceptual) cause of *P*? No. Many of *b*'s properties are exemplified in its interior or at its backside. These are not causally relevant, at least in visual perception. (3A) must therefore be construed as saying that P is (perceptually) caused by *b*'s having (jointly) *all* the members of *J*, and leaving open which, among these members, are individually causally relevant. It follows, however, that (3A) does not require that *b*'s-having-F, in particular, is a (perceptual) cause of *P*, and this omission might be regarded as objectionable. 'Surely,' it will be argued, 'S perceptually knows *b* to have *F* only if *b*'s-having-F (perceptually) causes the percept.' The reason I omit this requirement is the following. Suppose *F* is the property of being a dog. Can we say that *b*'s-being-a-dog is a cause of certain light waves' being reflected? This is very dubious. It is the molecular properties of the surface of the animal that are causally responsible for this transmission of light, and hence for the percept.

One might say that, even if the percept needn't be (perceptually) caused by *b*'s-having-F it must at least be caused by microstructural properties of *b* that *ensure b*'s-having-F. As the dog example again illustrates, however, this is too strong. The surface properties of the dog that reflect the light waves do not *ensure* that the object is a dog, either logically or nomologically. Something could have that surface (on one side) and still have a non-dog interior and backside. The problem should

(B) *P* noninferentially causes *S* at *t* to believe (or sustains *S* in believing) of
object *b* that it has property *F* and

(C) there is no alternative state of affairs $\langle c,K,R^* \rangle$ such that
   (i) $\langle c,K,R^* \rangle$ is a relevant perceptual equivalent of $\langle b,J,R \rangle$ for *S* at *t* relative
       to property *F*, and
   (ii) F does not belong to K.

Conditions 1 and 2 jointly entail the truth condition for knowledge: *S* knows *b* to
have *F* (at *t*) only if *b* does have *F* (at *t*). Condition 3B contains the belief condition
for knowledge, restricted, of course, to (noninferential) perceptual belief. The main
work of the conditions is done by 3C. It requires that there be no relevant alternative that is (i) a perceptual equivalent to the actual state of affairs relative to property *F*, and (ii) a state of affairs in which the appropriate object lacks *F* (and
hence *S*'s *F*-belief is false).

How does this analysis relate to my theme of a 'reliable discriminative mechanism'? A perceptual cognizer may be thought of as a two-part mechanism. The first
part constructs percepts (a special class of internal states) from receptor stimulation. The second part operates on percepts to produce beliefs. Now, in order for the
conditions of the analysans to be satisfied, each part of the mechanism must be
sufficiently discriminating, or 'finely tuned.' If the first part is not sufficiently
discriminating, patterns of receptor stimulation from quite different sources would
result in the same (or very similar) percepts, percepts that would generate the same
beliefs. If the second part is not sufficiently discriminating, then even if different
percepts are constructed by the first part, the same beliefs will be generated by the
second part. To be sure, even an undiscriminating bipartite mechanism may produce a belief that, luckily, is true; but there will be other, counterfactual, situations
in which such a belief would be false. In this sense, such a mechanism is unreliable.
What our analysis says is that *S* has perceptual knowledge if and only if not only
does his perceptual mechanism produce true belief, but there are no relevant counterfactual situations in which the same belief would be produced via an equivalent
percept and in which the belief would be false.

Let me now illustrate how the analysis is to be applied to the barn example,
where there are facsimiles in Henry's district. Let *S*=Henry, *b*=the barn Henry
actually sees, and *F*=the property of being a barn. Conditions 1 through 3B are met
by letting *J* take as its value the set of all nonrelational properties actually possessed
by the barn at *t*, *R* take as its value the actual DOE relation the barn bears to Henry
at *t*, and *P* take as its value the actual (visual) percept caused by the barn. Condition
3C is violated, however. There *is* a relevant triple that meets subclauses (i) and (ii),
i.e., the triple where *c*=a suitable barn facsimile, K=a suitable set of properties
(excluding, of course, the property of being a barn), and R^*=approximately the

---

be solved, I think, by reliance on whether there are relevant perceptual equivalents. If there are no
relevant perceptual equivalents in which *K* excludes being a dog, then the properties of the actual
object that are causally responsible for the percept suffice to yield knowledge. We need not require
either that the percept be (perceptually) caused by *b*'s-having-*F*, nor by any subset of *J* that
'ensures' *b*'s-having-*F*.

same DOE relation as the actual one. Thus, Henry does not (noninferentially) perceptually *know* of the barn that it has the property of being a barn.

In the dachshund-wolf case, S=Oscar, b=Dack the dachshund, and F=being a dog. The first several conditions are again met. Is 3C met as well? There is a relevant alternative state of affairs in which Wiley the wolf is believed by Oscar to be a dog, but lacks that property. This state of affairs doesn't violate 3C, however, since it isn't a *perceptual equivalent* of the actual situation relative to being a dog. So this alternative doesn't disqualify Oscar from knowing Dack to be a dog.

Is there another alternative that *is* a perceptual equivalent of the actual situation (relative to being a dog)? We can imagine a DOE relation in which fancy devices between Wiley and Oscar distort the light coming from Wiley and produce in Oscar a Dack-like visual percept. The question here, however, is whether this perceptual equivalent is *relevant*. Relevance is determined not only by the hypothetical object and its properties, but also by the DOE relation. Since the indicated DOE relation is highly unusual, this will count (at least for a nonskeptic) against the alternative's being relevant and against its disqualifying Oscar from knowing.[16]

The following 'Gettierized' example, suggested by Marshall Swain, might appear to present difficulties. In a dark room there is a candle several yards ahead of S which S sees and believes to be ahead of him. But he sees the candle only indirectly, via a system of mirrors (of which he is unaware) that make it appear as if he were seeing it directly.[17] We would surely deny that S knows the candle to be ahead of him. (This case does not really fit our intended analysandum, since the believed property F is relational. This detail can be ignored, however.) Why? If we say, with Harman, that all perceptual belief is based on inference, we can maintain that S infers that the candle is ahead of him from the premise that he sees whatever he sees *directly*. This premise being false, S's knowing is disqualified on familiar grounds.

My theory suggests another explanation, which makes no unnecessary appeal to inference. We deny that S knows, I suggest, because the system of mirrors draws our attention to a perceptual equivalent in which the candle is *not* ahead of S, i.e., a state of affairs where the candle is behind S but reflected in a system of mirrors so that it

---

16. It is the 'unusualness' of the DOE relation that inclines us not to count the alternative as relevant; it is not the mere fact that the DOE relation differs from the actual one. In general, our analysis allows knowledge to be defeated or disqualified by alternative situations in which the DOE relation differs from the DOE relation in the actual state of affairs. Our analysis differs in this respect from Fred Dretske's analysis in 'Conclusive Reasons', *Australasian Journal of Philosophy*, 49, 1 (May 1971): 1–22 [Ch. 6 in this volume]. Dretske's analysis, which ours resembles on a number of points, considers only those counterfactual situations in which everything that is 'logically and causally independent of the state of affairs expressed by P' (7–8 [in this volume p. 48]) is the same as in the actual situation. (P is the content of S's belief.) This implies that the actual DOE relation cannot be counterfactualized, but must be held fixed. (It may also imply—depending what P is—that one cannot counterfactualize the perceived object nor the full set of properties J.) This unduly narrows the class of admissible alternatives. Many *relevant* alternatives, that do disqualify knowledge, involve DOE relations that differ from the actual DOE relation.

17. Harman has a similar case, in *Thought*, pp. 22–3. In that case, however, S does not see the candle; it is not a cause of his percept. Given our causal requirement for perceptual knowledge, that case is easily handled.

appears to be ahead of him. Since the actual state of affairs involves a system of reflecting mirrors, we are impelled to count this alternative as relevant, and hence to deny that S knows.

Even in ordinary cases, of course, where S sees a candle directly, the possibility of reflecting mirrors constitutes a perceptual equivalent. In the ordinary case, however, we would not count this as relevant; we would not regard it as a serious possibility. The Gettierized case impels us to take it seriously because there the actual state of affairs involves a devious system of reflecting mirrors. So we have an explanation of why people are credited with knowing in ordinary perceptual cases but not in the Gettierized case.

The following is a more serious difficulty for our analysis. S truly believes something to be a tree, but there is a relevant alternative in which an electrode stimulating S's optic nerve would produce an equivalent percept, which would elicit the same belief. Since this is assumed to be a relevant alternative, it ought to disqualify S from knowing. But it doesn't satisfy our definition of a perceptual equivalent, first because the electrode would not be a perceptual cause of the percept (we would not say that S *perceives* the electrode), and second because S would not believe *of the electrode* (nor *of* anything else) that it is a tree. A similar problem arises where the alternative state of affairs would involve S's having a hallucination.

To deal with these cases, we could revise our analysis of perceptual knowledge as follows. (A similar revision in the definition of perceptual equivalence would do the job equally well.) We could reformulate 3C to say that there must neither be a relevant perceptual equivalent of the indicated sort (using our present definition of perceptual equivalence) *nor* a relevant alternative situation in which an equivalent percept occurs and prompts a *de dicto* belief that something has F, but where there is nothing that *perceptually* causes this percept and nothing *of which* F is believed to hold. In other words, knowledge can be disqualified by relevant alternative situations where S doesn't perceive anything and doesn't have any *de re* (F-) belief at all. I am inclined to adopt this solution, but will not actually make this addition to the analysis.

Another difficulty for the analysis is this. Suppose Sam's 'schemata' of Judy and Trudy have hitherto been indistinct, so Judy-caused percepts sometimes elicit Judy-beliefs and sometimes Trudy-beliefs, and similarly for Trudy-caused percepts. Today Sam falls down and hits his head. As a consequence a new feature is 'added' to his Judy-schema, a mole-associated feature. From now on he will believe someone to be Judy only if he has the sort of percept that would be caused by a Judy-like person with a mole over the left eye. Sam is unaware that this change has taken place and will remain unaware of it, since he isn't conscious of the cues he uses. Until today, neither Judy nor Trudy has had a left-eyebrow mole; but today Judy happens to develop such a mole. Thus, from now on Sam can discriminate Judy from Trudy. Does this mean that he will *know* Judy to be Judy when he correctly identifies her? I am doubtful.

A possible explanation of Sam's not knowing (on future occasions) is that Trudy-with-a-mole is a relevant perceptual equivalent of Judy. This is not Trudy's actual condition, of course, but it might be deemed a relevant possibility. I believe, however, that the mole case calls for a further restriction, one concerning the *genesis* of a person's propensity to form a certain belief as a result of a certain percept. A merely fortuitous or accidental genesis is not enough to support knowledge. I do not know exactly what requirement to impose on the genesis of such a propensity. The mole case intimates that the genesis should involve certain 'experience' with objects, but this may be too narrow. I content myself with a very vague addition to our previous conditions, which completes the analysis:

(4) S's propensity to form an F-belief as a result of percept P has an appropriate genesis.

Of course this leaves the problem unresolved. But the best I can do here is identify the problem.

IV

A few words are in order about the intended significance of my analysis. One of its purposes is to provide an alternative to the traditional 'Cartesian' perspective in epistemology. The Cartesian view combines a theory of knowledge with a theory of justification. Its theory of knowledge asserts that S knows that p at t only if S is (fully, adequately, etc.) justified at t in believing that p. Its theory of justification says that S is justified at t in believing that p only if either (A) p is self-warranting for S at t or (B) p is (strongly, adequately, etc.) supported or confirmed by propositions each of which is self-warranting for S at t. Now propositions about the state of the external world at t are not self-warranting. Hence, if S knows any such proposition p at t, there must be some other propositions which strongly support p and which are self-warranting for S at t. These must be propositions about S's mental state at t and perhaps some obvious necessary truths. A major task of Cartesian epistemology is to show that there is some such set of self-warranting propositions, propositions that support external-world propositions with sufficient strength.

It is impossible to canvass all attempts to fulfill this project; but none have succeeded, and I do not think that any will. One can conclude either that we have no knowledge of the external world or that Cartesian requirements are too demanding. I presuppose the latter conclusion in offering my theory of perceptual knowledge. My theory requires no justification for external-world propositions that derives entirely from self-warranting propositions. It requires only, in effect, that beliefs in the external world be suitably caused, where 'suitably' comprehends a process or mechanism that not only produces true belief in the actual situation, but would not produce false belief in relevant counterfactual situations. If one wishes, one can so employ the term 'justification' that belief causation of *this* kind counts as justification. In this sense, of course, my theory does require justification. But this is entirely different from the sort of justification demanded by Cartesianism.

My theory protects the possibility of knowledge by making Cartesian-style justification unnecessary. But it leaves a door open to skepticism by its stance on relevant alternatives. This is not a failure of the theory, in my opinion. An adequate account of the term 'know' should make the temptations of skepticism comprehensible, which my theory does. But it should also put skepticism in a proper perspective, which Cartesianism fails to do.

In any event, I put forward my account of perceptual knowledge not primarily as an antidote to skepticism, but as a more accurate rendering of what the term 'know' actually means. In this respect it is instructive to test my theory and its rivals against certain metaphorical or analogical uses of 'know'. A correct definition should be able to explain extended and figurative uses as well as literal uses, for it should explain how speakers arrive at the extended uses from the central ones. With this in mind, consider how tempting it is to say of an electric-eye door that it 'knows' you are coming (at least that *something* is coming), or 'sees' you coming. The attractiveness of the metaphor is easily explained on my theory: the door has a reliable mechanism for discriminating between something being before it and nothing being there. It has a 'way of telling' whether or not something is there: this 'way of telling' consists in a mechanism by which objects in certain DOE relations to it have differential effects on its internal state. By contrast, note how artificial it would be to apply more traditional analyses of 'know' to the electric-eye door, or to other mechanical detecting devices. How odd it would be to say that the door has 'good reasons,' 'adequate evidence,' or 'complete justification' for thinking something is there; or that it has 'the right to be sure' something is there. The oddity of these locutions indicates how far from the mark are the analyses of 'know' from which they derive.

The trouble with many philosophical treatments of knowledge is that they are inspired by Cartesian-like conceptions of justification or vindication. There is a consequent tendency to overintellectualize or overrationalize the notion of knowledge. In the spirit of naturalistic epistemology,[18] I am trying to fashion an account of knowing that focuses on more primitive and pervasive aspects of cognitive life, in connection with which, I believe, the term 'know' gets its application. A fundamental facet of animate life, both human and infra-human, is telling things apart, distinguishing predator from prey, for example, or a protective habitat from a threatening one. The concept of knowledge has its roots in this kind of cognitive activity.

18. Cf. W. V. Quine, 'Epistemology Naturalized,' in *Ontological Relativity, and Other Essays* (New York: Columbia, 1969) [Ch. 20 in this volume].

Chapter 9

Précis of *Knowledge and the Flow of Information*

Fred Dretske

KNOWLEDGE *and the Flow of Information* (Dretske 1981; henceforth *Knowledge*) is an attempt to develop a philosophically useful theory of information. To be philosophically useful the theory should: (1) preserve enough of our common understanding of information to justify calling it a theory *of* information; (2) make sense of (or explain its failure to make sense of) the theoretically central role information plays in the descriptive and explanatory efforts of cognitive scientists; and (3) deepen our understanding of the baffling place of mind, the chief consumer of information, in the natural order of things.

A secondary motive in writing this book, and in organizing its approach to philosophical problems around the notion of information, was to build a bridge, if only a terminological one, to cognitive science. Even if we don't have the same problems (psychologists are no more interested in Descartes's Demon than philosophers are in Purkinje's twilight shift), we have the same subject, and both sides could profit from improved communication.

In pursuit of these ends, it was found necessary to think of information as an *objective* commodity, as something whose existence (as information) is (largely) independent of the interpretative activities of conscious agents. It is common among cognitive scientists to regard information as a creation of the mind, as something we conscious agents assign to, or impose on, otherwise meaningless events. Information, like beauty, is in the eye of the beholder. For philosophical purposes though, this puts things exactly backward. It assumes what is to be explained. For we want to know what this interpretative ability amounts to, why some physical systems (typically, those with brains) have this capacity and others do not. What makes *some* processors of information (persons, but not television sets) sources of meaning? If we *begin* our study by populating the world with fully developed cognitive systems, systems that can transform 'meaningless' stimuli into thoughts, beliefs, and knowledge (or whatever is involved in interpretation), we make the analysis of information more tractable, perhaps, but only by abandoning it as a tool in our quest to understand the nature of cognitive phenomena. We merely postpone the philosophical questions.

Part I of *Knowledge* develops a semantic theory of information, a theory of the propositional *content* of a signal (events, structure, or state of affairs). It begins by

Fred Dretske, 'Précis of *Knowledge and the Flow of Information*' in Behavioral Brain Sciences 6 (1983) pp. 55–63, reprinted by permission of Cambridge University Press.

rehearsing some of the elementary ideas of the mathematical theory of communication (Shannon and Weaver 1949). This theory, though developed for quite different purposes, and though having (as a result) only the remotest connection (some would say *none*) with the kinds of cognitive issues of concern to this study, does, nonetheless, provide a key that can be used to articulate a semantical theory of information. Chapters 2 and 3 are devoted to *adapting* and *extending* this theory's account of an information source and channel into an account of how much information a *particular* signal carries about a source and what (if any) information this is.

Part 2 applies this theory of information to some traditional problems in epistemology: knowledge, skepticism, and perception. Knowledge is characterized as information-produced belief. Perception is a process in which incoming information is coded in analog form in preparation for further selective processing by cognitive (conceptual) centers. The difference between seeing a duck and recognizing it *as* a duck (seeing *that* it is a duck) is to be found in the different way information about the duck is coded (analog vs. digital).

Part 2I is devoted to an information–theoretic analysis of what has come to be called our propositional attitudes—in particular, the belief that something is so. Belief, the *thinking* that something is so, is characterized in terms of the instantiation of structures (presumably neural) that have, through learning, acquired a certain information-carrying role. Instances of these structures (the types of which are identified as concepts) sometimes fail to perform satisfactorily. This is false belief.

1. Information

The mathematical theory of communication (Cherry 1951; Shannon and Weaver 1949) is concerned with certain statistical quantities associated with 'sources' and 'channels.' When a certain condition is realized at a source, and there are other possible conditions that might have been realized (each with its associated probability of occurring), the source can be thought of as a generator of information. The ensemble of possibilities has been reduced to a single reality, and the amount of information generated is a function of these possibilities and their associated probabilities. The die is cast. Any one of six faces might appear uppermost. A '3' appears. Six possibilities, all (let us say) equally likely, have been reduced to one. The source, in this case the throw of the die, generates 2.6 bits of information ($\log_2 6 = 2.6$).

But more important (for my purposes and for the purpose of understanding *communication*) is the measure of how much information is transmitted from one point to another, how much information there is at point r (receiver) about what is transpiring at s (source). Once again, communication theory is concerned with the statistical properties of the 'channel' connecting r and s, because, for most engineering purposes, it is this channel whose characteristics must be exploited in designing effective coding strategies. The theory looks at a statistical quantity that is a certain weighted average of the conditional probabilities of all signals that can be transmitted from s to r. It does not concern itself with the individual events (the particular signals) except as a basis for computing the statistical functions that define the quantities of interest.

I skip over these matters rather lightly here, because it should be obvious that, insofar as communication theory deals with quantities that are statistical *averages* (sometimes called *entropy* to distinguish them from real information), it is *not* dealing with information as it is ordinarily understood. For information as it is ordinarily understood, and as it must figure in semantic and cognitive studies, is something associated with, and *only* with, individual events (signals, structures, conditions). It is only the particular signal (utterance, track, print, gesture, sequence of neural discharges) that has a content that can be given propositional expression (the content, message, or information carried by the signal). *This* is the relevant commodity in semantic cognitive studies, and content—*what* information a signal carries—cannot be averaged. All one can do is average *how much* information is carried. There is no meaningful average for the information that my grandmother had a stroke and that my daughter is getting married. If we can say *how much* information these messages represent, then we can speak about their average. But this tells us nothing about *what* information is being communicated. Hence, the quantities of interest in engineering—and, of course, some psychophysical contexts (Attneave 1959; Garner 1962; Miller 1953)—are not the quantities of interest to someone, like myself, concerned to develop an account of *what* information travels from source to receiver (object to receptor, receptor to brain, brain to brain) during communication.

Nevertheless, though communication theory has its attention elsewhere, it does, as Sayre (1965) and others have noted, highlight the relevant objective relations on which the communication of genuine information depends. For what this theory tells us is that the amount of information at r about s is a function of the *degree of lawful (nomic) dependence* between conditions at these two points. If two conditions are statistically independent (the way the ringing of *your* telephone is independent of the ringing of *mine*), then the one event carries no information about the other. When there is a lawful regularity between two events, statistical or otherwise, as there is between your dialing my number and my phone's ringing, then we can speak of one event's carrying information about the other. And, of course, this is the way we *do* speak. The ring *tells me* (informs me) that someone is calling my number, just as fingerprints carry information about the identity of the person who handled the gun, tracks in the snow about the animals in the woods, the honeybee's dance about the location of nectar, and light from a distant star about the chemical constitution of that body. Such events are pregnant with information, because they depend, in some lawfully regular way, on the conditions about which they are said to carry information.

If things are working properly, the ringing of my phone *tells* me that someone has dialed my number. It delivers this piece of information. It does *not* tell me that your phone is ringing, even if (coincidentally) your phone happens to be ringing at the same time. Even if A dials B's number whenever C dials D's number (so that D's phone rings *whenever* A dials B's number), we cannot say that the ringing of D's phone carries information about A's dialing activities—*not* if this 'correlation' is a mere coincidence. We cannot say this, because the correlation, being (by hypothesis) completely fortuitous, does not affect the conditional *probability* of A's dialing B's number, given that D's phone is ringing. Of course, if we *know* about this (coincidental) correlation (though *how* one could know about its *persistence* is beyond me), we can predict one event from a knowledge of the other, but this doesn't change the fact that they are statistically independent. If I correctly describe your future by consulting tea leaves, this is not genuine communication *unless* the arrangement of tea leaves somehow depends on what you are going to do, in the way a barometer depends on meteorological conditions and, therefore, indirectly on the impending weather. To deny the existence of mental telepathy is not to deny the possibility of improbable cooccurrences (between what A thinks and what B thinks A is thinking); it is, rather, to deny that they are manifestations of *lawful* regularities.

Communication theory only makes sense if it makes sense to talk about the probability of certain specific conditions given certain specific signals. This is so because the quantities of interest to communication theory are statistical functions of these probabilities. It is this *presupposed* idea that I exploit to develop an account of a signal's content. These conditional probabilities determine how much, and indirectly *what*, information a particular signal carries about a remote source. One needs only to stipulate that the content of the signal, the information it carries, be expressed by a sentence describing the condition (at the source) on which the signal depends in some regular, lawful way. I express this theoretical definition of a signal's (structure's) informational content in the following way:

> A signal r carries the information that s is F = The conditional probability of s's being F, given r (and k), is 1 (but, given k alone, less than 1)

My gas gauge carries the information that I still have some gas left, if and only if the conditional probability of my having some gas left, given the reading on the gauge, is 1. For the same reason, the discharge of a photoreceptor carries the information that a photon has arrived (perhaps a photon of a certain wavelength), and the pattern of discharge of a cluster of ganglion cells carries the information that there is a sharp energy gradient (a line) in the optic array (Lindsay and Norman 1972; Rumelhart 1977). The following comments explain the main features of this definition.

1. There are, essentially, three reasons for insisting that the value of the conditional probability in this definition be 1—nothing less. They are:

a. If a signal could carry the information that s was F while the conditional probability (of the latter, given the former) was less than 1 (.9 say), then the signal could carry the information that s was F (probability=.91), the information that s was G (probability=.91), but *not* the information that s was F and G (because the probability of their *joint* occurrence might be less than .9). I take this to be an unacceptable result.

b. I accept something I call the xerox principle: If C carries the information that

B, and *B*'s occurrence carries the information that *A*, then *C* carries the information that *A*. You don't *lose* information about the original (*A*) by perfectly reproduced copies (*B* of *A and C* of *B*). Without the transitivity this principle describes, the *flow* of information would be impossible. If we put the threshold of information at anything less than 1, though, the principle is violated. For (using the same numbers) the conditional probability of *A* given *C*, could be .91, the conditional probability of *A*, given *B*, also .91, but the conditional probability of *A*, given *C*, less than .9. The noise (equivocation, degree of nomic *in*dependence, or nonlawful relation) between the end points of this communication channel is enough to break communication, even though every link in the chain passes along the information to its successor. Somehow the information fails to get through, despite the fact that it is nowhere lost.

c. Finally, there is no nonarbitrary place to put a threshold that will retain the intimate tie we all intuitively feel between knowledge and information. For, if information about *s*'s being *F* can be obtained from a signal that makes the conditional probability of this situation only (say) .94, then information loses its cognitive punch. Think of a bag with 94 red balls and 6 white balls. If one is pulled at random (probability of red = .94), can you *know* (just from the fact that it was drawn from a bag with that composition of colored marbles) that it was red? Clearly not. Then why suppose you have the information that it is red?

The only reason I know for *not* setting the required probability this high is worries (basically skeptical in character) that there are no (or precious few) conditional probabilities of 1—hence, that no information is ever communicated. I address these worries in chapter 5. They raise issues (e.g., the idea of a 'relevant alternative') that have received some attention in recent epistemology.

2. The definition captures the element that makes information (in contrast, say, to meaning) an important *epistemic* commodity. No structure can carry the information that *s* is *F* unless, in fact, *s* is *F*. False information, misinformation, and (grimace!) disinformation are not varieties of information—any more than a decoy duck is a kind of duck. A glance at the dictionary reveals that information is related to intelligence, news, instruction, and knowledge—things that have an important connection to *truth*. And so it should be with any theoretical approximation to this notion. Information *is* an important commodity: We buy it, sell it, torture people to get it, and erect booths to dispense it. It should not be confused with meaning, despite some people's willingness to speak of anything (true, false, or meaningless) stored on a magnetic disk as information.

3. Information, as defined above, is an objective commodity, the sort of thing that can be delivered to, processed by, and transmitted from instruments, gauges, computers, and neurons. It is something that can be *in* the optic array,[1] on the printed

---

1. Though I am sympathetic to some of the (earlier) views of the late James Gibson (1950; 1966), and though some of my discourse on information (e.g., its availability in the proximal stimulus) is reminiscent of Gibson's language, this work was not intended as support for Gibson's views—certainly not the more extravagant claims (1979). If criticized for getting Gibson wrong, I will plead 'no contest.' I wasn't trying to get him right. If we disagree, so much the worse for one of us at least.

page, carried by a temporal configuration of electrical pulses, and stored on a magnetic disk, and it exists there *whether or not anyone appreciates this fact or knows how to extract it.* It is something that was in this world before we got here. It was, I submit, the raw material out of which minds were manufactured.

The parenthetical *k* occurring in the definition above (and explained below) relativizes information to what the receiver already knows (if anything) about the possibilities at the source, but this relativization does not undermine the essential objectivity of the commodity so relativized (MacKay 1969). We still have the flow of information (perhaps not so much) without conscious agents who know things, but without a lawfully regular universe (no matter how much knowledge we assign the occupants), no information is ever communicated.

4. A signal's informational content is not unique. There is, generally speaking, no *single* piece of information in a signal or structure. For anything that carries the information that *s* is a square, say, also carries the information that it is a rectangle, a parallelogram, *not* a circle, a circle *or* a square, and so on. If the acoustic pattern reaching my ears carries the information that the doorbell is ringing, and the ringing of the bell carries the information that the doorbell button is being pressed, then the acoustic pattern also carries the information that the doorbell button is being pressed (xerox principle). The one piece of information is *nested* in the other. This, once again, is as it should be. The linguistic meaning of an utterance may be unique (distinguishable, for instance, from what it implies), but not the information carried by that utterance. Herman's statement that he won't come to my party means, simply, that he won't come to my party. It doesn't mean (certainly not in any linguistically relevant sense of 'meaning') that he doesn't like me or that he can speak English, although his utterance may well carry these pieces of information.

5. The definition of a signal's informational content has been relativized to *k*, what the receiver (in the event that we are talking about a communication system in which the receiver—organism or computer—already has knowledge about the possible conditions existing at the source) already knows. This is a minor concession to the way we think and talk about information. The *k* is dischargeable by recursive applications of the definition. So, for instance, if I receive the information that your knight is *not* on KB-3 (by some signal), this carries the information that it *is* on KB-5, *if* I already know that the other possible positions to which your knight could have moved are already occupied by your pieces. To someone lacking such knowledge, the same signal does not carry this information (though it still carries the information that your knight is not on KB-3). The less we know, the more pregnant with information must be the signals we receive if we are to learn.

6. There is, finally, the important fact, already mentioned, that the informational content of a signal is a function of the *nomic* (or law-governed) relations it bears to other conditions. Unless these relations are what philosophers like to call 'counterfactual supporting' relations (a symptom of a background, lawful regularity), the relations in question are not such as to support an assignment of informational content (Dretske 1977). The reason my thermometer carries information about the

temperature of *my* room (the information *that* it is 72° F. in the room), but not about your room though both rooms are at the same temperature, is that (given its location) the registration of my thermometer is such that it *would not* read 72° F. *unless* my room was at this temperature. This isn't true of your room.

This fact helps explain an (otherwise puzzling) feature of information and, ultimately, of the cognitive attitudes that depend on it (belief, knowledge). For it is by virtue of this fact that a structure (some neural state, say) can carry the information that *s* (a distal object) is *F* (spherical) without carrying the information that *s* is *G* (plastic), even though (let us suppose) all spheres (in the relevant domain) are plastic. If the fact that all spheres are plastic is sheer accident, not underwritten by any lawful constraint, then the neural state might depend on *s*'s being spherical without depending, in the same way, on its being plastic. Another way of expressing this fact (dear to the heart of philosophers) is to say that the informational content of a structure exhibits *intentional* properties. By saying that it exhibits intentional properties, I mean what philosophers typically mean by this technical term: that the informational content of a signal or structure (like the content of a belief, a desire, or knowledge) depends, not only on the reference (extension) of the terms used in its sentential expression, but on their *meaning* (intension). That is, in the sentential expression of a structure's informational content, one cannot substitute coreferring (i.e., referring to the same thing, coextensional) expressions without (possible) alteration in content. Just as a belief that this man is my cousin differs from a belief that he is Susan's husband, despite the fact that Susan's husband *is* my cousin (these expressions have the same reference), the information (as defined above) that he is my cousin differs from the information that he is Susan's husband. A signal can carry the one piece of information without carrying the other.

We have, then, an account of a signal's informational content that exhibits a degree of intentionality. We have, therefore, an account of information that exhibits some of the attributes we hope eventually to be able to explain in our account of our cognitive states. Perhaps, that is, one can know that *s* is *F* without knowing that *s* is *G*, despite the fact that all *F*s are *G*, *because* knowledge requires information, and one *can* get the information that *s* is *F* without getting the information that it is *G*. If intentionality is 'the mark of the mental,' then we already have, in the physically objective notion of information defined above (even without *k*), the traces of mentality. And we have it in a form that voltmeters, thermometers, and radios have. What distinguishes us from these more pedestrian processors of information is not our occupation of intentional states, but the sophisticated way we process, encode, and utilize the information we receive. It is our *degree* of intentionality.

2. Knowledge

Knowledge is defined (chapter 4) as information-caused (or causally sustained) belief. The analysis is restricted to perceptual knowledge of contingent states of affairs (conditions having an informational measure of something greater than 0) of a *de re* form: seeing (hence, knowing) that this (the perceptual object) is blue, moving, a dog, or my grandmother.

This characterization of knowledge is a version of what has come to be called the 'reliability analysis' of knowledge (Armstrong 1973 [Ch. 7 in this volume]; Dretske 1969; 1971 [Ch. 6 in this volume]). It is an attempt to get away from the philosopher's usual bag of tricks (justification, reasons, evidence, etc.) in order to give a more realistic picture of what perceptual knowledge is. One doesn't need reasons, evidence, or rational justification for one's belief that there is wine left in the bottle, if the bottle is sitting in good light directly in front of one. One can *see* that it is still half-full. And, rightly or wrongly, I wanted a characterization that would at least allow for the possibility that animals (a frog, rat, ape, or my dog) could know things without my having to suppose them capable of the more sophisticated intellectual operations involved in traditional analyses of knowledge.

What can it mean to speak of information as causing anything—let alone causing a belief? [...] Assuming that belief is some kind of internal state with a content expressible as *s* is *F*, this is said to be caused by the information that *s* is *F*, if and only if those physical properties of the signal by virtue of which it carries this information are the ones that are causally efficacious in the production of the belief. So, for instance, not just any knock on the door tells you it is your friend. The (prearranged) signal is three quick knocks, followed by a pause, and then another three quick knocks. It is that particular signal, that particular temporal pattern, that constitutes the information-carrying property of the signal. The amplitude and pitch are irrelevant. When it is this pattern of knocks that causes you to believe that your friend has arrived, then (it is permissible to say that) the *information* that your friend has arrived causes you to believe he has arrived. The knocks might also frighten away a fly, cause the windows to rattle, and disturb the people upstairs. But what has these effects is not the information, because, presumably, the fly would have been frightened, the windows rattled, and the neighbors disturbed by *any* sequence of knocks of roughly the same amplitude. Hence, the information is not the cause.

In most ordinary situations, there is no explanatory value in talking about the information (in an event) as the cause of something, because there is some easily identifiable physical (nonrelational) property of the event that can be designated as the cause. Why talk of the information (that your friend has arrived) as the cause, when it is clear enough that it is the particular temporal patterns of knocks (or acoustic vibrations) that was the effective agent?

The point of this definition is not to *deny* that there are physical properties of the signal (e.g., the temporal pattern of knocks in the above example) that cause the belief, but to say *which* of these properties must be responsible for the effect if the resultant belief is to qualify as knowledge.[2] If the belief that your friend has arrived is caused by the knock, but the pattern of knocks is irrelevant, then (assuming that

---

2. This is not so much a denial of Fodor's (1980) formality condition as it is an attempt to say *which* syntactical (formal) properties of the representations must figure in the computational processes if the resulting transformations are to mirror faithfully our ordinary ways of describing them to terms of their semantic relations.

someone else could be knocking at your door), though you are caused to believe it by the knock on the door, you do not *know* your friend has arrived. Those properties of the signal that carry the information (that your friend has arrived) are not the ones that are causally responsible for your belief.

The need to speak in this more abstract way—of information (rather than the physical event carrying this information) as the cause of something—becomes much more compelling as we turn to more complex information processing systems. For we then discover that there are an indefinitely large number of different sensory inputs, having no identifiable physical (nonrelational) property in common, that all have the same cognitive outcome. The only way we can capture the relevant causal regularities is by retreating to a more abstract characterization of the cause, a characterization in terms of its relational (informational) properties. We often do this sort of thing in our ordinary descriptions of what we see. Why did he stop? He could see that he was almost out of gas. We speak here of the information (that he was almost out of gas) that is contained in (carried by) the fuel gauge pointer and *not* the fuel gauge pointer itself (which, of course, is what we actually see), because it is a property of this pointer (its position, not its size or color) carrying this vital piece of information that is relevantly involved in the production of the belief. We, as it were, ignore the messenger bringing the information (the fuel gauge indicator) in order to focus on what information the messenger brings. We also ignore the infinite variety of optical inputs (all of varying size, shape, orientation, intensity) in order to focus on the information they carry. Often we have no choice. The only thing they have in common is the information they bear.[3]

A belief that *s* is *F* may not itself carry the information that *s* is *F* just because it is caused by this information (thereby qualifying as knowledge). A gullible person may believe almost anything you tell him—for example, that there are three elephants in your backyard. His beliefs may not, as a result, have any reliable relation to the facts (this is why we don't believe him when he tells us something). Yet this does not prevent him from knowing something he observes firsthand. When he *sees* the elephants in your backyard, he *knows* they are there, whatever other signal (lacking the relevant information) might have caused him to believe this. If the belief is caused by the appropriate information, it qualifies as knowledge whatever *else* may be capable of causing it.

This definition of knowledge accords, I think, with our ordinary, intuitive judgments about when someone knows something. You can't know that Jimmy is home by seeing him come through the door, if it could be his twin brother Johnny. Even if it is extremely unlikely to be Johnny (for Johnny rarely comes home this early in the afternoon), as long as this remains a relevant possibility, it prevents one from seeing (hence, knowing) *that* it is Jimmy (though one may be caused to *believe* it is Jimmy). The information that it is Jimmy is missing. The optical input is equivocal.

---

3. I skip here a discussion of information's *causally sustaining* a belief. The idea is simply that one may already believe something when one receives the relevant supporting information. In this case, the belief is not caused or produced by the information. It nonetheless—after acquisition of the relevant information—qualifies as knowledge if it is, later, causally sustained by this information.

Furthermore, this account of knowledge neatly avoids some of the puzzles that intrigue philosophers (and bore everyone else to death). For example, Gettier-like difficulties (Gettier 1963 [Ch. 2 in this volume]) arise for any account of knowledge that makes knowledge a product of some justificatory relationship (having good evidence, excellent reasons, etc.) that *could* relate one to something false. For on all these accounts (unless special ad hoc devices are introduced to prevent it), one can be justified (in a way appropriate to knowledge) in believing something that is, in fact, false (hence, not know it); also know that Q (which happens to be true) is a logical consequence of what one believes, and come to believe Q as a result. On some perfectly natural assumptions, then, one is justified (in a way appropriate to knowledge) in believing the truth (Q). But one obviously doesn't *know* Q is true. This is a problem for justificational accounts. The problem is evaded in the information-theoretic model, because one can get into an appropriate justificational relationship to something false, but one cannot get into an appropriate informational relationship to something false.

Similarly, the so-called lottery paradox (Kyburg 1961; 1965) is disarmed. If one could know something without the information (as here defined), one should be able to know *before the drawing* that the 999,999 eventual losers in a (fair) lottery, for which a million tickets have been sold, are going to lose. For they all *are* going to lose, and one knows that the probability of each one's (not, of course, *all*) losing is negligibly less than 1. Hence, one is perfectly justified in believing (truly) that each one is going to lose. But, clearly, one cannot know this. The paradox is avoided by acknowledging what is already inherent in the information—theoretical analysis—that one cannot know one is going to lose in such a lottery no matter how many outstanding tickets there may be. And the reason one cannot is (barring a fixed drawing) the information that one is going to lose is absent. There remains a small, but nonetheless greater than 0, amount of equivocation for each outcome.

There are further, technical advantages to this analysis (discussed in chapter 4), but many will consider these advantages purchased at too great a price. For the feeling will surely be that one never gets the required information. *Not* if information requires a conditional probability of 1. The stimuli are *always* equivocal to some degree. Most of us know about Ames's demonstrations, Brunswik's ecological and functional validities, and the fallibility of our own sensory systems. If knowledge requires information, and information requires 0 equivocation, then precious little, if anything, is ever known.

These concerns are addressed in chapter 5, a chapter that will prove tedious to almost everyone but devoted epistemologists (i.e., those who take skepticism seriously). An example will have to suffice to summarize this discussion.

A perfectly reliable instrument (or one *as* reliable as modern technology can make it) has its output reliably correlated with its input. The position of a mobile pointer on a calibrated scale carries information about the magnitude of the quantity being measured. Communication theorists would (given certain tolerances) have no trouble in describing this as a noiseless channel. If we ask about the conditional probabilities, we note that these are determined by regarding certain parameters as fixed (or simply ignoring them). The spring *could* weaken, it *could* break, its coefficient of elasticity *could* fluctuate unpredictably. The electrical resistance of the leads (connecting the instrument to the apparatus on which measurements are being taken) *could* change. Error would be introduced if any of these possibilities was realized. And who is to say they are not *possibilities*? There *might* even be a prankster, a malevolent force, or a god who chooses to interfere. Should all these possibilities go into the reckoning in computing the noise, equivocation, and information conveyed? To do so, of course, would be to abandon communication theory altogether. For this theory requires for its application a system of fixed, stable, enduring conditions *within* which the degree of covariation in other conditions can be evaluated. If every logical possibility is deemed a possibility, then everything is noise. Nothing is communicated. In the same manner, if everything is deemed a *thing* for purposes of assessing the emptiness of containers (dust? molecules? radiation?), then no room, pocket, or refrigerator is ever empty. The framework of fixed, stable, enduring conditions within which one reckons the flow of information is what I call 'channel conditions.' Possible variations in these conditions are excluded. They are what epistemologists call 'irrelevant alternatives' (Dretske 1970; Goldman 1976 [Ch. 8 in this volume]).

And so it is with our sensory systems. Certainly, in some sense of the word *could*, Herman, a perfectly normal adult, could be hallucinating the entire football game. There is no logical contradiction in this supposition; it is the same sense in which a voltmeter's spring *could* behave like silly putty. But this is not a sense of *could* that is relevant to cognitive studies or the determination of what information these systems are capable of transmitting. The probability of these things happening is set at 0. If they remain possibilities in some sense, they are not possibilities that affect the flow of information.

This discussion merely accentuates the way our talk of information *presupposes* a stable, regular world in which some things can be taken as fixed for the purpose of assessing the covariation in other things. There is here a certain arbitrary or pragmatic element (in what may be taken as permanent and stable enough to qualify as a channel condition), but this element (it is argued) is precisely what we find when we put our cognitive concepts under the same analytical microscope. It is not an objection to regarding the latter as fundamentally information-dependent notions.

3. Perception

Perception itself is often regarded as a cognitive activity: a form of recognizing, identifying, categorizing, distinguishing, and classifying the things around us (R. N. Haber 1969). But there is what philosophers (at least *this* philosopher) think of as an *extensional* and an *intensional* way of describing our perceptions (Dretske 1969). We see the duck (extensional: a concrete noun phrase occurs as object of the verb) and we recognize it (see it) as a duck—see *that* it is a duck (intensional: typically taking a factive nominal as complement of the verb). Too many people (both philosophers and psychologists) tend to think about perception *only* in the latter form, and in so doing they systematically ignore one of the most salient aspects of our mental life: the *experiences* we have when we see, hear, and taste things. The experience in question, the sort of thing that occurs in you when you see a duck (without necessarily recognizing it *as* a duck), the internal state without which (though you may be looking at the duck) you don't *see* the duck, is a stage in the processing of sensory information in which information about the duck is coded in what I call analog form, in preparation for its selective utilization by the cognitive centers (where the *belief* that it is a duck may be generated).

To describe what object you see is to describe what object you are getting information about; to describe what you recognize it as (see it to be) is to describe what information (about that object) you have succeeded in cognitively processing (e.g., that it is a duck). You can see a duck, get information *about* a duck, without getting, let alone cognitively processing, the information that it is a duck. Try looking at one in dim light at such a distance that you can barely see it. To confuse seeing a duck with recognizing it (either as a duck or as something else) is simply to confuse sentience with sapience.

Our experience of the world is rich in information in a way that our consequent beliefs (if any) are not. A normal child of two can *see* as well as I can (probably better). The child's experience of the world is (I rashly conjecture) as rich and as variegated as that of the most knowledgeable adult. What is lacking is a capacity to exploit these experiences in the generation of reliable beliefs (knowledge) about what the child sees. I, my daughter, and my dog can all see the daisy. I see it as a daisy. My daughter sees it simply as a flower. And who knows about my dog?

There are severe limits to our information-processing capabilities (Miller 1956), but most of these limitations affect our ability to cognitively process the information supplied in such profusion by our sensory systems (Rock 1975). More information *gets in* than we can manage to digest and get out (in some appropriate response). Glance around a crowded room, a library filled with books, or a garden ablaze with flowers. How much do you see? Is all the information embodied in the sensory representation (experience) given a cognitive form? No. You saw 28 people in a single brief glance (the room was well lit, all were in easy view, and none was occluded by other objects or people). Do you believe you saw 28 people? No. You didn't count and you saw them so briefly that you can only guess. That there were 28 people in the room is a piece of information that was contained *in* the sensory representation without receiving the kind of cognitive transformation (what I call digitalization) associated with conceptualization (belief). This homely example illustrates what is more convincingly demonstrated by masking experiments with brief visual displays (Averbach and Coriell 1961; Neisser 1967; Sperling 1960).

Although it is misleading to put it this way, our sensory experience encodes information in the way a photograph encodes information about the scene at which the camera is pointed. This is *not* to say that our sensory experience is pictorial (consists of sounds, sights, smells, etc.). I don't think there are daisy replicas inside the head, although I *do* think there is information about—and in *this* sense a representation of—daisies in the head. Nor do I mean to suggest (by the picture metaphor) that we are *aware of* (somehow perceive) these internal sensory representations. On the contrary, what we perceive (what we are aware *of*) are the things represented by these internal representations (not the representations themselves), the things *about which* they carry information (see section on 'The Objects of Perception' in chapter 6).

I see a red apple in a white bowl surrounded by a variety of other objects. I recognize it as an apple. I come to believe that it is an apple. The belief has a content that we express with the words, 'That is an apple.' The content of this belief does not represent the apple as red, as large, or as lying next to an orange. I may have (other) beliefs about these matters, but the belief in question abstracts from the concreteness of the sensory representation (icon, sensory information store, experience) in order to represent it simply as an apple. However, these additional pieces of information *are* contained in the sensory experience of the apple. As Haber and Hershenson (1973) put it (in commenting on a specific experimental setup), 'It appears as if all of the information in the retinal projection is available in the iconic storage, since the perceiver can extract whichever part is asked for.'

In passing from the sensory to the cognitive representation (from seeing the apple to realizing that it is an apple), there is a systematic stripping away of components of information (relating to size, color, orientation, surroundings), which makes the experience of the apple the phenomenally rich thing we know it to be; in order to feature *one* component of this information—the information that it is an apple. Digitalization (of, for example, the information that *s* is an apple) is a process whereby a piece of information is taken from a richer matrix of information in the sensory representation (where it is held in what I call 'analog' form) and featured to the exclusion of all else. The difference between the analog and digital coding of information is illustrated by the way a picture of an apple (that carries the information that it is an apple) differs from a statement that it is an apple. Both represent it *as* an apple, but the one embeds this information in an informationally richer representation. Essential to this process of digitalization (the essence of conceptualization) is the *loss* of this excess information.

Digitalization is, of course, merely the information—theoretic version of stimulus generalization. Until information is deleted, nothing corresponding to recognition, classification, or identification has occurred. Nothing distinctively cognitive or conceptual has occurred. To design a pattern-recognition routine for a digital computer, for example, is to design a routine in which information *inessential* to *s*'s being an instance of the letter A (information about its specific size, orientation, color) is systematically discarded (treated as noise) in the production of some single type of internal structure, which, in turn, will produce some identificatory output label (Uhr 1973). If all the computer could do was pass along the information it received, it could not be credited with recognizing anything at all. It would not be responding to the essential sameness of different inputs. It would be merely a sophisticated transducer. Learning, the acquisition of concepts, is a process whereby we acquire the ability to extract, in this way, information from the sensory representation. Until that happens, we can see but we do not believe.

References

Armstrong, D. M. 1973. *Belief, Truth and Knowledge*, Cambridge, Cambridge University Press.

Attneave, F. 1959. *Applications of Information Theory to Psychology: A Summary of Basic Concepts, Methods and Results*, New York, Henry Holt & Co.

Averbach, E. and Coriell, A. S. 1961. 'Short-Term Memory in Vision', *Bell System Technical Journal* 40, pp. 309–28.

Cherry, E. C. 1951. 'A History of the Theory of Information', *Proceedings of the Institute of Electrical Engineers* 98, pp. 383–93.

Dretske, F. 1969. *Seeing and Knowing*, Chicago, Chicago University Press.

Dretske, F. 1970. 'Epistemic Operators', *Journal of Philosophy* 67, pp. 1007–23.

Dretske, F. 1971. 'Conclusive Reasons', *Australasian Journal of Philosophy* 49, pp. 1–22 [Ch. 6 in this volume].

Dretske, F. 1977. 'Laws of Nature', *Philosophy of Science* 44, pp. 248–68.

Dretske, F. 1981. *Knowledge and the Flow of Information*, Cambridge/MA, MIT Press.

Fodor, J. 1980. 'Methodological Solipsism Considered as a Research Strategy in Cognitive Psychology', *Behavioral and Brain Sciences* 3, pp. 63–110.

Garner, W. 1962. *Uncertainty and Structure as Psychological Concepts*, New York, Wiley.

Gettier, E. 1963. 'Is Justified True Belief Knowledge?' *Analysis* 23, pp. 121–3 [Ch. 2 in this volume].

Gibbons, J. J. 1950. *The Perception of the Visual World*, New York, Houghton Mifflin.

Gibbons, J. J. 1966. *The Senses Considered as a Perceptual System*, Boston, Houghton Mifflin.

Gibbons, J. J. 1979. *The Ecological Approach to Visual Perception*, Boston, Houghton Mifflin.

Goldman, A. I. 1976. 'Discrimination and Perceptual Knowledge', *Journal of Philosophy* 73, pp. 771–91 [Ch. 8 in this volume].

Haber, R. N. 1969. *Information-Processing Approaches to Visual Perception*, New York, Holt, Rinehart & Winston.

Haber, R. N. and Hershenson, M. 1973. *The Psychology of Visual Perception*, New York, Holt, Rinehart & Winston.

Kyburg, H. 1961. *Probability and the Logic of Rational Belief*, Middletown, Wesleyan University Press.

Kyburg, H. 1965. 'Probability, Rationality, and the Rule of Detachment', *Proceedings of the 1964 International Congress for Logic, Methodology, and the Philosophy of Science*, Amsterdam, North-Holland.

Lindsay, P. H. and Norman, D. A. 1972. *Human Information Processing*, New York, Academic Press.

MacKay, D. M. 1969. *Information, Mechanism and Meaning*, Cambridge/MA, MIT Press.

Miller, G. A. 1953. 'What is Information Measurement?', *The American Psychologist* 8, pp. 3–11.

Miller, G. A. 1956. 'The Magical Number Seven. Plus or Minus Two: Some Limits on Our Capacity for Processing Information', *Psychological Review* 63, pp. 81–97.

Neisser, U. 1967. *Cognitive Psychology*, New York, Appleton-Century-Crofts.

Rock, I. 1975. *An Introduction to Perception*, New York, Macmillan.

Rumelhart, D. E. 1977. *Introduction to Human Information Processing*, New York, Wiley.

Sayre, K. 1965. *Recognition: A Study in the Philosophy of Artificial Intelligence*, South Bend, University of Notre Dame Press.

Shannon, C. and Weaver, W. 1949. *The Mathematical Theory of Communication*, Urbana, University of Illinois Press.

Sperling, G. 1960. 'The Information Available in Brief Visual Presentations', *Psychological Monographs* 74, pp. 1–29.

Uhr, L. 1973. *Pattern Recognition, Learning, and Thought*, Englewood Cliffs/NJ, Prentice-Hall.

Internalism

Chapter 10

The indispensability of internal justification

Roderick M. Chisholm

> All knowledge is knowledge of someone; and ultimately, no one can have any
> ground for his beliefs which does not lie within his own experience.
>
> C. I. Lewis[1]

1. Introduction

THERE is a dispute within traditional epistemology, or theory of knowledge, between those who would interpret epistemic justification 'internally' and those who would interpret it 'externally'.[2] The dispute concerns the proper analysis of the concept of epistemic justification; it presupposes, therefore, that the internalists and externalists share a common concept of justification—the one that distinguishes knowledge from true belief that isn't knowledge.

We must be on guard, however, in interpreting contemporary literature that professes to be about 'internalism' or 'externalism'. Some of those authors who profess to view knowledge and epistemic justification 'externally' are not concerned with traditional theory of knowledge. That is to say, they are not concerned with the Socratic questions, 'What can I know?', 'How can I be sure that my beliefs are justified?' and 'How can I improve my present stock of beliefs?'. Indeed, many

Roderick M. Chisholm, 'The Indispensability of Internal Justification', in *Synthese* 74, (1988), pp. 285–96, reprinted by permission of Kluwer Academic Publishers, Dordrecht, The Netherlands.

1. C. I. Lewis: 1946, *An Analysis of Knowledge and Valuation*, The Open Court Publishing Company, La Salle, p. 236.
2. For early statements of the distinction, see Alvin Goldman: 1980, 'The Internalist Conception of Justification', in *Midwestern Studies in Philosophy* 5, 27–51, and by Laurence BonJour: 1980, 'Externalist Theories of Empirical Knowledge', in *Midwestern Studies in Philosophy* 5, 53–74 [Ch. 14 in this volume].

such philosophers are not concerned with the analysis of any ordinary concept of knowledge or of epistemic justification. Therefore their enterprise, whatever it may be, is not that of traditional theory of knowledge. My concern in what follows pertains only to the epistemological dispute: is the concept of epistemic justification to be analysed internally or externally?

I will begin by saying what I understand by 'internalism'.

2. What is 'internalism'?

The usual approach to the traditional questions of theory of knowledge is properly called 'internal' or 'internalistic'. The internalist assumes that, merely by reflecting upon his own conscious state, he can formulate a set of epistemic principles that will enable him to find out, with respect to any possible belief he has, whether he is justified in having that belief. The epistemic principles that he formulates are principles that one may come upon and apply merely by sitting in one's armchair, so to speak, and without calling for any outside assistance. In a word, one needs only consider one's own state of mind. I will argue that the approach to the traditional questions of theory of knowledge can thus only be internalistic. To be sure, we can assess the beliefs that *other* people have without examining *their* states of mind. And we can assess the beliefs that we ourselves have had at other times without examining the states of mind that we had at those other times. But these arguments, although 'external' in one sense, are 'internal' in another.

Suppose we are considering the beliefs that some other person had yesterday. After the fact, we can assess his beliefs and note just where he made his mistakes and where he did not. The principles we use need not be principles that were 'internal' for him at the time that he had the beliefs in question. That is to say, they need not be principles that *he* could then have applied by reflecting upon his own state of mind. For they make use of information that is now available to *us* and was not then available to him. Hence they do not tell us anything about what *he* was then justified in believing about himself. So far as he was then concerned they were 'external'; he could not have applied the principles merely by reflecting upon his state of mind. But if we are able to use them in appraising his beliefs, then they do presuppose something about what we are externally justified in believing about him.

According to this traditional conception of 'internal' epistemic justification, there is no logical connection between epistemic justification and truth. A belief may be internally justified and yet be false. The externalist feels that an adequate account of epistemic justification should exhibit *some* logical connection between epistemic justification and truth.

In recent years there have been many proposals concerning how epistemic justification might be explicated externally. But these suggestions, so far as I have been able to see, are of two sorts: either (1) they are empty or (2) they can be made to work only if they are supplemented by *internal* justification concepts. If this is true, then it has not yet been shown that internal concepts may be replaced by external ones.

I will consider, then, a number of possible explications of 'S is epistemically justified in believing p'. I will suggest that some of them are empty (an 'empty' explication being one that reduces justified belief to true belief). Then I will ask, with respect to those external explications that are not empty, whether they are adequate as they stand or whether they require supplementation by some epistemic concept that has not been shown to be externalistic.

3. The non-theory

I begin with a definition of external justification that is obviously unsatisfactory. I will use it to measure other possible definitions, for we may ask whether they tell us anything more than it does. We consider, then, theory (N)—'the non-theory':

(N) S is externally justified in believing p = Df. p is true; and S is a thinking subject.

The effect of this definition is to equate 'external justification' with truth. Or, more exactly, the definition makes no distinction between the *true* beliefs that a person has and those beliefs that he is *justified* in having. I think it is fair to call this theory empty, since it does not contribute anything of significance to the theory of knowledge.

Can we, then, find a concept of 'external' justification which does not thus reduce external justification to truth? Two types of external theory have been proposed—*reliability* theories and *causal* theories. And these may be combined into mixed reliability and causal theories.

I now turn to reliability theories.

4. Reliability theories of external justification

A common 'reliability' definition of 'external justification' is the following:[3]

(R1) S is externally justified in believing p = Df. The process by means of which S was led to believe p is reliable.

One serious difficulty with the definition, as it stands, is that it does not allow us to say, of a person who does not believe p, that he is justified in believing p. But conceivably, by making judicious use of counter-factuals, one could repair the definition to provide for this possibility.

A more serious difficulty has to do with the interpretation of the expression 'reliable process'. If we take 'process' in its broadest sense, then we may say that a process by means of which one is led to a belief is a series of activities that result in one's acquiring or retaining that belief. If we understand 'process' this way and if 'reliable process' means no more than 'process that is productive of true belief', then (R1) does not differ from (N)—that is to say, the present version of the reliability theory does not differ from the non-theory. For if the belief is true, then the process that led to it, however bizarre the process may have been, produced a belief that is true.

---

3. Compare Alvin Goldman: 'beliefs are justified if and only if they are produced by (relatively) reliable belief-forming processes,' op cit., p. 47.

One may now want to say:

(R2) S is externally justified in believing p = Df. The process by means of which S was led to believe p is a process which generally leads to true belief.

Does this add anything to (N)? If S has acquired a true belief, then once again, no matter how bizarre the situation may be, he has followed some procedure which is such that following that procedure always leads to true belief.[4] Let us consider this point in more detail.

If a person S has arrived at a true belief on a particular occasion, then S will have followed some procedure which was unique to that occasion. For example, S could have arrived at his belief by reading the tea-leaves on a Friday afternoon twenty-seven minutes after having visited his uncle. If necessary we may add further specifications—say, something about what S has just eaten or about the clothes that he is wearing. Since he has used this successful procedure only on *one* occasion, we may say:

(e) S has arrived at the belief that p by means of a belief-forming process which is such that, whenever he arrives at a belief by means of that process, the belief he thus arrives at is true.

If what we have said is correct, then *every* belief that S has arrived at will be one that has been arrived at by a unique process of the sort that (e) describes. Hence there is a process which is equivalent to the disjunction of all those successful belief-forming processes and which have provided S with as many justified beliefs as he has true beliefs.

We have, then, a counter-example to the analysis set forther in R2. It may seem, at first consideration, that a simple repair will save the definition. To see that this is so, consider the following dialogue between the reliabilist (R) and the internalist (I):

(R) 'You need only specify that the process not be a disjunctive process.'
(I) 'A *disjunction* is a type of sentence; but what is it for a *process* to be disjunctive?'
(R) 'A process is disjunctive if it can be described using disjunctive sentences.'
(I) 'But *every* process can be described using disjunctive sentences; therefore, if what you say is right, every process is disjunctive.'
(R) 'No, what I mean is that a disjunctive process is a process that can be described *only* by using disjunctive sentences.'[5]

---

4. See the discussion of this general question in Richard Feldman: 1985, 'Reliability and Justification', *The Monist* 68, 159–74.

5. In *Epistemology and Cognition*, Harvard University Press, Cambridge (1985), Alvin Goldman suggests other moves that the reliabilist might make to repair (R2). Thus the somewhat bizarre example of the tea-leaf reader could be avoided if we restricted our description of belief-forming processes to *organic processes* within the body of the believer (see p. 50). But here, too, there will be a unique bodily process for every belief-acquisition. We can all now truly say: 'I never was in exactly *this* bodily state before and I never will be in it again'. Should we add, then, that the processes be processes that are *relevant* to the acquisition or retention of belief? This move, of course, transfers the problem to that of finding a suitable analysis of 'relevant'.

(I) 'But there is *no* process which can be described *only* by using disjunctive sentences . . . .'

The problem is that the following two propositions are true: (1) any disjunction of particular-procedures is such that, if we know enough about it, we can show it also to be a particular-procedure; and (2) any particular-procedure is such that, if we know enough about it, we can show it also to be a disjunction of particular-procedures. If you describe for me a procedure which you think is a disjunction of particular procedures, I can add details which will entitle us to call it a particular procedure, and if you describe for me a procedure which you think is a particular procedure, I can add details which will entitle us to call it a disjunction of particular procedures.

These observations are not intended to belittle the concept of a reliable belief-forming process. They are intended, rather, to belittle the suggestion that epistemic justification can be defined merely by reference to such processes. Obviously one should try to know what belief-forming processes one is following and one should try to find out which of those processes are reliable; then one should try as far as possible to follow them. But this is to say that we should be concerned to follow those processes which are such that we are *justified* in believing them to be reliable.

Consider, now, the following definition:

(R3)   *S* is externally justified in believing p = Df. The process by means of which *S* was led to believe p is one which is such that it is evident to *S* that that process generally leads to true belief.

Since 'evident' expresses one of the internalist's epistemic concepts and since no externalistic explication of the concept of *being evident* is at hand, we may say this of (R3): It is an analysis of external justification which combines internal and external justification concepts. We could replace 'evident' in (R3) by 'knows', and say that the process is one which is such that *S knows* that it generally leads to true belief. If no externalistic explication of knowledge is added, then, once again, we have a definition that combines internal and external concepts.

Another possibility is to construe a reliable process as a process which is *probably* such that it leads to truth.[6] Then we might have:

(R4)   *S* is externally justified in believing p = Df. The process by means of which *S* was led to believe p is a process which is probably such as to lead to true belief.

---

6. Laurence BonJour writes: '. . . if finding epistemically justified beliefs did not substantially increase the likelihood of finding true ones, then epistemic justification would be irrelevant to our main cognitive goal and of dubious worth'; *The Structure of Empirical Knowledge*, Harvard University Press, Cambridge, (1985), p. 8. Compare Ernest Sosa: 'Faculty *F* is *more reliable* than faculty *F'* if the *likelihood* with which *F* would enable one to discriminate truth from falsehood in $f(F')$ is higher than the likelihood with which *F'* would enable one to make such discrimination in $f(F')$'. I have italicized 'likelihood'. It should be noted that Sosa here speaks of faculties instead of belief-yielding processes. See Ernest Sosa: 1985, 'Knowledge and Intellectual Virtue', *The Monist* 68, 226–47; the quotation is on p. 238.

Would this help the reliabilist? The answer is, I think that it simply transfers the problem. We may see this if we consider the two principal uses of 'probable'—the *statistical* use and the *relational* use.[7]

Statements in which 'probable' is taken merely *statistically* are rewordings of statements about statistical frequencies; they state what proportion of the members of one class are also members of another class. For example, 'The probability that any given A is a B is n' might be interpreted as telling us: 'n percent of the members of the class of A's are also members of the class of B's'. How are we to apply this type of interpretation to our example? (Statisticians make use of interpretations that are considerably more complex, but the added complexity does not affect the points that are here at issue.)

The statement (e) above entitles us to say that, in arriving at the belief that p, S followed a belief-forming process which was such that *all* the beliefs that he arrived at by using that process are true. Hence the statistical probability of that process yielding a true belief would be a probability of 1. Taking explication (R4) this way, we do not progress beyond the original explication (N).

Statements in which 'probable' is used in its *relational* sense are statements about the confirmation relation—that relation which is variously expressed as 'e confirms h', 'e makes h probable', 'h is probable in relation to e', and 'e tends to confirm h'. May we say of the proposition p, *which* S has arrived at as a result of his bizarre belief-forming process, that there is some true proposition which is such that p is more probable than not in relation to that proposition? Obviously we can; one such proposition is our earlier proposition (e):

(e) S has arrived at the belief that p by means of a belief-forming process which is such that, whenever he arrives at a belief by means of that process, the belief he thus arrives at is true.

But we may take relational probability more narrowly and relate p, not merely to a true proposition which tends to make p probable, but to a true proposition which is a part of someone's evidence-base. For example, if I investigate S's procedures, I may conclude: 'My body of evidence (i.e., the set of all the propositions that are evident to me) is such that p is probable in relation to it.' Variants would be: 'S's body of evidence is such that . . .' and 'There is a scientist having a body of evidence which is such that . . .' But these interpretations make use of the concept of S's *evidence* without providing any externalistic explication of that concept. Hence they cannot be said to provide us with any 'externalistic' explication of reliability.

There are, of course, other statistical and relational interpretations of

7. See Rudolf Carnap: 1950, *Logical Foundations of Probability*, The University of Chicago Press, Chicago, pp. 300 ff. Carnap speaks of statistical probability statements as statements about 'probability[2]' and of relational probability statements as statements about 'probability[1].' He notes that 'under certain conditions, probability[1] may be regarded as an estimate of probability[2]' (p. 300). But in the theory of knowledge, statements of relational probability are not concerned merely with estimates of relative frequencies; a typical statement of relational probability would be: 'Thinking that one remembers p tends to make p probable'.

'probable', but, so far as I have been able to see, none of them is of any help to the externalist.[8]

5. Causal theories of external justification

Another way of establishing a connection between epistemic justification and truth is the concept of justification by reference to that of causation. Consider, for example, those true propositions which are such that their *being true* is what causes us to *believe* that they are true.[9] Could it be that these are the propositions we are 'externally' justified in believing? At best, this suggestion gives us a very restricted account of epistemic justification. For it is not applicable as it stands to propositions about the future. And it is doubtful whether it would be applicable to propositions that are logically true. Are there, however, *some* propositions that may be said to be justified in this way?

The locution '*A* causes *B*' may be taken in two quite different ways: (1) as telling us that *A* is *the cause* of *B*, or (2) as telling us that *A contributes causally* to *B* (that *A* is one of the *causal factors* that leads to *B*). We have, then, two causal definitions to consider.

The first is this:

(C1)   *S* is externally justified in believing *p* = Df. *S* believes *p*; and *p*'s being true is *the cause* of *S*'s believing *p*.

The phrase 'the cause' is certainly one that is in common use; indeed it is suggested by the familiar propositional connective, 'because'. Thus many people like to think that, of the various events that contribute causally to a given event, there is just one of them that may properly be singled out as *the* cause of that event. Such a view is especially tempting when we are looking for a scape-goat.[10] But, as we know from the study of the nature of causation, the expression '*A* is *the cause* of *B*' is one that is applicable only in very restricted circumstances and is not likely to be of use in

---

8. Some would interpret the relational sense of 'probability' without appeal to the concept of evidence and would say that a proposition is probable for a given person provided only that the proposition is probable in relation to what that person happens to *believe*. But it is difficult to see how *this* way of construing probability would provide us with an account of epistemic justification.

9. Alvin Goldman has suggested that such propositions provide us with the clue that we need for solving the Gettier problem. In Gettier's best known example, a subject *S*, for whom the false proposition *Jones owns a Ford* is evident, picks some place-names at random and deduces the true proposition (*p*) *Either Jones owns a Ford or Brown is in Barcelona*; and *S* has no idea at all that Brown is in Barcelona. Goldman says: 'one thing that seems to be missing in this example is a causal connection between the fact that makes *p* true [or simply: the fact that *p*] and *S*'s belief that *p*'. Alvin Goldman: 1978, 'A Causal Theory of Knowing', in George S. Pappas and Marshall Swain (eds.), *Essays on Knowledge and Justification*, Cornell University Press, Ithaca, pp. 67–86 (the quotation is on page 68) [in this volume p. 19].

10. We might say of the expression 'the cause' what William James said of 'cause'—namely that it is 'an altar to an unknown God, an empty pedestal still marking the place of a hoped for statue'. William James: 1893, *The Principles of Psychology*, Vol. 2, Henry Holt and Company, New York, p. 671.

connection with the present problem. If p, for example, is the proposition that there are mountains on the other side of the moon, then it is doubtful whether one could pick out *any* situation in which p's being true could be said to be *the cause* of anyone's belief that p. That event which is p's being true is just one of many factors which, working together, contribute causally to the belief that p.

What if we were to define 'A is *the cause* of B' by saying: 'Of those events that contribute causally to E, A is the sole change that immediately preceded the occurrence of E'?[11] If we take 'the cause' this way, then the cause of the acquisition of a belief might be some other psychological event (the occurrence, say, of a certain thought) or it might be some neuro-physiological event. Application of (C1), therefore, would be restricted to those beliefs which are about such psychological or neuro-physiological events.

Does the causal theory fare better if we replace 'is the cause of' by 'causally contributes to'? Then we would have:

(C2) S is externally justified in believing p = Df. S believes p; and p's being true *contributes causally* to S's believing p.

Now the definition is subject to Rube Goldberg counter-examples. Consider a person who is working in the garden and who suddenly becomes tired; his fatigue leads him to go inside and read the newspaper; he reads that some of the people who suffer from a certain internal disorder have red hair; since *he* has red hair and is also a hypochondriac, he concludes: 'I've got that disorder!' If, now, his having that disorder was one of the many factors that contributed causally to his fatigue, then we may say that, according to (C2), he is externally justified in believing that he has that disorder.[12] *This* concept of justification is not likely to be of use in investigating the theory of knowledge.

Could one overcome such difficulties by specifying a type of causation that is not transitive, such as direct causation? (Roughly: 'A is a direct causal contributor to B, if and only if: A contributes causally to B, and A does not contribute causally to anything that contributes causally to B.) The direct contributor to a belief attribution would then presumably be either another psychological state or an internal physiological state. This move, then, has the same difficulties as '*the* cause' move considered above.

Our example above may suggest that the subject S should be *aware of* the

11. C. J. Ducasse proposed that 'the cause of a change K' is that change which 'alone occurred in the immediate environment of K immediately before'; *Truth, Knowledge and Causation*, Routledge & Kegan Paul, London, (1968), p. 4. Ducasse's definition, unlike the one proposed above, did not make use of the concept of causal contribution (causal factor).

12. If we are thus reduced to speaking of causal contribution instead of 'the cause', then it is not likely that Goldman's move, referred to above, will help us with the Gettier problem. S has picked a number of place-names including 'Barcelona' at random and was then led to deduce the true proposition (p) *Either Jones owns a Ford or Brown is in Barcelona*. Brown's being in Barcelona was not *the cause* of S's belief that p, but it could have *contributed causally* to his having the belief. One could add the following to Gettier's example: Brown had written a letter to Robinson from Barcelona; this fact contributed causally to Robinson's uttering 'Barcelona' in S's presence; and the latter fact, in turn, contributed causally to S's thinking of p.

causal role that is played by p in the formation of his belief. And so one might suggest:

(C3) *S* is externally justified in believing p = Df. *S believes p; p's being true contributes causally to S's believing p; and it is evident to S that p's being true contributes causally to his belief that p.*

This proposal is like (R3) above: it *combines* internal and external justification concepts.[13]

6. Mixed theories

The reliability and causal theories that we have considered may be combined in various ways.[14] We need consider only two possibilities:

(M1) *S* is externally justified in believing p = Df. *S believes that p; and the cause of S's believing that p is that S follows a belief-forming process that generally leads to true belief.*

This combines (R2) and (C1) and obviously has the difficulties of each.

(M2) *S* is externally justified in believing p = Df. *S* believes that p; and one of the facts that *contribute causally* to his believing p is the fact that he followed a belief-forming process which, *more probably than not*, yields true belief.

This combines (R4) and (C2) and obviously has the difficulties of each.

7. Conclusion

The 'externalistic' explications of epistemic justification that we have considered are all such that either they are empty or they make use of internal concepts. Hence there is no indication that externalistic justification concepts may *replace* internal concepts.

There are externalists, I think, who might grant the critical points that have been made here and who would draw a quite different conclusion from the one that I have drawn. They would say: 'But I cannot follow you in your internalism. You seem to agree with Keynes that "probability begins and ends with probabilities".[15] And you have said that there is no logical connection between the fact that a proposition is internally justified and the truth of that proposition. I must confess that I simply cannot understand what you are talking about.'

What kind of 'reply' can be made to this? I would quote C. I. Lewis:

13. This type of theory is suggested by Marshall Swain who proposes a causal theory that makes use of such internalistic expressions as the following: '*S's evidence*' and '*renders evident.*' See Marshall Swain: 'Knowledge, Causality and Justification', in Pappas and Swain, pp. 87–99.
14. '*Reliabilism* is the view that a belief is epistemically justified if and only if it is produced or sustained by a cognitive process that reliably yields truth and avoids error.' Sosa, p. 239.
15. See John Maynard Keynes: 1952, *A Treatise on Probability*, Macmillan, Basingstoke, p. 322.

For one who should lack a primordial sense of probable events, every attempted explication of a categorical probability statement must fail. Any who should perversely insist upon reduction of its meaning to terms of some presently ascertained factuality—other than the data giving rise to it—must simply be left behind in the discussion. He denies a category of cognition which is fundamental and as different from theoretically certain knowledge as apprehension of the future is different from observation of the past.[16]

16. Lewis. p. 320.

Chapter 11

The elements of coherentism

Laurence BonJour

1. The very idea of a coherence theory

IN light of the failure of foundationalism, it is time to look again at the apparent alternatives with regard to the structure of empirical justification which were distinguished in the discussion of the epistemic regress problem [in an earlier section]. If the regress of empirical justification does not terminate in basic empirical beliefs, then it must either (1) terminate in unjustified beliefs, (2) go on infinitely (without circularity), or (3) circle back upon itself in some way. As discussed earlier, alternative (1) is clearly a version of skepticism and as such may reasonably be set aside until all other alternatives have been seen to fail. Alternative (2) may also be a version of skepticism, though this is less clear. But the more basic problem with alternative (2) is that no one has ever succeeded in amplifying it into a developed position (indeed, it is not clear that anyone has even attempted to do so); nor do I see any plausible way in which this might be done. Failing any such elaboration which meets the objections tentatively developed earlier, alternative (2) may also reasonably be set aside. This then leaves alternative (3) as apparently the only remaining possibility for a nonskeptical account of empirical knowledge.

We are thus led to a reconsideration of the possibility of a coherence theory of empirical knowledge. If there is no way to justify empirical beliefs apart from an appeal to other justified empirical beliefs, and if an infinite sequence of distinct justified beliefs is ruled out, then the presumably finite system of justified empirical beliefs can only be justified from within, by virtue of the relations of its component beliefs to each other—if, that is, it is justified at all. And the idea of *coherence* should for the moment be taken merely to indicate whatever property (or complex set of properties) is requisite for the justification of such a system of beliefs.

Obviously this rather flimsy argument by elimination carries very little weight by itself. The analogous argument in the case of foundationalism lead to an untenable result; and that failure, when added to the already substantial problems with coherence theories which were briefly noted above, makes the present version even less compelling. At best it may motivate a more open-minded consideration of coherence theories than they have usually been accorded, such theories having usually been treated merely as dialectical bogeymen and only rarely as serious epistemological alternatives.

BonJour, Laurence, 'The Elements of Coherentism' in *The Structure of Empirical Knowledge* (Cambridge, MA., Harvard University Press, 1985) pp. 87–110, 239–41, reprinted by permission of Laurence BonJour.

It will be useful to begin by specifying more precisely just what sort of coherence theory is at issue here. In the first place, our concern is with coherence theories of empirical justification and not coherence theories of truth; the latter hold that truth is to be simply identified with coherence (presumably coherence with some specified sort of system). The classical idealist proponents of coherence theories in fact generally held views of both these sorts and unfortunately failed for the most part to distinguish clearly between them. And this sort of confusion is abetted by views which use the phrase 'theory of truth' to mean a theory of the criteria of truth, that is, a theory of the standards or rules which should be appealed to in deciding or judging whether or not something is true; if, as is virtually always the case, such a theory is meant to be an account of the criteria which can be used to arrive at a rational or warranted judgment of truth or falsity, then a coherence theory of truth in that sense would seem to be indiscernible from what is here called a coherence theory of justification, and quite distinct from a coherence theory of the very nature or meaning of truth.[1] But if such confusions are avoided, it is clear that coherence theories of empirical justification are both distinct from and initially a good deal more plausible than coherence theories of empirical truth and moreover that there is no manifest absurdity in combining a coherence theory of justification with a correspondence theory of truth. Whether such a combination is in the end dialectically defensible is of course a further issue and one to which I will return in the final chapter of this book.

Second, it is also worth emphasizing at the outset that I am concerned here only with coherence theories which purport to provide a response to skepticism. My view thus differs from those of several recent coherence theorists, most notably Michael Williams but also, to a lesser extent, Gilbert Harman and Keith Lehrer, who depart from foundationalism not only in their account of the structure of empirical justification but also with regard to the goals or purposes of an epistemological theory, by holding that such a theory need not attempt to provide a 'global' account of justification or to answer 'global' varieties of skepticism.

Third, the dialectical motive for coherentism depends heavily on the unacceptability of the externalist position. It is thus crucially important that a coherentist view itself avoid tacitly slipping into a nonfoundationalist version of externalism. If coherentism is to be even a dialectically interesting alternative, the coherentist justification must, in principle at least, be accessible to the believer himself.

The aim of this chapter is to begin the task of formulating a coherence theory which satisfied the foregoing structures by, first, considering in detail some of the main ingredients of such a view, including the idea of nonlinear or holistic justification, the concept of coherence itself, and the presumption concerning one's grasp of one's own system of beliefs; and, second, elaborating the leading objections which such a position must face. The upshot of the chapter will be the hardly

---

1. Rescher's 'coherence theory of truth' in Rescher (1973) is a coherence theory of the criteria of truth, not of the nature of truth. Though leaving the connection with justification somewhat obscure, this book contains an excellent discussion of the distinction between the two sorts of theories of truth.

surprising conclusion that a central, very likely decisive, issue with respect to coherence theories is whether they can somehow make room for a viable concept of *observation*.

2. Linear versus nonlinear justification

The initial problem is whether and how a coherence theory constitutes even a *prima facie* solution to the epistemic regress problem. Having rejected both foundationalism and the actual-infinite-regress position, a coherentist must hold, as we have seen, that the regress of empirical justification moves in a circle—or, more plausibly, some more complicated and multidimensional variety of closed curve. But this response to the regress will seem obviously and utterly inadequate to one who approaches the issue with foundationalist preconceptions. Surely, his argument will go, such a resort to circularity fails to solve or even adequately confront the problem. Each step in the regress is a justificatory argument whose premises must be justified *before* they can confer justification on the conclusion. To say that the regress moves in a circle is to say that at some point one (or more) of the beliefs which figured earlier as a conclusion is now appealed to as a justifying premise. And this response, far from solving the problem, seems to yield the patently absurd result that the justification of such a belief depends, indirectly but still quite inescapably, on *its own* logically prior justification: it cannot be justified unless it is already justified. And thus, assuming that it is not justified in some independent way, neither it nor anything which depends upon it can be genuinely justified. Since empirical justification is always ultimately circular in this way according to coherence theories, there can on such a view be in the end no empirical justification and no empirical knowledge.

   The crucial, though tacit, assumption which underlies this seemingly devastating line of argument is the idea that inferential justification is essentially *linear* in character, that it involves a one-dimensional sequence of beliefs, ordered by the relation of epistemic priority, along which epistemic justification is passed from the earlier to the later beliefs in the sequence via connections of inference. It is just this linear conception of justification which generates the regress problem in the first place. So long as it remains unchallenged, the idea that justification moves in a circle will seem obviously untenable, and only moderate or strong foundationalism will be left as an alternative: even weak foundationalism cannot accept a purely linear view of justification, since its initially credible beliefs are not sufficiently justified on that basis alone to serve as linear first premises for everything else. Thus the primary coherentist response to the regress problem cannot be merely the idea that justification moves in a circle, for this would be quite futile by itself; rather such a position must repudiate the linear conception of justification in its entirety.

   But what is the alternative? What might a nonlinear conception of justification amount to? Briefly, the main idea is that inferential justification, despite its linear appearance, is essentially systematic or holistic in character: beliefs are justified by being inferentially related to other beliefs in the overall context of a coherent system.

The best way to clarify this view is to distinguish two importantly different levels at which issues of empirical justification can be raised. The epistemic issue on a particular occasion will usually be merely the justification of a single empirical belief, or small set of such beliefs, within the context of a cognitive system whose overall justification is (more or less) taken for granted; we may call this the *local* level of justification. But it is also possible, at least in principle, to raise the issue of the overall justification of the entire system of empirical beliefs; we may call this the *global* level of justification. For the sort of coherence theory which will be developed here—and indeed, I would argue, for any comprehensive, nonskeptical epistemology—it is the issue of justification as it arises at the latter, global, level which is in the final analysis decisive for the determination of empirical justification in general.[2] This tends to be obscured in practice, I suggest, because it is only issues of the former, local, sort which tend to be explicitly raised in actual cases. (Indeed, it may well be that completely global issues are never in fact raised outside the context of explicitly epistemological discussion; but I cannot see that this in any way shows that there is something illegitimate about them.)

It is at the local level of justification that inferential justification *appears* linear. A given justification belief is shown to be justified by citing other premise-beliefs from which it correctly follows via some acceptable pattern of inference. Such premise-beliefs may themselves be challenged, of course, with justification being offered for them in the same fashion. But there is no serious danger of an infinite regress at this level, since the justification of the overall system of empirical beliefs, and thus of most of its constituent beliefs, is *ex hypothesi* not at issue. One quickly reaches premise-beliefs which are dialectically acceptable in that particular context and which can thus function there rather like the foundationalist's basic beliefs. (But these *contextually basic beliefs*, as they might be called, are unlikely to be only or even primarily beliefs which would be classified as basic by any plausible version of foundationalism.)

If, on the other hand, no dialectically acceptable stopping point were reached, if the new premise-beliefs offered as justification continued to be challenged in turn, then (according to the sort of coherence theory with which I am concerned) the epistemic dialogue would if ideally continued eventually circle back upon itself, giving the appearance of a linear regress and in effect challenging the entire system of empirical beliefs. At this global level, however, the previously harmless illusion of linearity becomes a serious mistake. According to the envisaged coherence theory, the relation between the various particular beliefs is correctly to be conceived, not as one of linear dependence, but rather as one of mutual or reciprocal support. There is no ultimate relation of epistemic priority among the members of such a system and consequently no basis for a true regress. Rather the component beliefs of such a coherent system will ideally be so related that each can be justified in

---

2. As already noted, some theories combine an appeal to coherence with a rejection of the global issue of justification. See, for example, Sklar (1975) and Williams (1980). Because I see no warrant for dismissing the global issue in this way, such views seem to me to constitute merely complicated versions of skepticism.

terms of the others, with the direction of argument on a particular occasion of local justification depending on which belief (or set of beliefs) has actually been challenged in the particular situation. And hence, a coherence theory will claim, the apparent circle of justification is not in fact vicious *because* it is not *genuinely a circle*: the justification of a particular empirical belief finally depends, not on other particular beliefs as the linear conception of justification would have it, but instead on the overall system and its coherence.

According to this conception, the fully explicit justification of a particular empirical belief would involve four distinct main steps or stages of argument, as follows:

(1) The inferability of that particular belief from other particular beliefs and further relations among particular empirical beliefs.
(2) The coherence of the overall system of empirical beliefs.
(3) The justification of the overall system of empirical beliefs.
(4) The justification of the particular belief in question, by virtue of its membership in the system.

The claim of a coherence theory of empirical justification is that each of these steps depends on the ones which precede it. It is the neglecting of steps (2) and (3), the ones pertaining explicitly to the overall cognitive system, that lends plausibility to the linear conception of justification and thus generates the regress problem. And this is a very seductive mistake: since the very same inferential connections between particular empirical beliefs are involved in both step (1) and step (4), and since the issues involved in the intervening steps are very rarely (if ever) raised in practical contexts, it becomes much too easy to conflate steps (1) and (4), thus leaving out any explicit reference to the cognitive system and its coherence. The picture which results from such an omission is vastly more simple; but the price of this simplicity, according to coherence theories, is a radical distortion of the very concept of epistemic justification—and also, in the end, skepticism or something tantamount to it.

How tenable is such a nonlinear conception of empirical justification? Of the three crucial transitions represented in this obviously quite schematic account, only the third, from step (3) to step (4), is reasonably unproblematic, depending as it does on the inferential relations that obtain between the justificandum belief and the other beliefs of the system; in effect it is this transition which is made when an inferential justification is offered in an ordinary context of local justification, with the other steps being taken for granted. But the other two transitions are highly problematic, and the issues that they raise are crucial for understanding and assessing the very conception of a coherence theory.

The transition from step (1) to step (2), from the relations obtaining between particular beliefs to the attribution of the holistic property of coherence to the empirical system as a whole, is rendered problematic by the obscurity of the central concept of coherence itself. A fully adequate explication of coherence is unfortunately not possible within the scope of this book (nor, one may well suspect, within the scope of any work of manageable length). But I will attempt to render the concept manageably clear in the next section, where I will also suggest that the clarity of the concept of coherence is not, surprisingly enough, a very crucial issue in assessing the plausibility of coherence theories *vis-à-vis* their nonskeptical opponents.

The problems relating to the other problematic transition in the schematic account, that from step (2) to step (3), are, in contrast, more serious, indeed critical. What is at issue here is the question of the connection between coherence and epistemic justification: why, if a system of empirical beliefs is coherent (and more coherent than any rival system), is it thereby justified *in the epistemic sense*, that is, why is it thereby likely to be true? I will address this question in section 5, where the standard set of objections to coherence theories will be developed in further detail.

3. The concept of coherence

What, then, is coherence? Intuitively, coherence is a matter of how well a body of beliefs 'hangs together': how well its component beliefs fit together, agree or dove-tail with each other, so as to produce an organized, tightly structured system of beliefs, rather than either a helter-skelter collection or a set of conflicting sub-systems. It is reasonably clear that this 'hanging together' depends on the various sorts of inferential, evidential, and explanatory relations which obtain among the various members of a system of beliefs, and especially on the more holistic and systematic of these. Thus various detailed investigations by philosophers and logi-cians of such topics as explanation, confirmation, probability, and so on, may be reasonably taken to provide some of the ingredients for a general account of coher-ence. But the main work of giving such an account, and in particular one which will provide some relatively clear basis for *comparative* assessments of coherence, has scarcely been begun, despite the long history of the concept.

My response to this problem, for the moment at least, is a deliberate—though, I think, justified—evasion. It consists in pointing out that the task of giving an adequate explication of the concept of coherence is not uniquely or even primarily the job of coherence theories. This is so because coherence—or something resem-bling it so closely as to be subject to the same sort of problem—is, and seemingly must be, a basic ingredient of virtually all rival epistemological theories as well. We have already seen that weak foundationalism essentially involves an appeal to coherence. And it seems clear that even moderate and strong foundationalisms cannot avoid an appeal to something like coherence in giving an account of know-ledge of the past, theoretical knowledge, and other types of knowledge which (on any view) go beyond direct experience. Thus it is not surprising that virtually all of the leading proponents of comprehensive foundationalist views, whether weak, moderate, or strong, employ the notion of coherence in their total epistemological accounts—though sometimes under other names, such as 'congruence' (Lewis) or 'concurrence' (Chisholm).[3] Even 'contextualist' views, which attempt to repudiate the whole issue of global justification, make a similar appeal. The conclusion

3. See Lewis (1946, chap. 2); and Chisholm (1977, chap. 4).

strongly suggested is that something like coherence is indispensable to any non-skeptical epistemological position which is even *prima facie* adequate. And if this is so, the absence of an adequate explication of coherence does not count against coherence theories any more than against their rivals.

The foregoing response is dialectically cogent in defending coherence theories against other, nonskeptical epistemologies, but it must be admitted that it is of little use *vis-à-vis* the skeptic, who may well argue that what it shows is that all nonskeptical epistemologies are fundamentally flawed by virtue of their dependence on this inadequately explicated concept. But although this challenge must be taken seriously, it is far from obvious that it is even close to being decisive. A better account of coherence is beyond any doubt something devoutly to be sought; but it is, I think, quite plausible to say, as Ewing does, that what proponents of coherence 'are doing is to describe an ideal that has never yet been completely clarified but is none the less immanent in all our thinking,'[4] and to hold on this basis that our intuitive grasp of this notion, though surely not ideally satisfactory, will suffice so long as the only alternative is skepticism—which itself carries, after all, a significant burden of implausibility.

In any case, however, there is little point in talking at length about coherence without a somewhat clearer idea of what is involved. Thus I will attempt to provide in this section a reasonable outline of the concept of coherence, while recognizing that it falls far short of what would be ideal. The main points are: first, coherence is not to be equated with mere consistency; second, coherence, as already suggested, has to do with the mutual inferability of the beliefs in the system; third, relations of explanation are one central ingredient in coherence, though not the only one; and, fourth, coherence may be enhanced through conceptual change.

First. A serious and perennial mistake in discussing coherence, usually committed by critics but occasionally also by would-be proponents of coherence theories, is to assume that coherence means nothing more than logical consistency, the absence of explicit contradiction.[5] It is true that consistency is one requirement for coherence, that inconsistency is obviously a very serious sort of incoherence. But it is abundantly clear, as many coherentists have pointed out, that a system of beliefs might be perfectly consistent and yet have no appreciable degree of coherence.

There are at least two ways in which this might be so. The more obvious is what might be called *probabilistic inconsistency*. Suppose that my system of beliefs contains both the belief that P and also the belief that it is extremely improbable that P. Clearly such a system of beliefs may perfectly well be logically consistent. But it is equally clear from an intuitive standpoint that a system which contains two such

4. Ewing (1934, p. 231).
5. Perhaps the clearest example of this rather pervasive mistake is Scheffler (1967, chap. 5). Another interesting case is Rescher (1973): the 'coherence criterion of truth' advocated there uses consistency to segregate propositions into maximally consistent subsets, and then chooses among those subsets on a variety of different bases, none of which have much to do with the standard idea of coherence. (Rescher's later development of the same view does, however, employ a more traditional notion of coherence, though in a different place.) See Rescher (1977), and also BonJour (1976).

beliefs is significantly less coherent than it would be without them and thus that probabilistic consistency is a second factor determining coherence.

Probabilistic consistency differs from straightforward logical consistency in two important respects. First, it is extremely doubtful that probabilistic inconsistency can be entirely avoided. Improbable things do, after all, sometimes happen, and sometimes one can avoid admitting them only by creating an even greater probabilistic inconsistency at another point.[6] Second, probabilistic consistency, unlike logical consistency, is plainly a matter of degree, depending on (a) just how many such conflicts the system contains and (b) the degree of improbability involved in each case. Thus we have two initial conditions for coherence, which we may formulate as follows:

(1) A system of beliefs is coherent only if it is logically consistent.[7]
(2) A system of beliefs is coherent in proportion to its degree of probabilistic consistency.

But these two requirements are still not enough. Imagine a set of beliefs, each member of which has simply no bearing at all on the subject matter of any of the others, so that they make no effective contact with each other. This lack of contact will of course assure that the set is both logically and probabilistically consistent by ruling out any possibility of conflict; but it will also assure that the members of the set fail to hang together in any very significant way. Thus consider the following two sets of propositions, A and B. A contains 'this chair is brown,' 'electrons are negatively charged,' and 'today is Thursday.' B contains 'all ravens are black,' 'this bird is a raven,' and 'this bird is black.' Clearly both sets of propositions are free of contradiction and are also probabilistically consistent. But in the case of A, this consistency results from the fact that its component propositions are almost entirely irrelevant to each other; though not in conflict, they also fail to be positively related in any significant way. And for this reason, set A possesses only a very low degree of coherence. In the case of set B, in contrast, consistency results from the fact that the component propositions, rather than being irrelevant to each

---

6. One pervasive case of this sort is worth explicit notice: it often happens that my system of beliefs makes it extremely probable that an event of a certain general description will occur, while providing no guidance as to which of a very large number of alternative, more specific possibilities will realize this description. If there is nothing more to be said, each of the specific possibilities will be very improbable, simply because there are so many, while at the same time it will be highly probable that one of them will occur. In such a case, adding a new belief (arrived at through observation or in some other way) that one of the possible specific events has actually occurred will bring with it a measure of probabilistic inconsistency—but less than would result from excluding all such specific beliefs, thereby coming into conflict with the more general one.

7. It might be questioned whether it is not an oversimplification to make logical consistency in this way an absolutely necessary condition for coherence. In particular, some proponents of relevance logics may want to argue that in some cases a system of beliefs which was sufficiently rich and complex but which contained some trivial inconsistency might be preferable to a much less rich system which was totally consistent. And there are also worries such as the Preface Paradox. But while I think there may be something to be said for such views, the issues they raise are too complicated and remote to be entered into here.

other, fit together and reinforce each other in a significant way; from an epistemic standpoint, any two of them would lend a degree of positive support to the third (though only very weak support in two out of the three cases). Thus set B, though obviously much too small to have a really significant degree of coherence, is much more coherent than set A. As the classical proponents of coherence have always insisted, coherence must involve some sort of positive connection among the beliefs in question, not merely the absence of conflict.

Second. But what sort of positive connection is required and how strong must it be? The obvious answer to the first question is that the connections in question are inference relations namely, any sort of relation of content which would allow one belief or set of beliefs, if justified, to serve as the premise(s) of a cogent epistemic-justificatory argument for a further belief. The basic requirement for such an inference relation, as suggested in the earlier discussion of epistemic justification, is that it be to some degree truth-preserving; any sort of relation which meets this requirement will serve as an appropriate positive connection between beliefs, and no other sort of connection seems relevant here.

This much would be accepted by most, if not all, proponents of coherence theories. The main thing that divides them is the issue of how close and pervasive such inferential connections are required to be. One pole with regard to this issue is represented by the classical absolute idealists. Blanshard's formulation is typical:

Fully coherent knowledge would be knowledge in which every judgment entailed, and was entailed by, the rest of the system.[8]

(In interpreting this formulation it is important to remember that Blanshard, like many others in this tradition, believes in synthetic entailments and indeed holds the admittedly dubious view that causal connections are one species of entailment.) The main problem with this view is that it is quite impossible even to imagine a system of beliefs which would satisfy such a requirement; as Blanshard himself admits, even such a system as Euclidean geometry, often appealed to as a paradigm of coherence, falls far short.[9] Thus it is plausible to weaken the requirement for coherence at least to the degree advocated by Ewing, who requires only that each proposition in a coherent system be entailed by the rest taken together, not that the reciprocal relation hold.[10] (We will see shortly that weakening the requirement in this way creates a problem which forces Ewing to add a further, related requirement.)

At the opposite extreme is Lewis's account of 'congruence,' a concept which plays a crucial role in his account of memory knowledge:

A set of statements . . . will be said to be congruent if and only if they are so related that the antecedent probability of any one of them will be increased if the remainder of the set can be assumed as given premises.[11]

This is obviously an extremely weak requirement. A system of beliefs which satis-

---

8. Blanshard (1939, p. 264).
9. Ibid., p. 265.
10. Ewing (1934, p. 229).
11. Lewis (1946, p. 338), Chisholm's definition of 'concurrence' in Chisholm (1977) is very similar.

fied it at only the most minimal level would possess a vastly lower degree of systematic interconnection than that envisaged by the idealists, in two significantly different respects. First, reducing the requirement from entailment to merely some increase in probability obviously allows a weakening of the inferential connections which constitute coherence. But this is no objection to Lewis's account, so long as it is understood that coherence is a matter of degree, and that a lower degree of inferential interconnection carries with it only a lower degree of coherence. Second, however, Lewis's account, and indeed Ewing's as well, by making the inferential connection between the individual belief in question and the rest of the system one-way rather than reciprocal, creates the possibility that a system of beliefs could count as coherent to as high a degree as one likes by being composed of two or more subsystems of beliefs, each internally connected by strong inference relations but none having any significant connection with the others. From an intuitive standpoint, however, it is clear that such a system, though coherent to some degree, would fall very far short of ideal coherence. Ideal coherence requires also that the entire system of beliefs form a unified structure, that there be laws and principles which underlie the various subsystems of beliefs and provide a significant degree of inferential connection between them. We are obviously very close here to the ideal of a 'unified science,' in which the laws and terms of various disparate disciplines are reduced to those of some single master discipline, perhaps physics; while such a specific result is not essential for coherence, it would represent one way in which a high degree of coherence could be achieved, and something in this general direction seems to be required.

Ewing attempts to meet this difficulty by adding as a separate requirement for coherence the condition that no set of beliefs smaller than the whole system be logically independent of the rest of the system,[12] and a similar requirement could be added to Lewis's account as well. It would be better, however, to make this further aspect of coherence also a matter of degree, since there are obviously many intermediate cases between a completely unified system and a system with completely isolated subsystems. Putting all of this together results in the following two additional conditions for coherence:

(3) The coherence of a system of beliefs is increased by the presence of inferential connections between its component beliefs and increased in proportion to the number and strength of such connections.

(4) The coherence of a system of beliefs is diminished to the extent to which it is divided into subsystems of beliefs which are relatively unconnected to each other by inferential connections.

It should be noted that condition (3), in addition to summarizing the preceding discussion, includes one important idea which did not emerge explicitly there: each individual belief can be involved in many different inferential relations, and the degree to which this is so is also a determinant of coherence.

Third. The foregoing account, though it seems to me to be on the right track, is

12. Ewing (1934, pp. 229–30).

obviously still extremely sketchy. One way to reduce this sketchiness somewhat is to consider the major role which the idea of *explanation* plays in the overall concept of coherence. As I have already suggested by mentioning the ideal of unified science, the coherence of a system of beliefs is enhanced by the presence of explanatory relations among its members.

Indeed, if we accept something like the familiar Hempelian account of explanation, this claim is to some extent a corollary of what has already been said. According to that account, particular facts are explained by appeal to other facts and general laws from which a statement of the explanandum fact may be deductively or probabilistically inferred; and lower-level laws and theories are explained in an analogous fashion by showing them to be deducible from more general laws and theories.[13] Thus the presence of relations of explanation within a system of beliefs enhances the inferential interconnectedness of the system simply because explanatory relations *are* one species of inference relations.

Explanatory connections are not just additional inferential connections among the beliefs of a system, however; they are inferential connections of a particularly pervasive kind. This is so because the basic goal of scientific explanation is to exhibit events of widely differing kinds as manifestations of a relatively small number of basic explanatory principles. As Hempel remarks: 'what scientific explanation, especially theoretical explanation, aims at is . . . an objective kind of insight that is achieved by a systematic unification, by exhibiting the phenomena as manifestations of common underlying structures and processes that conform to specific, testable, basic principles.'[14] What Hempel calls 'systematic unification' is extremely close to the concept of coherence.

One helpful way to elaborate this point is to focus on the concept of *anomaly*. For my purposes, an anomaly is a fact or event, especially one involving some sort of recurring pattern, which is claimed to obtain by one or more of the beliefs in the system of beliefs, but which is incapable of being explained (or would have been incapable of being predicted) by appeal to the other beliefs in the system.[15] (Obviously such a status is a matter of degree.) The presence of such anomalies detracts from the coherence of the system to an extent which cannot be accounted for merely by appeal to the fact that the belief in an anomalous fact or event has fewer inferential connections to the rest of the system than would be the case if an explanation were available. In the context of a coherentist position, such beliefs will have to be inferentially connected to the rest of the system in other, nonexplanatory ways if there is to be any justification for accepting them (see the discussion of observation in Chapter 6), and such connections may be very extensive. The distinctive significance of anomalies lies rather in the fact that they undermine the claim of the allegedly basic explanatory principles to be genuinely basic, and thus

13. For refinements, see, e.g., the title essay in Hempel (1965).
14. Hempel (1967, p. 83).
15. On the Hempelian view, explanation and prediction involve the same sorts of inferential relations within the system of beliefs, differing only as to whether the fact in question is known prior to drawing the appropriate inference. Although this view is not uncontroversial, I will assume that it is at least approximately correct.

threaten the overall coherence of the system in a much more serious way. For this reason, it seems advisable to add one more condition to our list of conditions for coherence:

(5) The coherence of a system of beliefs is decreased in proportion to presence of the unexplained anomalies in the believed content of the system.[16]

Having insisted on the close connection between coherence and explanation, we must nonetheless resist the idea that explanatory connections are all there is to coherence. Certain proponents of coherentist views, notably Sellars and Harman, have used phrases like 'explanatory coherence' in speaking of coherence, seeming to suggest (though I doubt whether any of those using it really intend such a suggestion) that coherence depends *entirely* on explanatory connections.[17] One could of course adopt a conception of coherence which is restricted in this way, but there is no reason at all—from an epistemological standpoint—to do so. The epistemologically significant concept of coherence is bound up with the idea of *justification*, and thus any sort of inference relation which could yield some degree of justification also enhances coherence, whether or not such a relation has any explanatory force.

A simple example (borrowed from Lehrer who in turn borrowed it from Bromberger) may help to illustrate this point.[18] Suppose that I am standing three feet from a pole which is four feet high. Next to my foot is a mouse, and on top of the pole is perched an owl. From these conditions I may obviously infer, using the Pythagorean theorem, that the mouse is five feet from the owl. This inference is surely adequate to justify my believing that the mouse is five feet from the owl, assuming that I am justified in believing these other propositions. And intuitively speaking, this inferential connection means that the belief that the mouse is five feet from the owl coheres with the rest of my beliefs to quite a significant extent. But none of this has any apparent connection with explanation. In particular, as Lehrer points out, this inference does not in any way help to *explain* why the mouse is so close to the owl. Thus it is a mistake to tie coherence too closely to the idea of explanation. Of course, it is still true that the coherence of the system in question would be enhanced by adding an explanation for the presence of the mouse in such close proximity to the owl: given the usual behavior of mice around owls, the presence of the mouse at that distance is an explanatory and predictive anomaly. The point is simply that coherence is also enhanced by inferential connections of a nonexplanatory sort.

Fourth. The final point is really just a corollary of the one just made. To the extent that coherence is closely bound up with explanation and systematic unification, achieving a high degree of coherence may well involve significant conceptual

16. Such a situation of anomaly may of course involve probabilistic inconsistency in the sense explained above, but it need not do so in any very straightforward way; the set of basic explanatory principles does not normally include an explicit rider to the effect that anything which it cannot subsume is thereby rendered improbable.

17. For a version of such a position, see Lehrer (1974, chap. 7). (The position in question is one which Lehrer is criticizing, not one he wishes to advocate.)

18. Lehrer (1974, pp. 166–7).

change. This point is most clear in the area of theoretical science, though it has much broader application. A typical situation of theoretical explanation involves one or more anomalies at the 'observational' level: apparently well-established facts formulated in the available system of concepts for which no adequate explanation seems to be available in those terms. By devising a new system of theoretical concepts the theoretician makes an explanation available and thus enhances the coherence of the system. In this way the progress of theoretical science may be plausibly viewed as a result of the search for greater coherence.[19]

The foregoing account of coherence is a long way from being as definitive as desirable. I submit, however, that it does indeed identify a concept which, in Ewing's phrase, is 'immanent in all our thinking,' including all our most advanced scientific thinking; and also that the concept thus identified, though vague and sketchy in many ways, is nonetheless clear enough to make it reasonable to use it, albeit with caution, in dealing with the sorts of epistemological issues under discussion here. In particular, it seems clear that the concept is not so vague as to be at all easy to satisfy.

4. The doxastic presumption

I have so far considered two of the elements which are arguably essential to a viable coherence theory: the idea of nonlinear justification and the concept of coherence itself. A third essential element is the presumption regarding one's grasp of one's own system of beliefs which I mentioned briefly at the end of the previous chapter; this is required, I will suggest, if our coherence theory is to avoid a relapse into externalism. (A fourth ingredient is the coherentist conception of observation; and a fifth, on a somewhat different level, is the metajustificatory argument for such a theory.)

It will be useful, before attempting to say in detail what the presumption in question amounts to and what it is supposed to do, to see more clearly why it is needed in the first place. According to a coherence theory of empirical justification, as so far characterized, the epistemic justification of an empirical belief derives entirely from its coherence with the believer's overall system of empirical beliefs and not at all from any sort of factor outside that system. What we must now ask is whether and how the fact that a belief coheres in this way is cognitively accessible to the believer himself, so that it can give *him* a reason for accepting the belief.

It would be possible, of course, to adopt an externalist version of coherentism. Such a view would hold that the person whose belief is justified need himself have no cognitive access to the fact of coherence, that his belief is justified if it in fact coheres with his system of beliefs, whether or not such coherence is cognitively accessible to him (or, presumably, to anyone). But such a view is unacceptable for essentially the same reasons which were offered against foundationalist versions of

19. For an elaboration of this view of scientific theories, see Wilfrid Sellars, 'The Language of Theories', reprinted in Sellars (1963, pp. 106–26).

externalism and, as discussed earlier, seems to run counter to the whole rationale for coherence theories. (If externalism were acceptable in general, the foundationalist versions would obviously be far simpler and more plausible.) But if the fact of coherence is to be accessible to the believer, it follows that he must somehow have an adequate grasp of his total system of beliefs, since it is coherence with this system which is at issue. One problem which we will eventually have to confront is that it seems abundantly clear that no actual believer possesses an *explicit* grasp of his overall belief system; if such a grasp exists at all, it must be construed as tacit or implicit, which creates obvious problems for the claim that he is actually, as opposed to potentially, justified.

The problem at issue in this section is, however, more immediate and more serious. For whether the believer's grasp of his own system of beliefs is construed as explicit or implicit, of what can that grasp possibly consist except a set of empirical metabeliefs, *themselves in need of justification*, to the effect that he has such and such specific beliefs? How then are these metabeliefs themselves to be justified? If a return to foundationalism is to be avoided, the answer must apparently be that these metabeliefs too are justified by virtue of their coherence with the rest of my system of beliefs. And the problem is that it is absolutely clear that such an answer is unacceptable: it is beyond any doubt viciously circular to claim that the metabeliefs which constitute the believer's grasp of his system of beliefs are themselves justified by virtue of their coherence with that system—even if the nonlinear view of justification articulated earlier is accepted in its entirety. How can my metabelief B_2 that I have a certain other belief B_1 be justified for me by appeal to the fact that B_2 coheres with my total system of beliefs if my very grasp of that system depends on the justification of B_2 and other similar beliefs? How, that is, can my reason for accepting B_2 be its coherence with my total system of beliefs when I have no justification apart from the appeal to B_2 and similar beliefs for thinking that I even have that system of beliefs? The shift to holism is of no help here, since the very possibility of a nonexternalist holism depends on my having a cognitive grasp of my total system of beliefs and its coherence which is prior to the justification of the particular beliefs in the system. It is quite clear, therefore, that this grasp, upon which any nonexternalist appeal to coherence must depend, cannot itself be justified by appeal to coherence.[20] And thus the very idea of a coherence theory of empirical justification threatens to collapse.

Is there any solution to this problem. Most proponents of coherence theories seem, surprisingly enough, either to take the believer's grasp of his own system of beliefs entirely for granted, or simply to ignore the issue of whether their envisaged coherentist justification is accessible to the believer himself. And the obvious conclusion, suggested by some foundationalists in passing, is that this problem shows

20. A coherence theory, at least as construed here, does not somehow reject any notion of epistemic priority. Its claim is rather that what look superficially like relations of epistemic priority and posteriority among individual beliefs turn out to be relations of reciprocal support in relation to a system of beliefs which is genuinely prior. Thus no appeal to the nonlinear conception of justification will help if it is the very existence of such a system which is in question.

that even an intended coherence theory must involve an irreducibly foundationalist element, that one's grasp of one's own system of beliefs must be justified in a foundationalist manner, even if everything else depends on coherence. But if the antifoundationalist arguments offered in an earlier chapter are genuinely cogent, no such retreat to foundationalism is available here, and skepticism looms as the only conclusion unless a further alternative can be found.

It was suggested earlier that an a priorist version of foundationalism (or quasi-foundationalism) might attempt to solve the problem of how the empirical claim that I have a certain belief is to be justified by maintaining that the existence of the justificandum belief is *presupposed* by the very raising of the issue of justification, so that the metabelief in question is not in need of justification, while still being available as a justifying premise. The normal justificatory issue, on this view, is whether the believer is justified in holding a certain belief *which he does in fact hold*, not whether such a belief would be somehow justified in the abstract independently of whether he holds it, nor even the hypothetical issue of whether it would be justified *if* he held it (though these other questions can, of course, also be asked). But since the basic unit of justification for a coherence theory is an entire system of beliefs, the analogous claim within the context of such a position is that the raising of an issue of empirical justification *presupposes* the existence of some specifiable *system* of empirical beliefs—or rather, as I will explain below, of *approximately* that system; the primary justificatory issue is whether or not, under the presumption that I do indeed hold approximately the system of beliefs which I believe myself to hold, those beliefs are justified. And thus the suggested solution to the problem raised in this section is that the grasp of my system of beliefs which is required if I am to have cognitive access to the fact of coherence is dependent, in a sense yet to be adequately clarified, on this *Doxastic Presumption*, as I will call it, rather than requiring further justification.

But how exactly is this presumption to be understood? Three issues need to be considered: First, what is the significance of the qualifier 'approximately' as it occurs in the above formulations of the presumption? Second, how exactly is this presumption supposed to function within the overall system of empirical knowledge? How exactly is it supposed to certify or secure (even the choice of word here is uncertain) one's grasp of one's system of beliefs? And third, what is the bearing of the Doxastic Presumption on issues pertaining to skepticism?—does it not amount to begging the question against a certain perhaps unusual, but nonetheless quite possible, version of skepticism? I will consider each of these questions in turn.

First. I have noted that the Doxastic Presumption is only that my representation of my overall system of beliefs is *approximately* correct. The point of the qualifier is that although assessments of coherence can be made only relative to a system of beliefs of which one has some prior grasp or representation, this does not mean that no aspect of that representation can be questioned. On the contrary, it is perfectly possible to raise the issue of whether I have a certain particular belief or reasonably small set of beliefs which I believe myself to have, and then to answer this question by appeal to the coherence or lack of coherence between the meta-belief that I have the specific belief(s) in question and the rest of the system as I represent it—the existence of the rest of the system, but not of those particular beliefs, being presupposed. What is *not* possible is to question whether my grasp of my system of beliefs might be wholly or largely mistaken and then resolve *this* question by appeal to coherence: the raising of this issue would leave me with no sufficiently ample grasp of my system of beliefs which would not beg the question and relative to which coherence might be judged.

Second. It might seem plausible, at first glance, to construe the Doxastic Presumption as constituting a further *premise* to be employed in the justificatory arguments or at least as functioning like such a premise. But only a little reflection will show that such an interpretation is quite untenable. For what might such a premise say? The only apparent possibility is that it would say that my metabeliefs to the effect that I have certain beliefs may be presumed to be true, without requiring justification. And it is immediately obvious that such a premise would do me no good relative to the problem under discussion here. For to apply it in any useful fashion, I would need further premises to the effect that I do in fact believe myself to have such and such specific beliefs, and the justification of these further premises would obviously be just as problematic as before.

Thus the Doxastic Presumption, if it is to solve the problem, cannot function like a premise. It is rather a characterization of something which is, from the standpoint of a coherence theory, a basic and unavoidable feature of cognitive *practice*. Epistemic reflection, according to such a theory, *begins* from a (perhaps tacit) representation of myself as having (approximately) such and such a specific system of beliefs: only relative to such a representation can questions of justification be meaningfully raised and answered. This representation is presumably a product of something like ordinary introspection (as understood from within the system), but whereas most introspective beliefs can be justified by appeal to coherence, the metabeliefs which constitute this representation cannot be thus justified in general for the reasons already considered. The issue of their justification can be raised and answered in particular, relatively confined cases which are for some reason especially problematic; but apart from such cases, such metabeliefs must be presumed to be correct in order for the process of justification to even get started. And this is what the Doxastic Presumption says.

Thus the Doxastic Presumption does not, strictly speaking, function at all in the normal workings of the cognitive system. Rather it simply describes or formulates, from the outside, something that I unavoidably *do*: I assume that the beliefs constituting my overall grasp of my system of beliefs are, by and large, correct.

Third. But does not the Doxastic Presumption, or rather the aspect of cognitive practice which it reflects, amount to begging the question against a certain form of skepticism, namely, that form which would question whether my representation of my own system of beliefs is in fact accurate? The answer is that it would be begging the question if it purported to be an answer to such a skeptical challenge but that as proposed here no such answer is intended. It would be possible, of course, to argue that if it is correct that empirical justification is only possible relative to a specific system of beliefs whose existence is presumed, then it follows that skepticism of the sort in question simply makes no sense; the underlying idea would be that a question is meaningful only if there is some way, at least in principle, in which it can be answered. But I can see no reason to accept such a view, amounting as it does to a version of verificationism. What the discussion leading up to the Doxastic *Presumption* shows is precisely that a coherence theory of empirical justification cannot, in principle, answer this form of skepticism; and this seems to me to count in favor of the skeptic, not against him.

Thus the position advocated here holds that such a version of skepticism, though certainly unusual, is perfectly coherent (and thus that it would be desirable to be able to answer it) but also concedes that such an answer is unfortunately in principle not available for a coherence theory. However, the failure to answer one version of skepticism does not in any way mean that there is no point in attempting to answer others. The effect of the Doxastic Presumption is precisely to distinguish a version of skepticism which cannot be successfully answered from others which perhaps can. Even if it is not possible in general to justify my representation of my own system of beliefs, it may yet be possible to argue successfully relative to the presumption that this representation is (approximately) correct that the beliefs which I hold are justified in a sense which makes them genuinely likely to be true; and this would be a significant epistemological result, even if not quite the one which would be ideally desirable.

There is one more important point about the Doxastic Presumption to be noted here. Obviously a person's system of beliefs changes and develops over time as new beliefs are added and old ones abandoned or forgotten. And it is clear on reflection that one's grasp of these changes is just as incapable of being justified in general by appeal to coherence as is one's grasp of the system at a moment. Thus the Doxastic Presumption must be understood to include the presumption that one's grasp of this temporal dimension of one's system of beliefs is also approximately correct.

The foregoing will suffice for an initial discussion of the Doxastic Presumption. For the moment the central point is that something like this presumption seems to be unavoidable if a coherentist position is to even get started. Nothing like a justification for the presumption has been offered for the simple reason that if it is properly understood, none is required: there can obviously be no objection to asking what follows about the justification of the rest of my beliefs from the presumption that my representation of my own system of beliefs is approximately correct. The only questions needing to be asked are: first, whether it is possible to justify my representation of my own system of beliefs, rather than having to presume that it is correct (I have argued that it is not); and, second, whether the epistemological issue which results from this presumption is still worth bothering with (I have suggested that it is).

5. The standard objections

There is obviously much which is problematic in the very tentative and fragmentary picture of a coherence theory of empirical justification which has so far emerged in this chapter, and many important questions and problems remain to be considered. But even if the conception were otherwise acceptable, there would still remain the three standard and extremely forceful objections to coherence theories—objections which have usually been thought to destroy any plausibility which such a view might possess. As will become clear, these objections are not entirely independent of one another and indeed might be plausibly regarded as merely different facets of one basic point. But each of them possesses enough independent plausibility and intuitive force to warrant separate consideration.

(I) The alternative coherent systems objection. According to a coherence theory of empirical justification, at least as so far characterized, the system of beliefs which constitutes empirical knowledge is epistemically justified *solely* by virtue of its internal coherence. But such an appeal to coherence will never even begin to pick out one uniquely justified system of beliefs, since on any plausible conception of coherence, there will always be many, probably infinitely many, different and incompatible systems of belief which are equally coherent. No nonarbitrary choice between such systems can be made solely on the basis of coherence, and thus all such systems, and the beliefs they contain, will be equally justified. And this will mean in turn, since all or virtually all consistent beliefs will belong to some such system, that we have no more reason to think that the beliefs we actually hold are true than we have for thinking that any arbitrarily chosen alternative belief is true—a result which is surely tantamount to skepticism and which obviously vitiates entirely the concept of epistemic justification by destroying its capacity to discriminate between different empirical beliefs.

A clear conception of this objection requires that it not be exaggerated, as it frequently is. Sometimes it is said that if one has an appropriately coherent system, an alternative coherent system can be produced simply by negative all of the components of the first system. This would be so if coherence amounted simply to consistency; but once it is seen that such a conception of coherence is much too limited, there is no reason to accept such a claim. Nor is it even minimally plausible that, as is sometimes suggested, a 'well written novel,' or indeed anything remotely resembling an actual novel, would have the degree of coherence required to be a serious alternative to anyone's actual system of beliefs. What would be missing in both cases is the pervasive inferential and especially explanatory connections needed for a high degree of coherence.

But even without these exaggerations, the objection is obviously very forceful. One suggestive way to elaborate it is by appeal to the idea of alternative possible worlds. Without worrying about whether there are infinitely many possible worlds or whether all possible worlds are capable of being given equally coherent descriptions, it seems enormously obvious that there are at least very many possible worlds, differing in major ways from the actual world, which are capable of being described in equally coherent ways. But then a standard of justification which appeals only to internal coherence has no way of choosing among the various systems of beliefs which would correctly describe these various possible worlds; such a standard is apparently impotent to justify believing in one of these worlds as opposed to any of the others. The skeptic need ask for nothing more.

(II) The input objection. The second objection is somewhat more elusive, but also perhaps more fundamental. Coherence is purely a matter of the *internal* relations between the components of the belief system; it depends in no way on any sort of relation between the system of beliefs and anything external to that system. Hence if, as a coherence theory claims, coherence is the sole basis for empirical justification, it follows that a system of empirical beliefs might be adequately justified, indeed might constitute empirical knowledge, in spite of being utterly out of contact with the world that it purports to describe. Nothing about any requirement of coherence dictates that a coherent system of beliefs need receive any sort of *input* from the world or be in any way causally influenced by the world. But this is surely an absurd result. Such a self-enclosed system of beliefs, entirely immune from any external influence, cannot constitute empirical knowledge of an independent world, because the achievement of even minimal descriptive success in such a situation would have to be either an accident or a miracle, not something which anyone could possibly have any reason to expect—which would mean that the beliefs involved would not be epistemically justified, even if they should somehow happen to be true. This objection is most obviously forceful against a coherentist position, like my own, which adopts a realist conception of independent reality. But in fact it is cogent *vis-à-vis* any position, including at least most versions of idealism, which does not simply identify the individual believer's limited cognitive system with its object: how can a system of beliefs be justified in a sense which carries with it likelihood of truth, while at the same time being entirely isolated from the reality, however that be understood, which it purports to describe?

Though intuitively forceful, this objection is also rather vague—mainly because of the vagueness of the crucial notion of 'input.' It would, however, be a mistake to attempt too precise a specification here, prior to the development of a more specific theory. The rough idea is that some of the elements in the cognitive system must be somehow shaped or influenced by the world outside the system;[21] and that this must be not just something which might or might not happen to occur, but rather in some way an essential requirement for the justification of the system. But just what precise form such input might take is a matter to be specified by a particular theory.[22]

(III) The problem of truth. The final objection of the three is the most fundamental of all. Recall that one crucial part of the task of an adequate epistemological theory is to show that there is an appropriate connection between its proposed account of epistemic justification and the cognitive goal of *truth*. That is, it must be somehow shown that justification as conceived by the theory is *truth-conducive*, that one who seeks justified beliefs is at least likely to find true ones. All this is by now quite familiar. The objection is simply that a coherence theory will be unable to accomplish this part of the epistemological task unless it also adopts a

---

21. I will ignore here the alternative possibility that a person's system of beliefs might be likely to be true because those beliefs shape reality rather than the other way around.

22. Many foundationalist views also fail to address this issue in any clear way, either by offering no real account of the status of the foundational beliefs or by merely appealing to the commonsensical belief that certain beliefs are somehow justified.

coherence theory of truth and the idealistic metaphysics which goes along with it—an expedient which is both commonsensically absurd and also dialectically unsatisfactory.

Historically, the appeal to a coherence theory of truth was made by the absolute idealists and, in a slightly different but basically parallel way, by Peirce. These philosophers attempted to solve the problem of the relation between justification and truth by in effect construing truth as simply *identical* with justification-in-the-long-run. Thus an idealist, having adopted a coherence theory of epistemic justification, might argue that only by adopting a coherence theory of truth could the essential link between justification and truth be secured: obviously if truth is long-run, ideal coherence, it is plausible to suppose that it will be truth-conducive to seek a system of beliefs which is as coherent as one can manage to make it at the moment.[23] Something like this seems also to be the essential motivation behind Peirce's version of the pragmatic conception of truth in which truth is identified with the ideal, long-run outcome of scientific inquiry; whether this amounts to precisely a coherence theory of truth depends on just how Peirce's rather obscure account of justification is properly to be understood, but it is at least similar. The same underlying motivation also seems present, albeit less clearly, in other versions of pragmatism.

Obviously, given such a construal of truth, there will be no difficulty of principle in arguing successfully that one who accepts justified beliefs will in the long run be likely to find true ones. But such a gambit is nonetheless quite unsatisfactory in relation to the basic problem at issue, even if the intuitive and commonsensical objections to such accounts of truth are discounted. The whole point, after all, of seeking an argument connecting justification and truth is to provide a rationale or metajustification for the proposed standard of epistemic justification by showing that adopting it leads or is likely to lead to the attainment of truth. But the force of such a metajustification depends on the independent claim to acceptance of the concept of truth which is invoked. If—as seems to be the case both historically and dialectically with respect to the specific concepts of truth under discussion here—the only rationale for the chosen concept of truth is an appeal to the related standard of justification, then the proposed metajustification loses its force entirely. It is clearly circular to argue both (1) that a certain standard of epistemic justification is correct because it is conducive to finding truth, conceived in a certain way, and (2) that the conception of truth in question is correct because only such a conception can connect up in this way with the original standard of justification. Such a defense would obviously be available to the proponent of *any* proposed standard of epistemic justification, no matter how silly or counterintuitive or arbitrary it might be: all he has to do is adopt his own nonstandard conception of truth as justification-in-the-long-run (in his idiosyncratic sense of justification). The moral of the story is that although any adequate epistemological theory must confront the task of bridging the gap between justification and truth, the adoption of a nonstandard conception of truth, such as a coherence theory of truth, will do

---

23. For the clearest version of this approach, see Blanshard (1939, chs. 25 and 26).

no good unless that conception is independently motivated.[24] Therefore, it seems that a coherence theory of justification has no acceptable way of establishing the essential connection with truth. A coherentist standard of justification, it is claimed, can be a good test only for a coherentist conception of truth, so that to reject the coherence theory of truth commits one also to the rejection of any such account of justification.[25]

Of these three objections, (2I) is the most basic and (I) is the most familiar. It is (2), however, which must be dealt with first, since the answer to it turns out, not surprisingly, to be essential for answering the other two objections. My view is that the point advanced in (2) must in the end simply be accepted: a cognitive system which is to contain empirical knowledge must somehow receive input of some sort from the world. And this means that the purest sort of coherence theory turns out, as the objections claim, to be indeed unacceptable. I will argue, however, that this need not mean a return to foundationalism (which has already been shown to be hopeless), that a theory which is recognizably coherentist—and more important, which is free of any significant foundationalist ingredients—can allow for such input.

24. A related objection also afflicts currently fashionable verificationist accounts of truth.
25. It is worth noting, however, that foundationalist views seem to face at least a somewhat analogous problem if it is true that they must appeal to coherence or something like it in their accounts of knowledge of the past, theoretical knowledge, and so on.

References

Blanshard, Brand (1939). *The Nature of Thought.* London: Allen and Unwin.

BonJour, Laurence (1976). 'Rescher's Idealistic Pragmatism.' *Review of Metaphysics* 29: 702–26.

Chisholm, Roderick (1977). *Theory of Knowledge,* 2nd edn. Englewood Cliffs, NJ: Prentice-Hall.

Ewing, A. C. (1934). *Idealism.* London: Methuen

Hempel, Carl G. (1965). *Aspects of Scientific Explanation.* New York: Free Press.

—— (1967). *Philosophy of Natural Science.* Englewood Cliffs, NJ: Prentice-Hall.

Lehrer, Keith (1974). *Knowledge.* Oxford: Oxford University Press.

Lewis, C. I. (1946). *An Analysis of Knowledge and Valuation.* La Salle, IL.: Open Court.

Rescher, Nicholas (1973). *The Coherence Theory of Truth.* Oxford: Oxford University Press.

—— (1977). *Methodological Pragmatism.* New York: New York University Press.

Scheffler, Israel (1967). *Science and Subjectivity.* New York: Bobbs-Merrill.

Sellars, Wilfred (1963). *Science, Perception and Reality.* London: Routledge and Kegan Paul.

Sklar, Lawrence (1975). 'Methodological Conservatism.' *Philosophical Review* 84: 374–400.

Williams, Michael (1980). 'Coherence, Justification, and Truth.' *Review of Metaphysics* 34: 243–72.

Chapter 12

The coherence theory of knowledge*

Keith Lehrer

M Y research program has been the articulation of a coherence theory of knowledge.[1] The analysis of knowledge embedded in the theory is traditional in
form but not in content. It is in the tradition of undefeated justified true belief
analyses. Such analyses were introduced in my earlier research with Paxson.[2] The
salient character of the theory of knowledge is contained in the theory of justification. Justification is the intersection of the subjective, the mental operations of the
knower, and the objective, the truth about reality. Justification thus effects what
Cohen and I have referred to as the truth connection.[3] The coherence theory of
justification on which the coherence theory of knowledge rests effects the truth
connection and explains the intersection between the mind and the world. The
explanation depends on our conception of ourselves as trustworthy with respect to
some matters in some circumstances and untrustworthy about other matters in
other circumstances. If we are as trustworthy as we think we are, then we are
justified in what we accept.

Reid remarked that it is the first principle of the human mind that our faculties
are trustworthy and not fallacious.[4] Our knowledge of the world depends on our
capacity to discern when we are trustworthy and when we are not. It is a fundamental feature of human knowledge that we have the capacity to discern when the
information we receive by means of our senses is to be trusted, when the probability

Keith Lehrer, 'The Coherence Theory of Knowledge' in *Philosophical Topics* 14 (1986) pp. 5–25, reprinted
by permission of Keith Lehrer.

* Research on this project was supported by a fellowship from the John Simon Guggenheim
Memorial Foundation and a grant from the National Science Foundation.

1. Lehrer, K., *Knowledge* Oxford, 1974, paperback edition, 1979; 'The Gettier Problem and the Analysis
of Knowledge', in *Justification and Knowledge*, G. Pappas, ed., Dordrecht, 1979; 'A Self Profile,' in
Keith Lehrer, R. Bogdan, ed., Dordrecht, 1981, pp. 74–98; and several articles, most recently, 'Coherence and the Hierarchy of Method,' in *Philosophie als Wissenschaft/Essay in Scientific Philosophy*,
E. Morscher *et al* eds., Bad Reichenhall, 1981, 25–56; 'Knowledge, Truth and Ontology', in *Language
and Ontology*, Dordrecht, 1982, pp. 201–11; and 'Justification, Truth and Coherence,' with S. Cohen,
Synthese, 1983, 55, 191–208.
2. Lehrer, K. and Paxson T. Jr., 'Knowledge: Undefeated Justified True Belief,' in *Journal of Philosophy*,
66, 1969, pp. 285–97, reprinted in *Essays on Knowledge and Justification*, G. S. Pappas and M. Swain
eds., Ithaca, 1978, pp. 146–54 [Ch. 5 in this volume].
3. Cohen and Lehrer, op. cit.
4. Reid, T., *Inquiry and Essays*, R. Beanblossom and K. Lehrer eds., Bobbs-Merrill, Indianapolis, 1975,
new edition, Hackett, Indianapolis, 1984.

of veracity is high and the probability of error is small. Such evaluation is essential to human knowledge and distinguishes human knowledge from the mere possession or exhibition of information. It is not merely the acquisition of information but the certification of that information as trustworthy in terms of background information by the central system that is the hallmark of human knowledge. Such knowledge involves, therefore, higher order processing of lower order information. The essential feature of human knowledge is that it is metaknowledge. The essential feature of the human mind is that it is a metamind.

1. **General Features of the Coherence Theory.** There are two principal features of the coherence theory of justification that are to be noticed at the outset. First of all, such justification is embedded in a perfectly traditional analysis of knowledge. The analysis which I still advocate, with some variation of detail, is the one I proposed in *Knowledge*. Where 'S' is a variable replaced by the name or description of a knowing subject and 'p' is replaced by a declarative sentence

S knows that p = df
  (i) p
 (ii) S accepts that p
(iii) S is completely justified in accepting that p and
(iv) S is justified in accepting that p in a way that does not depend essentially on any false statement.

Condition (iv) could be interpreted in such a way as to incorporate the third condition. I shall not be concerned with condition (iv) here, and, consequently, it will simplify exposition to separate condition (iii). I shall also not be concerned here with condition (i), though I shall assume that it is understood. It implies, for instance, that Brand knows that Lehrer wrote the present article only if Lehrer wrote the present article. No matter how convincing the evidence might be that Lehrer wrote the present article, nobody, Brand included, knows that Lehrer wrote it, if Lehrer did not write it. With these admittedly cursory remarks concerning conditions (i) and (iv), I turn to those conditions that are the focus of my present effort.

2. **Acceptance.** Condition (ii) is only unusual in that the notion of acceptance rather than belief is employed. It is clear that mere conception or representation that p is not adequate in that a person may conceive that p or represent that p without affirming that p. A special sort of positive attitude toward what is conceived or represented is required for knowledge. Acceptance is the notion that I have adopted for several reasons. In the first place, the notion is essentially relative to some purpose. What one accepts for one purpose, to be congenial, for example, one may not accept for another, to solve an intellectual or scientific problem. It is acceptance of something for the purposes of obtaining truth and eschewing error with respect to just the thing one accepts that is a condition of knowledge. That notion of acceptance is what is intended by condition (ii). I add the qualification 'with respect to just the thing one accepts' because it is possible that accepting something that the evidence indicates is false might serve the general purpose of accepting as much as one can of what is true and accepting as little as one can of what is false. Accepting that one falsehood might be bountifully fecund with respect

to accepting other truths. It is clear, however, that accepting something that the evidence indicates is false for such a generally worthwhile purpose is not the sort of acceptance that is required to know that the thing in question is true.

The second reason that acceptance seems to be the appropriate notion is that acceptance does not imply any long term disposition to recall or to act as though the thing accepted is true. In my opinion, belief does not imply this either, but there is a long tradition in philosophy that identifies belief with a long term disposition to act as though the thing believed were true, or, at least, to think that the thing believed is true. It seems clear to me, however, that one may know things for an instant and immediately forget. The experimental evidence concerning short term memory clearly supports this, and anyone who has been told the name of a person at a party knows that what one knows for an instant, the name of a person, may be immediately forgotten.

The third reason for preferring this notion is that acceptance, like judgment, is a notion more closely connected with decision and optionality. A person may decide to accept something, and, though such a decision may lead one to believe something, such a decision does not constitute belief. Note here that if I say to a person, 'I accept what you said,' I have accepted what the person said whatever I feel about it, but if I say instead 'I believe what you said,' whether I believed what the person said depends, not on what I said, but on what I feel about it. The locution 'I accept. . .' is akin to performatives, but 'I believe. . .' is not. One may come to know that what one believes is false when one accepts that it is false and is appropriately justified in doing so. In such instances, belief and acceptance conflict, belief and knowledge conflict. It should be noted, however, that the ordinary use of terms such as 'belief' and 'accept' is not perfectly consistent. For example, a person may say that she cannot accept something which she knows to be true, but, though this is said, it is clear that the person has accepted what she says she cannot accept. I think this is to be interpreted as hyperbole. We say we cannot do things when they are difficult or painful—even as we do them. 'I really can't stay any longer,' he says, staying longer.

3. **Justification.** Justification divides into a subjective and an objective component. A person may be justified in accepting something in terms of other things he accepts when he is not justified in accepting it in some more objective sense. Both senses of justification may be explicated in terms of coherence with some background system. Whether the person is subjectively or objectively justified depends on the character of the system. I call what a person accepts in the sense specified above an acceptance system, and I say that a person is *subjectively* justified in believing that p if and only if p coheres with the acceptance system of the person. An acceptance system, though motivated by the purpose of obtaining truth and eschewing error in each thing that is accepted, may, given human fallibility, be rife with error. To be objectively justified in accepting that p, the coherence of p with the acceptance system must be sustained when all error is removed. I call the system resulting from the diminution of the acceptance system when all acceptance of false things is expunged the *verific* system of the person. It is a subsystem of the acceptance system.

We thus obtain the following definitions of justification culminating in a definition of complete justification. I use the term *personally* justified to represent subjective justification and the term *verifically* justified to represent the objective notion. I acknowledge the technical character of even the defined notions.

(iip) S is *personally* justified in accepting that p if and only if p coheres with the acceptance system of S.

(iiv) S is *verifically* justified in accepting that p if and only if p coheres with the verific system of S.

(iic) S is *completely* justified in accepting that p if and only if S is personally justified in accepting that p and S is verifically justified in accepting that p.

The significance of (iic) is that it expresses the idea that a person is justified in accepting something in the manner required for human knowledge only if there is a coincidence between the background system of things that a person accepts in the attempt to obtain truth and avoid error and the subsystem of that system that would remain when it is cleansed of error. More precisely articulated, the acceptance system of a person is a set of propositions of the form 'S accepts that p', 'S accepts that q', 'S accepts that r' and so forth, articulating the things S accepts in the attempt to accept something true and eschew accepting what is false with respect to just the thing one accepts. The verific system is the subset of the acceptance system that results when all those propositions of the subsystem are deleted if the thing S is said to accept, that is, p, q, or r and so forth, is false.

4. **Coherence and Reasonableness.** A number of philosophers have noted that justification is a normative notion. My proposal is that coherence is also implicitly normative. Whether something coheres with some system of a person depends on how reasonable it is for the person to accept it on the basis of the system in question. One achieves coherence by reducing conflict, and so I propose that something coheres with a system of a person if it is more reasonable to accept it than to accept anything with which it conflicts on the basis of the system. For example, it is more reasonable for me to accept that I now see a monitor than that I am hallucinating, and here the former conflicts with the latter. When it is more reasonable to accept one thing than a second with which it conflicts, I shall say that the first beats the second. It is sufficient for something to cohere with a system that it beats anything with which it conflicts with respect to the system. It is not, however, necessary. The reason is that conflict may be a subtle affair. One thing may conflict with a second even though they are logically consistent with each. The notion of conflict may also be explicated in terms of one thing being more reasonable to accept than a second. Thus, it is more reasonable for me to accept that I now see a monitor on the condition that I am not now hallucinating than on the condition that I am now hallucinating, though, in fact, it is not contradictory to suppose that I really now see a monitor and that I am now hallucinating. People do sometimes see things that are real even when they are hallucinating and also see things that are not real. It is not that the assumption that I am now hallucinating contradicts that I now see a monitor, but the former assumption does render it less reasonable for me to accept that I now see a monitor than the denial of that assumption.

In order to explicate the notion of coherence, I shall employ the undefined locution 'it is more reasonable for S to accept that p on the assumption that c than to accept that q on the assumption that d on the basis of system A.' Chisholm developed his system taking the simpler locution 'it is more reasonable for S to accept p than to accept q' as primitive, and I am clearly indebted to him.[5] I choose the more complicated locution because it makes explicit the fact that our judgments of reasonableness are implicitly relative to some assumptions and system that we unreflectively take for granted. The nonrelativized notion may, of course, be defined in terms of the more complex one by selecting assumptions and a system that are irrelevant to the comparative reasonableness of accepting p and q. Thus, we may say that it is more reasonable for S to accept p than to accept q on the basis of A if and only if it is more reasonable for S to accept p on the assumption that t than to accept q on the assumption that t on the basis of A, where t is some trivial tautology. The reference to A becomes similarly otiose when A is null. It is less clear that the relativized notion may be defined in terms of the nonrelativized notion.

I would then define the notion of conflict or competition as follows.

(vc) p competes with q for S on the basis of system A if and only if it is more reasonable for S to accept p on the assumption that not q than on the assumption that q on the basis of system A.

With conflict defined, it is then possible to define the notion of something beating a competitor, when beating a competitor is sufficient for justification. The definition is as follows.

(vib) p beats q for S on the basis of system A if and only if p competes with q for S on the basis of system A and it is more reasonable for S to accept p than to accept q on the basis of system A.

It is important to notice, however, that beating all competitors, though sufficient for justification, is not necessary. The reason is that some competitors, though not beaten, may be dispensed with in another manner. The suggestion of a skeptic that I am now hallucinating when I accept that I now see a monitor may be beaten. It is more reasonable for me to accept what I do than what he suggests. But the skeptic may be more subtle and only insinuate that I may be hallucinating by noting that people sometimes hallucinate. Now the claim that people sometimes hallucinate does compete with the claim that I am now seeing a monitor. It is more reasonable for me to accept that I now see a monitor on the assumption that people never hallucinate than on the assumption that they sometimes do hallucinate. Moreover, it is not clear that it is more reasonable for me to accept that I see a monitor than that people sometimes hallucinate. I am, of course, quite certain that the former is true, but I am also quite certain that the latter is true.

It would be best to reply to the skeptic in another manner in this case. The right reply would be to neutralize the innuendo rather than refute his claim. For, even though people sometimes hallucinate, I am not hallucinating, and, therefore, his

5. Chisholm, R. M., *Theory of Knowledge*, 2nd ed., Prentice-Hall, Englewood Cliffs, 1977, esp. pp. 6–7.

innuendo is beside the point. The competition is not beaten but neutralized. We may define the required notion of neutralization as follows.

> (ivn) n neutralizes q as a competitor of p for S on the basis of system A if and only if q competes with p for S on the basis of system A, and n is such that the conjunction of q and n does not compete with p for S on the basis of system A when it is as reasonable for S to accept the conjunction of q and n as to accept q alone on the basis of system A.

This definition is somewhat baroque, but the idea is simple and may be illustrated by our example. If the skeptic attempts to undermine my claim that I see a monitor by pointing out that people sometimes hallucinate, thus suggesting that I may be hallucinating, the way to neutralize the suggestion is for me to point out that I am not hallucinating. The conjunction of the statements that people sometimes hallucinate and that I am not now hallucinating is as reasonable for me to accept as the single statement that people sometimes hallucinate. The conjunction does not compete with the statement that I now see a monitor. Consequently, the statement that I am not now hallucinating neutralizes the competitor that people sometimes hallucinate. The competitor of my claim that I see a monitor is thus neutralized.

It might be objected to this that there is a greater chance of the conjunction being false than a single conjunct. My reply is that the increase in risk of error in accepting the conjunction is negligible and the gain in perspicuity in accepting the conjunction is considerable. The objectives of obtaining truth and avoiding error pull in opposite directions. To avoid error it is always better to withhold acceptance, but that strategy works against the objective of accepting truths. When the acceptance of a more informative statement involves only a negligibly greater risk of error than accepting a less informative one, then it is as reasonable to accept the more informative as the less informative one. I admit that the problem of specifying when a greater risk of error is negligible is difficult.

We may now define coherence and, therefore, indirectly personal and verific justification as follows.

> (viic) p coheres with the system A of S if and only if, for every q that competes with p for S on the basis of the system A, q is either beaten or neutralized for S on the basis of the system A.

Personal justification results when the acceptance system is specified and verific justification results when the verific system is specified. This completes the formal analysis of justification. What is now necessary is to say something about what makes it more reasonable to accept one thing rather than another on the basis of a system and to provide the material motivation for adopting this formal account.

5. **Reasonableness and Probability**. The foregoing analyses adopt a comparative notion of reasonableness as a basic or primitive notion. What is required for a development of the theory is some indication of characteristics or conditions that make one thing more or less reasonable to accept than another. Without proposing any analysis of reasonableness, I shall propose some criteriological conditions, sufficient conditions, for the application of the notion. The most obvious criterion is one of probability. The acceptance in question has the avoidance of error as an

objective and, therefore, the risk of error is a determinant of the reasonableness of such acceptance. The probability of a statement is a measure of the risk of error. The more probable the truth of the statement the smaller the risk of error in accepting it. The risk of error is, however, not the only determinant of reasonableness, and, therefore, the avoidance of error is not the only objective of acceptance. The acceptance of truth is another.

The relation between reasonableness and probability may be articulated by saying that, other things being equal, the more probable a statement is, the more reasonable it is to accept it, and, conversely, the less probable a statement is the less reasonable it is to accept it. I call this the *correspondence* principle. The reason that the qualification, other things being equal, is added is that, as noted, the risk of error is only one determinant of epistemic reasonableness. It is important to notice, however, that the principle is sufficient to solve an epistemological problem of some interest. The lottery paradox of Kyburg is resolved by the principle.[6]

The lottery paradox arises when one assumes that there is some degree of probability less than one that is sufficient for reasonable or justified acceptance. Leaving aside the niceties, the paradox is that once a level of probability less than unity is specified as sufficient for acceptance, the set of accepted statements is a logically inconsistent set. If, for example, one picked 0.99, then one need only consider a fair lottery with a hundred tickets numbered from 1 to 100, the winning ticket having been selected but not examined, and reflect on the probability that a ticket numbered N has been drawn. Whatever number N is, the probability that it has not been drawn is 0.99, and, consequently, by the rule in question, one would be justified in accepting each hypothesis to the effect that ticket number N has not been drawn, where N takes the values from 1 to 100. This set of hypotheses taken together with the background knowledge that one of the tickets numbered 1 to 100 has been drawn is logically inconsistent. Kyburg and others have argued that the paradox depends on a conjunctive principle to the effect that if one is justified in accepting p and one is justified in accepting q, then one is justified in accepting the conjunction of p and q, which they then repudiate.[7] It is important to notice, however, the logical inconsistency of the *set* of accepted statements is not avoided by denying the conjunctivity principle. For this reason, I have argued that to avoid paradox we must deny that any degree of probability less than 1 is sufficient for justified acceptance. This solution is a consequence of the assumption concerning the relation between probability and reasonable acceptance.

The correspondence principle is sufficient to resolve the paradox. The hypothesis that a given ticket has not been drawn, say the number 6 ticket, has a lower probability on the condition that another ticket, say the number 5 ticket, has not been drawn than on the denial of the latter. The various negative hypotheses are negatively relevant to each. In this instance, other things are obviously equal. Hence, the various negative hypotheses compete with each other, and, since they are all equally

---

6. Kyburg, H. E. Jr., *Probability and the Logic of Rational Belief*, Wesleyan Press, Middleton, 1961. p. 197.
7. Hempel, C. G., 'Deductive-Nomological vs. Statistical Explanation', in *Minnesota Studies in the Philosophy of Science*, vol. 3, H. Feigl and G. Maxwell eds., Minneapolis, 1962, and Kyburg, H. E. Jr., 'Conjunctivitis,' in *Induction, Acceptance, and Rational Belief*, M. Swain, ed., Dordrecht, 1970.

probable, no such competitor of a negative hypothesis can be beaten, nor, for that matter, can it be neutralized. This result is, moreover, intuitive rather than *ad hoc*. In a lottery, people may sometimes say that they know that they will not win, especially if the lottery is very large, but surely that is mere hyperbole. Though it is very improbable that they will win, they do not by any means know that they will lose. The reason is that whatever ticket is, in fact, the winner is just as improbable. Indeed, there is exact cognitive symmetry between the winning ticket and any other, that is, there is no relevant difference that is discernible in advance. The analysis yields the result that we do not know that any specific ticket will lose before the winner is revealed.

6. **Probability and the Background System.** The second condition concerning probability is that probability is conditional on some background system, in the case of personal justification, the acceptance system. This naturally raises the question of whether conditionalizing on the acceptance system commits us to assigning a probability of 1 to the statements in the acceptance system. Were this required, the requirement would be that a subject S assign a probability of 1 to statement of the form 'S accepts that p' which is, perhaps, not an unrealistic requirement. In favor of such a policy, one might appeal to the optionality of acceptance and argue that if a person has decided to accept something, then she might well assign a probability of 1 to what is thus accepted.

It is, however, not necessary to assign a probability of unity to a statement in order to conditionalize on such probabilities, as Jeffrey has shown.[8] The crux of Jeffrey's proposal is that one can regard certain statements as the focus for assigning probabilities to other statements. To conditionalize on statements, one assigns probabilities to the focal statements and then uses those statements as the basis for distributing probabilities to other statements. Formally, supposing A to a focal statement, for example, a statement to the effect that S accepts that p, then the formula for assigning a new probability, p_N, to any other statement H, assuming an original probability assignment, p_O, is as follows.

$$p_N(H) = p_N(A)p_O(H/A) + p_N(\sim A)p_O(H/\sim A).$$

This contrasts with the simpler formula of traditional Bayesian conditionalization which is as follows.

$$p_N(H) = p_O(H/A)$$

The latter formula has the consequence that

$$p_N(A) = p_O(A/A) = 1$$

which amounts to assigning a probability of 1 to all statements that one uses as the basis of conditionalization.

If one is a falliblist, and the present author is favorably disposed toward falliblism, then one might hold that there is always some chance of error, even if negligible, attached to accepting any statement, even the statement that one accepts something or other. Hence, the more complicated Jeffrey formula is the superior

8. Jeffrey, R. C., *The Logic of Decision*, New York, 1965.

formula for articulating probabilities conditional on an acceptance system. Neither a statement to effect that one has accepted, need be assigned a probability of unity conditional on the acceptance system.

It is especially important to distinguish between accepting a statement and assigning that statement a probability of 1. Various probability assignments are reasonable depending on the background beliefs that one has concerning the trustworthiness of the statement one has accepted. Thus, for example, if someone tells me that he will have some work done by tomorrow, the construction of a class schedule, I might accept what he says, that he will have the work done, but what probability I assign to the statement that I accept will depend how reliable I consider my informant to be. If I see an automobile which I think is a Plymouth, and I accordingly accept that there is a Plymouth before me, the probability that I assign to that statement will depend on how trustworthy I consider myself to be in identifying such an automobile in the present circumstances.

Finally, if I merely accept that I hear some external thing buzzing, the probability I assign to the statement I accept will depend on how trustworthy I take my senses to be in their present condition to discern a buzzing in my ears from one in the external world. In general, then, how probable I take something to be, what probability is assigned on the basis of the acceptance system, depends on and is determined by what I accept within that system concerning how trustworthy I am in judging such matters on the basis of the information that I thus possess.

When I take myself to be in circumstances that are highly deceptive, or in which I consider myself to be highly unreliable, then I assign probabilities accordingly. This implies that the acceptance system uses probabilities to assign probabilities. If I accept that it is quite probable that a person in circumstances C would err concerning the truth of p, then if I accept that p, I would not assign very high probabilities to the proposition that p. This assignment of probabilities on the basis of an acceptance system that contains probabilities could, of course, lead to paradox. Kyburg has shown how such paradox may be avoided, and Skyrms has also made such proposals.[9] Ordinary thought about probabilities like ordinary thought about sets proceeds from assumptions that could lead to paradox. It need not, however.

7. **Coherence and Higher Order Evaluation.** The consideration of reliability leads to higher order evaluation and especially to higher order probabilities. Incoming information is evaluated and assigned probabilities depending on what one accepts about the reliability of the information. Those probabilities are also evaluated and assigned probabilities depending on what one accepts about the reliability of the first level probabilities. This is most clear from Keynes' example.[10] Suppose I see a coin that looks quite ordinary lying on a table. I assign a probability of 0.5 to the coin falling heads on a fair toss coming to rest on one side or the other. I have not checked on the coin at all carefully, however, and, consequently, I am less certain about the probability than I might be. By contrast, suppose that I have tossed the coin a few hundred times and checked on it with instruments to insure that it is

9. Kyburg, *Probability*, and Brian Skyrms, *Causal Necessity*, New Haven, 1980.
10. Keynes, J. M., *A Treatise on Probability*, London, 1952.

well balanced with positive results. In that case, I am much more certain that the probability of 0.5 of falling heads is correct. Thus, I would give much greater weight to the probability on the extended evidence than on the initial evidence. This situation arises, moreover, in much more common cases. In ordinary perception, for example, one accepts perceptual hypotheses about what one sees quickly and without careful observation. Careful observation might not alter the probabilities that one assigns, but it would alter the weight one attaches to the probabilities originally assigned. Thus, it is not only probabilities but the weights that one assigns to those probabilities that influences how reasonable it is to accept a statement.

8. **Probability and Reliability**. There is a question that immediately arises about the connection between probability and reliability. Suppose a person is generally reliable in some matter, say judging color with normal vision, who is in unusual circumstances that are highly deceptive, say ones involving the play of colored lights on the objects. As a result, she is not reliable in these circumstances. Here there might seem to be a conflict between reliability and probability. Though she is not in this instance reliable, it is highly probable that her judgment is correct because the circumstances in which she finds herself are, though deceptive, highly improbable. A more fanciful philosophical case, discussed by myself and Cohen, is one in which an evil demon is bent on deceiving us in all of our perceptual judgments. In this case, we would all be very unreliable, though our judgments would have a high probability of being true, because the demon hypothesis, even if true, is a highly improbable one.

This apparent division between reliability and probability is easily explained. The probability is either a prior probability or a conditional probability. The prior probability of error is low in the cases considered because the unusual circumstances have a small prior probability. On the other hand, the conditional probability, the probability of error given what the circumstances are like, is high. Similarly, in both cases we may say that a person has a high general reliability, but, in the special circumstances, her reliability is low. An objection in the evil demon case would seem to be that, given the activity of the evil demon, there is no reliability in the sense of a high frequency of truth. The reply to this is, of course, counterfactual. The people are highly reliable in the absence of the demon.

9. **Higher Level Evaluation and Convergence**. The higher level evaluation of probabilities may also be essential to convergence and coherence when it eliminates lower level conflict. There is reason to believe that more than one probability value for a given statement may be suggested by experience. The value that one would assign on the basis of background information may conflict with testimony from another which in turn may conflict with visual perception. This conflict between background information, testimony of others and visual perception may result in three different assignments of probability from differing perspectives. We might designate then as P_B, P_T and P_V. The obvious resolution of the conflict would be a weighted average of the probabilities, $wp_B + wp_T + wp_V = p_I$, where the latter is the probability that integrates the lower level conflict. This weighted average assumes that the weights fall between 0 and 1. Indeed, the weight of 0 may also be neglected

as merely a limiting case. A probability to which one gives no weight is a probability that is ignored.

The weighted average involves higher order evaluation of first level probabilities and, once again, is essentially a metamental activity. There is, however, the problem of the conflict recurring at a still higher level. Just as probabilities may be assigned from the point of view of background knowledge, testimony and visual perception, so weights may be assigned from these perspectives. We may find ourselves, there-fore, with a matrix of weights as follows, where the weight w_{XY} is the weight that is assigned to the probability of perspective Y from the perspective X.

$$W = \begin{matrix} w_{BB} & w_{BT} & w_{BV} \\ w_{TB} & w_{TT} & w_{TV} \\ w_{VB} & w_{VT} & w_{VV} \end{matrix}$$

which may be multiplied by the vector of original probabilities

$$p^O = \begin{matrix} p_B^{\ O} \\ p_T^{\ O} \\ p_V^{\ O} \end{matrix}$$

to obtain a new stage one vector of three probabilities, $p_B^{\ 1}, p_T^{\ 1}, p_V^{\ 1}$, each of which is a weighted average of the original probabilities from one perspective. This is the result of multiplying the matrix times the column vector, $W_p^{\ O}$, of original prob-abilities. Each stage on probability is an average of the original probabilities from each perspective by the formula

$$p_X^{\ 1} = w_{XB}p_B^{\ O} + w_{XT}p_T^{\ O} = w_{XV}p_V^{\ O}$$

This process of averaging or aggregating the original, or stage 0 probabilities, to arrive at the new, or stage 1 probabilities, does not insure convergence. The result of averaging may be three new but divergent probabilities in the column vector p^1. If, however, the new probabilities are again averaged using the same weights, and this process of averaging is repeated, then convergence will be obtained. This means that the probabilities calculated from the three perspectives will converge toward a single probability. Mathematically expressed, the values of the three probabilities in the column vector resulting from multiplying W^N times p^O converge toward a single probability value as N goes to infinity. That convergence represents the integration of the information articulated in the assignment of weights and original probabilities. Weighted averaging is, therefore, a method for obtaining a coherent probability assignment from conflicting information.[11]

An interest in obtaining integration and coherence from divergence and a con-flict suffices as an argument for averaging. There is, however, another argument for averaging, one of consistency. Notice that the refusal to aggregate from one perspec-tive is mathematically equivalent to assigning weights of 0 to the other prob-abilities and averaging. If, therefore, some positive weight is assigned to other probabilities from a perspective, then the refusal to average is inconsistent with the

11. Lehrer, K. and Wagner, C., *Rational Consensus in Science and Society: A Philosophical and Mathe-matical Study*, Dordrecht, 1981.

information motivating the assignment of those positive weights. This argument for averaging suffices from stage to stage so as long as positive weight is assigned to probabilities from other perspectives. The argument for averaging as opposed to some other use of the weights is given by Wagner in Lehrer and Wagner.[12] The argument is, essentially, that very intuitive axioms lead to the consequence that an aggregation method that yields coherence must be averaging. I have argued that the same axioms used to justify the method described above may also be used to justify the application of Jeffrey's method and Bayes' Theorem.[13] It is important to notice that the assumptions that the weights are all positive and that they remain constant through the various stages are sufficient but not necessary for convergence. Convergence will also result when some 0 weights are assigned and weights shift from stage to stage. These conditions for convergence are described in detail in Lehrer and Wagner.[14]

It is also important to notice that higher order evaluation and aggregation is here proposed as a normative model. The model permits us to determine how *reasonable* it is to accept some statement or hypothesis. It is, however, testable as an empirical model of the integration of conflicting information. The input of probabilities and weights has a mathematical rate of convergence, some initial inputs converging more rapidly than others. Some will not converge at all. The empirical applicability of the model might, therefore, be tested in terms of the time required to resolve conflicting sources of information. If there was a correspondence between the rate of mathematical convergence and the time required by a subject to resolve conflict, that would confirm the empirical applicablity of the model. It is also worth noting that weighted averaging of input is one standard model of information processing at the neural level. This is outlined in some detail by Palm.[15] In general, there is reason to think that higher level processing mimics or resembles lower level processing. Thus, weighted averaging, and, at the higher level, weighted averaging of weighted averages converging toward integrated values, provides us with a unified model of information processing in the human mind.

It should also be noticed that weighted averaging of probabilities may be mathematically interpreted as the probability of probabilities. If a person assigns weights to conflicting probabilities by dividing a unit weight of 1 among the conflicting probabilities, the set of weights, summing to unity, constitutes a probability vector. The weight thus assigned to a probability could not reasonably be construed as a simple second order probability of the first order probability. The weight may, however, be construed as a proportional or comparative second order probability of the first order probability in comparison to the other first order probabilities. If, moreover, one first obtained second order probabilities of the first order probabilities, one could obtain the comparative second order probabilities or weights by normalization. One could sum the second order probabilities assigned to all first

---

12. Lehrer and Wagner, *Rational Consensus.*
13. Lehrer, K., 'Rationality as Weighted Averaging', *Synthese,* 57 (1983), pp. 283–95.
14. Lehrer and Wagner, *Rational Consensus.*
15. Palm, G., *Neural Assemblies,* Berlin, 1982.

level probabilities and assign the ratio of the second order probability over that sum as the weight or comparative probability of a first order probability.

Thus, given the cogency of a theory of second order probability, as proposed by Skyrms for example, weights could be obtained from second order probabilities.[16] There is, moreover, a point of some philosophical interest to be gleaned from this discussion. Hume argued, in his early work, that if we assign probabilities to probabilities, then the probability of first order probability being less than unity would diminish the first order probability. The third order probability of the second order probability being less than unity would diminish the first order probability yet further, and, as we proceed infinitely, the first order probability would be diminished to 0.[17] Hume did not repeat this argument, and it is clearly fallacious on the grounds that diminishing values need not converge toward 0.

In terms of the present model, however, the result of considering the higher order probabilities, even a very low second order probability, may have the consequence of increasing rather than diminishing the first order probability. If, for example, the first order probability of a hypothesis is 0.6, and the second order probability of that first order probability is low, with the result that a low weight is assigned, 0.3, for example, averaging may result in a higher first order probability than 0.6. For example, if another higher first order probability, 0.8, had a higher second order probability, and correspondingly a greater weight, 0.7, the averaged first order probability would be 0.74. In short, if second order probabilities are normalized and used as weights for averaging, we obtain the result that the convergent probability value as aggregation goes to infinity will fall between the lowest and the highest first order probability. The idea that higher order probabilities will result in an infinite regress that will reduce all first order probabilities to 0 is as fallacious as Zeno's argument that an infinite regress of motion will reduce all motion to 0 and for the same reason. Infinite aggregation may yield positive values.

10. Justification under Risk. The foregoing is a brief account of the theory I have advanced as a coherence theory of justification and knowledge. It is an information processing model of human knowledge. Unlike other such models, Dretske's for example, it assumes that justification and knowledge are the result of higher order evaluation of first level information in terms of some acceptance system constituting background information.[18] One part of that acceptance system is an integrated system of probabilities. Input beliefs are evaluated in terms of such probabilities. The probabilities in the acceptance system are personal, those in the verific alternative objective. Personal and objective justification are based, in part, on probabilities, and neither requires a probability of unity. Justification and knowledge are, on this account, compatible with some risk of error, provided that the risk is justified in the quest for truth. This theory of justification might, therefore, be called a theory of justification under risk, and it contrasts with theories like those of

16. Skyrms, B., 'Higher Order Degrees of Belief', in *Prospects for Pragmatism—Essays in Honor of F. P. Ramsey*, D. H. Mellor ed., Cambridge, 1980.
17. Hume, D. *The Treatise of Human Nature*, London, 1739, Book I, Part IV, Section I.
18. Dretske, F., *Knowledge and the Flow of Information*, Cambridge, Mass. 1981.

Dretske and Armstrong which are theories of justification with certainty.[19] In order to exhibit the advantages of such a theory it will be useful to compare it with other theories of knowledge.

11. Comparison with the Foundation and Causal Theories. The *foundation* theory of knowledge and justification is one that postulates certain principles of justification affirming that certain mental states, sensory or belief states, for example, yield justified beliefs. This conception is articulated with precision by Chisholm who also postulates that some very cautious perceptual beliefs are evident.[20] The problem with the foundation theory is that it does not provide us with any explanation of why we should accept the postulates, when, in fact, it is perfectly clear why we accept those postulates. The reason is that we think that the beliefs in question are very probably true or, what is the same, very unlikely to be false. That is why we find the postulates of the foundation theory plausible, why we think, for example, that it is more reasonable to postulate that very cautious perceptual beliefs are evident than to postulate that all perceptual beliefs are evident. The cautious ones are less likely to be in error.

Van Cleve has argued that the foundation theory can provide some justification for the foundationary principles, but such justification does not explain why we accept them initially.[21] The needed explanation depends on a background system of beliefs concerning the conditions under which beliefs are trustworthy and those in which the beliefs are unreliable. This explanation is easy to provide within the context of the coherence theory on the basis of an acceptance system, and, so far as I can ascertain, impossible to provide within the constraints of the foundation theory.

It is, however, important not to confuse the explanation of justification in terms of coherence with inferential justification. If I believe that I see something red, this belief may be justified because it coheres with my acceptance system, but that does not mean that it is justified because I infer it from my acceptance system. On the contrary, the belief may be immediate and noninferential, though the justification of the belief depends on coherence with the acceptance system. Coherence does not depend on inference. Thomas Reid said that there are some beliefs that are justified in themselves without argument.[22] The coherence theory is compatible with this claim. Though argument does not generate the justification, an argument based on beliefs in the acceptance system may, nevertheless, explain the immediate justification. The explanation explicates a justification it does not generate.

Consider an example. Suppose I argue from the premises that I am almost always right about the color of objects seen with normal vision in daylight, that I am in those conditions, and that I believe that I see something red, to the conclusion that all competitors to the latter belief are either beaten or neutralized. That would explain why the belief is justified. Chisholm has noted that such argumentation is

19. Ibid.; and Armstrong, D., *Belief, Truth, and Knowledge*, London, 1973.
20. Chisholm, R. M., *Theory*, p. 84.
21. Van Cleve, J., 'Foundationalism, Epistemic Principles, and the Cartesian Circle', *Philosophical Review* 88, 1979, pp. 55–91.
22. Reid, T. *Inquiry*, passim, e.g., p. 89.

ultimately circular.[23] It is. But that does not prevent it from being explicative. The circle of our beliefs, what we accept in the interest of obtaining truth and avoiding error, explains what is justified and what is not. Some of what is justified does not depend on inference but is immediate. This immediacy arises within the circle of our beliefs. Within that circle, particular perceptual beliefs are justified, in part, because they cohere with general principles and theories, and those theories and principles are justified, in part, because they cohere with particular perceptual beliefs. Justification cycles to yield knowledge. Knowledge that is immediate may supply the premises for the inference of further knowledge, but even immediate knowledge depends on coherence.

12. **Causal Theories: An Objection.** Causal theories of knowledge are vulnerable to another objection, to wit, that they neglect the effect of background beliefs and higher order evaluation on justification and knowledge. It is characteristic of such theories, in their primitive forms, to maintain that beliefs that arise in a particular causal manner, from perception or from communication, for example, constitute knowledge simply because of the etiology of the beliefs. This sort of theory seems to me to be defective. In the first place, a true belief can arise in circumstances that are highly deceptive, and, in the second place, a true belief can arise in circumstances that are not deceptive but believed to be so. In neither instance do those beliefs constitute knowledge.

Consider a simple belief. A person sees a red patch, and her seeing a red patch causes her to believe that she sees a red patch. That is a paradigmatic instance of the appropriate etiology to yield knowledge. But does she know that she sees a red patch? Her conviction may fall short of knowledge. Suppose that she is looking at a painted red patch on a white wall in a room where there appear to be several such red patches which are quite indistinguishable from each other in quality. Suppose, moreover, some of the patches are painted red patches while others are the result of projecting a red light on the wall. If the person seeing the painted red patch cannot tell a red patch from a spot that is merely illuminated with red light, then she does not know that she sees a painted red patch when she sees one for she cannot tell a painted red patch from an illusion in this context. We may imagine, furthermore, that the person has no idea that she is confronted with any illuminated spots. The problem is that the person assumes, incorrectly, that circumstances are those in which she can tell the real thing when she sees one.

Another instance is one in which the circumstances are in no way deceptive but the person believes them to be, she believes, perhaps quite groundlessly, that the circumstances are deceptive, that the wall is illuminated by colored lights. She finds, however, that in spite of her belief about the deceptiveness of the circumstances that she cannot help but believe that she sees a painted red patch, which, in fact, she does. Nature and habit triumph over doubt, but she retains the view that it is no more likely that she is correct in her belief about what she sees than in error. Even though she does see a painted red patch and her seeing causes her to believe that she sees one, she does not *know* that she sees one. She thinks that her beliefs are

23. Chisholm, R. M., *Perceiving: A Philosophical Study*, Ithaca, 1957.

untrustworthy, and, whether she is right or wrong, this is sufficient to deprive her of knowledge.

13. Reliablism: An Objection. These objections may be combined to provide an objection to a somewhat different theory that makes justification a matter of eiology, namely, the reliablism of Goldman.[24] According to Goldman, justified belief is belief that is an output of a reliable belief forming process. The coherence theory incorporates the idea that one must believe that one is trustworthy with respect to what one accepts and be right in that belief in order to be completely justified in accepting what one does. Reliablism requires that one be reliable, but it does not entail that one believes that one is. The result is that, according to reliablism, when one believes one sees something red, as in the second example above, as the result of a reliable belief forming process, though one believes that it is not reliable, then one is justified in believing what one does. It seems, on the contrary, that, given the incoherence involved in believing something when one, at the same time, believes that one is not trustworthy in believing it, one is not justified in what one believes.

Now a reliablist may, as Goldman notes, argue that a belief forming process is not a reliable belief forming process in the relevant sense if one does not believe that it is. But that seems to me to be in error. There may be belief forming processes that are perfectly reliable even though one does not believe that they are, for example, when one mistakenly believes, as in the second example, that the belief forming process is not reliable. The crux is that one may have a false belief to the effect that some belief is the outcome of a belief forming process that is not reliable. In such a case, the belief forming process is reliable, though one believes that it is not, and, therefore, one is not completely justified in what one believes. The problem is not unreliability. It is coherence. A reliablist might, of course, add a coherence condition as a condition of justification, but that would be to abandon pure reliablism for a hybrid theory.

14. The Coherence Theory: A Reply. The coherence theory treats the examples in the following manner. In the case of the second example, the fact that the person accepts that she is in circumstances that render her belief untrustworthy means that what she believes cannot beat a competitor—the negation of what she believes, for example. In the first case, the person is personally justified in believing that she sees a red patch, but she is not completely justified because of the nature of the verific system. Since it is false that the circumstances are ones in which she is trustworthy in what she accepts, relative to the verific system the person does not accept that she is trustworthy in accepting that she sees a painted red patch. Hence, relative to the verific system, competitors cannot be beaten or neutralized. There is no neutralizing proposition for the competitor that says that she is seeing a white patch illuminated with red light, nor can that competitor be beaten. So the person is not completely justified in believing that she sees a red patch.

It might be objected to this line of argumentation that the coherence theory has incorporated reliablism as a component and is itself a hybrid theory. The objection

24. Goldman, A. I., 'What is Justified Belief?', in *Justification and Knowledge*, G. Pappas, ed., pp. 1–24. In the same volume, see also Swain, M., 'Justification and the Basis of Belief', pp. 25–49.

would be that an acceptance system might contain nothing concerning when a person is trustworthy and when not, and, therefore, the supposition that it contains assumptions about when we are trustworthy is an *ad hoc* way of smuggling reliabilism into coherence. The reply is twofold. First that, as a matter of fact, people do make assumptions about when they are trustworthy. So the assumption is psychologically well grounded. An analysis of completely justified belief should be based on a realistic psychology of belief.

15. **Coherence, Justification, and Higher Order Evaluation.** This brings us to the most fundamental observation concerning the coherence theory of knowledge and justification. It is that human knowledge and justification involves higher order evaluation and certification of information. One may receive information from various sources, but the mere possession of information does not constitute knowledge. The thermometer, as Armstrong noted, contains information, but, contrary to his suggestion, the thermometer does not know anything.[25] The ignorance of the thermometer is a result of the fact that it does not know that the reading is a temperature much less whether it is a correct temperature. The thermometer is an ignorant source of information. To know, one must understand and evaluate the information one receives. To do that, one must have a background system to evaluate the trustworthiness of the incoming information. It is such higher order evaluation of information that yields knowledge. There is no knowledge without such evaluation. Knowledge without metaknowledge is an impossibility.

25. Armstrong, D. M., *Belief, Truth, and Knowledge*, p. 166 [in this volume p. 75].

Criticisms and Compromises

Chapter 13

What's wrong with reliabilism?

Richard Foley

I

Aₙ increasing number of epistemologists claim that having beliefs which are reliable is a prerequisite of having epistemically rational beliefs. Alvin Goldman, for instance, defends a view he calls 'historical reliabilism.' According to Goldman, a person S rationally believes a proposition p only if his belief is caused by a reliable cognitive process. Goldman adds that a proposition p is epistemically rational for S, whether or not it is believed by him, only if there is available to S a reliable cognitive process which if used would result in S's believing p.[1] Likewise, Marshall Swain, Ernest Sosa, and William Alston all claim that reliability is a prerequisite of epistemic rationality. Swain claims that S rationally believes p only if he has reasons for p which are reliable indicators that p is true.[2] Sosa says S rationally believes p only if the belief is the product of an intellectual virtue, where intellectual virtues are stable dispositions to acquire truths.[3] And, Alston says that S rationally believes p only if the belief is acquired or held in such a way that beliefs held in that way are reliable, i.e., mostly true.[4]

Richard Foley, 'What's Wrong with Reliabilism?' in *The Monist* 68 (1985), pp. 188–202 reprinted by permission of The Hegeler Institute.

1. Alvin Goldman, 'What Is Justified Belief?' in *Justification and Knowledge*, ed. G. Pappas (Dordrecht: D. Reidel, 1979), pp. 1–23.
2. Marshall Swain, 'Justification and the Basis of Belief,' in *Justification and Knowledge*, ed. Pappas, pp. 25–49.
3. Ernest Sosa, 'The Raft and the Pyramid,' in *Midwest Studies in Philosophy*, vol. 5, eds. French, Uehling, and Wettstein (Minneapolis: University of Minnesota Press, 1980), pp. 3–25.
4. William Alston, 'Self-Warrant; A Neglected Form of Privileged Access,' *American Philosophical Quarterly*, 13 (1976), pp. 257–72, especially p. 268.

Each of these philosophers is suggesting that there is some sort of logical, or conceptual, tie between epistemic rationality and truth. The exact nature of this tie depends on what it means for a cognitive process, or a reason, or an intellectual virtue, to be reliable. But, at least for the moment, let us set aside this question. I will return to it shortly. In particular, let us simply assume that each of the above positions suggests (even if each doesn't strictly imply) the thesis that if one gathered into a set all the propositions it is epistemically rational for a person *S* to believe it would be impossible for the set to contain more falsehoods than truths. Or short of this, let us assume that each suggests the thesis that if one gathered into a set all the propositions which *both are epistemically rational for S and are believed by him*, it would be impossible for the set to contain more falsehoods than truths.

Since this amounts to saying that what a person rationally believes, or what it is rational for him to believe, must be a reliable indicator of what is true, any position which implies such a thesis can be regarded as a version of reliabilism.

This is somewhat broader than the usual use of the term 'reliabilism'. With respect to accounts of rational belief (I will discuss reliabilist accounts of knowledge later), the term often is reserved for accounts which require that a belief be *caused*, or *causally sustained*, by a reliable cognitive process. But, for purposes here I want to distinguish between the causal component of such accounts and the reliability component. The causal component requires a belief to have an appropriate causal ancestry in order to be rational. The reliability component requires a belief to have an appropriate relation to truth in order to be rational; in particular, on the present interpretation of reliability, it requires that more of a person's rational beliefs be true than false.

The advantage of isolating these components is that it makes obvious the possibility of endorsing a reliability requirement for rationality without endorsing a causal requirement, and vice-versa. It is possible, for example, to endorse noncausal versions of reliabilism. Consider a foundationalist position which implies that *S* rationally believes *p* only if either his belief *p* is incorrigible for him or propositions which are incorrigibly believed by him support *p* in a way which guarantees that most propositions so supported are true. A position of this sort is plausibly regarded as a reliabilist position, since it implies that a person's rational beliefs must be mostly true. It implies, in other words, that the set of such beliefs is a reliable indicator of what is true. Yet, it is not a causal position. It does not insist that *S*'s belief *p* be caused or causally sustained in an appropriate way in order to be rational.[5]

So, in my broad sense of 'reliabilism' both causal and noncausal accounts of rational belief can be versions of reliabilism. Indeed in my broad sense, Hume and Descartes might be plausibly interpreted as reliabilists.

My use of 'reliabilism' is weak in one other way. It requires only that there be a very loose connection between epistemic rationality and truth. In order for an account to be a version of reliabilism, it need not guarantee that a huge percentage

5. I discuss causal, reliabilist accounts of knowledge in Section 2. The arguments there also will apply to causal, reliabilist accounts of rational belief. See especially footnote 14.

of the propositions a person S rationally believes are true. It need only guarantee that one more such proposition is true than is false.

Unfortunately, even when reliabilism is understood in this very weak way, it is too strong; it is possible for more propositions which S rationally believes to be false than true. Consider how this might be so. Consider a world in which S believes, seems to remember, experiences, etc., just what he in this world believes, seems to remember, experiences, etc., but in which his beliefs are often false. Suppose further that in this other world the confidence with which he believes, and the clarity with which he seems to remember, and the intensity with which he experiences is identical with the actual world. Suppose even that what he would believe on reflection (about, e.g., what arguments are likely to be truth preserving) is identical with what he would believe on reflection in this world. So, if S somehow were to be switched instantaneously from his actual situation to the corresponding situation in this other world, he would not distinguish any difference, regardless of how hard he tried. To use the familiar example, suppose that a demon insures that this is the case. Call such a demon world 'w' and then consider this question: Could some of the propositions which a person S believes in w be epistemically rational for him? For example, could some of the propositions which S perceptually believes be epistemically rational? The answer is 'yes'. If we are willing to grant that in our world some of the propositions S perceptually believes are epistemically rational, then these same propositions would be epistemically rational for S in w as well. After all, world w by hypothesis is one which from S's viewpoint is indistinguishable from this world. So, if given S's situation in this world his perceptual belief p is rational, his belief p would be rational in w as well.

In one sense this is not a particularly surprising result, but in another sense it can seem somewhat surprising. Notice that the possibility of there being such a world w follows from the fact that our being in the epistemic situation we are is compatible with our world being w. This in no way shows that it is not epistemically rational for us to believe what we do. But, and this is what might seem somewhat surprising, if the mere possibility of our world being a demon world is not sufficient to defeat the epistemic rationality of our believing what we do, then neither should the actuality. Even if, contrary to what we believe, our world is world w, it still can be epistemically rational for us to believe many of the propositions we do, since the epistemic situation in world w is indistinguishable from the epistemic situation in a world which has the characteristics we take our world to have.

The point here is a simple one. In effect, I am asking you: aren't some of the propositions you believe epistemically rational for you to believe? And wouldn't whatever it is that makes those propositions epistemically rational for you also be present in a world where these propositions are regularly false, but where a demon hid this from you by making the world from your viewpoint indistinguishable from this world (so that what you believed, and what you would believe on reflection, and what you seemed to remember, and what you experienced were identical to this world)?

I think that the answer to each of these questions is 'yes' and I think you do too. But, a 'yes' answer to these questions suggests that the real lesson illustrated by the possibility of demon worlds is not a skeptical lesson as is sometimes thought, but rather an anti-reliabilist lesson. It suggests, in other words, that the demon by his deceits may cause us to have false beliefs, but he does not thereby automatically cause us to be irrational. And so, the possibility of such demon worlds illustrates that it is possible for more of what we rationally believe to be false than to be true, and it also illustrates that it is possible for more of what it is epistemically rational for us to believe (regardless of what we do in fact believe) to be false than to be true. Correspondingly, it illustrates that any version of reliabilism which implies that these are not genuine possibilities ought to be rejected.

Indeed, in one sense the claim that it is possible for more of what we rationally believe to be false than to be true is not even very controversial. It is but an extension of the claim that it is possible to rationally believe a falsehood. For if we admit that there are situations in which the conditions making a proposition epistemically rational are present but the conditions making it true are not, we will be hard-pressed to avoid the conclusion that it is possible for this to happen frequently. To put the matter metaphorically, if we allow the possibility of a crack developing between epistemic rationality and truth, such that some of what is epistemically rational can be false, we will be hard-pressed to avoid at least the possibility of a chasm developing, such that more of what is epistemically rational can be false than true. This is the lesson of demon examples, brain-in-the-vat examples, etc.

Moreover, examples of this sort also can be used to illustrate the implausibility of variations of what I have defined as reliabilism. Consider a version of reliabilism which implies not that more of S's current rational beliefs must be true than false but rather that more of S's current and past rational beliefs must be true than false. Perhaps, for example, one might try arguing for such a version of reliabilism with the help of a causal thesis which implies that S's belief p is rational only if it is the product of a reliable cognitive process, where a reliable cognitive process is one which *is and has* produced mostly true beliefs for S.[6]

It is not difficult to extend the demon example in order to illustrate the inadequacy of this version of reliabilism. Simply imagine a world which both *is and has been* indistinguishable from the actual world given S's viewpoint. Then, imagine that in this world a demon arranges things so that what S believes and has believed is regularly false. In particular, imagine that more of the propositions which he rationally believes in the actual world are false than are true in this demon world.

6. Although this causal thesis does not strictly imply that more of S's current and past rational beliefs are true than are false (since it proposes only a necessary condition of rational belief), the causal thesis might plausibly be used to support this kind of reliabilism. Think of it this way: suppose we gather into a set all of S's current and past beliefs which are the products of a reliable cognitive process and then use the other necessary conditions of rational belief to create a subset, consisting of S's current and past *rational* beliefs. If we assume that in creating this subset we have not lessened the percentage of true beliefs, then the subset, like the original set, will contain more true beliefs than false beliefs. So, although the causal thesis does not imply this version of reliabilism, it can be thought of as being closely related to it—i.e., close enough that the inadequacy of this version of reliabilism will suggest, even if it does not imply, the inadequacy of the causal thesis. (The discussion in Section 2 of causal accounts of knowledge will provide additional, and equally telling, reasons to reject *causal* reliabilist theses about rational belief; see footnote 14.)

Despite this, what he rationally believes in the actual world he also rationally believes in the demon world, since the two worlds from his viewpoint are indistinguishable in every way.

Consider other variations of reliabilism. Suppose it is claimed that more of S's rational beliefs have to be true than false *in the long-run*, or suppose it is claimed that the total set of rational beliefs in the long-run— S's as well as everyone else's rational beliefs—must contain more truths than falsehoods. Suppose, for instance, one tried defending this kind of reliabilism with the help of a causal thesis which implies that a person S's belief is rational only if it is produced by a cognitive process which in the long-run will produce more true beliefs than false beliefs.[7]

To illustrate the inadequacy of this version of reliabilism, imagine a world which is and has been from our viewpoint indistinguishable from our world. Imagine even that in this second world the percentage of truths which we have believed up until now or are now believing is about the same as in this world. But then, imagine that in the second world there is a demon who unbeknownst to us insures that our cognitive processes in the long-run give rise to more false beliefs than true beliefs.

Or, consider counterfactual versions of reliabilism, which imply that more of the rational beliefs S *would have* in appropriate counterfactual situations must be true than false if S's actual belief p is to be rational. One might try to defend this version with the help of the causal thesis which implies that S's belief p is rational only if it is the product of a cognitive process which in close counterfactual situations would produce mostly true beliefs for S.

For this kind of reliabilism, again imagine a world which from S's viewpoint is indistinguishable from the actual world. Only now imagine that in this world there is an anti-reliabilist demon—one who does not interfere with S but who was and is prepared to do so were things to be even a little different than they in fact are.

The problem with all these versions of reliabilism is essentially the same. They all assume that in the demon worlds described it would be impossible for us to have rational beliefs. The assumption, in other words, is that the deceiving activities of the demon *no matter how cleverly* they are carried out—even if we have no indication that we are (or have been, or will be, or would be) so deceived—preclude even the *possibility* of our beliefs being epistemically rational. So, the mere fact that we do have, or have had, or will have, or would have false beliefs, implies that we cannot be epistemically rational.

But, to make such an assumption is counterintuitive. In everyday situations we do not regard deception as precluding rationality. Likewise, we do not regard the fact that we have been deceived, or will be deceived, or would be deceived, as precluding rationality. Suppose I play an elaborate practical joke on you in order to get you to believe that I have left town. I tell you I am leaving town, I leave my car with you, I have someone send you a postcard signed by me, etc. My deceits may get you to believe the false proposition that I have left town, but from this it does not

7. The causal thesis here supports this version of reliabilism in much the same way that the previous version of reliabilism is supported by the causal thesis mentioned there. See n6. The remaining versions of reliabilism I discuss in this section can be supported in a corresponding way by corresponding causal theses.

follow that the proposition is not rational for you to believe. And one way to emphasize this point is to imagine (as I have done with the demon cases) a situation in which you have not been deceived and which in addition from your viewpoint is indistinguishable from the situation in which you have been deceived. In other words, imagine an ordinary situation. If in this ordinary situation it is possible for you to rationally believe that I have left town, it also is possible for you to rationally believe this in the situation in which I have deceived you. Everyone who allows rational beliefs to be false should agree to this. But then, it is natural to wonder why, if relatively modest deceits of this sort need not preclude the possibility of your having rational beliefs, more elaborate deceits of the sort a demon engages in should preclude you from having rational beliefs?

The intuitive answer is that they should not. The demon by his deceits may get you to have mostly false beliefs but this need not indicate that these beliefs also are irrational. This answer, moreover, illustrates something about the way we think of rationality. Namely, we think that what it is rational for a person to believe is a function of what it is appropriate for him to believe given his perspective. More exactly, it is a function of what it is appropriate for him to believe given his perspective *and* insofar as his goal is to believe truths and not to believe falsehoods.[8]

Precisely what makes reliabilist account of rational belief unacceptable is that they underemphasize this perspectival element. They imply that it is impossible for our beliefs to be rational if they are not in an appropriate sense reliable indicators of truths. And they imply that this is so regardless of what our perspective might be—even if, for example, it is indistinguishable from current perspective.

Can reliabilist accounts of rational belief be made acceptable by including some such perspectival element in them? Alvin Goldman, for one, hints that he might be willing to include such an element in his account. Goldman's willingness to consider such an element is motivated by his recognizing that it is possible for there to be a benevolent being who, although lazy until now, will shortly start arranging things so that our wishes come true. If there were such a benevolent demon, wishful thinking would be a reliable cognitive process in the long-run, and then given Goldman's account it might seem as if the beliefs produced by such wishful thinking would be rational. Goldman, however, rejects this consequence, saying that what matters 'is what we *believe* about wishful thinking, not what is true (in the long run) about wishful thinking.'[9] What matters if a belief is to be rational, Goldman seems to be suggesting, is not that the belief be produced by a process which in fact is reliable in the long-run; what matters is that it be produced by a process which *we take to be reliable* in the long-run.

If this suggestion is taken seriously,[10] however, it represents not a way of

---

8. This, of course, leaves open the question of what exactly makes it appropriate for a person S to believe a proposition given his perspective and given his goal of believing truths and not believing falsehoods.

9. Goldman, 'What Is Justified Belief?', p. 18.

10. It perhaps is best not to regard even Goldman himself as taking the problem here and his suggestion for how to handle it seriously. His final analysis of rational belief makes reference only to cognitive processes which in fact are reliable (and not to cognitive processes we think to be reliable).

amending reliabilism but rather a way of abandoning it. Any account of rational belief which incorporates such a suggestion will not be an account which requires that the set of rational beliefs be reliable indicators of what is true. It only will require that we believe this of them.

But if so, so be it; reliabilist accounts of rational belief ought to be abandoned.[11] Reliability is not in any plausible sense a necessary condition of epistemic rationality. In order for S's belief p to be rational, it neither is necessary for most rational beliefs of all people everywhere to be true, nor for most of S's current rational beliefs to be true, nor for most of S's rational beliefs over his lifetime to be true, nor for most of the rational beliefs S would have in close counterfactual situations to be true.

II

I would guess that for many philosophers (but certainly not all) the remarks I have been making about the relationship between rationality and reliability will not seem surprising. The remarks might even strike them as obvious albeit unimportant. For, they would claim that the epistemic significance of reliability has to do not with beliefs which are merely rational but rather with beliefs which are instances of knowledge. So, they would argue that even if reliability is not a prerequisite of rationality, it is a prerequisite of knowledge. Thus, Goldman, Sosa, Alston, Swain, and others with reliabilist sympathies might be willing to agree with me that there is a sense of rationality for which reliability is not a prerequisite. But, they would go on to insist either that rationality is not a prerequisite of knowledge (i.e., it is possible to know p without rationally believing it) or that the kind of rational belief needed for knowledge is more restrictive than the kind with which I have been concerned. Both of these options leave room for the claim that reliability is a prerequisite of knowledge even it is is not a prerequisite of mere rational belief (or of a certain kind of rational belief).

Even so, reliabilist theses about knowledge in the end fare no better than reliabilist theses about rational belief. More exactly, significant, or nontrivial, reliabilist theses about knowledge fare no better. A reliabilist thesis is not significant if it is a thesis which almost any kind of account of knowledge would imply. Thus, suppose it is claimed that reliability is a prerequisite of knowledge in the following sense: Most beliefs which are instances of knowledge have to be true. This thesis about knowledge is true but insignificant; any account of knowledge which requires a belief to be true if it is to be an instance of knowledge implies it. The problem, then, is to find a *true and significant* reliabilist account of knowledge. I claim it cannot be done; there is no such reliabilist account of knowledge.

11. This is not to say, however, that there are no problems with the above suggestion that S rationally believes p only if *he believes* of the process which causes his belief that it is reliable. To the contrary, it is no more plausible than causal, reliabilist theses: Just as S's belief p can be rational and yet not be the product of a reliable cognitive process, so too S's belief p can be rational and yet not be the product of a process which S *regards* as reliable. See n14, below.

To see this, consider how one might try to formulate a reliabilist account of knowledge. The most common approach is by describing a requirement upon knowledge which has both a causal aspect and a reliabilist aspect. In particular, the most common approach is to insist that if S's belief is to be an instance of knowledge, it must be the product of a reliable cognitive process.[12] But as is the case with reliabilist accounts of rational belief, it also is possible to describe noncausal, reliabilist accounts of knowledge. One might insist, for example, that S knows p only if his belief p is supported by evidence to such a degree that most of his beliefs supported to this degree are true. For convenience however, let us restrict discussion here to causal, reliabilist accounts, since they are the most common. (In any event, the remarks I make about causal accounts will apply *mutatis mutandis* to noncausal accounts as well.)[13]

Given this causal approach, then, the problem facing a proponent of a reliabilist account of knowledge is to explicate the notion of a reliable cognitive process in such a way that it is both true and significant that being the product of such a process is a necessary condition of a belief being an instance of knowledge.

So, suppose that a reliable cognitive process is understood to be one which produces more true beliefs than false beliefs. The claim, then, is that S's belief p is an instance of knowledge only if it is produced (or sustained) by a process which is reliable in this sense. But, the problem with this claim is that S can *know* that the kind of cognitive process (say, a perceptual one) which causes him to believe generates mostly false beliefs in other people. Indeed S might be a deceiver who is responsible for this. If so, then S's belief p is produced by a cognitive process which is unreliable. And yet, in this situation it is at least possible for S to know p. To claim otherwise is to claim that by perceptually deceiving other people S inevitably prevents himself from having perceptual knowledge. But, why should this be so?

Suppose, then, that a reliable cognitive process is one which is relativized to persons. Suppose it is understood to be one which *has produced* mostly true beliefs for person S. But then, it is possible for S to *know* that a demon has been deceiving him perceptually but not longer is. And if S does know this, he might very well now know p perceptually even though he also knows that the perceptual process which causes him to believe p is unreliable. The fact that a demon has deceived him perceptually need not make it impossible for him now to have perceptual knowledge. Or, suppose a reliable cognitive process is thought to be one which will in the long-run produce mostly true beliefs for S. But, it is possible for S to *know* that

---

12. See Alvin Goldman, 'What Is Justified Belief?'

13. It is worth noting that it also is possible for there to be causal accounts of knowledge which are not reliabilist accounts. Suppose, for instance, it is claimed that S knows p only if the fact that p causes S to believe p (or only if the fact that p in some appropriate sense is nomologically related to S's believing p). See Alvin Goldman, 'A Causal Theory of Knowing,' *The Journal of Philosophy*, 64 (1967), pp. 355–72 [Ch. 4 in this volume]. This kind of thesis, as Goldman himself now admits, faces numerous difficulties; it is not a particularly plausible thesis. But, putting aside the question of its plausibility, what is of interest here is that one can endorse this thesis without endorsing any significant reliabilist thesis. (This causal thesis does imply that all beliefs which are instances of knowledge must be true, but this does not indicate that the thesis commits one to a *significant* reliabilist thesis since this is a consequence which almost any account of knowledge implies.)

although he is not now under the control of a deceiving demon, he shortly will be. And if he does know this, he might now perceptually *know p* even though he also knows that the process which causes him to believe *p* is unreliable in this sense. For, the fact that a demon will deceive him perceptually need not make it impossible for him now to have perceptual knowledge. Or, suppose a reliable cognitive process is one which would produce mostly true beliefs in appropriately close counterfactual situations. But then, *S* might *know* that there is an anti-reliabilist demon who is not now deceiving him but is (and was) prepared to do so had the situation been even a little different. And, knowing that there is such a demon who is poised to act but who does not is compatible with now knowing *p*. The fact that a demon is prepared to deceive him perceptually does not make it impossible for him to have perceptual knowledge.

The same general lesson even applies to a demon who is now deceiving *S* perceptually. But there is a wrinkle here, since it may be impossible for *S* to believe (and hence to know) that due to the actions of a deceiving demon more of his current perceptual beliefs are false than are true. This may be impossible because it may be impossible for *S* to believe a proposition if he also genuinely believes that *p* is more likely to be false than true. But even if this is impossible, it nonetheless is possible for *S* to have adequate evidence for the claim that more of his current perceptual beliefs are false than are true (even if he does not believe it to be true) and yet for him to have perceptual knowledge *p*. Suppose, for example, he has adequate evidence for the truth that a demon is deceiving him with respect to most objects in his visual field but not those directly in front of him and within two feet of him. If proposition *p* concerns an object of this latter sort, *S* might very well know *p* even though he may have adequate reasons for believing the true proposition that the visual process which causes him to believe *p* is unreliable— i.e., even though more of the *S*'s current visual beliefs are false than true. The fact that a demon is deceiving him perceptually about objects not directly in front of him or not within two feet of him does not make it impossible for him to have perceptual knowledge about objects which are in front of him and within two feet of him.[14]

It may be tempting in this last case to insist that *S*'s belief *p is* the product of a reliable cognitive process—namely, *a process as it operates on objects within two feet of him and directly in front of him.* In other words, it may be tempting to insist that this last case only illustrates that we must allow the notion of a reliable cognitive process to be narrowly specified. In the case here, for example, once we specify the process which causes *S* to believe *p* as a visual process as operating on objects directly in front of *S* and within two feet of him, it by hypothesis is true that his belief *p* is caused by a reliable process. Indeed, in the case here, perhaps the only

14. Since in all of the preceding examples *S* can be assumed to rationally believe *p* (as well as to know *p*), the examples also can be used to illustrate the inadequacy of various theses about rational belief. For example, they illustrate that *S*'s believing or having adequate reason to believe that his belief is caused by a reliable process is not a prerequisite of *S*'s rationally believing *p*. Likewise, they illustrate that *S*'s belief actually having been caused by a reliable process is not a prerequisite at *S*'s rationally believing *p*.

beliefs produced by this narrowly specified process are the belief that p and beliefs in other propositions implied by p. And of course, by hypothesis all these propositions are true.

However, any attempt to save a reliabilist account of knowledge by this kind of maneuver is an attempt to save it by destroying it. For any reliabilist account which results from such a rescue maneuver will be an account which is insignificant. Indeed, it will be as insignificant as a reliabilist account which insists that most beliefs which are instances of knowledge must be true, and it will be insignificant for the same reason. Namely, *any* proponent of *any* kind of account of knowledge can endorse a reliabilism of this sort. Or, at least anyone who thinks knowledge requires true belief can endorse a reliabilism of this sort. After all, on any occasion where a person has a true belief p, there will be *some*, narrowly specified cognitive process which causes S to believe p and which in addition is reliable, if only because it is so narrowly specified that it produces only belief p and beliefs in propositions implied by p. So, insofar as a reliabilist resorts to such maneuvers to defend his account, his account will lose whatever distinctive character it was intended to have.

Reliabilist accounts of knowledge, then, face a dilemma. One horn of the dilemma is to allow the notion of a reliable cognitive process to be specified so narrowly that reliabilism is no longer an interesting thesis. It becomes true but trivial, since any true belief can be construed as being the product of a reliable cognitive process. The other horn is not to allow the notion of a reliable cognitive process to be so narrowly specified, in which case it becomes susceptible to demon counterexamples and the like. In other words, it becomes an interesting but false thesis.

III

I have not discussed every possible reliabilist thesis concerning rational belief and knowledge. But, I have discussed a number of representative theses, and neither they nor any other reliabilist thesis I can think of can avoid the difficulties raised for them by demon situations and the like. And so, I conclude that reliability is neither a necessary condition of rational belief (i.e., it is not necessary for more of a person's rational beliefs to be true than false) nor a necessary condition of knowledge (i.e., a belief in order to be an instance of knowledge need not be the product of a reliable cognitive process—provided 'reliable' is used in a nontrivial way).

In order to avoid this conclusion, one might be tempted, I suppose, to claim that the counterexamples I have described are not really possible. In arguing against reliabilist theses of knowledge, I have imagined situations in which a person S *knows* that he has been deceived by a demon but no longer is, and situations in which S *knows* that he shortly will be deceived by a demon but is not now, and situations in which S *knows* that in close counterfactual situations he would be deceived by a demon even though he is not being deceived by the demon in the actual situation. Accordingly, in order to save reliabilism, one might try claiming that S cannot know such propositions.

But why not? If such propositions can be true, why might not *S* be in a position to know that they are true? What is it about knowledge, or about these situations, or about *S* which is supposed to preclude even the *possibility* of *S*'s knowing such propositions? On the face of it, knowledge of such propositions would seem possible. And if it is possible, it is possible for *S*'s belief *p* to be an instance of knowledge even though it is not the product of a reliable cognitive process.

But, perhaps the objection here is that it is not possible for such propositions even to be true, and thus *a fortiori* it is not possible for *S* to know them. In particular, perhaps the objection is that it is not possible for a demon to deceive us so systematically that much of what we believe is false. Several philosophers recently have at least suggested this; they have tried to defend the surprising thesis that it is not possible for most of our beliefs to be false. Both Donald Davidson and Hilary Putnam, for example, recently have defended accounts of belief which imply that this is not possible.[15] Their accounts imply that although it may be possible for there to be evil demons or for us to be brains-in-a-vat, it is not possible for us to be in the grip of an evil demon, or for us to be brains-in-a-vat, *and* for us to believe what we now believe about the external world (assuming that we neither *now* are in the clutches of such a demon nor *now* are in a vat). The reason Davidson claims this (and Putnam claims it for a closely related reason) is because he thinks that the object of a belief at least in a majority of cases is the cause of the belief. So, according to Davidson, if we are brains-in-a-vat hooked up to a machine, it is not ordinary objects in the external world (such as tables, chairs, etc.) which cause our mental states. Rather, it is the inner workings of the machine which causes us to be in the mental states we are. But then, says Davidson, most of our beliefs are about these inner workings of the machine and not about tables, chairs, etc. Moreover, most of these beliefs are true.

I am not inclined to think that an account of belief of this rough sort is very plausible, but for purposes here such qualms can be put aside. For, even if the account is plausible and even if as a result it is impossible for most of a person's beliefs to be false, this does not do the reliabilist any good. To the contrary, it makes reliabilism pointless. At the heart of reliabilist accounts of rational belief is the idea that one crucial difference between rational beliefs and other beliefs is that the former are more intimately related to truth. More of them must be true than false. And, a similar idea lies at the heart of reliabilist accounts of knowledge. Beliefs which are instances of knowledge must be reliably produced, so that most beliefs so produced are true; this supposedly is a crucial element in what distinguishes beliefs which are eligible to be instances of knowledge from those which are not. But if it is impossible for more of a person's beliefs to be false than true, all of this is beside the

---

15. Hilary Putnam, 'Realism and Reason.' *Proceedings and Addresses of the American Philosophical Association* 20 (1977), pp. 483–98; Hilary Putnam, *Reason, Truth, and History* (Cambridge: Cambridge University Press, 1981), especially ch. 1 [Ch. 27 in this volume]; Donald Davidson, 'On the very Idea of a Conceptual Scheme,' *Proceedings and Addresses of the American Philosophical Association* 1717 (1974), pp. 5–20. Donald Davidson, 'A Coherence Theory of Truth and Knowledge,' in *Kant oder Hegel?* ed. Dieter Henrich (Klett-Cotta, Stuttgart, 1981), 423–33 [Ch. 29 in this volume].

point. A person's beliefs regardless of what they are—whether or not any of them are instances of knowledge and whether or not any of them are rational—must be mostly true. So, contrary to what is suggested by reliabilist accounts of rational belief and knowledge, reliability is not a significant criterion which can be used to distinguish these epistemically valuable kinds of beliefs from other kinds of beliefs.

All this, however, is not to say that considerations of reliability are altogether unimportant epistemically. As I suggested earlier, epistemic rationality is best understood to be a function of what it is appropriate for a person to believe given his perspective and given the goal of his having true beliefs and not having false beliefs. So, the goal in terms of which epistemic rationality can be understood is the goal of having reliable beliefs—i.e., mostly true beliefs. But, to say that reliability is the goal in terms of which epistemic rationality is to be understood is not to say that achieving that goal is a prerequisite of being epistemically rational. If a person, given his situation, believes what it is appropriate for him to believe with respect to the goal of his having true beliefs and not having false beliefs, then his beliefs can be epistemically rational even if they are mostly false. This is the lesson of demon examples and the like.

Likewise, nothing I have said implies that reliability is not an important consideration in understanding knowledge. Indeed, I think that reliability can be a crucial part of a set of conditions *sufficient* for knowledge. Recall D. H. Lawrence's story of the boy who when he rides his rocking horse is able unfailingly to pick the winners at a local race track. It is plausible to think that such a boy *somehow* knows who the winners will be,[16] and it is plausible to suppose this even if we also suppose that the boy has not been told that his picks are always correct. In other words, it is plausible to suppose that the boy somehow knows who the winners will be even if he lacks adequate evidence for his picks. Two lessons are suggested by such cases. First, in order to have knowledge it is not necessary to have a rational belief as has been traditionally claimed. At the very least, this is not necessary in one important sense of rational belief—one which makes rational belief a function of having adequate evidence. Second, having a true belief which is caused by a highly reliable cognitive process can be *sufficient* for knowledge. Or at least, it can be sufficient with the addition of a few other relatively minor conditions.[17] The mistake reliabilists tend to make is to try to draw a third lesson from such cases. Namely, they try to conclude that a necessary condition of a person S's knowing p is that his belief p be reliably produced.

16. The story is cited by Roderick Firth, 'Are Epistemic Concepts Reducible to Ethical Ones,' in *Values and Morals*, eds. A. Goldman and J. Kim (Dordrecht, Holland: D. Reidel, 1978), pp. 215–29.

17. Perhaps, for example, it would not be plausible to say that the boy on the rocking horse knows who the winners will be if he has adequate evidence for the (false) proposition that the process which causes him to think some horse will win is unreliable. Thus, perhaps something at last roughly resembling the following conditions are sufficient for S's knowing p: S belief p is true, it is caused by a highly reliable process R, and S does not have adequate evidence for believing R is not highly reliable.

Chapter 14

Externalist theories of empirical knowledge

Laurence BonJour

OF the many problems that would have to be solved by a satisfactory theory of empirical knowledge, perhaps the most central is a general structural problem which I shall call *the epistemic regress problem*: the problem of how to avoid an infinite and presumably vicious regress of justification in one's account of the justification of empirical beliefs. *Foundationalist* theories of empirical knowledge, as we shall see further below, attempt to avoid the regress by locating a class of empirical beliefs whose justification does not depend on that of other empirical beliefs. *Externalist* theories, the topic of the present paper, represent one species of foundationalism.

I

I begin with a brief look at the epistemic regress problem. The source of the problem is the requirement that beliefs that are to constitute knowledge must be *epistemically justified*. Such a requirement is of course an essential part of the 'traditional' conception of knowledge as justified true belief, but it also figures in at least most of the revisions of that conception which have been inspired by the Gettier problem. Indeed, if this requirement is understood in a sufficiently generic way as meaning roughly that the acceptance of the belief must be epistemically rational that it must not be epistemically irresponsible, then it becomes hard to see how any adequate conception of knowledge can fail to include it.

How then are empirical beliefs epistemically justified? Certainly the most obvious way to *show* that such a belief is justified is by producing a justificatory argument in which the belief to be justified is shown to follow inferentially from some other (perhaps conjunctive) belief, which is thus offered as a reason for accepting it. Beliefs whose justification would, if made explicit, take this form may be said to be *inferentially justified*. (Of course, such a justificatory argument would usually be explicitly rehearsed only in the face of some specific problem or challenge. Notice

Laurence BonJour, 'Externalist Theories of Empirical Knowledge' in P. A. French., T. E. Uehling, Jr., H. K. Wettstein (eds.), *Midwest Studies in Philosophy 5: Studies in Epistemology* (Minneapolis, University of Minnesota Press, 1980), pp. 53–73 reprinted by permission of Laurence BonJour and University of Minnesota Press.

also that an inferentially justified belief need not have been *arrived at* through inference, though it often will have been.)

The important point about inferential justification, however, is that if the justificandum belief is to be genuinely justified by the proffered argument, then the belief that provides the premise of the argument must itself be justified in some fashion. This premise belief might of course itself be inferentially justified, but this would only raise a new issue of justification with respect to the premise(s) of this new justificatory argument, and so on, so that empirical knowledge is threatened by an infinite and seemingly vicious regress of epistemic justification, with a thorough-going skepticism as the eventual outcome. So long as each new step of justification is inferential, it appears that justification can never be completed, indeed can never really even get started, and hence that there is no justification and no knowledge. Thus the epistemic regress problem.

What is the eventual outcome of this regress? There are a variety of possibilities, but the majority of philosophers who have considered the problem have believed that the only outcome that does not lead more or less directly to skepticism is *foundationalism*: the view that the regress terminates by reaching empirical beliefs (a) that are genuinely justified, but (b) whose justification is not inferentially dependent on that of any further empirical belief(s), so that no further issue of empirical justification is thereby raised. These non-inferentially justified beliefs, or *basic beliefs* as I shall call them, are claimed to provide the foundation upon which the edifice of empirical knowledge rests. And the central argument for foundationalism is simply that all other possible outcomes of the regress lead inexorably to skepticism.[1]

This argument has undeniable force. Nonetheless, the central concept of foundationalism, the concept of a basic belief, is itself by no means unproblematic. The fundamental question that must be answered by any acceptable version of foundationalism is: *how are basic beliefs possible*? How, that is, is it possible for there to be an empirical belief that is epistemically justified in a way completely independent of any believed premises that might provide reasons for accepting it? As Chisholm suggests, a basic belief seems to be in effect an epistemologically unmoved (or perhaps self-moved) mover. But such a status is surely no less paradoxical in epistemology than it is in theology.

This intuitive difficulty with the idea of a basic empirical belief may be elaborated by considering briefly the fundamental concept of epistemic justification. There are two points to be made. First, the idea of justification is generic, admitting in principle of many different species. Thus, for example, the acceptance of an empirical belief might be morally justified, or pragmatically justified, or justified in some still different sense. But a belief's being justified in one of these other senses will not satisfy the justification condition for knowledge. What knowledge requires is *epistemic* justification. And the distinguishing characteristic of this particular

---

1. For a fuller discussion of the regress argument, including a discussion of other possible outcomes of the regress, see my paper 'Can Empirical Knowledge Have a Foundation?' *American Philosophical Quarterly* 15 (1978): 1–13. That paper also contains a brief anticipation of the present discussion of externalism.

species of justification is, I submit, its internal relationship to the cognitive goal of *truth*. A cognitive act is epistemically justified, on this conception, only if and to the extent that is aimed at this goal—which means at a minimum that one accepts only beliefs that there is adequate reason to think are true.

Second, the concept of epistemic justification is fundamentally a normative concept. It has to do with what one has a duty or obligation to do, from an epistemic or intellectual standpoint. As Chisholm suggests, one's purely intellectual duty is to accept beliefs that are true, or likely to be true, and reject beliefs that are false, or likely to be false. To accept beliefs on some other basis is to violate one's epistemic duty—to be, one might say, *epistemically irresponsible*—even though such acceptance might be desirable or even mandatory from some other, non-epistemic standpoint.

Thus if basic beliefs are to provide a suitable foundation for empirical knowledge, if inference from them is to be the sole basis for the justification of other empirical beliefs, then that feature, whatever it may be, in virtue of which an empirical belief qualifies as basic, must also constitute an adequate reason for thinking that the belief is true. And now if we assume, plausibly enough, that the person for whom a belief is basic must *himself* possess the justification for that belief if *his* acceptance of it is to be epistemically rational or responsible, and thus apparently that he must believe *with justification* both (a) that the belief has the feature in question and (b) that beliefs having that feature are likely to be true, then we get the result that this belief is not basic after all, since its justification depends on that of these other beliefs. If this result is correct, then foundationalism is untenable as a solution to the regress problem.[2]

What strategies are available to the foundationalist for avoiding this objection? One possibility would be to grant that the believer must be in possession of the reason for thinking that his basic belief is true but hold that the believer's cognitive grasp of that reason does not involve further *beliefs*, which would then require justification, but instead cognitive states of a different and more rudimentary kind: *intuitions* or *immediate apprehensions*, which are somehow capable of conferring justification upon beliefs without themselves requiring justification. Some such view as this seems implicit in most traditional versions of foundationalism.[3]

My concern in the present paper, however, is with an alternative foundationalist strategy, one of comparatively recent innovation. One way, perhaps somewhat tendentious, to put this alternative approach is to say that according to it, though there must in a sense be a reason why a basic belief is likely to be true, the person for whom such a belief is basic need not have any cognitive grasp of this reason. On this view, the epistemic justification or reasonableness of a basic belief depends on the obtaining of an appropriate relation, generally causal or nomological in

2. It could, of course, still be claimed that the belief in question was *empirically* basic, so long as both the needed justifying premises were justifiable on an *a priori* basis. But this would mean that it was an *a priori* truth that a particular empirical belief was likely to be true. In the present paper, I shall simply assume, without further discussion, that this seemingly unlikely state of affairs does not in fact obtain.

3. For criticism of this view, see the paper cited in note 1.

character, between the believer and the world. This relation, which is differently characterized by different versions of the view, is such as to make it either nomologically certain or else highly probable that the belief is true. It would thus provide, *for anyone who knew about it*, an undeniably excellent reason for accepting such a belief. But according to proponents of the view under discussion, the person for whom the belief is basic need not (and in general will not) have any cognitive grasp of any kind of this reason or of the relation that is the basis for it in order for this basic belief to be justified; all these matters may be entirely *external* to the person's subjective conception of the situation. Thus the justification of a basic belief need not involve any further beliefs (or other cognitive states) so that no further regress of justification is generated. D. M. Armstrong calls this an 'externalist' solution to the regress problem, and I shall adopt this label.

My purpose in this paper is to examine such externalist views. I am not concerned with problems of detail in formulating a view of this kind, though some of these will be mentioned in passing, but rather with the overall acceptability of an externalist solution to the regress problem and thus of an externalist version of foundationalism. I shall attempt to argue that externalism is not acceptable. But there is a methodological problem with respect to such an argument which must be faced at the outset, since it determines the basic approach of the paper.

When viewed from the general standpoint of the western epistemological tradition, externalism represents a very radical departure. It seems safe to say that until very recent times, no serious philosopher of knowledge would have dreamed of suggesting that a person's belief might be epistemically justified simply in virtue of facts or relations that were external to his subjective conception. Descartes, for example, would surely have been quite unimpressed by the suggestion that his problematic beliefs about the external world were justified if only they were in fact reliably related to the world—whether or not he had any reason for thinking this to be so. Clearly his conception, and that of generations of philosophers who followed, was that such a relation could play a justificatory role only if the believer possessed adequate reason for thinking that it obtained. Thus the suggestion embodied in externalism would have been regarded by most epistemologists as simply irrelevant to the main epistemological issue, so much so that the philosopher who suggested it would have been taken either to be hopelessly confused or to be simply changing the subject (as I note below, this may be what some externalists in fact intend to be doing). The problem, however, is that this very radicalism has the effect of insulating the externalist from any very direct refutation: any attempt at such a refutation is almost certain to appeal to premises that a thoroughgoing externalist would not accept. My solution to this threatened impasse will be to proceed on an intuitive level as far as possible. By considering a series of examples, I shall attempt to exhibit as clearly as possible the fundamental intuition about epistemic rationality that externalism seems to violate. Although this intuition may not constitute a conclusive objection to the view, it is enough, I believe, to shift the burden of proof decisively to the externalist. In the final section of the paper, I shall consider briefly whether he can discharge this burden.

II

Our first task will be the formulation of a clear and relatively adequate version of externalism. The recent epistemological literature contains a reasonably large number of externalist and quasi-externalist views. Some of these, however, are not clearly relevant to our present concerns, either because they are aimed primarily at the Gettier problem, so that their implications for a foundationalist solution of the regress problem are not made clear, or because they *seem* on the surface at least, to involve a repudiation of the very conception of epistemic justification or reasonableness as a requirement for knowledge. Views of the latter sort seem to me to be very difficult to take seriously; but if they are seriously intended, they would have the consequence that the regress problem, at least in the form discussed here, would simply not arise, so that there would be no need for any solution, foundationalist or otherwise. My immediate concern here is with versions of externalism that claim to *solve* the regress problem and thus that also claim that the acceptance of beliefs satisfying the externalist conditions is epistemically justified or rational or warranted. Only such an externalist position genuinely constitutes a version of foundationalism, and hence the more radical views, if any such are in fact seriously intended, may safely be left aside for the time being.

The most completely developed externalist view of the sort we are interested in is that of Armstrong, as presented in his book, *Belief, Truth and Knowledge.*[4] Armstrong is explicitly concerned with the regress problem, though he formulates it in terms of knowledge rather than justification. And it seems reasonably clear that he wants to say that beliefs satisfying his externalist criterion are epistemically justified or rational, though he is not as explicit as one might like on this point.[5] In what follows, I shall in any case assume such an interpretation of Armstrong and formulate his position accordingly.

Another version of externalism, which fairly closely resembles Armstrong's except for being limited to knowledge derived from visual perception, is offered by Dretske in *Seeing and Knowing.*[6] Goldman, in several papers, also suggests views of

---

4. D. M. Armstrong, *Belief, Truth and Knowledge* (London, Press, 1973). Bracketed references in the text will be to the pages of this book.

5. The clearest passages are at p. 183 [in this volume p. 85], where Armstrong says that a belief satisfying his externalist condition, though not 'based on reasons,' nevertheless 'might be said to be reasonable (justifiable), because it is a sign, a completely reliable sign, that the situation believed to exist does in fact exist'; and at p. 189, where he suggests that the satisfaction of a slightly weaker condition, though it does not yield knowledge, may still yield rational belief. There is no reason to think that any species of rationality or reasonableness other than the epistemic is at issue in either of these passages. But though these passages seem to me to adequately support my interpretation of Armstrong, the strongest support may well derive simply from the fact that he at no point *disavows* a claim of epistemic rationality. (See also the parenthetical remark in the middle of p. 77.)

6. Fred Dretske, *Seeing and Knowing* (London, 1969), chap. 3. Dretske also differs from Armstrong in requiring in effect that the would-be knower also believe that the externalist condition is satisfied, but not of course that this belief be justified.

an externalist sort,[7] and the view that Alston calls 'Simple Foundationalism' and claims to be the most defensible version of foundationalism seems to be essentially externalist in character.[8] The most extreme version of externalism would be one that held that the external condition required for justification is simply the *truth* of the belief in question. Such a view could not be held in general, of course, without obliterating the distinction between knowledge and mere true belief, thereby turning every lucky guess into knowledge. But it might be held with respect to some more limited class of beliefs. Such a view is mentioned by Alston as one possible account of privileged access,[9] and seems, surprisingly enough, to be advocated by Chisholm (though it is very hard to be sure that this is what Chisholm really means).[10]

Here I shall concentrate mainly on Armstrong's view. Like all externalists, Armstrong makes the acceptability of a basic belief depend on an external relation between the believer and his belief, on the one hand, and the world, on the other, specifically a law-like connection: 'there must be a *law-like connection* between the state of affairs *Bap* [i.e., *a*'s believing that *p*] and the state of affairs which makes "*p*" true, such that, given *Bap*, it must be the case that *p*.' [166] [in this volume p. 75] This is what Armstrong calls the 'thermometer-model' of non-inferential knowledge: just as the readings of a reliable thermometer lawfully reflect the temperature, so one's basic beliefs lawfully reflect the states of affairs that make them true. A person whose beliefs satisfy this condition is in effect a reliable cognitive instrument; and it is, according to Armstrong, precisely in virtue of this reliability that these basic beliefs are justified.

Of course, not all thermometers are reliable, and even a reliable one may be accurate only under certain conditions. Similarly, it is not a requirement for the justification of a basic belief on Armstrong's view that all beliefs of that general kind or even all beliefs of that kind held by that particular believer be reliable. Thus

7. Goldman does this most clearly in 'Discrimination and Perceptual Knowledge,' *Journal of Philosophy* 73 (1976): 771–91 [Ch. 8 in this volume]; and in 'What is Justified Belief?' *Justification and Knowledge*, G. S. Pappas, ed., Dordrecht, 1979. See also 'A Causal Theory of Knowing,' *Journal of Philosophy* 64 (1967): 355–72 [Ch. 4 in this volume], though this last paper is more concerned with the Gettier problem than with a general account of the standards of epistemic justification.

8. William P. Alston, 'Two Types of Foundationalism,' *Journal of Philosophy* 73 (1976): 165–85; see especially p. 168.

9. Alston, 'Varieties of Privileged Access,' in Roderick Chisholm and Robert Swartz, *Empirical Knowledge* (Englewood Cliffs, N.J., 1973), pp. 396–9. Alston's term for this species of privileged access is 'truth sufficiency.'

10. See Chisholm, *Theory of Knowledge*, 2nd ed. (Englewood Cliffs, N.J., 1977), p. 22 [in this volume p. 250], where Chisholm offers the following definition of the concept of a state of affairs being *self-presenting*:

   h is *self-presenting* for *S* at *t* =Df *h* occurs at *t*; and necessarily, if *h* occurs at *t* then *h* is evident [i.e., justified] for *S* at *t*.

Despite the overtones of the term 'self-presentation,' nothing in this passage seems to require that the believer have any sort of immediate awareness of the state in question; all that is required is that it actually occur, i.e., that his belief be true. On the other hand, Chisholm also, in the section immediately preceding this definition, quotes with approval a passage from Leibniz which appeals to the idea of 'direct awareness' and of the absence of mediation 'between the understanding and its objects,' thus suggesting the non-externalist variety of foundationalism (pp. 20–1) [in this volume p. 248].

the law linking the having of the belief with the state of affairs that makes it true will have to mention properties, including relational properties, of the believer beyond his merely having that belief. Incorporating this modification yields the following schematic formulation of the conditions under which a non-inferential belief is justified and therefore basic: a non-inferential belief is justified if and only if there is some property H of the believer, such that it is a law of nature that whenever a person satisfies H and has that belief, then the belief is true. [197][11] Here H may be as complicated as one likes and may include facts about the believer's mental processes, sensory apparatus, environment, and so on. But presumably, though Armstrong does not mention this point, H is not to include anything that would entail the truth of the belief; such a logical connection would not count as a law of nature.

Armstrong adds several qualifications to this account, aimed at warding off various objections, of which I shall mention only two. First, the nomological connection between the belief and the state of affairs that makes it true is to be restricted to 'that of *completely reliable sign* to thing signified.' [182] What this is intended to exclude is the case where the belief itself *causes* the state of affairs that makes it true. In such a case, it seems intuitively that the belief is not a case of knowledge even though it satisfies the condition of complete reliability formulated above. Second, the property H of the believer which is involved in the law of nature must not be 'too specific'; there must be a 'real possibility' of a recurrence of the situation described by the law. What Armstrong is worried about here is the possibility of a 'veridical hallucination,' i.e., a case in which a hallucinatory belief happens to be correct. In such a case, if the state of affairs that makes the belief true happens to be part of the cause of the hallucination and if the believer and his environment are described in enough detail, it might turn out to be nomologically necessary that such a state of affairs obtain, simply because all alternative possible causes for the hallucinatory belief have been ruled out by the specificity of the description. Again, such a case intuitively should not count as a case of knowledge, but it would satisfy Armstrong's criterion in the absence of this additional stipulation. (Obviously this requirement of non-specificity or repeatability is extremely vague and seems in fact to be no more than an *ad hoc* solution to this problem; but I shall not pursue this issue here.)

There are various problems of detail, similar to those just discussed, which could be raised about Armstrong's view, but these have little relevance to the main theme of the present paper. Here I am concerned with the more fundamental issue of whether Armstrong's view, or any other externalist view of this general sort, is acceptable as a solution to the regress problem and the basis for a foundationalist account of empirical knowledge. When considered from this perspective, Armstrong's view seems at the very least to be in need of considerable refinement in the face of fairly obvious counterexamples. Thus our first task will be to develop some

---

11. Armstrong actually formulates the criterion as a criterion of knowledge, rather than merely of justification; the satisfaction of the belief condition is built into the criterion and this, with the satisfaction of the indicated justification condition, entails that the truth condition is satisfied.

of these counterexamples and suggest modifications in the view accordingly. This discussion will also lead, however, to a fundamental intuitive objection to all forms of externalism.

III

Although it is formulated in more general terms, the main concern of an externalist view like Armstrong's is obviously those non-inferential beliefs which arise from ordinary sources like sense-perception and introspection. For it is, of course, these beliefs which will on any plausible foundationalist view provide the actual foundations of empirical knowledge. Nevertheless, cases involving sense-perception and introspection are not very suitable for an intuitive assessment of externalism, since one central issue between externalism and other foundationalist and non-foundationalist views is precisely whether in such cases a further basis for justification beyond the externalist one is typically present. Thus it will be useful to begin by considering the application of externalism to other possible cases of non-inferential knowledge, cases of a less familiar sort where it will be easier to stipulate in a way that will be effective on an intuitive level that only the externalist sort of justification is present. Specifically, in this section and the next, our focus will be on possible cases of clairvoyant knowledge. Clairvoyance, the alleged psychic power of perceiving or intuiting the existence and character of distant states of affairs without the aid of any sensory input, remains the subject of considerable scientific controversy. Although many would like to dismiss out of hand the very idea of such a cognitive power, there remains a certain amount of evidence in favor of its existence which it is difficult to entirely discount. But in any case, the actual existence of clairvoyance does not matter at all for present purposes, so long as it is conceded to represent a coherent possibility. For externalism, as a general philosophical account of the foundations of empirical knowledge, must of course apply to all possible modes of non-inferential empirical knowledge, and not just to those that in fact happen to be realized.

The intuitive difficulty with externalism that the following discussion is intended to delineate and develop is this: on the externalist view, a person may be ever so irrational and irresponsible in accepting a belief, when judged in light of his own subjective conception of the situation, and may still turn out to be epistemically justified, i.e., may still turn out to satisfy Armstrong's general criterion of reliability. This belief may in fact be reliable, even though the person has no reason for thinking that it is reliable—or even though he has good reason to think that it is not reliable. But such a person seems nonetheless to be thoroughly irresponsible from an epistemic standpoint in accepting such a belief, and hence not justified, contrary to externalism. The following cases may help bring out this problem more clearly.

Consider first the following case:

Case I. Samantha believes herself to have the power of clairvoyance, though she has no reasons for or against this belief. One day she comes to believe, for no apparent reason, that the President is in New York City. She maintains this belief, appealing to her alleged clairvoyant power, even though she is at the same time aware of a massive amount of apparently cogent evidence, consisting of news reports, press releases, allegedly live television pictures, etc., indicating that the President is at that time in Washington, D.C. Now the President is in fact in New York City, the evidence to the contrary being part of a massive official hoax mounted in the face of an assassination threat. Moreover, Samantha does in fact have completely reliable clairvoyant power, under the conditions that were then satisfied, and her belief about the President did result from the operation of that power.

In this case, it is clear that Armstrong's criterion of reliability is satisfied. There will be some complicated description of Samantha, including the conditions then operative, from which it will follow, by the law describing her clairvoyant power, that her belief is true.[12] But it seems intuitively clear nevertheless that this is not a case of justified belief or of knowledge: Samantha is being thoroughly irrational and irresponsible in disregarding cogent evidence that the President is not in New York City on the basis of a clairvoyant power which she has no reason at all to think that she possesses; and this irrationality is not somehow canceled by the fact that she happens to be right. Thus, I submit, Samantha's irrationality and irresponsibility prevent her belief from being epistemically justified.

This case and others like it suggest the need for a further condition to supplement Armstrong's original one: not only must it be true that there is a law-like connection between a person's belief and the state of affairs that makes it true, such that given the belief, the state of affairs cannot fail to obtain, but it must also be true that the person in question does not possess cogent reasons for thinking that the belief in question is false. For, as this case seems to show, the possession of such reasons renders the acceptance of the belief irrational in a way that cannot be overridden by a purely externalist justification.

Nor is this the end of the difficulty for Armstrong. Suppose that the clairvoyant believer, instead of having evidence against the particular belief in question, has evidence against his possession of such a cognitive power, as in the following case:

Case II. Casper believes himself to have the power of clairvoyance, though he has no reasons for this belief. He maintains his belief despite the fact that on the numerous occasions on which he has attempted to confirm one of his allegedly clairvoyant beliefs, it has always turned out apparently to be false. One day Casper comes to believe, for no apparent reason, that the President is in New York City, and he maintains this belief, appealing to his alleged clairvoyant power. Now in fact the President is in New York City; and Casper does, under the conditions that were then satisfied, have completely reliable clairvoyant power, from which this belief in fact resulted. The apparent falsity of his other clairvoyant beliefs was due in some cases to his being in the wrong conditions for the operation of his power and in other cases to deception and misinformation.

Is Casper justified in believing that the President is in New York City, so that he then knows that this is the case? According to Armstrong's account, even with the modification just suggested, we must apparently say that the belief is justified and

---

12. This assumes that clairvoyant beliefs are caused in some distinctive way, so that an appropriately complete description of Samantha will rule out the possibility that the belief is a mere hunch and will connect appropriately with the law governing her clairvoyance.

hence a case of knowledge: the reliability condition is satisfied, and Casper possesses no reason for thinking that the President is not in New York City. But this result still seems mistaken. Casper is being quite irrational and irresponsible from an epistemic standpoint in disregarding evidence that his beliefs of this sort are not reliable and should not be trusted. And for this reason, the belief in question is not justified.

In the foregoing case, Casper possessed good reasons for thinking that he did not possess the sort of cognitive ability that he believed himself to possess. But the result would be the same, I believe, if someone instead possessed good reasons for thinking that *in general* there could be no such cognitive ability, as in the following case:

Case III. Maud believes herself to have the power of clairvoyance, though she has no reasons for this belief. She maintains her belief despite being inundated by her embarrassed friends and relatives with massive quantities of apparently cogent scientific evidence that no such power is possible. One day Maud comes to believe, for no apparent reason, that the President is in New York City, and she maintains this belief, despite the lack of any independent evidence appealing to her alleged clairvoyant power. Now in fact the President is in New York City, and Maud does, under the conditions then satisfied have completely reliable clairvoyant power. Moreover, her belief about the President did result from the operation of that power.

Again, Armstrong's criterion of reliability seems to be satisfied. But it also seems to me that Maud, like Casper, is not justified in her belief about the President and does not have knowledge. Maud has excellent reasons for thinking that no cognitive power such as she believes herself to possess is possible, and it is irrational and irresponsible of her to maintain her belief in that power in the face of that evidence and to continue to accept and maintain beliefs on this dubious basis.

Cases like these two suggest the need for a further modification of Armstrong's account: in addition to the law-like connection between belief and truth and the absence of any reasons against the particular belief in question, it must also be the case that the believer in question has no cogent reasons, either relative to his own case or in general, for thinking that such a law-like connection does *not* exist, i.e., that beliefs of that kind are not reliable.

IV

So far the modifications suggested for Armstrong's criterion are consistent with the basic thrust of externalism as a response to the regress problem. What emerges is in fact a significantly more plausible externalist position. But these cases and the modifications made in response to them also suggest an important moral which leads to a basic intuitive objection to externalism: external or objective reliability is not enough to offset subjective irrationality. If the acceptance of a belief is seriously unreasonable or unwarranted from the believer's own standpoint, then the mere fact that unbeknownst to the believer its existence in those circumstances lawfully guarantees its truth will not suffice to render the belief epistemically justified and thereby an instance of knowledge. So far we have been concerned only with situations in which the believer's subjective irrationality took the form of ignoring positive grounds in his possession for questioning either that specific belief or beliefs arrived at in that way. But now we must ask whether even in a case where these positive reasons for a charge of irrationality are not present, the acceptance of a belief where only an externalist justification is available cannot still be said to be subjectively irrational in a sense that rules out its being epistemically justified.

We may begin by considering one further case of clairvoyance, in which Armstrong's criterion with all the suggested modifications is satisfied:

Case IV. Norman, under certain conditions that usually obtain, is a completely reliable clairvoyant with respect to certain kinds of subject matter. He possesses no evidence or reasons of any kind for or against the general possibility of such a cognitive power, or for or against the thesis that he possesses it. One day Norman comes to believe that the President is in New York City, though he has no evidence either for or against this belief. In fact the belief is true and results from his clairvoyant power, under circumstances in which it is completely reliable.

Is Norman epistemically justified in believing that the President is in New York City, so that his belief is an instance of knowledge? According to the modified externalist position, we must apparently say that he is. But is this the right result? Are there not still sufficient grounds for a charge of subjective irrationality to prevent Norman's being epistemically justified?

One thing that might seem relevant to this issue, which I have deliberately omitted from the specification of the case, is whether Norman *believes* himself to have clairvoyant power, even though he has no justification for such a belief. Let us consider both possibilities. Suppose, first, that Norman does have such a belief and that it contributes to his acceptance of his original belief about the President's whereabouts in the sense that were Norman to become convinced that he did not have this power, he would also cease to accept the belief about the President.[13] But is it not obviously irrational, from an epistemic standpoint, for Norman to hold such a belief when he has no reasons at all for thinking that it is true or even for thinking that such a power is possible? This belief about his clairvoyance fails after all to possess even an externalist justification. And if we say that the belief about his clairvoyance is epistemically irrational and unjustified, must we not say the same thing about the belief about the President which *ex hypothesi* depends upon it?[14]

A possible response to this challenge would be to add one further condition to our modified externalist position, *viz.*, that the believer not even *believe* that the law-like connection in question obtains, since such a belief will not in general be justified (or at least that his continued acceptance of the particular belief that is at issue not depend on his acceptance of such a general belief). In our present case, this would mean that Norman must not believe that he has the power of clairvoyance (or at least that his acceptance of the belief about the President's whereabouts

13. This further supposition does not prevent the belief about the President's whereabouts from being non-inferential, since it is not in any useful sense Norman's reason for accepting that specific belief.
14. This is the basic objection to Dretske's version of externalism, mentioned above. Dretske's condition requires that one have an analogously unjustified (though true) belief about the reliability of one's perceptual belief.

not depend on his having such a general belief). But if this specification is added to the case, it now becomes more than a little puzzling to understand what Norman thinks is going on. From his standpoint, there is apparently no way in which he *could* know the President's whereabouts. Why then does he continue to maintain the belief that the President is in New York City? Why is not the mere fact that there is no way, as far as he knows or believes, for him to have obtained this information a sufficient reason for classifying this belief as an unfounded hunch and ceasing to accept it? And if Norman does not do this, is he not thereby being epistemically irrational and irresponsible?

For these reasons, I submit, Norman's acceptance of the belief about the President's whereabouts is epistemically irrational and irresponsible and thereby unjustified, whether or not he believes himself to have clairvoyant power so long as he has no justification for such a belief. Part of one's epistemic duty is to reflect critically upon one's beliefs, and such critical reflection precludes believing things to which one has, to one's knowledge, no reliable means of epistemic access.[15]

We are now face-to-face with the fundamental—and seemingly obvious—intuitive problem with externalism: *why* should the mere fact that such an external relation obtains mean that Norman's belief is epistemically justified, when the relation in question is entirely outside his ken? As remarked earlier, it is clear that one who knew that Armstrong's criterion was satisfied would be in a position to construct a simple and quite cogent justifying argument for the belief in question: if Norman has property H (being a completely reliable clairvoyant under the existing conditions and arriving at the belief on that basis), then he holds the belief in question only if it is true; Norman does have property H and does hold the belief in question; therefore, the belief is true. But Norman himself is by stipulation not in a position to employ this argument, and it is unclear why the mere fact that it is, so to speak, potentially available in the situation should justify *his* acceptance of the belief. Precisely what generates the regress problem in the first place, after all, is the requirement that for a belief to be justified for a particular person, not only is it necessary that there be true premises somehow available in the situation which could in principle provide a basis for a justification, but also that the believer in question know or at least justifiably believe some such set of premises and thus be in a position to employ the corresponding argument. The externalist position seems to amount merely to waiving this general requirement in a certain class of cases, and the question is why this should be acceptable in these cases when it is not acceptable generally. (If it were acceptable generally, then it seems likely that *any* true belief would be justified, unless some severe requirement is imposed as to how immediately available such premises must be. But any such requirement seems utterly arbitrary, once the natural one of actual access by the believer is abandoned.) Thus externalism looks like a purely *ad hoc* solution to the epistemic regress problem.

One reason why externalism may seem initially plausible is that if the external relation in question genuinely obtains, then Norman will in fact not go wrong in

---

15. The only apparent answer here would be to claim that the reasonable presumption is in favor of one's having such reliable means of access, unless there is good reason to the contrary. But it is hard to see why such a presumption should be thought reasonable.

accepting the belief, and it is, *in a sense*, not an accident that this is so. But how is this supposed to justify Norman's belief? From his subjective perspective, it is an accident that the belief is true. Of course, it would not be an accident from the standpoint of our hypothetical external observer who knows all the relevant facts and laws. Such an observer, having constructed the justifying argument sketched above, would be thereby in a position to justify *his own* acceptance of the belief. Thus Norman, as Armstrong's thermometer image suggests, could serve as a useful epistemic instrument for such an observer, a kind of cognitive thermometer; and it is to this fact, as we have seen, that Armstrong appeals in arguing that a belief like Norman's can be correctly said to be reasonable or justifiable. [183] [in this volume p. 85] But none of this seems in fact to justify Norman's *own* acceptance of the belief, for Norman, unlike the hypothetical external observer, has no reason at all for thinking that the belief is true. And the suggestion here is that the rationality or justifiability of Norman's belief should be judged from Norman's own perspective, rather than from one that is unavailable to him.[16]

This basic objection to externalism seems to me to be intuitively compelling. But it is sufficiently close to being simply a statement of what the externalist wants to deny to make it helpful to buttress it a bit by appealing to some related intuitions.

First, we may consider an analogy with moral philosophy. The same conflict between perspectives which we have seen to arise in the process of epistemic assessment can also arise with regard to the moral assessment of a person's action: the agent's subjective conception of what he is doing may differ dramatically from that which would in principle be available to an external observer who had access to facts about the situation that are beyond the agent's ken. And now we can imagine an approximate moral analogue of externalism which would hold that the moral justifiability of an agent's action was, in certain cases at least, properly to be determined from the external perspective, entirely irrespective of the agent's own conception of the situation.

Consider first the moral analogue of Armstrong's original, unmodified version of externalism. If we assume, purely for the sake of simplicity, a utilitarian moral theory, such a view would say that an action might on occasion be morally justified simply in virtue of the fact that in the situation then obtaining, it would as a matter of objective fact lead to the best overall consequences—even if the agent planned and anticipated that it would lead to very different, perhaps extremely undesirable, consequences. But such a view seems plainly mistaken. There is no doubt a

16. Mark Pastin, in a critical study of Armstrong, has suggested that ascriptions of knowledge depend on the epistemic situation of the ascriber rather than on that of the ascribee at this point, so that I am correct in ascribing knowledge to Norman so long as *I* know that his belief is reliable (and hence also that the other conditions of knowledge are satisfied), even if Norman does not. But I can see no very convincing rationale for this claim. See Pastin, 'Knowledge and Reliability: A Study of D. M. Armstrong's *Belief, Truth and Knowledge*,' *Metaphilosophy* 9 (1978): 150–62. Notice further that if the epistemic regress problem is in general to be dealt with along externalist lines, then my knowledge that Norman's belief is reliable would depend on the epistemic situation of a further external observer, who ascribes knowledge to me. And similarly for the knowledge of that observer, etc., *ad infinitum*. I do not know whether this regress of external observers is vicious, but it seems clearly to deprive the appeal to such an observer of any value as a practical criterion.

point to the objective, external assessment: we can say correctly that it turns out to be objectively a good thing that the agent performed the action. But this is not at all inconsistent with saying that his action was morally unjustified and reprehensible, given his subjective conception of the likely consequences.

Thus our envisaged moral externalism must at least be modified in a way that parallels the modifications earlier suggested for epistemological externalism. Without attempting to make the analogy exact, it will suffice for our present purposes to add to the original requirement for moral justification, *viz.*, that the action will in fact lead to the best overall consequences, the further condition that the agent not believe or intend that it lead to undesirable consequences. Since it is also, of course, not required by moral externalism that the agent believe that the action will lead to good consequences, the sort of case we are now considering is one in which an agent acts in a way that will in fact produce the best overall consequences, but has *no belief at all* about the likely consequences of his action. Although such an agent is no doubt preferable to one who acts in the belief that his action will lead to undesirable consequences, surely he is not morally justified in what he does. On the contrary, he is being highly irresponsible, from a moral standpoint, in performing the action in the absence of any evaluation of what will result from it. His moral duty, from our assumed utilitarian standpoint, is to do what will lead to the best consequences, but this duty is not satisfied by the fact that he produces this result willy-nilly, without any idea that he is doing so.[17] And similarly, the fact that a given sort of belief is objectively reliable, and thus that accepting it is in fact conducive to arriving at the truth, need not prevent our judging that the epistemic agent who accepts it without any inkling that this is the case violates his epistemic duty and is epistemically irresponsible and unjustified in doing so.

Second, we may appeal to the connection between knowledge and rational action. Suppose that Norman, in addition to the clairvoyant belief described earlier also believes that the Attorney-General is in Chicago. This latter belief, however, is not a clairvoyant belief but is based upon ordinary empirical evidence in Norman's possession, evidence strong enough to give the belief some fairly high degree of reasonableness, but *not* strong enough to satisfy the requirement for knowledge.[18] Suppose further that Norman finds himself in a situation where he is forced to bet

17. Of course there are cases in which one must act, even though one has no adequate knowledge of the likely consequences; and one might attempt to defend epistemic externalism by arguing that in epistemic contexts the analogous situation *always* obtains. But there are several problems with such a response. First, to simply assume that this is always so seems to be question-begging, and the externalist can argue for this claim only by refuting all alternatives to his position. Second, notice that in ethical contexts this situation usually, perhaps always, obtains only when not acting will lead definitely to bad consequences, not just to the failure to obtain good ones; and there seems to be no parallel to this in the epistemic case. Third, and most important, the justification for one's action in such a case would depend not on the external fact, if it is a fact, that the action leads to good consequences, but simply on the fact that one could do no better, given the unfortunate state of one's knowledge; thus this position would not be genuinely a version of moral externalism, and analogously for the epistemic case.

18. I am assuming here, following Chisholm, that knowledge requires a degree of justification stronger than that required to make a belief merely reasonable.

a very large amount, perhaps even his life or the life of someone else, on the whereabouts of either the President or the Attorney-General. Given his epistemic situation as described, which bet is it more reasonable for him to make? It seems relatively clear that it is more reasonable for him to bet the Attorney-General is in Chicago than to bet that the President is in New York City. But then we have the paradoxical result that from the externalist standpoint it is more rational to act on a merely reasonable belief than to act on one that is adequately justifed to qualify as knowledge (and which in fact *is* knowledge). It is very hard to see how this could be so. If greater epistemic reasonableness does not carry with it greater reasonableness of action, then it becomes most difficult to see why it should be sought in the first place. (Of course, the externalist could simply bite the bullet and insist that it is in fact more reasonable for Norman to bet on the President's whereabouts than the Attorney-General's, but such a view seems very implausible.)

I have been attempting in this section to articulate the fundamental intuition about epistemic rationality, and rationality generally, that externalism seems to violate. This intuition the externalist would of course reject, and thus my discussion does not constitute a refutation of the externalist position on its own ground. Nevertheless it seems to me to have sufficient intuitive force at least to place the burden of proof squarely on the externalist. In the final section of the paper, I shall consider briefly some of the responses that seem to be available to him.

V

One possible defense for the externalist in the face of the foregoing intuitive objection would be to narrow his position by restricting it to those commonsensical varieties of non-inferential knowledge which are his primary concern, *viz.*, sense-perception and introspection, thereby rendering the cases set forth above strictly irrelevant. Such a move seems, however, utterly *ad hoc*. Admittedly it is more difficult to construct intuitively compelling counterexamples involving sense-perception and introspection, mainly because our intuitions that beliefs of those kinds are in fact warranted in *some* way or other are very strong. But this does nothing to establish that the externalist account of their warrant is the correct one. Thus unless the externalist can give some positive account of why the same conclusion that seems to hold for non-standard cases like clairvoyance does not also hold for sense-perception and introspection, this narrowing of his position seems to do him no good.

If the externalist cannot escape the force of the objection in this way, can he perhaps balance it with positive arguments in favor of his position? Many attempts to argue for externalism are in effect arguments by elimination and depend on the claim that alternative accounts of empirical knowledge are unacceptable, either because they cannot solve the regress problem or for some other reason. Most such arguments, depending as they do on a detailed consideration of the alternatives, are beyond the scope of the present paper. But one such argument depends only on very general features of the competing positions and thus can usefully be considered here.

The basic factual premise of this argument is that in very many cases that are commonsensically instances of justified belief and of knowledge, there seem to be no justifying factors explicitly present beyond those appealed to by the externalist. An ordinary person in such a case may have no idea at all of the character of his immediate experience, of the coherence of his system of beliefs, etc., and yet may still have knowledge. Alternative theories, so the argument goes, may describe correctly cases of knowledge involving a knower who is extremely reflective and sophisticated, but they are obviously too demanding and too grandiose when applied to these more ordinary cases. In these cases, *only* the externalist condition is satisfied, and this shows that no more than that is necessary for justification and for knowledge, though more might still be epistemically desirable.

Although the precise extent to which it holds could be disputed, in the main this factual premise must be simply conceded. Any non-externalist account of empirical knowledge that has any plausibility will impose standards for justification which very many beliefs that seem commonsensically to be cases of knowledge fail to meet in any full and explicit fashion. And thus on such a view, such beliefs will not *strictly speaking* be instances of adequate justification and of knowledge. But it does not follow that externalism must be correct. This would follow only with the addition of the premise that the judgments of common sense in this area are sacrosanct, that any departure from them is enough to demonstrate that a theory of knowledge is inadequate. But such a premise seems entirely too strong. There seems in fact to be no basis for more than a reasonably strong presumption in favor of the correctness of common sense, but one which is still quite defeasible. And what it would take to defeat this presumption depends in part on how great a departure from common sense is being advocated. Thus, although it would take very strong grounds to justify a very strong form of skepticism, not nearly so much would be required to make acceptable the view that what common sense regards as cases of justification and of knowledge are in fact only rough approximations to an epistemic ideal which *strictly speaking* they do not satisfy.

Of course, a really adequate reply to the externalist would have to spell out in some detail the precise way in which such beliefs really do approximately satisfy some acceptable alternative standard, a task which obviously cannot be attempted here. But even without such elaboration, it seems reasonable to conclude that this argument in favor of externalism fails to carry very much weight as it stands and would require serious buttressing in order to give it any chance of offsetting the intuitive objection to externalism: either the advocacy and defense of a quite strong presumption in favor of common sense, or a detailed showing that alternative theories cannot in fact grant to the cases favored by common sense even the status of approximations to justification and to knowledge.

The other pro-externalist argument I want to consider does not depend in any important way on consideration of alternative positions. This argument is hinted at by Armstrong [185–8], among others, but I know of no place where it is developed very explicitly. Its basic claim is that only an externalist theory can handle a certain version of the lottery paradox.

The lottery paradox is standardly formulated as a problem confronting accounts of inductive logic that contain a rule of acceptance or detachment, but we shall be concerned here with a somewhat modified version. This version arises when we ask how much or what degree of epistemic justification is required for a belief to qualify as knowledge, given that the other necessary conditions for knowledge are satisfied. Given the intimate connection, discussed earlier, between epistemic justification and likelihood of truth, it seems initially reasonable to take likelihood or probability of truth as a measure of the degree of epistemic justification, and thus to interpret the foregoing question as asking how likely or probable it must be, relative to the justification of one's belief, that the belief be true, in order for that belief to satisfy the justification requirement for knowledge. Most historical theories of knowledge tended to answer that knowledge requires *certainty* of truth, relative to one's justification. But more recent epistemological views have tended to reject this answer, for familiar reasons, and to hold instead that knowledge requires only a reasonably high likelihood of truth. And now, if this high likelihood of truth is interpreted in the obvious way as meaning that, relative to one's justification, the numerical probability that one's belief is true must equal or exceed some fixed value, the lottery paradox at once rears its head.

Suppose, for example, that we decide that a belief is adequately justified to satisfy the requirement for knowledge if the probability of its truth, relative to its justification, is 0.99 or greater. Imagine now that a lottery is to be held, about which we know the following facts: exactly 100 tickets have been sold, the drawing will indeed be held, it will be a fair drawing, and there will be only one winning ticket. Consider now each of the 100 propositions of the form:

Ticket number *n* will lose

where *n* is replaced by the number of one of the tickets, Since there are 100 tickets and only one winner, the probability of each such proposition is 0.99; and hence if we believe each of them, our individual beliefs will be adequately justified to satisfy the requirement for knowledge. And then, given only the seemingly reasonable assumptions, first, that if one has adequate justification for believing each of a set of propositions, one also has adequate justification for believing the conjunction of the members of the set, and, second, that if one has adequate justification for believing a proposition, one also has adequate justification for believing any further proposition entailed by the first proposition, it follows that we are adequately justified in believing that no ticket will win, contradicting our other information.

Clearly this is a mistaken result, but how is it to be avoided? In the first place, it will plainly do no good to simply increase the level of numerical probability required for adequate justification. For no matter how high it is raised, short of certainty, it will obviously be possible to duplicate the paradoxical result by simply choosing a large enough lottery. Nor do the standard responses to the lottery paradox, whatever their merits may be in dealing with other versions of the paradox, seem to be of much help here. Most of them are ruled out simply by insisting that we do know that empirical propositions are true, not merely that they are probable, and that such knowledge is not in general relative to particular contexts of inquiry. This leaves only the possibility of avoiding the paradoxical result by rejecting the two assumptions stated in the preceding paragraph. But this would be extremely implausible—involving in effect a denial that one may always justifiably deduce conclusions from one's putative knowledge—and in any case would still leave the intuitively unacceptable result that one could on this basis come to know separately the 99 true propositions about various tickets losing (though not of course the false one). In fact, it seems intuitively clear that I do not *know* any of these propositions to be true: if I own one of the tickets, I do not know that it will lose, even if in fact it will, and would not know no matter how large the total number of tickets might be.

At this stage, it may seem that the only way to avoid the paradox is to return to the traditional idea that any degree of probability or likelihood of truth less than certainty is insufficient for knowledge, that only certainty, relative to one's justification, will suffice. The standard objection to such a view is that it seems to lead at once to the skeptical conclusion that we have little or no empirical knowledge. For it seems quite clear that there are no empirical beliefs, with the possible and extremely problematic exception of beliefs about one's own mental states, for which we have justification adequate to exclude all possibility of error. Such a solution seems as bad as the original problem.

It is at this point that externalism may seem to offer a way out. For an externalist position allows one to hold that the justification of an empirical belief must make it certain that the belief is true, while still escaping the clutches of skepticism. This is so precisely because the externalist justification need not be within the cognitive grasp of the believer or indeed of anyone. It need only be true that there is *some* description of the believer, however complex and practically unknowable it may be, which, together with *some* true law of nature, ensures the truth of the belief. Thus, e.g., my perceptual belief that there is a cup on my desk is not certain, on any view, relative to the evidence or justification that is in my possession; I might be hallucinating or there might be an evil demon who is deceiving me. But it seems reasonable to suppose that if the belief is indeed true, then there is *some* external description of me and my situation and *some* true law of nature, relative to which the truth of the belief is guaranteed, and if so it would satisfy the requirement for knowledge.

In some ways, this is a neat and appealing solution to the paradox. Nonetheless, it seems doubtful that it is ultimately satisfactory. In the first place, there is surely something intuitively fishy about solving the problem by appealing to an in-principle guarantee of truth which will almost certainly in practice be available to no one. A second problem, which cannot be elaborated here, is that insisting on this sort of solution seems likely to create insuperable difficulties for knowledge of general and theoretical propositions. But in any case, the externalist solution seems to yield intuitively incorrect results in certain kinds of cases. A look at one of these may also suggest the beginnings of a more satisfactory solution.

Consider then the following case:

Case V. Agatha, seated at her desk, believes herself to be perceiving a cup on the desk. She also knows, however, that she is one of a group of 100 people who have been selected for a philosophical experiment by a Cartesian evil demon. The conditions have been so arranged that all 100 will at this particular time seem to themselves to be perceiving a cup upon their respective desks, with no significant differences in the subjective character of their respective experiences. But in fact, though 99 of the people will be perceiving a cup in the normal way, the last one will be caused by the demon to have a complete hallucination (including perceptual conditions, etc.) of a non-existent cup. Agatha knows all this, but she does not have any further information as to whether she is the one who is hallucinating, though as it happens she is not.

Is Agatha epistemically justified in her belief that there is a cup on the desk and does she know this to be so? According to the externalist view, we must say that she is justified and does know. For there is, we may assume, an external description of Agatha and her situation relative to which it is nomologically certain that her belief is true. (Indeed, according to Armstrong's original, unmodified view, she would be justified and would know even if she also knew instead that 99 of the 100 persons were being deceived by the demon, so long as she was in fact the odd one who was perceiving normally.) But this result is, I submit, intuitively mistaken. If Agatha knows that she is perceiving a cup, then she also knows that she is not the one who is being deceived. But she does not know this, for reasons that parallel those operative in the lottery case.

Is there then no way out of the paradox? The foregoing case and others like it seem to me to suggest the following approach to at least the present version of the paradox, though I can offer only an exceedingly brief sketch here. Intuitively, what the lottery case and the case of Agatha have in common is the presence of a large number of relevantly similar, alternative possibilities, all individually very unlikely, but such that the person in question *knows* that at least one of them will in fact be realized. In such a case, since there is no relevant way of distinguishing among these possibilities, the person cannot believe with adequate justification and *a fortiori* cannot know that any particular possibility will not be realized, even though the probability that it will not be realized maybe made as high as one likes by simply increasing the total number of possibilities. Such cases do show that high probability is not by itself enough to satisfy the justification condition for knowledge. They do not show, however, that certainty is required instead. For what rules out knowledge in such a case is not merely the fact that the probability of truth is less than certainty but also the fact that the person *knows* that at least one of these highly probable propositions is false. It is a necessary condition for justification and for knowledge that this not be so. But there are many cases in which a person's justification for a belief fails to make it certain that the belief is true, but in which the person also does not know that some possible situation in which the belief would be false is one of a set of relevantly similar, alternative possibilities, at least one of which will definitely be realized. And in such a case, the lottery paradox provides no reason to think that the person does not know.[19]

An example may help to make this point clear. Consider again my apparent

19. I do not, alas, have any real account to offer here of the notion of *relevant similarity*. Roughly, the idea is that two possibilities are relevantly similar if there is no known difference between them that has a bearing on the likelihood that they will be realized. But this will not quite do. For consider a lottery case in which there are two tickets bearing each even number and only one for each odd number. Intuitively, it seems to me, this difference does not prevent all the tickets, odd and even, from being relevantly similar, despite the fact that it is twice as likely that an even ticket will be drawn.

perception of the cup on my desk. I think that I do in fact know that there is a cup there. But the justification that is in my possession surely does not make it certain that my belief is true. Thus, for example, it seems to be possible, relative to my subjective justification, that I am being deceived by an evil demon, who is causing me to have a hallucinatory experience of the cup, together with accompanying conditions of perception. But it does not follow from this that I do not know that there is a cup on the desk, because it does not follow and I do not know that there is some class of relevantly similar cases in at least one of which a person is in fact deceived by such a demon. Although it is only probable and not certain that there is no demon, it is still possible for all I *know* that never in the history of the universe, past, present, or future, is there a case in which someone in a relevantly similar situation is actually deceived by such a demon. And as far as I can see, the same thing is true of all the other ways in which it is possible that my belief might be mistaken. If this is so, then the lottery paradox provides no obstacle to my knowledge in this case.[20]

This response to the lottery paradox seems to me to be on the right track. It must be conceded, however, that it is in considerable need of further development and may turn out to have problems of its own. But that is a subject for another paper.[21]

There is one other sort of response, mentioned briefly above, which the externalist might make to the sorts of criticisms developed in this paper. I want to remark on it briefly, though a full-scale discussion is impossible here. In the end it may be possible to make intuitive sense of externalism only by construing the externalist as simply abandoning the traditional idea of epistemic justification or rationality and along with it anything resembling the traditional conception of knowledge. I have already mentioned that this may be precisely what the proponents of externalism intend to be doing, though most of them are anything but clear on this point.[22]

20. But if this account is correct, I may still fail to know in many other cases in which common sense would say fairly strongly that I do. E.g., do I know that my house has not burned down since I left it this morning? Ordinarily we are inclined to say that we do know such things. But if it is true, as it might well be, that I also know that of the class of houses relevantly similar to mine, at least one will burn down at some point, then I do not, on the present account, *know* that my house has not burned down, however improbable such a catastrophe may be. (On the other hand, knowledge would not be ruled out by the present principle simply because I knew that certain specific similar houses, *other than mine*, have in the past burned down or even that they will in the future burn down. For I know, *ex hypothesi*, that my house is not one of those. The force of the principle depends on my knowing that at least one possibility *which might for all I know be the one I am interested in* will be realized, not just on descriptively similar possibilities being realized.)

21. This response to the lottery paradox derives in part from discussions with C. Anthony Anderson.

22. The clearest example of such a position is in Goldman's paper 'Discrimination and Perceptual Knowledge,' [Ch. 8 in this volume] cited above, where he rejects what he calls 'Cartesian-style justification' as a requirement for perceptual knowledge, in favor of an externalist account. He goes on to remark, however, that one could use the term 'justification' in such a way that satisfaction of his externalist conditions 'counts as justification,' though a kind of justification 'entirely different from the sort of justification demanded by Cartesianism' (p. 790) [in this volume p. 101]. What is unclear is whether this is supposed to be a purely verbal possibility, which would then be of little interest, or whether it is supposed to connect with something like the concept of epistemic rationality explicated in section I. Thus it is uncertain whether Goldman means to repudiate the whole idea of epistemic rationality, or only some more limited view such as the doctrine of the given (reference to which provides his only explanation of what he means by 'Cartesianism' in epistemology).

Against an externalist position that seriously adopts such a gambit, the criticisms developed in the present paper are of course entirely ineffective. If the externalist does not want even to claim that beliefs satisfying his conditions are epistemically justified or reasonable, then it is obviously no objection that they seem in some cases to be quite unjustified and unreasonable. But, as already noted, such a view, though it may possess some sort of appeal, constitutes a solution to the epistemic regress problem or to any problem arising out of the traditional conception of knowledge only in the radical and relatively uninteresting sense that to reject that conception entirely is also, of course, to reject any problems arising out of it. Such 'solutions' would seem to be available for any philosophical problem at all, but it is hard to see why they should be taken seriously.

Chapter 15

A rationale for reliabilism

Kent Bach

W<small>HAT</small> bothers people about reliabilism as a theory of justified belief? It as yet to be formulated adequately, but most philosophical theories have that problem. People seem to be bothered by the very idea of reliabilism, with its apparent disregard for believers' rationality and responsibility. Yet its supporters can't seem to understand its opponents' complaints. I believe that the conflict can be clarified, if not resolved, by drawing certain important distinctions. Indeed the fundamental distinction, about justification itself, suggests that the two sides are not really talking about the same thing. After drawing these distinctions, I will offer some positive suggestions about the relation of reasoning to reliability. These suggestions will depend on a certain conception of the nature of reasoning itself. The conception I will sketch departs dramatically from common philosophical views but is akin to the notion of *default reasoning* currently influential in Artificial Intelligence.

1. Some preliminary distinctions

I am concerned with reliabilism only as a theory of justified belief. Originally, as with David Armstrong's and Alvin Goldman's versions,[1] reliabilism was a theory of knowledge. *Epistemological* reliabilism was designed to solve the Gettier problem not by augmenting but by replacing the justification condition in the traditional analysis of knowledge as justified true belief. The problem was to find a suitable conception of reliability. Armstrong's conception, for example, was too strong, seeming to entail that a reliably formed belief must be true. At any rate, it wasn't long before reliabilism took the form of a theory of justified belief itself, thanks mainly to Marshall Swain and again to Goldman.[2] The idea, roughly, is that to be justified a belief must be formed as the result of reliable processes,[3] where now

Kent Bach, 'A Rationale for Reliabilism' in *The Monist* 68 (1985), pp. 246–63 reprinted by permission of The Hegeler Institute.

1. D. M. Armstrong, *Belief, Truth, and Knowledge* (London: Cambridge University Press, 1973); Alvin I. Goldman, 'Discrimination and Perceptual Knowledge,' *Journal of Philosophy* 73 (1976): 771–91 [Ch. 8 in this volume].
2. Marshall Swain, 'Justification and Reliable Belief,' *Philosophical Studies* 40 (1981) 389–407; Alvin I. Goldman, 'What Is Justified Belief?,' in George S. Pappas, ed., *Justification and Knowledge* (Dordrecht, Holland: D. Reidel, 1979), pp. 1–23.
3. Swain presents his view as the 'reliable indicator' theory of justified belief, and his formulations strongly suggest that reliability is to be predicated of individual beliefs, but he does maintain that being a reliable indicator just is being the result of a reliable process (p. 405). However, Swain's formulation, which I will not take up here, is quite different in detail from Goldman's.

reliability does not entail truth. I take it that what is under dispute today is *justificational* reliabilism, and hereafter that is what I will mean by 'reliabilism.'

The difference between epistemological and justificational reliabilism has been obscured, I suspect, by an ambiguity in the notion of reliability itself, at least insofar as it is understood, as it often is, in terms of the notion of relevant alternatives. On that understanding, a process is reliable not just if it generally leads to true beliefs but only if it generally results in the ruling out of all relevant alternatives. The trouble is that what counts as a relevant alternative depends on whether we are talking about knowledge or merely about justified belief. So there are really two different notions of relevance involved here, but in the literature these are not explicitly distinguished. A *justificationally relevant* alternative is one that must be ruled out if a belief is to be justified, while an *epistemologically relevant* alternative must be ruled out if a justified (and true) belief is to qualify as knowledge. In other words, JRA's but not ERA's are alternatives that, under the circumstances, one has reason to consider.[4] No alternative can be both an ERA and a JRA in the same situation, and so the difference between the two must be kept in mind when the notion of relevant alternatives is invoked to explicate reliabilism of either sort, justificational or epistemological.

There is also confusion about the notion of justification that reliabilism is supposed to explicate. People on both sides of the dispute assume that this is not the traditional notion. Mark Pastin, for example, calls it a 'nouveau-justification or justification-surrogate concept.'[5] And Goldman seems to agree when he says he is not retracting his earlier view, the aforementioned version of epistemological reliabilism, on which justification is not necessary for knowledge. He insists that he then meant classical, 'Cartesian' accounts of justification and that in now maintaining that justified belief is necessary for knowledge, he means justified belief as understood in reliabilist terms.[6] Pastin and Goldman both view the traditional notion of justified belief as inherently regulative, hence as not explicable by the obviously descriptive notion of reliability. Thus they do not regard reliabilism as an account of the traditional notion. However, as I will suggest, reliabilism is a nontraditional

4. For example, if there appears to be a sleeping hippopotamus on your front lawn, before believing that one is there you have reason, considering you don't live in a hippo habitat, to rule out the JRA's that a stuffed, papier-mache, or robot hippo is out there. But if there appeared to be a puppy on your front lawn, normally you would have no reason to consider the analogous alternatives. They would be JRA's only if you believed or had evidence that there were stuffed, papier-mache, or robot puppies around. But such an alternative could still be an ERA. For example, if Martians had placed some lifelike puppy robots in the neighborhood and you were unaware of this and had no reason to suspect it, you would not know that there is a puppy on your lawn even if you justifiably believed this and were in fact looking at a real puppy. In the circumstances, knowing this would require ruling out the ERA that what you are looking at is a robot. However, you have no reason to rule it out—it is not a JRA.

5. Mark Pastin, 'The Multi-Perspectival Theory of Knowledge,' *Midwest Studies in Philosophy* 5 (1980): 97–111, p. 97.

6. 'What Is Justified Belief?,' p. 1. In 'The Internalist Conception of Justification,' *Midwest Studies in Philosophy* 5 (1980): 27–51, Goldman remarks that many epistemologists have '[mistakenly] assumed that a regulative notion of justification is the same notion of justification as the one that appears in the analysis of propositional knowledge' (p. 29).

account of the traditional notion, insofar as this is the notion that figures in the traditional definition of knowledge as justified true belief.

2. Two conceptions of justified belief

Be that as it may, there surely are two conceptions of justified belief involved in the debate, the *internalist* and the *externalist* conceptions. Laurence BonJour has contrasted them nicely.[7] Internalism requires that a person have 'cognitive grasp' of whatever makes his belief justified. Being justified depends on how rational and 'epistemically responsible' (whatever these mean precisely) he is in coming to hold the belief. In contrast, the externalist (reliabilist) conception allows that the source of justification can be 'external to the person's subjective conception of the situation.' On this conception epistemic rationality/responsibility is neither sufficient nor even necessary for justified belief. Since a believer can reasonably and responsibly rely on false principles it is not sufficient. It is not necessary because certain beliefs, such as perceptual and introspective beliefs, can be justified even though for them the question of rationality/responsibility generally does not arise.

Put most simply, externalism is simply the denial of internalism. But it can be put more informatively, if tendentiously, as holding that being justified is that property, whatever it may be, which a true, 'ungettiered' belief must possess in order to qualify as knowledge. Put in this way it is not explicitly committed to denying that justifiedness is regulative but leaves that question open. Still, the externalist conception of justified belief does *seem* descriptive, whereas the internalist conception is explicitly regulative.[8]

3. Arguments against reliabilism

Intuitively, what seems right about internalism is the idea that the epistemic merit of a belief depends on the performance of the person who arrived at it. Just as we do not downgrade an action because it has unforeseeable bad consequences, so we

---

7. Laurence BonJour, 'Externalist Theories of Empirical Knowledge,' *Midwest Studies in Philosophy*, 5 (1980): 53–73, p. 55 [in this volume p. 180].

8. Note that the issue here is not the proper *standards* of justification. Internalism may require that what makes a belief justified be available to the believer, but it does not insist that a justified belief be certain, much less true. Like Descartes, BonJour and most contemporary internalists accept the first condition on justified belief, but unlike Descartes they reject the second. They recognize that justification is fallible: a belief does not have to be true to be justified. This point is relevant here, since the infallibilist conception of justified belief rules out the possibility of Gettier examples, contrary to what both externalists and most internalists take for granted. Gettier examples are justified true beliefs that qualify as knowledge in one situation but not in another, though justified in the same way. By Cartesian standards a belief can qualify as knowledge only if completely or conclusively justified, so that it is certain and cannot be false. As the infallibilist Robert Almeder argues in 'The Invalidity of Gettier-type Counterexamples,' *Philosophia* 13 (1983): 67–74, any putative Gettier example is incompletely justified, since there is always some relevant feature of the situation that the justification of the (true) belief must have failed to take into account.

do not downgrade a belief because it is based on something that the believer had no reason to question. We assess his rationality and responsibility in forming the belief. Innocent ignorance does not change the assessment. This can be seen, the internalist argues, by comparing two subjectively identical situations in which a person forms the same belief on the basis of the same supposition, but such that the supposition is true in one situation but false in the other. The internalist would hold that the two beliefs are equally justified.

How can the externalist answer this internalist argument? Suppose that the pair of situations just described make up a Gettier example, so that in both situations the belief in question is true and justified. Then in the first situation the belief would qualify as knowledge, since it is based on a true supposition, whereas in the second the belief would not so qualify, since the supposition is false. Now recall that for the externalist being justified is whatever property an 'ungettiered' true belief must have to qualify as knowledge. Besides the difference in truth value between the two underlying suppositions, which seems irrelevant to questions of justification, there is no difference in the justifications for the two beliefs. So must not the externalist grant that the belief is just as justified in the second situation as it is in the first?

However, the externalist must concede this point only if the supposition in question is specific in content. For only then could it, if false, 'gettier' a justified true belief. If the false supposition were a broad generalization (or a general principle), the externalist would insist that reasoning which relies on it not only could not give one knowledge but could not, no matter how rational and responsible the agent, yield justified beliefs.[9] Any true, rationally/responsibly acquired belief based on some false generalization fails to qualify as knowledge but not because it has been gettiered. It is not the situation that keeps the belief from qualifying. The culprit is the falsity of the supporting generalization, not its local inapplicability. Thus it seems that the real conflict between internalism and externalism concerns whether there is an empirical side to what it is for a belief to be justified. Clearly internalism cannot allow that beliefs formed rationally and responsibly can fail to be justified because they are based on what is in fact a false generalization. Later I will try to resolve this conflict by suggesting that even though relying on a false generalization cannot give one justified beliefs, one can be justified in so doing.

In perhaps the most thoroughgoing critique of externalism to date, Laurence BonJour'[10] charges it with violating the requirement that 'beliefs that are to constitute knowledge must be epistemically . . . justified . . . meaning roughly that the

9. Here the internalist might invoke the alleged distinction between 'objectively' and 'subjectively' justified beliefs and say that his argument, indeed his very conception of justification, applies only to subjectively justified beliefs. The trouble is, however, that this distinction is bogus. Subjectively 'justified' beliefs that are not 'objectively' justified are reasonable or 'excusable,' as Goldman puts it ('The Internalist Conception of Justification,' pp. 37–8), but that does not make them genuinely justified, any more than two lines that are 'subjectively equal' (i.e., look equal) because of an optical illusion, are genuinely equal.

10. In 'Externalist Theories of Empirical Knowledge.' In what follows the page references to BonJour are to this article.

acceptance of the belief must be epistemically rational, that it must not be epistemically irresponsible' (p. 53 [in this volume p. 178]). He maintains that any belief meeting this requirement must be based on 'a justificatory argument,' hence be 'inferentially justified' by other beliefs.

This requirement implausibly rules out noninferential or 'basic beliefs,' since those beliefs are not justified on the basis of other beliefs. Yet BonJour cheerfully concedes this, as in the context of his diagnosis of the strategy behind externalism (reliabilism in particular). Taking it to be foundationalist as opposed to coherentist, BonJour views it as designed to avoid the 'epistemic regress of justification' by 'locating a class of empirical beliefs whose justification does not depend on that of other empirical beliefs' (p. 53 [in this volume p. 178]). The problem is that noninferentially justified beliefs obviously cannot meet the justification requirement mentioned above. There must be something that makes them justified, but it cannot be necessary for the believer himself to recognize this feature and take it to make the belief justified. For that would render the 'belief not basic after all, since its justification depends on that of these other beliefs' (p. 55 [in this volume p. 180]). So if externalism is to solve the regress problem, 'though there must in a sense be a reason why a basic belief is likely to be true, the person for whom such a belief is basic need not have any cognitive grasp of this reason' (p. 55 [in this volume p. 180]). BonJour goes on to give an example, which I will consider later, designed to bring out 'the fundamental intuition about epistemic rationality that externalism seems to violate,' hoping if not to refute externalism then at least 'to shift the burden of proof decisively to the externalist' (p. 56 [in this volume p. 181]).

Unfortunately, BonJour has not shifted the burden. As he himself admits,

Any non-externalist account of empirical knowledge that has any plausibility will impose standards for justification which very many beliefs that seem commonsensically to be cases of knowledge fail to meet in any full and explicit fashion. And thus on such a view, such beliefs will not strictly speaking be instances of adequate justification and of knowledge. But it does not follow that externalism must be correct. This would follow only with the addition of the premise that the judgments of common sense in this area are sacrosanct, that any departure from them is enough to demonstrate that a theory of knowledge is inadequate. (p. 66 [in this volume p. 193])

However, BonJour is well aware that according to foundationalism, basic beliefs 'provide the foundation upon which the edifice of empirical knowledge rests' (p. 54 [in this volume p. 179]). Therefore, if he is going to deny that they really are justified and really do provide such a foundation, he needs to defend coherentism, something he does not do. Until he does that, he has not shifted the burden of proof to the externalist.

Moreover, BonJour should distinguish *epistemologically basic* from *psychologically basic* beliefs. A belief is epistemologically basic if it is justified without any support from the believer's other beliefs; it is psychologically basic if not actually inferred from other beliefs. Clearly a belief can be psychologically basic without being epistemologically basic (the converse seems false). Perhaps there are no epistemologically basic beliefs (at least no empirical ones) but plenty of psychologically basic ones, such as ordinary memory and perceptual beliefs. This would be so if any belief formed without inference from other beliefs could conceivably be disconfirmed by others that were brought to bear against it. In particular, as my proposed conception of reasoning will suggest, psychologically basic beliefs can result from processes that occur only if not blocked by other processes that reliably lead to the occurrence of thoughts of reasons against the belief.

The point of mentioning the distinction between epistemologically and psychologically basic beliefs is that the reliabilist does not have to regard beliefs that are merely psychologically basic as 'sacrosanct.' It is enough that they generally be justified, i.e., have what it takes generally to qualify as knowledge. Even if they are not formed by inference from other beliefs, their justification could still depend on other beliefs. So I think BonJour is wrong to assume that externalism must be motivated by the foundationalist need to escape the epistemic regress. Indeed, if justifiedness is ultimately to be explained in coherentist terms, reliabilism is a solution to a different epistemic regress problem, a problem that internalism cannot solve. This is the problem of justifying everything on which our purportedly justified beliefs depend. Internalism cannot solve it because it treats justifiedness as a purely internal matter: if p is justified for S, then S must be aware (or at least be immediately capable of being aware) of what makes it justified and why. Reliabilism requires no such thing. Instead, it requires only that the generalizations and principles that cognitive processes follow be true in order for the beliefs that result from these processes to be justified and, if true and ungettiered, to qualify as knowledge.

4. Justified Beliefs and Justified Believers

Curiously enough, some internalists and some externalists allow that theirs is not the only legitimate conception of justification. For example, Hilary Kornblith, an internalist, acknowledges that his notion of justified belief as a product of epistemically responsible action is not the only legitimate notion of justified belief.[11] And Goldman the externalist distinguishes between 'theoretical and regulative justification principles.'[12] Regulative principles are for epistemic agents to follow; theoretical principles are for epistemologists to discover. Of course, this distinction would be trivial if it turned out that for every valid regulative principle there is a corresponding theoretical principle, namely one asserting the validity of the regulative principle, but clearly Goldman would reject such a suggestion outright.[13] At any

11. Hilary Kornblith, 'Justified Belief and Epistemically Responsible Action,' *Philosophical Review* 92 (1983): 33–48.
12. 'The Internalist Conception of Justification,' p. 28.
13. Goldman does not argue explicitly against this correspondence, but his rejection of it is evident from the nontrivial differences between the various plausible principles of each sort that he examines. It seems to me that a decisive reason for rejecting the correspondence claim is that the same theoretical principles can dictate different regulative principles in different sorts of worlds. For example, a source of error that is worth taking into account in one world might not be worth bothering with in another, save for some special reason for considering it. Moreover, which regulative principles are validated by the theoretical principles may depend on how and how well the cognitive processes to be regulated actually work.

rate, I believe there to be a distinction that provides a place for principles of both sorts and, further, that captures the difference between the internalist and externalist conceptions of justification.

I propose that we distinguish between a person being justified in holding a belief and the belief itself being justified. What makes a person justified in holding a belief resides in the quality of his epistemic action. There is much that this can involve, including asking fruitful questions, considering plausible alternatives, and properly evaluating evidence. Without trying to spell out precisely what good epistemic action involves, let's just say that a *person* is justified in believing something to the extent that he holds the belief rationally and responsibly. However, a *belief* can be justified even in the absence of any action on the part of the believer, as in the case of beliefs formed automatically or routinely, without any deliberate consideration. Indeed, I suggest that most of our beliefs are of this sort, including run-of-the-mill perceptual, memory, and introspective beliefs. The distinction is clearest in the case of psychologically basic (noninferential) beliefs, since whatever would make someone justified in holding such a belief would also render that belief psychologically nonbasic. If a basic belief is justified at all, because it is basic there is nothing one does in order to be justified in holding it. Nothing counts as being rational or epistemically responsible in holding such a belief. This is why BonJour conceded that psychologically basic beliefs cannot satisfy the internalist conception of justification. If only he distinguished between people being justified in believing and beliefs being justified, he would not have to make such a skeptical concession.

This distinction defuses an internalist argument offered by Kornblith.[14] Insisting

14. It also undercuts two otherwise plausible objections to reliabilism recently put forth by John Pollock ('Reliability and Justified Belief,' *Canadian Journal of Philosophy* 14 (1984): 103–14). Space does not permit giving them the attention they deserve, but the first objection, in a nutshell, is that since reliability is a probabilistic notion, reliabilism leads to the lottery paradox. I cannot rehearse Pollock's argument here, but clearly it depends on the assumption that reliabilism sanctions a purely probabilistic rule of acceptance. Such a rule leads to the lottery paradox, as Gilbert Harman noted in *Thought* (Princeton: Princeton University Press, 1973), pp. 118–19. Now Harman exposes a further trouble with such a rule, arguing that 'given any evidence, some false conclusion will be highly probable on that evidence' (p. 22) and that 'purely probabilistic rules are incompatible with the natural account of Gettier examples by means of principle P' (p. 124). Fortunately, as we have seen, reliabilism is a theory of justified belief in the sense relevant to the analysis of knowledge, not in the sense of being justified in believing. Rules of acceptance are relevant to the latter, not the former, and Pollock makes no attempt to show that reliabilism sanctions any purely probabilistic rule of acceptance.

Pollock also argues against reliability as a necessary condition for justified belief.

We often become justified in believing a conclusion by reasoning to it from other beliefs we are already justified in holding. But from the fact that our premises are reliable, it does not follow that our conclusion is reliable. In general, by conjoining a number of beliefs which are both justified and reliable, we can arrive at a conclusion which is justified but as improbable and hence unreliable as we desire. (p. 106)

This argument can be disposed of quickly. For one thing, reliabilism invokes the notion of reliability of belief-forming processes, not that of beliefs themselves. Moreover, we may 'often become justified in believing a conclusion by reasoning to it from other beliefs we are already justified in holding,' but not when our conclusion is 'improbable and hence unreliable.' Reliabilism can account for this straightforwardly. Any reasoning process that is insensitive to such probabilistic considerations is unreliable and therefore does not lead to justified beliefs.

that 'justified belief cannot be identified with reliably produced belief,' Kornblith argues,

Since epistemically responsible action may result in something less than reliably produced belief, an agent may be justified in holding a belief without that belief being reliably produced. Beliefs produced by unreliable processes, where the extent of the unreliability would not be detected by epistemically responsible agent, are nonetheless justified.[15]

In effect, Kornblith is equating a belief being justified with an agent being justified in holding it. If he distinguished the two, he could then say that an agent can be justified in holding an unreliably produced belief even if the belief itself is not justified. And, of course, he could say that a belief is justified even if it is not the case that the believer is justified in holding it (which does not mean that the believer would be justified in not holding it).

So I think that our distinction captures what is right about both conceptions of justification. They are conceptions of two different things! Taking rationality and responsibility as the marks of justification, internalism can maintain that whatever makes a person justified in holding a belief must be available to him. And external-ism can maintain that being justified is whatever property a true, ungettiered belief must possess to qualify as knowledge. As we have seen, a belief need not be justified in that sense in order for a person to be justified in holding it. For since he can rationally and responsibly rely on some false generalization or principle, reliance on which cannot give him knowledge, he can be justified in holding a belief that is itself not justified.

Finally, our distinction undercuts a seemingly decisive counterexample to exter-nalism put forth by BonJour. He describes the case of a completely reliable clair-voyant who 'possesses no evidence or reasons of any kind for or against the general possibility of such a cognitive power, or for or against the thesis that he possesses it,' and asks, 'Is Norman epistemically justified in believing that the President is in New York City?' (p. 62 [in this volume p. 188]). Now Norman either does or does not believe that he is a reliable clairvoyant, but by hypothesis he has no reason to believe that he is. So if he does, this belief is unjustified and thus cannot help justify his belief about the President's whereabouts. But if Norman has no belief about the reliability of his clairvoyance, his belief about the President's whereabouts is, according to BonJour, 'epistemically irrational and irresponsible, and thereby unjustified,' since 'part of one's epistemic duty is to reflect critically upon one's beliefs' (p. 63 [in this volume p. 189]). Now even if fulfilling this 'duty' is necessary for Norman to be justified in believing, that leaves open the question, once our distinction is drawn, whether the belief itself is justified. The reliabilist could main-tain that it is. Given the reliability of the process that leads to such beliefs, this process gives Norman knowledge whenever it results in a true belief (unless, of course, the belief has been 'gettiered').

Since he uses it to criticize Goldman, presumably BonJour would take the example to show that simple reliability is not enough even for justified belief. Yet

---

15. 'Justified Belief and Epistemically Responsible Action,' p. 44.

Goldman himself recognizes that simple reliability is not enough and requires in addition to the reliability of the process leading to the belief that there not be available a reliable defeating process. Thus Goldman could explain why Norman's belief is not justified, though the result of a reliable cognitive process, by the fact that Norman fails to reflect on the reliability of his clairvoyance. The process of doing so, which surely would incorporate inductive principles generally relied on by Norman, would lead him to doubt or even deny the reliability of his clairvoyance. After all, BonJour has stipulated that Norman does not have inductive support for believing himself clairvoyant. If he did have such support, contrary to BonJour's description of the case, his belief that he is reliably clairvoyant would be justified.[16]

Let's go further and suppose that it does not occur to Norman to reflect on his powers of clairvoyance. Now it doesn't occur to most people to reflect on their powers of perception, and yet perception can give them knowledge, hence justified beliefs. So why couldn't clairvoyance do the same for Norman? It might seem that Norman is required to reflect on his clairvoyant powers in a way that ordinary people are not required to reflect on their perceptual powers, but what is the relevant difference? I think there is no relevant difference, and that there seems to be one only because of our doubts about clairvoyance in real life (what if we were all clairvoyant?). So if Norman really is reliably clairvoyant and has no reason to believe otherwise, it seems that his beliefs based on that power are as justified as ordinary perceptual beliefs.

One way to appreciate this is to imagine that what we take to be the perception of physical objects is not a matter of their affecting our sense organs. Instead, a benign Cartesian demon, recognizing the unbridgeable mind/body barrier, has arranged the world so that our sensory experiences are generally veridical, just as they are (presumably) in fact. But our knowledge of physical objects would be by clairvoyance, not perception. Then we would all be in Norman's position, except there would be now a way to check the reliability of our clairvoyance. Indeed, in this hypothetical circumstance the situation with clairvoyance would be just like our actual situation with perception, where simple reliability generally *is* enough for justified belief![17]

5. The default conception of reasoning

BonJour gives the impression that the dispute between internalism and externalism is solely about basic beliefs, but it goes further than that. This is evident from Goldman's formulation.[18] His recursive definition of justified belief distinguishes *categorically* from *conditionally* reliable belief-forming processes. Categorical

16. Indeed, sometimes simple reliability is enough, as with unreflective agents. After all, such people are capable of knowledge, hence of justified beliefs. So even if it is 'part of one's epistemic duty to reflect critically upon one's beliefs,' they lack the psychological resources to do this.

17. Later I will qualify this statement by adding that reliable belief-forming perceptual processes be backed by reliable processes for detecting when the situation is out of the ordinary.

18. See, in particular, the formulations on pp. 13, 14, and 20 of 'What Is Justified Belief?'

reliability is defined for belief-independent processes, which lead to beliefs not based on other beliefs, i.e., to psychologically basic beliefs. Conditional reliability is defined for belief-dependent processes, which lead to beliefs based (at least partly) on other beliefs. Reliability here is conditional since what comes out of the process depends on what goes into it. Now why doesn't Goldman content himself with reliabilism about basic beliefs and let the internalists have their way with inferential beliefs? As we saw, Goldman is skeptical about the prospects of identifying and adequately formulating regulative doxastic principles. Moreover, he observes that 'doxastic habits' not only do but must precede 'the choice of a doxastic principle,' since otherwise 'there would be an infinite regress of choices [of doxastic principles].'[19] I agree with Goldman, but I think the issue goes even deeper than this. It concerns the very nature of reasoning.

I have been supposing (contrary to BonJour) that most of our everyday, garden-variety beliefs qualify as knowledge, and that to do so they must be justified. Accordingly, a reasonable theory of justified belief (hence of knowledge) must take into account real-life limitations on our everyday reasoning. Now philosophers tend to focus on reasoning at its most explicit and deliberate. Yet such reasoning is exceptional: most of the reasoning that gives us knowledge is largely inexplicit. It is what in Artificial Intelligence is called *default reasoning*.[20] It is so called because it contains steps that are taken by default. That is, each such step is based on some generalization or stereotype which is overridden only if there occurs the thought of an alternative or of a reason to the contrary. The stereotypical assumption is like the default value assigned to a variable in a computer program. When a value needs to be assigned, the default value is assigned automatically if no alternative is provided, and the program runs from there.

The simplest case of default reasoning is when a question comes up and we believe the first thing that comes into our heads. This pervasive phenomenon can lead to justified beliefs insofar as it is reliable. Its reliability depends, as I will explain later, on how reliable we are at knowing when to think twice. Jumping to conclusions enables us to form beliefs much more freely than explicit consideration would allow. This does not mean that they are less justified (or are governed by lower standards of justifiedness), for in most cases explicit consideration would yield the same result—after considerable time and attention.

More elaborate reasoning, containing a number of steps, can still be (and generally is) default reasoning, for there can be an implicit assumption at any step along the way. We implicitly assume a proposition whenever we reason in a way that is sensitive to it: drawing inferences consistent with it and not drawing ones inconsistent with it. Ordinarily we do not question such an assumption unless there occurs to us some reason to do so. We rely on our ability to detect or to think of reasons, when worth considering, for challenging our assumptions. For example, we often apply generalizations automatically and yet, relying on our ability to detect

---

19. 'The Internalist Conception of Justification,' p. 47.
20. The conception of reasoning sketched here is developed more fully in my 'Default Reasoning: Jumping to Conclusions and Knowing When to Think Twice,' *Pacific Philosophical Quarterly* 65 (1984): 37–58.

exceptions, we often know when not to apply them. These abilities can become highly refined, as with experts like detectives and doctors (as modeled by expert systems in AI), but we are all experts about many aspects of the world around us.

When our reasoning to a conclusion is sufficiently complex, we do not survey the entire argument for validity. We go more or less step by step, and as we proceed, we assume that if each step follows from what precedes, nothing has gone wrong. That is not always so, for an implausible conclusion along the way may lead us to question some previous step (either a premise or a bit of reasoning). An intermediate conclusion will seem implausible if it conflicts with other beliefs. Of course there is no guarantee that we will detect every such conflict, but we implicitly assume that when there is one, we will detect it and go back over our reasoning. Here we rely on our ability to detect such conflicts. Even if our lines of reasoning were always perspicuous, so that we could view them as a whole, there would still be points at which we do not actually check for validity but simply 'go along' with the reasoning at that point. We just 'see' that the next step follows. In any case, to lead to justified belief reasoning does not have to be evaluated in every evaluable respect. It can include steps that are not explicitly evaluated and implicit assumptions that would become explicit only if such steps were evaluated explicitly. Their implicit 'evaluation' consists simply in their not being questioned. Such an evaluation is reliable insofar as the person is reliable at detecting good reasons for questioning steps in his reasoning. Moreover, generally a person is not aware of what validates his reasoning and might not even be able to be aware of all of it. Even if he were aware of what must be true for his reasoning to be valid, he might have no idea how to establish these underlying presuppositions. That would require, in effect, knowing how to answer the skeptic, and that's too much to ask of the ordinary cognizer (not to mention the seasoned epistemologist!).

Since justified beliefs commonly result from default reasoning, the internalist conception of justification is psychologically unrealistic and epistemologically inadequate, even when restricted to inferential beliefs. Even if all aspects of reasoning, however complex, could be evaluated explicitly, it would be absurd to require reasoning to be evaluated in every evaluable respect in order to lead to justified belief. To be sure, no internalist I know of holds that such thoroughgoing evaluation is necessary for justified belief, but I don't see how an internalist can consistently settle for less. To impose the requirement merely that the believer be able to perform such an evaluation would be plausible only if coupled with the requirement that the believer know when actually to perform the evaluation. However, the latter is a reliabilist requirement, not an internalist one. And even if it were plausible to require merely that the believer be able to perform a thoroughgoing evaluation, that would divorce what justifies a belief from the process actually leading to it.[21]

Finally, the default conception of ordinary reasoning suggests that what makes a belief justified is not merely the actual reasoning that leads to the belief. Would-be reasoning is relevant too, reasoning that would take place if thoughts of certain

---

21. See Harman (cited in n14, above), pp. 26–32.

possibilities occurred to the person. This means that how justified the belief is depends on the reliability of the process of thinking of relevant possibilities (JRA's) and even on the reliability of the process whereby they are evaluated. As we shall see next, this is true even in the case of psychologically basic beliefs.

6. Taking things for granted

The default conception of everyday reasoning has an interesting application to Gilbert Harman's approach to the Gettier problem, an approach which has been charged, in my view unjustly, with being psychologically implausible. He proposes a psychologistic strategy of using intuitions about knowledge 'to decide when reasoning has occurred and what reasoning there has been.'[22] The strategy is based on the principle (P) that reasoning can give one knowledge only if it contains no false steps. Harman suggests that what distinguishes a gettiered justified true belief from its normal counterpart is that the reasoning leading to it contains (essentially) something false. Now if principle P is to distinguish the two cases, the reasoning leading to the gettiered belief must be elaborate enough to contain the requisite false step. But then the reasoning in the normal case, where there is genuine knowledge, has to contain a counterpart of that step. Thus Harman's strategy can seem psychologically unrealistic, in that it requires attributing implausibly elaborate reasoning to the normal believer. If I may allude to a few well-known examples, the believer seems not even to consider, much less affirm, that what he takes to be a barn is not a papier-mache facade, that the candle he seems to see directly is not really being reflected through a system of mirrors, or that Havit (or anyone other than Nogot) is not the student who owns a Ford. I suggest that the step required in the normal case corresponding to the false step in the gettiered case concerns a proposition which is not explicitly considered but is merely taken for granted.

Let us look at the second case, Harman's perceptual Gettier example. A person has a justified true belief that there is a candle in front of him. He does not know this, though, for he is unaware (and has no reason to suppose) that what he sees is really the reflection in a mirror of another candle off to the side. However, he does not seem to be explicitly thinking any such thing when he infers that there is a candle in front of him. For this reason Michael Williams argues that there is no evidence to warrant ascribing reasoning that does include this supposition.[23] There is the further consideration that the belief about the candle is but one of countless beliefs continuously being formed as a person contemplates his surroundings or navigates about them. It seems highly unlikely that for each and every object a person takes to be before him, he draws a distinct intermediate conclusion like the one Harman suggests for the case of the candle. That seems not only implausible but highly inefficient. Much more plausible to ascribe and efficient to use would be a generalization like this: ordinarily things are as they seem, because they seem as

22. See Harman (cited in n14, above), p. 47.

23. Michael Williams, 'Inference, Justification, and the Analysis of Knowledge,' *Journal of Philosophy* 75 (1978): 249–63.

they do because of the way they are. This generalization could be used over and over, as countless perceptual judgments are made. It would function as an intermediate step each time one infers the presence of something, but a new intermediate step would not be needed for each new inference. There is no reason to suppose, Harman's strategy notwithstanding, that this same step explicitly occurs over and over, as each succeeding judgment is made. And yet such truncated reasoning, though lacking an element corresponding to the intermediate step, could be both explicable and justified, provided it makes sense to say that the required intermediate step is at least *implicit* in the reasoning. I suggest that we can make sense of this with the help of the following psychological distinction, which can serve further to defend Harman's strategy against the charge of psychological implausibility.

Let us distinguish between reasoning *realizing* an inference pattern and its merely *instantiating* that pattern. A piece of reasoning realizes an abstract pattern of inference if it contains psychologically real elements corresponding to all the steps of that pattern. It merely instantiates that pattern if there is some step that is not explicitly included but merely implicitly assumed. This distinction makes sense, I suggest, if we suppose that our ordinary, routine reasoning, as in perceptual judgment, operates according to something like the following rule, which I call the *taking-for-granted rule*.

(TFG) If it seems to me that p, then infer that p, provided no reason to the contrary occurs to me.

If our routine reasoning relies on the TFG, this reliance leads to justified beliefs insofar as we are able to detect abnormal circumstances. I must be pretty good at knowing when not to infer that things are as they seem in order to be justified, when the situation is normal, in supposing that things are as they seem. If I were insensitive to abnormal situations, I would directly infer that p even when I should not. In following TFG, whenever I directly infer that things are as they seem, i.e., without considering reasons to the contrary, I implicitly rely on my reliability at detecting indications of abnormality.

I am suggesting that we jump to conclusions except when we look before we leap. That's obviously efficient, but how reliable is it? Offhand, jumping to conclusions seems to gain speed at the risk of error. It looks as though it could get us into lots of trouble. But don't forget, drawing inferences is, as Mill observed, 'the only occupation in which the mind never ceases to be engaged.' We can't avoid trading off possible error for speed, for there are always more inferences to be made. If we didn't generally jump to conclusions, we wouldn't make most of the inferences that need to be made. In any case, it seems that when we do jump to conclusions, we are generally right. We are generally right in our snap judgments about the kinds and qualities of things we perceive around us, right in our recollections of our prior experiences, right about persons, places, and things we seem to recognize, right about what people mean when they talk to us. Perceptual judgment, recall, recognition, and understanding utterances[24] are all clear cases of generally reliable jumping

24. See Kent Bach and Robert M. Harnish, *Linguistic Communication and Speech Acts* (Cambridge, MA: The MIT Press, 1979), pp. 84–96.

to conclusions. Since this is not a monumental coincidence, somehow our inferences must take relevant information into account without getting bogged down in irrelevancies. But how? How do we resolve the tension between efficiency and reliability? After all, reliability requires ruling out alternatives to the tempting conclusion. The way this tension is resolved, I suggest, is that alternatives can be effectively and legitimately ruled out without even being considered, at least not consciously. This can occur if our reasoning processes have the following feature: we consider an alternative only when there is special reason to do so. Otherwise, without explicitly thinking that the alternative does not obtain, we reason as if it does not.

Obviously our reasoning can work like this only if we are equipped somehow to detect the presence of reasons for considering alternatives that we ordinarily take for granted not to obtain. A belief resulting from such a process is justified to the extent that the process not only leads to true beliefs, at least generally, but also guards against forming false beliefs, by means of precautionary subroutines that are generally activated when and only when they need to be. For it is only to that extent that following TFG can lead to justified beliefs. In the ungettiered case of the candle, for example, I couldn't know that there is a candle in front of me simply by inferring this from how things appear if I did so on the basis that objects are as they appear. That is, if I followed the preposterous appearance-is-reality rule (AIR), 'If it appears to me that *p*, then infer that *p*,' then when I inferred that something is as it appears my reasoning would instantiate an obviously invalid inference pattern and could not lead to justified beliefs. Fortunately, my reasoning follows a different rule, TFG, and generally instantiates a valid inference pattern, one that is validated, I suggest, by what we might call the *take-for-granted principle*:

> (TFGP) Its appearing to one that *p* justifies directly inferring that *p* provided that
> (a) it does not occur to one that the situation
> might be out of the ordinary, and
> (b) if the situation were out of the ordinary,
> it probably would occur to one that the
> situation might be out of the ordinary.

(The force of 'ordinary' here is to exclude sources of illusion, distortion, and hallucination.) When TFGP applies, I am justified in taking for granted that the situation is ordinary, unless it occurs to me that perhaps my perception is being affected abnormally, say by bad lighting or by devious psychologists. Thus, as clause (b) provides, TFGP licenses my implicit use of TFG to the extent that I am able to detect abnormal circumstances. I must be pretty good at knowing when not to infer that things are as they seem in order to be justified, when the situation is normal, in supposing that things are as they seem. If I were insensitive to abnormal situations, I would directly infer that *p* even when I should not.

TFGP licenses me to jump to conclusions if I don't think of a reason not to. Thus, the justification of such an inference is conditional on the nonoccurrence of a certain thought. In the case of visual belief, for example, ordinarily I assume that things are as they look, unless it occurs to me that my vision is being affected abnormally. Similarly, in the case of recall, as of somebody's name or the spelling of a certain word, I take for granted that the first thought that comes to mind is the right one—unless it occurs to me that it might not be, say because some other possibility comes to mind.

If this picture of ordinary reasoning and its justification is at all correct, it has a fundamental consequence for the dispute between internalism and externalism. Since making inferences according to TFG requires the nonoccurrence of a certain thought, TFG has the remarkable feature that it cannot be explicitly followed. For if TFG occurred to me while I was following it, then I would have to consider whether there are occurring to me any thoughts to the contrary of my prospective conclusion, in which case I would no longer be drawing that conclusion directly. Instead, my reasoning would contain the additional thought that there are no reasons contrary to that conclusion. But that's not the way jumping to conclusions goes, or at least not the way it seems to go. I don't seem to draw my conclusion after noting that no contrary possibility has occurred to me, and if I did reason in that way, undoubtedly plenty of such possibilities would occur to me.

Only externalism is compatible with the supposition that in everyday we employ default reasoning and that this reasoning generally leads to justified beliefs and gives us knowledge. Internalism may be appropriate as a conception of what it is for a person to be justified in holding a belief, but not as a conception of justified belief itself. Now I have not addressed the problem of precisely how to formulate externalism, reliabilism in particular. Solving it would require finding a suitable way to individuate cognitive processes[25] and specifying the precise role of back-up processes. Whether this can be done remains to be seen, for I have tried to show only that in principle there is nothing wrong with reliabilism.

25. Goldman recognizes this problem in 'What Is Justified Belief', pp. 12 and 20. Robert Nozick takes up the analogous problem for this theory, a form of epistemological reliabilism, in *Philosophical Explanations* (Cambridge, MA: Harvard University Press, 1981), 179–85 [in this volume pp. 354–5].

Chapter 16

An internalist externalism*

William P. Alston

I

In this paper I will explain, and at least begin to defend, the particular blend of internalism and externalism in my view of epistemic justification. So far as I know, this is my own private blend;[1] many, I'm afraid, will not take that as a recommendation. Be that as it may, it's mine, and it's what I will set forth in this paper. I will first have to present the general contours of the position, basis for specifying the points at which we have an internalism–externalism issue. I won't have time to defend the general position, or even to present more than a sketch. Such defence as will be offered will be directed to the internalist and externalist features.

In a word, my view is that to be justified in believing that *p* is for that belief *to be based on an adequate ground*. To explain what I mean by this I will have to say something about the correlative terms 'based' on and 'ground' and about the *adequacy* of grounds.

The ground of a belief is what it is based on. The notion of *based on* is a difficult one. I am not aware that anyone has succeeded in giving an adequate and illuminating general explanation of it. It seems clear that some kind of causal dependence is involved, whether the belief is based on other beliefs or on experience. If my belief that it rained last night is based on my belief that the streets are wet, then I hold the former belief *because* I hold the latter belief; my holding the latter belief *explains* my holding the former. Similarly, if my belief that the streets are wet is based on their looking wet, I believe that they are wet *because* of the way they look, and their looking that way *explains* my believing that they are wet. And presumably these are relations of causal dependence. But, equally clearly, not just any kind of causal dependence will do. My belief that *p* is causally dependent on a certain physiological state of my brain, but the former is not based on the latter. How is *being*

William P. Alston, 'An Internalist Externalism' in *Synthese* 74 (1988) pp. 265–83, reprinted by permission of Kluwer Academic Publishers, Dordrecht, The Netherlands.

* An earlier version of this paper was delivered at a Conference on Epistemic Justification, honoring Roderick Chisholm, at Brown University in November, 1986. I am grateful to the participants in that conference for many penetrating remarks, and especially to my commentator, Marshall Swain. Those comments have been expanded into his essay 'Alston's Internalistic Externalism', *Philosophical Perspectives* 2 (1988).

1. The position does, however, bear a marked family resemblance to that put forward in Marshall Swain's *Reasons and Knowledge* (Ithaca, Cornell University Press, 1981).

based on distinguished from other sorts of causal dependence? We have a clear answer to this question for cases of maximally explicit inference, where I come to believe that p because I see (or at least take it) that it is adequately supported by the fact that q (which I believe). And where the ground is experiential we can also come to believe that p because we take its truth to be adequately indicated by the experience from which it arises. In these cases the belief forming process is *guided* by our belief in the adequate support relation, and this marks them out as cases of a belief's being based on a ground, rather than just causally depending on something.[2] A belief, however, may be based on other beliefs or on experiences, where no such guiding belief in support relations is in evidence.[3] My belief that you are upset may be based on various aspects of the way you look and act without my consciously believing that these features provide adequate support for that belief; in a typical case of this sort I have no such belief simply because I am not consciously aware of which features these are; I do not consciously discriminate them. And even where I am more explicitly aware of the ground I may not consciously believe anything at all about support relations. It is very dubious that very small children, e.g., ever have such support beliefs; and yet surely a small child's belief that the kitten is sick can be based on her belief that the kitten is not running around as usual. But then what feature is common to all cases of a belief's being *based on* something and serves to distinguish this kind of causal dependence from other kinds? Here I will have to content myself with making a suggestion. Wherever it is clear that a belief is *based on* another belief or on an experience, the belief forming 'process' or 'mechanism' is *taking account* of that ground or features thereof, being *guided* by it, even if this does not involve the conscious utilisation of a belief in a support relation. To say that my belief that the streets are wet is based on the way they look is to say that in forming a belief about the condition of the streets I (or the belief forming 'mechanism') am differentially sensitive to the way the streets look; the mechanism is so constituted that the belief formed about the streets will be some, possibly very complex, function of the visual experience input. Even where an explicit belief in a support relation is absent, the belief formation is the result of a *taking account* of features of the experience and forming the belief *in the light of* them, rather than just involving some sub-cognitive transaction.[4] Much more could and should be said about this, but the foregoing will have to suffice for now. In any event, whether or not this suggestion is along the right line, I shall take it that we have an adequate working grasp of the notion of a belief's being based on something, and that this suffices for the concerns of this paper.

2. For an elaborate development of this idea, along with much else relevant to the notion of believing for a reason, see Robert Audi's 'Belief, Reason, and Inference,' *Philosophical Topics*, 14, no. 1 (1986), 27–65.

3. Audi in the article referred to in the previous note alleges that there are such 'connecting beliefs', as he calls them, in every case of 'believing for a reason' (what I am calling beliefs based on other beliefs). However I do not find his arguments for this compelling.

4. It may be contended that where such 'taking account' is involved, this amounts to the subject's having and using a belief in a support relation. And perhaps this is right, for a minimal, low-level grade of belief possession and use. However one could 'have' and 'use' the belief in this way without the belief's being available for conscious entertainment, assertion, or use in inference.

In the foregoing I was speaking of the ground of a belief as playing a role in its *formation*. That is not the whole story. It is often pointed out that a belief may acquire a new basis after its initial acquisition. However the role of post-origination bases in justification is a complex matter, one not at all adequately dealt with in the epistemological literature. To keep things manageable for this short conspectus of my view, I shall restrict myself to bases on which a belief is originally formed. That means, in effect, that the discussion will be limited to what it takes for a belief to be justified at the moment of its acquisition.

In taking the justification of a belief to be determined by what it is based on, I am reflecting the subject-relative character of justification. I may be justified in believing that *p* while you are not. Indeed, justification is time as well as subject relative; I may be justified in believing that *p* at one time but not at another.[5] Whether I am justified in believing that *p* is a matter of how I am situated vis-à-vis the content of that belief. In my view, that is cashed out in terms of what the subject was 'going on' in supposing the proposition in question to be true, on what basis she supposed *p* to be the case.[6]

What sorts of thing do subjects go on in holding beliefs? The examples given above suggest that the prime candidates are the subject's other beliefs and experiences; and I shall consider grounds to be restricted to items of those two categories. Though I will offer no a priori or transcendental argument for this, I will adopt the plausible supposition that where the input to a belief forming mechanism is properly thought of as *what the belief is based on*, it will be either a belief or an experience. But we must tread carefully here. Where a philosopher or a psychologist would say that *S*'s belief that it rained last night is based on *S*'s *belief* that the streets are wet, *S* would probably say, if he were aware of the basis of his belief, that his ground, basis, or reason for believing that it rained last night is the *fact* that the streets are wet. The ordinary way of talking about reasons specifies the (putative) fact believed as the reason rather than the belief.[7] I think we can set up the matter either way. I choose to use 'ground' for the psychological input to the belief forming mechanism, that is, the belief or experience, thus deviating from the most ordinary way of speaking of these matters.

I need to be more explicit about how grounds are specified in my account. I can best approach this by considering a difficulty raised by Marshall Swain in his comments on this paper at the Brown conference. Swain wrote as follows:

Suppose two subjects, Smith and Jones, who have the same evidence (grounds) for the belief

---

5. For simplicity of exposition I shall omit temporal qualifiers from my formulations, but they are to be understood. Thus, a tacit 'at *t*' qualifies '*S* is justified in believing that *p*'.

6. Admittedly there are other ways of cashing out this general idea of subject-relativity, e.g., by making justification hang on what the subject 'had to go on' by way of support, rather than on what the subject actually went on, but I won't have time to go into those alternatives.

7. With experiential grounds we do not have the same problem, for, at least as I am thinking of it, an experiential ground is not, *qua* experiential ground, a propositional attitude, or set thereof, like a belief, so that here there is no propositional or factive object to serve as a ground rather than the experience itself. One who does take experiences to be essentially propositional attitudes will find the same problem as with doxastic grounds.

that p, where the evidence consists of the proposition $p \vee (p \& q)$. Both subjects come to believe that p on this basis of the evidence (and no other evidence). In the case of Smith, the mechanism for generating the belief is an inference which instantiates a tendency to invalidly infer p from any sentence of the form '$p \vee q$'. In the case of Jones, the mechanism is an inference which is based on an internalized valid inference schema (of which several are possible). It seems clear to me that only Jones has a justified belief that p, even though they have the same grounds.

Such cases can be proliferated indefinitely. For an example involving experiential grounds, consider two persons, A and B, who come to believe that a collie is in the room on the basis of qualitatively identical visual experiences. But A recognizes the dog as a collie on the basis of distinctively collie features, whereas B would take any largish dog to be a collie. Again, it would seem that A is justified in his belief while B is not, even though they have the same grounds for a belief with the same propositional content.[8] Swain takes it that such cases show that characteristics of the subject must be brought into the account in addition to what we have introduced.

However, I believe that unwanted applications like these can be excluded just by giving a sufficiently discriminating specification of grounds. As I am using the term, the 'ground' for a belief is not what we might call the total concrete input to the belief forming mechanism, but rather those features of that input that are actually taken account of in forming the belief, in, so to say, 'choosing' a propositional content for a belief. In Swain's case, the only feature of the belief input taken account of by Smith was that its propositional object was of the form '$p \vee q$'. No further features of the input were playing a role in that belief formation; no further features were 'guiding' the operation of the belief forming mechanism. In Jones' case, however, the belief formation was guided by the fact that the input belief had a propositional content of the form '$p \vee (p \& q)$'. In Smith's case any input of the '$p \vee q$' form would have led to the same doxastic output, whereas for Jones many other inputs of that form would *not* have led to the formation of a belief that p. Thus, strictly speaking, the grounds were different. Similarly in the canine identification case, for A the ground was the object's visually presenting certain features that are in fact distinctively collie-like, whereas for B the ground was the object's visually presenting itself as a largish dog.

We may sum this up by saying that the ground of a belief is made up of those features of the input to the formation of that belief that were actually taken account of in the belief formation. (Again, remember that our discussion is restricted to the bases of beliefs when formed.)

Not every grounded belief will be justified, but only one that has an *adequate* ground. To get at the appropriate criterion of adequacy, let's note that a belief's *being justified* is a favorable status vis-à-vis the basic aim of believing or, more generally, of cognition, viz., to believe truly rather than falsely. For a ground to be favorable relative to this aim it must be 'truth conducive'; it must be sufficiently

---

8. This is similar to problem cases involving perceptual discrimination introduced in Alvin Goldman's 'Discrimination and Perceptual Knowledge,' *Journal of Philosophy*, 73 (1976), 771–91 [Ch. 8 in this volume].

indicative of the truth of the belief it grounds. In other terms, the ground must be such that the *probability* of the belief's being true, given that ground, is very high. It is an objective probability that is in question here. The world is such that, at least in the kinds of situations in which we typically find ourselves, the ground is a reliable indication of the fact believed. In this paper I will not attempt to spell out the kind of objective probability being appealed to. So far as I am aware, no adequate conception of this sort of probability (or perhaps of any other sort) has been developed. Suffice it to say that I am thinking in terms of some kind of 'tendency' conception of probability, where the lawful structure of the world is such that one state of affairs renders another more or less probable.

The ambiguity noted earlier as to what constitutes a ground has to be dealt with here as well. Suppose that the ground of my belief that p is my belief that q. In order that the former belief be justified is it required that the belief that q be a reliable indication of the truth of the belief that p, or is it required that the fact that q be a reliable indication? The latter is the ordinary way of thinking about the matter. If my belief that Jones is having a party is based on my belief that there are a lot of cars around his house, then just as I would ordinarily cite the *fact* that there are a lot of cars around his house as my reason for supposing that he is having a party, so I would think that my reason is an adequate one because the former *fact* is a reliable indication of the latter one. The adequacy requirement, however, could be set up in either way. To appreciate this let's first note that in either case the belief that p will be justified only if the grounding belief be justified (a stronger requirement would be that the grounding belief constitute knowledge, but I won't go that far). Even if the fact that q is a highly reliable indication that p, that won't render my belief that p justified by virtue of being based on a belief that q unless I am justified in believing that q. An unjustified belief cannot transfer justification to another belief via the basis relation. But if I am justified in believing that q and if q is a reliable indication of p, then my belief that q will also be a (perhaps slightly less) reliable indication that q provided a belief cannot be justified unless its ground renders it likely to be true. For in that case my having a justified belief that q renders it likely that q, which in turn renders it likely that p. And so if q is a strong indication of the truth of p, so is my belief that q (assuming that we don't lose too much of the strength of indication in the probabilistic relation between the justified belief that q and q). This being the case, I will simplify matters for purposes of this paper by taking the adequacy of a ground to depend on *its* being a sufficiently strong indication of the truth of the belief grounded.

II

Now we are in a position to say what is internalist and what is externalist about this position, and to make a start, at least, in defending our choices. The view is internalist most basically, and most minimally, by virtue of the requirement that there be a ground of the belief. As we have made explicit, the ground must be a psychological state of the subject and hence 'internal' to the subject in an important sense. Facts that obtain independently of the subject's psyche, however favorable to the truth of the belief in question, cannot be *grounds* of the belief in the required sense.

But this is only a weak form of internalism, one that would hardly be deemed worthy of the name by those who flaunt the label. There are, in fact, several constraints on justification that have gone under this title. In 'Internalism and Externalism in Epistemology' I distinguish two main forms: Perspectival Internalism (PI), according to which only what is within the subject's perspective in the sense of being something the subject knows or justifiably believes can serve to justify; and Accessibility Internalism (AI), according to which only that to which the subject has cognitive access in some specially strong form can be a justifier. However, it is now clear to me that I should have added at least one more version, Consciousness Internalism (CI), according to which only those states of affairs of which the subject is actually conscious or aware can serve to justify.[9]

In 'Internalism and Externalism in Epistemology' I argued against PI, partly on the grounds that its only visible means of support is from an unacceptable deontological conception of justification that makes unrealistic assumptions about the voluntary control of belief, and partly on the grounds that it rules out the possibility of immediate justification by experience of such things as introspective and perceptual beliefs. CI has the crushing disability that one can never complete the formulation of a sufficient condition for justification. For suppose that we begin by taking condition C to be sufficient for the justification of S's belief that p. But then we must add that S must be aware of C (i.e., the satisfaction of condition C) in order to be justified. Call this enriched condition C_1. But then C_1 is not enough by itself either; S must be aware of C_1. So that must be added to yield a still richer condition C_2. And so on ad infinitum. Any thesis that implies that it is in principle impossible to complete a statement of conditions sufficient for justification is surely unacceptable.[10]

I find AI to be much more promising. To be sure, many formulations are, I believe, much too strong to be defensible. Thus Carl Ginet's version is in terms of what he calls being 'directly recognizable':

Every one of every set of facts about S's position that minimally suffices to make S, at a given time, justified in being confident that p must be *directly recognizable* to S at that time. By 'directly recognizable' I mean this: if a certain fact obtains, then it is directly recognizable to S at a given time if and only if, provided that S at that time has the concept of that sort of fact, S needs at that time only to reflect clear-headedly on the question of whether or not that fact obtains in order to know that it does. (1975, p. 34)

But there are very plausible conditions for justification that are not directly

---

9. For an example of CI see Paul Moser, *Empirical Justification* (Dordecht, D. Reidel, 1985), p. 174.
10. The proponent of CI might seek to avoid this consequence by construing the awareness requirement not as part of the condition for justification but as a constraint on what can be a sufficient condition for justification. Indeed this is the way Moser, *ibid.*, formulates it on p. 174 '. . . we should require that one have some kind of awareness of the justifying conditions of one's given-beliefs'. The suggestion is that the awareness does not itself form part of the justifying conditions. But I take this to be a shuffling evasion. If the awareness of condition C is required for justification, then it is an essential part of a sufficient condition for justification, whatever the theorist chooses to call it.

recognizable in this sense. Consider, for example, the familiar situation in which I recognize something or someone on the basis of subtle perceptual cues I am unable to specify, even on careful reflection. Here it seems correct to say that my belief that the person before me is John Jones is justified, if it is, by virtue of being based on a visual experience with such-and-such features, where the experience's having those features is crucial for its providing justification. But those features are not 'directly recognizable' by me. Or again consider the familiar situation of a belief, for example, that Republicans are unlikely to be tough on big business, that is based on a wide diversity of evidence, most of which I cannot specify even after careful reflection. Ginet's form of AI is too stringent to be suited to our condition.[11]

However, I believe that it is possible to support a more moderate version of AI. To determine just what sort of accessibility is required I had better make explicit what I see as the source of the requirement. I find widely shared and strong intuitions in favor of some kind of accessibility requirement for justification. We expect that if there is something that justifies my belief that p I will be able to determine what it is. We find something incongruous, or conceptually impossible, in the notion of my being justified in believing that p while totally lacking any capacity to determine what is responsible for that justification. Thus when reliability theorists of justification maintain that any reliably formed belief is ipso facto justified, most of us balk. For since it is possible for a belief to be reliably formed without the subject's having any capacity to determine this, and, indeed, without there being anything accessible to the subject on which the belief is based—as when invariably correct beliefs about the future of the stock market seem to pop out of nowhere—it seems clear to many of us that reliable belief formation cannot be sufficient for justification.

Why these intuitions? Why is some kind of accessibility required for justification? Is this just a basic constituent of the concept? Or can it be derived from other more basic components? I myself do not see any way to argue from other 'parts' of the concept to this one. Hence I will not attempt to *prove* that accessibility is required for justification. But I believe that we can get some understanding of the presence of this accessibility requirement by considering the larger context out of which the concept of epistemic justification has developed and which gives it its distinctive importance. Thus I will attempt to *explain* the presence of the requirement.

First I want to call attention to a view of justification I do not accept. Suppose, with pragmatists like Peirce and Dewey and other contextualists, we focus on the *activity* of *justifying* beliefs to the exclusion of the *state* of *being justified* in holding a belief. The whole topic of epistemic justification will then be confined to the question of what it takes to successfully carry out the activity of justifying a belief, *showing* it to be something one is entitled to believe, establishing its credentials, responding to challenges to its legitimacy, and so on. But then the only considerations that can have any bearing on justification (i.e., on the successful outcome of such an activity) are those that are cognitively accessible to the subject. For only those can be appealed to in order to justify the belief.

---

11. I might also add that AI is typically supported by inconclusive arguments from an unacceptable deontological conception of justification. For details see Alston 'Internalism and Externalism in Epistemology', *Philosophical Topics* 14 (1986), 79–221.

Now I have no temptation to restrict the topic of epistemic justification to the activity of justifying. Surely epistemology is concerned with the epistemic status of beliefs with respect to which no activity of justifying has been carried on. We want to know whether people are justified in holding normal perceptual beliefs, normal memory beliefs, beliefs in generalizations concerning how things generally go in the physical world, beliefs about the attitudes of other people, religious beliefs, and so on, even where, as is usually the case, such beliefs have not been subjected to an attempt to justify. It is quite arbitrary to ban such concerns from epistemology.

But though the activity of responding to challenges is not the whole story, I do believe that in a way it is fundamental to the concept of *being justified*. Why is it that we have this concept of *being justified in holding a belief* and why is it important to us? I suggest that the concept was developed, and got its hold on us, because of the practice of critical reflection on our beliefs, of challenging their credentials and responding to such challenges—in short the practice of attempting to *justify* beliefs. Suppose there were no such practice; suppose that no one ever challenges the credentials of anyone's beliefs; suppose that no one ever critically reflects on the grounds or basis of one's own beliefs. In that case would we be interested in determining whether one or another belief *is* justified? I think not. It is only because we participate in such activities, only because we are alive to their importance, that the question of whether someone is in a state of *being justified* in holding a belief is of live interest to us. I am not suggesting that being justified is a matter of engaging in, or successfully engaging in, the activity of justifying. I am not even affirming the less obviously false thesis that being justified in believing that *p* is a matter of *being able to* successfully justify the belief. Many persons are justified in many beliefs without possessing the intellectual or verbal skills to exhibit what justifies those beliefs. Thus the *fact* of being justified is not dependent on any particular actual or possible activity of justifying. What I am suggesting is that those facts of justification would not have the interest and importance for us that they do have if we were not party to a social practice of demanding justification and responding to such demands.

Now for the bearing of this on AI. I want to further suggest that this social practice has strongly influenced the development of the *concept* of being justified. What has emerged from this development is the concept of *what would have to be specified to carry out a successful justification of the belief*. Our conception of what a belief needs in the way of a basis in order to *be justified* is the conception of that the specification of which in answer to a challenge would suffice to answer that challenge. But then it is quite understandable that the concept should include the requirement that the justifier be accessible to the subject. For only what the subject can ascertain can be cited by that subject in response to a challenge. This, I believe, provides the explanation for the presence of the AI constraint on justification.

Now that we have a rationale for an AI constraint, let's see just what form of the constraint is dictated by that rationale. There are at least two matters to be decided: (a) what is required to be accessible; (b) what degree of accessibility is to be required.

As for (a), the most important distinction is between (1) the 'justifier', i.e., the ground of the belief, and (2) its adequacy or justificatory efficacy: its 'truth-conduciveness'. I'm going to save adequacy for the next section and concentrate here on the justifier. But there are still choices. Should we say that in order for S's belief that p to be justified by being based on a ground, G, G itself, that very individual ground, must be accessible to S? Or is it enough that G is the sort of thing that is typically accessible to normal human subjects? The latter, weaker requirement would allow a justifying ground in a particular case to be a belief that is not in fact accessible to the subject's consciousness, because of repression, a cognitive overload, or whatever, provided beliefs are in general the sort of thing to which subjects have cognitive access. The rationale offered above for AI would not demand of every justifying ground that it itself be available for citation, but only that it be the *sort* of thing that is, in general, so available. We were not arguing that it is conceptually necessary, or even universally true, that a justifying ground can be cited in response to a challenge. We were only contending that the concept of being justified in believing that p (including the concept of a justifying ground for a belief) has been developed against the background of the practice of citing grounds in defence of assertions. This looser sort of relationship of justifying grounds to the activity of justifying supports at most the weaker requirement that a justifying ground is the sort of thing that, in general or when nothing interferes, is available for citation by the subject. And it is just as well that only this weaker requirement is mandated, for, because of the considerations adduced in criticizing Ginet's form of AI, it seems that we must allow cases in which the basis of a belief is blocked from consciousness through some special features of that situation. Thus we are free to recognize cases of justification in which the complexity of the grounds or the rapidity of their appearance and disappearance renders the subject unable to store and retrieve them as she would have to in order to cite them in answer to a challenge.

Now for degree. Just *how* does a kind of state have to be generally accessible to its subject in order to be a candidate for a justifying ground? I have already argued that Ginet's version of AI is too demanding to be realistic. On the other hand, if we simply require that justifiers be the sorts of things that are knowable in principle by the subject, somehow or other, that is too weak. That would allow anything to count as a justifier that it is not *impossible* for the subject to come to know about. That would not even rule out neurophysiological states of the brain about which no one knows anything now. What is needed here is a concept of something like 'fairly direct accessibility'. In order that justifiers be generally available for presentation as the legitimizers of the belief, they must be fairly readily available to the subject through some mode of access much quicker than lengthy research, observation, or experimentation. It seems reasonable to follow Ginet's lead and suggest that to be a justifier an item must be the sort of thing that, in general, a subject can explicitly note the presence of just by sufficient reflection on his situation. However the amount and depth of reflection needed for this will vary in different cases. I want to avoid the claim that justifiers can always be spotted right away, just by raising the question. I don't know how to make this notion of 'fairly direct accessibility' precise, and I suspect that it may be impossible to do so. Perhaps our concept of justification is not itself precise enough to require a precise degree of ease or rapidity of access. Let's just say that to be a justifier of a belief, its ground must be the sort of thing whose instances are fairly directly accessible to their subject on reflection.

I am going to just mention in passing another internalist feature of this position. Being based on an adequate ground is sufficient only for prima facie justification, justification that can be overridden by sufficient reasons to the contrary from the subject's stock of knowledge and justified belief.[12] Reasons that override a given justification for a belief that p are of two sorts. First there are sufficient reasons for supposing p to be false; call them *rebutters*. Second, there are reasons such that the combination of them with the initial ground fails to be sufficiently indicative of the truth of p; call them *neutralizers*. Thus even if my current visual experience is, in itself, a strong indication that there is a tree in front of me, I will not be, all things considered, justified in believing that there is a tree in front of me provided I have even stronger reasons for supposing there to be no tree there (rebutter), or provided I have strong reasons for supposing my visual apparatus not to be working properly at the moment (neutralizer). The effect of the requirement (for unqualified justification) of no sufficient overriders is to make unqualified justification sensitive to the totality of what the subject knows and justifiably believes. I am unqualifiedly justified in believing that p only if the totality of my knowledge, justified belief, and experience constitutes an adequate ground for that belief. Since the fate of prima facie justification is determined by what is in the subject's perspective on the world, rather than by the way the world is, this is an additional internalist factor, though as the last footnote makes explicit, not of the AI sort.

III

So much for internalism. Now where is the externalism? To see where that comes in we must move from the existence of grounds to their adequacy. An internalist position on this point will make it a condition of justification that the adequacy of the ground be internal to the subject in some way or other. The externalism of my position will consist in the rejection of all such rquirements. We can distinguish here between making the internality of adequacy a *necessary* condition of justification and making it sufficient for justification, along with the belief's being based on the ground in question. I shall consider these in turn.

Go back to the distinction between PI and AI. (We may ignore CI in this connection, since we are unlikely to find a plausible way of construing the notion of an 'awareness' or 'consciousness' of the *adequacy* of a ground.) A PI necessary condition in this area would presumably run as follows.

(I) One is justified in believing that p only if one knows or is justified in believing that the ground of that belief is an adequate one.

Let's focus on the justified belief alternative. This requirement labors under the very considerable disadvantage of requiring an infinite hierarchy of justified beliefs in

12. More generally, the points made in this paper specifically concern prima facie justification. For example the accessibility constraint on grounds does not apply to the subject's perspective as a whole, from which overriders emerge. Or, to put the point more modestly, nothing I say in this paper gives any support to the idea that in order for something the subject knows or justifiably believes to override a prima facie justification that something has to be fairly readily accessible to the subject.

order to be justified in any belief. For the requirement will also apply to the higher level belief that the ground of the belief that p is adequate. (Call the propositional content of this higher level belief 'q'.) To be justified in the belief that q one must be justified in believing that *its* ground is adequate. Call the propositional object of this still higher level belief 'r'. Then to be justified in believing that r one must be justified in the still higher level belief that the ground of one's belief that r is an adequate one . . . Since it seems clear that no human being is capable of possessing all at once an infinite hierarchy of beliefs, it is equally clear that this requirement allows no one to have any justified beliefs. And that should be a sufficient basis for rejecting it.

The story with AI is somewhat different. First we have to decide on what is to count as 'accessibility to the adequacy of the ground'. The most obvious suggestion would be that accessibility consists in the capacity of the subject to come into the state required by the *PI* requirement, viz., being justified in believing that the ground of the target belief that p is adequate. We can then add the specification of the required degree and mode of accessibility. This will give us the following.

(II) S is justified in believing that p only if S is capable, fairly readily on the basis of reflection, to acquire a justified belief that the ground of S's belief p is an adequate one.

Clearly (II), unlike (I), does not imply that S has an infinite hierarchy of justified beliefs. For (II) does not require that S actually have a justified higher level belief for each belief in the hierarchy, but only that, for each justified belief she actually has, it is possible for her to acquire, by a certain route, an appropriately related justified higher level belief. To be sure, this does imply that S has, as we might say, an infinite hierarchy of possibilities for the acquisition of justified beliefs. But it is not at all clear that this is impossible, in the way it is clearly impossible for one of us to have an infinite hierarchy of actually justified beliefs. Thus I will have to find some other reason for rejecting (II).

That reason can be found by turning from possibility to actuality. Though it may well be within the limits of human capacity, it is by no means always the case that the subject of a justified belief is capable of determining the adequacy of his ground, just by careful reflection on the matter, or, indeed, in any other way. For one thing, many subjects are not at the level of conceptual sophistication to even raise the question of adequacy of ground, much less determine an answer by reflection. One thinks here of small children and, I fear, many adults as well. The maximally unsophisticated human perceiver is surely often justified in believing that what he sees to be the case is the case, even though he is in no position to even raise a question about the adequacy of his grounds. But even if capable of raising the question, he may not be able to arrive at a justified answer. Our judgment on this will depend both on what we take to be required for adequacy and what we regard as necessary for the justification of a belief that certain grounds are adequate. The two are, of course, intimately connected. I have already made it explicit that I take a ground, G, of belief B to be adequate if and only if it is sufficiently indicative of the truth of B. And this being the case, it seems clear that for me to be justified in believing G to be an adequate basis for belief, B, I must have sufficient *reasons* for supposing that this truth-indication relation does hold. (And, on my view, the belief in adequacy must be based on those reasons.) And many, or most, subjects are just not up to this. Consider, for instance, all the things we believe on authority. If we have been trained properly we generally recognize the marks of competence in an area, and when we believe the pronouncements of one who exhibits those marks we are believing on adequate grounds, proceeding aright in our belief formation, and so epistemically justified. But how many of us can, on reflection, come up with adequate evidence on which to base the belief that a given putative authority is to be relied on? Very few of us. (2) would imply that we are rarely justified in believing on authority, even when we are utilising what we have been trained to recognize as marks of authority, marks that are indeed reliable indications of expertise.

A weaker *AI* condition on adequacy of grounds would be the following.

(III) *S* is justified in believing that *p* only if *S* has adequate grounds for a judgment that the grounds for *S*'s belief that *p* are adequate.

This is weaker than (2) because it does not require that *S* actually be able to acquire a justified belief about adequacy, whether just on reflection or otherwise. It only requires that she 'have' the grounds (evidence, experiences, or whatever) that would serve to justify such a belief if that belief were based on those grounds. A subject could conceivably satisfy (2I) even if she lacked the conceptual equipment to formulate the issue of adequacy. Nevertheless, the considerations I have advanced make it dubious that even this condition is met by all or most justified believers. Do I have the evidence it would take to adequately support a belief that my present perceptual grounds for believing that there is a maple tree near my study window are adequate? I very much doubt it. Even if we can overcome problems of circularity (relying on other perceptual beliefs to support the claim that this perceptual ground is adequate), as I believe we can,[13] it seems very dubious that we store enough observational evidence to constitute adequate evidence for the thesis that normal sensory experience is an adequate ground for our beliefs about the physical environment. No doubt our experience reinforces our tendency to believe this, but that is another matter. For these and other reasons, I very much doubt that all or most justified believers satisfy (2I).

We must, of course, be alive to the point that our *AI* principle concerning the presence of the ground did not require that the ground be fairly directly accessible to the subject in each case, but only that it be the sort of thing that is typically so accessible. This suggests a weakening of (I)–(2I) so that the requirement is not that so-and-so be true in each case, but only that it be generally or normally the case. But if the above contentions are sound, these weaker principles would be excluded also. For I have argued that it is not even generally or typically the case that, taking (2) as our example, one who has a justified belief that *p* is capable of arriving fairly readily at a justified belief that the ground of his belief that *p* is an adequate one.

13. See W. P. Alston 'Epistemic Circularity', *Philosophical and Phenomenological Research* 47 (1986), 1–30 for a defence of this view.

What about an internalist *sufficient* condition of adequacy (sufficient along with the belief's being based on the ground question)? Here again we will have both *PI* and *AI* versions. Let's say that the *PI* version takes it as sufficient for the justification of *S*'s belief that *p* that:

(IV) *S*'s belief that *p* is based on an accessible ground that *S* is justified in supposing to be adequate.

The *AI* version can be construed as taking the condition to consist in the appropriate sort of possibility of *S*'s satisfying (IV). More explicitly:

(V) *S*'s belief that *p* is based on an accessible ground such that *S* can fairly readily come to have a justified belief that this ground is an adequate one.

Since the *PI* condition is stronger, it will suffice to show that it is not strong enough.[14]

The crucial question here is whether (IV) insures truth conducivity, which we saw at the beginning of the paper to be an essential feature of epistemic justification. And this boils down to the question of whether *S*'s being justified in supposing the ground of his belief in *p* to be adequate guarantees that the belief that *p* is likely to be true. This depends on both the concept of adequacy and the concept of justification used in (IV). If (IV) employs a non-truth-indicative concept of adequacy, the game is up right away. Suppose, e.g., that an adequate ground for a belief that *p* is one on which a confident belief of this sort is customarily based. In that case likelihood of truth is not ensured even by the ground's *being* adequate, much less by *S*'s being justified in supposing it to be adequate. Let's take it, then, that our *PI* internalist is using our concept of a ground's *being* adequate; his difference from us is simply that where we require for justification that the ground *be* adequate, he takes it sufficient that *S* be justified in supposing it to be adequate. But then we must ask what concept of justification he is using. If he were using our concept of justification in (IV), the satisfaction of that condition would imply that *p* is likely to be true. For if *S* is justified in believing the ground to be adequate, on our concept of justification, then the belief that the ground is adequate is thereby likely to be true; and so, if there is not too much leakage in the double probabilification, the likelihood that the ground of the belief that *p* is adequate implies in turn that it is likely that *p*. But this would mean that our internalist opponent avoids our concept of justification (requiring actual adequacy of ground) at the first level only to embrace it at the second and, presumably, at all higher levels. The only effect of this is that the implication of truth-conducivity at the first level is somewhat weaker than on our view; since whereas we flat-out require adequacy at the first level, his view only requires the likelihood of adequacy. But this difference lacks motivation, and in any event it certainly

14. Note that if the condition is asserted only as sufficient and not also as necessary, no infinite hierarchy can be shown to follow even from the *PI* version. Since the claim is compatible with there being other sufficient conditions of justification, it does not imply that one can be justified in believing that *p* only if one has an infinite hierarchy of justified beliefs. But, of course, if other sufficient conditions are countenanced the position would lose its distinctively internalist clout.

doesn't give his view a distinctively *internalist* cast in contrast to ours, since he uses our concept of justification at all higher levels. Hence if our opponent is to be more than a paper internalist, he will have to be using some non-truth-conducive conception of justification at the higher levels;[15] and in that case the fact that S is justified in believing that the ground of his belief that p is adequate has no tendency to imply that the ground *is* adequate, and hence no tendency to imply that p is (likely to be) true. And therefore (IV) cannot be sufficient for epistemic justification.

Thus it would seem that internalist conditions concerning adequacy are neither necessary nor sufficient for justification. And so the view here being defended is resolutely and uncompromisingly externalist, so far as adequacy of grounds is concerned. In order for my belief that p, which is based on ground G, to be justified, it is quite sufficient, as well as necessary, that G be sufficiently indicative of the truth of p. It is in no way required that I know anything, or be justified in believing anything, about this relationship. No doubt, we sometimes do have justified beliefs about the adequacy of our grounds, and that is certainly a good thing. But that is icing on the cake.

IV

In this paper I have proposed an account of the prima facie epistemic justification of beliefs according to which that amounts to a belief's having an adequate ground. The justification will be ultima facie provided there are not sufficient overriders from within the subject's knowledge and justified belief. I have given reasons for placing a (rather weak) AI constraint on something's being a ground that could justify a belief, but I have resisted attempts to put any internalist constraint on what constitutes the adequacy of a ground. There I have insisted that it is both necessary and sufficient that the world be such that the ground be 'sufficiently indicative of the truth' of the belief, both necessary and sufficient that this actually be the case, and neither necessary nor sufficient that the subject have any cognitive grasp of this fact. Thus my position has definite affinities with reliabilism, especially with that variant thereof sometimes called a 'reliable indication' view, as contrasted with a 'reliable process' view.[16] But it differs from a pure reliabilism by holding that the justification of a belief requires that the belief be based on a 'ground' that satisfies an AI constraint, as well as by letting the subject's perspective on the world

---

15. We have not ruled out the possibility that our opponent is using, in (IV), some truth-conducive concept of justification other than ours, e.g., a straight reliability concept according to which it is sufficient for the justification of a belief that it have been acquired in some reliable way. But if that's what he's doing, he turns out to be even less internalist than if he had used our concept.

16. To be sure, in explaining early on in the paper the way in which I pick out grounds, I appealed to features of the *process* of belief formation. (I am indebted to Hilary Kornblith and Alvin Goldman for calling this to my attention.) Nevertheless, reliability enters into my formulation of what is necessary and sufficient for justification by way of the truth indicativeness of the ground, rather than by way of the reliability of any belief forming process.

determine whether overriding occurs.[17] Beliefs that, so far as the subject can tell, just pop into his head out of nowhere would not be counted as justified on this position. I do hold that mere reliable belief production, suitably construed, is sufficient for knowledge, but that is another story.

17. I would suggest that much of the plausibility of some prominent attacks on externalism in general and reliabilism in particular stems from a failure to distinguish externalism with respect to the ground and with respect its adequacy. See, e.g., Laurence BonJour, *The Structure of Empirical Knowledge* (Cambridge, Harvard University Press, 1985), Ch. 3, and Richard Foley, 'What's Wrong with Reliabilism?', *The Monist*, 68 (1985), 188–202 [Ch. 13 in this volume].

Part III

Foundations and Norms

Introduction

MOST of the things we know are based on other things we know. I know that I got a telephone call while I was out of the office because I can see the blinking 'new message' light on my answering machine. I believe, reasonably enough, that she is asleep because I can hear her snoring. And we learn a lot from newspapers, television, books, teachers, and friends. In each of these cases, one belief—that the 'new message' light is blinking, that she is snoring, that the newspaper (teacher, friend) *said* so-and-so—is more basic than the other. One belief stands under or supports another. This naturally raises the question whether this hierarchy of beliefs has a bottom, a foundation, a level which is not itself based on any more basic beliefs. Are there, in other words, unjustified (by other beliefs) justifiers, unsupported supporters.

Foundationalism is the view that there is—indeed, that there must be—such an ultimate level of non-inferentially justified beliefs. All other beliefs are derived from them or demonstrated by appeal to them. Foundationalism divides our beliefs into two classes: those which need support from others and those which do not. We thus get the picture of our beliefs forming a pyramid with non-basic beliefs being supported by reasoning that traces back ultimately to the basic beliefs. Perhaps an upside down pyramid would be a more appropriate model since there are comparatively few basic beliefs compared to the vast number of beliefs in commonsense and in science that stand in need of justification. The driving force behind foundationalism has always been the threat of an *infinite regress*: if every justified belief could be justified only by inferring it from some further justified belief, the justificational regress would go on forever. To avoid the regress, a foundationalist argues that we are forced to suppose that in tracing back the inferential chain we arrive at one or more immediately justified beliefs that stop the regress. These immediately (non-inferentially) justified beliefs are not based on other beliefs. They qualify as knowledge (or at least as fully justified) not because we have reasons to support them, but because they address a special realm of facts to which the mind has direct access. These facts constitute 'the Given'.

A first impression might be that the only beliefs that are not held on the basis of reasoning are perceptual beliefs. We do not infer that the light is on. We can *see* that it is on. As we all know, though, such beliefs can be mistaken. Given that perceptual beliefs are fallible (things are not always what they seem) they stand as much in need of justification as any other belief and therefore cannot provide an ultimate stopping point. In response, classical foundationalism maintains that the basic beliefs are not ordinary perceptual beliefs about physical objects but beliefs about our own sensory states or immediate experiences—how things seem or appear to us. We can be wrong about whether the lights are on, but not about the fact that they appear to be on. Beliefs about how the world appears to us would thus seem to be a more basic level of belief than perceptual beliefs about the world.

Price (Chapter 17) gives a classical statement of foundationalism. He can, he says, doubt whether there really is a tomato he is seeing, but there is something he cannot doubt, something that is absolutely indubitable and certain—that he is experiencing a red patch of a round and somewhat bulgy character. This, for Price, is *the given*, the sort of datum of sense (hence, sense datum) that is directly present to consciousness and which provides the certain foundation for all empirical knowledge. With physical reality there is a distinction between how things are and how they appear to be, but in the case of sense data the distinction collapses. In the sphere of the given, what *appears* to be, *is*. Mistakes are impossible.

Chisholm (Chapter 18) is another foundationalist. He uses different terminology than Price, but his point is the same. He speaks not of 'the given' but of 'the directly evident'. The directly evident consists of those self-presenting states which justify a belief in them. Seeming to have a headache (a self-presenting state) justifies the belief that you seem to have one. Thinking about Socrates justifies the belief that you are thinking about Socrates. That something looks red and bulgy (Price's example) also justifies the belief that something looks red and bulgy.

Chisholm carefully distinguishes various senses of such words as 'look', 'appear', and 'seem'. What is directly evident is how things seem in what Chisholm calls the phenomenological or descriptive (non-comparative) sense. In this descriptive sense, to believe that something *looks* red is not to believe it looks, say, the way ripe tomatoes look in normal light; for that is a comparison of the way the object looks to the way tomatoes look and one could be wrong about the way tomatoes look in normal light. In this comparative sense of 'look', the fact that the object looks red is *not* directly evident. Since Chisholm's notion of what is directly evident depends so critically on the existence of a non-comparative, a phenomenological, sense of 'appear', this idea has come in for heavy criticism from other philosophers. Chisholm spends some time answering these objections. He closes with a list of statements that express what is directly evident. It is worth noting that everything on this list describes what is going on in the mind of the believer. No statement describing an independent (of the self) reality is directly evident. This is typical of foundationalism. The foundation exists within the self.

Sellars' essay (Chapter 19) is an influential attack on the myth of the given embodied in classical foundationalism. The target of Sellars' criticism is the view that sense-data reports such as 'something appears red to me' are self-justifying and infallible and can serve as foundations for other beliefs. According to Sellars, this view involves a confusion between having sense experiences, which is non-epistemic, and having non-inferential knowledge of propositions referring to sense experiences. While the former is a necessary condition for the latter, it is not itself a kind of knowledge. The fact that having sense experiences is non-epistemic renders it infallible, but also unsuitable for providing the foundation for other beliefs. Having non-inferential knowledge of propositions referring to sense experiences, however, is epistemic and hence suitable for epistemological foundations; but it is fallible, requiring concepts acquired through trained responses to public physical objects.

Quine (Chapter 20) argues that the classical foundationalist project was a failure, both in its details and its conception. Classical foundationalism contends that there is a privileged class of self-justifying and infallible truths sufficient for deducing all other truths. First Quine denies the privileged status of any such alleged truths and second he denies that even if there were such, they would be sufficient for deducing all other truths.

Moreover, Quine rejects the more general conception of foundationalism according to which an epistemological account of how we should arrive at our beliefs must precede a commitment to any substantive belief about the world around us. Epistemology, on Quine's view, is a branch of natural science; it should not be based on ideal abstract conditions but on scientific research in the processes underlying human perception and cognition. In other words, epistemology should not concern itself with how we *should* form beliefs but with how we *do* in fact form them.

Kim (Chapter 21) objects to Quine's rejection of the normative dimension of epistemological theorizing. The concept of justification is absolutely central to epistemology, and this concept, Kim argues, is essentially normative. Since you cannot get norms—how things should be—from facts about how things are, epistemology cannot be reduced to cognitive psychology. We can stop doing epistemology if we like, but we should not fool ourselves into thinking we are doing it by studying the causal processes at work in belief acquisition.

Further reading

Austin, J. L., *Sense and Sensibilia*, Oxford, Clarendon Press, 1962.

Ayer, A. J., *The Foundations of Empirical Knowledge*, New York, St. Martin's Press, 1955.

Brandom, R., 'Study Guide' in W. Sellars, *Empiricism and the Philosophy of Mind*, Cambridge/MA, Harvard University Press, 1997, pp. 119–81

Chisholm, R. M., *The Foundations of Knowing*, Brighton, Harvester Press, 1982, Chs. 1, 10.

Chisholm, R. M. and Swartz, R. J., eds., *Empirical Knowledge*, Englewood Cliffs/NJ, Prentice-Hall, 1973.

Dancy, J., *An Introduction to Contemporary Epistemology*, Oxford, Basil Blackwell, 1985, Part 2.

Gibons, R. F., Jr., *Enlightened Empiricism. An Examination of W.V. Quine's Theory of Knowledge*, Tampa, University of South Florida Press, 1988.

Goldman, A. H., *Empirical Knowledge*, Berkeley, University of California Press, 1988, Part 2.

Harman, G., *Change in View*, Cambridge/MA, MIT Press, 1986.

Kornblith, H., ed., *Naturalizing Epistemology*, 2nd edition, Cambridge/MA, MIT Press, 1994.

Kornblith, H., 'In Defense of a Naturalized Epistemology', in J. Greco and F. Sosa, eds., *The Blackwell Guide to Epistemology*, Oxford, Basil Blackwell, 1999, pp. 158–69.

Lewis, C. I., *An Analysis of Knowledge and Valuation*, La Salle, Open Court, 1946.

McGrew, T. J., *The Foundations of Knowing*, Lanham/MD, Littlefield Adams, 1995.

Pollock, J. L., *Knowledge and Justification*, Princeton, Princeton University Press, 1974, Ch. 2.

Pollock, J. L., 'A Plethora of Epistemological Theories', in G. S. Pappas, ed., *Justification and Knowledge*, Dordrecht, Reidel, 1979, pp. 93–113.

Quine, W. V., 'The Nature of Natural Knowledge', in S. Guttenplan, ed., *Mind and Language*, Oxford, Clarendon Press, 1975, pp. 67–81.

Rorty, R., *Philosophy and the Mirror of Nature*, Princeton, Princeton University Press, 1979.

Sellars, W., 'Givenness and Explanatory Coherence', *The Journal of Philosophy* 70 (1973), pp. 612–24.

Stich, S. P., *The Fragmentation of Reason*, Cambridge/MA, MIT Press, 1990.

Swartz, R. J., ed., *Perceiving, Sensing, and Knowing*, Garden City/NY, Doubleday Anchor, 1965.

Synthese 55, No. 1 (1983), special issue on 'Naturalized Epistemology and Foundationalism'.

Williams, M., *Groundless Belief*, Oxford, Basil Blackwell, 1977.

In addition consult the 'Further reading' sections at the end of Part II and at the end of Part V (perception).

Foundations and Norms

Chapter 17
The given
H. H. Price

Every man entertains a great number of beliefs concerning material things, e.g. that there is a square-topped table in this room, that the earth is a spheroid, that water is composed of hydrogen and oxygen. It is plain that all these beliefs are based on sight and on touch (from which organic sensation cannot be separated): based upon them in the sense that if we had not had certain particular experiences of seeing and touching, it would be neither *possible* nor *reasonable* to entertain these beliefs. Beliefs about imperceptibles such as molecules or electrons or X-rays are no exception to this. Only they are based not directly on sight and touch, but indirectly. Their direct basis consists of certain other beliefs concerning scientific instruments, photographic plates, and the like. Thus over and above any intrinsic uncertainty that they themselves may have, whatever uncertainty attaches to these more basic beliefs is communicated to them. It follows that in any attempt either to analyse or to justify our beliefs concerning material things, the primary task is to consider beliefs concerning perceptible or 'macroscopic' objects such as chairs and tables, cats and rocks. It follows, too, that no theory concerning 'microscopic' objects can possibly be used to throw doubt upon our beliefs concerning chairs or cats or rocks, so long as these are based directly on sight and touch. Empirical Science can never be more trustworthy than perception, upon which it is based; and it can hardly fail to be *less* so, since among its non-perceptual premises there can hardly fail to be some which are neither self-evident nor demonstrable. Thus the not uncommon view that the world which we perceive is an illusion and only the 'scientific' world of protons and electrons is real, is based upon a gross fallacy, and would destroy the very premises upon which Science itself depends.

My aim in this book is to examine those experiences in the way of seeing and touching upon which our beliefs concerning material things are based, and to inquire in what way and to what extent they justify these beliefs. Other modes of

H. H. Price, 'The Given' in *Perception* (2nd revised edition) (London, Methuen, 1950) pp. 1–12, 18–20, reprinted by permission of the author.

sense-experience, e.g. hearing and smelling, will be dealt with only incidentally. For it is plain that they are only auxiliary. If we possessed them, but did not possess either sight or touch, we should have no beliefs about the material world at all, and should lack even the very conception of it. Possessing sight or touch or both, we can use experiences of these other senses as signs of obtainable but not at the moment actual experiences of seeing or touching, and thereby gain indirectly information which these inferior senses in themselves provide no hint of.

It may appear to some people that Science, particularly Physiology, can answer these questions for us. But it should already be clear that this is a mistake. Thus if it be said that when a man sees something, e.g. a tomato, light rays emanating from the object impinge upon his retina and this stimulates the optic nerve, which in turn causes a change in the optic centres in his brain, which causes a change in his mind: there are two comments to be made. 1. No doubt this is in fact a perfectly true account, but what are our *grounds* for believing it? Obviously they are derived from observation, and mainly if not entirely from visual observation. Thus the Physiologist has not explained in the least how visual observation justifies a man in holding a certain belief about a tomato, e.g. that it is spherical. All he has done is to put forward certain *other* beliefs concerning a retina and a brain. Those other beliefs have themselves to be justified in exactly the same way as the first belief, and we are as far as ever from knowing what way that is. Instead of answering our question, we have found another instance of it. Nor is this result surprising. Since the premises of Physiology are among the propositions into whose validity we are inquiring, it is hardly likely that its conclusions will assist us. 2. In any case, Science only professes to tell us what are the *causes* of seeing and touching. But we want to know what seeing and touching themselves *are*. This question lies outside the sphere of Science altogether.

Thus there is no short cut to our goal. We must simply examine seeing and touching for ourselves and do the best we can. What, then, is it to see or to touch something? Let us confine ourselves to sight for the moment and return to the instance of the tomato.

When I see a tomato there is much that I can doubt. I can doubt whether it is a tomato that I am seeing, and not a cleverly painted piece of wax. I can doubt whether there is any material thing there at all. Perhaps what I took for a tomato was really a reflection; perhaps I am even the victim of some hallucination. One thing however I cannot doubt: that there exists a red patch of a round and somewhat bulgy shape standing out from a background of other colour-patches, and having a certain visual depth, and that this whole field of colour is directly present to my consciousness. What the red patch is, whether a substance, or a state of a substance, or an event, whether it is physical or psychical or neither, are questions that we may doubt about. But that something is red and round then and there[1] I cannot doubt. Whether the something persists even for a moment before and after it is present to my consciousness, whether other minds can be conscious of it as well as I, may be doubted. But that it now *exists*, and that *I* am conscious of it—by me at

---

1. 'There' means 'In spatial relations to other colour-patches present to my consciousness at the same time'.

least who am conscious of it this cannot possibly be doubted. And when I say that it is 'directly' present to my consciousness, I mean that my consciousness of it is not reached by inference, nor by any other intellectual process (such as abstraction or intuitive induction), nor by any passage from sign to significate. There obviously must be some sort or sorts of presence to consciousness which can be called 'direct' in this sense, else we should have an infinite regress. Analogously, when I am in the situations called 'touching something', 'hearing it', 'smelling it', etc., in each case there is something which at that moment indubitably exists—a pressure (or pre-ment patch), a noise, a smell; and that something is directly present to my consciousness.

This peculiar and ultimate manner of being present to consciousness is called *being given*, and that which is thus present is called a *datum*. The corresponding mental attitude is called *acquaintance, intuitive apprehension*, or sometimes *having*. Data of this special sort are called *sense-data*. And the acquaintance with them is conveniently called *sensing*; though sometimes, I think, this word is used in another sense. It is supposed by some writers that sense-data are mental events, and these writers appear to think that the word 'sensing', if used at all, ought to mean the coming-into-being of sense-data, not the intuitive apprehension of them. (For their coming-into-being will then be a mental process.) This seems to be a very inconvenient usage. We need some word for the intuitive apprehension of sense-data. We cannot say 'perceiving' (for that, as we shall see, has at least two other meanings already). And 'sensing' is the obvious word to use. At any rate in this book we shall always use it in this sense. When we have occasion to speak of the process which is the coming-into-being of a sense-datum we shall call it *sense-datum-genesis*.

It is true that the term 'given' or 'datum' is sometimes used in a wider and looser sense to mean 'that, the inspection of which provides a premise for inference'. Thus the data of the historian are the statements which he finds in documents and inscriptions; the data of the general are the facts reported by his aircraft and his intelligence service: the data of the detective are the known circumstances and known results of the crime; and so on. But it is obvious that these are only data relatively and for the purpose of answering a certain question. They are really themselves the results of inference, often of a very complicated kind. We may call them data *secundum quid*. But eventually we must get back to something which is a datum *simpliciter*, which is not the result of any previous intellectual process. It is with data *simpliciter*, or rather with one species of them, that we are concerned.

How do sense-data differ from other data, e.g. from those of memory or intro-spection? We might be tempted to say, in the manner in which they come to be given, viz. as a result of the stimulation of a sense-organ. This will not do. For first, the sense-organs are themselves material things, and it seems quite likely that the term 'material thing' cannot be defined except by reference to sense-data; and if so we should have a vicious circle. And secondly, even though we doubted the exist-ence of all material things, including our own body and its organs, it would still be perfectly obvious that sense-data differ from other sorts of data. The only describ-able differentia that they seem to have is this, that they lead us to conceive of and believe in the existence of certain material things, whether there are in fact any such things or not. (Visual and tactual sense-data do this directly, the others indirectly, as explained above.) But it seems plain that there is also another characteristic common and peculiar to them, which may be called 'sensuousness'. This is obvious on inspection, but it cannot be described.

Does sensing differ from other forms of intuitive apprehension? Or is there only one sort of intuitive apprehension, and does the difference between (say) sensing, remembering and the contemplation of mental images lie only in the nature of the apprehensa? The question is difficult, nor does it seem very important. Perhaps we may say that there are two sorts of intuitive apprehension, one directed upon *facts,* e.g. the fact that I am puzzled or was puzzled or again the fact that $2 + 2 = 4$, or that courage is good: another directed upon *particular existents,* e.g. this colour-patch or this noise or that visual image, or again upon this feeling of disgust and that act of wondering. The first is apprehension *that,* the second is apprehension *of.* The term *acquaintance* is properly reserved for the second, and we shall so use it in future.

Are there several different sorts of acquaintance, e.g. sensing, self-consciousness, and contemplation of mental images? I cannot see that there are. The difference seems to be wholly on the side of the data. If so, *a fortiori* there are not different kinds of sensing. Visual sensing will simply be the acquaintance with colour-patches, auditory sensing the acquaintance with sounds, and so on; the acquaintance being the same in each case. No doubt there will be different kinds of *sense-datum-genesis,* just as there are different kinds of sense-data. And if any one likes to use the term 'visual sensing'[2] to mean the genesis of colour-patches and 'auditory sensing' to mean the genesis of noises, he may; and of course he is then entitled to say that there *are* different kinds of sensing. But this has not the slightest tendency to show that there are different kinds of sensing in *our* sense of the word (which is also the usual one).

If the term sense-datum is taken in the strictly limited meaning that we have given it, I do not see how any one can doubt that there are sense-data. Yet it is certain that many philosophers do profess to doubt this and even to deny it. Indeed the sense-datum has come in for a good many hard words. It has been compared to the Wild Goose which we vainly chase: or again it is the Will o' the Wisp which lures the Realist further and further from Reality. According to an eminent Idealist philosopher,[3] our modern interest in the sense-datum is just one more manifestation (among so many others) of the degeneracy of an age which prefers the childish, the easy, and the barbarous to the laborious achievement of Intelligence and Civilization. Or again—charge hardly compatible with this—it is derided as the invention of sophisticated philosophers, as no datum at all. Nor are our opponents

---

2. The substitution of 'seeing' for visual sensing, 'hearing' for auditory sensing, etc., would make confusion even worse confounded. For in the ordinary sense of the word *see,* what I see is not a colour-patch, but a material thing, e.g. a table or a tomato. Likewise *hear, smell* etc., are in ordinary usage ambiguous. I hear the train, or I hear a noise. I smell the rose, or I smell a smell.

3. Professor H. J. Paton. 'The Idea of the Self' in *The Nature of Ideas. Lectures Delivered before the Philosophical Union, University of California, 1925–6.*

content with brilliant metaphors. They have plausible arguments to put forward, and these we must try to answer. It is obvious that we cannot do more than this. It is impossible from the nature of the case to *prove* that there are sense-data or data of any other sort. The utmost we can do is to remove misunderstandings which prevent people from searching for them and from acknowledging them when found. After that, we can only appeal to every man's own consciousness.

The doctrine that there are no sense-data may take two forms, a wider and a narrower, which are not always clearly separated.

1. It is said that the very notion of givenness is an absurd and self-contradictory notion, that from the nature of the case nothing can ever be given at all. This is the most radical criticism that we have to meet. It may be called the *A priori* Thesis.

2. There is also what may be called the Empirical Thesis. This does not say that there is an absurdity in the very notion of givenness. It only says that we can never in fact find anything which is given. And it concludes that either there is no Given at all, or if there is any, it is found only in the experience of new-born children, idiots, and people falling into or just coming out of fainting fits: in which case (it is urged) the Given is clearly of no importance to the philosopher, for it is quite beyond the reach of investigation, and therefore cannot be appealed to as evidence for anything.

Either of these theses if established would be very damaging. The *A priori* Thesis is the most radical, but also the easier to answer. The Empirical Thesis is the really difficult one to meet, and we shall have to make some concessions to it. Nevertheless, the arguments by which it is ordinarily supported are open to very grave objections.

The 'A priori' Thesis. The main argument in favour of this may be summed up as follows:

It is impossible to apprehend something without apprehending some at least of its qualities and relations. In the language of Cambridge logicians, what we apprehend is always a *fact*—something of the form 'that A is B' or 'the B-ness of A'. You cannot apprehend just A. For instance, you cannot apprehend a round red patch without apprehending that it is red and round and has certain spatial relations. But if we apprehend that it has these qualities and relations, we are not passively 'receiving' or (as it were) swallowing; we are actively thinking—judging or classifying—and it is impossible to do less than this.

To this I answer, it is very likely true, but it is irrelevant. The argument only proves that nothing stands *merely* in the relation of givenness to the mind, without also standing in other relations: i.e. that what is given is always also 'thought about' in some sense or other of that ambiguous phrase. But this does not have the slightest tendency to prove that *nothing is given at all*. The fact that A and B are constantly conjoined, or even necessarily connected, does not have the slightest tendency to prove that A does not exist.[4] How could it, since it itself presupposes

---

4. A stands here for 'Givenness' and B for 'thought-of-ness'. The argument is the one commonly used against what is called *vicious abstraction*. Sometimes the conclusion is not that A does not exist but that A is identical with B: but here again it is presupposed in the premises that they are different— else how could they be necessarily connected?

the existence of A? That arguments of this sort should be so frequently used, and should be thought so conclusive, is one of the curiosities of philosophical controversy.

Secondly, we may attack the enemy on his own ground and ask him how we can think without having something to think about. This *subject* or *subject-matter*, about which we think must be somehow brought before the mind, if we are to think about it, and it cannot always be brought there by previous thinking, or we should have an infinite regress, This means that something must be *given*. And sensing is one of the ways (I do not say the only one) in which subject-matters for thought are given to us. No doubt it is important to insist that this intuitive 'receiving' of a datum is never more than an element in our total state of mind. But still it *is* an element, and an essential one.

The Empirical Thesis. This maintains that it is in fact impossible to discover any data. For if we try to point to an instance, it is said, we shall have to confess that the so-called datum is not really given at all, but is the product of interpretation.

This doctrine is put forward both in the interests of Subjective Idealism, which holds that each mind lives in a private world of it own, and in the interests of that Objective Rationalistic Idealism which holds that the world is entirely constructed by 'Thought', or by 'Mind' with a capital M. But it may be suspected that sometimes the one party uses arguments which are only appropriate to the other.

We must begin by protesting, with Professor G. E. Moore, against the word 'interpretation', which is used to cover several quite different processes and is at best only a metaphor. For instance, it may mean either *association of ideas*, or some form of *thinking*. We shall begin with the first.

Effects of Association. We can easily find cases where the Given seems to have been contaminated, as it were, by the effects of association. Thus it would be said that Visual Depth beyond a pretty short range is plainly not given, but is due to the revival, by association, of the traces of past kinaesthetic and tactual experience. Or again a distant snowy peak looks cold, but is it not obvious that its coldness cannot be given? The sounds of a foreign language, say Italian, sound quite different when I have learned to speak the language myself. They then fall apart, as it were, into words and word-groups, which they never did before. (At first I heard just one continuous sound.) This is due to the traces of the kinaesthetic experiences experienced in speaking the language oneself, and further to one's newly-acquired knowledge of what the words mean—for this knowledge too has left its 'traces'. But neither the kinaestheta nor the meanings can be *heard*. Both are 'read into' what we hear. Proof-reading and Psychic Blindness also provide instances. But here the effect of the traces is negative instead of positive. Instead of seeing what is not there, we fail to see what is there.

Objections to the Argument. Let us first take the argument on its own ground, without criticizing its premises. We must then answer that no doubt the facts are as stated, but they do not prove what is wanted. Indeed, if anything, they prove the very opposite, viz. that there *are* data and that we know what they are.

1. If nothing whatever is given to me when I look at the mountain or hear the

sounds, the phrase 'due to association' loses all sense. Association is a relation, and if we speak of it, we imply that there are at least two terms to be associated: what is associated must be associated *with something*. When the mountain looks cold to me, the presence of the coldness to my mind is due to association. But with what is the coldness associated? Obviously with the colour and shape. These then *are* given: *their* presence cannot be explained by association, for they are what the associated qualities join on to. And if, preferring another metaphor, you say that what I see is 'contaminated by' the traces of past experiences, or 'overlaid with' them: I answer, that where there is contamination there must be something which is contaminated, and where there is overlaying there must be something which is overlaid.

2. Is it not dangerous to specify *what* characteristics are due to association? We are told 'What you see looks cold, distant and solid; and obviously coldness, distance and solidity cannot be given to sight'. But how does the critic know that they are not given to sight? The only answer must be: 'Because colour and two-dimensional shape are the only qualities that *are* given to sight'. But in that case there is after all a datum of sight, and the critic knows what it is.

3. Is it not dangerous to give a name to the associations, to speak of them, for instance, as *tactual* associations, *kinaesthetic* associations and the like? For this presupposes that the associated characteristics, though not given now, have been given in the past. For instance, if you say that the apparent coldness and solidity of the seen mountain-peak are due to tactual associations, and therefore are not given to sight at this moment, you admit that they have been given to touch in the past. Otherwise what is the sense of using the word 'tactual'? And even if, more wary, you merely say that the presence of these qualities is due just to the traces of past experience, we must press you to specify what kind of past experience. And you will be obliged to say, past *sense*-experience, and so you will have admitted that these qualities have been given in the past. Thus in order to prove that A *is* not given, one has to assume that B *has been* given.

So far we have been attacking the critics of the Given upon their own ground. And that ground is this. They begin by assuming that there is a distinction between 'the real given' or the given-as-it-is-in-itself on the one hand, and 'what the given seems to be' on the other. And they then argue that we cannot know what this given-as-it-is-in-itself is. That the argument when we pursue it into detail is incoherent, and proves the very opposite of what it is supposed to prove, we have seen. We must now attack the initial assumption and point out:

4. That the distinction between the Given as it really is and what the Given seems to be[5] is altogether untenable. I scarcely know how to prove this. Is it not just obvious that if something seems to be given, it is given? For in the sphere of the given (as in that of pleasure and pain) what seems, is. Indeed we might go farther. We might say that the notion of seeming has no *application* to the given: and that, by the very definitions of 'seeming' and of 'given'. When A seems to be B, this really

5. In his *Philosophical Studies* [London, Routledge & Kegan Paul, 1922], pp. 243–7, Professor G. E. Moore has suggested that sense-data may seem to be what they are not. But he admits that this suggestion may be 'sheer nonsense'.

means that some mind unreflectively believes A to be B, or as we say 'takes' it to be B. Now if so, there must be some *evidence* upon which this taking is (however hastily and unreflectively) based. Thus if it seems to me to be raining, the evidence is that I hear a pitter-patter sound. This does not *seem* to be a pitter-patter sound; it *is* one. And only because there *is* this sound can it seem to have a certain cause, viz. rain falling on the roof. And though the rain which there seems to be may not after all exist (for it may have been a shower of gravel or peas) the sound none the less exists, and does have a pitter-patter character. In short, the Given is by definition that which by being itself actual and intuitively apprehended, makes it possible for something else to seem to exist or to have a certain quality. Of course certain characteristics may be given which some philosopher thinks *ought not* to be given, e.g. solidity. So much the worse for him, that is all. He must have held a false theory of what is 'giveable'. If something is given, it is given, and we must just make the best of it. In a matter of this kind we cannot and will not accept the dictation of theorists.

To clinch my point, I will try to show how these errors may have arisen. They arise, I think, from a confusion between two standpoints or modes of investigation, (*a*) the physiological and (*b*) the immanent or phenomenological. The physiologist finds that many of the characteristics of the visual field are not due to the electro-magnetic stimulus which affects the retina; or even that none of its characteristics are entirely due to this. He therefore concludes that those characteristics are not given. But we must point out that he is using the term 'given' in an utterly different sense from ours, a *causal* sense: he is using it to mean 'due to a physical stimulus external to the organism'—or he may even be meaning that this stimulus *is* what is given.

But our standpoint is quite a different one. We are asking what is *given to consciousness*, or presented to the mind. We are not inquiring into the causes which may have led to its being given. Further (as has been shown already), our standpoint is the more fundamental one. For the physiologist's only evidence for believing that there is an organism, and physical stimuli affecting it, is derived from observation: that is, from the presentation to him—to him, not to his organism—of data in *our* sense of the word.

To sum up this rather intricate discussion:

1. It is true that what is given now to a certain mind depends to a surprisingly large extent upon what has been given to that mind in the past. But this, so far from disproving the existence either of present or of past data, asserts the existence of both, and enables us to describe their nature in a way we could not do before.

2. It is true that the facts concerning association adduced by our critics do make the causal explanation of the datum more complicated than one might expect. But to say that they prove that there are no data is to deny the very fact of association itself, which presupposes the existence of past data. And to say that the causal explanation of something is complicated is to assert, not to deny, the existence of the something to be explained.

3. The facts adduced do not hinder but help the Realist, that is, the man who wishes to use his data to gain knowledge or true belief about a Real which exists

whether known and believed about or not. For the datum, it turns out, gives information not only about the present or the immediate past, but also—*via* earlier data—about the remote past. And the past is as much a part of the real world as the present, and quite as interesting. Moreover, the datum, we have found, gives information not merely about the non-mental, but also about the mind to which it is presented (e.g. a psycho-analyst can argue from the peculiarities of a man's data, say the hallucinations from which he suffers, to the existence of such and such a suppressed complex in the man's mind). Why should it be supposed that this would upset the Realist? The mind is just as much a part of the Real, and just as fit an object for inquiry, as any mountain-top or teacup. And if we can collect information about it from the given, so much the better for us. We ought to be glad that the given is so full of a number of things, and accept the gift in the spirit in which it is offered.

[. . .]

We may sum up this discussion as follows. When I am in the situation which is described as seeing something, touching something, hearing something, etc., it is certain in each case that a colour-patch, or a pressure, or a noise exists at that moment and that I am acquainted with this colour-patch, pressure or noise. Such entities are called sense-data, and the acquaintance with them is conveniently called sensing; but it differs from other instances of acquaintance only in its object, not in its nature, and it has no species. The usual arguments against the reality and against the knowability of sense-data break down on examination. They only prove at most that there is no sense-datum which is not the object of other sorts of consciousness besides sensing, and that the causes of most sense-data are more complicated than might have been expected: and in these conclusions there is nothing to disturb us.

In conclusion we may point out that the admission that there are sense-data is not a very large one; it commits us to very little. It maybe worth while to mention explicitly a number of things which we are *not* committed to.

1. We are not committed to the view that sense-data *persist*[6] through the intervals when they are not being sensed. We have only to admit that they *exist* at the times when they are being sensed.

2. We are not committed to the view that several minds can be acquainted with the *same* sense-datum. We have only to admit that every mind is acquainted with *some* sense-data from time to time.

3. We are not committed to any view about what is called 'the status' of sense-data in the Universe, either as regards the *category* they fall under, or as regards their relations with other types of existent entities. They may be events, or substances, or states of substances. They may be physical; i.e. they may be parts of, or events, in material objects such as chairs and tables or (in another theory) brains. They may

---

6. Or more strictly, that there are persistent *sensibilia* which become sense-data temporarily when they are sensed. Cf. Mr. Bertrand Russell's *Mysticism and Logic* [New York, Longmans, Green & Co. 1918], p. 148.

be mental, as Berkeley and many others have held. They may be neither mental nor physical.

4. We are not committed to any view about their *origin*. They may originate as a result of processes in material objects, or of mental processes, or of both. Or again, it may be that the boot is on the other leg: it may be that they are the ultimate constituents of the Universe, and material things (perhaps minds as well) may be just collections of them; in which case they 'just are', and have no origin and no explanation, since everything else is explained by reference to them.

Thus the term sense-datum is meant to be a *neutral* term. The use of it does not imply the acceptance of any particular theory. The term is meant to stand for something whose existence is indubitable (however fleeting), something from which all theories of perception ought to start, however much they may diverge later.

And I think that all past theories have in fact started with sense-data. The Ancients and the Schoolmen called them *sensible species*. Locke and Berkeley called them *ideas of sensation*, Hume *impressions*, Kant *Vorstellungen*. In the nineteenth century they were usually known as *sensations*, and people spoke of visual and auditory sensations when they meant colour-patches and noises; while many contemporary writers, following Dr. C. D. Broad, have preferred to call them *sensa*.

All these terms have the defect of begging questions. If we speak of *sensible species* we assume that sense-data are physical, a sort of effluences flying off the external objects into our sense-organs. If we use terms like *idea, impression*, and *sensation* we commit ourselves to the view that sense-data are mental events. *Sensum* is very much the best. But it is generally used to mean a, 'third kind' of entity, neither mental nor physical. And although we are not at present in a position to assert that sense-data are physical or that they are mental, neither are we in a position to deny either of these alternatives. (Thus 'sense-data are sensa' is not a tautology, but a synthetic proposition.)

An incidental virtue of the term *sense-datum* is that it enables us to give a brief and intelligible account of the traditional theories concerning perception and the external world, and so to make use of the work of our predecessors without wasting time in tedious historico-lexicographical investigations.

Chapter 18

The directly evident

Roderick M. Chisholm

1. Socratic questions

IN investigating the theory of evidence from a philosophical—Socratic—point of view, we make three general presuppositions.

We presuppose, first, that there is something that we know and we adopt the working hypothesis that *what* we know is pretty much that which, on reflection, we think we know. This may seem the wrong place to start. But where else *could* we start? [. . .]

We presuppose, second, that the things we know are justified for us in the following sense: *we* can know what it is, on any occasion, that constitutes our grounds, or reason, or evidence for thinking that we know. If I think that I know that there is now snow on the top of the mountain, then, as the quotation from Wittgenstein suggests, I am in a position to say what ground or reason I have for thinking that there is now snow on the top of the mountain. (Of course, from the fact that there *is* ground for thinking that there is now snow there, from the fact, say, that you have been there and seen it, it doesn't follow that *I* now have any ground or reason for the belief.)

And we presuppose, third, that if we do thus have grounds or reasons for the things we think we know, then there are valid general principles of evidence—principles stating the general conditions under which we may be said to have grounds or reasons for what we believe. And, [. . .] our concern, in investigating the theory of evidence, is to find out what these general principles are.

In order to formulate, or make explicit, our rules of evidence, we will do well to proceed as we do in logic, when formulating the rules of inference, or in moral philosophy, when formulating rules of action. We suppose that we have at our disposal certain instances which the rules should countenance or permit and other instances which the rules should reject or forbid; and we suppose that by investigating these instances we can formulate criteria which any instance must satisfy if it is to be accepted or permitted, as well as criteria which any instance must satisfy if it is to be rejected or forbidden. To obtain the instances we need if we are to formulate rules of evidence, we may proceed in the following way.

We consider certain things that we know to be true, or think we know to be true,

Roderick M. Chisholm, 'The Directly Evident' in *Theory of Knowledge* (2nd edition) (Englewood Cliffs, NJ., Prentice-Hall, 1977) pp. 16–33 © Roderick M. Chisholm 1977, reprinted by permission of Prentice-Hall, Inc., Upper Saddle River, NJ.

or certain things which, upon reflection, we would be willing to call *evident*. With respect to each of these, we then try to formulate a reasonable answer to the question, 'What justification do you have for thinking you know this thing to be true?' or 'What justification do you have for counting this thing as something that is evident?' In beginning with what we think we know to be true, or with what, after reflection, we would be willing to count as being evident, we are assuming that the truth we are seeking is 'already implicit in the mind which seeks it, and needs only to be elicited and brought to clear reflection'.[1]

There are philosophers who point out, with respect to some things that are quite obviously known to be true, that questions concerning their justification 'do not arise,' for (they say) to express a doubt concerning such things is to 'violate the rules of our language.' But their objections do not apply to the type of question that we are discussing here; for these questions need not be taken to express any doubts or to indicate any attitude of skepticism. Designed only to elicit information, the questions are not challenges and they do not imply or presuppose that there is any ground for doubting, or for suspecting, that to which they pertain.[2] When Aristotle considered an invalid mood and asked himself 'What is wrong with this?' he was trying to learn; he need not have been suggesting to himself that perhaps nothing was wrong with the mood.

It should be also noted that when we ask ourselves, concerning what we may think we know to be true, 'What *justification* do I have for believing this?' or 'What justification do I have for thinking I know that this is something that is true?' we are not asking any of the following questions: 'What *further evidence* can I find in support of this?' 'How did I *come to believe* this or find out that it is true? How would I go about *persuading* some other reasonable person that it is true?' We must not expect, therefore, that answers to these latter questions will be, *ipso facto*, answers to the questions that we are asking. Our questions are Socratic and therefore not at all of the type that one ordinarily asks.[3]

1. Lewis, *Mind and the World-Order* (New York: Charles Scribner's Sons, 1929) p. 19.

2. These remarks also apply to Leonard Nelson's statement, 'If one asks whether one possesses objectively valid cognitions at all, one thereby presupposes that the objectivity of cognition is questionable at first . . .'; *Socratic Method and Critical Philosophy* (New Haven: Yale University Press, 1949), p. 190. One of the unfortunate consequences of the work of Descartes and, in the present century, the work of Bertrand Russell and Edmund Husserl, is the widely accepted supposition that questions about the justification for counting evident statements *as* evident must be *challenges* or expressions of *doubts*. See Bertrand Russell's *Problems of Philosophy* (New York: Holt Rinehart & Winston, Inc., 1912) and his many other writings on the theory of knowledge, and E. Husserl's *Meditations Cartesiennes* (Paris: J. Vrin, 1931), also published as *Cartesianische Meditationen und Pariser Vorträge* (The Hague: Martinus Nijhoff, 1950). The objections to this approach to the concept of the evident were clearly put forth by A. Meinong; see his *Gesammelte Abhandlungen*, 2 (Leipzig: Johann Ambrosius Barth, 1913). p. 191. The papers by Nelson and Meinong that are here referred to are reprinted in *Empirical Knowledge: Readings from Contemporary Sources*, Roderick M. Chisholm and Robert J. Swartz, eds. (Englewood Cliffs, NJ.: Prentice-Hall, Inc., 1973).

3. According to Xenophon, Charicles said to Socrates: 'You generally ask questions when you know quite well how the matter stands; these are the questions you are not to ask.' [*Memorabilia*, I, 2, 36]

2. Stopping place

In many instances the answers to our questions will take the following form: 'What justifies me in thinking that I know that a is F is the fact that it is evident to me that b is G.' For example: 'What justifies me in thinking I know that he has that disorder is the fact that it is evident to me that he has those symptoms.' Such an answer, therefore, presupposes an epistemic principle, what we might call a 'rule of evidence.' The rule would have the form:

If it is evident to me that b is G, then it is evident to me that a is F.

'If it *is* evident that he has those symptoms, then it is also evident that he has that disorder' and so we should distinguish the answer to our Socratic question from its epistemic presupposition. The answer to our Socratic question is a proposition to the effect that our justification for counting one thing as evident is the fact that something else is evident. And the epistemic presupposition of our answer is a rule of evidence: It is a proposition to the effect that if certain conditions obtain, then something may be said to be evident. One could say of such a rule that it tells us that one thing *serves to make another thing evident.*

This type of answer to our Socratic questions shifts the burden of justification from one claim to another. For we may now ask, 'What justifies me in counting it as evident that b is G?' or 'What justifies me in thinking I know that b is G?' And possibly we will formulate, once again, an answer of the first sort: 'What justifies me in counting it, as evident that b is G is the fact that it is evident that c is H.' ('What justifies me in counting it as evident that he has those symptoms is the fact that it is evident that his temperature is recorded as being high . . .') And this answer will presuppose still another rule of evidence: 'If it is evident that c is H, then it is evident that b is G.' How long can we continue in this way?

We might try to continue *ad indefinitum,* justifying each new claim that we elicit by still another claim. Or we might be tempted to complete a vicious circle: in such a case, having justified 'a is F' by appeal to 'b is G', and 'b is 'G' by reference to 'c is H,' we would then justify 'c is H by reference to 'a is F.' But if we are rational beings, we will do neither of these things. For we will find that our Socratic questions lead us to a proper stopping place.

How are we to recognize such a stopping place?

Sextus Empiricus remarked that every object of apprehension seems to be apprehended either through itself or through another object.[4] Those things, if there are any, that are 'apprehended through themselves' might provide us with a stopping place. But what could they be? The form of our Socratic questions suggests a way of finding an answer. Let us say provisionally that we have found a proper stopping place when the answer to our question may take the following form:

4. Sextus Empiricus, *Outlines of Pyrrhonism,* Book I, Chapter 6, in *Sextus Empiricus,* Vol. I, The Loeb Classical Library (Cambridge: Harvard University Press, 1933).

What justifies me in thinking I know that *a* is *F* is simply the fact that *a* is *F.*

Whenever this type of answer is appropriate, we have encountered what is *directly evident.*

3. An improper stopping place

At first consideration, one might suppose that those statements that correctly describe our 'experience,' or formulate our 'perceptions' or 'observations,' are statements expressing what is directly evident in the sense described. But what is expressed by such statements does not satisfy the criteria we have just set forth.

In answer to the question, 'What is my justification for thinking I know that Mr. Smith is here?' one may say, 'I see that he is here.' But 'I see that he is here' does not pick out the kind of stopping place we have just described in reply to the question, 'What is my justification for counting it as evident that it is Mr. *Smith* that I see?' A reasonable man will *not* say, 'What justifies me in counting it as evident that I see Mr. Smith is simply the fact that I do see Mr. Smith.' If he understands the Socratic question, he will say instead something like: 'I know that Mr. Smith is a tall man with red hair; I see a tall man with red hair; I know that no one else satisfying that description would be in this room now ... Each of these propositions in turn, including 'I see a tall man with red hair,' would be justified by reference to still other propositions. And this is true of any other perceptual proposition. Hence, we cannot say that what we know by means of perception or observation is itself something that is directly evident.

There are those who will say, 'What justifies me in counting it as evident that Mr. Smith is here (or that I see Mr. Smith) is simply my present *experience*; but the experience itself cannot be said to be evident, much less to have evidence conferred upon it.' But this reply seems clearly to make room for further Socratic questioning. For we may ask, 'What justifies me in counting it as evident that my experience is of such a sort that experiences of that sort make it evident to me that Mr. Smith is here, or that I see that Mr. Smith is here?' And to this question one could reasonably reply in the way described above.

4. States that present themselves

The following quotation from Leibniz points to what is directly evident: 'Our direct awareness of our own existence and of our own thoughts provides us with the primary truths *a posteriori*, the primary truths of fact, or, in other words, our primary experiences; just as identical propositions constitute the primary truths *a priori*, the primary truths of reason, or, in other words, our primary insights. Neither the one nor the other is capable of being demonstrated and both can be called *immediate*—the former, because there is no mediation between the understanding and its objects, and the latter, because there is no mediation between the subject and the predicate.'[5] We are here concerned with Leibniz's 'primary truths of fact.' The 'primary truths of reason' will be discussed in the next chapter.

Thinking and believing provide us with paradigm cases of the directly evident. Consider a reasonable man who is thinking about a city he takes to be Albuquerque, or who believes that Albuquerque is in New Mexico, and suppose him to reflect on the philosophical question, 'What is my justification for thinking that I know that I am thinking about a city I take to be Albuquerque, or that I believe that Albuquerque is in New Mexico?' (This strange question would hardly arise, of course, on any practical occasion, for the man is not asking, 'What is my justification for thinking that Albuquerque is in New Mexico? The question is a Socratic question and therefore a philosophical one.) The man could reply in this way: 'My justification for thinking I know that I am thinking about a city I take to be Albuquerque, or that I believe that Albuquerque is in New Mexico, is simply the fact that I *am* thinking about a city I take to be Albuquerque, or that I *do* believe that it is in New Mexico.' And this reply fits our formula for the directly evident:

What justifies me in thinking I know that a is F is simply the fact that a is F.

Our man has stated his justification for a proposition merely by reiterating that proposition. This type of justification is *not* appropriate to the questions that were previously discussed. Thus, in answer to 'What justification do you have for counting it as evident that there can be no life on the moon?' it would be inappropriate—and presumptuous—simply to reiterate, 'There can be no life on the moon.' But we can state our justification for certain propositions about our *beliefs* and certain propositions about our *thoughts*, merely by reiterating those propositions. They may be said, therefore, to pertain to what is directly evident.

Borrowing a technical term from Meinong, let us say that if there is something that is directly evident to a man, then there is some state of affairs that 'presents itself to him.' Thus, my believing that Socrates is mortal is a state of affairs that is 'self-presenting' to me. If I do believe that Socrates is mortal, then, *ipso facto*, it is evident to me that I believe that Socrates is mortal; the state of affairs is 'apprehended through itself.'[6]

Other states that may be similarly self-presenting are those described by 'thinking that one remembers that ...' or 'seeming to remember that ...' (as distinguished from 'remembering that ...') and 'taking,' or 'thinking that one perceives' (as distinguished from 'perceiving'). Desiring, hoping, wondering, wishing, loving, hating may also be self-presenting. These states are what Leibniz intended by the term 'thoughts' in the passage quoted above.

5. G. W. Leibniz, *New Essays Concerning Human Understanding* (La Salle, Ill.: Open Court Publishing Company, 1916) Book IV, Chapter 9.

6. See A. Meinong, *On Emotional Presentation*, ed. and trans. M. S. Kalsi (Evanston: Northwestern University Press. 1972), sec. 1. Cf. Franz Brentano, *Psychology from an Empirical Standpoint* (London: Routledge & Kegan Paul, 1972), Chapter 2, sec. 2; C. J. Ducasse, 'Propositions, Truth, and the Ultimate Criterion of Truth,' *Philosophy and Phenomenological Research*, 4 (1944), 317–40; William J. Alston, 'Varieties of Privileged Access,' in *Empirical Knowledge*, Chisholm and Swartz, eds., pp. 376–410; and Thomas J. Steel, 'Knowledge and the Self-Presenting' in *Analysis and Metaphysics*, ed. Keith Lehrer (Dordrecht: D. Reidel, 1975), pp. 145–50.

5. The nature of self-presentation

Let us now try to characterize self-presentation more exactly. If seeming to have a headache is a state of affairs that is self-presenting for S at the present moment, then S does now seem to have a headache and, moreover, it is evident to him that he seems to have a headache.[7] And so may formulate the definition this way:

D2.1 h is *self-presenting* for S at t = Df h occurs at t; and necessarily, if h occurs at t, then h is evident for S at t.

An alternative formulation would be this.

> h is self-presenting for S at t = Df h is true at t; and necessarily, if h is true at t, then h is evident for S *at t.*

The difference between the two types of formulation will be discussed in Chapter 5. For the moment, we will assume that they are inter-changeable, sometimes saying that *states of affairs* are what is self-presenting and at other times saying that *propositions* are what is self-presenting.

We should note that what follows logically from what is self-presenting need not itself be self-presenting. It will be instructive to consider three different examples of this fact.

1. The proposition expressed by 'I seem to have a headache' logically implies that expressed by '2 and 2 are 4.' But even if the former is self-presenting, the latter is not. For the latter is not necessarily such that if it is true then it is evident for me; it could be true even if I didn't exist.

2. The proposition expressed by 'I seem to have a headache' logically implies that expressed by 'Either I seem to have a headache or all crows are black.' But the latter proposition is not necessarily such that if it is true then it is evident to me; it could be true even if I didn't exist.

3. The proposition expressed by 'I seem to have a headache' logically implies that expressed by 'I exist.' But the latter proposition is not necessarily such that if it is true then it is evident for me; it could be true if I were asleep and such that nothing is evident to me.

The negations of self-presenting propositions will not be self-presenting, for they may all be true when no one exists and hence when nothing is evident. What of the proposition expressed by 'I am thinking but I do not seem to see a dog.' Is this necessarily such that, if it is true, then it is evident? No. For it could be true, even though I didn't have the concept of a dog and therefore didn't understand the proposition 'I am thinking but I do not seem to see a dog.' But if the proposition is one that could be true when I didn't understand it, then it is one that could be true without being evident to me. For, according to what we said in the previous chapter,

---

7. For other approaches to the concept of self-presentation, compare: Roderick Firth, 'The Anatomy of Certainty,' in *Empirical Knowledge,* Chisholm and Swartz, eds., pp. 203–223; Wilfrid Sellars, 'Givenness and Explanatory Coherence,' *Journal of Philosophy,* 70 (1973), 612–24; and Alston, 'Varieties of Privileged Access,' referred to above.

a proposition cannot be evident to a person unless it is one that he is able to grasp or to understand. (More exactly, we said that, if believing one proposition is more reasonable than believing another for any given person S, then S is able to grasp or understand the first proposition.)

One may object: 'But isn't it directly evident to me now both that I am thinking and that I do not see a dog?' The answer is yes. But the concept of the directly evident is not the same as that of the self-presenting.

6. A definition of the directly evident

The concept of the directly evident is considerably broader than that of the self-presenting. A self-presenting state of affairs for S is one which is necessarily such that, if it occurs, then it is evident to S. Hence we could say that the Cartesian statement 'I am thinking' expresses what is self-presenting for S—provided he *is* thinking. For it would be impossible for S to be thinking unless it were evident to him that he was thinking. But what of the statement 'There is someone who is thinking'? If we adhere to the tradition of Descartes and Leibniz, we will want to say that, if 'I am thinking' expresses what is directly evident for S, then so, too, does 'There is someone who is thinking.' But the latter is not self-presenting by our definition above. For it is not *necessary* that, if there is someone who is thinking, then that fact is then evident to S. (If someone is thinking while S is asleep, the fact that someone is thinking need not be evident to S.) But, we may assume, it is not possible for anyone to accept the proposition he would express by 'I am thinking' unless he also accepts the proposition that someone is thinking. And so let us say:

D2.2   h is *directly evident* for S =Df h is logically contingent; and there is an e such that (i) e is self-presenting for S and (ii) necessarily, whoever accepts e accepts h.

Those propositions which are themselves self-presenting, of course, will also be directly evident by this definition.

What of *negative* propositions? Isn't it directly evident to me that I do not now seem to see a dog? If such propositions were never directly evident, it would be difficult to see what would ever justify any contingent judgments of nonexistence. Yet we noted above that 'I do not now seem to see a dog' cannot be said to be self-presenting—for it may be true without being evident. From what self-presenting proposition, then, may one deduce the proposition expressed by 'I do not now seem to see a dog?' The answer would seem to be this: 'I am considering the proposition that I seem to see a dog, and I do not seem to see a dog.' (This example illustrates the fact that negative apprehension is more complex than positive apprehension.)

7. An alternative description

'Surely,' one may object, 'it makes no sense to speak of evidence in the kind of cases you describe. What sense does it make to ask whether or not it is *evident* to me that I believe that Socrates is mortal?'[8]

To one who feels that such questions 'make no sense,' we need not reply by trying to show him that they do. It is enough to make two points: (1) If he is right, then such propositions as 'I believe that Socrates is mortal' and 'I am thinking about the moon' differ in one very important respect from such propositions as 'Socrates is mortal' and 'There can be no life on the moon.' The former propositions, if our critic is right, are such that it 'makes no sense' to ask, with respect to them, 'What is my justification for thinking I know that they are true?' (2) Yet they resemble propositions which *are* known to be true in that they may function as *evidence*. My evidence that you and I think alike with respect to the mortality of Socrates cannot consist solely of the evidence I have concerning *your* beliefs about Socrates. It must also consist of the fact that *I* believe that Socrates is mortal. And these two points provide us with an alternative way of characterizing the directly evident.

We could say paradoxically that a proposition is *directly evident* to a man, provided (1) that it makes no sense to say of him that he knows the proposition to be true, and (2) that the proposition is evidence for him of something else.

If we use our original characterization of the directly evident, we might think of the directly evident as that which 'constitutes its own evidence,' for we have characterized it in terms of what is self-presenting—in terms of that which is 'apprehended through itself.' But if we use the alternative characterization, we may think paradoxically of the directly evident as being that which is 'evidence but not evident.'[9] In the one case, we are reminded of the prime mover that moves itself, and in the other, of the prime mover unmoved.[10]

It will be convenient to continue with the terms of our original characterization, but what we shall say can readily be translated into those of the second.

---

8. Compare John V. Canfield, ' "I Know that I Am in Pain" Is Senseless,' in *Analysis and Metaphysics*, ed. Keith Lehrer, pp. 129–44.
9. The second method of characterization is in the spirit of the following observations by Ludwig Wittgenstein: (1) 'It can't be said of me at all (except perhaps as a joke) that I *know* I'm in pain' and (2) 'Justification by experience comes to an end. If it did not it would not be justification.' *Philosophical Investigations* (Oxford: Basil Blackwell, 1953), pp. 89e, 136e. From the fact that it can't be said of me that I know I'm that in pain, it will not follow, of course, that it *can* be said of me that I do *not* know—i.e., that I am ignorant of the fact—that I am in pain.
10. Compare Rudolf Haller, "Concerning the So-called "Munchhausen Trilemma."' *Ratio*, 16 (1974), 119–40.

8. A skeptical objection

Before listing still other types of self-presenting states, we should consider an objection that might be made to *any* item on our list.

We have said, for example, that seeming to have a headache is self-presenting. Suppose now the skeptic asks: 'But how do you *know* that seeming to have a headache is self-presenting? How do you know that seeming to have a headache is necessarily such that, if you do seem to have a headache, then it is evident to you that you do?'

One possible move—and one that would please the skeptic—would be this. We would try to think of some *additional* feature of self-presenting states, some feature the presence of which would guarantee us that a given state *is a* self-presenting state. And then we would go on to note that this feature is shared by such self-presenting states as seeming to have a headache and believing that all men are mortal.

But whatever features we might thus find—let us call it '*F*'—the skeptic will be ready with his answer: 'But how do you know that only self-presenting states have *F*? And how do you know that seeming to have a headache and believing that all men are mortal have *F*?'

And if we were foolish enough to take on these additional questions, then the skeptic would be ready for us once again: 'Yes, but how do you know . . . ?'

To the questions 'How do you know that you seem to have a headache?' and "How do you know that you believe that all men are mortal?' the only possible answers are, 'I do seem to have a headache' and 'I do believe that all men are mortal.' And to the philosophical questions 'How do you know that seeming to have a headache is self-presenting?' and 'How do you know that believing that all men are mortal is self-presenting?' the only possible answers are, 'I know that seeming to have a headache is self-presenting' and 'I know that believing that all men are mortal is self-presenting.'[11]

One would like to think that there is a better way of dealing with the skeptic's objection. But what could it possibly be? We will return to this general problem in the final chapter.

9. Seeming and appearing

We have yet to consider the most interesting—and controversial—examples of the directly evident.

In the second of his *Meditations*, Descartes offers what he takes to be good

---

11. See Franz Brentano, *Psychology from an Empirical Standpoint*, pp. 139–140. Compare Leonard Nelson's *Über das sogenannte Erkenntnisproblem* (Göttingen: Verlag 'Öffentliches Leben,' 1930), reprinted from *Abhandlungen der Fries'schen Schule* 2 (Göttingen: Verlag 'Öffentliches Leben,' 1908), especially pp. 479–485, 502–503, 521–528, 525. Compare 'The Impossibility of the "Theory of Knowledge,"' in his *Socratic Method and Critical Philosophy*, and reprinted in *Empirical Knowledge*, Chisholm and Swartz, eds.

reasons for doubting whether, on any occasion, he sees light, hears noise, or feels heat, and he then observes: 'Let it be so, still it is at least quite *certain that it seems to me that* I see light, that I hear noise, and that I feel heat'.[12] This observation about seeming should be contrasted with what St. Augustine says, in his *Contra Academicos*, about appearing.

I do not see how the Academician can refute him who says: 'I know that this appears white to me, I know that my hearing is delighted with this, I know that this has an agreeable odor, I know that this tastes sweet to me, I know that this feels cold to me.' . . . I say this that, when a person tastes something, he can honestly swear that he knows it is sweet to his palate or the contrary, and that no trickery of the Greeks can dispossess him of that knowledge.[13]

These two passages remind us that such words as 'seem' or 'appear' have different uses in different contexts.

Thus, Descartes' expression, 'It seems to me that I see light,' when uttered on any ordinary occasion, might be taken to be performing one or the other of two quite different functions. (1) The expression might be used simply to report one's belief; in such a case, 'It seems to me that I see light' could be replaced by 'I believe that I see light.' Taken in this way, the 'seems' statement expresses what is directly evident, but since it is equivalent to a belief-statement, it does not add anything to the cases we have ready considered. (2) 'It seems to me'—or better, 'It seems to *me*'—may be used not only to report a belief, but also to provide the speaker with a way out, a kind of hedge, in case the statement prefixed by 'It seems to me' should turn out to be false. This function of 'It seems' is thus the contrary of the performative use of 'I know' to which J. L. Austin has called attention. In saying 'I know,' I give my hearers a kind of guarantee and, as Austin says, stake my reputation; but in saying 'It seems to *me*'—I play it safe, indicating to them that what I say carries no guarantee at all and that if they choose to believe what I say they do so entirely at their own risk.[14] 'It seems to me,' used in this way, cannot be said to describe what is directly evident for it cannot be said to describe anything at all.

But the word 'appear' as it is used in the translation from St. Augustine—'This appears white to me'—performs still another function. (3) It may be used to describe a certain state of affairs which is not itself a belief. When 'appear' is used in this descriptive, 'phenomenological' way, one may say consistently and without any incongruity, 'That thing appears white to me in this light, but I know that it is really gray.' One may also say, again, consistently and without any incongruity, 'It appears white to me in this light and I know that, as a matter of fact, it *is* white.'

The latter statement illustrates two points overlooked by many contemporary

---

12. E. S. Haldane and G. R. T. Ross, eds., *The Philosophical Works of Descartes*, I (London: Cambridge University Press, 1934), p. 155 [my italics]. The French reads: ' . . . il est certain qu'il me semble que je vois de la lumière, que j'entend du bruit et que je sens de la chaleur.'

13. *Against the Academicians* (*Contra Academicos*), ed. and trans. Sister Mary Patricia Garvey (Milwaukee: Marquette University Press. 1942), para. 26, p. 68 of translation.

14. Austin discussed this use of 'seems' in considerable detail in his posthumous *Sense and Sensibilia* (Oxford: The Clarendon Press, 1962). Compare the essay 'Other Minds' in Austin's *Philosophical Papers* (Oxford: The Clarendon Press, 1961), pp. 44–84.

philosophers. The first is that in such a statement, 'appear' cannot have the hedging use just referred to, for if it did, the statement would be incongruous (which it is not); the second part of the statement ('I know that it is white') would provide a guarantee which the first part ('This appears white') withholds. The second point is that the descriptive, phenomenological use of 'appears' is not restricted to the description of *illusory experiences.*

The following translation from Sextus Empiricus reminds us that 'seems,' as well as a number of other verbs, has this descriptive, phenomenological use:

The same water which feels very hot when poured on inflamed spots seems lukewarm to us. And the same air seems chilly to the old but mild to those in their prime, and similarly the same sound seems to the former faint, but to the latter clearly audible. The same wine which seems sour to those who have previously eaten dates or figs seems sweet to those who have just consumed nuts or chickpeas; and the vestibule of the bathhouse which warms those entering from the outside chills those coming out.[15]

Sextus is here using certain appear-words to indicate a fact about our experience that is familiar to us all—namely, the fact that by varying the state of the subject or perceiver, or of the intervening medium, or of other conditions of observation, we may also vary the ways in which the objects that the subject perceives will appear to him. Sextus' appear-statements are simply descriptive of experience.

Some of these descriptive 'appear' and 'seem' statements may describe what is self-presenting, and when they do, what they express is directly evident. We can single out such a class of directly evident 'appear' statements by referring to what Aristotle called the 'proper objects' of the various senses and to what he called the 'common sensibles.'[16] The 'proper objects' may be illustrated by the following: visual characteristics such as blue, green, yellow, red, white, black; auditory characteristics such as sounding or making a noise; somesthetic characteristics such as rough, smooth, hard, soft, heavy, light, hot, cold; gustatory characteristics such as sweet, sour, salt, bitter; and olfactory characteristics, such as fragrant, spicy, putrid, burned. The 'common sensibles' are those characteristics such as movement, rest, number, figure, and magnitude, which, as Aristotle says, 'are not peculiar to any one sense, but are common to all.'

If for any such characteristic *F*, I can justify a claim to knowledge by saying of something that it *appears F* (by saying of the wine that it now *looks* red, or *tastes* sour, to me), where the verb is intended in the descriptive, phenomenological sense just indicated, then the *appearing* in question is self-presenting and my statement expresses what is directly evident. The claim that I thus justify, by saying of something that it appears *F*, may be the claim that the thing *is F*, but as we have seen, it may also be some other claim. To the question 'What justification do I have for thinking I know, or for counting it as evident, that something now *looks* red to me,

15. *Outlines of Pyrrhonism*, Book I, Chapter 14; abridged from Vol. I of *Sextus Empiricus*, The Loeb Classical Library, pp. 55, 63, 65. Cf. K. Lykos, 'Aristotle and Plato on "Appearing,"' *Mind*, 73 (1964), 496–514.

16. See Aristotle's *De Anima*, Book 2, Chapters 6 and 7.

or *tastes* sour?' I could reply only by reiterating that something does now look red or taste sour.[17]

Strictly speaking, 'The *wine* tastes sour to me' and '*Something* looks red to me' do not express what is directly evident in our sense of this term. For the first statement implies that I am tasting *wine* and the second that there *is* a certain thing that is appearing red to me, and 'I am tasting wine' and 'There is a certain thing that is appearing red to me' do not express what is directly evident. What justifies me in counting it as evident that I am tasting wine is *not* simply the fact that I am tasting wine, and what justifies me in counting it as evident that a certain thing is appearing red to me (and that I am not, say, merely suffering from a hallucination) is not simply the fact that a certain thing *is* appearing red to me. To arrive at what is directly evident in these cases, we must remove the reference to wine in 'The wine tastes sour to me' and we must remove the reference to the appearing thing in 'That thing appears red to me.' This, however, is very difficult to do, since our language was not developed for any such philosophical purpose.

Many philosophers and psychologists would turn verbs into substantives, saying in the one case, 'I have a sour taste,' and in the other 'I am experiencing a red appearance.' Such a procedure has the advantage of enabling us to assimilate these seemings and appearings to other types of sensuous experience—to feelings, imagery, and the sensuous content of dreams and hallucinations, all of which may be 'self-presenting' in the sense we have described. But in introducing the substantive 'appearance,' we may seem to be multiplying entities beyond necessity; for now we seem to be saying that *appearances*, as well as fences and houses, may be counted among the entities that are red. 'I have a sour taste' may suggest, similarly, that *tastes*, like wine and fruit, are among the entities that may be sour. It is clear that we must proceed with great care if we are to employ this substantival terminology.[18]

Let us consider another way of describing these self-presenting states. In our examples, 'appear' requires a grammatical subject and thus requires a term that purports to refer not merely to a way of appearing, but also to a thing that is said to appear in that way. We may eliminate the reference to the thing that appears, however, if we *convert* our appear-sentences. Instead of saying 'Something appears white to me,' we may say, more awkwardly, 'I am appeared white to by something.' We may then eliminate the substantival 'something' merely by dropping the final phrase and saying, 'I am appeared white to.'[19] The verbs 'tastes' and 'sounds' do not

17. Or if the directly evident is to be viewed in analogy with the prime mover unmoved instead of with the prime mover that moves itself, I could say (1) that it 'makes no sense' to say 'It is evident to me that something now looks red or tastes sour' and (2) 'Something now looks red' or 'Something now tastes sour' may yet formulate my *evidence* for something else.

18. One of the first philosophers to note the pitfalls which this substantival, or 'sense datum,' terminology involves was Thomas Reid; see his *Inquiry into the Human Mind* (1764), Chapter 6, sec. 20, and *Essays on the Intellectual Powers* (1785), Essay 2, Chapter 16. Cf. H. A. Prichard, *Kant's Theory of Knowledge* (Oxford: The Clarendon Press, 1909), and 'Appearances and Reality,' *Mind* (1906): the latter is reprinted in *Realism and the Background of Phenomenology*, ed. Roderick M. Chisholm (New York: Free Press of Glencoe, Inc., 1960).

19. But the substantive 'I' remains. Recall the beginning of our quotation from Leibniz: 'Our direct awareness of our own existence and of our thoughts provides us with the primary truths *a posteriori*. . . .'

allow a similar conversion of 'This tastes sour' and 'That sounds loud' but 'is appeared to' could replace such verbs: We could say 'I am appeared loud to' and 'I am appeared sour to,' just as we have said 'I am appeared white to.' The words 'loud,' 'sour,' and 'white,' in these sentences, do not function as adjectives; the sentences do not say, of any entity, that that entity *is* loud, sour, or white. The words are used here to describe *ways* of appearing, or of being appeared to, just as 'swift' and 'slow' may be used to describe ways of running. They function as adverbs and our sentences would be more correct, therefore, if they were put as 'I am appeared sourly to,' 'I am appeared whitely to' and 'I am appeared loudly to.'

The awkwardness of the 'appears to' terminology could be avoided if, at this point, we were to introduce another verb, say, 'sense,' using it in a technical way as a synonym for 'is appeared to.' In such a case, we would say 'I sense sourly,' 'I sense whitely,' and 'I sense loudly.' But even this procedure will introduce ambiguities, as 'I sense loudly' may suggest.

Once these terminological difficulties have been removed, is there ground for doubt concerning the directly evident character of what is expressed by statements about appearing? Doubts have been raised in recent years and we should consider these briefly.

10. Some misconceptions

There are *some* descriptive appear-statements that do not express what is directly evident—for example, 'He looks just the way his uncle did fifteen years ago.' If we describe a way of appearing by *comparing* it with the way in which some physical thing happens to have appeared in the past, or with the way in which some physical thing is thought normally to appear, then the justification for what we say about the way of appearing will depend in part upon the justification for what we say about the physical thing; and what we say about the physical thing will not now be directly evident. Now it has been argued that the types of appear-statements we have just been considering *also* involve some comparison with previously experienced objects, and hence, that what they express cannot ever be said to be directly evident. It has been suggested, for example, that if I say 'This appears white,' then I am making a 'comparison between a present object and a formerly seen object.'[20] What justification is there for saying this?

It is true that the expression 'appears white' may be used to abbreviate 'appears the way in which white things normally appear.' But this should not prevent us from seeing that things may also be the other way around: 'white thing' can be used to abbreviate 'thing having the color of things that normally appear white.' In such a case, the expression, 'appear white,' as it is used in the latter sentence, is *not* used to abbreviate 'appear the way in which white things normally appear.' For in saying that 'white thing' may be used to abbreviate 'thing having the color of things that normally appear white,' we are *not* saying simply that 'white thing' may be used to

20. Hans Reichenbach, *Experience and Prediction* (Chicago: University of Chicago Press, 1938), p. 176.

abbreviate 'thing having the color of things which ordinarily appear the way in which *white things* normally appear.' Therefore, when we say that 'white thing' may be used to abbreviate 'thing having the color of things that ordinarily appear white,' the point of 'appear white' is not to compare a way of appearing with anything. In this use of 'appear white,' we may say significantly and without redundancy, 'Things that *are* white normally *appear* white.' And this is the way in which we should interpret 'This appears white to me' in the quotation above from St. Augustine. More generally, it is in terms of this descriptive, noncomparative use of our other 'appear' and 'seem' words (including 'looks,' 'tastes,' 'sounds,' and the like) that we are to interpret those appear-statements that are said to be directly evident.

But philosophers have offered three different arguments to show that appear-words cannot be used in this noncomparative way. Each of the three arguments, I believe, is quite obviously invalid.

1. The first argument may be summarized in this way: '(a) Sentences such as "This appears white" are "parasitical upon" sentences such as "This *is* white"; that is to say, in order to understand "This appears white," one must *first* be able to understand "This is white." Therefore (b) "This appears white" ordinarily means the same as "This appears in the way in which white things ordinarily appear." Hence (c) "This is white" *cannot* be used to mean the same as "This is the sort of thing that ordinarily appears white," where "appears white" is used in the way you have just described. And so (d) then there is no clear sense in which what is expressed by "This appears white" can be said to be directly evident.'

There is an advantage in thus making the argument explicit. For to see what the conclusion (d) does not follow from the premise (a), we have only to note that (c) does not follow from (b). From the fact that a linguistic expression is ordinarily used in one way, it does not follow that that expression may not also sometimes be used in another way. And so even if the linguistic hypothesis upon which the argument is based were true, the conclusion does not follow from the premise.

2. It has also been argued: '(a) If the sentence "I am appeared white to" does not express a comparison between a present way of appearing and anything else, then the sentence is completely empty and says nothing at all about a present way of appearing. But (b) if "I am appeared white to" expresses what is directly evident, then it cannot assert a comparison between a present way of appearing and anything else, Therefore, (c) either "I am appeared white to" is empty or it does not express what is directly evident.'

Here the difficulty lies in the first premise. It may well be true that if an appear-sentence is to be used to communicate anything to another person, it must assert some comparison of things. Thus if I wish *you* to know the way in which I am appeared to now, I must relate this way of being appeared to with something that is familiar to you. ('Describe the taste? It's something like the taste of a mango.') But our question is not: 'If you are to understand me when I say something about the way in which I am appeared to, must I be comparing that way of appearing with the way in which some object, familiar to you, happens to appear?' The question is, more simply: 'Can I apprehend the way in which I am now appeared to without thereby supposing, with respect to some object, that the way I am being appeared to is the way in which that object sometimes appears or has sometimes appeared?' From the fact that the first of these two questions must be answered in the negative, it does not follow that the second must also be answered in the negative.

The argument, moreover, presupposes an absurd thesis about the nature of thought or predication. This thesis might be expressed by saying that 'all judgments are comparative.' To see that this is absurd, we have only to consider more carefully what it says. It tells us that in order to assert or to believe, with respect to any particular thing x, that x has a certain property F, one must *compare* x with some other thing y and thus assert or believe of x that it has something in common with the other thing y. But clearly, we cannot derive 'x is F' from 'x resembles y' unless, among other things, we can say or believe *noncomparatively* that y is F.

3. The final argument designed to show that appear-statements cannot express what is directly evident, may be put as follows: '(a) In saying "Something appears white," you are making certain assumptions about language; you are assuming, for example, that the word "white," or the phrase "appears white," is being used in the way in which you have used it on other occasions, or in the way in which other people have used it. Therefore (b) when you say "This appears white," you are saying something not only about your present experience, but also about all of these other occasions. But (c) what you are saying about these other occasions is not directly evident. And therefore (d) "This is white" does not express what is directly evident.'

The false step in this argument is the inference from (a) to (b). We must distinguish the belief that a speaker has about the words that he is using from the belief that he is using those words to express. What holds true for the former need not hold true for the latter. A Frenchman, believing that 'potatoes' is English for apples, may use, 'There are potatoes in the basket' to express the belief that there are apples in the basket; from the fact that he has a mistaken belief about 'potatoes' and 'apples,' it does not follow that he has a mistaken belief about potatoes and apples. Similarly, it may be that what a man believes about his own use of the expression 'appears white' is something that is not directly evident to him—indeed what he believes about his own language may even be false and unreasonable; but from these facts it does not follow that what he intends to assert when he utters 'This appears white to me' is something that cannot be directly evident.[21]

We have, then, singled out various types of statements expressing what is directly evident. Most of these statements, as Leibniz said, refer to our *thoughts*; they may say what we are thinking, believing, hoping, fearing, wishing, wondering, desiring, loving, hating; or they may say what we think we know, or think we are remembering, or think we are perceiving. Some of them will refer to our *actions*, at least to the extent of saying what we are trying or undertaking to do at any particular time. And some of them will refer to ways in which we *sense*, or are *appeared* to.

21. For a further defense of this way of looking at appearing, compare John Pollock, *Knowledge and Justification* (Princeton: Princeton University Press, 1974), pp. 71–9.

Chapter 19

Does empirical knowledge have a foundation?

Wilfrid Sellars

1. ONE of the forms taken by the Myth of the Given is the idea that there is, indeed *must be*, a structure of particular matter of fact such that (*a*) each fact can not only be noninferentially known to be the case, but presupposes no other knowledge either of particular matter of fact, or of general truths; and (*b*) such that the noninferential knowledge of facts belonging to this structure constitutes the ultimate court of appeals for all factual claim—particular and general—about the world. It is important to note that I characterized the knowledge of fact belonging to this stratum as not only noninferential, but as presupposing no knowledge of other matter of fact, whether particular or general. It might be thought that this is a redundancy, that knowledge (not belief or conviction, but knowledge) which logic-ally presupposes knowledge of other facts *must* be inferential. This, however, as I hope to show, is itself an episode in the Myth.

Now, the idea of such a privileged stratum of fact is a familiar one, though not without its difficulties. Knowledge pertaining to this level is *noninferential*, yet it is, after all, *knowledge*. It is *ultimate*, yet it has *authority*. The attempt to make a consistent picture of these two requirements has traditionally taken the following form:

Statements pertaining to this level, in order to 'express knowledge' must not only be made, but, so to speak, must be worthy of being made, *credible*, that is, in the sense of worthy of credence. Furthermore, and this is a crucial point, they must be made in a way which *involves* this credibility. For where there is no connection between the making of a statement and its authority, the assertion may express *conviction*, but it can scarcely be said to express knowledge.

The authority—the credibility—of statements pertaining to this level cannot exhaustively consist in the fact that they are supported by *other* statements, for in that case all *knowledge* pertaining to this level would have to be inferential, which not only contradicts the hypoth-esis, but flies in the face of good sense. The conclusion seems inevitable that if some statements pertaining to this level are to express *noninferential* knowledge, they must have a credibility which is not a matter of being supported by other statements. Now there does seem to be a class of statements which fill at least part of this bill, namely such statements as would be said to *report observations*, thus, 'This is red.' These statements, candidly made,

Wilfrid Sellars, 'Does Empirical Knowledge have a Foundation?' in *Science, Perception and Reality* (London, Routledge & Kegan Paul, 1963), pp. 164–70 reprinted by permission of Taylor & Francis.

have authority. Yet they are not expressions of inference. How, then, is this authority to be understood?

Clearly, the argument continues, it springs from the fact that they are made in just the circumstances in which they are made, as is indicated by the fact that they characteristically, though not necessarily or without exception, involve those so-called token-reflexive expressions which, in addition to the tenses of verbs, serve to connect the circumstances in which a statement is made with its sense. (At this point it will be helpful to begin putting the line of thought I am developing in terms of the *fact-stating* and *observation-reporting* roles of certain sentences.) Roughly, two verbal performances which are tokens of a non-token-reflexive sentence can occur in widely different circumstances and yet make the same statement; whereas two tokens of a token-reflexive sentence can make the same statement only if they are uttered in the same circumstances (according to a relevant criterion of sameness). And two tokens of a sentence, whether it contains a token-reflexive expression—over and above a tensed verb—or not, can make the same *report* only if, made all candour, they express the *presence*—in *some* sense of 'presence'—of the state of affairs that is being reported; if, that is, they stand in that relation to the state of affairs, whatever the relation may be, by virtue of which they can be said to formulate observations of it.

It would appear, then, that there are two ways in which a sentence token can have credibility: (1) The authority may accrue to it, so to speak, from above, that is, as being a token of a sentence type *all* the token of which, in a certain use, have credibility, e.g. '2+2=4'. In this case, let us say that token credibility is inherited from type authority. (2) The credibility may accrue to it from the fact that it came to exist in a certain way in a certain set of circumstances, e.g. 'This is red.' Here token credibility is not derived from type credibility.

Now, the credibility of *some* sentence types appear to be *intrinsic*—at least in the limited sense that it is *not* derived from other sentences, type or token. This is, or seems to be, the case with certain sentences used to make analytic statements. The credibility of *some* sentence types accrues to them by virtue of their logical relations to other sentence types, thus by virtue of the fact that they are logical consequences of more basic sentences. It would seem obvious, however, that the credibility of empirical sentence types cannot be traced without remainder to the credibility of other sentence types. And since no empirical sentence type appears to have *intrinsic* credibility, this means that credibility must accrue to *some* empirical sentence types by virtue of their logical relations to certain sentence tokens, and, indeed, to sentence tokens the authority of which is not derived, in its turn, from the authority of sentence types.

The picture we get is that of their being two *ultimate* modes of credibility: (1) The intrinsic credibility of analytic sentences, which accrues to tokens as being tokens of such a type; (2) the credibility of such tokens as 'express observations', a credibility which flows from tokens to types.

2. Let us explore this picture, which is common to all traditional empiricisms, a bit further. How is the authority of such sentence tokens as 'express observational knowledge' to be understood? It has been tempting to suppose that in spite of the obvious differences which exist between 'observation reports' and 'analytic statements', there is an essential similarity between the ways in which they come by their authority. Thus, it has been claimed, not without plausibility, that whereas *ordinary* empirical statements can be *correctly* made without being *true*, observation reports resemble analytic statements in that being correctly made is a sufficient as well as

necessary condition of their truth. And it has been inferred from this—somewhat hastily, I believe—that 'correctly making' the report 'This is green' is a matter of 'following the rules for the use of "this", "is", and "green".'

Three comments are immediately necessary:

(1) First a brief remark about the term 'report'. In ordinary usage a report is a report made *by* someone *to* someone. To make a report is to *do* something. In the literature of epistemology, however, the word 'report' or *'Konstatierung'* has acquired a technical use in which a sentence token can play a reporting role (*a*) without being an *overt* verbal performance, and (*b*) without having the character of being 'by someone to someone'—even oneself. There is, of course, such a thing as 'talking to *oneself'—in foro interno*—but, as I shall be emphasizing in the closing stages of my argument, it is important not to suppose that all 'covert' verbal episodes are of this kind.

(2) My second comment is that while *we* shall not assume that because 'reports' *in the ordinary sense* are actions, 'reports' in the sense of *Konstatierungen* are also actions, the line of thought we are considering treats them as such. In other words, it interprets the correctness of *Konstatierungen* as analogous to the rightness of actions. Let me emphasize, however, that not all *ought* is *ought to do*, nor all correctness the correctness of *actions*.

(3) My third comment is that if the expression 'following a rule' is taken seriously, and is not weakened beyond all recognition into the bare notion of exhibiting a uniformity—in which case the lightning–thunder sequence would 'follow a rule'—then it is the knowledge or belief that the circumstances are of a certain kind, and not the mere fact that they *are* of this kind, which contributes to bringing about the action.

3. In the light of these remarks it is clear that *if* observation reports are construed as *actions*, *if* their correctness is interpreted as the correctness of an *action* and *if* the authority of an observation report is construed as the fact that making it is 'following a rule' in the proper sense of this phrase, *then* we are face to face with givenness in its most straightforward form. For these stipulations commit one to the idea that the authority of *Konstatierungen* rests on nonverbal episodes of a awareness—awareness *that* something is the case, e.g. *that this is green*—which nonverbal episodes have an intrinsic authority (they are, so to speak, 'self-authenticating') which the *verbal* performances (the *Konstatierungen*) properly performed 'express'. One is committed to a stratum of authoritative nonverbal episodes ('awarenesses'), the authority of which accrues to a superstructure of *verbal actions*, provided that the expressions occurring in these actions are properly *used*. These self-authenticating episodes would constitute the tortoise on which stands the elephant on which rests the edifice of empirical knowledge. The essence of the view is the same whether these intrinsically authoritative episodes are such items as the awareness that a certain sense content is green or such items as the awareness that a certain physical object looks to oneself to be green.

4. But what is the alternative? We might begin by trying something like the following: An overt or covert token of 'This is green' in the presence of a green item is a *Konstatierung* and expresses observational knowledge if and only if it is a

manifestation of a tendency to produce overt or covert tokens of 'This is green'—given a certain set—if and only if a green object is being looked at in standard conditions. Clearly on this interpretation the occurrence of such tokens of 'This is green' would be 'following a rule' only in the sense that they are instances of a uniformity, a uniformity differing from the lightning–thunder case in that it is an acquired causal characteristic of the language user. Clearly the above suggestion, which corresponds to the 'thermometer view' criticized by Professor Price, and which we have already rejected, won't do as it stands. Let us see, however, if it cannot be revised to fit the criteria I have been using for 'expressing observational knowledge'.

The first hurdle to be jumped concerns the *authority* which, as I have emphasized, a sentence token must have in order that it may be said to express knowledge. Clearly, on this account the only thing that can remotely be supposed to constitute such authority is the fact that one can infer the presence of a green object from the fact that someone makes this report. As we have already noticed, the correctness of a report does not have to be construed as the rightness of an *action*. A report can be correct as being an instance of a general mode of behaviour which, in a given linguistic community, it is reasonable to sanction and support.

The second hurdle is, however, the decisive one. For we have seen that to be the expression of knowledge, a report must not only *have* authority, this authority must *in some sense* be recognized by the person whose report it is. And this is a steep hurdle indeed. For if the authority of the report 'This is green' lies in the fact that the existence of green items appropriately related to the perceiver can be inferred from the occurrence of such reports, it follows that only a person who is able to draw this inference, and therefore who has not only the concept *green*, but also the concept of uttering 'This is green'—indeed, the concept of certain conditions of perception, those which would correctly be called 'standard conditions'—could be in a position to token 'This is green' in recognition of its authority. In other words, for a *Konstatierung* 'This is green' to 'express observational knowledge', not only must it be a *symptom* or *sign* of the presence of a green object in standard conditions, but the perceiver must know that tokens of 'This is green' *are* symptoms of the presence of green objects in conditions which are standard for visual perception.

5. Now it might be thought that there is something obviously absurd in the idea that before a token uttered by, say, Jones could be the expression of observational knowledge, Jones would have to know that overt verbal episodes of this kind are reliable indicators of the existence, suitably related to the speaker, of green objects. I do not think that it is. Indeed, I think that something very like it is true. The point I wish to make now, however, is that if it *is* true, then it follows, as a matter of simple logic, that one could not have observational knowledge of *any* fact unless one knew many *other* things as well. And let me emphasize that the point is not taken care of by distinguishing between *knowing how* and *knowing that*, and admitting that observational knowledge requires a lot of 'know how'. For the point is specifically that observational knowledge of any particular fact, e.g. that this is green, presupposes that one knows general facts of the form *X is a reliable symptom of Y*. And to

admit this requires an abandonment of the traditional empiricist idea that obser-vational knowledge 'stands on its own feet'. Indeed, the suggestion would be anath-ema to traditional empiricists for the obvious reason that by making observational knowledge *presuppose* knowledge of general facts of the form X *is a reliable symp-tom of Y*, it runs counter to the idea that we come to know general facts of this form only *after* we have come to know by observation a number of particular facts which support the hypothesis that X is a symptom of Y.

And it might be thought that there is an obvious regress in the view we are examining. Does it not tell us that observational knowledge at time t presupposes knowledge of the form X *is a reliable symptom of Y*, which presupposes *prior* observational knowledge, which presupposes *other* knowledge of the form X *is a reliable symptom of Y*, which presupposes still other, and *prior*, observational know-ledge, and so on? This charge, however, rests on too simple, indeed a radically mistaken, conception of what one is saying of Jones when one says that he *knows* that p. It is not just that the objection supposes that knowing is an *episode*; for clearly there are episodes which we can correctly characterize as knowings, in particular, *observings*. The essential point is that in characterizing an episode or a state as that of *knowing*, we are not giving an empirical description of that episode or state; we are placing it in the logical space of reasons, of justifying and being able to justify what one says.

6. Thus, all that the view I am defending requires is that no tokening by S *now* of 'This is green' is to count as 'expressing observational knowledge' unless it is also correct to say of S that he *now* knows the appropriate fact of the form X *is a reliable symptom of Y*, namely that (and again I oversimplify) utterances of 'This is green' are reliable indicators of the presence of green objects in standard conditions of perception. And while the correctness of this statement about Jones requires that Jones could *now* cite prior particular facts as evidence for the idea that these utterances *are* reliable indicators, it requires only that it is correct to say that Jones *now* knows, thus remembers,[1] that these particular facts *did* obtain. It does not require that it be correct to say that at the time these facts did obtain he *then knew* them to obtain. And the regress disappears.

Thus, while Jones's ability to give inductive reasons *today* is built on a long history of acquiring and manifesting verbal habits in perceptual situations, and, in particular, the occurrence of verbal episodes, e.g. 'This is green', which is super-ficially like those which are later properly said to express observational knowledge, it does not require that any episode in this prior time be characterizeable as express-ing knowledge. [. . .]

7. The idea that observation 'strictly and properly so-called' is constituted by certain self-authenticating nonverbal episodes, the authority of which is transmit-ted to verbal and quasi-verbal performances when these performances are made 'in conformity with the semantical rules of the language', is, of course, the heart of the

---

1. (Added 1963) My thought was that one can have direct (noninferential) knowledge of a past fact which one did not or even (as in the case envisaged) *could* not conceptualize at the time it was present.

Myth of the Given. For the *given*, in epistemological tradition, is what is *taken* by these self-authenticating episodes. These 'takings' are, so to speak, the unmoved movers of empirical knowledge, the 'knowings in presence' which are presupposed by all other knowledge, both the knowledge of general truths and the knowledge 'in absence' of other particular matters of fact. Such is the framework in which traditional empiricism makes its characteristic claim that the perceptually given is the foundation of empirical knowledge.

Let me make it clear, however, that if I reject this framework, it is not because I should deny that observings are *inner* episodes, nor that *strictly speaking* they are *nonverbal* episodes. It will be my contention, however, that the sense in which they are nonverbal—which is also the sense in which thought episodes are nonverbal—is one which gives no aid or comfort to epistemological givenness. In the concluding sections of this paper I shall attempt to explicate the logic of inner episodes, and show that we can distinguish between observations and thoughts, on the one hand, and their verbal expression on the other, without making the mistakes of traditional dualism. I shall also attempt to explicate the logical status of *impressions* or *immediate experiences*, and thus bring to a successful conclusion the quest with which my argument began.

One final remark before I begin this task. If I reject the framework of traditional empiricism, it is not because I want to say that empirical knowledge has *no* foundation. For to put it this way is to suggest that it is really 'empirical knowledge so-called', and to put it in a box with rumours and hoaxes. There is clearly *some* point to the picture of human knowledge as resting on a level of propositions—observation reports—which do not rest on other propositions in the same way as other propositions rest on them. On the other hand, I do wish to insist that the metaphor of 'foundation' is misleading in that it keeps us from seeing that if there is a logical dimension in which other empirical propositions rest on observation reports, there is another logical dimension in which the latter rest on the former.

Above all, the picture is misleading because of its static character. One seems forced to choose between the picture of an elephant which rests on a tortoise (What supports the tortoise?) and the picture of a great Hegelian serpent of knowledge with its tail in its mouth (Where does it begin?). Neither will do. For empirical knowledge, like its sophisticated extension, science, is rational, not because it has a *foundation* but because it is a self-correcting enterprise which can put *any* claim in jeopardy, though not *all* at once.

Normativity

Chapter 20

Espistemology naturalized

W. V. Quine

EPISTEMOLOGY is concerned with the foundations of science. Conceived thus broadly, epistemology includes the study of the foundations of mathematics as one of its departments. Specialists at the turn of the century thought that their efforts in this particular department were achieving notable success: mathematics seemed to reduce altogether to logic. In a more recent perspective this reduction is seen to be better describable as a reduction to logic and set theory. This correction is a disappointment epistemologically, since the firmness and obviousness that we associate with logic cannot be claimed for set theory. But still the success achieved in the foundations of mathematics remains exemplary by comparative standards, and we can illuminate the rest of epistemology somewhat by drawing parallels to this department.

Studies in the foundations of mathematics divide symmetrically into two sorts, conceptual and doctrinal. The conceptual studies are concerned with meaning, the doctrinal with truth. The conceptual studies are concerned with clarifying concepts by defining them, some in terms of others. The doctrinal studies are concerned with establishing laws by proving them, some on the basis of others. Ideally the obscurer concepts would be defined in terms of the clearer ones so as to maximize clarity, and the less obvious laws would be proved from the more obvious ones so as to maximize certainty. Ideally the definitions would generate all the concepts from clear and distinct ideas, and the proofs would generate all the theorems from self-evident truths.

The two ideals are linked. For, if you define all the concepts by use of some favored subset of them, you thereby show how to translate all theorems into these favored terms. The clearer these terms are, the likelier it is that the truths couched in them will be obviously true, or derivable from obvious truths. If in particular the concepts of mathematics were all reducible to the clear terms of logic, then all the truths of mathematics would go over into truths of logic; and surely the truths of logic are all obvious or at least potentially obvious, i.e., derivable from obvious truths by individually obvious steps.

This particular outcome is in fact denied us, however, since mathematics reduces only to set theory and not to logic proper. Such reduction still enhances clarity, but only because of the interrelations that emerge and not because the end terms of the analysis are clearer than others. As for the end truths, the axioms of set theory, these have less obviousness and certainty to recommend them than do most of the mathematical theorems that we would derive from them. Moreover, we know from Gödel's work that no consistent axiom system can cover mathematics even when we renounce self-evidence. Reduction in the foundations of mathematics remains mathematically and philosophically fascinating, but it does not do what the epistemologist would like of it: it does not reveal the ground of mathematical knowledge, it does not show how mathematical certainty is possible.

Still there remains a helpful thought, regarding epistemology generally, in that duality of structure which was especially conspicuous in the foundations of mathematics. I refer to the bifurcation into a theory of concepts, or meaning, and a theory of doctrine, or truth; for this applies to the epistemology of natural knowledge no less than to the foundations of mathematics. The parallel is as follows. Just as mathematics is to be reduced to logic, or logic and set theory, so natural knowledge is to be based somehow on sense experience. This means explaining the notion of body in sensory terms; here is the conceptual side. And it means justifying our knowledge of truths of nature in sensory terms; here is the doctrinal side of the bifurcation.

Hume pondered the epistemology of natural knowledge on both sides of the bifurcation, the conceptual and the doctrinal. His handling of the conceptual side of the problem, the explanation of body in sensory terms, was bold and simple: he identified bodies outright with the sense impressions. If common sense distinguishes between the material apple and our sense impressions of it on the ground that the apple is one and enduring while the impressions are many and fleeting, then, Hume held, so much the worse for common sense; the notion of its being the same apple on one occasion and another is a vulgar confusion.

Nearly a century after Hume's *Treatise*, the same view of bodies was espoused by the early American philosopher Alexander Bryan Johnson.[1] 'The word iron names an associated sight and feel,' Johnson wrote.

What then of the doctrinal side, the justification of our knowledge of our truths about nature? Here, Hume despaired. By his identification of bodies with impressions he did succeed in construing some singular statements about bodies as indubitable truths, yes; as truths about impressions, directly known. But general statements, also singular statements about the future, gained no increment of certainty by being construed as about impressions.

On the doctrinal side, I do not see that we are farther along today than where

---

1. A. B. Johnson, *A Treatise on Language* (New York, 1836; Berkeley, 1947).

Hume left us. The Humean predicament is the human predicament. But on the conceptual side there has been progress. There the crucial step forward was made already before Alexander Bryan Johnson's day, although Johnson did not emulate it. It was made by Bentham in his theory of fictions. Bentham's step was the recognition of contextual definition, or what he called paraphrasis. He recognized that to explain a term we do not need to specify an object for it to refer to, nor even specify a synonymous word or phrase; we need only show, by whatever means, how to translate all the whole sentences in which the term is to be used. Hume's and Johnson's desperate measure of identifying bodies with impressions ceased to be the only conceivable way of making sense of talk of bodies, even granted that impressions were the only reality. One could undertake to explain talk of bodies in terms of talk of impressions by translating one's whole sentences about bodies into whole sentences about impressions, without equating the bodies themselves to anything at all.

This idea of contextual definition, or recognition of the sentence as the primary vehicle of meaning, was indispensable to the ensuing developments in the foundations of mathematics. It was explicit in Frege, and it attained its full flower in Russell's doctrine of singular descriptions as incomplete symbols.

Contextual definition was one of two resorts that could be expected to have a liberating effect upon the conceptual side of the epistemology of natural knowledge. The other is resort to the resources of set theory as auxiliary concepts. The epistemologist who is willing to eke out his austere ontology of sense impressions with these set-theoretic auxiliaries is suddenly rich: he has not just his impressions to play with, but sets of them, and sets of sets, and so on up. Constructions in the foundations of mathematics have shown that such set-theoretic aids are a powerful addition; after all, the entire glossary of concepts of classical mathematics is constructible from them. Thus equipped, our epistemologist may not need either to identify bodies with impressions or to settle for contextual definition; he may hope to find in some subtle construction of sets upon sets of sense impressions a category of objects enjoying just the formula properties that he wants for bodies.

The two resorts are very unequal in epistemological status. Contextual definition is unassailable. Sentences that have been given meaning as wholes are undeniably meaningful, and the use they make of their component terms is therefore meaningful, regardless of whether any translations are offered for those terms in isolation. Surely Hume and A. B. Johnson would have used contextual definition with pleasure if they had thought of it. Recourse to sets, on the other hand, is a drastic ontological move, a retreat from the austere ontology of impressions. There are philosophers who would rather settle for bodies outright than accept all these sets, which amount, after all, to the whole abstract ontology of mathematics.

This issue has not always been clear, however, owing to deceptive hints of continuity between elementary logic and set theory. This is why mathematics was once believed to reduce to logic, that is, to an innocent and unquestionable logic, and to inherit these qualities. And this is probably why Russell was content to resort to sets as well as to contextual definition when in *Our Knowledge of the External World* and elsewhere he addressed himself to the epistemology of natural knowledge, on its conceptual side.

To account for the external world as a logical construct of sense data—such, in Russell's terms, was the program. It was Carnap, in his *Der logische Aufbau des Welt* of 1928, who came nearest to executing it.

This was the conceptual side of epistemology; what of the doctrinal? There the Humean predicament remained unaltered. Carnap's constructions, if carried successfully to completion, would have enabled us to translate all sentences about the world into terms of sense data, or observation, plus logic and set theory. But the mere fact that a sentence is *couched* in terms of observation, logic, and set theory does not mean that it can be *proved* from observation sentences by logic and set theory. The most modest of generalizations about observable traits will cover more cases than its utterer can have had occasion actually to observe. The hopelessness of grounding natural science upon immediate experience in a firmly logical way was acknowledged. The Cartesian quest for certainty had been the remote motivation of epistemology, both on its conceptual and its doctrinal side; but that quest was seen as a lost cause. To endow the truths of nature with the full authority of immediate experience was as forlorn a hope as hoping to endow the truths of mathematics with the potential obviousness of elementary logic.

What then could have motivated Carnap's heroic efforts on the conceptual side of epistemology, when hope of certainty on the doctrinal side was abandoned? There were two good reasons still. One was that such constructions could be expected to elicit and clarify the sensory evidence for science, even if the inferential steps between sensory evidence and scientific doctrine must fall short of certainty. The other reason was that such constructions would deepen our understanding of our discourse about the world, even apart from questions of evidence; it would make all cognitive discourse as clear as observation terms and logic and, I must regretfully add, set theory.

It was sad for epistemologists, Hume and others, to have to acquiesce in the impossibility of strictly deriving the science of the external world from sensory evidence. Two cardinal tenets of empiricism remained unassailable, however, and so remain to this day. One is that whatever evidence there *is* for science *is* sensory evidence. The other, to which I shall recur, is that all inculcation of meanings of words must rest ultimately on sensory evidence. Hence the continuing attractiveness of the idea of a *logischer Aufbau* in which the sensory content of discourse would stand forth explicitly.

If Carnap had successfully carried such a construction through, how could he have told whether it was the right one? The question would have had no point. He was seeking what he called a *rational reconstruction*. Any construction of physicalistic discourse in terms of sense experience, logic, and set theory would have been seen as satisfactory if it made the physicalistic discourse come out right. If there is one way there are many, but any would be a great achievement.

But why all this creative reconstruction, all this make-believe? The stimulation of his sensory receptors is all the evidence anybody has had to go on, ultimately, in arriving at his picture of the world. Why not just see how this construction really proceeds? Why not settle for psychology? Such a surrender of the epistemological burden to psychology is a move that was disallowed in earlier times as circular reasoning. If the epistemologist's goal is validation of the grounds of empirical science, he defeats his purpose by using psychology or other empirical science in the validation. However, such scruples against circularity have little point once we have stopped dreaming of deducing science from observations. If we are out simply to understand the link between observation and science, we are well advised to use any available information, including that provided by the very science whose link with observation we are seeking to understand.

But there remains a different reason, unconnected with fears of circularity, for still favoring creative reconstruction. We should like to be able to *translate* science into logic and observation terms and set theory. This would be a great epistemological achievement, for it would show all the rest of the concepts of science to be theoretically superfluous. It would legitimize them—to whatever degree the concepts of set theory, logic, and observation are themselves legitimate—by showing that everything done with the one apparatus could in principle be done with the other. If psychology itself could deliver a truly translational reduction of this kind, we should welcome it; but certainly it cannot, for certainly we did not grow up learning definitions of physicalistic language in terms of a prior language of set theory, logic, and observation. Here, then, would be good reason for persisting in a rational reconstruction: we want to establish the essential innocence of physical concepts, by showing them to be theoretically dispensable.

The fact is, though, that the construction which Carnap outlined in *Der logische Aufbau der Welt* does not give translational reduction either. It would not even if the outline were filled in. The crucial point comes where Carnap is explaining how to assign sense qualities to positions in physical space and time. These assignments are to be made in such a way as to fulfill, as well as possible, certain desiderata which he states, and with growth of experience the assignments are to be revised to suit. This plan, however illuminating, does not offer any key to *translating* the sentences of science into terms of observation, logic, and set theory.

We must despair of any such reduction. Carnap had despaired of it by 1936, when, in 'Testability and meaning,'[2] he introduced so-called *reduction forms* of a type weaker than definition. Definitions had shown always how to translate sentences into equivalent sentences. Contextual definition of a term showed how to translate sentences containing the term into equivalent sentences lacking the term. Reduction forms of Carnap's liberalized kind, on the other hand, do not in general give equivalences; they give implications. They explain a new term, if only partially, by specifying some sentences which are implied by sentences containing the term, and other sentences which imply sentences containing the term.

It is tempting to suppose that the countenancing of reduction forms in this liberal sense is just one further step of liberalization comparable to the earlier one, taken by Bentham, of countenancing contextual definition. The former and sterner kind of rational reconstruction might have been represented as a fictitious history

---

2. *Philosophy of Science* 3 (1936), 419–71; 4 (1937), 1–40.

in which we imagined our ancestors introducing the terms of physicalistic discourse on a phenomenalistic and set-theoretic basis by a succession of contextual definitions. The new and more liberal kind of rational reconstruction is a fictitious history in which we imagine our ancestors introducing those terms by a succession rather of reduction forms of the weaker sort.

This, however, is a wrong comparison. The fact is rather that the former and sterner kind of rational reconstruction, where definition reigned, embodied no fictitious history at all. It was nothing more nor less than a set of directions—or would have been, if successful—for accomplishing everything in terms of phenomena and set theory that we now accomplish in terms of bodies. It would have been a true reduction by translation, a legitimation by elimination. *Definire est eliminare.* Rational reconstruction by Carnap's later and looser reduction forms does none of this.

To relax the demand for definition, and settle for a kind of reduction that does not eliminate, is to renounce the last remaining advantage that we supposed rational reconstruction to have over straight psychology; namely, the advantage of translational reduction. If all we hope for is a reconstruction that links science to experience in explicit ways short of translation, then it would seem more sensible to settle for psychology. Better to discover how science is in fact developed and learned than to fabricate a fictitious structure to a similar effect.

The empiricist made one major concession when he despaired of deducing the truths of nature from sensory evidence. In despairing now even of translating those truths into terms of observation and logico-mathematical auxiliaries, he makes another major concession. For suppose we hold, with the old empiricist Peirce, that the very meaning of a statement consists in the difference its truth would make to possible experience. Might we not formulate, in a chapter-length sentence in observational language, all the difference that the truth of a given statement might make to experience, and might we not then take all this as the translation? Even if the difference that the truth of the statement would make to experience ramifies indefinitely, we might still hope to embrace it all in the logical implications of our chapter-length formulation, just as we can axiomatize an infinity of theorems. In giving up hope of such translation, then, the empiricist is conceding that the empirical meanings of typical statements about the external world are inaccessible and ineffable.

How is this inaccessibility to be explained? Simply on the ground that the experiential implications of a typical statement about bodies are too complex for finite axiomatization, however lengthy? No; I have a different explanation. It is that the typical statement about bodies has no fund of experiential implications it can call its own. A substantial mass of theory, taken together, will commonly have experiential implications; this is how we make verifiable predictions. We may not be able to explain why we arrive at theories which make successful predictions, but we do arrive at such theories.

Sometimes also an experience implied by a theory fails to come off; and then, ideally, we declare the theory false. But the failure falsifies only a block of theory as a whole, a conjunction of many statements. The failure shows that one or more of those statements is false, but it does not show which. The predicted experiences, true and false, are not implied by any one of the component statements of the theory rather than another. The component statements simply do not have empirical meanings, by Peirce's standard; but a sufficiently inclusive portion of theory does. If we can aspire to a sort of *logischer Aufbau der Welt* at all, it must be to one in which the texts slated for translation into observational and logico-mathematical terms are mostly broad theories taken as wholes, rather than just terms or short sentences. The translation of a theory would be a ponderous axiomatization of all the experiential difference that the truth of the theory would make. It would be a queer translation, for it would translate the whole but none of the parts. We might better speak in such a case not of translation but simply of observational evidence for theories; and we may, following Peirce, still fairly call this the empirical meaning of the theories.

These considerations raise a philosophical question even about ordinary unphilosophical translation, such as from English into Arunta or Chinese. For, if the English sentences of a theory have their meaning only together as a body, then we can justify their translation into Arunta only together as a body. There will be no justification for pairing off the component English sentences with component Arunta sentences, except as these correlations make the translation of the theory as a whole come out right. Any translations of the English sentences into Arunta sentences will be as correct as any other, so long as the net empirical implications of the theory as a whole are preserved in translation. But it is to be expected that many different ways of translating the component sentences, essentially different individually, would deliver the same empirical implications for the theory as a whole; deviations in the translation of one component sentence could be compensated for in the translation of another component sentence. Insofar, there can be no ground for saying which of two glaringly unlike translations of individual sentences is right.[3]

For an uncritical mentalist, no such indeterminacy threatens. Every term and every sentence is a label attached to an idea, simple or complex, which is stored in the mind. When on the other hand we take a verification theory of meaning seriously, the indeterminacy would appear to be inescapable. The Vienna Circle espoused a verification theory of meaning but did not take it seriously enough. If we recognize with Peirce that the meaning of a sentence turns purely on what would count as evidence for its truth, and if we recognize with Duhem that theoretical sentences have their evidence not as single sentences but only as larger blocks of theory, then the indeterminacy of translation of theoretical sentences is the natural conclusion. And most sentences, apart from observation sentences, are theoretical. This conclusion, conversely, once it is embraced, seals the fate of any general notion of propositional meaning or, for that matter, state of affairs.

Should the unwelcomeness of the conclusion persuade us to abandon the verification theory of meaning? Certainly not. The sort of meaning that is basic to

---

3. W. V. Quine, 'Speaking of Objects' in his *Ontological Relativity and Other Essays* (New York 1969), pp. 2 ff.

translation, and to the learning of one's own language, is necessarily empirical meaning and nothing more. A child learns his first words and sentences by hearing and using them in the presence of appropriate stimuli. These must be external stimuli, for they must act both on the child and on the speaker from whom he is learning.[4] Language is socially inculcated and controlled; the inculcation and control turn strictly on the keying of sentences to shared stimulation. Internal factors may vary *ad libitum* without prejudice to communication as long as the keying of language to external stimuli is undisturbed. Surely one has no choice but to be an empiricist so far as one's theory of linguistic meaning is concerned.

What I have said of infant learning applies equally to the linguist's learning of a new language in the field. If the linguist does not lean on related languages for which there are previously accepted translation practices, then obviously he has no data but the concomitances of native utterance and observable stimulus situation. No wonder there is indeterminacy of translation—for of course only a small fraction of our utterances report concurrent external stimulation. Granted, the linguist will end up with unequivocal translations of everything; but only by making many arbitrary choices—arbitrary even though unconscious—along the way. Arbitrary? By this I mean that different choices could still have made everything come out right that is susceptible in principle to any kind of check.

Let me link up, in a different order, some of the points I have made. The crucial consideration behind my argument for the indeterminacy of translation was that a statement about the world does not always or usually have a separable fund of empirical consequences that it can call its own. That consideration served also to account for the impossibility of an epistemological reduction of the sort where every sentence is equated to a sentence in observational and logico-mathematical terms. And the impossibility of that sort of epistemological reduction dissipated the last advantage that rational reconstruction seemed to have over psychology.

Philosophers have rightly despaired of translating everything into observational and logico-mathematical terms. They have despaired of this even when they have not recognized, as the reason for this irreducibility, that the statements largely do not have their private bundles of empirical consequences. And some philosophers have seen in this irreducibility the bankruptcy of epistemology. Carnap and the other logical positivists of the Vienna Circle had already pressed the term 'metaphysics' into pejorative use, as connoting meaninglessness; and the term 'epistemology' was next. Wittgenstein and his followers, mainly at Oxford, found a residual philosophical vocation in therapy: in curing philosophers of the delusion that there were epistemological problems.

But I think that at this point it may be more useful to say rather that epistemology still goes on, though in a new setting and a clarified status. Epistemology, or something like it, simply falls into place as a chapter of psychology and hence of natural science. It studies a natural phenomenon, viz., a physical human subject. This human subject is accorded a certain experimentally controlled input—certain

4. W. V. Quine, 'Ontological Relativity' in his *Ontological Relativity and Other Essays* (New York 1969), p. 28.

patterns of irradiation in assorted frequencies, for instance—and in the fullness of time the subject delivers as output a description of the three-dimensional external world and its history. The relation between the meager input and the torrential output is a relation that we are prompted to study for somewhat the same reasons that always prompted epistemology; namely, in order to see how evidence relates to theory, and in what ways one's theory of nature transcends any available evidence.

Such a study could still include, even, something like the old rational reconstruction, to whatever degree such reconstruction is practicable; for imaginative constructions can afford hints of actual psychological processes, in much the way that mechanical simulations can. But a conspicuous difference between old epistemology and the epistemological enterprise in this new psychological setting is that we can now make free use of empirical psychology.

The old epistemology aspired to contain, in a sense, natural science; it would construct it somehow from sense data. Epistemology in its new setting, conversely, is contained in natural science, as a chapter of psychology. But the old containment remains valid too, in its way. We are studying how the human subject of our study posits bodies and projects his physics from his data, and we appreciate that our position in the world is just like his. Our very epistemological enterprise, therefore, and the psychology wherein it is a component chapter, and the whole of natural science wherein psychology is a component book—all this is our own construction or projection from stimulations like those we were meting out to our epistemological subject. There is thus reciprocal containment, though containment in different senses: epistemology in natural science and natural science in epistemology.

This interplay is reminiscent again of the old threat of circularity, but it is all right now that we have stopped dreaming of deducing science from sense data. We are after an understanding of science as an institution or process in the world, and we do not intend that understanding to be any better than the science which is its object. This attitude is indeed one that Neurath was already urging in Vienna Circle days, with his parable of the mariner who has to rebuild his boat while staying afloat in it.

One effect of seeing epistemology in a psychological setting is that it resolves a stubborn old enigma of epistemological priority. Our retinas are irradiated in two dimensions, yet we see things as three-dimensional without conscious inference. Which is to count as observation—the unconscious two-dimensional reception or the conscious three-dimensional apprehension? In the old epistemological context the conscious form had priority, for we were out to justify our knowledge of the external world by rational reconstruction, and that demands awareness. Awareness ceased to be demanded when we gave up trying to justify our knowledge of the external world by rational reconstruction. What to count as observation now can be settled in terms of the stimulation of sensory receptors, let consciousness fall where it may.

The Gestalt psychologists' challenge to sensory atomism, which seemed so relevant to epistemology forty years ago, is likewise deactivated. Regardless of whether sensory atoms or Gestalten are what favor the forefront of our consciousness, it is simply the stimulations of our sensory receptors that are best looked upon as the input to our cognitive mechanism. Old paradoxes about unconscious data and inference, old problems about chains of inference that would have to be completed too quickly—these no longer matter.

In the old anti-psychologistic days the question of epistemological priority was moot. What is epistemologically prior to what? Are Gestalten prior to sensory atoms because they are noticed, or should we favor sensory atoms on some more subtle ground? Now that we are permitted to appeal to physical stimulation, the problem dissolves; A is epistemologically prior to B if A is causally nearer than B to the sensory receptors. Or, what is in some ways better, just talk explicitly in terms of causal proximity to sensory receptors and drop the talk of epistemological priority.

Around 1932 there was debate in the Vienna Circle over what to count as observation sentences, or *Protokollsätze*.[5] One position was that they had the form of reports of sense impressions. Another was that they were statements of an elementary sort about the external world, e.g., 'A red cube is standing on the table.' Another, Neurath's, was that they had the form of reports of relations between percipients, and external things: 'Otto now sees a red cube on the table.' The worst of it was that there seemed to be no objective way of settling the matter: no way of making real sense of the question.

Let us now try to view the matter unreservedly in the context of the external world. Vaguely speaking, what we want of observation sentences is that they be the ones in closest causal proximity to the sensory receptors. But how is such proximity to be gauged? The idea may be rephrased this way: observation sentences are sentences which, as we learn language, are most strongly conditioned to concurrent sensory stimulation rather than to stored collateral information. Thus let us imagine a sentence queried for our verdict as to whether it is true or false; queried for our assent or dissent. Then the sentence is an observation sentence if our verdict depends only on the sensory stimulation present at the time.

But a verdict cannot depend on present stimulation to the exclusion of stored information. The very fact of our having learned the language evinces much storing of information, and of information without which we should be in no position to give verdicts on sentences however observational. Evidently then we must relax our definition of observation sentence to read thus: a sentence is an observation sentence if all verdicts on it depend on present sensory stimulation and on no stored information beyond what goes into understanding the sentence.

This formulation raises another problem: how are we to distinguish between information that goes into understanding a sentence and information that goes beyond? This is the problem of distinguishing between analytic truth, which issues from the mere meanings of words, and synthetic truth, which depends on more than meanings. Now I have long maintained that this distinction is illusory. There is one step toward such a distinction, however, which does make sense: a sentence that is true by mere meanings of words should be expected, at least if it is simple, to be subscribed to by all fluent speakers in the community. Perhaps the controversial notion of analyticity can be dispensed with, in our definition of

---

5. Carnap 'Protokollsätze' and Neurath 'Protokollsätze' in *Erkenntnis* 3 (1932), 204–28.

observation sentence, in favor of this straightforward attribute of community-wide acceptance.

This attribute is of course no explication of analyticity. The community would agree that there have been black dogs, yet none who talk of analyticity would call this analytic. My rejection of the analyticity notion just means drawing no line between what goes into the mere understanding of the sentences of a language and what else the community sees eye-to-eye on. I doubt that an objective distinction can be made between meaning and such collateral information as is community-wide.

Turning back then to our task of defining observation sentences, we get this: an observation sentence is one on which all speakers of the language give the same verdict when given the same concurrent stimulation. To put the point negatively, an observation sentence is one that is not sensitive to differences in past experience within the speech community.

This formulation accords perfectly with the traditional role of the observation sentence as the court of appeal of scientific theories. For by our definition the observation sentences are the sentences on which all members of the community will agree under uniform stimulation. And what is the criterion of membership in the same community? Simply general fluency of dialogue. This criterion admits of degrees, and indeed we may usefully take the community more narrowly for some studies than for others. What count as observation sentences for a community of specialists would not always so count for a larger community.

There is generally no subjectivity in the phrasing of observation sentences, as we are now conceiving them; they will usually be about bodies. Since the distinguishing trait of an observation sentence is intersubjective agreement under agreeing stimulation, a corporeal subject matter is likelier than not.

The old tendency to associate observation sentences with a subjective sensory subject matter is rather an irony when we reflect that observation sentences are also meant to be the intersubjective tribunal of scientific hypotheses. The old tendency was due to the drive to base science on something firmer and prior in the subject's experience; but we dropped that project.

The dislodging of epistemology from its old status of first philosophy loosed a wave, we saw, of epistemological nihilism. This mood is reflected somewhat in the tendency of Polányi, Kuhn, and the late Russell Hanson to belittle the role of evidence and to accentuate cultural relativism. Hanson ventured even to discredit the idea of observation, arguing that so-called observations vary from observer to observer with the amount of knowledge that the observers bring with them. The veteran physicist looks at some apparatus and sees an x-ray tube. The neophyte, looking at the same place, observes rather 'a glass and metal instrument replete with wires, reflectors, screws, lamps, and pushbuttons.'[6] One man's observation is another man's closed book or flight of fancy. The notion of observation as the impartial and objective source of evidence for science is bankrupt. Now my answer

---

6. N. R. Hanson, 'Observation and interpretation,' in S. Morgenbesser, ed., *Philosophy of Science Today* (New York: Basic Books, 1966).

to the x-ray example was already hinted a little while back: what counts as an observation sentence varies with the width of community considered. But we can also always get an absolute standard by taking in all speakers of the language, or most.[7] It is ironical that philosophers, finding the old epistemology untenable as a whole, should react by repudiating a part which has only now moved into clear focus.

Clarification of the notion of observation sentence is a good thing, for the notion is fundamental in two connections. These two correspond to the duality that I remarked upon early in this lecture: the duality between concept and doctrine, between knowing what a sentence means and knowing whether it is true. The observation sentence is basic to both enterprises. Its relation to doctrine, to our knowledge of what is true, is very much the traditional one: observation sentences are the repository of evidence for scientific hypotheses. Its relation to meaning is fundamental too, since observation sentences are the ones we are in a position to learn to understand first, both as children and as field linguists. For observation sentences are precisely the ones that we can correlate with observable circumstances of the occasion of utterance or assent, independently of variations in the past histories of individual informants. They afford the only entry to a language.

The observation sentence is the cornerstone of semantics. For it is, as we just saw, fundamental to the learning of meaning. Also, it is where meaning is firmest. Sentences higher up in theories have no empirical consequences they can call their own; they confront the tribunal of sensory evidence only in more or less inclusive aggregates. The observation sentence, situated at the sensory periphery of the body scientific, is the minimal verifiable aggregate; it has an empirical content all its own and wears it on its sleeve.

The predicament of the indeterminacy of translation has little bearing on observation sentences. The equating of an observation sentence of our language to an observation sentence of another language is mostly a matter of empirical generalization; it is a matter of identity between the range of stimulations that would prompt assent to the one sentence and the range of stimulations that would prompt assent to the other.[8]

It is no shock to the preconceptions of old Vienna to say that epistemology now becomes semantics. For epistemology remains centered as always on evidence, and meaning remains centered as always on verification; and evidence is verification. What is likelier to shock preconceptions is that meaning, once we get beyond observation sentences, ceases in general to have any clear applicability to single sentences; also that epistemology merges with psychology, as well as with linguistics.

This rubbing out of boundaries could contribute to progress, it seems to me, in philosophically interesting inquiries of a scientific nature. One possible area is

---

7. This qualification allows for occasional deviants such as the insane or the blind. Alternatively, such cases might he excluded by adjusting the level of fluency of dialogue whereby we define sameness of language. (For prompting this note and influencing the development of this paper also in more substantial ways I am indebted to Burton Dreben.)

8. W. V. Quine, *Word and Object* (Cambridge/MA 1960), pp. 31–46, 68.

perceptual norms. Consider, to begin with, the linguistic phenomenon of phonemes. We form the habit, in hearing the myriad variations of spoken sounds, of treating each as an approximation to one or another of a limited number of norms—around thirty altogether—constituting so to speak a spoken alphabet. All speech in our language can be treated in practice as sequences of just those thirty elements, thus rectifying small deviations. Now outside the realm of language also there is probably only a rather limited alphabet of perceptual norms altogether, toward which we tend unconsciously to rectify all perceptions. These, if experimentally identified, could be taken as epistemological building blocks, the working elements of experience. They might prove in part to be culturally variable, as phonemes are, and in part universal.

Again there is the area that the psychologist Donald T. Campbell calls evolutionary epistemology.[9] In this area there is work by Hüseyin Yilmaz, who shows how some structural traits of color perception could have been predicted from survival value.[10] And a more emphatically epistemological topic that evolution helps to clarify is induction, now that we are allowing epistemology the resources of natural science.[11]

9. D. T. Campbell, 'Methodological suggestions from a comparative psychology of knowledge processes,' *Inquiry*, 2 (1959), 152–82.

10. Hüseyin Yilmaz, 'On color vision and a new approach to general perception,' in E. E. Bernard and M. R. Kare, eds., *Biological Prototypes and Synthetic Systems* (New York: Plenum, 1962); 'Perceptual invariance and the psychophysical law,' *Perception and Psychophysics* 2 (1967), 533–38.

11. W. V. Quine, 'Natural Kinds' in his *Ontological Relativity and Other Essays* (New York 1969), pp. 114–38.

Chapter 21

What is 'naturalized epistemology?'

Jaegwon Kim

1. Epistemology as a normative inquiry

DESCARTES' epistemological inquiry in the *Meditations* begins with this question: What propositions are worthy of belief? In the *First Meditation* Descartes canvasses beliefs of various kinds he had formerly held as true and finds himself forced to conclude that he ought to reject them, that he ought not to accept them as true. We can view Cartesian epistemology as consisting of the following two projects: to identify the criteria by which we ought to regulate acceptance and rejection of beliefs, and to determine what we may be said to know according to those criteria. Descartes' epistemological agenda has been the agenda of Western epistemology to this day. The twin problems of identifying criteria of justified belief and coming to terms with the skeptical challenge to the possibility of knowledge have defined the central tasks of theory of knowledge since Descartes. This was as true of the empiricists, of Locke and Hume and Mill, as of those who more closely followed Descartes in the rationalist path.[1]

It is no wonder then that modern epistemology has been dominated by a single concept, that of *justification*, and two fundamental questions involving it: What conditions must a belief meet if we are justified in accepting it as true? and What beliefs are we in fact justified in accepting? Note that the first question does not ask for an 'analysis' or 'meaning' of the term 'justified belief'. And it is generally assumed, even if not always explicitly stated, that not just any statement of a necessary and sufficient condition for a belief to be justified will do. The implicit requirement has been that the stated conditions must constitute 'criteria' of justified belief, and for this it is necessary that the conditions be stated *without the use of epistemic terms*. Thus, formulating, conditions of justified belief in such terms as 'adequate evidence', 'sufficient ground', 'good reason', 'beyond a reasonable doubt', and so on, would be merely to issue a promissory note redeemable only when these

Jaegwon Kim, 'What is Naturalized Epistemology?' in J. E Tomberlin (ed.) *Philosophical Perspectives 2: Epistemology* (Atascadero/CA, Ridgeview Publishing Co., 1988), pp. 381–405 reprinted by permission of the author.

1. In making these remarks I am only repeating the familiar textbook history of philosophy; however, what *our* textbooks say about the history of a philosophical concept has much to do with *our* understanding of that concept.

epistemic terms are themselves explained in a way that accords with the requirement.[2]

This requirement, while it points in the right direction, does not go far enough. What is crucial is this: *the criteria of justified belief must be formulated on the basis of descriptive or naturalistic terms alone, without the use of any evaluative or normative ones, whether epistemic or of another kind.*[3] Thus, an analysis of justified belief that makes use of such terms as 'intellectual requirement'[4] and 'having a right to be sure'[5] would not satisfy this generalized condition; although such an analysis can be informative and enlightening about the inter-relationships of these normative concepts, it will not, on the present conception, count as a statement of *criteria* of justified belief, unless of course these terms are themselves provided with non-normative criteria. What is problematic, therefore, about the use of epistemic terms in stating criteria of justified belief is not its possible circularity in the usual sense; rather it is the fact that these epistemic terms are themselves essentially normative. We shall later discuss the rationale of this strengthened requirement.

As many philosophers have observed,[6] the two questions we have set forth, one about the criteria of justified belief and the other about what we can be said to know according to those criteria, constrain each other. Although some philosophers have been willing to swallow skepticism just because what we regard as correct criteria of justified belief are seen to lead inexorably to the conclusion that none, or very few, of our beliefs are justified, the usual presumption is that our answer to the first question should leave our epistemic situation largely unchanged. That is to say, it is expected to turn out that according to the criteria of justified belief we come to accept, we know, or are justified in believing, pretty much what we reflectively think we know or are entitled to believe.

2. Alvin Goldman explicitly states this requirement as a desideratum of his own analysis of justified belief in 'What is Justified Belief?', in George S. Pappas (ed.), *Justification and Knowledge* (Dordrecht: Reidel, 1979), p. 1. Roderick M. Chisholm's definition of 'being evident' in his *Theory of Knowledge*, 2nd ed. (Englewood Cliffs, N.J.: Prentice-Hall, 1977) does not satisfy this requirement as it rests ultimately on an unanalyzed epistemic concept of one belief being *more reasonable than* another. What does the real 'criteriological' work for Chisholm is his 'principles of evidence'. See especially (A) on p. 73 of *Theory of Knowledge*, which can usefully be regarded as an attempt to provide nonnormative, descriptive conditions for certain types of justified beliefs.

3. The basic idea of this stronger requirement seems implicit in Roderick Firth's notion of 'warrant-increasing property' in his 'Coherence, Certainty, and Epistemic Priority', *Journal of Philosophy* 61 (1964): 545–57. It seems that William P. Alston has something similar in mind when he says, '. . . like any evaluative property, epistemic justification is a supervenient property, the application of which is based on more fundamental properties' (at this point Alston refers to Firth's paper cited above), in 'Two Types of Foundationalism', *Journal of Philosophy* 73 (1976): 165–85 (the quoted remark occurs on p. 170). Although Alston doesn't further explain what he means by 'more fundamental properties', the context makes it plausible to suppose that he has in mind nonnormative, descriptive properties. See Section 7 below for further discussion.

4. See Chisholm, ibid., p. 14. Here Chisholm refers to a 'person's responsibility or duty *qua* intellectual being'.

5. This term was used by A. J. Ayer to characterize the difference between lucky guessing and knowing; see *The Problem of Knowledge* (New York & London: Penguin Books, 1956), p. 33.

6. Notably by Chisholm in *Theory of Knowledge* 1st ed., ch. 4.

Whatever the exact history, it is evident that the concept of justification has come to take center stage in our reflections on the nature of knowledge. And apart from history, there is a simple reason for our preoccupation with justification: it is the only specifically epistemic component in the classic tripartite conception of knowledge. Neither belief nor truth is a specifically epistemic notion: belief is a psychological concept and truth a semantical-metaphysical one. These concepts may have an implicit epistemological dimension, but if they do, it is likely to be through their involvement with essentially normative epistemic notions like justification, evidence, and rationality. Moreover, justification is what makes knowledge itself a normative concept. On surface at least, neither truth nor belief is normative or evaluative (I shall argue below, though, that belief does have an essential normative dimension). But justification manifestly is normative. If a belief is justified for us, then it is *permissible* and *reasonable*, from the epistemic point of view, for us to hold it, and it would be *epistemically irresponsible* to hold beliefs that contradict it. If we consider believing or accepting a proposition to be an 'action' in an appropriate sense, belief justification would then be a special case of justification of action, which in its broadest terms is the central concern of normative ethics. Just as it is the business of normative ethics to delineate the conditions under which acts and decisions are justified from the moral point of view, so it is the business of epistemology to identify and analyze the conditions under which beliefs, and perhaps other propositional attitudes, are justified from the epistemological point of view. It probably is only an historical accident that we standardly speak of 'normative ethics' but not of 'normative epistemology'. Epistemology is a normative discipline as much as, and in the same sense as, normative ethics.

We can summarize our discussion thus far in the following points: that justification is a central concept of our epistemological tradition, that justification, as it is understood in this tradition, is a normative concept, and in consequence that epistemology itself is a normative inquiry whose principal aim is a systematic study of the conditions of justified belief. I take it that these points are uncontroversial, although of course there could be disagreement about the details—for example, about what it means to say a concept or theory is 'normative' or 'evaluative'.

2. The foundationalist strategy

In order to identify the target of the naturalistic critique—in particular, Quine's—it will be useful to take a brief look at the classic response to the epistemological program set forth by Descartes. Descartes' approach to the problem of justification is a familiar story, at least as the textbook tells it: it takes the form of what is now commonly called 'foundationalism'. The foundationalist strategy is to divide the task of explaining justification into two stages: first, to identify a set of beliefs that are 'directly' justified in that they are justified without deriving their justified status from that of any other belief, and then to explain how other beliefs may be 'indirectly' or 'inferentially' justified by standing in an appropriate relation to those already justified. Directly justified beliefs, or 'basic beliefs', are to constitute the foundation upon which the superstructure of 'non-basic' or 'derived' beliefs is to rest. What beliefs then are directly justified, according to Descartes? Subtleties aside, he claimed that beliefs about our own present conscious states are among them. In what does their justification consist? What is it about these beliefs that make them directly justified? Somewhat simplistically again, Descartes' answer is that they are justified because they are *indubitable*, that the attentive and reflective mind *cannot but assent* to them. How are non-basic beliefs justified? By 'deduction'—that is, by a series of inferential steps, or 'intuitions', each of which is indubitable. If, therefore, we take Cartesian indubitability as a psychological notion, Descartes' epistemological theory can be said to meet the desideratum of providing nonepistemic, naturalistic criteria of justified belief.

Descartes' foundationalist program was inherited, in its essential outlines, by the empiricists. In particular, his 'mentalism', that beliefs about one's own current mental state are epistemologically basic, went essentially unchallenged by the empiricists and positivists, until this century. Epistemologists have differed from one another chiefly in regard to two questions: first, what else belonged in our corpus of basic beliefs, and second, how the derivation of the non-basic part of our knowledge was to proceed. Even the Logical Positivists were, by and large, foundationalists, although some of them came to renounce Cartesian mentalism in favor of a 'physicalistic basis'.[7] In fact, the Positivists were foundationalists twice over: for them 'observation', whether phenomenological or physical, served not only as the foundation of knowledge but as the foundation of all 'cognitive meaning'—that is, as both an epistemological and a semantic foundation.

3. Quine's arguments

It has become customary for epistemologists who profess allegiance to a 'naturalistic' conception of knowledge to pay homage to Quine as the chief contemporary provenance of their inspiration—especially to his influential paper 'Epistemology Naturalized'.[8] Quine's principal argument in this paper against traditional epistemology is based on the claim that the Cartesian foundationalist program has failed—that the Cartesian 'quest for certainty' is 'a lost cause'. While this claim about the hopelessness of the Cartesian 'quest for certainty' is nothing new, using it

7. See Rudolf Carnap, 'Testability and Meaning', *Philosophy of Science* 3 (1936), and 4 (1937). We should also note the presence of a strong coherentist streak among some positivists; see, e.g., Carl G. Hempel, 'On the Logical Positivists' Theory of Truth', *Analysis* 2 (1935) 49–59, and 'Some Remarks on "Facts" and Propositions', *Analysis* 2 (1935): 93–6.
8. In W. V. Quine, *Ontological Relativity and Other Essays* (New York: Columbia University Press, 1969) [Ch. 20 in this volume]. Also see his *Word and Object* (Cambridge: MIT Press, 1960); *The Roots of Reference* (La Salle Ill.: Open Court, 1973); (with Joseph Ullian) *The Web of Belief* (New York: Random House, 1970); and especially 'The Nature of Natural Knowledge' in Samuel Guttenplan (ed.), *Mind and Language* (Oxford: Clarendon Press, 1975). See Frederick F. Schmitt's excellent bibliography on naturalistic epistemology in Hilary Kornblith (ed.), *Naturalizing Epistemology* (Cambridge: MIT/Bradford, 1985).

to discredit the very conception of normative epistemology is new, something that any serious student of epistemology must contend with.

Quine divides the classic epistemological program into two parts: *conceptual reduction* whereby physical terms, including those of theoretical science, are reduced, via definition, to terms referring to phenomenal features of sensory experience, and *doctrinal reduction* whereby truths about the physical world are appropriately obtained from truths about sensory experience. The 'appropriateness' just alluded to refers to the requirement that the favored epistemic status ('certainty' for classic epistemologists, according to Quine) of our basic beliefs be transferred, essentially undiminished, to derived beliefs, a necessary requirement if the derivational process is to yield knowledge from knowledge. What derivational methods have this property of preserving epistemic status? Perhaps there are none, given our proneness to err in framing derivations as in anything else, not to mention the possibility of lapses of attention and memory in following lengthy proofs. But logical deduction comes as close to being one as any; it can at least be relied on to transmit truth, if not epistemic status. It could perhaps be argued that no method can preserve certainty unless it preserves (or is known to preserve) truth; and if this is so, logical deduction is the only method worth considering. I do not know whether this was the attitude of most classic epistemologists; but Quine assumes that if deduction doesn't fill their bill, nothing will.

Quine sees the project of conceptual reduction as culminating in Carnap's *Der Logische Aufbau der Welt*. As Quine sees it, Carnap 'came nearest to executing' the conceptual half of the classic epistemological project. But coming close is not good enough. Because of the holistic manner in which empirical meaning is generated by experience, no reduction of the sort Carnap and others so eagerly sought could in principle be completed. For definitional reduction requires point-to-point meaning relations[9] between physical terms and phenomenal terms, something that Quine's holism tells us cannot be had. The second half of the program, doctrinal reduction, is in no better shape; in fact, it was the one to stumble first, for, according to Quine, its impossibility was decisively demonstrated long before the *Aufbau*, by Hume in his celebrated discussion of induction. The 'Humean predicament' shows that theory cannot be logically deduced from observation; there simply is no way of deriving theory from observation that will transmit the latter's epistemic status intact to the former.

I don't think anyone wants to disagree with Quine in these claims. It is not possible to 'validate' science on the basis of sensory experience, if 'validation' means justification through logical deduction. Quine of course does not deny that our theories depend on observation for evidential support; he has said that sensory evidence is the only evidence there is. To be sure, Quine's argument against the possibility of conceptual reduction has a new twist: the application of his 'holism'. But his conclusion is no surprise; 'translational phenomenalism' has been moribund for many years.[10] And, as Quine himself notes, his argument against the

9. Or confirmational relations, given the Positivists' verificationist theory of meaning.
10. I know of no serious defense of it since Ayer's *The Foundations of Empirical Knowledge* (London: Macmillan, 1940).

doctrinal reduction, the 'quest for certainty', is only a restatement of Hume's 'skep-tical' conclusions concerning induction: induction after all is not deduction. Most of us are inclined, I think, to view the situation Quine describes with no great alarm, and I rather doubt that these conclusions of Quine's came as news to most epistemologists when 'Epistemology Naturalized' was first published. We are tempted to respond: of course we can't define physical concepts in terms of sense-data; of course observation 'underdetermines' theory. That is why observation is observation and not theory.

So it is agreed on all hands that the classical epistemological project, conceived as one of deductively validating physical knowledge from indubitable sensory data, cannot succeed. But what is the moral of this failure? What should be its philo-sophical lesson to us? Having noted the failure of the Cartesian program, Quine goes on:[11]

The stimulation of his sensory receptors is all the evidence anybody has had to go on, ultimately, in arriving at his picture of the world. Why not just see how this construction really proceeds? Why not settle for psychology? Such a surrender of the epistemological burden to psychology is a move that was disallowed in earlier times as circular reasoning. If the epistemologist's goal is validation of the grounds of empirical science, he defeats his purpose by using psychology or other empirical science in the validation. However, such scruples against circularity have little point once we have stopped dreaming of deducing science from observation. If we are out simply to understand the link between observation and science, we are well advised to use any available information, including that provided by the very science whose link with observation we are seeking to understand.

And Quine has the following to say about the failure of Carnap's reductive program in the *Aufbau*:[12]

To relax the demand for definition, and settle for a kind of reduction that does not eliminate, is to renounce the last remaining advantage that we supposed rational reconstruction to have over straight psychology; namely, the advantage of translational reduction. If all we hope for is a reconstruction that links science to experience in explicit ways short of transla-tion, then it would seem more sensible to settle for psychology. Better to discover how science is in fact developed and learned than to fabricate a fictitious structure to a similar effect.

If a task is entirely hopeless, if we know it cannot be executed, no doubt it is rational to abandon it; we would be better off doing something else that has some hope of success. We can agree with Quine that the 'validation'—that is, logical deduction—of science on the basis of observation cannot be had; so it is rational to abandon this particular epistemological program, if indeed it ever was a program that anyone seriously undertook. But Quine's recommendations go further. In particular, there are two aspects of Quine's proposals that are of special interest to us: first, he is not only advising us to quit the program of 'validating science', but urging us to take up another specific project, an empirical psychological study of our cognitive processes; second, he is also claiming that this new program replaces

11. 'Epistemology Naturalized', pp. 75–6 [in this volume pp. 269–70].
12. Ibid., p. 78 [in this volume p. 271].

the old, that both programs are part of something appropriately called 'epistemology'. Naturalized epistemology is to be a kind of epistemology after all, a 'successor subject'[13] to classical epistemology.

How should we react to Quine's urgings? What should be our response? The Cartesian project of validating science starting from the indubitable foundation of first-person psychological reports (perhaps with the help of certain indubitable first principles) is not the whole of classical epistemology—or so it would seem at first blush. In our characterization of classical epistemology, the Cartesian program was seen as one possible response to the problem of epistemic justification, the two-part project of identifying the criteria of epistemic justification and determining what beliefs are in fact justified according to those criteria. In urging 'naturalized epistemology' on us, Quine is not suggesting that we give up the Cartesian foundationalist solution and explore others within the same framework[14]—perhaps, to adopt some sort of 'coherentist' strategy, or to require of our basic beliefs only some degree of 'initial credibility' rather than Cartesian certainty, or to permit some sort of probabilistic derivation in addition to deductive derivation of nonbasic knowledge, or to consider the use of special rules of evidence, like Chisholm's 'principles of evidence',[15] or to give up the search for a derivational process that transmits undiminished certainty in favor of one that can transmit diminished but still useful degrees of justification. Quine's proposal is more radical than that. He is asking us to set aside the entire framework of justification-centered epistemology. That is what is new in Quine's proposals. Quine is asking us to put in its place a purely descriptive, causal-nomological science of human cognition.[16]

How should we characterize in general terms the difference between traditional epistemological programs, such as foundationalism and coherence theory, on the one hand and Quine's program of naturalized epistemology on the other? Quine's stress is on the *factual* and *descriptive* character of his program; he says, 'Why not see how [the construction of theory from observation] *actually proceeds*? Why not settle for psychology?';[17] again, 'Better to *discover how science is in fact developed and learned than ...*'[18] We are given to understand that in contrast traditional epistemology is not a descriptive, factual inquiry. Rather, it is an attempt at a 'validation' or 'rational reconstruction' of science. Validation, according to Quine,

---

13. To use an expression of Richard Rorty's in *Philosophy and the Mirror of Nature* (Princeton: Princeton University Press, 1979), p. 11.
14. Elliott Sober makes a similar point: 'And on the question of whether the failure of a foundationalist programme shows that questions of justification cannot be answered, it is worth noting that Quine's advice "Since Carnap's foundationalism failed, why not settle for psychology" carries weight only to the degree that Carnapian epistemology exhausts the possibilities of epistemology', in 'Psychologism', *Journal of Theory of Social Behaviour* 8 (1978): 165–91.
15. See Chisholm, *Theory of Knowledge*, 2nd ed., ch. 4.
16. 'If we are seeking only the causal mechanism of our knowledge of the external world, and not a justification of that knowledge in terms prior to science ...', Quine, 'Grades of Theoreticity', in L. Foster and J. W. Swanson (eds.), *Experience and Theory* (Amherst: University of Massachusetts Press, 1970), p. 2.
17. Ibid., p. 75. Emphasis added [in this volume pp. 269–70].
18. Ibid., p. 78. Emphasis added [in this volume p. 271].

proceeds via deduction, and rational reconstruction via definition. However, their *point* is justificatory—that is, to rationalize our sundry knowledge claims. So Quine is asking us to set aside what is 'rational' in rational reconstruction.

Thus, it is normativity that Quine is asking us to repudiate. Although Quine does not explicitly characterize traditional epistemology as 'normative' or 'prescriptive', his meaning is unmistakable. Epistemology is to be 'a chapter of psychology', a law-based predictive-explanatory theory, like any other theory within empirical science; its principal job is to see how human cognizers develop theories (their 'picture of the world') from observation ('the stimulation of their sensory receptors'). Epistemology is to go out of the business of justification. We earlier characterized traditional epistemology as essentially normative; we see why Quine wants us to reject it. Quine is urging us to replace a normative theory of cognition with a descriptive science.

4. Losing knowledge from epistemology

If justification drops out of epistemology, knowledge itself drops out of epistemology. For our concept of knowledge is inseparably tied to that of justification. As earlier noted, knowledge itself is a normative notion. Quine's nonnormative, naturalized epistemology has no room for our concept of knowledge. It is not surprising that, in describing naturalized epistemology, Quine seldom talks about knowledge; instead, he talks about 'science' and 'theories' and 'representations'. Quine would have us investigate how sensory stimulation 'leads' to 'theories' and 'representation' of the world. I take it that within the traditional scheme these 'theories' and 'representations' correspond to beliefs, or systems of beliefs; thus, what Quine would have us do is to investigate how sensory stimulation leads to the formation of beliefs about the world.

But in what sense of 'lead'? I take it that Quine has in mind a causal or nomological sense. He is urging us to develop a theory, an empirical theory, that uncovers lawful regularities governing the processes through which organisms come to develop beliefs about their environment as a causal result of having their sensory receptors stimulated in certain ways. Quine says:[19]

[Naturalized epistemology] studies a natural phenomenon, viz., a physical human subject. This human subject is accorded experimentally controlled input—certain patterns of irradiation in assorted frequencies, for instance—and in the fullness of time the subject delivers as output a description of the three-dimensional external world and its history. *The relation between the meager input and torrential output* is a relation that we are prompted to study for somewhat the same reasons that always prompted epistemology; namely, in order to see *how evidence relates to theory*, and in what ways one's theory of nature transcends any available evidence.

The relation Quine speaks of between 'meager input' and 'torrential output' is a causal relation; at least it is qua causal relation that the naturalized epistemologist

19. Quine, 'Grades of Thoreticity', p. 83. Emphasis added [in this volume pp. 273–4].

investigates it. It is none of the naturalized epistemologist's business to assess whether, and to what degree, the input 'justifies' the output, how a given irradiation of the subject's retinas makes it 'reasonable' or 'rational' for the subject to emit certain representational output. His interest is strictly causal and nomological: he wants us to look for patterns of lawlike dependencies characterizing the input–output relations for this particular organism and others of a like physical structure.

If this is right, it makes Quine's attempt to relate his naturalized epistemology to traditional epistemology look at best lame. For in what sense is the study of causal relationships between physical stimulation of sensory receptors and the resulting cognitive output a way of 'seeing how evidence relates to theory' in an epistemologically relevant sense? The causal relation between sensory input and cognitive output is a relation between 'evidence' and 'theory'; however, it is not an *evidential relation*. This can be seen from the following consideration: the nomological patterns that Quine urges us to look for are certain to vary from species to species, depending on the particular way each biological (and possibly non-biological) species processes information, but the evidential relation in its proper normative sense must abstract from such factors and concern itself only with the degree to which evidence supports hypothesis.

In any event, the concept of evidence is inseparable from that of justification. When we talk of 'evidence' in an epistemological sense we are talking about justification: one thing is 'evidence' for another just in case the first tends to enhance the reasonableness or justification of the second. And such evidential relations hold in part because of the 'contents' of the items involved, not merely because of the causal or nomological connections between them. A strictly nonnormative concept of evidence is not our concept of evidence; it is something that we do not understand.[20]

None of us, I think, would want to quarrel with Quine about the interest or importance of the psychological study of how our sensory input causes our epistemic output. This is only to say that the study of human (or other kinds of) cognition is of interest. That isn't our difficulty; our difficulty is whether, and in what sense, pursuing Quine's 'epistemology' is a way of doing epistemology—that is, a way of studying 'how evidence relates to theory'. Perhaps, Quine's recommendation that we discard justification-centered epistemology is worth pondering; and his exhortation to take up the study of psychology perhaps deserves to be heeded also. What is mysterious is why this recommendation has to be coupled with the rejection of normative epistemology (if normative epistemology is not a possible inquiry, why shouldn't the would-be epistemologist turn to, say, hydrodynamics or ornithology rather than psychology?). But of course Quine is saying more; he is saying that an understandable, if misguided, motivation (that is, seeing 'how

20. But aren't there those who advocate a 'causal theory' of evidence or justification? I want to make two brief points about this. First, the nomological or causal input/output relations are not in themselves evidential relations, whether these latter are understood causally or otherwise. Second, a causal theory of evidence attempts to state *criteria* for 'e is evidence for h' in causal terms; even if this is successful, it does not necessarily give us a causal 'definition' or 'reduction' of the concept of evidence. For more details see section 6 below.

evidence relates to theory') does underlie our proclivities for indulgence in normative epistemology, but that we would be better served by a scientific study of human cognition than normative epistemology.

But it is difficult to see how an 'epistemology' that has been purged of normativity, one that lacks an appropriate normative concept of justification or evidence, can have anything to do with the concerns of traditional epistemology. And unless naturalized epistemology and classical epistemology share some of their central concerns, it's difficult to see how one could *replace* the other, or be a way (a better way) of doing the other.[21] To be sure, they both investigate 'how evidence relates to theory'. But putting the matter this way can be misleading, and has perhaps misled Quine: the two disciplines do not investigate the same relation. As lately noted, normative epistemology is concerned with the evidential relation properly so-called—that is, the relation of justification—and Quine's naturalized epistemology is meant to study the causal-nomological relation. For epistemology to go out of the business of justification is for it to go out of business.

5. Belief attribution and rationality

Perhaps we have said enough to persuade ourselves that Quine's naturalized epistemology, while it may be a legitimate scientific inquiry, is not a kind of epistemology, and, therefore, that the question whether it is a better kind of epistemology cannot arise. In reply, however, it might be said that there was a sense in which Quine's epistemology and traditional epistemology could be viewed as sharing a common subject matter, namely this: they both concern beliefs or 'representations'. The only difference is that the former investigates their causal histories and connections whereas the latter is concerned with their evidential or justificatory properties and relations. This difference, if Quine is right, leads to another (so continues the reply): the former is a feasible inquiry, the latter is not.

I now want to take my argument a step further: I shall argue that the concept of belief is itself an essentially normative one, and in consequence that if normativity is wholly excluded from naturalized epistemology it cannot even be thought of as being about beliefs. That is, if naturalized epistemology is to be a science of beliefs properly so called, it must presuppose a normative concept of belief.

Briefly, the argument is this. In order to implement Quine's program of naturalized epistemology, we shall need to identify, and individuate, the input and output of cognizers. The input, for Quine, consists of physical events ('the stimulation of sensory receptors') and the output is said to be a 'theory' or 'picture of the world'—that is, a set of 'representations' of the cognizer's environment. Let us focus on the output. In order to study the sensory input-cognitive output relations for the given cognizer, therefore, we must find out what 'representations' he has formed as a result of the particular stimulations that have been applied to his sensory

---

21. I am not saying that Quine is under any illusion on this point. My remarks are directed rather at those who endorse Quine without, it seems, a clear appreciation of what is involved.

transducers. Setting aside the jargon, what we need to be able to do is to attribute *beliefs*, and other contentful intentional states, to the cognizer. But belief attribution ultimately requires a 'radical interpretation' of the cognizer, of his speech and intentional states; that is, we must construct an 'interpretive theory' that simultaneously assigns meanings to his utterances and attributes to him beliefs and other propositional attitudes.[22]

Even a cursory consideration indicates that such an interpretation cannot begin—we cannot get a foothold in our subject's realm of meanings and intentional states—unless we assume his total system of beliefs and other propositional attitudes to be largely and essentially rational and coherent. As Davidson has emphasized, a given belief has the content it has in part because of its location in a network of other beliefs and propositional attitudes; and what at bottom grounds this network is the evidential relation, a relation that regulates what is reasonable to believe given other beliefs one holds. That is, unless our cognizer is a 'rational being', a being whose cognitive 'output' is regulated and constrained by norms of rationality—typically, these norms holistically constrain his propositional attitudes in virtue of their contents—we cannot intelligibly interpret his 'output' as consisting of beliefs. Conversely, if we are unable to interpret our subject's meanings and propositional attitudes in a way that satisfies a minimal standard of rationality, there is little reason to regard him as a 'cognizer', a being that form's representations and constructs theories. This means that there is a sense of 'rational' in which the expression 'rational belief' is redundant; every belief must be rational in certain minimal ways. It is not important for the purposes of the present argument what these minimal standards of rationality are; the only point that matters is that unless the output of our cognizer is subject to evaluation in accordance with norms of rationality, that output cannot be considered as consisting of beliefs and hence cannot be the object of an epistemological inquiry, whether plain or naturalized.

We can separate the core of these considerations from controversial issues involving the so-called 'principle of charity', minimal rationality, and other matters in the theory of radical interpretation. What is crucial is this: for the interpretation and attribution of beliefs to be possible, not only must we assume the overall rationality of cognizers, but also we must continually evaluate and re-evaluate the putative beliefs of a cognizer in their evidential relationship to one another and other propositional attitudes. It is not merely that belief attribution requires the umbrella assumption about the overall rationality of cognizers. Rather, the point is that *belief attribution requires belief evaluation*, in accordance with normative standards of evidence and justification. If this is correct, rationality in its broad and fundamental sense is not an optional property of beliefs, a virtue that some beliefs may enjoy and others lack; it is a precondition of the attribution and individuation of belief—that is, a property without which the concept of belief would be unintelligible and pointless.

22. Here I am drawing chiefly on Donald Davidson's writings on radical interpretation. See Essays 9, 10, and 11 in his *Inquiries into Truth and Interpretation* (Oxford: Clarendon Press, 1984). See also David Lewis, 'Radical Interpretation', *Synthese* 27 (1974): 331–44.

Two objections might be raised to counter these considerations. First, one might argue that at best they show only that the normativity of belief is an epistemological assumption—that we need to assume the rationality and coherence of belief systems when we are trying to *find out* what beliefs to attribute to a cognizer. It does not follow from this epistemological point, the objection continues, that the concept of belief is itself normative.[23] In replying to this objection, we can by-pass the entire issue of whether the rationality assumption concerns only the epistemology of belief attribution. Even if this premise (which I think is incorrect) is granted, the point has already been made. For it is an essential part of the business of naturalized epistemology, as a theory of how beliefs are formed as a result of sensory stimulation, to *find out* what particular beliefs the given cognizers have formed. But this is precisely what cannot be done, if our considerations show anything at all, unless the would-be naturalized epistemologist continually evaluates the putative beliefs of his subjects in regard to their rationality and coherence, subject to the overall constraint of the assumption that the cognizers are largely rational. The naturalized epistemologist cannot dispense with normative concepts or disengage himself from valuational activities.

Second, it might be thought that we could simply avoid these considerations stemming from belief attribution by refusing to think of cognitive output as consisting of 'beliefs', namely as states having propositional contents. The 'representations' Quine speaks of should be taken as appropriate neural states, and this means that all we need is to be able to discern neural states of organisms. This requires only neurophysiology and the like, not the normative theory of rational belief. My reply takes the form of a dilemma: either the 'appropriate' neural states are identified by seeing how they correlate with beliefs,[24] in which case we still need to contend with the problem of radical interpretation, or beliefs are entirely by-passed. In the latter case, belief, along with justification, drops out of Quinean epistemology, and it is unclear in what sense we are left with an inquiry that has anything to do with knowledge.[25]

6. The 'psychologistic' approach to epistemology

Many philosophers now working in theory of knowledge have stressed the importance of systematic psychology to philosophical epistemology. Reasons proffered for this are various, and so are the conceptions of the proper relationship between psychology and epistemology.[26] But they are virtually unanimous in their rejection

---

23. Robert Audi suggested this as a possible objection.
24. For some considerations tending to show that these correlations cannot be lawlike see my 'Psychophysical Laws', in Ernest LePore and Brian McLaughlin (eds.), *Actions and Events: Perspectives on the Philosophy of Donald Davidson* (Oxford: Blackwell, 1985).
25. For a more sympathetic account of Quine than mine, see Hilary Kornblith's introductory essay, 'What is Naturalistic Epistemology?', in Kornblith (ed.), *Naturalizing Epistemology*.
26. See for more details Alvin I. Goldman, *Epistemology and Cognition* (Cambridge: Harvard University Press, 1986).

of what they take to be the epistemological tradition of Descartes and its modern embodiments in philosophers like Russell, C. I. Lewis, Roderick Chisholm, and A. J. Ayer; and they are united in their endorsement of the naturalistic approach of Quine we have been considering. Traditional epistemology is often condemned as 'aprioristic', and as having lost sight of human knowledge as a product of natural causal processes and its function in the survival of the organism and the species. Sometimes, the adherents of the traditional approach are taken to task for their implicit antiscientific bias or indifference to the new developments in psychology and related disciplines. Their own approach in contrast is hailed as 'naturalistic' and 'scientific', better attuned to significant advances in the relevant scientific fields such as 'cognitive science' and 'neuroscience', promising philosophical returns far richer than what the aprioristic method of traditional epistemology has been able to deliver. We shall here briefly consider how this new naturalism in epistemology is to be understood in relation to the classic epistemological program and Quine's naturalized epistemology.

Let us see how one articulate proponent of the new approach explains the distinctiveness of his position vis-à-vis that of the traditional epistemologists. According to Philip Kitcher, the approach he rejects is characterized by an 'apsychologistic' attitude that takes the difference between knowledge and true belief—that is, justification—to consist in 'ways which are independent of the causal antecedents of a subject's states'.[27] Kitcher writes:[28]

> ... we can present the heart of [the apsychologistic approach] by considering the way in which it would tackle the question of whether a person's true belief that p counts as knowledge that p. The idea would be to disregard the psychological life of the subject, looking just at the various propositions she believes. If p is 'connected in the right way' to other propositions which are believed, then we count the subject as knowing that p. Of course, apsychologistic epistemology will have to supply a criterion for propositions to be 'connected in the right way' ... but proponents of this view of knowledge will emphasize that the criterion is to be given in *logical* terms. We are concerned with logical relations among propositions, not with psychological relations among mental states.

On the other hand, the psychologistic approach considers the crucial difference between knowledge and true belief—that is, epistemic justification—to turn on 'the factors which produced the belief', focusing on 'processes which produce belief, processes which will always contain, at their latter end, psychological events'.[29]

It is not entirely clear from this characterization whether a psychologistic theory of justification is to be *prohibited* from making *any* reference to logical relations

---

27. *The Nature of Mathematical Knowledge* (New York: Oxford University Press, 1983), p. 14.
28. Ibid.
29. Ibid., p. 13. I should note that Kitcher considers the apsychologistic approach to be an aberration of the twentieth century epistemology, as represented by philosophers like Russell, Moore, C. I. Lewis, and Chisholm, rather than an historical characteristic of the Cartesian tradition. In 'The Psychological Turn', *Australasian Journal of Philosophy* 60 (1982): 238–53, Hilary Kornblith gives an analogous characterization of the two approaches to justification; he associates 'justification-conferring processes' with the psychologistic approach and 'epistemic rules' with the apsychologistic approach.

among belief contents (it is difficult to believe how a theory of justification respecting such a blanket prohibition could succeed); nor is it clear whether, conversely, an apsychologistic theory will be permitted to refer at all to beliefs qua psychological states, or exactly what it is for a theory to do so. But such points of detail are unimportant here; it is clear enough, for example, that Goldman's proposal to explicate justified belief as belief generated by a reliable belief-forming process[30] nicely fits Kitcher's characterization of the psychologistic approach. This account, one form of the so-called 'reliability theory' of justification, probably was what Kitcher had in mind when he was formulating his general characterization of epistemological naturalism. However, another influential form of the reliability theory does not qualify under Kitcher's characterization. This is Armstrong's proposal to explain the difference between knowledge and true belief, at least for non-inferential knowledge, in terms of 'a *law-like connection* between the state of affairs [of a subject's believing that *p*] and the state of affairs that makes '*p*' true such that, given the state of affairs [of the subject's believing that *p*], it must be the case that *p*'.[31] There is here no reference to the causal *antecedents* of beliefs, something that Kitcher requires of apsychologistic theories.

Perhaps, Kitcher's preliminary characterization needs to be broadened and sharpened. However, a salient characteristic of the naturalistic approach has already emerged, which we can put as follows: justification is to be characterized in terms of *causal* or *nomological* connections involving beliefs as *psychological states* or *processes*, and not in terms of the *logical* properties or relations pertaining to the *contents* of these beliefs.[32]

If we understand current epistemological naturalism in this way, how closely is it related to Quine's conception of naturalized epistemology? The answer, I think, is obvious: not very closely at all. In fact, it seems a good deal closer to the Cartesian tradition than to Quine. For, as we saw, the difference that matters between Quine's epistemological program and the traditional program is the former's total renouncement of the latter's normativity, its rejection of epistemology as a normative inquiry. The talk of 'replacing' epistemology with psychology is irrelevant and at best misleading, though it could give us a momentary relief from a sense of deprivation. When one abandons justification and other valuational concepts, one abandons the entire framework of normative epistemology. What remains is a descriptive empirical theory of human cognition which, if Quine has his way, will be entirely devoid of the notion of justification or any other evaluative concept.

As I take it, this is not what most advocates of epistemological naturalism are aiming at. By and large they are not Quinean eliminativists in regard to justification, and justification in its full-fledged normative sense continues to play a central

30. See Goldman, 'What is Justified Belief?'.
31. David M. Armstrong, *Truth, Belief and Knowledge* (London: Cambridge University Press, 1973), p. 166 [in this volume p. 75].
32. The aptness of this characterization of the 'apsychologistic' approach for philosophers like Russell, Chisholm, Keith Lehrer, John Pollock, etc., can be debated. Also, there is the issue of 'internalism' vs. 'externalism' concerning justification, which I believe must be distinguished from the psychologistic vs. apsychologistic division.

role in their epistemological reflections. Where they differ from their nonnaturalist adversaries is the specific way in which criteria of justification are to be formulated. Naturalists and nonnaturalists ('apsychologists') can agree that these criteria must be stated in descriptive terms—that is, without the use of epistemic or any other kind of normative terms. According to Kitcher, an apsychologistic theory of justification would state them primarily in terms of *logical* properties and relations holding for propositional contents of beliefs, whereas the psychologistic approach advocates the exclusive use of *causal* properties and relations holding for beliefs as events or states. Many traditional epistemologists may prefer criteria that confer upon a cognizer a position of special privilege and responsibility with regard to the epistemic status of his beliefs, whereas most self-avowed naturalists prefer 'objective' or 'externalist' criteria with no such special privileges for the cognizer. But these differences are among those that arise within the familiar normative framework, and are consistent with the exclusion of normative terms in the statement of the criteria of justification.

Normative ethics can serve as a useful model here. To claim that basic ethical terms, like 'good' and 'right', are *definable* on the basis of descriptive or naturalistic terms is one thing; to insist that it is the business of normative ethics to provide *conditions* or *criteria* for 'good' and 'right' in descriptive or naturalistic terms is another. One may properly reject the former, the so-called 'ethical naturalism', as many moral philosophers have done, and hold the latter; there is no obvious inconsistency here. G. E. Moore is a philosopher who did just that. As is well known, he was a powerful critic of ethical naturalism, holding that goodness is a 'simple' and 'nonnatural' property. At the same time, he held that a thing's being good 'follows' from its possessing certain naturalistic properties. He wrote:[33]

I should never have thought of suggesting that goodness was 'non-natural', unless I had supposed that it was 'derivative' in the sense that, whenever a thing is good (in the sense in question) its goodness ... 'depends on the presence of certain non-ethical characteristics' possessed by the thing in question: I have always supposed that it did so 'depend', in the sense that, if a thing is good (in my sense), then that it is so *follows* from the fact that it possesses certain natural intrinsic properties ...

It makes sense to think of these 'natural intrinsic properties' from which a thing's being good is thought to follow as constituting naturalistic criteria of goodness, or at least pointing to the existence of such criteria. One can reject ethical naturalism, the doctrine that ethical concepts are definitionally eliminable in favor of naturalistic terms, and at the same time hold that ethical properties, or the ascription of ethical terms, must be governed by naturalistic criteria. It is clear, then, that we are here using 'naturalism' ambiguously in 'epistemological naturalism' and 'ethical naturalism'. In our present usage, epistemological naturalism does not include (nor does it necessarily exclude) the claim that epistemic terms are definitionally reducible to naturalistic terms. (Quine's naturalism is eliminative, though it is not a definitional eliminativism.)

33. Moore, 'A Reply to My Critics', in P. A. Schilpp (ed.), *The Philosophy of G. E. Moore* (Chicago & Evanston: Open Court, 1942), p. 588.

If, therefore, we locate the split between Quine and traditional epistemology at the descriptive vs. normative divide, then currently influential naturalism in epistemology is not likely to fall on Quine's side. On this descriptive vs. normative issue, one can side with Quine in one of two ways: first, one rejects, with Quine, the entire justification-based epistemological program; or second, like ethical naturalists but unlike Quine, one believes that epistemic concepts are naturalistically definable. I doubt that very many epistemological naturalists will embrace either of these alternatives.[34]

7. Epistemic supervenience—or why normative epistemology is possible

But why should we think that there *must* be naturalistic criteria of justified belief and other terms of epistemic appraisal? If we take the discovery and systematization of such criteria to be the central task of normative epistemology, is there any reason to think that this task can be fruitfully pursued, that normative epistemology is a possible field of inquiry? Quine's point is that it is not. We have already noted the limitation of Quine's negative arguments in 'Epistemology Naturalized', but is there a positive reason for thinking that normative epistemology is a viable program? One could consider a similar question about the possibility of normative ethics.

I think there is a short and plausible initial answer, although a detailed defense of it would involve complex general issues about norms and values. The short answer is this: we believe in the supervenience of epistemic properties on naturalistic ones, and more generally, in the supervenience of all valuational and normative properties on naturalistic conditions. This comes out in various ways. We think, with R. M. Hare,[35] that if two persons or acts coincide in all descriptive or naturalistic details, they cannot differ in respect of being good or right, or any other valuational aspects. We also think that if something is 'good'—a 'good car', 'good drop shot', 'good argument'—then that must be so 'in virtue of' its being a 'certain way', that is, its having certain 'factual properties'. Being a good car, say, cannot be a brute and ultimate fact: a car is good *because* it has a certain contextually indicated set of properties having to do with performance, reliability, comfort, styling, economy, etc. The same goes for justified belief: if a belief is justified, that must be so *because* it has certain factual, nonepistemic properties, such as perhaps that it is

34. Richard Rorty's claim, which plays a prominent role in his arguments against traditional epistemology in *Philosophy and the Mirror of Nature*, that Locke and other modern epistemologists conflated the normative concept of justification with causal-mechanical concepts is itself based, I believe, on a conflation of just the kind I am describing here. See Rorty, ibid., pp. 139 ff. Again, the critical conflation consists in not seeing that the view, which I believe is correct, that epistemic justification, like any other normative concept, must have factual, naturalistic criteria, is entirely consistent with the rejection of the doctrine, which I think is incorrect, that justification itself *is*, or is *reducible* to, a naturalistic nonnormative concept.

35. *The Language of Morals* (London: Oxford University Press, 1952), p. 145.

'indubitable', that it is seen to be entailed by another belief that is independently justified, that it is appropriately caused by perceptual experience, or whatever. That it is a justified belief cannot be a brute fundamental fact unrelated to the kind of belief it is. There must be a *reason* for it, and this reason must be grounded in the factual descriptive properties of that particular belief. Something like this, I think, is what we believe.

Two important themes underlie these convictions: first, values, though perhaps not reducible to facts, must be 'consistent' with them in that objects that are indiscernible in regard to fact must be indiscernible in regard to value; second, there must be nonvaluational 'reasons' or 'grounds' for the attribution of values, and these 'reasons' or 'grounds' must be *generalizable*—that is, they are covered by *rules* or *norms*. These two ideas correspond to 'weak supervenience' and 'strong supervenience' that I have discussed elsewhere.[36] Belief in the supervenience of value upon fact, arguably, is fundamental to the very concepts of value and valuation.[37] Any valuational concept, to be significant, must be governed by a set of criteria, and these criteria must ultimately rest on factual characteristics and relationships of objects and events being evaluated. There is something deeply incoherent about the idea of an infinitely descending series of valuational concepts, each depending on the one below it as its criterion of application.[38]

It seems to me, therefore, that epistemological supervenience is what underlies our belief in the possibility of normative epistemology, and that we do not need new inspirations from the sciences to acknowledge the existence of naturalistic criteria for epistemic and other valuational concepts. The case of normative ethics is entirely parallel: belief in the possibility of normative ethics is rooted in the belief that moral properties and relations are supervenient upon non-moral ones. Unless we are prepared to disown normative ethics as a viable philosophical inquiry, we had better recognize normative epistemology as one, too.[39] We should note, too, that epistemology is likely to parallel normative ethics in regard to the degree to

36. See 'Concepts of Supervenience', *Philosophy and Phenomenological Research* 65 (1984): 153–76.

37. Ernest Sosa, too, considers epistemological supervenience as a special case of the supervenience of valuational properties on naturalistic conditions, in 'The Foundation of Foundationalism', *Nous* 14 (1980): 547–64; especially p. 551. See also James Van Cleve's instructive discussion in his 'Epistemic Supervenience and the Circle of Belief', *The Monist* 68 (1985): 90–104; especially, pp. 97–9.

38. Perhaps one could avoid this kind of criteriological regress by embracing directly apprehended valuational properties (as in ethical intuitionism) on the basis of which criteria for other valuational properties could be formulated. The denial of the supervenience of valuational concepts on factual characteristics, however, would sever the essential connection between value and fact on which, it seems, the whole point of our valuational activities depends. In the absence of such supervenience, the very notion of valuation would lose its significance and relevance. The elaboration of these points, however, would have to wait for another occasion; but see Van Cleve's paper cited in the preceding note for more details.

39. Quine will not disagree with this: he will 'naturalize' them both. For his views on values see 'The Nature of Moral Values' in Alvin I. Goldman and Jaegwon Kim (eds.), *Values and Morals* (Dordrecht: Reidel, 1978). For a discussion of the relationship between epistemic and ethical concepts see Roderick Firth, 'Are Epistemic Concepts Reducible to Ethical Concepts?' in the same volume.

which scientific results are relevant or useful to its development.[40] Saying this of course leaves large room for disagreement concerning how relevant and useful, if at all, empirical psychology of human motivation and action can be to the development and confirmation of normative ethical theories.[41] In any event, once the normativity of epistemology is clearly taken note of, it is no surprise that epistemology and normative ethics share the same metaphilosophical fate. Naturalized epistemology makes no more, and no less, sense than naturalized normative ethics.[42]

40. For discussions of this and related issues see Goldman, *Epistemology and Cognition.*
41. For a detailed development of a normative ethical theory that exemplifies the view that it is crucially relevant, see Richard B. Brandt, *A Theory of the Good and the Right* (Oxford: The Clarendon Press, 1979).
42. An early version of this paper was read at a meeting of the Korean Society for Analytic Philosophy in 1984 in Seoul. An expanded version was presented at a symposium at the Western Division meetings of the American Philosophical Association in April, 1985, and at the epistemology conference at Brown University in honor of Roderick Chisholm in 1986. I am grateful to Richard Foley and Robert Audi who presented helpful comments at the APA session and the Chisholm Conference respectively. I am also indebted to Terence Horgan and Robert Meyers for helpful comments and suggestions.

References

Alston, William P., 'Two Types of Foundationalism' *Journal of Philosophy* 73 (1976): 165–85.

Armstrong, David M., *Truth, Belief and Knowledge* (London: Cambridge University Press, 1973).

Ayer, A. J., *The Foundations of Empirical Knowledge* (London: Macmillan, 1940).

Ayer, A. J., *The Problem of Knowledge* (New York & London: Penguin Books, 1956).

Brandt, Richard B., *A Theory of the Good and the Right* (Oxford: The Clarendon Press, 1979).

Carnap, Rudolf, 'Testability and Meaning', *Philosophy of Science* 3 (1936), and 4 (1937).

Chisholm, Roderick M., *Theory of Knowledge*, 2nd ed. (Englewood Cliffs, N.J.: Prentice-Hall, 1977).

Davidson, Donald, *Inquiries into Truth and Interpretation* (Oxford: Clarendon Press, 1984).

Firth, Roderick, 'Coherence, Certainty, and Epistemic Priority', *Journal of Philosophy* 61 (1964): 545–57.

Firth, Roderick, 'Are Epistemic Concepts Reducible to Ethical Concepts?' in Goldman, Alvin I. and Jaegwon Kim (eds.), *Values and Morals* (Dordrecht: Reidel, 1978).

Goldman, Alvin I., 'What is Justified Belief?', in George S. Pappas (ed.), *Justification and Knowledge* (Dordrecht: Reidel, 1979).

Goldman, Alvin I., *Epistemology and Cognition* (Cambridge: Harvard University Press, 1986).

Hare, R. M., *The Language of Morals* (London: Oxford University Press, 1952)

Hempel, Carl G., 'On the Logical Positivists' Theory of Truth', *Analysis* 2 (1935): 49–59.

Hempel, Carl G., 'Some Remarks on "Facts" and Propositions', *Analysis* 2 (1935): 93–6.

Kim, Jaegwon, 'Concepts of Supervenience', *Philosophy and Phenomenological Research* 65 (1984): 153–76.

Kim, Jaegwon, 'Psychophysical Laws', in Ernest Lepore and Brian McLaughlin (eds.), *Actions and Events: Perspectives on the Philosophy of Donald Davidson* (Oxford: Blackwell, 1985).

Kitcher, Phillip, *The Nature of Mathematical Knowledge* (New York: Oxford University Press, 1983).

Kornblith, Hilary, 'The Psychological Turn', *Australasian Journal of Philosophy* 60 (1982): 238–53.

Kornblith, Hilary, (ed.), *Naturalizing Epistemology* (Cambridge: MIT/Bradford, 1985).

Kornblith, Hilary, 'What is Naturalistic Epistemology?', in Kornblith (ed.), *Naturalizing Epistemology*.

Lewis, David, 'Radical Interpretation', *Synthese* 27 (1974): 331–44.

Moore, G. E., 'A Reply to My Critics', in P. A. Schilpp (ed.), *The Philosophy of G. E. Moore* (Chicago & Evanston: Open Court, 1942).

Quine, W. V., *Word and Object* (Cambridge: MIT Press, 1960).

Quine, W. V., *Ontological Relativity and Other Essays* (New York: Columbia University Press, 1969).

Quine, W. V., (with Joseph Ullian), *The Web of Belief* (New York: Random House, 1970).

Quine, W. V., 'Grades of Theoreticity', in L. Foster and J. W. Swanson (eds.), *Experience and Theory* (Amherst: University of Massachusetts Press, 1970).

Quine, W. V., *The Roots of Reference* (La Salle, IL,: Open Court, 1973).

Quine, W. V., 'The Nature of Natural Knowledge' in Samuel Guttenplan (ed.), *Mind and Language* (Oxford: Clarendon Press, 1975).

Quine, W. V., 'The Nature of Moral Values' in Alvin I. Goldman and Jaegwon Kim (eds.), *Values and Morals* (Dordrecht: Reidel, 1978).

Rorty, Richard, *Philosophy and the Mirror of Nature* (Princeton: Princeton University Press, 1979).

Sober, Elliott, 'Psychologism', *Journal of Theory of Social Behavior* 8 (1978): 165–91.

Sosa, Ernest, 'The Foundation of Foundationalism', *Nous* 14 (1980): 547–64.

Van Cleve, James, 'Epistemic Supervenience and the Circle of Belief', *The Monist* 68 (1985): 90–104.

Part IV

Scepticism

Introduction

ALMOST nobody thinks that scepticism is true. That does not mean scepticism is not important. Its relevance is methodological. By understanding whether and how sceptical arguments fail, we learn something about knowledge.

Scepticism comes in many shapes and colors. *Academic* (from Plato's academy in ancient Greece) scepticism embodies a positive claim: we do not know there is a reality (and, if there is, what its nature might be) independent of our own immediate experience. *Pyrrhonian* (Pyrrho was an ancient sceptic) scepticism is more cautious. It does not deny that we have knowledge. Instead, it recommends suspension of judgement. The readings in this part are concerned with academic scepticism only.

Academic sceptics differ among themselves in the scope of their scepticism. A global sceptic maintains we can know *nothing* or next to nothing about *anything*. Local sceptics, on the other hand, maintain that even if knowledge is possible elsewhere, it is, for special reasons, not available in this or that selected area. Favourite areas for local scepticism are knowledge of the external world, of other minds, of the past, of God, or moral truths. The readings are primarily concerned with scepticism about the external world.

Scepticisms differ not only in scope, but in theme. Sceptical arguments can either be directed against knowledge (you cannot know propositions of type P) or justification (it is not even reasonable to believe propositions of type P) or both at once. Still another difference concerns the order or level of one's scepticism. First-order (or direct) scepticism is the thesis that you cannot know that propositions of type P (e.g., propositions about the external world) are true. Second-order (or iterative) scepticism is the weaker thesis that we cannot know (or justifiably believe) that we have (first-order) knowledge of P-type propositions. Maybe you know P, maybe you do not, but you cannot know that you know P. Second-order scepticism is true if first-order scepticism is, but not vice versa. Readings in this part focus on first-order scepticism.

Scepticism about the external world is the thesis that the evidence we have for our beliefs about the external world falls short of what is needed for knowledge (or even justification in more aggressive forms of scepticism). The evidence is never logically conclusive. Error is always possible. So in order to minimize the possibility of mistake, it seems reasonable to demand that someone, in order to know, must be able to exclude sources of error and deception. According to the sceptic, though, this is exactly what we cannot do. There is no sure way of telling that we are causally hooked up (via perception, say) to the facts in the way we think we are. It might all be a dream. The rationality of our beliefs about an independently existing world might be nothing but the coherence of a dream or (as Descartes suggested) a clever deception by some malevolent demon. To put a more contemporary spin on these sceptical hypotheses, our perceptual evidence for an external world is consistent with our being disembodied brains wired to a properly programmed computer. If the computer stimulated us to have exactly the experiences we now have, our beliefs would be false but our evidence would none the less be the same. How can we know this is *not* the case?

The point of sceptical hypotheses such as these is to highlight the fact that all our evidence for an external world resides in the subjective character of our experience. Everything in our experience could be exactly the way it now is even if the world were completely different from the way we judge it to be. Experience is our only source of information about the world, but experience does not rule out alternative possibilities. It would seem, therefore, that nothing can be known for certain on the basis of this experience. If we cannot, by appealing to experience, show we are not dreaming, then experience is not a sufficiently secure basis for knowing we are not dreaming. And if we cannot know we are not dreaming, we cannot know we are perceiving a mind-independent reality.

Stroud (Chapter 22) and Unger (Chapter 23) explain the sceptical challenge and provide arguments in support of scepticism. Unger begins by pointing out a category of what he calls 'absolute terms' (e.g., 'flat', 'full', 'wet', 'important'). Being flat means being perfectly flat—not at all bumpy—a standard which, for all we know, quite likely nothing whatever achieves. A necessary condition of knowing, Unger then argues, is being certain. 'Certain' is another absolute term. For a person to know some proposition, P, she has to be absolutely certain that P, and since no person is ever absolutely certain of (hardly) anything, Unger concludes that no person ever knows (hardly) anything. Scepticism is right but of no practical importance.

In contemporary epistemology, one can distinguish three strategies to rebut scepticism: (1) epistemological externalism, (2) the so-called 'relevant alternative account of knowledge', and (3) semantic externalism. Each strategy is represented by one or more readings.

Epistemological externalism (cf. Chapters 7–9) is the view that to know something the subject needs reliable, non-accidentally produced, true belief but she need not know that she has non-accidental true belief. The externalist definition of knowledge promises to avoid the justificatory regress that seems to be an inevitable ingredient of scepticism. The sceptic typically asks how one can know that sense experience, say, is an accurate, reliable, guide to what is going on in the rest of the world. The externalist acknowledges that she does not know that it is, but this does not matter; this does not undermine her knowledge. To know something on the basis of experience a person does not have to know that experience is a reliable indicator of the truth. It just has to *be* a reliable indicator of the truth. If experience is reliable, it gives us knowledge. If it is not, then it does not. Thus, second-level scepticism may be in order (we cannot know whether we know), but arguments for first-order scepticism, arguments designed to show that we *cannot* know there is an external world, are refuted. We *do* know if our experience is related in the appropriate way to the reality it causes us to believe in. Stroud (Chapter 22) argues that this response to scepticism is not satisfactory for it only shows that it is possible that our beliefs about the external world amount to knowledge. A satisfactory response to scepticism, he feels, must establish that we *in fact* possess knowledge.

The second category of response to scepticism is known as the 'relevant alternative account of knowledge'. The sceptic argues that we have no way of knowing that the sceptical hypotheses are false and concludes, therefore, we do not know anything about the external world. This reasoning typically employs the principle of closure under known entailment: if S knows that P, and S knows that P entails Q, then S knows Q. The proposition that you are now reading a book (P) logically implies the falsity of the sceptical counter-possibility that you are a brain in a vat (Q). If you are aware of this implication, the closure principle yields the consequence that if you know that P, then you know Q; and since you cannot rule out the possibility that you are a brain in a vat, you do not know Q. So you do not know P—that you are reading. Conclusion: scepticism is true.

Some epistemologists think that the closure principle is too strict to be convincing. If knowing that P would require the elimination of every known alternative to P, as suggested by the closure principle, we could never know anything about the world around us. A more plausible view might be that knowledge requires the elimination of only relevant alternatives and that sceptical alternatives are normally not relevant. In an ordinary case of claiming to know that some animals in the zoo are zebras, for example, the possibility that they are cleverly painted mules is not relevant. Thus, one can truthfully claim to know that they are zebras despite one's inability to rule out this fanciful alternative. But in some extraordinary cases, the painted mules hypothesis *is* a relevant alternative; and then we have to eliminate this alternative to know that what we are seeing are really zebras. Since sceptical alternatives are ordinarily not relevant, the fact that our evidence cannot eliminate them does not lead to a sceptical result.

What makes an alternative relevant? On one view (Goldman, Chapter 8, Nozick, Chapter 25), relevant alternatives consist in certain features of the subject's circumstances beyond the evidence that she has. Among such features are the availability of unpossessed misleading counter-evidence and the objective probability of being wrong. If there are hoaxing zoos in one's vicinity, then this could render it a relevant alternative that what looks like a zebra is in fact a disguised mule. On another view (Austin, Chapter 24, Lewis, Chapter 26), relevance consist in certain features of the conversational context in which the knowledge attribution is made. The latter view is sometimes called 'contextualism'.

Austin (Chapter 24) was the major figure of the movement known as 'ordinary language' philosophy which holds that the significance of concepts is fixed by the actual use of words associated with these concepts. Consequently, Austin is more interested in classifying the use of 'know' in ordinary language than in providing a definition of knowledge in terms of necessary and sufficient conditions. If I claim to know that there is a goldfinch in the garden, I am expected to provide reasons which specify those features of the situation which enable me to recognize that it is a goldfinch. These reasons have to rule out possibilities compatible with everything I have said but which, if actual, would imply that I do not know that there is a goldfinch. I cannot know that it is a goldfinch based only on the red color of its head since woodpeckers also have red heads. Austin emphasizes that justificatory reasons do not have to rule out every counter-possibility, only those which are relevant in ordinary contexts. For example, I do not have to show that it is not a stuffed animal to know that it is a goldfinch.

In a selection from his book *Philosophical Explanation*, Nozick (Chapter 25) challenges scepticism by denying the closure principle. The denial of closure follows from his reliabilist account of knowledge. According to Nozick, a subject's belief that P counts as knowledge when the following counterfactuals hold: (1) if P were not true, the subject would not believe that P; (2) and if P were (contrary to fact) true, the subject would believe that P. When these conditions hold, the subject is said to '*track*' the fact that P. One knows that

P when one's belief that P tracks the fact that P. Nozick realizes that, as it stands, this is too strong (it rules out some obvious cases of knowledge) so he relativizes it to a particular method. Furnished with this and other amendments, Nozick's analysis assures that a knower's belief be non-accidentally connected with the fact that makes it true.

In the second part of his paper, Nozick argues that sceptics are in no position to assume the closure principle once they accept his reliabilist account of knowledge. If the tracking conditions (1) and (2) are necessary for knowledge, then closure is false. The reason is that the tracking conditions themselves are not closed under known entailment. That is, it is quite possible to track one fact without tracking another fact even if the second is a (known) consequence of the first. I can, for example, track the fact that I am reading a book (P) without tracking the fact that I am not a brain in a vat (Q), even though I know that P implies Q.

Like Austin, Lewis (Chapter 26) maintains that for a subject to know that P her reasons have to eliminate only relevant possibilities in which not-P is the case. Since, on Lewis' view, relevance depends on the conversational context, the standards of justification cannot be fixed once and for all. Knowledge is elusive. Nevertheless, Lewis develops rules which determine, for all contexts, which counter-possibilities are relevant. Unlike Nozick, Lewis does not reject scepticism for its reliance on the closure principle. According to Lewis, the illegitimate move of the sceptic is to start out from the ordinary context of knowledge claims and then to raise the scrutiny to a level which is impossible to meet. The context and the justification-standards are thereby switched midway.

The third category of response to external-world scepticism relies on *semantic* externalism, a view about meaning and the nature of concepts. We have seen that scepticism assumes that everything in our experience could be exactly the way it is now, even if the world were completely different from the way we take it to be. A person living in a normal environment and a brain in a vat are imagined as having the *same* beliefs—that, for example, they are reading a book. Semantic externalists reject this assumption. A semantic externalist insists that what we take things to be, what we actually believe about the world, depends on what concepts we have, and the concepts we have depends on what kind of world we live in. It depends on the actual (external) environment we inhabit. Persons who live in much different worlds (e.g., a normal human being and a brain in a vat) will therefore end up believing much different things. If this is so, then we cannot automatically assume that a brain in a vat *could* believe what we, normal human beings, believe when we believe such things as that we are reading a book. If a brain in a vat could not (as we could) believe she was reading a book, then she could not, contrary to scepticism, be mistaken about it.

The chief motivating factor for semantic externalism are Twin Earth thought-experiments which go back to Putnam. Suppose Bert is an English speaker who uses the word 'water' much as anyone in his linguistic community. He does not have any considerable knowledge of the chemical properties of water. Let's suppose that there exists somewhere in a nearby galaxy a planet called 'Twin Earth' that is a duplicate of Earth. The only difference between the two planets is that Twin Earth does not have any water; instead there is a liquid that superficially resembles water but which has the chemical formula XYZ. This liquid plays the role on Twin Earth that H_2O plays on Earth. Like each of us, Bert has a molecular duplicate on Twin Earth. When Bert utters 'water is wet', Twin

Bert does likewise—but both mean something different. In contrast to Bert, Twin Bert's word 'water' does not refer to water (H_2O). It refers to XYZ which is not water. If we want to express Twin Bert's thought in English we have to coin a word—'twater', say—to translate his word 'water'. Bert and Twin Bert mean different things despite the fact that all of their internal properties as well as their utterances are the same. The difference in their thoughts is due to the difference in their physical and social environments.

Putnam (Chapter 27) discusses the sceptical hypothesis that we might be disembodied brains in a vat being fed electrical signals by a computer that is programmed to stimulate our nerve endings as to induce in us experiences indistinguishable from the ones we actually have. He uses semantic externalism to argue that there is a certain sense in which we cannot be brains in a vat. The key is supposed to be that though brains in a vat can 'say' or 'think' anything we can, as far as their subjective experiences go, they cannot mean what we mean. When they say 'We are brains in a vat', they do not say (as we do) that they are brains in a vat but rather that they are brains in the image (or whatever it is their word 'vat' refers to). Therefore, if the hypothesis that we are brains in a vat is true, then we say something false when we say 'We are brains in a vat'; if we are brains in a vat, we are not brains in the image. Thus, if we are not brains in a vat, it is epistemically impossible that we are brains in a vat. Semantic externalism refutes the external-world sceptical claim that we *might* be brains in a vat.

By examining the general conditions in which a structure could come to represent another state of affairs, Dretske (Chapter 28) develops a similar argument. He argues that beliefs, a special class of representations, have their contents limited by the sort of information the system in which they occur can pick up and process. If a system—a measuring instrument, animal or human being—cannot process information to the effect that something is Q, it cannot represent something as Q. From this it follows (for simple, ostensively acquired concepts at least) that if an organism has the concept Q, if it can believe that things are Q, then it is the kind of organism that has the information-processing capabilities for knowing that something is Q. In other words, just as we can only know what we have the resources of believing, we can only believe what we have (or have had) the resources of knowing. Since sceptics do not challenge that we have beliefs, the argument shows that the view that nothing can be known is demonstrably false.

Davidson's (Chapter 29) version of semantic externalism is centred around the notion of radical interpretation. A radical interpreter is defined to be someone who faces the problem of attributing content to a speaker's sentences based only on knowledge of the correlations between the speaker's environment and the sentences that the speaker holds true. Since thought contents are extrinsic rather than intrinsic properties, Davidson takes it to be a necessary truth that any content-bearing state can be interpreted under these epistemological conditions. There is no way, he argues, the radical interpreter can be largely wrong about the world. For the interpreter cannot but interpret the sentences held true according to events in the environment that causes the sentences to be held true. The speaker's sentences must be true (by the interpreter's light). But, the sceptic might object, this only shows that the sentences the speaker holds true must be true according to the interpreter. It is however possible that what the interpreter holds to be true is generally false. To complete the argument Davidson imagines an interpreter who is omniscient about the world and about what causes a speaker to hold any sentence true. Like the fallible interpreter, the omniscient interpreter finds the fallible speaker largely consistent and correct, by his standards. But since his standards *are* objectively correct, the fallible speaker is largely correct by objective standards. Hence, radical interpretation implies the falsity of scepticism.

Further reading

Brueckner, A., 'Skepticism and Epistemic Closure', *Philosophical Topics* 13 (1985), pp. 89–117.

Burnyeat, M., ed., *The Skeptical Tradition*, Berkeley, University of California Press, 1983.

Clay, M. and Lehrer, K., eds., *Knowledge and Skepticism*, Boulder, Westview Press, 1989.

Cornman, J. W., Lehrer, K. and Pappas, G. S., *Philosophical Problems and Arguments*, 4th edition, Indianapolis, Hackett, 1992. Part II.

DeRose, K., 'Solving the Skeptical Puzzle', *The Philosophical Review* 104 (1995), pp. 1–52.

Descartes, R., *Meditations on First Philosophy* (1641), trans. by J. Cottingham, R. Stoothoff, and D. Murdoch, *Descartes Selected Philosophical Writings*, Cambridge, Cambridge University Press, 1988.

Dretske, F., 'Epistemic Operators,' *The Journal of Philosophy* 24 (1970), pp. 1007–23.

Dupré, J., *The Disorder of Things*, Cambridge/MA, Harvard University Press, 1993.

Fogelin, R.J., *Pyrrhonian Reflections on Knowledge and Justification*, New York, Oxford University Press, 1994.

Fumerton, R., *Metaepistemology and Skepticism*, Lanham/MD, Rowman & Littlefield, 1995.

Godfrey-Smith, P., 'Misinformation', *Canadian Journal of Philosophy* 19 (1989), pp. 533–50.

Greco, J. and Sosa, E., eds., *The Blackwell Guide to Epistemology*, Oxford, Basil Blackwell, 1999, Chs. 1, 2, 5, 8.

Hookway, C., *Skepticism*, London, Routledge, 1990.

Klein, P., *Certainty. A Refutation of Scepticism*, Minneapolis, University of Minnesota Press, 1981.

LePore, E. ed., *Truth and Interpretation. Perspectives on the Philosophy of Donald Davidson*, Oxford, Basil Blackwell, 1986.

Ludwig, K., 'Skepticism and Interpretation', *Philosophy and Phenomenological Research* 52 (1992), pp. 317–39.

Luper-Foy, S., *The Possibility of Knowledge. Nozick and his Critics*, Totowa, Rowman & Littlefield, 1987.

McGinn, C., *Mental Content*, Oxford, Basil Blackwell, 1989.

Roth, M. D. and Ross, G., eds., *Doubting*, Dordrecht, Kluwer, 1990.

Strawson, P. F., *Skepticism and Naturalism*, London, Methuen, 1985.

Stroud, B., *The Significance of Philosophical Scepticism*, Oxford, Oxford University Press, 1984.

Synthese 55, No. 2 (1983), special issue on 'Skepticism and Relevant Alternatives'.

Unger, P., *Ignorance: A Case for Scepticism*, Oxford, Clarendon Press, 1975.

Warfield, T. A., 'Knowing the World and Knowing Our Minds', *Philosophy and Phenomenological Research* 55 (1995), pp. 525–45.

Williams, M., *Unnatural Doubts*, Oxford, Basil Blackwell, 1991.

Wittgenstein, L., *On Certainty*, Oxford, Basil Blackwell, 1969.

Motivations

Chapter 22

Understanding human knowledge in general

Barry Stroud

THE philosophical study of human knowledge seeks to understand what knowledge is and how it comes to be. A long tradition of reflection on these questions suggests that we can never get the kind of satisfaction we seek. Either we reach the skeptical conclusion that we do not know the things we thought we knew, or we cannot see how the state we find ourselves in is a state of knowledge.

Most philosophers today still deny, or at the very least resist, the force of such reflections. In their efforts to construct a positive theory of knowledge they operate on the not-unreasonable assumption that since human perception, belief, and knowledge are natural phenomena like any other, there is no more reason to think they cannot be understood and explained than there is to think that digestion or photosynthesis cannot be understood and explained. Even if there is still much to be learned about human cognition, it can hardly be denied that we already know a great deal, at least in general, about how it works. Many see it now as just a matter of filling in the details, either from physiology or from something called 'cognitive science'. We might find that we understand much less than we think we do, but even so it would seem absurd simply to deny that there is such a thing as human knowledge at all, or that we can ever understand how it comes to be. Those traditional skeptical considerations, whatever they were, therefore tend to be ignored. They will be refuted in any case by a successful theory that explains how we do in fact know the things we do.

It would be as absurd to cast doubt on the prospects of scientific investigation of human knowledge and perception as it would be to declare limits to our understanding of human digestion. But I think that what we seek in epistemology—in the philosophical study of human knowledge—is not just anything we can find

Barry Stroud, 'Understanding Human Knowledge in General' in M. Clay, K. Lehrer (eds) *Knowledge and Skepticism* (Boulder, Westview Press, 1989), pp. 31–50 reprinted by permission of Westview Press.

about how we know things. We try to understand human knowledge in general, and to do so in a certain special way. If the philosophical investigation of knowledge is something distinctive, or sets itself certain special or unique goals, one might question whether those goals can really be reached without thereby casting any doubt on investigations of human knowledge which lack those distinctive philosophical features. That is what I shall try to do. I want to raise and examine the possibility that, however much we came to learn about this or that aspect of human knowledge, thought, and perception, there might still be nothing that could satisfy us as a philosophical understanding of how human knowledge is possible.

When I say nothing could satisfy us I do not mean that it is a very difficult task and that we will never finish the job. It *is* very difficult, and we *will* never finish the job, but I assume that is true of most of our efforts to understand anything. Rather, the threat I see is that once we really understand what we aspire to in the philosophical study of knowledge, and we do not deviate from the aspiration to understand it in that way, we will be forever unable to get the kind of understanding that would satisfy us.

That is one reason I think skepticism is so important in epistemology. It is the view that we do not, or perhaps cannot, know anything, and it is important because it seems to be the inevitable consequence of trying to understand human knowledge in a certain way. Almost nobody thinks for a moment that skepticism could be correct. But that does not mean it is not important. If skepticism really is the inevitable outcome of trying to understand human knowledge in a certain way, and we think it simply could not be correct, that should make us look much more critically at that way of trying to understand human knowledge in the first place. But that is not what typically happens in philosophy. The goal itself is scarcely questioned, and for good reason. We feel human knowledge ought to be intelligible in that way. The epistemological project feels like the pursuit of a perfectly comprehensible intellectual goal. We know that skepticism is no good; it is an answer, but it is not satisfactory. But being constitutionally unable to arrive at an answer to a perfectly comprehensible question is not satisfactory either. We therefore continue to acquiesce in the traditional problem and do not acknowledge that there is no satisfactory solution. We proceed as if it must be possible to find an answer, so we deny the force, and even the interest, of skepticism.

What we seek in the philosophical theory of knowledge is an account that is completely general in several respects. We want to understand how any knowledge at all is possible—how anything we currently accept amounts to knowledge. Or, less ambitiously, we want to understand with complete generality how we come to know anything at all in a certain specified domain.

For example, in the traditional question of our knowledge of the material bodies around us we want to understand how we know anything at all about any such bodies. In the philosophical problem of other minds we want to understand how any person ever comes to know anything at all about what is going on in the mind of any other person, or even knows that there are any other minds at all. In the case of induction we want to understand how anyone can ever have any reason at all to believe anything beyond what he himself has so far observed to be true. I take it to be the job of a positive philosophical theory of knowledge to answer these and similarly general questions.

One kind of generality I have in mind is revealed by what we would all regard as no answer at all to the philosophical problem. The question of other minds is how anyone can know what someone else thinks or feels. But it would be ludicrous to reply that someone can know what another person thinks or feels by asking a good friend of that person's. That would be no answer at all, but not because it is not true. I *can* sometimes find out what someone else thinks by asking his best friend. But that would not contribute to the solution to the philosophical problem of other minds. We are not simply looking for a list of all the ways of knowing. If we were, that way of knowing would go on the list. But in fact we seek a more inclusive description of all our ways of knowing that would explain our knowledge in general.

What is wrong with that particular way of knowing the mind of another is not that it is only one way among others. The trouble is that it explains how we know some particular fact in the area we are interested in by appeal to knowledge of some other fact in that same domain. I know what Smith thinks by knowing that Jones told me what Smith thinks. But knowing that Jones told me something is itself a bit of knowledge about the mind of another. So that kind of answer could not serve as, nor could it be generalized into, a satisfactory answer to the question how we know anything at all about any other minds. Not because it does not mention a legitimate way of knowing something about the mind of another. It does. Coming to know what Smith thinks by asking Jones is a perfectly acceptable way of knowing, and it is a different way of getting that knowledge from having Smith tell me himself, or from reading Smith's mail. There is nothing wrong with it in itself as an explanation. It is only for the general philosophical task that it is felt to be inadequate.

The same holds for everyday knowledge of the objects around us. One way I can know that my neighbor is at home is by seeing her car in front of her house, where she parks it when and only when she is at home. That is a perfectly good explanation of how I know that fact about one of the things around me. It is a different way of knowing where my neighbor is from seeing her through the window or hearing her characteristic fumblings on the piano. But it could not satisfy us as an explanation of how I know anything at all about any objects around me. It explains how I know something about one object around me—my neighbor—by knowing something about another object around me—her car. It could not answer the philosophical question as to how I know anything about any objects around me at all.

The kind of generality at stake in these problems takes its characteristic philosophical form when we come to see, on reflection, that the information available to us for knowing things in a particular domain is systematically less than we might originally have thought. Perhaps the most familiar instance of this is the *First Meditation* of Descartes,[1] in which he asks about knowledge of the material world

---

1. R. Descartes, *Meditations on First Philosophy* in *The Philosophical Writings of Descartes*, vol. I, tr. J. Cottingham, R. Stoothoff, D. Murdoch (Cambridge, 1985).

by means of the senses. It apparently turns out on reflection that the senses give us less than we might have thought; there is no strictly sensory information the possession of which necessarily amounts to knowledge of the material world. We could perceive exactly what we perceive now even if there were no material world at all. The problem then is to see how we ever come to get knowledge of the material world on that sensory basis.

In the case of other minds we find on reflection that the only evidence we can ever have or even imagine for the mental states of other people is their bodily behavior, including the sounds coming out of their mouths, or even the tears coming out of their eyes. But there is no strictly physical or behavioral information the possession of which necessarily amounts to knowledge of another person's mind or feelings. With induction the general distinction is perhaps even more obvious. The only reason we could ever have for believing anything about what we are not observing at the moment is something we have observed in the past or are observing right now. The problem then is how any knowledge of strictly past or even present fact amounts to knowledge of, or reasonable belief in, some unobserved or future fact.

These apparently simple, problem-generating moves come right at the beginning of epistemology. They are usually taken as so obvious and undeniable that the real problems of epistemology are thought to arise only after they have been made. In this paper I simply assume familiarity with them and with how easily they work. They are the very moves I think we eventually must examine more carefully if we are ever going to understand the real source of the dissatisfaction we are so easily driven to in philosophy. But for now I am concerned with the structure of the plight such reflections appear to leave us in.

If we start by considering a certain domain of facts or truths and ask how anyone could come to know anything at all in that domain, it will seem that any other knowledge that might be relevant could not be allowed to amount to already knowing something in the domain in question. Knowledge of anything at all in that domain is what we want to explain, and if we simply assume from the outset that the person has already got some of that knowledge we will not be explaining all of it. Any knowledge we do grant to the person will be of use to him only if he can somehow get from that knowledge to some knowledge in the domain in question. Some inference or transition would therefore appear to be needed—for example, some way of going from what he is aware of in perception to knowledge of the facts he claims to know. But any such inference will be a good one, and will lead the person to knowledge, only if it is based on something the person also knows or has some reason to believe. He cannot just be making a guess that he has got good evidence. He has to know or at least have reason to believe something that will help get him from his evidential base to some knowledge in the domain in question. That 'something' that he needs to know cannot simply be part of his evidential base, since it has to get him beyond that base. But it cannot go so far beyond that base as to imply something already in the domain in question either, since the knowledge of anything at all in that domain is just what we are trying to explain. So it would seem that on either possibility we cannot explain with the proper generality how the kind of knowledge we want to understand is possible. If the person does know what he needs to know, he has already got some knowledge in the domain in question, and if he does not, he will not be able to get there from his evidential base alone.

This apparent dilemma is a familiar quandary in traditional epistemology. I think it arises from our completely general explanatory goal. We want to explain a certain kind of knowledge, and we feel we must explain it on the basis of another, prior kind of knowledge that does not imply or presuppose any of the knowledge we are trying to explain. Without that, we will not be explaining the knowledge in question in the proper, fully general way. This felt need is what so easily brings into the epistemological project some notion or other of what is usually called 'epistemic priority'—one kind of knowledge being prior to another. I believe it has fatal consequences for our understanding of our knowledge. It is often said that traditional epistemology is generated by nothing more than a misguided 'quest for certainty,' or a fruitless search for absolutely secure 'foundations' for knowledge, and that once we abandon such a will-o'-the-wisp we will no longer be threatened by skepticism, or even much interested in it.[2] But that diagnosis seems wrong to me—in fact, completely upside down. What some philosophers see as a poorly motivated demand for 'foundations' of knowledge looks to me to be the natural consequence of seeking a certain intellectual goal, a certain kind of understanding of human knowledge in general.

In the philosophical problem of other minds, for example, we pick out observable physical movements or 'behavior' and ask how on that basis alone, which is the only basis we have, we can ever know anything about the mind behind the 'behavior'. Those observable facts of 'behavior' are held to be 'epistemically prior' to any facts about the mind in the sense that it is possible to know all such facts about others' 'behavior' without knowing anything about their minds. We insist on that condition for a properly general explanation of our knowledge of other minds. But in doing so we need not suppose that our beliefs about that 'behavior' are themselves indubitable or incorrigible 'foundations' of anything. Levels of relative epistemic priority are all we need to rely on in pressing the epistemological question in that way.

In the case of our knowledge of the material objects around us we single out epistemically prior 'sensations' or 'sense data' or 'experiences' or whatever it might be, and then ask how on that basis alone, which is the only basis we have, we can know anything of the objects around us. We take it that knowledge of objects comes to us somehow by means of the senses, but if we thought of sensory knowledge as itself knowledge of material objects around us we would not get an appropriately general explanation of how any knowledge of any objects at all is possible by means of the senses. We would be explaining knowledge of some material objects only on the basis of knowledge of some others. 'Data,' 'the given,' 'experiences,' and so on,

2. This charge has been laid against traditional epistemology at least since Dewey's *The Quest for Certainty* and is by now, I suppose, more or less philosophical orthodoxy. For more recent expressions of it see, for example, Michael Williams, *Groundless Belief* (Oxford, 1977), and Richard Rorty, *Philosophy and the Mirror of Nature* (Princeton, 1979).

which traditional epistemologists have always trafficked in, therefore look to me much more like inevitable products of the epistemological enterprise than elusive 'foundations,' the unmotivated quest for which somehow throws us into epistemology in the first place.

But once we accept the idea of one kind of knowledge being prior to another as an essential ingredient in the kind of philosophical understanding we seek, it immediately becomes difficult even to imagine, let alone to find, anything that could satisfy us. How *could* we possibly know anything about the minds of other people on the basis only of truths about their 'behavior' if those truths do not imply anything about any minds? If we really are restricted in perception to 'experiences' or 'sense data' or 'stimulations' which give us information that is prior to any knowledge of objects, how *could* we ever know anything about what goes on beyond such prior 'data'? It would seem to be possible only if we somehow knew of some connection between what we are restricted to in observation and what is true in the wider domain we are interested in. But then knowing even that there was such a connection would be knowing something about that wider domain after all, not just about what we are restricted to in observation. And then we would be left with no satisfactorily general explanation of our knowledge.

In short, it seems that if we really were in the position the traditional account in terms of epistemic priority describes us as being in, skepticism would be correct. We could not know the things we think we know. But if, in order to resist that conclusion, we no longer see ourselves in that traditional way, we will not have a satisfactorily general explanation of all our knowledge in a certain domain.

Theorists of knowledge who accept the traditional picture of our position in the world obviously do not acknowledge what I see as its skeptical or otherwise unsatisfactory consequences. Some philosophers see their task as that of exhibiting the general structure of our knowledge by making explicit what they think are the 'assumptions' or 'postulates' or 'epistemic principles' that are needed to take us from our 'data' or evidence in a particular area to some richer domain of knowledge we want to explain.[3] The fact that certain 'postulates' or 'principles' can be shown to be precisely what is needed for the knowledge in question is somehow taken to count in their favour. Without those 'principles,' it is argued, we wouldn't know what we think we know.

However illuminating such 'rational reconstructions' of our knowledge might be, they cannot really satisfy us if we want to understand how we actually do know the things we think we know. If it had been shown that there is a certain 'postulate' or 'principle' which we have to have some reason to accept if we are to know anything about, say, the world around us, we would not thereby have come to understand how we do know anything about the world around us. We would have identified something we need, but its indispensability would not show that we do in

---

3. Perhaps the best example of this, with a list of metaphysical and epistemological 'postulates' deemed to be necessary, is B. Russell, *Human Knowledge: Its Scope and Limits* (London, 1948). For a more recent version of the same project concentrating only on 'epistemic principles' see the epistemological writings of R. Chisholm, e.g., *Theory of Knowledge* (Englewood Cliffs, N.J., 1977) or *The Foundations of Knowing* (Minneapolis, 1980).

fact have good reason to accept it. We would be left with the further question whether we know that that 'principle' is true, and if so how. And all the rest of the knowledge we wanted to explain would then be hanging in the balance, since it would have been shown to depend on that 'principle.' Trying to answer the question of its justification would lead right back into the old dilemma. If the 'principle' involved says or implies something richer than anything to be found in the prior evidential base—as it seems it must if it is going to be of any help—there will be nothing in that base alone that could give us reason to accept it. But if we assume from the outset that we do know or have some reason to accept that 'principle,' we will be assuming that we already know something that goes beyond our prior evidential base, and that knowledge itself will not have been explained. We would therefore have no completely general explanation of how we get beyond that base to any knowledge of the kind in question.

The threat of a regress in the support for any such 'principles' leads naturally to the idea of two distinct sources or types of knowledge. If the 'principles' or presuppositions of knowledge could be known independently, not on the basis of the prior evidence, but in some other way, it might seem that the regress could be avoided. This might be said to be what Kant learned from Hume:[4] if all our knowledge is derived from experience, we can never know anything. But Kant did not infer from that conditional proposition the categorical skeptical conclusion he thought Hume drew from it. For Kant the point was that if we do have knowledge from experience we must also have some knowledge that is independent of experience. Only in that way is experiential knowledge possible. We must know some things *a priori* if we know anything at all.

As a way of explaining how we know the things we do, this merely postpones or expands the problem. It avoids the skeptical regress in sensory knowledge of the world by insisting that the basic 'principles' or presuppositions needed for such empirical knowledge do not themselves depend on empirical, sensory support. But that says only that those 'principles' are *not* known by experience; it does not explain how they are known. Merely being presupposed by our empirical knowledge confers no independent support. It has to be explained how we know anything at all *a priori*, and how in particular we know those very things we need for empirical knowledge. And then the old dilemma presents itself again. If our *a priori* knowledge of those 'principles' is derived from something prior to them which serves as their evidential base, it must be shown how the further 'principles' needed to take us from that base to the 'principles' in question could themselves be supported. If we assume from the outset that we do know some 'principles' *a priori*, not all of our *a priori* knowledge in general will have been explained. It would seem that *a priori* knowledge in general could be explained only in terms of something that is not itself *a priori* knowledge. But empirical knowledge cannot explain *a priori* knowledge—and it would be no help here even if it could—so either we must simply accept the unexplained fact that we know things *a priori* or we must try to explain it without appealing to any other knowledge at all.

4. See, e.g., I. Kant, *Critique of Pure Reason*, tr. N. Kemp Smith (New York, 1965), B 19–20.

I do not want to go further into the question of *a priori* knowledge. Not because it is not difficult and important in its own right, but because many theorists of knowledge would now argue that it is irrelevant to the epistemological project of explaining our knowledge of the world around us. They find they can put their finger precisely on the place where the traditional philosophical enterprise turns inevitably towards skepticism. And they hold that that step is wrong, and that without it there is no obstacle to finding a satisfactory account of our epistemic position that avoids any commitment to skepticism. This claim for a new 'enlightened' theory of knowledge that does not take that allegedly skeptical step is what I want to question.

I have already sketched the hopeless plight I think the old conception leaves us in. The trouble in that conception is now thought to enter at just the point at which the regress I have described apparently gets started. To get from his 'evidence' to any of the knowledge in question the person was said to need some 'principle' or assumption that would take him from that 'evidence' to that conclusion. But he would also need some reason for accepting that 'principle'—he would have to know something else that supports it. And then he would need some reason for accepting that 'something else,' and it could not be found either in his evidential base or in the 'principles' he originally needed to take him beyond that base. It must be found in something else in turn—another 'something else'—and so on *ad infinitum*. What is wrong in this, it is now thought, is not the idea that the person cannot find such reasons, or that he can only find them somehow mysteriously *a priori*. What is wrong is the requirement that he himself has to find such reasons, that he has to be able to support his 'principles,' at all. The new 'enlightened' approach to knowledge insists that there is a clear sense in which he does not.

The objection can be put another way. What is wrong with the traditional epistemological project that leads so easily to skepticism, it is said, is that the whole thing assumes that anyone who knows something must know that he knows it. He must himself know that his reasons are good ones, or that his prior 'evidence' is adequate to yield knowledge of the kind in question. And then, by that same assumption, he must know that he knows that, and so on. But that assumption, it is argued, is not correct. It is obviously possible for someone to know something without knowing that he knows it. The theory of knowledge asks simply whether and how people know things. If that can be explained, that is enough. The fact that people sometimes do not know that they know things should not make us deny that they really do know those things—especially if we have a satisfactory theory that explains that knowledge.

Now it certainly seems right to allow that someone can know something even when we recognize that he does not know that he knows it. Think of the simplest ordinary examples. Someone is asked if he knows who won the battle of Hastings, and when it took place, and he tentatively replies 'William the Conqueror, 1066.' He knew the answer. He had learned it in school, perhaps, and had never forgotten it, but at the time he was asked he did not know whether he had really retained that information. He was not sure about the state of his knowledge, but as for the winner and the date of the battle of Hastings, he knew that all along. He knew more than he thought he did. So whether somebody knows something is one thing; whether he knows that he knows it is something else. That seems to be a fact about our everyday assessments of people's knowledge.

The question is not whether that is a fact, but what significance it has for the prospects of the philosophical theory of knowledge. Obviously it turns on what a satisfactory philosophical account is supposed to do. The goal as I have presented it so far is to take ourselves and our ways of knowing on the one hand, and a certain domain of truths that we want to know about on the other, and to understand how we know any of those truths at all on the basis of prior knowledge that does not amount to already knowing something in the domain we are interested in. The question was what support we could find for the bridge that would be needed to get us from that prior basis to the knowledge in question. The present suggestion amounts in effect to saying that no independent or *a priori* support is needed on the part of the knower. All that is needed is that a certain proposition should be true; the person doesn't have to know that it is true in order to know the thing in question. If he has the appropriate prior knowledge or experience, and there is in fact a truth linking his having that knowledge or experience with his knowing something in the domain in question, then he does in fact know something in that domain, even if he is not aware of the favorable epistemic position he is in.

The truth in question will typically be one expressing the definition of knowledge, or of having reason to believe something. The search for such definitions is what many philosophers regard as the special job of the philosophical theory of knowledge. If knowing something could be defined solely in terms of knowledge or experience in some unproblematic, prior domain, then that definition could be fulfilled even if you didn't know that you knew anything in that domain. You yourself would not have to find a 'bridge' from your evidential basis to the knowledge in question. As long as there actually was a 'bridge' under your feet, whether you knew of it or not, there would be no threat of a skeptical regress.

In one form, this anti-skeptical strategy has been applied to the problem of induction. Hume had argued that if a long positive correlation observed to hold between two sorts of things in the past is going to give you some reason now to expect a thing of the second sort, given an observed instance of the first, you will also have to have some reason to think that what you have observed in the past gives you some reason to believe something about the future. P. F. Strawson replied that you need no such thing. Having observed a long positive correlation between two sorts of things under widely varied circumstances in the past is just what it is— what it means—to have reason to expect a thing of the second sort, given that a thing of the first sort has just appeared.[5] If that is a necessary truth about reasonable belief it will guarantee that you do in fact have a reasonable belief in the future as long as you have had the requisite experience of the past and present. You do not have to find some additional reason for thinking that what you have observed in the past gives you good reason to believe something about the future.

This has come to be called an 'externalist' account of knowledge or reasonable

5. P. F. Strawson, *Introduction to Logical Theory* (London, 1952), pp. 256–7.

belief. It would explain knowledge in terms of conditions that are available from an 'external,' third-person point of view, independent of what the knower's own attitude towards the fulfillment of those conditions might be. It is not all smooth sailing. To give us what we need, it has to come up with an account of knowledge or reasonable belief that is actually correct—that distinguishes knowledge from lack of knowledge in the right way. I think the account just given of inductive reasons does not meet that test. As it stands, it does not state a necessary truth about reasons to believe.[6] To come closer to being right, it would have to define the difference between a 'law-like' generalization and a merely 'accidental' correlation which does not give reason to believe it will continue. That task is by no means trivial, and it faces a 'new riddle of induction' all over again.[7] But if we do draw a distinction between having good reasons and not having them it would seem that there must be some account that captures what we do. It is just a matter of finding what it is.

The same goes for definitions of knowledge. One type of view says that knowing that p is equivalent to something like having acquired and retained a true belief that p as a result of the operation of a properly functioning, reliable belief-forming mechanism.[8] That general scheme still leaves many things unexplained or undefined, and it is no trivial task to get it to come out right. But I am not concerned here with the details of 'externalist' definitions of knowledge. My reservations about the philosophical theory of knowledge are not just that it is difficult. I have doubts about the satisfactoriness of what you would have even if you had an 'externalist' account of knowledge which as far as you could tell matched up completely with those cases in which we think other people know things and those in which we think they do not.

Here we come up against another, and perhaps the most important, dimension of generality I think we seek in the theory of knowledge. We want an account that explains how human knowledge in general is possible, or how anyone can know anything at all in a certain specified domain. The difficulty arises now from the fact that we as human theorists are ourselves part of the subject-matter that we theorists of human knowledge want to understand in a certain way. If we merely study another group and draw conclusions only about them, no such difficulty presents itself. But then our conclusions will not be completely general. They will be known to apply only to those others, and we will be no closer to understanding how our own knowledge is possible. We want to be able to apply what we find out about knowledge to ourselves, and so to explain how our own knowledge is possible.

I have already suggested why I think we cannot get a satisfactory explanation along traditional Cartesian lines. The promise of the new 'externalist' strategy is that it would avoid the regress that seems inevitable in that project. A person who

6. I have made the point in more detail in my *Hume* (London, 1977), pp. 64–6.

7. See N. Goodman, 'The New Riddle of Induction,' in *Fact, Fiction, and Forecast* (Cambridge, Mass., 1955) [Ch. 39 in this volume].

8. What the mechanism is, how its reliability is to be defined, and what other conditions are necessary vary from one 'externalist' theory to another. See, e.g., F. Dretske, *Knowledge and the Flow of Information* (Cambridge, Mass., 1981), or A. Goldman, *Epistemology and Cognition* (Cambridge, Mass., 1986).

knows something does not himself have to know that what he has got in his prior evidential base amounts to knowledge in the domain in question. As long as he in fact satisfies the conditions of knowing something in the domain we are interested in, there is nothing more he has to do in order to know things in that domain. No regress gets started.

The question now is: can we find such a theory satisfactory when we apply it to ourselves? To illustrate what I find difficult here I return to Descartes, as we so often must do in this subject. Not to his skeptical argument in the *First Meditation*, but to the answer he gives to it throughout the rest of the *Meditations*. He eventually comes to think that he does know many of the things that seemed to be thrown into doubt by his earlier reflections on dreaming and the evil demon. He does so by proving that God exists and is not a deceiver and that everything in us, including our capacity to perceive and think, comes from God. So whatever we clearly and distinctly perceive to be true is true. God would not have it any other way. By knowing what I know about God I can know that He is not a deceiver and therefore that I do know the things I think I know when I clearly and distinctly perceive them. If I am careful, and keep God and his goodness in mind, I can know many things, and the threat of skepticism is overcome.

Many objections have been made to this answer to Descartes's question about his knowledge. One is the 'externalist' complaint that Descartes's whole challenge rests on the assumption that you don't know something unless you know that you know it. Not only do my clear and distinct perceptions need some guarantee, but on Descartes's view I have to know what that guarantee is. That is why he thinks the atheist or the person who denies God in his heart cannot really know those things that we who accept Descartes's proof of God's existence and goodness can know.[9] But according to 'externalism' that requirement is wrong; you don't have to know that you know in order to know something.

Another and perhaps the most famous objection is that Descartes's proof of the guarantee of his knowledge is no good because it is circular. The knowledge he needs in order to reach the conclusion of God's existence and goodness is available to him only if God's existence and goodness have already been proved. What he calls his clear and distinct perception of God's existence will be knowledge of God's existence only if whatever he clearly and distinctly perceives is true. But that is guaranteed only by God, so he can't know that it is guaranteed unless he already knows that God exists.

Taking these two objections together, we can see that if the first is correct, the second is no objection at all. If Descartes is assuming that knowing requires knowing that you know, and if that assumption is wrong, then the charge of circularity has no force against his view. If 'externalism' were correct, Descartes's inability to prove that God exists and guarantees the truth of our clear and distinct perceptions would be no obstacle to his knowing the truth of whatever he clearly and distinctly perceives. He would not have to know that he knows those things. As long as God

9. R. Descartes, 'Third Set of Objections with the Author's Replies' and 'Author's Replies to the Sixth Set of Objections,' in *The Philosophical Writings of Descartes*, vol. I, pp. 137, 289 (Cambridge, 1985).

did in fact exist and did in fact make sure that his clear and distinct perceptions were true, Descartes would have the knowledge he started out thinking he had, even if God's existence and nature remained eternally unknown to him. The soundness of his proof would not matter. All that would matter for the everyday knowledge Descartes is trying to account for is the truth of its conclusion—God's existence and goodness. If that conclusion is in fact true, his inability to know that it is true would be no argument against his account.

To develop this thought further we can try to imagine what an 'enlightened' or 'externalist,' but still otherwise Cartesian, theory might look like. It would insist that the knowing subject does not have to know the truth of the theory that explains his knowledge in order to have the knowledge that the theory is trying to account for. Otherwise, the theory would retain the full Cartesian story of God and his goodness and his guarantee of the truth of our clear and distinct perceptions. What would be wrong with accepting such an 'enlightened' theory? If we are willing to accept the kind of theory that says that knowing that p is having acquired the true belief that p by some reliable belief-forming mechanism, why would we not be equally or even more willing to accept a theory that says that knowing that p is having acquired the true belief that p by clearly and distinctly perceiving it—a method of belief formation that is reliable because God guarantees that whatever is clearly and distinctly perceived is true? It is actually more specific than a completely general form of 'externalism' or 'reliabilism.' It explains *why* the belief-forming mechanism is reliable. What, then, would be wrong with accepting it?

I think most of us simply don't believe it. We think that God does not in fact exist and is not the guarantor of the reliability of our belief-forming mechanisms. So we think that what this theory says about human knowledge is not true. Now that is certainly a defect in a theory, but is it the only thing standing in the way of our accepting it and finding it satisfactory? It seems to me it is not, and perhaps by examining its other defects, beyond its actual truth-value, we can identify a source of dissatisfaction with other 'externalist' theories as well.

We have to admit that if the imagined 'externalist' Cartesian theory were true, we would know many of the things we think we know. So skepticism would not be correct. But in the philosophical investigation of knowledge we want more than the falsity of skepticism and more than the mere possession of the knowledge we ordinarily think we've got. We want to understand how we know the things we know, how skepticism turns out not to be true. And even if this 'enlightened' Cartesian story were in fact true, if we didn't know that it was, or if we didn't have some reason to believe that it was, we would be no further along towards understanding our knowledge than we would be if the theory were false. So we need some reason to accept a theory of knowledge if we are going to rely on that theory to understand how our knowledge is possible. That is what I think no form of 'externalism' can give a satisfactory account of.

Suppose someone had said to Descartes, as they in effect did, 'Look, you have no reason to accept any of this story about God and his guarantee of the truth of your clear and distinct perceptions. Of course, if what you say were true you would have the knowledge you think you have, but your whole proof of it is circular. You could justify your explanation of knowledge only if you already knew that what you clearly and distinctly perceive is true.' Could an 'enlightened' 'externalist' Descartes reply: 'That's right. I suppose I have to admit that I can give no good reason to accept my explanation. But that doesn't really bother me any more, now that I am an "externalist." Circularity in my proofs is no objection to my theory if "externalism" is correct. I still do believe my theory, after all, and as long as that theory is in fact true—whether I can give any reason to accept it or not—skepticism will be false and I will in fact know the things that I clearly and carefully claim to know.'

I take it that that response is inadequate. The 'externalist' Descartes I have imagined would not have a satisfactory understanding of his knowledge. It is crucial to what I want to say about 'externalism' that we recognize some inadequacy in his position. It is admittedly not easy to specify exactly what the deficiency or the unsatisfactoriness of accepting that position amounts to. I think this much can be said: if the imagined Descartes responded only in that way he would be at best in the position of saying, 'If the story that I accept is true, I do know the things I think I know. But I admit that if it is false, and a certain other story is true instead, then I do not.' If 'externalism' is correct, what he would be saying here is true. His theory, if true, would explain his knowledge. The difficulty is that until he finds some reason to believe his theory rather than some other, he cannot be said to have explained how he knows the things he knows. That is not because he is assuming that a person cannot know something unless he knows that he knows it. He has explicitly abandoned that assumption. He admits that people know things whether they know the truth of his theory or not. The same of course holds for him. And he knows that implication. That is precisely what he is saying: if his theory is true he will know the things he thinks he knows. But he is, in addition, a theorist of knowledge. He wants to understand how he knows the things he thinks he knows. And he cannot satisfy himself on that score unless he can see himself as having some reason to accept the theory that he (and all the rest of us) can recognize would explain his knowledge if it were true. That is not because knowing implies knowing that you know. It is because having an explanation of something in the sense of understanding it is a matter of having good reason to accept something that would be an explanation if it were true.

The question now is whether an 'externalist' scientific epistemologist who rejects Descartes's explanation and offers one of his own is in any better position when he comes to apply his theory to his own knowledge than the imagined 'externalist' Descartes is in. He begins by asking about all knowledge in a specified domain. A philosophically satisfactory explanation of such knowledge must not explain some of the knowledge in the domain in question by appeal to knowledge of something else already in the domain. But the scientific student of human knowledge must know or have some reason to believe his theory of knowledge if he is going to understand how knowledge is possible. His theory about our belief-forming mechanisms and their reliability is a theory about the interactions between us and the world around us. It is arrived at by studying human beings, finding out how they get the beliefs they do, and investigating the sources of the reliability of those belief-forming mechanisms. Descartes claimed knowledge of God and his goodness, and of the relation between those supernatural facts and our earth-bound belief-forming mechanisms. A more naturalistic epistemologist's gaze does not reach so high. He claims knowledge of nothing more than the familiar natural world in which he thinks everything happens. But he will have an explanation of human knowledge, and so will understand how people know the things they do, only if he knows or has some reason to believe that his scientific story of the goings-on in that world is true.

If his goal was, among other things, to explain our scientific knowledge of the world around us, he will have an explanation of such knowledge only if he can see himself as possessing some knowledge in that domain. In studying other people, that presents no difficulty. It is precisely by knowing what he does about the world that he explains how others know what they do about the world. But if he had started out asking how anyone knows anything at all about the world, he would be no further along towards understanding how any of it is possible if he had not understood how he himself knows what he has to know about the world in order to have any explanation at all. He must understand himself as knowing or having reason to believe that his theory is true.

It might seem that he fulfills that requirement because his theory of knowledge is meant to identify precisely those conditions under which knowledge or good reason to believe something is present. If that theory is correct, and he himself fulfills those conditions in his own scientific investigations of human knowledge, he will in fact know that his theory of knowledge is true, or at least he will have good reason to believe it. He studies others and finds that they often satisfy the conditions his theory says are sufficient for knowing things about the world, and he believes that theory, and he believes that he too satisfies those same conditions in his investigations of those other people. He concludes that he does know how human beings know what they do, and he concludes that he therefore understands how he in particular knows the things he knows about the world. He is one of the human beings that his theory is true of. So the non-Cartesian scientific 'externalist' claims to be in a better position than the imagined 'externalist' Descartes because he claims to know by a reliable study of the natural world that his explanation of human knowledge is correct and Descartes's is wrong. In accepting his own explanation he claims to fulfill the conditions his theory asserts to be sufficient for knowing things.

I think this theorist would still be in no better position than the position the imagined 'externalist' Descartes is in. If his theory is true, he will in fact know that his explanation is correct. In that sense he could be said to possess an explanation of how human beings know the things they know. In that same sense the imagined 'externalist' Descartes would possess an explanation of his knowledge. He accepts something which, if true, would explain his knowledge. But none of this would be any help or consolation to them as epistemologists. The position of the imagined 'externalist' Descartes is deficient for the theory of knowledge because he needs some reason to believe that the theory he has devised is true in order to be said to understand how people know the things they think they know. The scientific 'externalist' claims he does have reason to believe his explanation of knowledge and so to be in a better position than the imagined 'externalist' Descartes. But the way in which he fulfills that condition, even if he does, is only in an 'externalist' way, and therefore in the same way that the imagined Descartes fulfills the conditions of knowledge, if he does. *If* the scientific 'externalist's' theory is correct about the conditions under which knowledge or reasonable belief is present, and if he does fulfill those conditions in coming to believe his own explanation of knowledge, then he is in fact right in thinking that he has good reason to think that his explanation is correct. But that is to be in the same position with respect to whether he has good reason to think his explanation is correct as the imagined 'externalist' Descartes was in at the first level with respect to whether he knows the things he thinks he knows.

It was admitted that if that imagined Descartes's theory were true he would know the things he thinks he knows, but he could not be said to see or to understand himself as possessing such knowledge because he had no reason to think that his theory was true. The scientific 'externalist' claims to have good reason to believe that his theory is true. It must be granted that if, in arriving at his theory, he did fulfill the conditions his theory says are sufficient for knowing things about the world, then if that theory is correct, he does in fact know that it is. But still, I want to say, he himself has no reason to think that he does have good reason to think that his theory is correct. He is at best in the position of someone who has good reason to believe his theory if that theory is in fact true, but has no such reason to believe it if some other theory is true instead. He can see what he *would* have good reason to believe if the theory he believes were true, but he cannot see or understand himself as knowing or having good reason to believe what his theory says.

I am aware that describing what I see as the deficiency in this way is not really satisfactory or conclusive. It encourages the 'externalist' to re-apply his theory of knowing or having good reason to believe at the next level up, and to claim that he can indeed understand himself to have good reason to believe his theory because he has good reason to believe that he does have good reason to believe his theory. That further belief about his reasons is arrived at in turn by fulfilling what his theory says are the conditions for reasonably believing something. But then he is still in the same position two levels up that we found the imagined 'externalist' Descartes to be in at the first level. If the imagined Descartes's claim to self-understanding was inadequate there, any similar claim will be equally inadequate at any higher level of knowing that one knows or having reason to believe that one has reason to believe. That is why our reaction to the original response of the imagined 'externalist' Descartes is crucial. Recognition of its inadequacy is essential to recognizing the inadequacy of 'externalism' that I have in mind. It is difficult to say precisely what is inadequate about that kind of response, especially in terms that would be acceptable to an 'externalist.' Perhaps it is best to say that the theorist has to see himself as having good reason to believe his theory in some sense of 'having good reason' that cannot be fully captured by an 'externalist' account.

So even if it is true that you can know something without knowing that you know it, the philosophical theorist of knowledge cannot simply insist on the point and expect to find acceptance of an 'externalist' account of knowledge fully satisfactory. If he could, he would be in the position of someone who says: 'I don't know whether I understand human knowledge or not. If what I believe about it is true and my beliefs about it are produced in what my theory says is the right way, I do know how human knowledge comes to be, so in that sense I do understand. But if my beliefs are not true, or not arrived at in that way, I do not.' I wonder which it is. I wonder whether I understand human knowledge or not. That is not a satisfactory position to arrive at in one's study of human knowledge—or of anything else.

It might be said that there can be such a thing as unwitting understanding, or understanding you don't know you've got, just as there can be unwitting knowledge, or knowledge you don't know you've got. Such 'unwitting understanding,' if there is such a thing, is the most that the 'externalist' philosophical theorist about human knowledge could be said to have of his own knowledge. But even if there is such a thing, it is not something it makes sense to aspire to, or something to remain content with having reached, if you happen to have reached it. We want witting, not unwitting, understanding. That requires knowing or having some reason to accept the scientific story you believe about how people know the things they know. And in the case of knowledge of the world around us, that would involve already knowing or having some reason to believe something in the domain in question. Not all the knowledge in that domain would thereby be explained.

I do not mean that there is something wrong with our explaining how people know certain things about the world by assuming that they or we know certain other things about it. We do it all the time. It is only within the general epistemological enterprise that that otherwise familiar procedure cannot give us what we want. And when I say that 'externalism' cannot give us what we want I do not mean that it possesses some internal defect which prevents it from being true. The difficulty I am pointing to is an unsatisfactoriness involved in *accepting* an 'externalist' theory and claiming to understand human knowledge in general in that way. And even that is too broad. It is not that there is any difficulty in understanding other people's knowledge in those terms. It is only with self-understanding that the unsatisfactoriness or loss of complete generality makes itself felt. 'Externalism,' if it got the conditions of knowledge right, would work fine for other people's knowledge. As a third-person, observational study of human beings and other animals, it would avoid the obstacles to human understanding apparently involved in the first-person Cartesian project. But the question is whether we can take up such an 'external' observer's position with respect to ourselves and our knowledge and still gain a satisfactorily general explanation of how we know the things we know. That is where I think the inevitable dissatisfaction comes in.

The demand for completely general understanding of knowledge in a certain domain requires that we see ourselves at the outset as not knowing anything in that domain and then coming to have such knowledge on the basis of some independent and in that sense prior knowledge or experience. And that leads us to seek a standpoint from which we can view ourselves without taking for granted any of that knowledge that we want to understand. But if we could manage to detach ourselves in that way from acceptance of any truths in the domain we are interested in, it seems that the only thing we could discover from that point of view is that we can never know anything in that domain. We could find no way to explain how that prior knowledge alone could yield any richer knowledge lying beyond it. That is the plight the traditional view captures. That is the truth in skepticism. If we think of our knowledge as arranged in completely general levels of epistemic priority in that way, we find that we cannot know what we think we know. Skepticism is the only answer.

But then that seems absurd. We realize that people do know many things in the domains we are interested in. We can even explain how they know such things, whether they know that they do or not. That is what the third-person point of view captures. That is the truth in 'externalism.' But when we try to explain how we know those things we find we can understand it only by assuming that we have got some knowledge in the domain in question. And that is not philosophically satisfying. We have lost the prospect of explaining and therefore understanding all of our knowledge with complete generality.

For these and other reasons I think we need to go back and look more carefully into the very sources of the epistemological quest. We need to see how the almost effortlessly natural ways of thinking embodied in that traditional enterprise nevertheless distort or misrepresent our position, if they do. But we should not think that if and when we come to see how the epistemological enterprise is not fully valid, or perhaps not even fully coherent, we will then possess a satisfactory explanation of how human knowledge in general is possible. We will have seen, at best, that we cannot have any such thing. And that too, I believe, will leave us dissatisfied.[10]

10. I would like to thank Janet Broughton, Thompson Clarke, Fred Dretske, Alvin Goldman, Samuel Guttenplan, and Christopher Peacocke for helpful comments on earlier versions of this paper.

Chapter 23

A defense of skepticism

Peter Unger

THE skepticism that I will defend is a negative thesis concerning what we know. I happily accept the fact that there is much that many of us correctly and reasonably believe, but much more than that is needed for us to know even a fair amount. Here I will not argue that nobody knows anything about anything, though that would be quite consistent with the skeptical thesis for which I will argue. The somewhat less radical thesis which I will defend is this one: every human being knows, at best, hardly anything to be so. More specifically, I will argue that hardly anyone knows that 45 and 56 are equal to 101, if anyone at all. On this skeptical thesis, no one will know the thesis to be true. But this is all right. For I only want to argue that it may be reasonable for us to suppose the thesis to be true, not that we should ever know it to be true.

Few philosophers now take skepticism seriously. With philosophers, even the most powerful of traditional skeptical argument has little force to tempt them nowadays. Indeed, nowadays, philosophers tend to think skepticism interesting only as a formal challenge to which positive accounts of our common-sense knowledge are the gratifying responses. Consequently, I find it at least somewhat natural to offer a defense of skepticism.[1]

My defense of skepticism will be quite unlike traditional arguments for this thesis. This is largely because I write at a time when there is a common faith that, so far as expressing truths is concerned, all is well with the language that we speak. Against this common, optimistic assumption, I shall illustrate how our language

Peter Unger, 'A Defense of Skepticism' in the *Philosophical Review* 80 (1971) pp. 198–219. Copyright 1971 Cornell University, reprinted by permission of the publisher.

1. Among G. E. Moore's most influential papers against skepticism are 'A Defense of Common Sense,' 'Four Forms of Scepticism,' and 'Certainty.' These papers are now available in Moore's *Philosophical Papers* (New York, 1962). More recent representatives of the same anti-skeptical persuasion include A. J. Ayer's *The Problem of Knowledge* (Baltimore, 1956) and two books by Roderick M. Chisholm: *Perceiving* (Ithaca, 1957) and *Theory of Knowledge* (Englewood Cliffs, N.J., 1966). Among the many recent journal articles against skepticism are three papers of my own: 'Experience and Factual Knowledge,' *Journal of Philosophy*, vol. 64 (1967), 'An Analysis of Factual Knowledge,' *Journal of Philosophy*, vol. 65 (1968), and 'Our Knowledge of the Material World,' *Studies in the Theory of Knowledge, American Philosophical Quarterly Monograph* No. 4 (1970). At the same time, a survey of the recent journal literature reveals very few papers where skepticism is defended or favored. With recent papers which do favor skepticism, however, I can mention at least two. A fledgling skepticism is persuasively advanced by Brian Skyrms in his 'The Explication of "*X* Knows that *p*," *Journal of Philosophy*, vol. 64 (1967). And in William W. Rozeboom's 'Why I Know So Much More Than You Do,' *American Philosophical Quarterly*, vol. 4 (1967), we have a refreshingly strong statement of skepticism in the context of recent discussion.

habits might serve us well in practical ways, even while they involve us in saying what is false rather than true. And this often does occur, I will maintain, when our positive assertions contain terms with special features of a certain kind, which I call *absolute* terms. Among these terms, 'flat' and 'certain' are *basic* ones. Due to these terms' characteristic features, and because the world is not so simple as it might be, we do not speak truly, at least as a rule, when we say of a real object, 'That has a top which is flat' or when we say of a real person, 'He is certain that it is raining.' And just as basic absolute terms generally fail to apply to the world, so other absolute terms, which are at least partially defined by the basic ones, will fail to apply as well. Thus, we also speak falsely when we say of a real object or person, 'That is a cube' or 'He knows that it is raining.' For an object is a cube only if it has surfaces which are flat, and, as I shall argue, a person knows something to be so only if he is certain of it.

1. Sophisticated worries about what skepticism requires

The reason contemporary sophisticated philosophers do not take skepticism seriously can be stated broadly and simply. They think that skepticism implies certain things which are, upon a bit of reflection, quite impossible to accept. These unacceptable implications concern the functioning of our language.

Concerning our language and how it functions, the most obvious requirement of skepticism is that some common terms of our language will involve us in error systematically. These will be such terms as 'know' and 'knowledge,' which may be called the 'terms of knowledge.' If skepticism is right, then while we go around saying 'I know,' 'He knows,' and so on, and while we believe what we say to be true, all the while what we say and believe will actually be false. If our beliefs to the effect that we know something or other are so consistently false, then the terms of knowledge lead us into error systematically. But if these beliefs really are false, should we not have experiences which force the realization of their falsity upon us, and indeed abandon these beliefs? Consequently, shouldn't our experiences get us to stop thinking in these terms which thus systematically involve us in error? So, as we continue to think in the terms of knowledge and to believe ourselves to know all sorts of things, this would seem to show that the beliefs are not false ones and the terms are responsible for no error. Isn't it only reasonable, then, to reject a view which requires that such helpful common terms as 'knows' and 'knowledge' lead us into error systematically?

So go some worrisome thoughts which might lead us to dismiss skepticism out of hand. But it seems to me that there is no real need for our false beliefs to clash with our experiences in any easily noticeable way. Suppose, for instance, that you falsely believe that a certain region of space is a vacuum. Suppose that, contrary to your belief, the region does contain some gaseous stuff though only the slightest trace. Now, for practical purposes, we may suppose that, so far as gaseous contents go, it is not important whether that region really is a vacuum or whether it contains whatever gaseous stuff it does contain. Once this is supposed, then it is reasonable to suppose as well that, for practical purposes, it makes no important difference whether you falsely believe that the region is a vacuum or truly believe this last thing—namely, that, for practical purposes, it is not important whether the region is a vacuum or whether it contains that much gaseous stuff.

We may notice that this supposed truth is entailed by what you believe but does not entail it. In other words, a region's being a vacuum entails that, for practical purposes, there is no important difference between whether the region is a vacuum or whether it contains whatever gaseous stuff it does contain. For, if the region *is* a vacuum, whatever gas it contains is nil, and so there is no difference at all, for any sort of purpose, between the region's being a vacuum and its having that much gaseous stuff. But the entailment does not go the other way, and this is where we may take a special interest. For while a region may not be a vacuum, it may contain so little gaseous stuff that, so far as gaseous contents go, for practical purposes there is no important difference between the region's being a vacuum and its containing whatever gaseous stuff it does contain. So if this entailed truth lies behind the believed falsehood, your false belief, though false, may not be harmful. Indeed, generally, it may even be helpful for you to have this false belief rather than having none and rather than having almost any other belief about the matter that you might have. On this pattern, we may have many false beliefs about regions being vacuums even while these beliefs will suffer no important clash with the experiences of life.

More to our central topic, suppose that, as skepticism might have it, you falsely believe that you *know* that there are elephants. As before, there is a true thing which is entailed by what you falsely believe and which we should notice. The thing here, which presumably you do not actually believe, is this: that, with respect to the matter of whether there are elephants, for practical purposes there is no important difference between whether you know that there are elephants or whether you are in that position with respect to the matter that you actually are in. This latter, true thing is entailed by the false thing you believe—namely, that you know that there are elephants. For if you do know, then, with respect to the matter of the elephants, there is no difference at all, for any purpose of any sort, between your knowing and your being in the position you actually are in. On the other hand, the entailment does not go the other way and, again, this is where our pattern allows a false belief to be helpful. For even if you do not really know, still, it may be that for practical purposes you are in a position with respect to the matter (of the elephants) which is not importantly different from knowing. If this is so, then it may be better, practically speaking, for you to believe falsely that you know than to have no belief at all here. Thus, not only with beliefs to the effect that specified regions are vacuums, but also with beliefs to the effect that we know certain things, it may be that there are very many of them which, though false, it is helpful for us to have. In both cases, the beliefs will not noticeably clash with the experiences of life. Without some further reason for doing so, then, noting the smooth functioning of our 'terms of knowledge' gives us no powerful reason for dismissing the thesis of skepticism.

There is, however, a second worry which will tend to keep sophisticates far from embracing skepticism, and this worry is, I think, rather more profound than the first. Consequently, I shall devote most of the remainder to treating this second worry. The worry to which I shall be so devoted is this: that, if skepticism is right, then the terms of knowledge, unlike other terms of our language, will never or hardly ever be used to make simple, positive assertions that are true. In other words, skepticism will require the terms of knowledge to be isolated freaks of our language. But even with familiar, persuasive arguments for skepticism, it is implausible to think that our language is plagued by an isolated little group of troublesome freaks. So, by being so hard on knowledge alone, skepticism seems implausible once one reflects on the exclusiveness of its persecution.

2. Absolute terms and relative terms

Against the worry that skepticism will require the terms of knowledge to be isolated freaks, I shall argue that, on the contrary, a variety of other terms is similarly troublesome. As skepticism becomes more plausible with an examination of the terms of knowledge, so other originally surprising theses become more plausible once their key terms are critically examined. When all of the key terms are understood to have essential features in common, the truth of any of these theses need not be felt as such a surprise.

The terms of knowledge, along with many other troublesome terms, belong to a class of terms that is quite pervasive, in our language. I call these terms *absolute terms*. The term 'flat,' in its central, literal meaning, is an absolute term. (With other meanings, as in 'His voice is flat' and 'The beer is flat,' I have no direct interest.) To say that something is flat is no different from saying that it is absolutely, or perfectly, flat. To say that a surface is flat is to say that some things or properties *which are matters of degree* are *not* instanced in the surface *to any degree at all*. Thus, something which is flat is not at all bumpy, and not at all curved. Bumpiness and curvature are matters of degree. When we say of a surface that it is bumpy, or that it is curved, we use the *relative terms* 'bumpy' and 'curved' to talk about the surface. Thus, absolute terms and relative terms go together, in at least one important way, while other terms, like 'unmarried,' have only the most distant connections with terms of either of these two sorts.

There seems to be a syntactic feature which is common to relative terms and to certain absolute terms, while it is found with no other terms. This feature is that each of these terms may be modified by a variety of terms that serve to indicate (matters of) degree. Thus, we find 'The table is *very* bumpy' and 'The table is *very* flat' but not 'The lawyer is *very* unmarried.' Among those absolute terms which admit such qualification are all those absolute terms which are *basic* ones. A basic absolute term is an absolute term which is not (naturally) defined in terms of some other absolute term, not even partially so. I suspect that 'straight' is such a term, and perhaps 'flat' is as well. But in its central (geometrical) meaning, 'cube' quite clearly is not a basic absolute term even though it is an absolute term. For 'cube' means, among other things,'having edges that are *straight* and surfaces which are *flat*': and 'straight' and 'flat' are absolute terms. While 'cube' does not admit of qualification of degree, 'flat' and 'straight' do admit of such qualification. Thus, all relative terms and all basic absolute terms admit of constructions of degree. While this is another way in which these two sorts of terms go together, we must now ask: how may we distinguish terms of the one sort from those of the other?

But is there now anything to distinguish here? For if absolute terms admit of degree construction, why think that any of these terms is not a relative term, why think that they do not purport to predicate things or properties which are, as they now look to be, matters of degree? If we may say that a table is very flat, then why not think flatness a matter of degree? Isn't this essentially the same as our saying of a table that it is very bumpy, with bumpiness being a matter of degree? So perhaps 'flat,' like 'bumpy' and like all terms that take degree constructions, is, fittingly, a relative term. But basic absolute terms may be distinguished from relatives even where degree constructions conspire to make things look otherwise.

To advance the wanted distinction, we may look to a procedure for paraphrase. Now, we have granted that it is common for us to say of a surface that it is pretty, or very, or extremely, flat. And it is also common for us to say that, in saying such things of surfaces, we are saying *how* flat the surfaces are. What we say here seems of a piece with our saying of a surface that it is pretty, or very, or extremely, bumpy, and our then saying that, in doing this, we are saying *how* bumpy the surface is. But, even intuitively, we may notice a difference here. For only with our talk about 'flat,' we have the idea that these locutions are only convenient means for saying how closely a surface approximates, or *how close it comes to being*, a surface which is (absolutely) flat. Thus, it is intuitively plausible, and far from being a nonsensical interpretation, to paraphrase things so our result with our 'flat' locutions is this: what we have said of a surface is that it is pretty *nearly* flat, or very *nearly* flat, or extremely *close to being* flat and, in doing that, we have said, not simply how flat the surface is, but rather *how close* the surface is *to being* flat. This form of paraphrase gives a plausible interpretation of our talk of flatness while allowing the term 'flat' to lose its appearance of being a relative term. How will this form of paraphrase work with 'bumpy,' where, presumably, a genuine relative term occurs in our locutions?

What do we say when we say of a surface that it is pretty bumpy, or very bumpy, or extremely so? Of course, it at least appears that we say *how* bumpy the surface is. The paraphrase has it that what we are saying is that the 'surface is pretty *nearly* bumpy, or very *nearly* bumpy, or extremely *close to being* bumpy. In other words, according to the paraphrase, we are saying *how close* the surface is *to being* bumpy. But anything of this sort is, quite obviously, a terribly poor interpretation of what we are saying about the surface. Unfortunately for the paraphrase, if we say that a surface is very bumpy it is entailed by what we say that the surface is bumpy, while if we say that the surface is very close to being bumpy it is entailed that the surface is *not* bumpy. Thus, unlike the case with 'flat,' our paraphrase cannot apply with 'bumpy.' Consequently, by means of our paraphrase we may distinguish between absolute terms and relative ones.

Another way of noticing how our paraphrase lends support to the distinction between absolute and relative terms is this: the initial data are that such terms as 'very,' which standardly serve to indicate that there is a great deal of something, serve with opposite effect when they modify terms like 'flat'—terms which I have called basic absolute terms. That is, when we say, for example, that something is (really) very flat, then, so far as flatness is concerned, we seem to say less of the thing than when we say, simply, that it is (really) flat. The augmenting function of 'very' is turned on its head so that the term serves to diminish. What can resolve this conflict? It seems that our paraphrase can. For on the paraphrase, what we are saying of the thing is that it is very *nearly* flat, and so, by implication, that it is *not* flat (but only very nearly so). Once the paraphrase is exploited, the term 'very' may be understood to have its standard augmenting function. At the same time, 'very' functions without conflict with 'bumpy.' Happily, the term 'very' is far from being unique here; we get the same results with other augmenting modifiers: 'extremely,' 'especially,' and so on.

For our paraphrastic procedure to be comprehensive, it must work with contexts containing explicitly comparative locutions. Indeed, with these contexts, we have a common form of talk where the appearance of relativeness is most striking of all. What shall we think of our saying, for example, that one surface is not *as* flat as another, where things strikingly look to be a matter of degree? It seems that we must allow that in such a suggested comparison, the surface which is said to be the *flatter* of the two may be, so far as logic goes, (absolutely) flat. Thus, we should *not* paraphrase this comparative context as 'the one surface is not as *nearly* flat as the other.' For this form of paraphrase would imply that the second surface is not flat, and so it gives us a poor interpretation of the original, which has no such implication. But then, a paraphrase with no bad implications is not far removed. Instead of simply inserting our 'nearly' or our 'close to being,' we may allow for the possibility of (absolute) flatness by putting things in a way which is only somewhat more complex. For we may paraphrase our original by saying: the first surface is *either not flat though the second is, or else it is* not as *nearly* flat as the second. Similarly, where we say that one surface is flatter than another, we may paraphrase things like this: the first surface is *either flat though the second is not or else it is closer to being flat* than the second. But in contrast to all this, with comparisons of bumpiness, no paraphrase is available. To say that one surface is not as bumpy as another is not to say either that the first surface is not bumpy though the second is, or else that it is not as nearly bumpy as the second one.

Our noting the availability of degree constructions allows us to class together relative terms and basic absolute terms, as against any other terms. And our noting that only with the absolute terms do our constructions admit of our paraphrase allows us to distinguish between the relative terms and the basic absolute terms. Now that these terms may be quite clearly distinguished, we may restate without pain of vacuity those ideas on which we relied to introduce our terminology. Thus, to draw the *connection* between terms of the two sorts we may now say this: every basic absolute term, and so every absolute term whatever, may be defined, at least partially, by means of certain relative terms. The defining conditions presented by means of the relative terms are negative ones; they say that what the relative term purports to denote is *not* present *at all,* or *in the least,* where the absolute term correctly applies. Thus, these negative conditions are logically necessary ones for basic absolute terms, and so for absolute terms which are defined by means of the basic ones. Thus, something is flat, in the central, literal sense of 'flat,' only if it is not at all, or not in the least, curved or bumpy. And similarly, something is a cube, in the central, literal sense of 'cube,' only if it has surfaces which are not at all, or not in the least, bumpy or curved. In noting these demanding *negative relative requirements,* we may begin to appreciate, I think, that a variety of absolute terms, if not all of them, might well be quite troublesome to apply, perhaps even failing consistently in application to real things.

In a final general remark about these terms, I should like to motivate my choice of terminology for them. A reason I call terms of the one sort 'absolute' is that, at least in the case of the basic ones, the term may always be modified, grammatically, with the term 'absolutely.' And indeed, this modification fits so well that it is, I think, always redundant. Thus, something is flat if and only if it is absolutely flat. In contrast, the term 'absolutely' never gives a standard, grammatical modification for any of our relative terms: nothing which is bumpy is absolutely bumpy. On the other hand, each of the relative terms takes 'relatively' quite smoothly as a grammatical modifier. (And, though it is far from being clear, it is at least arguable, I think, that this modifier is redundant for these terms. Thus, it is at least arguable that something is bumpy if and only if it is relatively bumpy.) In any event, with absolute terms, while 'relatively' is grammatically quite all right as a modifier, the construction thus obtained must be understood in terms of our paraphrase. Thus, as before, something is relatively flat if and only if it is relatively close to being (absolutely) flat, and so only if it is not flat.

In this terminology, and in line with our linguistic tests, I think that the first term of each of the following pairs is a relative term while the second is an absolute one: 'wet' and 'dry,' 'crooked' and 'straight,' 'important' and 'crucial,' 'incomplete' and 'complete,' 'useful' and 'useless,' and so on. I think that both 'empty' and 'full' are absolute terms, while 'good' and 'bad,' 'rich' and 'poor,' and 'happy' and 'unhappy' are all relative terms. Finally, I think that, in the sense defined by our tests, each of the following is neither an absolute term nor a relative one: 'married' and 'unmarried,' 'true' and 'false,' and 'right' and 'wrong.' In other plausible senses, though, some or all of this last group might be called 'absolute.'

3. On certainty and certain related things

Certain terms of our language are standardly followed by propositional clauses, and, indeed, it is plausible to think that wherever they occur they *must* be followed by such clauses on pain of otherwise occurring in a sentence which is elliptical or incomplete. We may call terms which take these clauses *propositional terms* and we may then ask: are some propositional terms absolute ones, while others are relative terms? By means of our tests, I will argue that 'certain' is an absolute term, while 'confident,' 'doubtful,' and 'uncertain' are all relative terms.

With regard to being certain, there are two ideas which are important: first, the idea of something's being certain, where that which is certain is *not* certain *of* anything, and, second, the idea of a being's being certain, where that which is certain *is* certain *of* something. A paradigm context for the first idea is the context 'It is certain that it is raining' where the term 'it' has no apparent reference. I will call such contexts *impersonal* contexts, and the idea of certainty which they serve to express, thus, the impersonal idea of certainty. In contrast, a paradigm context for the second idea is this one: 'He is certain that it is raining'—where, of course, the term 'he' purports to refer as clearly as one might like. In the latter context, which we may call the *personal* context, we express the personal idea of certainty. This last may be allowed, I think, even though in ordinary conversations we may speak of dogs as being certain; presumably, we treat dogs there the way we typically treat persons.

Though there are these two important sorts of context, I think that 'certain' must mean the same in both. In both cases, we must be struck by the thought that the presence of certainty amounts to the complete absence of doubt, or doubtfulness. This thought leads me to say that 'It is certain that p' means, within the bounds of nuance, 'It is not at all doubtful that p.' The idea of personal certainty may then be defined accordingly; we relate what is said in the impersonal form to the mind of the person, or subject, who is said to be certain of something. Thus, 'He is certain that p' means, within the bounds of nuance, '*In his mind*, it is not at all doubtful that p.' Where a man is certain of something, then, concerning that thing, all doubt is absent in that man's mind. With these definitions available, we may now say this: connected negative definitions of certainty suggest that, in its central, literal meaning, 'certain' is an absolute term.

But we should like firmer evidence for thinking that 'certain' is an absolute term. To be consistent, we turn to our procedure for paraphrase. I will exhibit the evidence for personal contexts and then say a word about impersonal ones. In any event, we want contrasting results for 'certain' as against some related relative terms. One term which now suggests itself for contrast is, of course, 'doubtful.' Another is, of course, 'uncertain.' And we will get the desired results with these terms. But it is, I think, more interesting to consider the term 'confident.'

In quick discussions of these matters, one might speak indifferently of a man's being confident of something and of his being certain of it. But on reflection there is a difference between confidence and certainty. Indeed, when I say that I am certain of something, I tell you that I am not confident of it but that I am *more than* that. And if I say that I am confident that so-and-so, I tell you that I am *not so much as* certain of the thing. Thus, there is an important difference between the two. At least part of this difference is, I suggest, reflected by our procedure for paraphrase.

We may begin to apply our procedure by resolving the problem of augmenting modifiers. Paradoxically, when I say that I am (really) very certain of something, I say *less* of myself, so far as certainty is concerned, than I do when I say, simply, that I am (really) certain of the thing. How may we resolve this paradox? Our paraphrase explains things as before. In the first case, what I am really saying is that I am very *nearly* certain, and so, in effect, that I am not really certain. But in the second case, I say that I really am. Further, we may notice that, in contrast, in the case of 'confident' and 'uncertain,' and 'doubtful' as well, no problem with augmenting arises in the first place. For when I say that I am very confident of something, I say more of myself, so far as confidence is concerned, than I do when I simply say that I am confident of the thing. And again our paraphrastic procedure yields us the lack of any problems here. For the augmented statement cannot be sensibly interpreted as saying that I am very nearly confident of the thing. Indeed, with any modifier weaker than 'absolutely,' our paraphrase works well with 'certain' but produces only a nonsensical interpretation with 'confident' and other contrasting terms. For example, what might it mean to say of someone that he was rather confident of something? Would this be to say that he was rather close to being confident of the thing? Surely not.

Turning to comparative constructions, our paraphrase separates things just as we should expect. For example, from 'He is more certain that p than he is that q' we get 'He is either certain that p while not certain that q, or else he is more nearly certain that p than he is that q.' But from 'He is more confident that p than he is that q' we do *not* get 'He is either confident that p while not confident that q, or else he is more nearly confident that p than he is that q.' For he may well already be confident of both things. Further comparative constructions are similarly distinguished when subjected to our paraphrase. And no matter what locutions we try, the separation is as convincing with impersonal contexts as it is with personal ones, so long as there are contexts which are comparable. Of course, 'confident' has no impersonal contexts; we cannot say 'It is confident that p,' where the 'it' has no purported reference. But where comparable contexts do exist, as with 'doubtful' and 'uncertain,' further evidence is available. Thus, we may reasonably assert that 'certain' is an absolute term while 'confident,' 'doubtful,' and 'uncertain' are relative terms.

4. The doubtful applicability of some absolute terms

If my account of absolute terms is essentially correct, then, at least in the case of some of these terms, fairly reasonable suppositions about the world make it somewhat doubtful that the terms properly apply. (In certain contexts, generally where what we are talking about divides into discrete units, the presence of an absolute term need cause no doubts. Thus, considering the absolute term 'complete,' the truth of 'His set of steins is now complete' may be allowed without hesitation, but the truth of 'His explanation is now complete' may well be doubted. It is with the latter, more interesting contexts, I think, that we shall be concerned in what follows.) For example, while we say of many surfaces of physical things that they are flat, a rather reasonable interpretation of what we do observe makes it at least somewhat doubtful that these surfaces actually *are* flat. When we look at a rather smooth block of stone through a powerful microscope, the observed surface appears to us to be rife with irregularities. And this irregular appearance seems best explained, not by being taken as an illusory optical phenomenon, but by taking it to be a finer, more revealing look of a surface which is, in fact, rife with smallish bumps and crevices. Further, we account for bumps and crevices by supposing that the stone is composed of much smaller things, molecules and so on, which are in such a combination that, while a large and sturdy stone is the upshot, no stone with a flat surface is found to obtain.

Indeed, what follows from my account of 'flat' is this: that, as a matter of logical necessity, if a surface is flat, then there never is any surface which is flatter than it is. For on our paraphrase, if the second surface is flatter than the first, then either the second surface is flat while the first is not, or else the second is more nearly flat than the first, neither surface being flat. So if there is such a second, flatter surface, then the first surface is not flat after all, contrary to our supposition. Thus there cannot be any second, flatter surface. Or in other words, if it is logically possible that there be a surface which is flatter than a given one, then that given surface is not really a flat one. Now, in the case of the observed surface of the stone, owing to the stone's irregular composition, the surface is *not* one such that it is logically impossible that there be a flatter one. (For example, we might veridically observe a surface through a microscope of the same power which did not appear to have any bumps or crevices.) Thus it is only reasonable to suppose that the surface of this stone is not really flat.

Our understanding of the stone's composition, that it is composed of molecules and so on, makes it reasonable for us to suppose as well that any similarly sized or larger surfaces will fail to be flat just as the observed surface fails to be flat. At the same time, it would be perhaps a bit rash to suppose that much smaller surfaces would fail to be flat as well. Beneath the level of our observation perhaps there are small areas of the stone's surface which are flat. If so, then perhaps there are small objects that have surfaces which are flat, like this area of the stone's surface: for instance, chipping off a small part of the stone might yield such a small object. So perhaps there are physical objects with surfaces which are flat, and perhaps it is not now reasonable for us to assume that there are no such objects. But even if this strong assumption is not now reasonable, one thing which does seem quite reasonable for us now to assume is this: we should at least suspend judgment on the matter of whether there are any physical objects with flat surfaces. That there are such objects is something it is not now reasonable for us to believe.

It is at least somewhat doubtful, then, that 'flat' ever applies to actual physical objects or to their surfaces. And the thought must strike us that if 'flat' has no such application, this must be due in part to the fact that 'flat' is an absolute term. We may then do well to be a bit doubtful about the applicability of any other given absolute term and, in particular, about the applicability of the term 'certain.' As in the case of 'flat,' our paraphrase highlights the absolute character of 'certain.' As a matter of logical necessity, if someone is certain of something, then there never is anything of which he is more certain. For on our paraphrase, if the person is more certain of any other thing, then either he is certain of the other thing while not being certain of the first, or else he is more nearly certain of the other thing than he is of the first; that is, he is certain of neither. Thus, if it is logically possible that there be something of which a person might be more certain than he now is of a given thing, then he is not really certain of that given thing.

Thus it is reasonable to suppose, I think, that hardly anyone, if anyone at all, is certain that 45 and 56 are 101. For it is reasonable to suppose that hardly anyone, if anyone at all, is so certain of that particular calculation that it is impossible for there to be anything of which he might be yet more certain. But this is not surprising; for hardly anyone feels certain that those two numbers have that sum. What, then, about something of which people commonly do feel absolutely certain—say, of the existence of automobiles?

Is it reasonable for us now actually to believe that many people are certain that there are automobiles? If it is, then it is reasonable for us to believe as well that for each of them it is not possible for there to be anything of which he might be more certain than he now is of there being automobiles. In particular, we must then believe of these people that it is impossible for any of them ever to be more certain of his own existence than all of them now are of the existence of automobiles. While these people *might* all actually be as certain of the automobiles as this, just as each of them *feels* himself to be, I think it somewhat rash for us actually to believe that they *are* all so certain. Certainty being an absolute and our understanding of people being rather rudimentary and incomplete, I think it more reasonable for us now to suspend judgment on the matter. And, since there is nothing importantly peculiar about the matter of the automobiles, the same cautious position recommends itself quite generally: so far as actual human beings go, the most reasonable course for us now is to suspend judgment as to whether any of them is certain of more than hardly anything, if anything at all.[2]

5. Does knowing require being certain?

One tradition in philosophy holds that knowing requires being certain. As a matter of logical necessity, a man knows something only if he is certain of the thing. In this tradition, certainty is not taken lightly; rather, it is equated with absolute certainty. Even that most famous contemporary defender of common sense, G. E. Moore, is willing to equate knowing something with knowing the thing with absolute certainty.[3] I am rather inclined to hold with this traditional view, and it is now my purpose to argue that this view is at least a fairly reasonable one.

To a philosopher like Moore, I would have nothing left to say in my defense of skepticism. But recently some philosophers have contended that not certainty, but only belief, is required for knowing.[4] According to these thinkers, if a man's belief

2. For an interesting discussion of impersonal certainty, which in some ways is rather in line with my own discussion while in other ways against it, one might see Michael Anthony Slote's 'Empirical Certainty and the Theory of Important Criteria,' *Inquiry*, vol. 10 (1967). Also, Slote makes helpful references to other writers in the philosophy of certainty.

3. See Moore's cited papers, especially 'Certainty,' p. 232.

4. An influential statement of this view is Roderick M. Chisholm's, to be found in the first chapter of each of his cited books. In 'Experience and Factual Knowledge,' I suggest a very similar view.

meets certain conditions not connected with his being certain, that mere belief may properly be counted as an instance or a bit of knowledge. And even more recently some philosophers have held that not even so much as belief is required for a man to know that something is so.[5] Thus, I must argue for the traditional view of knowing. But then what has led philosophers to move further and further away from the traditional strong assertion that knowing something requires being certain of the thing?

My diagnosis of the situation is this. In everyday affairs we often speak loosely, charitably, and casually; we tend to let what we say pass as being true. I want to suggest that it is by being wrongly serious about this casual talk that philosophers (myself included) have come to think it rather easy to know things to be so. In particular, they have come to think that certainty is not needed. Thus typical in the contemporary literature is this sort of exchange. An examiner asks a student when a certain battle was fought. The student fumbles about and, eventually, unconfidently says what is true: 'The Battle of Hastings was fought in 1066.' It is supposed, quite properly, that this correct answer is a result of the student's reading. The examiner, being an ordinary mortal, allows that the student knows the answer; he judges that the student knows that the Battle of Hastings was fought in 1066. Surely, it is suggested, the examiner is correct in his judgment even though this student clearly is not certain of the thing; therefore, knowing does not require being certain. But is the examiner really correct in asserting that the student knows the date of this battle? That is, do such exchanges give us good reason to think that knowing does not require certainty?

My recommendation is this. Let us try focusing on just those words most directly employed in expressing the concept whose conditions are our object of inquiry. This principle is quite generally applicable and, I think, quite easily applied. We may apply it by suitably juxtaposing certain terms, like 'really' and 'actually,' with the terms most in question (here, the term 'knows'). More strikingly, we may *emphasize* the terms in question. Thus, instead of looking at something as innocent as 'He knows that they are alive,' let us consider the more relevant 'He (really) *knows* that they are alive.'

Let us build some confidence that this principle is quite generally applicable, and that it will give us trustworthy results. Toward this end, we may focus on some thoughts about definite descriptions—that is, about expressions of the form 'the so-and-so.' About these expressions, it is a tradition to hold that they require uniqueness, or unique satisfaction, for their proper application. Thus, just as it is traditional to hold that a man knows something only if he is certain of it, so it is also traditional to hold that there is something which is the chair with seventeen legs only if there is exactly one chair with just that many legs. But, again, by being wrongly serious about our casual everyday talk, philosophers may come to deny the traditional view. They may do this by being wrongly serious, I think, about the

---

5. This view is advanced influentially by Colin Radford in 'Knowledge by Examples,' *Analysis*, 27 (October, 1966). In 'An Analysis of Factual Knowledge,' and especially in 'Our Knowledge of The Material World,' I suggest this view.

following sort of ordinary exchange. Suppose an examiner asks a student, 'Who is the father of Nelson Rockefeller, the present Governor of New York State?' The student replies, 'Nelson Rockefeller is the son of John D. Rockefeller, Jr.' No doubt, the examiner will allow that, by implication, the student got the right answer; he will judge that what the student said is true even though the examiner is correctly confident that the elder Rockefeller sired other sons. Just so, one might well argue that definite descriptions, like 'the son of X,' do not require uniqueness. But against this argument from the everyday flow of talk, let us insist that we focus on the relevant conception by employing our standard means for emphasizing the most directly relevant term. Thus, while we might feel nothing contradictory at first in saying, 'Nelson Rockefeller is the son of John D. Rockefeller, Jr., and so is Winthrop Rockefeller,' we must confess that even initially we would have quite different feelings about our saying 'Nelson Rockefeller is actually *the* son of John D. Rockefeller, Jr., and so is Winthrop Rockefeller.' With the latter, where emphasis is brought to bear, we cannot help but feel that what is asserted is inconsistent. And, with this, we feel differently about the original remark, feeling it to be essentially the same assertion and so inconsistent as well. Thus, it seems that when we focus on things properly, we may assume that definite descriptions do require uniqueness.

Let us now apply our principle to the question of knowing. Here, while we might feel nothing contradictory at first in saying 'He knows that it is raining, but he isn't certain of it,' we would feel differently about our saying 'He really *knows* that it is raining, but he isn't certain of it.' And, if anything, this feeling of contradiction is only enhanced when we further emphasize, 'He really *knows* that it is raining, but he isn't actually *certain* of it.' Thus it is plausible to suppose that what we said at first is actually inconsistent, and so that knowing does require being certain.

For my defense of skepticism, it now remains only to combine the result we have just reached with that at which we arrived in the previous section. Now, I have argued that each of two propositions deserves, if not our acceptance, at least the suspension of our judgment:

That, in the case of every human being, there is hardly anything, if anything at all, of which he is certain.
That (as a matter of necessity), in the case of every human being, the person knows something to be so only if he is certain of it.

But I think I have done more than just that. For the strength of the arguments given for this position on each of these two propositions is, I think, sufficient for warranting a similar position on propositions which are quite obvious consequences of the two of them together. One such consequential proposition is this:

That, in the case of every human being, there is hardly anything, if anything at all, which the person knows to be so.

And so this third proposition, which is just the thesis of skepticism, also deserves, if not our acceptance, at least the suspension of our judgment. If this thesis is not reasonable to accept, then neither is its negation, the thesis of 'common sense.'

6. A prospectus and a retrospective

I have argued that we know hardly anything, if anything, because we are certain of hardly anything, if anything. My offering this argument will strike many philosophers as peculiar, even many who have some sympathy with skepticism. For it is natural to think that, except for the requirement of the truth of what is known, the requirement of 'attitude,' in this case of personal certainty, is the *least* problematic requirement of knowing. Much more difficult to fulfill, one would think, would be requirements about one's justification, about one's grounds, and so on. And, quite candidly, I am inclined to agree with these thoughts. Why, then, have I chosen to defend skepticism by picking on what is just about the easiest requirement of knowledge? My thinking has been this: the requirement of being certain will, most likely, not be independent of more difficult requirements; indeed, any more difficult requirement will entail this simpler one. Thus one more difficult requirement might be that the knower be completely *justified* in being certain, which entails the requirement that the man be certain. And, in any case, for purposes of establishing some clarity, I wanted this defense to avoid the more difficult requirements because they rely on normative terms—for example, the term 'justified.' The application of normative terms presents problems which, while worked over by many philosophers, are still too difficult to handle at all adequately. By staying away from more difficult requirements, and so from normative terms, I hoped to raise doubts in a simpler, clearer context. When the time comes for a more powerful defense of skepticism, the more difficult requirements will be pressed. Then normative conditions will be examined and, for this examination, declared inapplicable. But these normative conditions will, most likely, concern one's being certain; no justification of mere belief or confidence will be the issue in the more powerful defenses. By offering my defense, I hoped to lay part of the groundwork for more powerful defenses of skepticism.

I would end with this explanation but for the fact that my present views contradict claims I made previously, and others have discussed critically these earlier claims about knowledge.[6] Before, I strove to show that knowledge was rather easy to come by, that the conditions of knowledge could be met rather easily. To connect my arguments, I offered a unified analysis:

For any sentential value of *p*, (at a time *t*) a man knows that *p* if and only if (at *t*) it is not at all accidental that the man is right about its being the case that *p*.

And, in arguing for the analysis, I tried to understand its defining condition just so liberally that it would allow men to know things rather easily. Because I did this, I

---

6. See my cited papers and these interesting discussions of them: Gilbert H. Harman, 'Unger on Knowledge,' *Journal of Philosophy*, 64 (1967), 353–9; Ruth Anna Putnam, 'On Empirical Knowledge,' *Boston Studies in the Philosophy of Science*, IV, 392–410; Arthur C. Danto, *Analytical Philosophy of Knowledge* (Cambridge, 1968), pp. 130 ff. and 144 ff.; Keith Lehrer and Thomas Paxson, Jr., 'Knowledge: Undefeated Justified True Belief,' *Journal of Philosophy*, 66 (1969), 225–37 [Ch. 5 in this volume]; J. L. Mackie, 'The Possibility of Innate Knowledge,' *Proceedings of the Aristotelian Society* (1970), pp. 245–57.

used the analysis to argue against skepticism—that is, against the thesis which I have just defended.

Given my present views, while I must find the criticisms of my earlier claims more interesting than convincing, I must find my analysis to be more accurate than I was in my too liberal application of it. For, however bad the analysis might be in various respects, it does assert that knowledge is an absolute. In terms of my currently favored distinctions, 'accidental' is quite clearly a relative term, as are other terms which I might have selected in its stead: 'coincidental,' 'matter of luck,' 'lucky,' and so on. Operating on these terms with expressions such as 'not at all' and 'not in the least degree' will yield us absolute expressions, the equivalent of absolute terms. Thus, the condition that I offered is not at all likely to be one that is easily met. My main error, then, was not that of giving too vague or liberal a defining condition, but rather that of too liberally interpreting a condition which is in fact strict.

But I am quite uncertain that my analysis is correct in any case, and even that one can analyze knowledge. Still, so far as analyzing knowledge goes, the main plea of this paper must be this: whatever analysis of knowledge is adequate, if any such there be, it must allow that the thesis of skepticism be at least fairly plausible. For this plea only follows from my broader one: that philosophers take skepticism seriously and not casually suppose, as I have often done, that this unpopular thesis simply must be false.[7]

7. Ancestors of the present paper were discussed in philosophy colloquia at the following schools: Brooklyn College of The City University of New York, The University of California at Berkeley, Columbia University, The University of Illinois at Chicago Circle, The Rockefeller University, Stanford University, and The University of Wisconsin at Madison. I am thankful to those who participated in the discussion. I would also like to thank each of these many people for help in getting to the present defense: Peter M. Brown, Richard Cartwright, Fred Dretske, Hartry Field, Bruce Freed, H. P. Grice, Robert Hambourger, Saul A. Kripke, Stephen Schiffer, Michael A. Slote, Sydney S. Shoemaker, Dennis W. Stampe, Julius Weinberg, and Margaret Wilson, *all* of whom remain at least somewhat skeptical. Finally, I would like to thank the Graduate School of The University of Wisconsin at Madison for financial assistance during the preparation of this defense.

Relative Alternatives

Chapter 24

Other minds

J. L. Austin

WHEN we make an assertion such as 'There is a goldfinch in the garden' or 'He is angry', there is a sense in which we imply that we are sure of it or know it ('But I took it you *knew*', said reproachfully), though what we imply, in a similar sense and more strictly, is only that we *believe* it. On making such an assertion, therefore, we are directly exposed to the questions (1) 'Do you *know* there is?' 'Do you *know* he is?' and (2) 'How do you know?' If in answer to the first question we reply 'Yes', we may then be asked the second question, and even the first question alone is commonly taken as an invitation to state not merely *whether* but also *how* we know. But on the other hand, we may well reply 'No' in answer to the first question: we may say 'No, but I think there is', 'No, but I believe he is'. For the implication that I know or am sure is not strict: we are not all (terribly or sufficiently) strictly brought up. If we do this, then we are exposed to the question, which might also have been put to us without preliminaries, 'Why do you believe that?' (or 'What makes you think so?', 'What induces you to suppose so?', etc.).

There is a singular difference between the two forms of challenge: '*How* do you know?' and '*Why* do you believe?' We seem never to ask '*Why* do you know?' or '*How* do you believe?' And in this, as well as in other respects to be noticed later, not merely such other words as 'suppose' 'assume', etc., but also the expressions 'be sure' and 'be certain', follow the example of 'believe', not that of 'know'.

Either question, 'How do you know?' or 'Why do you believe?', may well be asked only out of respectful curiosity, from a genuine desire to learn. But again, they may both be asked as *pointed* questions, and, when they are so, a further difference comes out. 'How do you know?' suggests that perhaps you *don't* know it at all, whereas 'Why do you believe?' suggests that perhaps you *oughtn't* to believe it. There is no suggestion[1] that you *ought* not to know or that you don't believe it. If

J. L. Austin, 'Other Minds' in *Proceedings of the Aristotelian Society* Suppl. Vol. 20 (1946), pp. 148–87 reprinted by kind permission of the author.

the answer to 'How do you know?' or to 'Why do you believe?' is considered unsatisfactory by the challenger, he proceeds rather differently in the two cases. His next riposte will be, on the one hand, something such as 'Then you *don't* know any such thing', or 'But that doesn't prove it: in that case you don't really know it at all', and on the other hand, something such as 'That's very poor evidence to go on: you oughtn't to believe it on the strength of that alone'.[2]

The 'existence' of your alleged belief is not challenged, but the 'existence' of your alleged knowledge *is* challenged. If we like to say that 'I believe', and likewise 'I am sure' and 'I am certain', are descriptions of subjective mental or cognitive states or attitudes, or what not, then 'I know' is not that, or at least not merely that: it functions differently in talking.

'But of course', it will be said, ' "I know" is obviously more than that, more than a description of my own state. If I *know*, I *can't be wrong.* You can always show I don't know by showing I am wrong, or may be wrong, or that I didn't know by showing that I might have been wrong. *That's* the way in which knowing differs even from being as certain as can be.' This must be considered in due course, but first we should consider the types of answer that may be given in answer to the question 'How do you know?'

Suppose I have said 'There's a bittern at the bottom of the garden', and you ask 'How do you know?' my reply may take very different forms:

(*a*) I was brought up in the fens
(*b*) I heard it
(*c*) The keeper reported it
(*d*) By its booming
(*e*) From the booming noise
(*f*) Because it is booming.

We may say, roughly, that the first three are answers to the questions 'How do you come to know?', 'How are you in a position to know?', or 'How do *you* know?' understood in different ways: while the other three are answers to 'How can you tell?' understood in different ways. That is, I may take you to have been asking:

(1)   How do I come to be in a position to know about bitterns?
(2)   How do I come to be in a position to say there's a bittern here and now?
(3)   How do (can) I tell bitterns?
(4)   How do (can) I tell the thing here and now as a bittern?

The implication is that in order to know this is a bittern, I must have:

(1)   been trained in an environment where I could become familiar with bitterns
(2)   had a certain opportunity in the current case
(3)   learned to recognize or tell bitterns
(4)   succeeded in recognizing or telling this as a bittern.

1. But in special senses and cases, there is—for example, if someone has announced some top secret information, we can ask, 'How do *you* know?', nastily.
2. An interesting variant in the case of knowing would be 'You *oughtn't to say* (you've no business to say) you know it at all'. But of course this is only superficially similar to 'You oughtn't to believe it': you ought *to say* you believe it, if you do believe it, however poor the evidence.

(1) and (2) mean that my experiences must have been of certain kinds, that I must have had certain opportunities: (3) and (4) mean that I must have exerted a certain kind and amount of acumen.[3]

The questions raised in (1) and (3) concern our *past* experiences, our opportunities and our activities in learning to discriminate or discern, and, bound up with both, the correctness or otherwise of the linguistic usages we have acquired. Upon these earlier experiences depends how *well* we know things, just as, in different but cognate cases of 'knowing', it is upon earlier experience that it depends how *thoroughly* or how *intimately* we know: we know a person by sight or intimately, a town inside out, a proof backwards, a job in every detail, a poem word for word, a Frenchman when we see one. 'He doesn't know what love (real hunger) is' means he hasn't had enough experience to be able to recognize it and to distinguish it from other things slightly like it. According to how well I know an item, and according to the kind of item it is, I can recognize it, describe it, reproduce it, draw it, recite it, apply it, and so forth. Statements like 'I know *very well* he isn't angry' or 'You know *very well* that isn't calico', though of course about the current case, ascribe the excellence of the knowledge to past experience, as does the general expression 'You are old enough to know better'.[4]

By contrast, the questions raised in (2) and (4) concern the circumstances of the current case. Here we can ask 'How *definitely* do you know?' You may know it for certain, quite positively, officially, on his own authority, from unimpeachable sources, only indirectly, and so forth.

Some of the answers to the question 'How do you know' are, oddly enough, described as 'reasons for knowing' or 'reasons to know', or even sometimes as 'reasons why I know', despite the fact that we do not ask 'Why do you know?' But now surely, according to the Dictionary, 'reasons' should be given in answer to the question 'Why?' just as we do in fact give reasons for believing in answer to the question 'Why do you believe?' However there is a distinction to be drawn here. 'How do you know that IG Farben worked for war?' 'I have every reason to know: I served on the investigating commission': here, giving my reasons for knowing is stating how I come to be in a position to know. In the same way we use the expressions 'I know *because* I saw him do it' or 'I know *because* I looked it up only ten minutes ago': these are similar to 'So it is: it *is* plutonium. How did you know?' 'I did quite a bit of physics at school before I took up philology', or to 'I ought to know: I was standing only a couple of yards away'. Reasons for *believing* on the other hand are normally quite a different affair (a recital of symptoms, arguments in support, and so forth), though there are cases where we do give as reasons for

---

3. 'I know, I *know*, I've seen it a hundred times, don't keep on telling me' complains of a super-abundance of opportunity: 'knowing a hawk from a handsaw' lays down a minimum of acumen in recognition or classification. 'As well as I know my own name' is said to typify something I *must* have experienced and *must* have learned to discriminate.

4. The adverbs that can be inserted in 'How ... do you know?' are few in number and fall into still fewer classes. There is practically no overlap with those that can be inserted in 'How ... do you believe?' (firmly, sincerely, genuinely, etc.).

believing our having been in a position in which we could get good evidence: 'Why do you believe he was lying?' 'I was watching him very closely.'

Among the cases where we give our reasons for knowing things, a special and important class is formed by those where we cite authorities. If asked 'How do you know the election is today?', I am apt to reply 'I read it in *The Times*', and if asked 'How do you know the Persians were defeated at Marathon?' I am apt to reply 'Herodotus expressly states that they were'. In these cases 'know' is correctly used: we know 'at second hand' when we can cite an authority who was in a position to know (possibly himself also only at second hand).[5] The statement of an authority makes me aware of something, enables me to know something, which I shouldn't otherwise have known. It is a source of knowledge. In many cases; we contrast such reasons for knowing with other reasons for believing the very same thing: 'Even if we didn't know it, even if he hadn't confessed, the evidence against him would be enough to hang him'.

It is evident, of course, that this sort of 'knowledge' is 'liable to be wrong', owing to the unreliability of human testimony (bias, mistake, lying, exaggeration, etc.). Nevertheless, the occurrence of a piece of human testimony radically alters the situation. We say 'We shall never know what Caesar's feelings were on the field of the battle of Philippi', because he did not pen an account of them: *if* he *had*, then to say 'We shall never know' won't do in the same way, even though we may still perhaps find reason to say 'It doesn't read very plausibly: we shall never really know the *truth*' and so on. Naturally, we are judicious: we don't say we know (at second hand) if there is any special reason to doubt the testimony: but there has to be *some* reason. It is fundamental in talking (as in other matters) that we are entitled to trust others, except in so far as there is some concrete reason to distrust them. Believing persons, accepting testimony, is the, or one main, point of talking. We don't play (competitive) games except in the faith that our opponent is trying to win: if he isn't, it isn't a game, but something different. So we don't talk with people (descriptively) except in the faith that they are trying to convey. information.[6]

It is now time to turn to the question 'How can you tell?', i.e. to senses (2) and (4) of the question 'How do you know?' If you have asked 'How do you know it's a goldfinch?' I may reply 'From its behaviour', 'By its markings', or, in more detail, 'By its red head', 'From its eating thistles'. That is, I indicate, or to some extent set out with some degree of precision, those features of the situation which enable me to recognize it as one to be described in the way I did describe it. Thereupon you may still object in several ways to my saying it's a goldfinch, without in the least 'disputing my facts', which is a further stage to be dealt with later. You may object:

5. Knowing at second hand, or on authority, is not the same as 'knowing indirectly', whatever precisely that difficult and perhaps artificial expression may mean. If a murderer 'confesses', then, whatever our opinion of the worth of the 'confession', we cannot say that 'we (only) know indirectly that he did it', nor can we so speak when a witness, reliable or unreliable, has stated that he saw the man do it. Consequently, it is not correct, either, to say that the murderer himself knows 'directly' that he did it whatever precisely 'knowing directly' may mean.

6. Reliance on the authority of others is fundamental, too, in various special matters, for example, for corroboration and for the correctness of our own use of words, which we learn from others.

(1)   But goldfinches *don't* have red heads

(1*a*) But that's not a *goldfinch*. From your own description I can recognize it as a gold*crest*

(2)   But that's not enough: plenty of other birds have red heads, What you say doesn't prove it. For all you know, it may be a woodpecker.

Objections (1) and (1*a*) claim that, in one way or another, I am evidently unable to recognize goldfinches. It may be (1*a*)—that I have not learned the right (customary, popular, official) name to apply to the creature ('Who taught you to use the word "goldfinch" ?'):[7] or it may be that my powers of discernment, and consequently of classification, have never been brought sharply to bear in these matters, so that I remain confused as to how to tell the various species of small British bird. Or, of course, it may be a bit of both. In making this sort of accusation, you would perhaps tend not so much to use the expression 'You don't know' or 'You oughtn't to say you know' as, rather, 'But that *isn't* a goldfinch (*goldfinch*)', or 'Then you're wrong to call it a goldfinch'. But still, if asked, you would of course deny the statement that I do know it is a goldfinch.

It is in the case of objection (2) that you would be more inclined to say right out 'Then you don't know'. Because it doesn't prove it, it's not enough to prove it. Several important points come out here:

(*a*) If you say 'That's not enough', then you must have in mind some more or less definite lack. 'To be a goldfinch, besides having a red head it must also have the characteristic eye-markings': or 'How do you know it isn't a woodpecker? Wood-peckers have red heads too'. If there is no definite lack, which you are at least prepared to specify on being pressed, then it's silly (outrageous) just to go on saying 'That's not enough'.

(*b*) Enough is enough: it doesn't mean everything. Enough means enough to show that (within reason, and for present intents and purposes) it 'can't' be any-thing else, there is no room for an alternative, competing, description of it. It does *not* mean, for example, enough to show it isn't a *stuffed* goldfinch.

(*c*) '*From* its red head', given as an answer to 'How do you know?' requires careful consideration: in particular it differs very materially from '*Because* it has a red head', which is also sometimes given as an answer to 'How do you know?', and is commonly given as an answer to 'Why do you believe?' It is much more akin to such obviously 'vague' replies as 'From its markings' or 'From its behaviour' than at first appears. Our claim, in saying we know (i.e. that we can tell) is to *recognize*: and recognizing, at least in this sort of case, consists in seeing, or otherwise sensing, a feature or features which we are sure are similar to something noted (and usually named) before, on some earlier occasion in our experience. But, this that we see, or

---

7. Misnaming is not a trivial or laughing matter: If I misname I shall mislead others, and I shall also misunderstand information given by others to me. 'Of course I knew all about his condition perfectly, but I never realized that was *diabetes*: I thought it was cancer, and all the books agree that's incurable: if I'd only known it was diabetes, I should have thought of insulin at once'. Knowing *what a thing is* is, to an important extent, knowing what the name for it, and the right name for it, is.

otherwise sense, is not necessarily *describable in words*, still less describable in detail, and in non-committal words, and by anybody you please. Nearly everybody can recognize a surly look or the smell of tar, but few can describe them non-committally, i.e. otherwise than as 'surly' or 'of tar': many can recognize, and 'with certainty', ports of different vintages, models by different fashion houses, shades of green, motor-car makes from behind, and so forth, without being able to say '*how they recognize them*', i.e. without being able to 'be more specific about it'—they can only say they can tell 'by the taste', 'from the cut', and so on. So, when I say I can tell the bird 'from its red head', or that I know a friend 'by his nose', I imply that there is something *peculiar* about the red head or the nose, something peculiar to gold-finches or to him, by which you can (always) tell them or him. In view of the fewness and crudeness of the classificatory words in any language compared with the infinite number of features which are recognized, or which could be picked out and recognized, in our experience, it is small wonder that we often and often fall back on the phrases beginning with 'from' and 'by', and that we are not able to *say*, further and precisely, *how* we can tell. Often we know things quite well, while scarcely able at all to say 'from' what we know them, let alone what there is so very special about them. Any answer beginning 'From' or 'By' has, intentionally, this saving 'vagueness'. But on the contary, an answer beginning 'Because' is dangerously definite. When I say I know it's a goldfinch 'Because it has a red head', that implies that all I have noted, or needed to note, about it is that its head is red (nothing special or peculiar about the shade, shape, etc. of the patch): so that I imply that there is no other small British bird that has any sort of red head except the goldfinch.

(*d*) Whenever I say I know, I am always liable to be taken to claim that, in a certain sense appropriate to the kind of statement (and to present intents and purposes), I am able to *prove* it. In the present, very common, type of case, 'proving' seems to mean stating what are the features of the current case which are enough to constitute it one which is correctly describable in the way we have described it, and not in any other way relevantly variant. Generally speaking, cases where I can 'prove' are cases where we use the 'because' formula: cases where we 'know but can't prove' are cases where we take refuge in the 'from' or 'by' formula.

I believe that the points so far raised are those most genuinely and normally raised by the question 'How do you know?' But there are other, further, questions sometimes raised under the same rubric, and especially by philosophers, which may be thought more important. These are the worries about 'reality' and about being 'sure and certain'.

Up to now, in challenging me with the question 'How do you know?', you are not taken to have *queried my credentials as stated*, though you have asked what they were: nor have you *disputed my facts* (the facts on which I am relying to prove it is a goldfinch), though you have asked me to detail them. It is this further sort of challenge that may now be made, a challenge as to the *reliability* of our alleged 'credentials' and our alleged 'facts'. You may ask:

(1) But do you know it's a real goldfinch? How do you know you're not dream-ing? Or after all, mightn't it be a stuffed one? And is the head really red? Couldn't it have been dyed, or isn't there perhaps an odd light reflected on it?

(2) But are you certain it's the *right* red for a goldfinch? Are you quite sure it isn't too orange? Isn't it perhaps rather too strident a note for a bittern?

These two sorts of worry are distinct, though very probably they can be combined or confused, or may run into one another: e.g. 'Are you sure it's really red?' may mean 'Are you sure it isn't orange?' or again 'Are you sure it isn't just the peculiar light?'

If you ask me, 'How do you know it's a real stick?' 'How do you know it's really bent?' ('Are you sure he's really angry?'), then you are querying my credentials or my facts (it's often uncertain which) in a certain special way. In various *special, recognized* ways, depending essentially upon the nature of the matter which I have announced myself to know, either my current experiencing or the item currently under consideration (or uncertain which) may be abnormal, *phoney*. Either I myself may be dreaming, or in delirium, or under the influence of mescal, etc.: or else the item may be stuffed, painted, dummy, artificial, trick, freak, toy, assumed, feigned, etc.: or else again there's an uncertainty (it's left open) whether *I* am to blame or *it* is—mirages, mirror images, odd lighting effects, etc.

These doubts are all to be allayed by means of recognized procedures (more or less roughly recognized, of course), appropriate to the particular type of case. There are recognized ways of distinguishing between dreaming and waking (how otherwise should we know how to use and to contrast the words?), and of deciding whether a thing is stuffed or live, and so forth. The doubt or question 'But is it a *real* one?' has always (*must* have) a special basis, there must be some 'reason for suggesting' that it isn't real, in the sense of some specific way, or limited number of specific ways, in which it is suggested that this experience or item may be phoney. Sometimes (usually) the context makes it clear what the suggestion is: the goldfinch might be stuffed but there's no suggestion that it's a mirage, the oasis might be a mirage but there's no suggestion it might be stuffed. If the context doesn't make it clear, then I am entitled to ask 'How do you mean? Do you mean it may be stuffed or what? *What are you suggesting?*' The wile of the metaphysician consists in asking 'Is it a real table?' (a kind of object which has no obvious way of being phoney) and not specifying or limiting what may be wrong with it, so that I feel at a loss 'how to prove' it *is* a real one.[8] It is the use of the word 'real' in this manner that leads us on to the supposition that 'real' has a single meaning ('the real world' 'material objects'), and that a highly profound and puzzling one. Instead, we should insist always on specifying with what 'real' is being contrasted—'not what' I shall have to show it is, in order to show it is 'real': and then usually we shall find some specific, less fatal, word, appropriate to the particular case, to substitute for 'real'.

Knowing it's a 'real' goldfinch isn't in question in the ordinary case when I say I know it's a goldfinch: reasonable precautions only are taken. But when it *is* called in question, in *special* cases, then I make sure it's a real goldfinch in ways essentially similar to those in which I made sure it was a goldfinch, though corroboration by other witnesses plays a specially important part in some cases. Once again the

8. Conjurers, too, trade on this. 'Will some gentleman kindly satisfy himself that this is a perfectly ordinary hat?' This leaves us baffled and uneasy: sheepishly we agree that it seems all right, while conscious that we have not the least idea what to guard against.

precautions cannot be more than reasonable, relative to current intents and purposes. And once again, in the special cases just as in the ordinary cases, two further conditions hold good:

(*a*) I don't by any means *always* know whether it's one or not. It may fly away before I have a chance of testing it, or of inspecting it thoroughly enough. This is simple enough: yet some are prone to argue that because I *sometimes* don't know or can't discover, I *never* can.

(*b*) 'Being sure it's real' is no more proof against miracles or outrages of nature than anything else is or, *sub specie humanitatis*, can be. If we have made sure it's a goldfinch, and a real goldfinch, and then in the future it does something outrageous (explodes, quotes Mrs. Woolf, or what not), we don't say we were wrong to say it was a goldfinch, *we don't know what to say*. Words literally fail us: 'What would you have said?' 'What are we to say now?' 'What would *you* say?' When I have made sure it's a real goldfinch (not stuffed, corroborated by the disinterested, etc.) then I am *not* 'predicting' in saying it's a real goldfinch, and in a very good sense I can't be proved wrong whatever happens. It seems a serious mistake to suppose that language (or most language, language about real things) is 'predictive' in such a way that the future can always prove it wrong. What the future *can* always do, is to make us *revise our ideas* about goldfinches or real goldfinches or anything else.

Perhaps the normal procedure of language could be schematized as follows. First, it is arranged that, on experiencing a complex of features C, then we are to say 'This is C' or 'This is a C'. Then subsequently, the occurrence either of the whole of C or of a significant and characteristic part of it is, on one or many occasions, accompanied or followed in definite circumstances by another special and distinctive feature or complex of features, which makes it seem desirable to revise our ideas: so that we draw a distinction between 'This looks like a C, but in fact is only a dummy, etc.' and 'This is a real C (live, genuine, etc.)'. *Henceforward*, we can only ascertain that it's a real C by ascertaining that the special feature or complex of features is present in the appropriate circumstances. The old expression 'This is a C' will tend as heretofore to fail to draw any distinction between 'real, live, etc.' and 'dummy, stuffed, etc.' If the special distinctive feature is one which does not have to manifest itself in *any* definite circumstances (on application of some specific test, after some limited lapse of time, etc.) then it is not a suitable feature on which to base a distinction between 'real' and 'dummy, imaginary, etc.' All we can then do is to say 'Some Cs are and some aren't, some do and some don't: and it may be very interesting or important whether they are or aren't, whether they do or don't, but they're all Cs, real Cs, just the same'.[9] Now if the special feature is one which must appear in (more or less) definite circumstances, then 'This is a real C' is not necessarily predictive: we can, in favourable cases, make sure of it.[10]

9. The awkwardness about some snarks being boojums.
10. Sometimes, on the basis of the new special feature, we distinguish, not between 'Cs' and 'real Cs', but rather between Cs and Ds. There is a reason for choosing the one procedure rather than the other: all cases where we use the 'real' formula exhibit (complicated and serpentine) likenesses, as do all cases where we use 'proper', a word which behaves in many ways like 'real', and is no less nor more profound.

Chapter 25

Knowledge and scepticism

Robert Nozick

You think you are seeing these words, but could you not be hallucinating or dreaming or having your brain stimulated to give you the experience of seeing these marks on paper although no such thing is before you? More extremely, could you not be floating in a tank while super-psychologists stimulate your brain electrochemically to produce exactly the same experiences as you are now having, or even to produce the whole sequence of experiences you have had in your lifetime thus far? If one of these other things was happening, your experience would be exactly the same as it now is. So how can you know none of them is happening? Yet if you do not know these possibilities don't hold, how can you know you are reading this book now? If you do not know you haven't always been floating in the tank at the mercy of the psychologists, how can you know anything—what your name is, who your parents were, where you come from?

The sceptic argues that we do not know what we think we do. Even when he leaves us unconverted, he leaves us confused. Granting that we do know, how *can* we? Given these other possibilities he poses, how is knowledge possible? [...] In answering this question, we do not seek to convince the sceptic, but rather to formulate hypotheses about knowledge and our connection to facts that show how knowledge can exist even given the sceptic's possibilities. These hypotheses must reconcile our belief that we know things with our belief that the sceptical possibilities are logical possibilities.

The sceptical possibilities, and the threats they pose to our knowledge, depend upon our knowing things (if we do) mediately, through or by way of something else. Our thinking or believing that some fact p holds is connected somehow to the fact that p, but is not itself identical with that fact. Intermediate links establish the connection. This leaves room for the possibility of these intermediate stages holding and producing our belief that p without the fact that p being at the other end. The intermediate stages arise in a completely different manner, one not involving the fact that p although giving rise to the appearance that p holds true. [...]

Are the sceptic's possibilities indeed logically possible? Imagine reading a science fiction story in which someone is raised from birth floating in a tank with psychologists stimulating his brain. The story could go on to tell of the person's reactions when he is brought out of the tank, of how the psychologists convince him of what had been happening to him, or how they fail to do so. This story is coherent, there is

Robert Nozick, 'Knowledge and Scepticism' in *Philosophical Explanations* (Cambridge, MA., Harvard University Press, 1981), pp. 167–9, 172–9, 197–211, 679–90 reprinted by permission of Robert Nozick.

nothing self-contradictory or otherwise impossible about it. Nor is there anything incoherent in imagining that you are now in this situation, at a time before being taken out of the tank. To ease the transition out, to prepare the way, perhaps the psychologists will give the person in the tank thoughts of whether floating in the tank is possible, or the experience of reading a book that discusses this possibility, even one that discusses their easing his transition. (Free will presents no insuperable problem for this possibility. Perhaps the psychologists caused all your experiences of choice, including the feeling of freely choosing; or perhaps you do freely choose to act while they, cutting the effector circuit, continue the scenario from there.)

Some philosophers have attempted to demonstrate there is no such coherent possibility of this sort.[1] However, for any reasoning that purports to show this sceptical possibility cannot occur, we can imagine the psychologists of our science fiction story feeding *it* to their tank-subject, along with the (inaccurate) feeling that the reasoning is cogent. So how much trust can be placed in the apparent cogency of an argument to show the sceptical possibility isn't coherent?

The sceptic's possibility is a logically coherent one, in tension with the existence of (almost all) knowledge; so we seek a hypothesis to explain how, even given the sceptic's possibilities, knowledge is possible. We may worry that such explanatory hypotheses are ad hoc, but this worry will lessen if they yield other facts as well, fit in with other things we believe, and so forth. Indeed, the theory of knowledge that follows was not developed in order to explain how knowledge is possible. Rather, the motivation was external to epistemology; only after the account of knowledge was developed for another purpose did I notice its consequences for scepticism, for understanding how knowledge is possible. So whatever other defects the explanation might have, it can hardly be called ad hoc.

[...]

1. Most recently, my colleague Hilary Putnam has used considerations from the theory of reference in an attempt toward formulating a transcendental argument that would undercut the skeptical possibility: if we can successfully describe the possibility, using constituent terms that refer, then it cannot hold true. (See his 'Realism and Reason', *Proceedings and Addresses of the American Philosophical Association*, Vol. 50, No. 6, 1977, pp. 483–98; he extends the argument in [his *Reason, Truth and History* (Cambridge, 1981), Ch. 1; Ch. 27 in this volume].) Recall another earlier attempt. The 'paradigm case argument' held that since some situations were the very type of situation wherein was taught the application of a term, 'free will' for example, the term must refer to that type of situation. This argument is now rightly discredited; one would expect Putnam's more sophisticated use of a theory of reference to fall before correspondingly more sophisticated versions of the earlier objections.

First, at best, Putnam's argument shows the terms have something they refer to, not that we are in any sort of direct contact with the referents. For all the argument shows, we could be floating in the tank using terms whose reference is parasitic on the terms of the psychologists, who are not. Second, we cannot tell from Putnam's argument which terms will have a referent that fits them; for the meaning of some can be built up out of other terms (for subatomic particles, say) which, while they do refer, are not explicitly mentioned in the sceptic's science fiction story. Third, though the 'tank' is a salient device to pose the problem, the story need not assume you are materially ensconced; then the mode of influence exerted by the other consciousnesses will not be mediated materially.

1. Conditions for Knowledge

Our task is to formulate further conditions to go alongside

(1) p is true
(2) S believes that p.

We would like each condition to be necessary for knowledge, so any case that fails to satisfy it will not be an instance of knowledge. Furthermore, we would like the conditions to be jointly sufficient for knowledge, so any case that satisfies all of them will be an instance of knowledge. We first shall formulate conditions that seem to handle ordinary cases correctly, classifying as knowledge cases which are knowledge, and as non-knowledge cases which are not; then we shall check to see how these conditions handle some difficult cases discussed in the literature. [. . .]

One plausible suggestion is causal, something like: the fact that p (partially) causes S to believe that p, that is, (2) because (1). But this provides an inhospitable environment for mathematical and ethical knowledge; also there are well-known difficulties in specifying the type of causal connection. If someone floating in a tank oblivious to everything around him is given (by direct electrical and chemical stimulation of the brain) the belief that he is floating in a tank with his brain being stimulated, then even though that fact is part of the cause of his belief, still he does not know that it is true.

Let us consider a different third condition:

(3) If p were not true, S would not believe that p.

Throughout this work, let us write the subjunctive 'if-then' by an arrow, and the negation of a sentence by prefacing 'not-' to it. The above condition thus is rewritten as:

(3) not-$p \rightarrow$ not-(S believes that p).

This subjunctive condition is not unrelated to the causal condition. Often when the fact that p (partially) causes someone to believe that p, the fact also will be causally necessary for his having the belief—without the cause, the effect would not occur. In that case, the subjunctive condition (3) also will be satisfied. Yet this condition is not equivalent to the causal condition. For the causal condition will be satisfied in cases of causal overdetermination, where either two sufficient causes of the effect actually operate, or a back-up cause (of the same effect) would operate if the first one didn't; whereas the subjunctive condition need not hold for these cases.[2] When the two conditions do agree, causality indicates knowledge because it acts in a manner that makes the subjunctive (3) true.

The subjunctive condition (3) serves to exclude cases of the sort first described by Edmund Gettier, such as the following. Two other people are in my office and I am justified on the basis of much evidence in believing the first owns a Ford car; though he (now) does not, the second person (a stranger to me) owns one. I believe

2. [. . .] I should note here that I assume bivalence throughout this chapter, and consider only statements that are true if and only if their negations are false.

truly and justifiably that someone (or other) in my office owns a Ford car, but I do not know someone does. Concluded Gettier, knowledge is not simply justified true belief.

The following subjunctive, which specifies condition (3) for this Gettier case, is not satisfied: if no one in my office owned a Ford car, I wouldn't believe that someone did. The situation that would obtain if no one in my office owned a Ford is one where the stranger does not (or where he is not in the office); and in that situation I still would believe, as before, that someone in my office does own a Ford, namely, the first person. So the subjunctive condition (3) excludes this Gettier case as a case of knowledge.

The subjunctive condition is powerful and intuitive, not so easy to satisfy, yet not so powerful as to rule out everything as an instance of knowledge. A subjunctive conditional 'if p were true, q would be true', $p \rightarrow q$, does not say that p entails q or that it is logically impossible that p yet not-q. It says that in the situation that would obtain if p were true, q also would be true. This point is brought out especially clearly in recent 'possible-worlds' accounts of subjunctives: the subjunctive is true when (roughly) in all those worlds in which p holds true that are closest to the actual world, q also is true. (Examine those worlds in which p holds true closest to the actual world, and see if q holds true in all these.) Whether or not q is true in p worlds that are still farther away from the actual world is irrelevant to the truth of the subjunctive. I do not mean to endorse any particular possible-worlds account of subjunctives, nor am I committed to this type of account.[3] I sometimes shall use it, though, when it illustrates points in an especially clear way. [. . .]

The subjunctive condition (3) also handles nicely cases that cause difficulties for the view that you know that p when you can rule out the relevant alternatives to p in the context. For, as Gail Stine writes, 'what makes an alternative relevant in one context and not another? . . . if on the basis of visual appearances obtained under optimum conditions while driving through the countryside Henry identifies an object as a barn, normally we say that Henry knows that it is a barn. Let us suppose, however, that unknown to Henry, the region is full of expertly made papier-mâché facsimiles of barns. In that case, we would not say that Henry knows that the object is a barn, unless he has evidence against it being a papier-mâché facsimile, which is now a relevant alternative. So much is clear, but what if no such facsimiles exist in Henry's surroundings, although they once did? Are either of these circumstances sufficient to make the hypothesis (that it's a papier-mâché object) relevant? Probably not; but the situation is not so clear.'[4] Let p be the statement that the object in the field is a (real) barn, and q the one that the object in the field is a papier-mâché barn. When papier-mâché barns are scattered through the area, if p were false, q would he true or might be. Since in this case (we are supposing) the person still would believe p, the subjunctive

3. See Robert Stalnaker, 'A Theory of Conditionals', in N. Rescher, ed., *Studies in Logical Theory* (Oxford 1968); David Lewis, *Counterfactuals* (Cambridge 1973); and Jonathan Bennett's critical review of Lewis, 'Counterfactuals and Possible Worlds', *Canadian Journal of Philosophy*, 4 (1974), pp. 381–402. Our purposes require, for the most part, no more than an intuitive understanding of subjunctives. [. . .]

4. G. C. Stine, 'Scepticism, Relevant Alternatives and Deductive Closure', *Philosophical Studies*, 29 (1976), p. 252, who attributes the example to Carl Ginet.

(3) not-$p \rightarrow$ not-(S believes that p)

is not satisfied, and so he doesn't know that p. However, when papier-mâché barns are or were scattered around another country, even if p were false q wouldn't be true, and so (for all we have been told) the person may well know that p. A hypothesis q contrary to p clearly is relevant when if p weren't true, q would be true; when not-$p \rightarrow q$. It clearly is irrelevant when if p weren't true, q also would not be true; when not-$p \rightarrow$ not-q. The remaining possibility is that neither of these opposed subjunctives holds; q might (or might not) be true if p weren't true. In this case, q also will be relevant, according to an account of knowledge incorporating condition (3) and treating subjunctives along the lines sketched above. Thus, condition (3) handles cases that befuddle the 'relevant alternatives' account; though that account can adopt the above subjunctive criterion for when an alternative is relevant, it then becomes merely an alternate and longer way of stating condition (3).[5]

Despite the power and intuitive force of the condition that if p weren't true the person would not believe it, this condition does not (in conjunction with the first two conditions) rule out every problem case. There remains, for example, the case of the person in the tank who is brought to believe, by direct electrical and chemical stimulation of his brain, that he is in the tank and is being brought to believe things in this way; he does not know this is true. However, the subjunctive condition is satisfied: if he weren't floating in the tank, he wouldn't believe he was.

The person in the tank does not know he is there, because his belief is not sensitive to the truth. Although it is caused by the fact that is its content, it is not sensitive to that fact. The operators of the tank could have produced any belief, including the false belief that he wasn't in the tank; if they had, he would have believed that. Perfect sensitivity would involve beliefs and facts varying together. We already have one portion of that variation, subjunctively at least: if p were false he wouldn't believe it. This sensitivity as specified by a subjunctive does not have the belief vary with the truth or falsity of p in all possible situations, merely in the ones that would or might obtain if p were false.

The subjunctive condition

(3) not-$p \rightarrow$ not-(S believes that p)

tells us only half the story about how his belief is sensitive to the truth-value of p. It tells us how his belief state is sensitive to p's falsity, but not how it is sensitive to p's truth; it tells us what his belief state would be if p were false, but not what it would be if were true.

To be sure, conditions (1) and (2) tell us that p is true and he does believe it, but it does not follow that his believing p is sensitive to p's being true. This additional sensitivity is given to us by a further subjunctive: if p were true, he would believe it.

---

5. This last remark is a bit too brisk, for that account might use a subjunctive criterion for when an alternative q to p is relevant (namely, when if p were not to hold, q would or might), and utilize some further notion of what it is to rule out relevant alternatives (for example, have evidence against them), so that it did not turn out to be equivalent to the account we offer.

(4) $p \rightarrow S$ believes that p.

Not only is p true and S believes it, but if it were true he would believe it. Compare: not only was the photon emitted and did it go to the left, but (it was then true that): if it were emitted it would go to the left. The truth of antecedent and consequent is not alone sufficient for the truth of a subjunctive; (4) says more than (1) and (2).[6] Thus, we presuppose some (or another) suitable account of subjunctives. According to the suggestion tentatively made above, (4) holds true if not only does he actually truly believe p, but in the 'close' worlds where p is true, he also believes it. He believes that p for some distance out in the p neighbourhood of the actual world; similarly, condition (3) speaks not of the whole not-p neighbourhood of the actual world, but only of the first portion of it. (If, as is likely, these explanations do not help, please use your own intuitive understanding of the subjunctives (3) and (4).)

The person in the tank does not satisfy the subjunctive condition (4). Imagine as actual a world in which he is in the tank and is stimulated to believe he is, and consider what subjunctives are true in that world. It is not true of him there that if he were in the tank he would believe it; for in the close world (or situation) to his own where he is in the tank but they don't give him the belief that he is (much less instil the belief that he isn't) he doesn't believe he is in the tank. Of the person actually in the tank and believing it, it is not true to make the further statement that if he were in the tank. [. . .] he would believe it—so he does not know he is in the tank.

The subjunctive condition (4) also handles a case presented by Gilbert Harman.[7] The dictator of a country is killed; in their first edition, newspapers print the story, but later all the country's newspapers and other media deny the story, falsely. Everyone who encounters the denial believes it (or does not know what to believe and so suspends judgement). Only one person in the country fails to hear any denial and he continues to believe the truth. He satisfies conditions (1)–(3) (and the causal condition about belief) yet we are reluctant to say he knows the truth. The reason is that if he had heard the denials, he too would have believed them, just like everyone else. His belief is not sensitively tuned to the truth, he doesn't satisfy the condition that if it were true he would believe it. Condition (4) is not satisfied.[8]

There is a pleasing symmetry about how this account of knowledge relates conditions (3) and (4), and connects them to the first two conditions. The account has the following form.

(1)

(2)

(3) not-1 $\rightarrow$ not-2

(4) 1 $\rightarrow$ 2

---

6. More accurately, since the truth of antecedent and consequent is not necessary for the truth of the subjunctive either, (4) says something different from (1) and (2).

7. Gilbert Harman, *Thought* (Princeton; 1973), ch. 9.

8. What if the situation or world where he too hears the later false denials is not so close, so easily occurring? Should we say that everything that prevents his hearing the denial easily could have not happened, and does not in some close world?

I am not inclined, however, to make too much of this symmetry, for I found also that with other conditions experimented with as a possible fourth condition there was some way to construe the resulting third and fourth conditions as symmetrical answers to some symmetrical looking questions, so that they appeared to arise in parallel fashion from similar questions about the components of true belief.

Symmetry, it seems, is a feature of a mode of presentation, not of the contents presented. A uniform transformation of symmetrical statements can leave the results non-symmetrical. But if symmetry attaches to mode of presentation, how can it possibly be a deep feature of, for instance, laws of nature that they exhibit symmetry? (One of my favourite examples of symmetry is due to Groucho Marx. On his radio programme he spoofed a commercial, and ended, 'And if you are not completely satisfied, return the unused portion of our product and we will return the unused portion of your money.') Still, to present our subject symmetrically makes the connection of knowledge to true belief especially perspicuous. It seems to me that a symmetrical formulation is a sign of our understanding, rather than a mark of truth. If we cannot understand an asymmetry as arising from an underlying symmetry through the operation of a particular factor, we will not understand why that asymmetry exists in that direction. (But do we also need to understand why the underlying asymmetrical factor holds instead of its opposite?)

A person knows that p when he not only does truly believe it, but also would truly believe it and wouldn't falsely believe it. He not only actually has a true belief, he subjunctively has one. It is true that p and he believes it; if it weren't true he wouldn't believe it, and if it were true he would believe it. To know that p is to be someone who would believe it if it were true, and who wouldn't believe it if it were false.

It will be useful to have a term for this situation when a person's belief is thus subjunctively connected to the fact. Let us say of a person who believes that p, which is true, that when (3) and (4) hold, his belief *tracks* the truth that p. To know is to have a belief that tracks the truth. Knowledge is a particular way of being connected to the world, having a specific real factual connection to the world: tracking it.

One refinement is needed in condition (4). It may be possible for someone to have contradictory beliefs, to believe p and also believe not-p. We do not mean such a person to easily satisfy (4), and in any case we want his belief-state, sensitive to the truth of p, to focus upon p. So let us rewrite our fourth condition as:

(4) $p \rightarrow S$ believes that p and not-(S believes that not-p).

As you might have expected, this account of knowledge as tracking requires some refinements and epicycles. [. . .]

2. Ways and Methods

The fourth condition says that if p were true the person would believe it. Suppose the person only happened to see a certain event or simply chanced on a book describing it. He knows it occurred. Yet if he did not happen to glance that way or encounter the book, he would not believe it, even though it occurred. As written, the fourth condition would exclude this case as one where he actually knows the event occurred. It also would exclude the following case. Suppose some person who truly believes that p would or might arrive at a belief about it in some other close situation where it holds true, in a way or by a method different from the one he (actually) used in arriving at his belief that p, and so thereby come to believe that not-p. In that (close) situation, he would believe not-p even though still p holds true. Yet, all this does not show he actually doesn't know that p, for actually he has not used this alternative method in arriving at his belief. Surely he can know that p, even though condition (4), as written, is not satisfied.

Similarly, suppose he believes that p by one method or way of arriving at belief, yet if p were false he wouldn't use this method but would use another one instead, whose application would lead him mistakenly to believe p (even though it is false). This person does not satisfy condition (3) as written; it is not true of him that if p were false he wouldn't believe it. Still, the fact that he would use another method of arriving at belief if p were false does not show he didn't know that p when he used this method. A grandmother sees her grandson is well when he comes to visit; but if he were sick or dead, others would tell her he was well to spare her upset. Yet this does not mean she doesn't know he is well (or at least ambulatory) when she sees him. Clearly, we must restate our conditions to take explicit account of the ways and methods of arriving at belief.

Let us define a technical locution, S knows, via method (or way of believing) M, that p:

(1) p is true.
(2) S believes, via method or way of coming to believe M, that p.
(3) If p weren't true and S were to use M to arrive at a belief whether (or not) p, then S wouldn't believe, via M, that p.
(4) If p were true and S were to use M to arrive at a belief whether (or not) p, then S would believe, via M, that p.

[. . .]

3. Scepticism

The sceptic about knowledge argues that we know very little or nothing of what we think we know, or at any rate that this position is no less reasonable than the belief in knowledge. The history of philosophy exhibits a number of different attempts to refute the sceptic: to prove him wrong or show that in arguing against knowledge he presupposes there is some and so refutes himself. Others attempt to show that accepting scepticism is unreasonable, since it is more likely that the sceptic's extreme conclusion is false than that all of his premises are true, or simply because reasonableness of belief just means proceeding in an anti-sceptical way. Even when these counter-arguments satisfy their inventors, they fail to satisfy others, as is shown by the persistent attempts against scepticism. [. . .] The continuing felt need to refute scepticism, and the difficulty in doing so, attests to the power of the sceptic's position, the depth of his worries.

An account of knowledge should illuminate sceptical arguments and show wherein lies their force. If the account leads us to reject these arguments, this had better not happen too easily or too glibly. To think the sceptic overlooks something obvious, to attribute to him a simple mistake or confusion or fallacy, is to refuse to acknowledge the power of his position and the grip it can have upon us. We thereby cheat ourselves of the opportunity to reap his insights and to gain self-knowledge in understanding why his arguments lure us so. Moreover, in fact, we cannot lay the spectre of scepticism to rest without first hearing what it shall unfold.

Our goal is not, however, to refute scepticism, to prove it is wrong or even to argue that it is wrong. In the introduction we have distinguished between philosophy that attempts to prove, and philosophy that attempts to explain how something is possible. Our task here is to explain how knowledge is possible, given what the sceptic says that we do accept (for example, that it is logically possible that we are dreaming or are floating in the tank). In doing this, we need not convince the sceptic, and we may introduce explanatory hypotheses that he would reject. What is important for our task of explanation and understanding is that *we* find those hypotheses acceptable or plausible, and that they show us how the existence of knowledge fits together with the logical possibilities the sceptic points to, so that these are reconciled within our own belief system. These hypotheses are to explain to ourselves how knowledge is possible, not to prove to someone else that knowledge *is* possible.[9]

4. Sceptical possibilities

The sceptic often refers to possibilities in which a person would believe something even though it was false: really, the person is cleverly deceived by others, perhaps by an evil demon, or the person is dreaming, or he is floating in a tank near Alpha Centauri with his brain being stimulated. In each case, the p he believes is false, and he believes it even though it is false.

How do these possibilities adduced by the sceptic show that someone does not know that p? Suppose that someone is you; how do these possibilities count against your knowing that p? One way might be the following. (I shall consider other ways later.) If there is a possible situation where p is false yet you believe that p, then in that situation you believe that p even though it is false. So it appears you do not satisfy condition (3) for knowledge.

(3) If p were false, S wouldn't believe that p.

For a situation has been described in which you do believe that p even though p is false. How then can it also be true that if p were false, you wouldn't believe it? If the

9. From the perspective of explanation rather than proof, the extensive philosophical discussion, deriving from Charles S. Peirce, of whether the sceptic's doubts are real is beside the point. The problem of explaining how knowledge is possible would remain the same, even if no one ever claimed to doubt that there was knowledge.

sceptic's possible situation shows that (3) is false, and if (3) is a necessary condition for knowledge, then the sceptic's possible situation shows that there isn't knowledge.

So construed, the sceptic's argument plays on condition (3); it aims to show that condition (3) is not satisfied. The sceptic may seem to be putting forth

R: Even if p were false, S still would believe p.[10]

This conditional, with the same antecedent as (3) and the contradictory consequent, is incompatible with the truth of (3). If (3) is true, then R is not. However, R is stronger than the sceptic needs in order to show (3) is false. For (3) is false when if p were false, S might believe that p. This last conditional is weaker than R, and is merely (3)'s denial:

T: not-$[$not-$p \rightarrow$ not-$(S$ believes that $p)]$.

Whereas R does not simply deny (3), it asserts an opposing subjunctive of its own. Perhaps the possibility the sceptic adduces is not enough to show that R is true, but it appears at least to establish the weaker T; since this T denies (3), the sceptic's possibility appears to show that (3) is false.[11]

However, the truth of (3) is not incompatible with the existence of a possible situation where the person believes p though it is false. The subjunctive

(3)   not-$p \rightarrow$ not-$(S$ believes $p)$

does not talk of all possible situations in which p is false (in which not-p is true). It does not say that in all possible situations where not-p holds, S doesn't believe p. To say there is no possible situation in which not-p yet S believes p, would be to say that not-p entails not-$(S$ believes $p)$, or logically implies it. But subjunctive conditionals differ from entailments; the subjunctive (3) is not a statement of entailment. So the existence of a possible situation in which p is false yet S believes p does not show that (3) is false;[12] (3) can be true even though there is a possible situation where not-p and S believes that p.

What the subjunctive (3) speaks of is the situation that would hold if p were false. Not every possible situation in which p is false is the situation that would hold if p were false. To fall into possible worlds talk, the subjunctive (3) speaks of the not-p world that is closest to the actual world, or of those not-p worlds that are closest to the actual world. And it is of this or these not-p worlds that it says (in them) S does not believe that p. What happens in yet other more distant not-p worlds is no concern of the subjunctive (3).

---

10. Subjunctives with actually false antecedents and actually true consequents have been termed by Goodman *semi-factuals*. R is the semi-factual not-$p \rightarrow$ S believes p.
11. Should one weaken condition (3), so that the account of knowledge merely denies the opposed subjunctive R? That would give us: not-(not-$p \rightarrow$ S believes p). This holds when (3) does not, in situations where if p were false, S might believe p, and also might not believe it. The extra strength of (3) is needed to exclude these as situations of knowledge.
12. Though it does show the falsity of the corresponding entailment, 'not-p entails not-(S believes that p)'.

The sceptic's possibilities (let us refer to them as SK), of the person's being deceived by a demon or dreaming or floating in a tank, count against the subjunctive

(3)   if *p* were false then *S* wouldn't believe that *p*

only if (one of) these possibilities would or might obtain if *p* were false; only if one of these possibilities is in the not-*p* neighbourhood of the actual world. Condition (3) says: if *p* were false, *S* still would not believe *p*. And this can hold even though there is some situation SK described by the sceptic in which *p* is false and *S* believes *p*. If *p* were false *S* still would not believe *p*, even though there is a situation SK in which *p* is false and *S* does believe *p*, provided that this situation SK wouldn't obtain if *p* were false. If the sceptic describes a situation SK which would not hold even if *p* were false then this situation SK doesn't show that (3) is false and so does not (in this way at least) undercut knowledge. Condition C acts to rule out sceptical hypotheses.

C: not-*p* → SK does not obtain.

Any sceptical situation SK which satisfies condition C is ruled out. For a sceptical situation SK to show that we don't know that *p*, it must fail to satisfy C which excludes it; instead it must be a situation that might obtain if *p* did not, and so satisfy C's denial:

not-(not-*p* → SK doesn't obtain).

Although the sceptic's imagined situations appear to show that (3) is false, they do not; they satisfy condition C and so are excluded.

The sceptic might go on to ask whether we know that his imagined situations SK are excluded by condition C, whether we know that if *p* were false SK would not obtain. However, typically he asks something stronger: do we know that his imagined situation SK does not actually obtain? Do we know that we are not being deceived by a demon, dreaming, or floating in a tank? And if we do not know this, how can we know that *p*? Thus we are led to the second way his imagined situations might show that we do not know that *p*.

5. Sceptical results

According to our account of knowledge, *S* knows that the sceptic's situation SK doesn't hold if and only if

(1)   SK doesn't hold
(2)   *S* believes that SK doesn't hold
(3)   If SK were to hold, *S* would not believe that SK doesn't hold
(4)   If SK were not to hold, *S* would believe it does not.

Let us focus on the third of these conditions. The sceptic has carefully chosen his situations SK so that if they held we (still) would believe they did not. We would believe we weren't dreaming, weren't being deceived, and so on, even if we were. He has chosen situations SK such that if SK were to hold, S would (still) believe that SK doesn't hold—and this is incompatible with the truth of (3).[13]

Since condition (3) is a necessary condition for knowledge, it follows that we do not know that SK doesn't hold. If it were true that an evil demon was deceiving us, if we were having a particular dream, if we were floating in a tank with our brains stimulated in a specified way, we would still believe we were not. So, we do not know we're not being deceived by an evil demon, we do not know we're not in that tank, and we do not know we're not having that dream. So says the sceptic, and so says our account. And also so we say—don't we? For how could we know we are not being deceived that way, dreaming that dream? If those things *were* happening to us, everything would seem the same to us. There is no way we can know it is not happening for there is no way we could tell if it were happening; and if it were happening we would believe exactly what we do now—in particular, we still would believe that it was not. For this reason, we feel, and correctly, that we don't know— how could we?—that it is not happening to us. It is a virtue of our account that it yields, and explains, this result.

The sceptic asserts we do not know his possibilities don't obtain, and he is right. Attempts to avoid scepticism by claiming we do know these things are bound to fail. The sceptic's possibilities make us uneasy because, as we deeply realize, we do not know they don't obtain; it is not surprising that attempts to show we do know these things leave us suspicious, strike us even as bad faith. [...] Nor has the sceptic merely pointed out something obvious and trivial. It comes as a surprise to realize that we do not know his possibilities don't obtain. It is startling, shocking. For we would have thought, before the sceptic got us to focus on it, that we did know those things, that we did know we were not being deceived by a demon, or dreaming that dream, or stimulated that way in that tank. The sceptic has pointed out that we do not know things we would have confidently said we knew. And if we don't know these things, what can we know? So much for the supposed obviousness of what the sceptic tells us.

Let us say that a situation (or world) is doxically identical for S to the actual situation when if S were in that situation, he would have exactly the beliefs (*doxa*) he actually does have. More generally, two situations are doxically identical for S if and only if he would have exactly the same beliefs in them. It might be merely a curiosity to be told there are non-actual situations doxically identical to the actual

13. If a person is to know that SK doesn't hold, then condition (3) for knowledge must be satisfied (with 'SK doesn't hold' substituted for p). Thus, we get

(3) not-(SK doesn't hold) $\rightarrow$ not-(S believes that SK doesn't hold).

Simplifying the antecedent, we have

(3) SK holds $\rightarrow$ not-(S believes that SK doesn't hold).

The sceptic has chosen a situation SK such that the following is true of it:

SK holds $\rightarrow$ S believes that SK doesn't hold.

Having the same antecedent as (3) and a contradictory consequent, this is incompatible with (3). Thus, condition (3) is not satisfied by the person's belief that SK does not hold.

one. The sceptic, however, describes worlds doxically identical to the actual world in which almost everything believed is false.[14]

Such worlds are possible because we know mediately, not directly. This leaves room for a divergence between our beliefs and the truth. It is as though we possessed only two-dimensional plane projections of three-dimensional objects. Different three-dimensional objects, oriented appropriately, have the same two-dimensional plane projection. Similarly, different situations or worlds will lead to our having the very same beliefs. What is surprising is how very different the doxically identical world can be—different enough for almost everything believed in it to be false. Whether or not the mere fact that knowledge is mediated always makes room for such a very different doxically identical world, it does so in our case, as the sceptic's possibilities show. To be shown this is non-trivial, especially when we recall that we do not know the sceptic's possibility doesn't obtain: we do not know that we are not living in a doxically identical world wherein almost everything we believe is false. [. . .]

What more could the sceptic ask for or hope to show? Even readers who sympathized with my desire not to dismiss the sceptic too quickly may feel this has gone too far, that we have not merely acknowledged the force of the sceptic's position but have succumbed to it.

The sceptic maintains that we know almost none of what we think we know. He has shown, much to our initial surprise, that we do not know his (non-trivial) possibility SK doesn't obtain. Thus, he has shown of one thing we thought we knew, that we didn't and don't. To the conclusion that we know almost nothing, it appears but a short step. For if we do not know we are not dreaming or being deceived by a demon or floating in a tank, then how can I know, for example, that I am sitting before a page writing with a pen, and how can you know that you are reading a page of a book?

However, although our account of knowledge agrees with the sceptic in saying that we do not know that not-SK, it places no formidable barriers before my knowing that I am writing on a page with a pen. It is true that I am, I believe I am, if I weren't I wouldn't believe I was, and if I were, I would believe it. Also, it is true that you are reading a page (please, don't stop now!), you believe you are, if you weren't reading a page you wouldn't believe you were, and if you were reading a page you would believe you were. So according to the account, I do know that I am writing on a page with a pen, and you do know that you are reading a page. The account does not lead to any general scepticism.

Yet we must grant that it appears that if the sceptic is right that we don't know we are not dreaming or being deceived or floating in the tank, then it cannot be that I know I am writing with a pen or that you know you are reading a page. So we must scrutinize with special care the sceptic's 'short step' to the conclusion that we don't know these things, for either this step cannot be taken or our account of knowledge is incoherent.

14. I say almost everything, because there still could be some true beliefs such as 'I exist.' More limited sceptical possibilities present worlds doxically identical to the actual world in which almost every belief of a certain sort is false, for example, about the past, or about other people's mental states. [. . .]

6. Non-closure

In taking the 'short step', the sceptic assumes that if S knows that p and he knows that 'p entails q' then he also knows that q. In the terminology of the logicians, the sceptic assumes that knowledge is closed under known logical implication; that the operation of moving from something known to something else known to be entailed by it does not take us outside of the (closed) area of knowledge. He intends, of course, to work things backwards, arguing that since the person does not know that q, assuming (at least for the purposes of argument) that he does know that p entails q, it follows that he does not know that p. For if he did know that p, he would also know that q, which he doesn't.

The details of different sceptical arguments vary in their structure, but each one will assume some variant of the principle that knowledge is closed under known logical implication. If we abbreviate 'knowledge that p' by 'Kp' and abbreviate 'entails' by the fishhook sign '$\dashv$', we can write this principle of closure as the subjunctive principle

P: $K(p \dashv q)$ & $Kp \rightarrow Kq$.

If a person were to know that p entails q and he were to know that p then he would know that q. The statement that q follows by *modus ponens* from the other two stated as known in the antecedent of the subjunctive principle P; this principle counts on the person to draw the inference to q.

You know that your being in a tank on Alpha Centauri entails your not being in place X where you are. (I assume here a limited readership.) And you know also the contrapositive, that your being at place X entails that you are not then in a tank on Alpha Centauri. If you knew you were at X you would know you're not in a tank (of a specified sort) at Alpha Centauri. But you do not know this last fact (the sceptic has argued and we have agreed) and so (he argues) you don't know the first. Another intuitive way of putting the sceptic's argument is as follows. If you know that two statements are incompatible and you know the first is true then you know the denial of the second. You know that your being at X and your being in a tank on Alpha Centauri are incompatible; so if you knew you were at X you would know you were not in the (specified) tank on Alpha Centauri. Since you do not know the second, you don't know the first.

No doubt, it is possible to argue over the details of principle P, to point out it is incorrect as it stands. Perhaps, though Kp, the person does not know that he knows that p (that is, not-KKp) and so does not draw the inference to q. Or perhaps he doesn't draw the inference because not-$KK(p \dashv q)$. Other similar principles face their own difficulties: for example, the principle that $K(p \rightarrow q) \rightarrow (Kp \rightarrow Kq)$ fails if Kp stops $p \rightarrow q$ from being true, that is, if $Kp \rightarrow$ not-$(p \rightarrow q)$; the principle that $K(p \dashv q) \rightarrow K(Kp \rightarrow Kq)$ faces difficulties if Kp makes the person forget that $(p \dashv q)$ and so he fails to draw the inference to q. We seem forced to pile K upon K until we reach something like $KK(p \dashv q)$ & $KKp \rightarrow Kq$; this involves strengthening considerably the antecedent of P and so is not useful for the sceptic's argument that is not known. (From a principle altered thus, it would follow at best that it is not known that p is known.)

We would be ill-advised, however, to quibble over the details of P. Although these details are difficult to get straight, it will continue to appear that something like P is correct. If S knows that 'p entails q', and he knows that p and knows that (p and p entails q) entails q' [. . .] and he does draw the inference to q from all this and believes q via the process of drawing this inference, then will he not know that q? And what is wrong with simplifying this mass of detail by writing merely principle P, provided we apply it only to cases where the mass of detail holds, as it surely does in the sceptical cases under consideration? For example, I do realize that my being in the Van Leer Foundation Building in Jerusalem entails that I am not in a tank on Alpha Centauri; I am capable of drawing inferences now; I do believe I am not in a tank on Alpha Centauri (though not solely via this inference, surely); and so forth. Won't this satisfy the correctly detailed principle, and shouldn't it follow that I know I am not (in that tank) on Alpha Centauri? The sceptic agrees it should follow; so he concludes from the fact that I don't know I am not floating in the tank on Alpha Centauri that I don't know I am in Jerusalem. Uncovering difficulties in the details of particular formulations of P will not weaken the principle's intuitive appeal; such quibbling will seem at best like a wasp attacking a steamroller, at worst like an effort in bad faith to avoid being pulled along by the sceptic's argument.

Principle P is wrong, however, and not merely in detail. Knowledge is not closed under known logical implication.[15] S knows that p when S has a true belief that p, and S wouldn't have a false belief that p (condition (3)) and S would have a true belief that p (condition 4)). Neither of these latter two conditions is closed under known logical implication.

Let us begin with condition

(3) if p were false, S wouldn't believe that p.

When S knows that p, his belief that p is contingent on the truth of p, contingent in the way the subjunctive condition (3) describes. Now it might be that p entails q (and S knows this), that S's belief that p is subjunctively contingent on the truth of p, that S believes q, yet his belief that q is not subjunctively dependent on the truth of q, in that it (or he) does not satisfy:

(3') if q were false, S wouldn't believe that q.

For (3') talks of what S would believe if q were false, and this may be a very different situation from the one that would hold if p were false, even though p entails q. That you were born in a certain city entails that you were born on earth.[16] Yet contemplating what (actually) would be the situation if you were not born in that city is very different from contemplating what situation would hold if you weren't born on earth. Just as those possibilities are very different, so what is believed in them may be very different. When p entails q (and not the other way around) p will be a stronger statement than q and so not-q (which is the antecedent of (3')) will

15. Note that I am not denying that Kp & K(p ⊰q) → Believes q.
16. Here again I assume a limited readership, and ignore possibilities such as those described in James Blish, *Cities in Flight* (New York, 1982).

be a stronger statement than not-p (which is the antecedent of (3)). There is no reason to assume you will have the same beliefs in these two cases, under these suppositions of differing strengths.

There is no reason to assume the (closest) not-p world and the (closest) not-q world are doxically identical for you, and no reason to assume, even though p entails q, that your beliefs in one of these worlds would be a (proper) subset of your beliefs in the other.

Consider now the two statements:

p = I am awake and sitting on a chair in Jerusalem;
q = I am not floating in a tank on Alpha Centauri being stimulated by electro-chemical means to believe that p.

The first one entails the second: p entails q. Also, I know that p entails q; and I know that p. If p were false, I would be standing or lying down in the same city, or perhaps sleeping there, or perhaps in a neighbouring city or town. If q were false, I would be floating in a tank on Alpha Centauri. Clearly these are very different situations, leading to great differences in what I then would believe. If p were false, if I weren't awake and sitting on a chair in Jerusalem, I would not believe that p. Yet if q were false, if I was floating in a tank on Alpha Centauri I would believe that q, that I was not in the tank, and indeed, in that case, I would still believe that p. According to our account of knowledge, I know that p yet I do not know that q, even though (I know) p entails q.

This failure of knowledge to be closed under known logical implication stems from the fact that condition (3) is not closed under known logical implication; condition (3) can hold of one statement believed while not of another known to be entailed by the first. [. . .] It is clear that any account that includes as a necessary condition for knowledge the subjunctive condition (3), not-$p \rightarrow$ not-(S believes that p), will have the consequence that knowledge is not closed under known logical implication.[17]

When p entails q and you believe each of them, if you do not have a false belief that p (since p is true) then you do not have a false belief that q. However, if you are to know something not only don't you have a false belief about it, but also you wouldn't have a false belief about it. Yet, we have seen how it may be that p entails q

---

17. Does this same consequence of nonclosure under known logical implication follow as well from condition (4): $p \rightarrow S$ believes that p? When p is not actually true, condition (4) can hold of p yet not of a q known to be entailed by p. For example, let p be the (false) statement that I am in Antarctica, and let q be the disjunction of p with some other appropriate statement; for example, let q be the statement that I am in Antarctica or I lost some object yesterday though I have not yet realized it. If p were true I would know it, p entails q, yet if q were true I wouldn't know it, for the way it would be true would be by my losing some object without yet realizing it, and if that happened I would not know it.

This example to show that condition (4) is not closed under known logical implication depends on the (actual) falsity of p. I do not think there is any suitable example to show this in the case where p is true, leaving aside the trivial situation when the person simply does not infer the entailed statement q.

and you believe each and you wouldn't have a false belief that p yet you might have a false belief that q (that is, it is not the case that you wouldn't have one). Knowledge is not closed under the known logical implication because 'wouldn't have a false belief that' is not closed under known logical implication.

If knowledge were the same as (simply) true belief then it would be closed under known logical implication (provided the implied statements were believed). Knowledge is not simply true belief, however; additional conditions are needed. These further conditions will make knowledge open under known logical implication, even when the entailed statement is believed, when at least one of the further conditions itself is open. Knowledge stays closed (only) if all of the additional conditions are closed. I lack a general non-trivial characterization of those conditions that are closed under known logical implication; possessing such an illuminating characterization, one might attempt to prove that no additional conditions of that sort could provide an adequate analysis of knowledge.

Still, we can say the following. A belief that p is knowledge that p only if it somehow varies with the truth of p. The causal condition for knowledge specified that the belief was 'produced by' the fact, but that condition did not provide the right sort of varying with the fact. The subjunctive conditions (3) and (4) are our attempt to specify that varying. But however an account spells this out, it will hold that whether a belief that p is knowledge partly depends on what goes on with the belief in some situations when p is false. An account that says nothing about what is believed in any situation when p is false cannot give us any mode of varying with the fact.

Because what is preserved under logical implication is truth, any condition that is preserved under known logical implication is most likely to speak only of what happens when p, and q, are true, without speaking at all of what happens when either one is false. Such a condition is incapable of providing 'varies with'; so adding only such conditions to true belief cannot yield an adequate account of knowledge. [. . .]

A belief's somehow varying with the truth of what is believed is not closed under known logical implication. Since knowledge that p involves such variation, knowledge also is not closed under known logical implication. The sceptic cannot easily deny that knowledge involves such variation, for his argument that we don't know that we're not floating in that tank, for example, uses the fact that knowledge does involve variation. ('If you were floating in the tank you would still think you weren't, so you don't know that you're not.') Yet, though one part of his argument uses that fact that knowledge involves such variation, another part of his argument presupposes that knowledge does not involve any such variation. This latter is the part that depends upon knowledge being closed under known logical implication, as when the sceptic argues that since you don't know that not-SK, you don't know you are not floating in the tank, then you also don't know, for example, that you are now reading a book. That closure can hold only if the variation does not. The sceptic cannot be right both times. According to our view he is right when he holds that knowledge involves such variation and so concludes that we don't know, for example, that we are not floating in that tank; but he is wrong when he assumes knowledge is closed under known logical implication and concludes that we know hardly anything.[18]

Knowledge is a real factual relation, subjunctively specifiable, whose structure admits our standing in this relation, tracking, to p without standing in it to some q which we know p to entail. Any relation embodying some variation of belief with the fact, with the truth (value), will exhibit this structural feature. The sceptic is right that we don't track some particular truths—the ones stating that his sceptical possibilities SK don't hold—but wrong that we don't stand in the real knowledge-relation of tracking to many other truths, including ones that entail these first mentioned truths we believe but don't know.

The literature on scepticism contains writers who endorse these sceptical arguments (or similar narrower ones), but confess their inability to maintain their sceptical beliefs at times when they are not focusing explicitly on the reasoning that led them to sceptical conclusions. The most notable example of this is Hume:

I am ready to reject all belief and reasoning, and can look upon no opinion even as more probable or likely than another . . . Most fortunately it happens that since reason is incapable

---

18. Reading an earlier draft of this chapter, friends pointed out to me that Fred Dretske already had defended the view that knowledge (as one among many epistemic concepts) is not closed under known logical implication. (See his 'Epistemic Operators', *Journal of Philosophy*, 67, (1970), 1007–23.) Furthermore, Dretske presented a subjunctive condition for knowledge in his 'Conclusive Reasons', *Australasian Journal of Philosophy* 49, (1971), 1–22 [Ch. 6 in this volume], holding that S knows that p on the basis of reasons R only if: R would not be the case unless p were the case. Here Dretske ties the evidence subjunctively to the fact, and the belief based on the evidence subjunctively to the fact through the evidence. (Our account of knowledge has not yet introduced or discussed evidence or reasons at all. While this condition corresponds to our condition (3), he has nothing corresponding to (4).) So Dretske has hold of both pieces of our account, subjunctive and nonclosure, and he even connects them in a passing footnote (*Journal of Philosophy*, Vol. 67, p. 1019, n. 4), noticing that any account of knowledge that relies on a subjunctive conditional will not be closed under known logical implication. Dretske also has the notion of a relevant alternative as 'one that might have been realized in the existing circumstances if the actual state of affairs had not materialized' (p. 1021), and he briefly applies all this to the topic of scepticism (pp. 1015–1016), holding that the sceptic is right about some things but not about others.

It grieves me somewhat to discover that Dretske also had all this, and was there first. It raises the question, also, of why these views have not yet had the proper impact. Dretske makes his points in the midst of much other material, some of it less insightful. The independent statement and delineation of the position here, without the background noise, I hope will make clear its many merits.

After Goldman's paper on a causal theory of knowledge, in *Journal of Philosophy*, 64, (1967), [Ch. 4 in this volume], an idea then already 'in the air', it required no great leap to consider subjunctive conditions. Some two months after the first version of this chapter was written, Goldman himself published a paper on knowledge utilizing counterfactuals ('Discrimination and Perceptual Knowledge', *Journal of Philosophy*, 78 (1976), pp. 771–91 [Ch. 8 in this volume]), also talking of relevant possibilities (without using the counterfactuals to identify which possibilities are relevant); and R. Shope has called my attention to a paper of L. S. Carrier ('An Analysis of Empirical Knowledge', *Southern Journal of Philosophy*, 9, (1971), pp. 3–11) that also used subjunctive conditions including our condition (3). Armstrong's reliability view of knowledge (*Belief Truth and Knowledge*, Cambridge, 1973, pp. 166, 169 [in this volume pp. 75, 77]) involved a lawlike connection between the belief that p and the state of affairs that makes it true. Clearly, the idea is one whose time has come.

of dispelling these clouds, nature herself suffices to that purpose, and cures me of this philosophical melancholy and delirium, either by relaxing this bent of mind, or by some chimeras. I dine, I play a game of backgammon, I converse, and am merry with my friends; and when after three or four hours' amusement, I would return to these speculations, they appear so cold, and strained, and ridiculous, that I cannot find in my heart to enter into them any farther. (*A Treatise of Human Nature*, Book I, Part IV, section VII.)

The great subverter of Pyrrhonism or the excessive principles of scepticism is action, and employment, and the occupations of common life. These principles may flourish and triumph in the schools; where it is, indeed, difficult, if not impossible, to refute them. But as soon as they leave the shade, and by the presence of the real objects, which actuate our passions and sentiments, are put in opposition to the more powerful principles of our nature, they vanish like smoke, and leave the most determined skeptic in the same condition as other mortals . . . And though a Pyrrhonian may throw himself or others into a momentary amazement and confusion by his profound reasonings; the first and most trivial event in life will put to flight all his doubts and scruples, and leave him the same, in every point of action and speculation, with the philosophers of every other sect, or with those who never concerned themselves in any philosophical researches. When he awakes from his dream, he will be the first to join in the laugh against himself, and to confess that all his objections are mere amusement. *(An Enquiry Concerning Human Understanding*, Section XII, Part II.)

The theory of knowledge we have presented explains why sceptics of various sorts have had such difficulties in sticking to their far-reaching sceptical conclusions 'outside the study', or even inside it when they are not thinking specifically about sceptical arguments and possibilities SK.

The sceptic's arguments do show (but show only) that we don't know the sceptic's possibilities SK do not hold; and he is right that we don't track the fact that SK does not hold. (If it were to hold, we would still think it didn't.) However, the sceptic's arguments don't show we do not know other facts (including facts that entail not-SK) for we do track these other facts (and knowledge is not closed under known logical entailment). Since we do track these other facts—you, for example, the fact that you are reading a book; I, the fact that I am writing on a page—and the sceptic tracks such facts too, it is not surprising that when he focuses on them, on his relationship to such facts, the sceptic finds it hard to remember or maintain his view that he does not know those facts. Only by shifting his attention back to his relationship to the (different) fact that not-SK, which relationship is not tracking, can he revive his sceptical belief and make it salient. However, this sceptical triumph is evanescent, it vanishes when his attention turns to other facts. Only by fixating on the sceptical possibilities SK can he maintain his sceptical virtue; otherwise, unsurprisingly, he is forced to confess to sins of credulity.

Chapter 26

Elusive knowledge*

David Lewis

W<small>E</small> know a lot. I know what food penguins eat. I know that phones used to ring, but nowadays squeal, when someone calls up. I know that Essendon won the 1993 Grand Final. I know that here is a hand, and here is another.

We have all sorts of everyday knowledge, and we have it in abundance. To doubt that would be absurd. At any rate, to doubt it in any serious and lasting way would be absurd; and even philosophical and temporary doubt, under the influence of argument, is more than a little peculiar. It is a Moorean fact that we know a lot. It is one of those things that we know better than we know the premises of any philosophical argument to the contrary.

Besides knowing a lot that is everyday and trite, I myself think that we know a lot that is interesting and esoteric and controversial. We know a lot about things unseen: tiny particles and pervasive fields, not to mention one another's underwear. Sometimes we even know what an author meant by his writings. But on these questions, let us agree to disagree peacefully with the champions of 'post-knowledgeism'. The most trite and ordinary parts of our knowledge will be problem enough.

For no sooner do we engage in epistemology—the systematic philosophical examination of knowledge—than we meet a compelling argument that we know next to nothing. The sceptical argument is nothing new or fancy. It is just this: it seems as if knowledge must be by definition infallible. If you claim that *S* knows that *P*, and yet you grant that *S* cannot eliminate a certain possibility in which not-*P*, it certainly seems as if you have granted that *S* does not after all know that *P*. To speak of fallible knowledge, of knowledge despite uneliminated possibilities of error, just *sounds* contradictory.

Blind Freddy can see where this will lead. Let your paranoid fantasies rip—CIA plots, hallucinogens in the tap water, conspiracies to deceive, old Nick himself—soon you find that uneliminated possibilities of error are everywhere. Those possibilities of error are far-fetched, of course, but possibilities all the same. They bite into even our most everyday knowledge. We never have infallible knowledge.

Never—well, hardly ever. Some say we have infallible knowledge of a few simple,

David Lewis, 'Elusive Knowledge' in *The Australasian Journal of Philosophy*, 74 (1996) pp. 549–67, reprinted by permission of the author.

* Thanks to many for valuable discussions of this material. Thanks above all to Peter Unger; and to Stewart Cohen, Michael Devitt, Alan Hajek, Stephen Hetherington, Denis Robinson, Ernest Sosa, Robert Stalnaker, Jonathan Vogel, and a referee for this Journal. Thanks also to the Boyce Gibson Memorial Library and to Ormond College.

axiomatic necessary truths; and of our own present experience. They say that I simply cannot be wrong that a part of a part of something is itself a part of that thing; or that it seems to me now (as I sit here at the keyboard) exactly as if I am hearing clicking noises on top of a steady whirring. Some say so. Others deny it. No matter; let it be granted, at least for the sake of the argument. It is not nearly enough. If we have only that much infallible knowledge yet knowledge is by defi-nition infallible, then we have very little knowledge indeed—not the abundant everyday knowledge we thought we had. That is still absurd.

So we know a lot; knowledge must be infallible; yet we have fallible knowledge or none (or next to none). We are caught between the rock of fallibilism and the whirlpool of scepticism. Both are mad!

Yet fallibilism is the less intrusive madness. It demands less frequent corrections of what we want to say. So, if forced to choose, I choose fallibilism. (And so say all of us.) We can get used to it, and some of us have done. No joy there—we know that people can get used to the most crazy philosophical sayings imaginable. If you are a contented fallibilist, I implore you to be honest, be naive, hear it afresh. 'He knows, yet he has not eliminated all possibilities of error.' Even if you've numbed your ears, doesn't this overt, explicit fallibilism *still* sound wrong?

Better fallibilism than scepticism; but it would be better still to dodge the choice. I think we can. We will be alarmingly close to the rock, and also alarmingly close to the whirlpool, but if we steer with care, we can—just barely—escape them both.

Maybe epistemology is the culprit. Maybe this extraordinary pastime robs us of our knowledge. Maybe we do know a lot in daily life; but maybe when we look hard at our knowledge, it goes away. But only when we look at it harder than the sane ever do in daily life; only when we let our paranoid fantasies rip. That is when we are forced to admit that there always are uneliminated possibilities of error, so that we have fallible knowledge or none.

Much that we say is context-dependent, in simple ways or subtle ways. Simple: 'it's evening' is truly said when, and only when, it is said in the evening. Subtle: it could well be true, and not just by luck, that Essendon played rottenly, the Easybeats played brilliantly, yet Essendon won. Different contexts evoke different standards of evaluation. Talking about the Easybeats we apply lax standards, else we could scarcely distinguish their better days from their worse ones. In talking about Essendon, no such laxity is required. Essendon won because play that is rotten by demanding standards suffices to beat play that is brilliant by lax standards.

Maybe ascriptions of knowledge are subtly context-dependent, and maybe epis-temology is a context that makes them go false. Then epistemology would be an investigation that destroys its own subject matter. If so, the sceptical argument might be flawless, when we engage in epistemology—and only then![1]

1. The suggestion that ascriptions of knowledge go false in the context of epistemology is to be found in Barry Stroud, 'Understanding Human Knowledge in General' in Marjorie Clay and Keith Lehrer (eds.), *Knowledge and Skepticism* (Boulder: Westview Press, 1989) [Ch. 22 in this volume]; and in Stephen Hetherington, 'Lacking Knowledge and Justification by Theorising About Them' (lecture at the University of New South Wales, August 1992). Neither of them tells the story just as I do, however it may be that their versions do not conflict with mine.

If you start from the ancient idea that justification is the mark that distinguishes knowledge from mere opinion (even true opinion), then you well might conclude that ascriptions of knowledge are context-dependent because standards for adequate justification are context-dependent. As follows: opinion, even if true, deserves the name of knowledge only if it is adequately supported by reasons; to deserve that name in the especially demanding context of epistemology, the arguments from supporting reasons must be especially watertight; but the special standards of justification that this special context demands never can be met (well, hardly ever). In the strict context of epistemology we know nothing, yet in laxer contexts we know a lot.

But I myself cannot subscribe to this account of the context-dependence of knowledge, because I question its starting point. I don't agree that the mark of knowledge is justification.[2] First, because justification is not sufficient: your true opinion that you will lose the lottery isn't knowledge, whatever the odds. Suppose you know that it is a fair lottery with one winning ticket and many losing tickets, and you know how many losing tickets there are. The greater the number of losing tickets, the better is your justification for believing you will lose. Yet there is no number great enough to transform your fallible opinion into knowledge—after all, you just might win. No justification is good enough—or none short of a watertight deductive argument, and all but the sceptics will agree that this is too much to demand.[3]

Second, because justification is not always necessary. What (non-circular) argument supports our reliance on perception, on memory, and on testimony?[4] And yet we do gain knowledge by these means. And sometimes, far from having supporting arguments, we don't even know how we know. We once had evidence, drew conclusions, and thereby gained knowledge; now we have forgotten our reasons, yet still we retain our knowledge. Or we know the name that goes with the face, or the sex of the chicken, by relying on subtle visual cues, without knowing what those cues may be.

The link between knowledge and justification must be broken. But if we break that link, then it is not—or not entirely, or not exactly—by raising the standards of justification that epistemology destroys knowledge. I need some different story.

To that end, I propose to take the infallibility of knowledge as my starting point.[5] Must infallibilist epistemology end in scepticism? Not quite. Wait and see. Anyway, here is the definition. Subject *S knows* proposition *P* iff *P* holds in every possibility

---

2. Unless, like some, we simply define 'justification' as 'whatever it takes to turn true opinions into knowledge' regardless of whether what it takes turns out to involve argument from supporting reasons.

3. The problem of the lottery was introduced in Henry Kyburg, *Probability and the Logic of Rational Belief* (Middletown, CT: Wesleyan University Press, 1961), and in Carl Hempel, 'Deductive-Nomological vs. Statistical Explanation' in Herbert Feigl and Grover Maxwell (eds.), *Minnesota Studies in the Philosophy of Science*, Vol. 2 (Minneapolis: University of Minnesota Press, 1962). It has been much discussed since, as a problem both about knowledge and about our everyday, non-quantitative concept of belief.

4. The case of testimony is less discussed than the others; but see C. A. J. Coady, *Testimony: A Philosophical Study* (Oxford: Clarendon Press, 1992) pp. 79–129.

5. I follow Peter Unger, *Ignorance: A Case for Skepticism* (New York: Oxford University Press, 1975). But I shall not let him lead me into scepticism.

left uneliminated by S's evidence; equivalently, if S's evidence eliminates every possibility in which not-P.

The definition is short; the commentary upon it is longer. In the first place, there is the proposition, P. What I choose to call 'propositions' are individuated coarsely, by necessary equivalence. For instance, there is only one necessary proposition. It holds in every possibility; hence in every possibility left uneliminated by S's evidence, no matter who S may be and no matter what his evidence may be. So the necessary proposition is known always and everywhere. Yet this known proposition may go unrecognised when presented in impenetrable linguistic disguise, say as the proposition that every even number is the sum of two primes. Likewise, the known proposition that I have two hands may go unrecognised when presented as the proposition that the number of my hands is the least number n such that every even number is the sum of n primes. (Or if you doubt the necessary existence of numbers, switch to an example involving equivalence by logic alone.) These problems of disguise shall not concern us here. Our topic is modal, not hyperintensional, epistemology.[6]

Next, there are the possibilities. We needn't enter here into the question whether these are concreta, abstract constructions, or abstract simples. Further, we needn't decide whether they must always be maximally specific possibilities, or whether they need only be specific enough for the purpose at hand. A possibility will be specific enough if it cannot be split into subcases in such a way that anything we have said about possibilities, or anything we are going to say before we are done, applies to some subcases and not to others. For instance, it should never happen that proposition P holds in some but not all subcases; or that some but not all subcases are eliminated by S's evidence.

But we do need to stipulate that they are not just possibilities as to how the whole world is; they also include possibilities as to which part of the world is oneself, and as to when it now is. We need these possibilities *de se et nunc* because the propositions that may be known include propositions *de se et nunc*.[7] Not only do I know that there are hands in this world somewhere and somewhen. I know that *I* have hands, or anyway I have them *now*. Such propositions aren't just made true or made false by the whole world once and for all. They are true for some of us and not for others, or true at some times and not others, or both.

Further, we cannot limit ourselves to 'real' possibilities that conform to the actual laws of nature, and maybe also to actual past history. For propositions about laws and history are contingent, and may or may not be known.

Neither can we limit ourselves to 'epistemic' possibilities for S—possibilities that S does not know not to obtain. That would drain our definition of content. Assume only that knowledge is closed under strict implication. (We shall consider the merits of this assumption later.) Remember that we are not distinguishing between equivalent propositions. Then knowledge of a conjunction is equivalent to knowledge of every conjunct. P is the conjunction of all propositions not-W, where W is

6. See Robert Stalnaker, *Inquiry* (Cambridge, MA: MIT Press, 1984) pp. 59–99.
7. See my 'Attitudes *De Dicto* and *De Se*', *The Philosophical Review* 88 (1979) pp. 513–43; and R. M. Chisholm, 'The Indirect Reflexive' in C. Diamond and J. Teichman (eds.), *Intention and Intentionality: Essays in Honour of G.E.M. Anscombe* (Brighton: Harvester, 1979).

a possibility in which not-P. That suffices to yield an equivalence: S knows that P iff, for every possibility W in which not-P, S knows that not-W. Contraposing and cancelling a double negation: iff every possibility which S does not know not to obtain is one in which P. For short: iff P holds throughout S's epistemic possibilities. Yet to get this far, we need no substantive definition of knowledge at all! To turn this into a substantive definition, in fact the very definition we gave before, we need to say one more thing: S's epistemic possibilities are just those possibilities that are uneliminated by S's evidence.

So, next, we need to say what it means for a possibility to be eliminated or not. Here I say that the uneliminated possibilities are those in which the subject's entire perceptual experience and memory are just as they actually are. There is one possibility that actually obtains (for the subject and at the time in question); call it *actuality*. Then a possibility W is *uneliminated* iff the subject's perceptual experience and memory in W exactly match his perceptual experience and memory in actuality. (If you want to include other alleged forms of basic evidence, such as the evidence of our extrasensory faculties, or an innate disposition to believe in God, be my guest. If they exist, they should be included. If not, no harm done if we have included them conditionally.)

Note well that we do not need the 'pure sense-datum language' and the 'incorrigible protocol statements' that for so long bedevilled foundationalist epistemology. It matters not at all whether there are words to capture the subject's perceptual and memory evidence, nothing more and nothing less. If there are such words, it matters not at all whether the subject can hit upon them. The given does not consist of basic axioms to serve as premises in subsequent arguments. Rather, it consists of a match between possibilities.

When perceptual experience E (or memory) eliminates a possibility W, that is not because the propositional content of the experience conflicts with W. (Not even if it is the narrow content.) The propositional content of our experience could after all be false. Rather, it is the existence of the experience that conflicts with W: W is a possibility in which the subject is not having experience E. Else we would need to tell some fishy story of how the experience has some sort of infallible, ineffable, purely phenomenal propositional content . . . Who needs that? Let E have propositional content P. Suppose even—something I take to be an open question—that E is, in some sense, fully characterized by P. Then I say that E eliminates W iff W is a possibility in which the subject's experience or memory has content different from P. I do *not* say that E eliminates W iff W is a possibility in which P is false.

Maybe not every kind of sense perception yields experience; maybe, for instance, the kinaesthetic sense yields not its own distinctive sort of sense-experience but only spontaneous judgements about the position of one's limbs. If this is true, then the thing to say is that kinaesthetic evidence eliminates all possibilities except those that exactly resemble actuality with respect to the subject's spontaneous kinaesthetic judgements. In saying this, we would treat kinaesthetic evidence more on the model of memory than on the model of more typical senses.

Finally, we must attend to the word 'every'. What does it mean to say that every possibility in which not-*P* is eliminated? An idiom of quantification, like 'every', is normally restricted to some limited domain. If I say that every glass is empty, so it's time for another round, doubtless I and my audience are ignoring most of all the glasses there are in the whole wide world throughout all of time. They are outside the domain. They are irrelevant to the truth of what was said.

Likewise, if I say that every uneliminated possibility is one in which *P*, or words to that effect, I am doubtless ignoring some of all the uneliminated alternative possibilities that there are. They are outside the domain, they are irrelevant to the truth of what was said.

But, of course, I am not entitled to ignore just any possibility I please. Else true ascriptions of knowledge, whether to myself or to others, would be cheap indeed. I may properly ignore some uneliminated possibilities; I may not properly ignore others. Our definition of knowledge requires a *sotto voce* proviso. *S knows* that *P* iff *S*'s evidence eliminates every possibility in which not-*P*—Psst!—except for those possibilities that we are properly ignoring.

Unger suggests an instructive parallel.[8] Just as *P* is known iff there are no uneliminated possibilities of error, so likewise a surface is flat iff there are no bumps on it. We must add the proviso: Psst!—except for those bumps that we are properly ignoring. Else we will conclude, absurdly, that nothing is flat. (Simplify by ignoring departures from flatness that consist of gentle curvature.)

We can restate the definition. Say that we *presuppose* proposition *Q* iff we ignore all possibilities in which not-*Q*. To close the circle: we *ignore* just those possibilities that falsify our presuppositions. *Proper* presupposition corresponds, of course, to proper ignoring. Then *S knows* that *P* iff *S*'s evidence eliminates every possibility in which not-*P*—Psst!—except for those possibilities that conflict with our proper presuppositions.[9]

The rest of (modal) epistemology examines the *sotto voce* proviso. It asks: what may we properly presuppose in our ascriptions of knowledge? Which of all the uneliminated alternative possibilities may not properly be ignored? Which ones are the 'relevant alternatives'?—relevant, that is, to what the subject does and doesn't know?[10] In reply, we can list several rules.[11] We begin with three prohibitions: rules to tell us what possibilities we may not properly ignore.

8. Peter Unger, *Ignorance*, chapter 2. I discuss the case, and briefly foreshadow the present paper in my 'Scorekeeping in a Language Game', *Journal of Philosophical Logic* 8 (1979) pp. 339–59, esp. pp. 353–5.

9. See Robert Stalnaker, 'Presuppositions', *Journal of Philosophical Logic* 2 (1973) pp. 447–57; and 'Pragmatic Presuppositions' in Milton Munitz and Peter Unger (eds.), *Semantics and Philosophy* (New York: New York University Press, 1974). See also my 'Scorekeeping in a Language Game'.
   The definition restated in terms of presupposition resembles the treatment of knowledge in Kenneth S. Ferguson, *Philosophical Scepticism* (Cornell University doctoral dissertation, 1980).

10. See Fred Dretske, 'Epistemic Operators', *The Journal of Philosophy* 67 (1970) pp. 1007–22, and 'The Pragmatic Dimension of Knowledge', *Philosophical Studies* 40 (1981) pp. 363–78; Alvin Goldman, 'Discrimination and Perceptual Knowledge', *The Journal of Philosophy* 73 (1976) pp. 771–91 [Ch. 8 in this volume]; G. C. Stine, 'Skepticism, Relevant Alternatives, and Deductive Closure', *Philosophical Studies* 29 (1976) pp. 249–61; and Stewart Cohen, 'How to be A Fallibilist', *Philosophical Perspectives* 2 (1988) pp. 91–123.

11. Some of them, but only some, taken from the authors just cited.

First, there is the *Rule of Actuality*. The possibility that actually obtains is never properly ignored; actuality is always a relevant alternative; nothing false may properly be presupposed. It follows that only what is true is known, wherefore we did not have to include truth in our definition of knowledge. The rule is 'externalist'— the subject himself may not be able to tell what is properly ignored. In judging which of his ignorings are proper, hence what he knows, we judge his success in knowing—not how well he tried.

When the Rule of Actuality tells us that actuality may never be properly ignored, we can ask: *whose* actuality? Ours, when we ascribe knowledge or ignorance to others? Or the subject's? In simple cases, the question is silly. (In fact, it sounds like the sort of pernicious nonsense we would expect from someone who mixes up what is true with what is believed.) There is just one actual world, we the ascribers live in that world, the subject lives there too, so the subject's actuality is the same as ours.

But there are other cases, less simple, in which the question makes perfect sense and needs an answer. Someone may or may not know who he is; someone may or may not know what time it is. Therefore I insisted that the propositions that may be known must include propositions *de se et nunc*; and likewise that the possibilities that may be eliminated or ignored must include possibilities *de se et nunc*. Now we have a good sense in which the subject's actuality may be different from ours. I ask today what Fred knew yesterday. In particular, did he then know who he was? Did he know what day it was? Fred's actuality is the possibility *de se et nunc* of being Fred on September 19th at such-and-such possible world; whereas my actuality is the possibility *de se et nunc* of being David on September 20th at such-and-such world. So far as the world goes, there is no difference: Fred and I are worldmates, his actual world is the same as mine. But when we build subject and time into the possibilities *de se et nunc*, then his actuality yesterday does indeed differ from mine today.

What is more, we sometimes have occasion to ascribe knowledge to those who are off at other possible worlds. I didn't read the newspaper yesterday. What would I have known if had read it? More than I do in fact know. (More and less: I do in fact know that I left the newspaper unread, but if I had read it, I would not have known that I had left it unread.) I-who-did-not-read-the-newspaper am here at this world, ascribing knowledge and ignorance. The subject to whom I am ascribing that knowledge and ignorance, namely I-as-I-would-have-been-if-I-had-read-the-newspaper, is at a different world. The worlds differ in respect at least of a reading of the newspaper. Thus the ascriber's actual world is not the same as the subject's. (I myself think that the ascriber and the subject are two different people: the subject is the ascriber's otherworldly counterpart. But even if you think the subject and the ascriber are the same identical person, you must still grant that this person's actuality *qua* subject differs from his actuality *qua* ascriber.)

Or suppose we ask modal questions about the subject: what must he have known, what might he have known? Again we are considering the subject as he is not here, but off at other possible worlds. Likewise if we ask questions about knowledge of knowledge: what does he (or what do we) know that he knows?

So the question 'whose actuality?' is not a silly question after all. And when the question matters, as it does in the cases just considered, the right answer is that it is the subject's actuality, not the ascriber's, that never can be properly ignored.

Next, there is the *Rule of Belief*. A possibility that the subject believes to obtain is not properly ignored, whether or not he is right to so believe. Neither is one that he ought to believe to obtain—one that evidence and arguments justify him in believing—whether or not he does so believe.

That is rough. Since belief admits of degree, and since some possibilities are more specific than others, we ought to reformulate the rule in terms of degree of belief, compared to a standard set by the unspecificity of the possibility in question. A possibility may not be properly ignored if the subject gives it, or ought to give it, a degree of belief that is sufficiently high, and high not just because the possibility in question is unspecific.

How high is 'sufficiently high'? That may depend on how much is at stake. When error would be especially disastrous, few possibilities may be properly ignored. Then even quite a low degree of belief may be 'sufficiently high' to bring the Rule of Belief into play. The jurors know that the accused is guilty only if his guilt has been proved beyond reasonable doubt.[12]

Yet even when the stakes are high, some possibilities still may be properly ignored. Disastrous though it would be to convict an innocent man, still the jurors may properly ignore the possibility that it was the dog, marvellously well-trained, that fired the fatal shot. And, unless they are ignoring other alternatives more relevant than that, they may rightly be said to know that the accused is guilty as charged. Yet if there had been reason to give the dog hypothesis a slightly less negligible degree of belief—if the world's greatest dog-trainer had been the victim's mortal enemy—then the alternative would be relevant after all.

This is the only place where belief and justification enter my story. As already noted, I allow justified true belief without knowledge, as in the case of your belief that you will lose the lottery. I allow knowledge without justification, in the cases of face recognition and chicken sexing. I even allow knowledge without belief, as in the case of the timid student who knows the answer but has no confidence that he has it right, and so does not believe what he knows.[13] Therefore any proposed converse to the Rule of Belief should be rejected. A possibility that the subject does not believe to a sufficient degree, and ought not to believe to a sufficient degree, may nevertheless be a relevant alternative and not properly ignored.

Next, there is the *Rule of Resemblance*. Suppose one possibility saliently resembles another. Then if one of them may not be properly ignored, neither may the other. (Or rather, we should say that if one of them may not properly be ignored *in virtue*

12. Instead of complicating the Rule of Belief as I have just done, I might equivalently have introduced a separate Rule of High Stakes saying that when error would be especially disastrous, few possibilities are property ignored.
13. A. D. Woozley, 'Knowing and Not Knowing', *Proceedings of the Aristotelian Society* 53 (1953) pp. 151–72; Colin Radford, 'Knowledge—By Examples', *Analysis* 27 (1966) pp. 1–11.

of rules other than this rule, then neither may the other. Else nothing could be properly ignored; because enough little steps of resemblance can take us from anywhere to anywhere.) Or suppose one possibility saliently resembles two or more others, one in one respect and another in another, and suppose that each of these may not properly be ignored (in virtue of rules other than this rule). Then these resemblances may have an additive effect, doing more together than any one of them would separately.

We must apply the Rule of Resemblance with care. Actuality is a possibility uneliminated by the subject's evidence. Any other possibility *W* that is likewise uneliminated by the subject's evidence thereby resembles actuality in one salient respect: namely, in respect of the subject's evidence. That will be so even if *W* is in other respects very dissimilar to actuality—even if, for instance, it is a possibility in which the subject is radically deceived by a demon. Plainly, we dare not apply the Rules of Actuality and Resemblance to conclude that any such *W* is a relevant alternative—that would be capitulation to scepticism. The Rule of Resemblance was never meant to apply to *this* resemblance! We seem to have an *ad hoc* exception to the Rule, though one that makes good sense in view of the function of attributions of knowledge. What would be better, though, would be to find a way to reformulate the Rule so as to get the needed exception without *ad hoc*ery. I do not know how to do this.

It is the Rule of Resemblance that explains why you do not know that you will lose the lottery, no matter what the odds are against you and no matter how sure you should therefore be that you will lose. For every ticket, there is the possibility that it will win. These possibilities are saliently similar to one another: so either every one of them may be properly ignored, or else none may. But one of them may not properly be ignored: the one that actually obtains.

The Rule of Resemblance also is the rule that solves the Gettier problems: other cases of justified true belief that are not knowledge.[14]

(1) I think that Nogot owns a Ford, because I have seen him driving one; but unbeknownst to me he does not own the Ford he drives, or any other Ford. Unbeknownst to me, Havit does own a Ford, though I have no reason to think so because he never drives it, and in fact I have often seen him taking the tram. My justified true belief is that one of the two owns a Ford. But I do not know it; I am right by accident. Diagnosis: I do not know, because I have not eliminated the possibility that Nogot drives a Ford he does not own whereas Havit neither drives nor owns a car. This third possibility may not properly be ignored. Because, first,

---

14. See Edmund Gettier, 'Is Justified True Belief Knowledge?', *Analysis* 23 (1963) pp. 121–3 [Ch. 2 in this volume]. Diagnoses have varied widely. The four examples below come from: (1) Keith Lehrer and Thomas Paxson Jr., 'Knowledge: Undefeated Justified True Belief', *The Journal of Philosophy* 66 (1969) pp. 225–37 [Ch. 5 in this volume]; (2) Bertrand Russell, *Human Knowledge: Its Scope and Limits* (London: Allen and Unwin, 1948) p. 154; (3) Alvin Goldman, 'Discrimination and Perceptual Knowledge', op. cit. [Ch. 8 in this volume]; (4) Gilbert Harman, *Thought* (Princeton, NJ: Princeton University Press, 1973) p. 143.

Though the lottery problem is another case of justified true belief without knowledge, it is not normally counted among the Gettier problems. It is interesting to find that it yields to the same remedy.

actuality may not properly be ignored; and, second, this possibility saliently resembles actuality. It resembles actuality perfectly so far as Nogot is concerned; and it resembles actuality well so far as Havit is concerned, since it matches actuality both with respect to Havit's carless habits and with respect to the general correlation between carless habits and carlessness. In addition, this possibility saliently resembles a third possibility: one in which Nogot drives a Ford he owns while Havit neither drives nor owns a car. This third possibility may not properly be ignored, because of the degree to which it is believed. This time, the resemblance is perfect so far as Havit is concerned, rather good so far as Nogot is concerned.

(2) The stopped clock is right twice a day. It says 4:39, as it has done for weeks. I look at it at 4:39; by luck I pick up a true belief. I have ignored the uneliminated possibility that I looked at it at 4:22 while it was stopped saying 4:39. That possibility was not properly ignored. It resembles actuality perfectly so far as the stopped clock goes.

(3) Unbeknownst to me, I am travelling in the land of the bogus barns; but my eye falls on one of the few real ones. I don't know that I am seeing a barn, because I may not properly ignore the possibility that I am seeing yet another of the abundant bogus barns. This possibility saliently resembles actuality in respect of the abundance of bogus barns, and the scarcity of real ones, hereabouts.

(4) Donald is in San Francisco, just as I have every reason to think he is. But, bent on deception, he is writing me letters and having them posted to me by his accomplice in Italy. If I had seen the phoney letters, with their Italian stamps and postmarks, I would have concluded that Donald was in Italy. Luckily, I have not yet seen any of them. I ignore the uneliminated possibility that Donald has gone to Italy and is sending me letters from there. But this possibility is not properly ignored, because it resembles actuality both with respect to the fact that the letters are coming to me from Italy and with respect to the fact that those letters come, ultimately, from Donald. So I don't know that Donald is in San Francisco.

Next, there is the *Rule of Reliability*. This time, we have a presumptive rule about what *may* be properly ignored; and it is by means of this rule that we capture what is right about causal or reliabilist theories of knowing. Consider processes whereby information is transmitted to us: perception, memory, and testimony. These processes are fairly reliable.[15] Within limits, we are entitled to take them for granted. We may properly presuppose that work without a glitch in the case under consideration. Defeasibly—*very* defeasibly!—a possibility in which they fail may properly be ignored.

My visual experience, for instance, depends causally on the scene before my eyes, and what I believe about the scene before my eyes depends in turn on my visual experience. Each dependence covers a wide and varied range of alternatives.[16] Of

15. See Alvin Goldman, 'A Causal Theory of Knowing', *The Journal of Philosophy* 64 (1967) pp. 357–72 [Ch. 4 in this volume]; D. M. Armstrong, *Belief, Truth and Knowledge* (Cambridge: Cambridge University Press, 1973).

16. See my 'Veridical Hallucination and Prosthetic Vision', *Australasian Journal of Philosophy* 58 (1980) pp. 239–49. John Bigelow has proposed to model knowledge-delivering processes generally on those found in vision.

course, it is possible to hallucinate—even to hallucinate in such a way that all my perceptual experience and memory would be just as they actually are. That possibility never can be eliminated. But it can be ignored. And if it is properly ignored—as it mostly is—then vision gives me knowledge. Sometimes, though, the possibility of hallucination is not properly ignored; for sometimes we really do hallucinate. The Rule of Reliability may be defeated by the Rule of Actuality. Or it may be defeated by the Rules of Actuality and of Resemblance working together, in a Gettier problem: if I am not hallucinating, but unbeknownst to me I live in a world where people mostly do hallucinate and I myself have only narrowly escaped, then the uneliminated possibility of hallucination is too close to actuality to be properly ignored.

We do not, of course, presuppose that nowhere ever is there a failure of, say, vision. The general presupposition that vision is reliable consists, rather, of a standing disposition to presuppose, concerning whatever particular case may be under consideration, that we have no failure in that case.

In similar fashion, we have two permissive *Rules of Method*. We are entitled to presuppose—again, very defeasibly—that a sample is representative; and that the best explanation of our evidence is the true explanation. That is, we are entitled properly to ignore possible failures in these two standard methods of non-deductive inference. Again, the general rule consists of a standing disposition to presuppose reliability in whatever particular case may come before us.

Yet another permissive rule is the *Rule of Conservatism*. Suppose that those around us normally do ignore certain possibilities, and it is common knowledge that they do. (They do, they expect each other to, they expect each other to expect each other to, . . .) Then—again, very defeasibly!—these generally ignored possibilities may properly be ignored. We are permitted, defeasibly, to adopt the usual and mutually expected presuppositions of those around us.

(It is unclear whether we need all four of these permissive rules. Some might be subsumed under others. Perhaps our habits of treating samples as representative, and of inferring to the best explanation, might count as normally reliable processes of transmission of information. Or perhaps we might subsume the Rule of Reliability under the Rule of Conservatism, on the ground that the reliable processes whereby we gain knowledge are familiar, are generally relied upon, and so are generally presupposed to be normally reliable. Then the only extra work done by the Rule of Reliability would be to cover less familiar—and merely hypothetical?—reliable processes, such as processes that relied on extrasensory faculties. Likewise, *mutatis mutandis*, we might subsume the Rules of Method under the Rule of Conservatism. Or we might instead think to subsume the Rule of Conservatism under the Rule of Reliability, on the ground that what is generally presupposed tends for the most part to be true, and the reliable processes whereby this is so are covered already by the Rule of Reliability. Better redundancy than incompleteness, though. So, leaving the question of redundancy open, I list all four rules.)

Our final rule is the *Rule of Attention*. But it is more a triviality than a rule. When we say that a possibility *is* properly ignored, we mean exactly that; we do not mean that it *could have been* properly ignored. Accordingly, a possibility not ignored at all is *ipso facto* not properly ignored. What is and what is not being ignored is a feature of the particular conversational context. No matter how far-fetched a certain possibility may be, no matter how properly we might have ignored it in some other context, if in *this* context we are not in fact ignoring it but attending to it, then for us now it is a relevant alternative. It is in the contextually determined domain. If it is an uneliminated possibility in which not-*P*, then it will do as a counter-example to the claim that *P* holds in every possibility left uneliminated by *S*'s evidence. That is, it will do as a counter-example to the claim that *S* knows that *P*.

Do some epistemology. Let your fantasies rip. Find uneliminated possibilities of error everywhere. Now that you are attending to them, just as I told you to, you are no longer ignoring them, properly or otherwise. So you have landed in a context with an enormously rich domain of potential counter-examples to ascriptions of knowledge. In such an extraordinary context, with such a rich domain, it never can happen (well, hardly ever) that an ascription of knowledge is true. Not an ascription of knowledge to yourself (either to your present self or to your earlier self, untainted by epistemology); and not an ascription of knowledge to others. That is how epistemology destroys knowledge. But it does so only temporarily. The pastime of epistemology does not plunge us forevermore into its special context. We can still do a lot of proper ignoring, a lot of knowing, and a lot of true ascribing of knowledge to ourselves and others, the rest of the time.

What is epistemology all about? The epistemology we've just been doing, at any rate, soon became an investigation of the ignoring of possibilities. But to investigate the ignoring of them was *ipso facto* not to ignore them. Unless this investigation of ours was an altogether atypical sample of epistemology, it will be inevitable that epistemology must destroy knowledge. That is how knowledge is elusive. Examine it, and straightway it vanishes.

Is resistance useless? If you bring some hitherto ignored possibility to our attention, then straightway we are not ignoring it at all, so *a fortiori* we are not properly ignoring it. How can this alteration of our conversational state be undone? If you are persistent, perhaps it cannot be undone—at least not so long as you are around. Even if we go off and play backgammon, and afterward start our conversation afresh, you might turn up and call our attention to it all over again.

But maybe you called attention to the hitherto ignored possibility by mistake. You only suggested that we ought to suspect the butler because you mistakenly thought him to have a criminal record. Now that you know he does not—that was the *previous* butler—you wish you had not mentioned him at all. You know as well as we do that continued attention to the possibility you brought up impedes our shared conversational purposes. Indeed, it may be common knowledge between you and us that we would all prefer it if this possibility could be dismissed from our attention. In that case we might quickly strike a tacit agreement to speak just as if we were ignoring it; and after just a little of that, doubtless it really would be ignored.

Sometimes our conversational purposes are not altogether shared, and it is a matter of conflict whether attention to some far-fetched possibility would advance them or impede them. What if some far-fetched possibility is called to our attention not by a sceptical philosopher, but by counsel for the defence? We of the jury may wish to ignore it, and wish it had not been mentioned. If we ignored it now, we would bend the rules of cooperative conversation; but we may have good reason to do exactly that. (After all, what matters most to us as jurors is not whether we can truly be said to know; what really matters is what we should believe to what degree, and whether or not we should vote to convict.) We would ignore the far-fetched possibility if we could—but can we? Perhaps at first our attempted ignoring would be make-believe ignoring, or self-deceptive ignoring; later, perhaps, it ought ripen into genuine ignoring. But in the meantime, do we know? There may be no definite answer. We are bending the rules, and our practices of context-dependent attributions of knowledge were made for contexts with the rules unbent.

If you are still a contented fallibilist, despite my plea to hear the sceptical argument afresh, you will probably be discontented with the Rule of Attention. You will begrudge the sceptic even his very temporary victory. You will claim the right to resist his argument not only in everyday contexts, but even in those peculiar contexts in which he (or some other epistemologist) busily calls your attention to far-fetched possibilities of error. Further, you will claim the right to resist without having to bend any rules of cooperative conversation. I said that the Rule of Attention was a triviality: that which is not ignored at all is not properly ignored. But the Rule was trivial only because of how I had already chosen to state the *sotto voce* proviso. So you, the contented fallibilist, will think it ought to have been stated differently. Thus, perhaps: 'Psst!—except for those possibilities we *could* properly have ignored'. And then you will insist that those far-fetched possibilities of error that we attend to at the behest of the sceptic are nevertheless possibilities we could properly have ignored. You will say that no amount of attention can, by itself, turn them into relevant alternatives.

If you say this, we have reached a standoff. I started with a puzzle: how can it be, when his conclusion is so silly, that the sceptic's argument is so irresistible? My Rule of Attention, and the version of the proviso that made that Rule trivial, were built to explain how the sceptic manages to sway us—why his argument seems irresistible, however temporarily. If you continue to find it eminently resistible in all contexts, you have no need of any such explanation. We just disagree about the explanandum phenomenon.

I say S knows that P iff P holds in every possibility left uneliminated by S's evidence—Psst!—except for those possibilities that *we* are properly ignoring. 'We' means: the speaker and hearers of a given context; that is, those of us who are discussing S's knowledge together. It is our ignorings, not S's own ignorings, that matter to what we can truly say about S's knowledge. When we are talking about our own knowledge or ignorance, as epistemologists so often do, this is a distinction without a difference. But what if we are talking about someone else?

Suppose we are detectives; the crucial question for our solution of the crime is whether *S* already *knew*, when he bought the gun, that he was vulnerable to black-mail. We conclude that he did. *We* ignore various far-fetched possibilities, as hard-headed detectives should. But *S* does not ignore them. *S* is by profession a sceptical epistemologist. He never ignores much of anything. If it is our own ignorings that matter to the truth of our conclusion, we may well be right that *S* already knew. But if it is *S*'s ignorings that matter, then we are wrong, because *S* never knew much of anything. I say we may well be right; so it is our own ignorings that matter, not *S*'s.

But suppose instead that we are epistemologists considering what *S* knows. If we are well-informed about *S* (or if we are considering a well-enough specified hypo-thetical case), then if *S* attends to a certain possibility, we attend to *S*'s attending to it. But to attend to *S*'s attending to it is *ipso facto* to attend to it ourselves. In that case, unlike the case of the detectives, the possibilities we are properly ignoring must be among the possibilities that *S* himself ignores. We may ignore fewer possi-bilities than *S* does, but not more.

Even if *S* himself is neither sceptical nor an epistemologist, he may yet be clever at thinking up far-fetched possibilities that are uneliminated by his evidence. Then again, we well-informed epistemologists who ask what *S* knows will have to attend to the possibilities that *S* thinks up. Even if *S*'s idle cleverness does not lead *S* him-self to draw sceptical conclusions, it nevertheless limits the knowledge that we can truly ascribe to him when attentive to his state of mind. More simply: his cleverness limits his knowledge. He would have known more, had he been less imaginative.[17]

Do I claim you can know *P* just by presupposing it?! Do I claim you can know that a possibility *W* does not obtain just by ignoring it? Is that not what my analysis implies, provided that the presupposing and the ignoring are proper? Well, yes. And yet I do not claim it. Or rather, I do not claim it for any specified *P* or *W*. I have to grant, in general, that knowledge just by presupposing and ignoring *is* knowledge; but it is an *especially* elusive sort of knowledge, and consequently it is an unclaim-able sort of knowledge. You do not even have to practice epistemology to make it vanish. Simply *mentioning* any particular case of this knowledge, aloud or even in silent thought, is a way to attend to the hitherto ignored possibility, and thereby render it no longer ignored, and thereby create a context in which it is no longer true to ascribe the knowledge in question to yourself or others. So, just as we should think, presuppositions alone are not a basis on which to *claim* knowledge.

In general, when *S* knows that *P* some of the possibilities in which not-*P* are eliminated by *S*'s evidence and others of them are properly ignored. There are some that can be eliminated, but cannot properly be ignored. For instance, when I look around the study without seeing Possum the cat, I thereby eliminate various possibilities in which Possum is in the study; but had those possibilities not been

17. See Catherine Elgin, 'The Epistemic Efficacy of Stupidity', *Synthese* 74 (1988) pp. 297–311. The 'efficacy' takes many forms; some to do with knowledge (under various rival analyses), some to do with justified belief. See also Michael Williams, *Unnatural Doubts: Epistemological Realism and the Basis of Scepticism* (Oxford: Blackwell, 1991) pp. 352–5, on the instability of knowledge under reflection.

eliminated, they could not properly have been ignored. And there are other possibilities that never can be eliminated, but can properly be ignored. For instance, the possibility that Possum is on the desk but has been made invisible by a deceiving demon falls normally into this class (though not when I attend to it in the special context of epistemology).

There is a third class: not-P possibilities that might either be eliminated or ignored. Take the far-fetched possibility that Possum has somehow managed to get into a closed drawer of the desk—maybe he jumped in when it was open, then I closed it without noticing him. That possibility could be eliminated by opening the drawer and making a thorough examination. But if uneliminated, it may nevertheless be ignored, and in many contexts that ignoring would be proper. If I look all around the study, but without checking the closed drawers of the desk, I may truly be said to know that Possum is not in the study—or at any rate, there are many contexts in which that may truly be said. But if I did check all the closed drawers, then I would know *better* that Possum is not in the study. My knowledge would be better in the second case because it would rest more on the elimination of not-P possibilities, less on the ignoring of them.[18, 19]

Better knowledge is more stable knowledge: it stands more chance of surviving a shift of attention in which we begin to attend to some of the possibilities formerly ignored. If, in our new shifted context, we ask what knowledge we may truly ascribe to our earlier selves, we may find that only the better knowledge of our earlier selves still deserves the name. And yet, if our former ignorings were proper at the time, even the worse knowledge of our earlier selves could truly have been called knowledge in the former context.

Never—well, hardly ever—does our knowledge rest entirely on elimination and not at all on ignoring. So hardly ever is it quite as good as we might wish. To that extent, the lesson of scepticism is right—and right permanently, not just in the temporary and special context of epistemology.[20]

What is it all for? Why have a notion of knowledge that works in the way I

---

18. Mixed cases are possible: Fred properly ignores the possibility W_1 which Ted eliminates; however Ted properly ignores the possibility W_2 which Fred eliminates. Ted has looked in all the desk drawers but not the file drawers, whereas Fred has checked the file drawers but not the desk. Fred's knowledge that Possum is not in the study is better in one way, Ted's is better in another.

19. To say truly that X is known, I must be properly ignoring any uneliminated possibilities in which not-X; whereas to say truly that Y is better known than X, I must be attending to some such possibilities. So I cannot say both in a single context. If I say 'X is known, but Y is better known', the context changes in mid-sentence: some previously ignored possibilities must stop being ignored. That can happen easily. Saying it the other way around—'Y is better known than X, but even X is known'—is harder, because we must suddenly start to ignore previously unignored possibilities. That cannot be done, really; but we could bend the rules and make believe we had done it, and no doubt we would be understood well enough. Saying 'X is flat, but Y is flatter' (that is, 'X has no bumps at all, but Y has even fewer or no bumps') is a parallel case. And again, 'Y is flatter, but even X is flat' sounds clearly worse—but not altogether hopeless.

20. Thanks here to Stephen Hetherington. While his own views about better and worse knowledge are situated within an analysis of knowledge quite unlike mine, they withstand transplantation.

described? (Not a compulsory question. Enough to observe that we do have it.) But I venture the guess that it is one of the messy short-cuts—like satisficing, like having indeterminate degrees of belief—that we resort to because we are not smart enough to live up to really high, perfectly Bayesian, standards of rationality. You cannot maintain a record of exactly which possibilities you have eliminated so far, much as you might like to. It is easier to keep track of which possibilities you have eliminated if you—Psst!—ignore many of all the possibilities there are. And besides, it is easier to list some of the propositions that are true in *all* the uneliminated, unignored possibilities than it is to find propositions that are true in *all and only* the uneliminated, unignored possibilities.

If you doubt that the word 'know' bears any real load in science or in metaphysics, I partly agree. The serious business of science has to do not with knowledge *per se*, but rather, with the elimination of possibilities through the evidence of perception, memory, etc., and with the changes that one's belief system would (or might or should) undergo under the impact of such eliminations. Ascriptions of knowledge to yourself or others are a very sloppy way of conveying very incomplete information about the elimination of possibilities. It is as if you had said:

The possibilities eliminated, whatever else they may also include, at least include all the not-P possibilities; or anyway, all of those except for some we are presumably prepared to ignore just at the moment.

The only excuse for giving information about what really matters in such a sloppy way is that at least it is easy and quick! But it *is* easy and quick; whereas giving full and precise information about which possibilities have been eliminated seems to be extremely difficult, as witness the futile search for a 'pure observation language'. If I am right about how ascriptions of knowledge work, they are a handy but humble approximation. They may yet be indispensable in practice, in the same way that other handy and humble approximations are.

If we analyse knowledge as a modality, as we have done, we cannot escape the conclusion that knowledge is closed under (strict) implication.[21] Dretske has denied that knowledge is closed under implication; further, he has diagnosed closure as the fallacy that drives arguments for scepticism. As follows: the proposition that I have hands implies that I am not a handless being, and *a fortiori* that I am not a handless being deceived by a demon into thinking that I have hands. So, by the closure principle, the proposition that I know I have hands implies that I know that I am not handless and deceived. But I don't know that I am not handless and deceived— for how can I eliminate that possibility? So, by *modus tollens*, I don't know that I have hands. Dretske's advice is to resist scepticism by denying closure. He says that

21. A proof-theoretic version of this closure principle is common to all 'normal' modal logics: if the logic validates an inference from zero or more premises to a conclusion, then also it validates the inference obtained by prefixing the necessity operator to each premise and to the conclusion. Further, this rule is all we need to take us from classical sentential logic to the least normal modal logic. See Brian Chellas, *Modal Logic: An Introduction* (Cambridge: Cambridge University Press, 1980) p. 114.

although having hands *does* imply not being handless and deceived, yet knowing that I have hands *does not* imply knowing that I am not handless and deceived. I do know the former, I do not know the latter.[22]

What Dretske says is close to right, but not quite. Knowledge *is* closed under implication. Knowing that I have hands *does* imply knowing that I am not handless and deceived. Implication preserves truth—that is, it preserves truth in any given, fixed context. But if we switch contexts midway, all bets are off. I say (1) pigs fly; (2) what I just said had fewer than three syllables (true); (3) what I just said had fewer than four syllables (false). So 'less than three' does not imply 'less than four'? No! The context switched midway, the semantic value of the context-dependent phrase 'what I just said' switched with it. Likewise in the sceptical argument the context switched midway, and the semantic value of the context-dependent word 'know' switched with it. The premise 'I know that I have hands' was true in its everyday context, where the possibility of deceiving demons was properly ignored. The mention of that very possibility switched the context midway. The conclusion 'I know that I am not handless and deceived' was false in *its* context, because that was a context in which the possibility of deceiving demons was being mentioned, hence was not being ignored, hence was not being properly ignored. Dretske gets the phenomenon right, and I think he gets the diagnosis of scepticism right; it is just that he misclassifies what he sees. He thinks it is a phenomenon of logic, when really it is a phenomenon of pragmatics. Closure, rightly understood, survives the test. If we evaluate the conclusion for truth not with respect to the context in which it was uttered, but instead with respect to the different context in which the premise was uttered, then truth is preserved. And if, *per impossibile*, the conclusion could have been said in the same unchanged context as the premise, truth would have been preserved.

A problem due to Saul Kripke turns upon the closure of knowledge under implication. *P* implies that any evidence against *P* is misleading. So, by closure, whenever you know that *P*, you know that any evidence against *P* is misleading. And you know that evidence is misleading, you should pay it no heed. Whenever we know—and we know a lot, remember—we should not heed any evidence tending to suggest that we are wrong. But that is absurd. Shall we dodge the conclusion by denying closure? I think not. Again, I diagnose a change of context. At first, it was stipulated that *S* knew, whence it followed that *S* was properly ignoring all possibilities of error. But as the story continues, it turns out that there is evidence on offer that points to some particular possibility of error. Then, by the Rule of Attention, that possibility is no longer properly ignored, either by *S* himself or by we who are telling the story of *S*. The advent of that evidence destroys *S*'s knowledge, and thereby destroys *S*'s licence to ignore the evidence lest he be misled.

There is another reason, different from Dretske's, why we might doubt closure. Suppose two or more premises jointly imply a conclusion. Might not someone who is compartmentalized in his thinking—as we all are?—know each of the premises but fail to bring them together in a single compartment? Then might he not fail to

22. See Fred Dretske, 'Epistemic Operators', *Journal of Philosophy* 67 (1970) pp. 1007–23.

know the conclusion? Yes; and I would not like to plead idealization-of-rationality as an excuse for ignoring such cases. But I suggest that we might take not the whole compartmentalized thinker, but rather each of his several overlapping compartments, as our 'subjects'. That would be the obvious remedy if his compartmentalization amounted to a case of multiple personality disorder; but maybe it is right for milder cases as well.[23]

A compartmentalized thinker who indulges in epistemology can destroy his knowledge, yet retain it as well. Imagine two epistemologists on a bushwalk. As they walk, they talk. They mention all manner of far-fetched possibilities of error. By attending to these normally ignored possibilities they destroy the knowledge they normally possess. Yet all the while they know where they are and where they are going! How so? The compartment in charge of philosophical talk attends to far-fetched possibilities of error. The compartment in charge of navigation does not. One compartment loses its knowledge, the other retains its knowledge. And what does the entire compartmentalized thinker know? Not an altogether felicitous question. But if we need an answer, I suppose the best thing to say is that S knows that P iff any one of S's compartments knows that P. Then we can say what we would offhand want to say: yes, our philosophical bushwalkers still know their whereabouts.

Context-dependence is not limited to the ignoring and non-ignoring of far-fetched possibilities. Here is another case. Pity poor Bill! He squanders all his spare cash on the pokies, the races, and the lottery. He will be a wage slave all his days. We know he will never be rich. But if he wins the lottery (if he wins big), then he will be rich. Contrapositively: his never being rich, plus other things we know, imply that he will lose. So, by closure, if we know that he will never be rich, we know that he will lose. But when we discussed the case before, we concluded that we cannot know that he will lose. All the possibilities in which Bill loses and someone else wins saliently resemble the possibility in which Bill wins and the others lose; one of those possibilities is actual; so by the Rules of Actuality and of Resemblance, we may not properly ignore the possibility that Bill wins. But there is a loophole: the resemblance was required to be salient. Salience, as well as ignoring, may vary between contexts. Before, when I was explaining how the Rule of Resemblance applied to lotteries, I saw to it that the resemblance between the many possibilities associated with the many tickets was sufficiently salient. But this time, when we were busy pitying poor Bill for his habits and not for his luck, the resemblance of the many possibilities was not so salient. At that point, the possibility of Bill's winning was properly ignored; so then it was true to say that we knew he would never be rich. Afterward I switched the context. I mentioned the possibility that Bill might win, wherefore that possibility was no longer properly ignored. (Maybe there were two separate reasons why it was no longer properly ignored, because maybe I also made the resemblance between the many possibilities more salient.) It was true at first that we knew that Bill would never be rich. And at that point it was also true that we knew he would lose—but that was only true so long as it remained unsaid! (And

---

23. See Stalnaker, *Inquiry*, pp. 79–99.

maybe unthought as well.) Later, after the change in context, it was no longer true that we knew he would lose. At that point, it was also no longer true that we knew he would never be rich.

But wait. Don't you smell a rat? Haven't I, by my own lights, been saying what cannot be said? (Or whistled either.) If the story I told was true, how have I managed to tell it? In trendyspeak, is there not a problem of reflexivity? Does not my story deconstruct itself?

I said: *S* knows that *P* iff *S*'s evidence eliminates every possibility in which not-*P*—Psst! —except for those possibilities that we are properly ignoring. That 'psst' marks an attempt to do the impossible—to mention that which remains unmentioned. I am sure you managed to make believe that I had succeeded. But I could not have done.

And I said that when we do epistemology, and we attend to the proper ignoring of possibilities, we make knowledge vanish. First we do know, then we do not. But I had been doing epistemology when I said that. The uneliminated possibilities were being ignored—not just then. So by what right did I say even that we used to know?[24]

In trying to thread a course between the rock of fallibilism and the whirlpool of scepticism, it may well seem as if I have fallen victim to both at once. For do I not say that there are all those uneliminated possibilities of error? Yet do I not claim that we know a lot? Yet do I not claim that knowledge is, by definition, infallible knowledge?

I did claim all three things. But not all at once! Or if I did claim them all at once, that was an expository shortcut, to be taken with a pinch of salt. To get my message across, I bent the rules. If I tried to whistle what cannot be said, what of it? I relied on the cardinal principle of pragmatics, which overrides every one of the rules I mentioned: interpret the message to make it make sense—to make it consistent, and sensible to say.

When you have context-dependence, ineffability can be trite and unmysterious. Hush! [moment of silence] I might have liked to say, just then, 'All of us are silent'. It was true. But I could not have said it truly, or whistled it either. For by saying it aloud, or by whistling, I would have rendered it false.

I could have said my say fair and square, bending no rules. It would have been tiresome, but it could have been done. The secret would have been to resort to 'semantic ascent'. I could have taken great care to distinguish between (1) the language I use when I talk about knowledge, or whatever, and (2) the second language that I use to talk about the semantic and pragmatic workings of the first language. If you want to hear my story told that way, you probably know enough to do the job for yourself. If you can, then my informal presentation has been good enough.

24. Worse still: by what right can I even say that we used to be in a position to say truly that we knew? Then, we were in a context where we properly ignored certain uneliminated possibilities of error. Now, we are in a context where we no longer ignore them. If *now* I comment retrospectively upon the truth of what was said, *then* which context governs: the context now or the context then? I doubt there is any general answer, apart from the usual principle that we should interpret what is said so as to make the message make sense.

Semantic Approaches

Chapter 27

Brains in a vat

Hilary Putnam

An ant is crawling on a patch of sand. As it crawls, it traces a line in the sand. By pure chance the line that it traces curves and recrosses itself in such a way that it ends up looking like a recognizable caricature of Winston Churchill. Has the ant traced a picture of Winston Churchill, a picture that *depicts* Churchill?

Most people would say, on a little reflection, that it has not. The ant, after all, has never seen Churchill, or even a picture of Churchill, and it had no intention of depicting Churchill. It simply traced a line (and even *that* was unintentional), a line that *we* can 'see as' a picture of Churchill.

We can express this by saying that the line is not 'in itself' a representation[1] of anything rather than anything else. Similarity (of a certain very complicated sort) to the features of Winston Churchill is not sufficient to make something represent or refer to Churchill. Nor is it necessary: in our community the printed shape 'Winston Churchill', the spoken words 'Winston Churchill', and many other things are used to represent Churchill (though not pictorially), while not having the sort of similarity to Churchill that a picture—even a line drawing—has. If *similarity* is not necessary or sufficient to make something represent something else, how can *anything* be necessary or sufficient for this purpose? How on earth can one thing represent (or 'stand for', etc.) a different thing?

The answer may seem easy. Suppose the ant had seen Winston Churchill, and

Hilary Putnam, 'Brains in a Vat' in *Reason, Truth and History* (Cambridge, Cambridge University Press, 1981, pp. 1–21 reprinted by permission of the publisher and the author.

1. In this essay the terms 'representation' and 'reference' always refer to a relation between a word (or other sort of sign, symbol, or representation) and something that actually exists (i.e. not just an 'object of thought'). There is a sense of 'refer' in which I can 'refer' to what does not exist; this is not the sense in which 'refer' is used here. An older word for what I call 'representation' or 'reference' is *denotation*.

   Secondly, I follow the custom of modern logicians and use 'exist' to mean 'exist in the past, present, or future'. Thus Winston Churchill 'exists', and we can 'refer to' or 'represent' Winston Churchill, even though he is no longer alive.

suppose that it had the intelligence and skill to draw a picture of him. Suppose it produced the caricature *intentionally*. Then the line would have represented Churchill.

On the other hand, suppose the line had the shape WINSTON CHURCHILL. And suppose this was just accident (ignoring the improbability involved). Then the 'printed shape' WINSTON CHURCHILL would *not* have represented Churchill, although that printed shape does represent Churchill when it occurs in almost any book today.

So it may seem that what is necessary for representation, or what is mainly necessary for representation, is *intention*.

But to have the intention that *anything*, even private language (even the words 'Winston Churchill' spoken in my mind and not out loud), should *represent* Churchill, I must have been able to *think about* Churchill in the first place. If lines in the sand, noises, etc., cannot 'in themselves' represent anything, then how is it that thought forms can 'in themselves' represent anything? Or can they? How can thought reach out and 'grasp' what is external?

Some philosophers have, in the past, leaped from this sort of consideration to what they take to be a proof that the mind is *essentially non-physical in nature*. The argument is simple; what we said about the ant's curve applies to any physical object. No physical object can, in itself, refer to one thing rather than to another; nevertheless, *thoughts in the mind* obviously do succeed in referring to one thing rather than another. So thoughts (and hence the mind) are of an essentially different nature than physical objects. Thoughts have the characteristic of *intentionality*—they can refer to something else; nothing physical has 'intentionality', save as that intentionality is derivative from some employment of that physical thing by a mind. Or so it is claimed. This is too quick; just postulating mysterious powers of mind solves nothing. But the problem is very real. How is intentionality, reference, possible?

1. Magical theories of reference

We saw that the ant's 'picture' has no necessary connection with Winston Churchill. The mere fact that the 'picture' bears a 'resemblance' to Churchill does not make it into a real picture, nor does it make it a representation of Churchill. Unless the ant is an intelligent ant (which it isn't) and knows about Churchill (which it doesn't), the curve it traced is not a picture or even a representation of anything. Some primitive people believe that some representations (in particular, names) have a necessary connection with their bearers; that to know the 'true name' of someone or something gives one power over it. This power comes from the *magical connection* between the name and the bearer of the name; once one realizes that a name *only* has a contextual, contingent, conventional connection with its bearer, it is hard to see why knowledge of the name should have any mystical significance.

What is important to realize is that what goes for physical pictures also goes for mental images, and for mental representations in general; mental representations no more have a necessary connection with what they represent than physical representations do. The contrary supposition is a survival of magical thinking.

Perhaps the point is easiest to grasp in the case of mental *images*. (Perhaps the first philosopher to grasp the enormous significance of this point, even if he was not the first to actually make it, was Wittgenstein.) Suppose there is a planet somewhere on which human beings have evolved (or been deposited by alien spacemen, or what have you). Suppose these humans, although otherwise like us, have never seen *trees*. Suppose they have never imagined trees (perhaps vegetable life exists on their planet only in the form of molds). Suppose one day a picture of a tree is accidentally dropped on their planet by a spaceship which passes on without having other contact with them. Imagine them puzzling over the picture. What in the world is this? All sorts of speculations occur to them: a building, a canopy, even an animal of some kind. But suppose they never come close to the truth.

For *us* the picture is a representation of a tree. For these humans the picture only represents a strange object, nature and function unknown. Suppose one of them has a mental image which is exactly like one of my mental images of a tree as a result of having seen the picture. His mental image is not a *representation of a tree*. It is only a representation of the strange object (whatever it is) that the mysterious picture represents.

Still, someone might argue that the mental image is *in fact* a representation of a tree, if only because the picture which caused this mental image was itself a representation of a tree to begin with. There is a causal chain from actual trees to the mental image even if it is a very strange one.

But even this causal chain can be imagined absent. Suppose the 'picture of the tree' that the spaceship dropped was not really a picture of a tree, but the accidental result of some spilled paints. Even if it looked exactly like a picture of a tree, it was, in truth, no more a picture of a tree than the ant's 'caricature' of Churchill was a picture of Churchill. We can even imagine that the spaceship which dropped the 'picture' came from a planet which knew nothing of trees. Then the humans would still have mental images qualitatively identical with my image of a tree, but they would not be images which represented a tree any more than anything else.

The same thing is true of *words*. A discourse on paper might seem to be a perfect description of trees, but if it was produced by monkeys randomly hitting keys on a typewriter for millions of years, then the words do not refer to anything. If there were a person who memorized those words and said them in his mind without understanding them, then they would not refer to anything when thought in the mind, either.

Imagine the person who is saying those words in his mind has been hypnotized. Suppose the words are in Japanese, and the person has been told that he understands Japanese. Suppose that as he thinks those words he has a 'feeling of understanding'. (Although if someone broke into his train of thought and asked him what the words he was thinking *meant*, he would discover he couldn't say.) Perhaps the illusion would be so perfect that the person could even fool a Japanese telepath! But if he couldn't use the words in the right contexts, answer questions about what he 'thought', etc., then he didn't understand them.

By combining these science fiction stories I have been telling, we can contrive a case in which someone thinks words which are in fact a description of trees in some language *and* simultaneously has appropriate mental images, but *neither* understands the words *nor* knows what a tree is. We can even imagine that the mental images were caused by paint-spills (although the person has been hypnotized to think that they are images of something appropriate to his thought—only, if he were asked, he wouldn't be able to say of what). And we can imagine that the language the person is thinking in is one neither the hypnotist nor the person hypnotized has ever heard of—perhaps it is just coincidence that these 'nonsense sentences', as the hypnotist supposes them to be, are a description of trees in Japanese. In short, everything passing before the person's mind might be qualitatively identical with what was passing through the mind of a Japanese speaker who was *really* thinking about trees—but none of it would refer to trees.

All of this is really impossible, of course, in the way that it is really impossible that monkeys should by chance type out a copy of *Hamlet*. That is to say that the probabilities against it are so high as to mean it will never really happen (we think). But it is not logically impossible, or even physically impossible. It *could* happen (compatibly with physical law and, perhaps, compatibly with actual conditions in the universe, if there are lots of intelligent beings on other planets). And if it did happen, it would be a striking demonstration of an important conceptual truth; that even a large and complex system of representations, both verbal and visual, still does not have an *intrinsic* built-in, magical connection with what it represents—a connection independent of how it was caused and what the dispositions of the speaker or thinker are. And this is true whether the system of representations (words and images, in the case of the example) is physically realized—the words are written or spoken, and the pictures are physical pictures—or only realized in the mind. Thought words and mental pictures do not *intrinsically* represent what they are about.

2. The case of the brains in a vat

Here is a science fiction possibility discussed by philosophers: imagine that a human being (you can imagine this to be yourself) has been subjected to an operation by an evil scientist. The person's brain (your brain) has been removed from the body and placed in a vat of nutrients which keeps the brain alive. The nerve endings have been connected to a super-scientific computer which causes the person whose brain it is to have the illusion that everything is perfectly normal. There seem to be people, objects, the sky, etc; but really all the person (you) is experiencing is the result of electronic impulses travelling from the computer to the nerve endings. The computer is so clever that if the person tries to raise his hand, the feedback from the computer will cause him to 'see' and 'feel' the hand being raised. Moreover, by varying the program, the evil scientist can cause the victim to 'experience' (or hallucinate) any situation or environment the evil scientist wishes. He can also obliterate the memory of the brain operation, so that the victim will seem to himself to have always been in this environment. It can even seem to the victim that he is sitting and reading these very words about the amusing but quite absurd supposition that there is an evil scientist who removes people's brains from their bodies and places them in a vat of nutrients which keep the brains alive. The nerve endings are supposed to be connected to a super-scientific computer which causes the person whose brain it is to have the illusion that . . .

When this sort of possibility is mentioned in a lecture on the Theory of Knowledge, the purpose, of course, is to raise the classical problem of scepticism with respect to the external world in a modern way. (*How do you know you aren't in this predicament?*) But this predicament is also a useful device for raising issues about the mind/world relationship.

Instead of having just one brain in a vat, we could imagine that all human beings (perhaps all sentient beings) are brains in a vat (or nervous systems in a vat in case some beings with just a minimal nervous system already count as 'sentient'). Of course, the evil scientist would have to be outside—or would he? Perhaps there is no evil scientist, perhaps (though this is absurd) the universe just happens to consist of automatic machinery tending a vat full of brains and nervous systems.

This time let us suppose that the automatic machinery is programmed to give us all a *collective* hallucination, rather than a number of separate unrelated hallucinations. Thus, when I seem to myself to be talking to you, you seem to yourself to be hearing my words. Of course, it is not the case that my words actually reach your ears—for you don't have (real) ears, nor do I have a real mouth and tongue. Rather, when I produce my words, what happens is that the efferent impulses travel from my brain to the computer, which both causes me to 'hear' my own voice uttering those words and 'feel' my tongue moving, etc., and causes you to 'hear' my words, 'see' me speaking, etc. In this case, we are, in a sense, actually in communication. I am not mistaken about your real existence (only about the existence of your body and the 'external world', apart from brains). From a certain point of view, it doesn't even matter that 'the whole world' is a collective hallucination; for you do, after all, really hear my words when I speak to you, even if the mechanism isn't what we suppose it to be. (Of course, if we were two lovers making love, rather than just two people carrying on a conversation, then the suggestion that it was just two brains in a vat might be disturbing.)

I want now to ask a question which will seem very silly and obvious (at least to some people, including some very sophisticated philosophers), but which will take us to real philosophical depths rather quickly. Suppose this whole story were actually true. Could we, if we were brains in a vat in this way, *say* or *think* that we were?

I am going to argue that the answer is 'No, we couldn't.' In fact, I am going to argue that the supposition that we are actually brains in a vat, although it violates no physical law, and is perfectly consistent with everything we have experienced, cannot possibly be true. *It cannot possibly be true*, because it is, in a certain way, self-refuting.

The argument I am going to present is an unusual one, and it took me several years to convince myself that it is really right. But it is a correct argument. What makes it seem so strange is that it is connected with some of the very deepest issues in philosophy. (It first occurred to me when I was thinking about a theorem in modern logic the 'Skolem–Löwenheim Theorem' and I suddenly saw a connection between this theorem and some arguments in Wittgenstein's *Philosophical Investigations*.)

A 'self-refuting supposition' is one whose truth implies its own falsity. For example, consider the thesis that *all general statements are false.* This is a general statement. So if it is true, then it must be false. Hence, it is false. Sometimes a thesis is called 'self-refuting' if it is *the supposition that the thesis is entertained or enunciated* that implies its falsity. For example, 'I do not exist' is self-refuting if thought by *me* (for any '*me*'). So one can be certain that one oneself exists, if one thinks about it (as Descartes argued).

What I shall show is that the supposition that we are brains in a vat has just this property. If we can consider whether it is true or false, then it is not true (I shall show). Hence it is not true.

Before I give the argument, let us consider why it seems so strange that such an argument can be given (at least to philosophers who subscribe to a 'copy' conception of truth). We conceded that it is compatible with physical law that there should be a world in which all sentient beings are brains in a vat. As philosophers say, there is a 'possible world' in which all sentient beings are brains in a vat. (This 'possible world' talk makes it sound as if there is a *place* where any absurd supposition is true, which is why it can be very misleading in philosophy.) The humans in that possible world have exactly the same experiences that *we* do. They think the same thoughts we do (at least, the same words, images, thought-forms, etc., go through their minds). Yet, I am claiming that there is an argument we can give that shows we are not brains in a vat. How can there be? And why couldn't the people in the possible world who really are brains in a vat give it too?

The answer is going to be (basically) this: although the people in that possible world can think and 'say' any words we can think and say, they cannot (I claim) *refer* to what we can refer to. In particular, they cannot think or say that they are brains in a vat (*even by thinking 'we are brains in a vat'*).

3. Turing's test

Observation is crucial in the equation of consciousness

Suppose someone succeeds in inventing a computer which can actually carry on an intelligent conversation with one (on as many subjects as an intelligent person might). How can one decide if the computer is 'conscious'?

The British logician Alan Turing proposed the following test:[2] let someone carry on a conversation with the computer and a conversation with a person whom he does not know. If he cannot tell which is the computer and which is the human being, then (assume the test to be repeated a sufficient number of times with different interlocutors) the computer is conscious. In short, a computing machine

2. A. M. Turing, 'Computing Machinery and Intelligence', *Mind* (1950), reprinted in A. R. Anderson (ed.), *Minds and Machines.*

Can computers observe

is conscious if it can pass the 'Turing Test'. (The conversations are not to be carried on face to face, of course, since the interlocutor is not to know the visual appearance of either of his two conversational partners. Nor is voice to be used, since the mechanical voice might simply sound different from a human voice. Imagine, rather, that the conversations are all carried on via electric typewriter. The interlocutor types in his statements, questions, etc., and the two partners—the machine and the person—respond via the electric keyboard. Also, the machine may *lie*— asked 'Are you a machine' it might reply, 'No, I'm an assistant in the lab here.')

The idea that this test is really a definitive test of consciousness has been criticized by a number of authors (who are by no means hostile in principle to the idea that a machine might be conscious). But this is not our topic at this time. I wish to use the general idea of the Turing test, the general idea of a *dialogic test of competence*, for a different purpose, the purpose of exploring the notion of *reference*.

Imagine a situation in which the problem is not to determine if the partner is really a person or a machine, but is rather to determine if the partner uses the words to refer as we do. The obvious test is, again, to carry on a conversation, and, if no problems arise, if the partner 'passes' in the sense of being indistinguishable from someone who is certified in advance to be speaking the same language, referring to the usual sorts of objects, etc., to conclude that the partner does refer to objects as we do. When the purpose of the Turing test is as just described, that is, to determine the existence of (shared) reference, I shall refer to the test as the *Turing Test for Reference*. And, just as philosophers have discussed the question whether the original Turing test is a *definitive* test for consciousness, i.e. the question of whether a machine which 'passes' the test not just once but regularly is *necessarily* conscious, so, in the same way, I wish to discuss the question of whether the Turing Test for Reference just suggested is a definitive test for shared reference.

The answer will turn out to be 'No'. The Turing Test for Reference is not definitive. It is certainly an excellent test in practice; but it is not logically impossible (though it is certainly highly improbable) that someone could pass the Turing Test for Reference and not be referring to anything. It follows from this, as we shall see, that we can extend our observation that words (and whole texts and discourses) do not have a necessary connection to their referents. Even if we consider not words by themselves but rules deciding what words may appropriately be produced in certain contexts—even if we consider, in computer jargon, *programs for using words*— unless those programs themselves *refer to something extra-linguistic* there is still no determinate reference that those words possess. This will be a crucial step in the process of reaching the conclusion that the Brain-in-a-Vat Worlders cannot refer to anything external at all (and hence cannot say that they are Brain-in-a-Vat Worlders).

Suppose, for example, that I am in the Turing situation (playing the 'Imitation Game', in Turing's terminology) and my partner is actually a machine. Suppose this machine is able to win the game ('passes' the test). Imagine the machine to be programmed to produce beautiful responses in English to statements, questions, remarks, etc. in English, but that it has no sense organs (other than the hookup to my electric typewriter), and no motor organs (other than the electric typewriter).

(As far as I can make out, Turing does not assume that the possession of either sense organs or motor organs is necessary for consciousness or intelligence.) Assume that not only does the machine lack electronic eyes and ears, etc., but that there are no provisions in the machine's program, the program for playing the Imitation Game, for incorporating inputs from such sense organs, or for controlling a body. What should we say about such a machine?

To me, it seems evident that we cannot and should not attribute reference to such a device. It is true that the machine can discourse beautifully about, say, the scenery in New England. But it could not recognize an apple tree or an apple, a mountain or a cow, a field or a steeple, if it were in front of one.

What we have is a device for producing sentences in response to sentences. But none of these sentences is at all connected to the real world. *If one coupled two of these machines and let them play the Imitation Game with each other, then they would go on 'fooling' each other forever, even if the rest of the world disappeared!* There is no more reason to regard the machine's talk of apples as referring to real world apples than there is to regard the ant's 'drawing' as referring to Winston Churchill.

What produces the illusion of reference, meaning, intelligence, etc., here is the fact that there is a convention of representation which *we* have under which the machine's discourse refers to apples, steeples, New England, etc. Similarly, there is the *illusion* that the ant has caricatured Churchill, for the same reason. But we are able to perceive, handle, deal with apples and fields. Our talk of apples and fields is intimately connected with our *non-verbal* transactions with apples and fields. There are 'language entry rules' which take us from experiences of apples to such utterances as 'I see an apple', and 'language exit rules' which take us from decisions expressed in linguistic form ('I am going to buy some apples') to actions other than speaking. Lacking either language entry rules or language exit rules, there is no reason to regard the conversation of the machine (or of the two machines, in the case we envisaged of two machines playing the Imitation Game with each other) as more than syntactic play. Syntactic play that *resembles* intelligent discourse, to be sure; but only as (and no more than) the ant's curve resembles a biting caricature.

In the case of the ant, we could have argued that the ant would have drawn the same curve even if Winston Churchill had never existed. In the case of the machine, we cannot quite make the parallel argument; if apples, trees, steeples and fields had not existed, then, presumably, the programmers would not have produced that same program. Although the machine does not *perceive* apples, fields, or steeples, its creator—designers did. There is *some* causal connection between the machine and the real world apples, etc., via the perceptual experience and knowledge of the creator—designers. But such a weak connection can hardly suffice for reference. Not only is it logically possible, though fantastically improbable, that the same machine *could* have existed even if apples, fields, and steeples had not existed; more important, the machine is utterly insensitive to the *continued* existence of apples, fields, steeples, etc. Even if all these things *ceased* to exist, the machine would still discourse just as happily in the same way. That is why the machine cannot be regarded as referring at all.

The point that is relevant for our discussion is that there is nothing in Turing's

Time machine

Test to rule out a machine which is programmed to do nothing *but* play the Imitation Game, and that a machine which can do nothing *but* play the Imitation Game is *clearly* not referring any more than a record player is.

4. Brains in a vat (again)

Let us compare the hypothetical 'brains in a vat' with the machines just described. There are obviously important differences. The brains in a vat do not have sense organs, but they do have *provision* for sense organs; that is, there are afferent nerve endings, there are inputs from these afferent nerve endings, and these inputs figure in the 'program' of the brains in the vat just as they do in the program of our brains. The brains in a vat are *brains*; moreover, they are *functioning* brains, and they function by the same rules as brains do in the actual world. For these reasons, it would seem absurd to deny consciousness or intelligence to them. But the fact that they are conscious and intelligent does not mean that their words refer to what our words refer. The question we are interested in is this: do their verbalizations containing, say, the word 'tree' actually refer to *trees*? More generally: can they refer to *external* objects at all? (As opposed to, for example, objects in the image produced by the automatic machinery.)

To fix our ideas, let us specify that the automatic machinery is supposed to have come into existence by some kind of cosmic chance or coincidence (or, perhaps, to have always existed). In this hypothetical world, the automatic machinery itself is supposed to have no intelligent creator–designers. In fact, as we said at the beginning of this chapter, we may imagine that all sentient beings (however minimal their sentience) are inside the vat.

This assumption does not help. For there is no connection between the *word* 'tree' as used by these brains and actual trees. They would still use the word 'tree' just as they do, think just the thoughts they do, have just the images they have, even if there were no actual trees. Their images, words, etc., are qualitatively identical with images, words, etc., which do represent trees in *our* world; but we have already seen (the ant again!) that qualitative similarity to something which represents an object (Winston Churchill or a tree) does not make a thing a representation all by itself. In short, the brains in a vat are not thinking about real trees when they think 'there is a tree in front of me' because there is nothing by virtue of which their thought 'tree' represents actual trees.

If this seems hasty, reflect on the following: we have seen that the words do not necessarily refer to trees even if they are arranged in a sequence which is identical with a discourse which (were it to occur in one of our minds) would unquestionably *be about trees* in the actual world. Nor does the 'program', in the sense of the rules, practices, dispositions of the brains to verbal behavior, necessarily refer to trees or bring about reference to trees through the connections it establishes between words and words, or *linguistic* cues and *linguistic* responses. If these brains think about, refer to, represent trees (real trees, outside the vat), then it must be because of the way the 'program' connects the system of language to *non-verbal* input and outputs. There are indeed such non-verbal inputs and outputs in the Brain-in-a-Vat world (those efferent and afferent nerve endings again!), but we also saw that the 'sense-data' produced by the automatic machinery do not represent trees (or anything external) even when they resemble our tree-images exactly. Just as a splash of paint might resemble a tree picture without *being* a tree picture, so, we saw, a 'sense datum' might be qualitatively identical with an 'image of a tree' without being an image of a tree. How can the fact that, in the case of the brains in a vat, the language is connected by the program with sensory inputs which do not intrinsically or extrinsically represent trees (or anything external) possibly bring it about that the whole system of representations, the language-in-use, *does* refer to or represent trees or anything external?

The answer is that it cannot. The whole system of sense-data, motor signals to the efferent endings, and verbally or conceptually mediated thought connected by 'language entry rules' to the sense-data (or whatever) as inputs and by 'language exit rules' to the motor signals as outputs, has no more connection to *trees* than the ant's curve has to Winston Churchill. Once we see that the *qualitative similarity* (amounting, if you like, to qualitative identity) between the thoughts of the brains in a vat and the thoughts of someone in the actual world by no means implies sameness of reference, it is not hard to see that there is no basis at all for regarding the brain in a vat as referring to external things.

5. The premisses of the argument

I have now given the argument promised to show that the brains in a vat cannot think or say that they are brains in a vat. It remains only to make it explicit and to examine its structure.

By what was just said, when the brain in a vat (in the world where every sentient being is and always was a brain in a vat) thinks 'There is a tree in front of me', his thought does not refer to actual trees. On some theories that we shall discuss it might refer to trees in the image, or to the electronic impulses that cause tree experiences, or to the features of the program that are responsible for those electronic impulses. These theories are not ruled out by what was just said, for there is a close causal connection between the use of the word 'tree' in vat-English and the presence of trees in the image, the presence of electronic impulses of a certain kind, and the presence of certain features in the machine's program. On these theories the brain is *right*, not *wrong* in thinking 'There is a tree in front of me.' Given what 'tree' refers to in vat-English and what 'in front of' refers to, assuming one of these theories is correct, then the truth-conditions for 'There is a tree in front of me' when it occurs in vat-English are simply that a tree in the image be 'in front of' the 'me' in question—in the image—or, perhaps, that the kind of electronic impulse that normally produces this experience be coming from the automatic machinery, or, perhaps, that the feature of the machinery that is supposed to produce the 'tree in front of one' experience be operating. And these truth-conditions are certainly fulfilled.

By the same argument, 'vat' refers to vats in the image in vat-English, or something related (electronic impulses or program features), but certainly not to real vats, since the use of 'vat' in vat-English has no causal connection to real vats (apart from the connection that the brains in a vat wouldn't be able to use the word 'vat', if it were not for the presence of one particular vat—the vat they are in; but this connection obtains between the use of *every* word in vat-English and that one particular vat; it is not a special connection between the use of the *particular* word 'vat' and vats). Similarly, 'nutrient fluid' refers to a liquid in the image in vat-English, or something related (electronic impulses or program features). It follows that if their 'possible world' is really the actual one, and we are really the brains in a vat, then what we now mean by 'we are brains in a vat' is that *we are brains in a vat in the image* or something of that kind (if we mean anything at all). But part of the hypothesis that we are brains in a vat is that we aren't brains in a vat in the image (i.e. what we are 'hallucinating' isn't that we are brains in a vat). So, if we are brains in a vat, then the sentence 'We are brains in a vat' says something false (if it says anything). In short, if we are brains in a vat, then 'We are brains in a vat' is false. So it is (necessarily) false.

The supposition that such a possibility makes sense arises from a combination of two errors: (1) taking *physical possibility* too seriously; and (2) unconsciously operating with a magical theory of reference, a theory on which certain mental representations necessarily refer to certain external things and kinds of things.

There is a 'physically possible world' in which we are brains in a vat—what does this mean except that there is a *description* of such a state of affairs which is compatible with the laws of physics? Just as there is a tendency in our culture (and has been since the seventeenth century) to take *physics* as our metaphysics, that is, to view the exact sciences as the long-sought description of the 'true and ultimate furniture of the universe', so there is, as an immediate consequence, a tendency to take 'physical possibility' as the very touchstone of what might really actually be the case. Truth is physical truth; possibility physical possibility; and necessity physical necessity, on such a view. But we have just seen, if only in the case of a very contrived example so far, that this view is wrong. The existence of a 'physically possible world' in which we are brains in a vat (and always were and will be) does not mean that we might really, actually, possibly *be* brains in a vat. What rules out this possibility is not physics but *philosophy*.

Some philosophers, eager both to assert and minimize the claims of their profession at the same time (the typical state of mind of Anglo-American philosophy in the twentieth century), would say: 'Sure. You have shown that some things that seem to be physical possibilities are really *conceptual* impossibilities. What's so surprising about that?'

Well, to be sure, my argument can be described as a 'conceptual' one. But to describe philosophical activity as the search for 'conceptual' truths makes it all sound like *inquiry about the meaning of words*. And that is not at all what we have been engaging in.

What we have been doing is considering the *preconditions* for *thinking about, representing, referring to,* etc. We have investigated these preconditions *not* by investigating the meaning of these words and phrases (as a linguist might, for example) but by *reasoning a priori*. Not in the old 'absolute' sense (since we don't claim that magical theories of reference are *a priori* wrong), but in the sense of inquiring into what is *reasonably* possible *assuming* certain general premises, or making certain very broad theoretical assumptions. Such a procedure is neither 'empirical' nor quite 'a priori', but has elements of both ways of investigating. In spite of the fallibility of my procedure, and its dependence upon assumptions which might be described as 'empirical' (e.g. the assumption that the mind has no access to external things or properties apart from that provided by the senses), my procedure has a close relation to what Kant called a 'transcendental' investigation; for it is an investigation, I repeat, of the *preconditions* of reference and hence of thought—preconditions built in to the nature of our minds themselves, though not (as Kant hoped) wholly independent of empirical assumptions.

One of the premises of the argument is obvious: that magical theories of reference are wrong, wrong for mental representations and not only for physical ones. The other premise is that one cannot refer to certain kinds of things, e.g. *trees*, if one has no causal interaction at all with them,[3] or with things in terms of which they can be described. But why should we accept these premises? Since these constitute the broad framework within which I am arguing, it is time to examine them more closely.

6. The reasons for denying necessary connections between representations and their referents

I mentioned earlier that some philosophers (most famously, Brentano) have ascribed to the mind a power, 'intentionality', which precisely enables it to *refer*. Evidently, I have rejected this as no solution. But what gives me this right? Have I, perhaps, been too hasty?

These philosophers did not claim that we can think about external things or properties without using representations at all. And the argument I gave above comparing visual sense data to the ant's 'picture' (the argument via the science fiction story about the 'picture' of a tree that came from a paint-splash and that gave rise to sense data qualitatively similar to our 'visual images of trees', but unaccompanied by any *concept* of a tree) would be accepted as showing that *images* do not necessarily refer. If there are mental representations that necessarily refer (to external things) they must be of the nature of *concepts* and not of the nature of images. But what are *concepts*?

When we introspect we do not perceive 'concepts' flowing through our minds as such. Stop the stream of thought when or where we will, what we catch are words,

3. If the Brains in a Vat will have causal connection with, say, trees *in the future*, then perhaps they can *now* refer to trees by the description 'the things I will refer to as "trees" at such-and-such a future time'. But we are to imagine a case in which the Brains in a Vat *never* get out of the vat, and hence *never* get into causal connection with trees, etc.

images, sensations, feelings. When I speak my thoughts out loud I do not think them twice. I hear my words as you do. To be sure it feels different to me when I utter words that I believe and when I utter words I do not believe (but sometimes, when I am nervous, or in front of a hostile audience, it feels as if I am lying when I know I am telling the truth); and it feels different when I utter words I understand and when I utter words I do not understand. But I can imagine without difficulty someone thinking just these words (in the sense of saying them in his mind) and having just the feeling of understanding, asserting, etc., that I do, and realizing a minute later (or on being awakened by a hypnotist) that he did not understand what had just passed through his mind at all, that he did not even understand the language these words are in. I don't claim that this is very likely; I simply mean that there is nothing at all unimaginable about this. And what this shows is not that concepts *are* words (or images, sensations, etc.), but that to attribute a 'concept' or a 'thought' to someone is quite different from attributing any mental 'presentation', any introspectible entity or event, to him. Concepts are not mental presentations that intrinsically refer to external objects for the very decisive reason that they are not mental presentations at all. Concepts are signs used in a certain way; the signs may be public or private, mental entities or physical entities, but even when the signs are 'mental' and 'private', the sign itself apart from its use is not the concept. And signs do not themselves intrinsically refer.

We can see this by performing a very simple thought experiment. Suppose you are like me and cannot tell an elm tree from a beech tree. We still say that the reference of 'elm' in my speech is the same as the reference of 'elm' in anyone else's, viz. elm trees, and that the set of all beech trees is the extension of 'beech' (i.e. the set of things the word 'beech' is truly predicated of) both in your speech and my speech. Is it really credible that the difference between what 'elm' refers to and what 'beech' refers to is brought about by a difference in our *concepts*? My concept of an elm tree is exactly the same as my concept of a beech tree (I blush to confess). (This shows that the determination of reference is social and not individual, by the way; you and I both defer to experts who *can* tell elms from beeches.) If someone heroically attempts to maintain that the difference between the reference of 'elm' and the reference of 'beech' in *my* speech is explained by a difference in my psychological state, then let him imagine a Twin Earth where the words are switched. Twin Earth is very much like Earth; in fact, apart from the fact that 'elm' and 'beech' are interchanged, the reader can suppose Twin Earth is exactly like Earth. Suppose I have a *Doppelgänger* on Twin Earth who is molecule for molecule identical with me (in the sense in which two neckties can be 'identical'). If you are a dualist, then suppose my *Doppelgänger* thinks the same verbalized thoughts I do, has the same sense data, the same dispositions, etc. It is absurd to think his psychological state is one bit different from mine: yet his word 'elm' represents *beeches*, and my word 'elm' represents elms. (Similarly, if the 'water' on Twin Earth is a different liquid — say, XYZ and not H_2O — then 'water' represents a different liquid when used on Twin Earth and when used on Earth, etc.) Contrary to a doctrine that has been with us since the seventeenth century, *meanings just aren't in the head.*

We have seen that possessing a concept is not a matter of possessing images (say, of trees – or even images, 'visual' or 'acoustic', of sentences, or whole discourses, for that matter) since one could possess any system of images you please and not possess the *ability* to use the sentences in situationally appropriate ways (considering both linguistic factors—what has been said before—and non-linguistic factors as determining 'situational appropriateness'). A man may have all the images you please, and still be completely at a loss when one says to him 'point to a tree', even if a lot of trees are present. He may even have the image of what he is supposed to do, and still not know what he is supposed to do. For the image, if not accompanied by the ability to act in a certain way, is just a *picture*, and acting in accordance with a picture is itself an ability that one may or may not have. (The man might picture himself pointing to a tree, but just for the sake of contemplating something logically possible; himself pointing to a tree after someone has produced the—to him meaningless—sequence of sounds 'please point to a tree'.) He would still not know that he was supposed to point to a tree, and he would still not *understand* 'point to a tree'.

I have considered the ability to use certain sentences to be the criterion for possessing a full-blown concept, but this could easily be liberalized. We could allow symbolism consisting of elements which are not words in a natural language, for example, and we could allow such mental phenomena as images and other types of internal events. What is essential is that these should have the same complexity, ability to be combined with each other, etc., as sentences in a natural language. For, although a particular presentation—say, a blue flash—might serve a particular mathematician as the inner expression of the whole proof of the Prime Number Theorem, still there would be no temptation to say this (and it would be false to say this) if that mathematician could not unpack his 'blue flash' into separate steps and logical connections. But, no matter what sort of inner phenomena we allow as possible *expressions* of thought, arguments exactly similar to the foregoing will show that it is not the phenomena themselves that constitute understanding, but rather the ability of the thinker to *employ* these phenomena, to produce the right phenomena in the right circumstances.

The foregoing is a very abbreviated version of Wittgenstein's argument in *Philosophical Investigations*. If it is correct, then the attempt to understand thought by what is called 'phenomenological' investigation is fundamentally misguided; for what the phenomenologists fail to see is that what they are describing is the inner *expression* of thought, but that the *understanding* of that expression—one's understanding of one's own thoughts—is not an *occurrence* but an *ability*. Our example of a man pretending to think in Japanese (and deceiving a Japanese telepath) already shows the futility of a phenomenological approach to the problem of *understanding*. For even if there is some introspectible quality which is present when and only when one *really* understands (this seems false on introspection, in fact), still that quality is only *correlated* with understanding, and it is still possible that the man fooling the Japanese telepath have that quality too and *still* not understand a word of Japanese.

On the other hand, consider the perfectly possible man who does not have any 'interior monologue' at all. He speaks perfectly good English, and if asked what his opinions are on a given subject, he will give them at length. But he never thinks (in words, images, etc.) when he is not speaking out loud; nor does anything 'go through his head', except that (of course) he hears his own voice speaking, and has the usual sense impressions from his surroundings, plus a general 'feeling of understanding'. (Perhaps he is in the habit of talking to himself.) When he types a letter or goes to the store, etc., he is not having an internal 'stream of thought'; but his actions are intelligent and purposeful, and if anyone walks up and asks him 'What are you doing?' he will give perfectly coherent replies.

This man seems perfectly imaginable. No one would hesitate to say that he was conscious, disliked rock and roll (if he frequently expressed a strong aversion to rock and roll), etc., just because he did not think conscious thoughts except when speaking out loud.

What follows from all this is that (a) no set of mental events—images or more 'abstract' mental happenings and qualities—*constitutes* understanding; and (b) no set of mental events is *necessary* for understanding. In particular, *concepts cannot be identical with mental objects of any kind.* For, assuming that by a mental object we mean something introspectible, we have just seen that whatever it is, it may be absent in a man who does understand the appropriate word (and hence has the full blown concept), and present in a man who does not have the concept at all.

Coming back now to our criticism of magical theories of reference (a topic which also concerned Wittgenstein), we see that, on the one hand, those 'mental objects' we *can* introspectively detect—words, images, feelings, etc.—do not intrinsically refer any more than the ant's picture does (and for the same reasons) while the attempts to postulate special mental objects, 'concepts', which *do* have a necessary connection with their referents, and which only trained phenomenologists can detect, commit a *logical* blunder; for concepts are (at least in part) *abilities* and not occurrences. The doctrine that there are mental presentations which necessarily refer to external things is not only bad natural science; it is also bad phenomenology and conceptual confusion.

Chapter 28

The epistemology of belief

Fred Dretske

BELIEVING is easy, knowing is hard. Believing is easy because it is just a way of saying something in the internal language of thought. No trick at all once you have the language. Talk is cheap. The real trick is getting things right or, even harder, securing some *guarantee* that one has got things right. This is knowledge and this is hard.

Such is the conventional contrast between knowledge and belief. Underlying this contrast is the idea that knowledge, unlike belief, requires special endowments. It takes something *more* to know because knowledge requires, besides mere belief, some reliable coordination of internal belief with external reality, and this coordination, being an extremely delicate matter, requires the exercise of special skills. If, though, one takes no thought for whether one's beliefs correspond to anything, no thought for whether they are true or false, reliable or unreliable, then believing itself is mere child's play—a form of mental doodling. Witness the fact that the ignorant believe as effortlessly as the learned—indeed, it seems, with far *less* effort. According to the conventional wisdom, then, the problem, at least for epistemology (but perhaps not for the philosophy of mind), is not one of understanding how we manage to *have* beliefs, but one of understanding the sources and extent of their reliability.

This picture, I submit, dominates philosophical thinking about knowledge and belief. It is what keeps epistemology a durable, if not exactly flourishing, industry. We can thank, or blame, Descartes for installing it as the centerpiece of philosophical debate about our cognitive predicament. I think, though, that this picture distorts the epistemological task by grossly underestimating the cognitive demands of simple belief. Knowing *is* hard, but believing is no piece of cake either. In fact, or so I wish to argue, believing something requires precisely the same skills involved in knowing. Anyone who believes something *thereby* exhibits the cognitive resources for knowing. There is, as we shall see, a gap between belief and knowledge, but it is not one that provides any comfort to the philosophical skeptic. If I may, for dramatic effect, overstate my case somewhat, if you can't know it, you can't believe it either.

1. Representation and misrepresentation

Let me organize my defense of this thesis by discussing representations in general, and, in particular, the representational powers we typically assign to measuring

Fred Dretske, 'The Epistemology of Belief' in *Synthese* 55 (1983) pp. 3–19, reprinted by permission of Kluwer Academic Publishers, Dordrecht, The Netherlands.

instruments. I shall return to beliefs, a special kind of representation, in a moment.

Consider, first, a fairly crude altimeter, a device used for measuring altitude or height above sea level. It operates basically as a pressure gauge, responding to changes in air pressure as altitude varies. As the instrument ascends, the diminished air pressure allows a diaphragm, to which a pointer is attached, to expand. The expanding diaphragm moves the pointer across a scale calibrated in feet above sea level.

We can, of course, fool this instrument. We can place it in a chamber from which air has been pumped. The partial vacuum in the chamber will cause the instrument to register, say, 35,000 feet when it is, in fact, only a few hundred feet above sea level. The instrument, it seems, misrepresents its own altitude. It 'says' it is at 35,000 feet when it is not. If altimeters had beliefs, this, surely, would qualify as a false belief.

But have we really fooled the instrument? This depends on what we take it to be representing or saying. I said above that the instrument misrepresented its own altitude. But why suppose it is *altitude* that the instrument represents or, in this case, misrepresents? *We*, after all, are the ones who printed 'feet above sea level' on the face of the instrument and called it an 'altimeter'. *We* are the ones making it 'say' this. The instrument itself (if I may take its part for the moment) might object to this way of describing its representational efforts. It is, it might say, a device for representing pressure, and its representation of the pressure, even in a vacuum chamber, is perfectly accurate. It is making no mistake. No one is fooling it. It believes the pressure is 5 pounds per square inch and the pressure *is* 5 pounds per square inch. If anyone is making a mistake (the instrument concludes) it is we who assigned it a representational capacity beyond its actual powers. One could as well print 'Gross National Product in Dollars' on its face and then complain that it misrepresented the state of the national economy.

It seems more reasonable to say that it is the instrument's job to register the pressure and that it is *our* job (the job of those who use the instrument) to see to it that a change in pressure is reliably correlated with altitude (or whatever other quantity we may use the instrument to measure)—to see to it, in other words, that the instrument is used in conditions where alterations in pressure carry information about the magnitudes we use the instrument to measure. If this is so, then the instrument is discharging *its* representational responsibilities in a perfectly satisfactory way. We aren't fooling the instrument; at most we are fooling ourselves.

Is the speedometer on a car misrepresenting the vehicle's speed if we jack up the car, engage the gears and run the engine? The drive shaft and wheels will turn, and the speedometer will, accordingly, register (say) 30 m.p.h. The car, of course, is stationary. Something is amiss, and if we have to place blame, the speedometer is the likely culprit. It is saying something false. Or is it? How do we decide what the speedometer is saying? Perhaps the speedometer is representing the only thing it is capable of representing, saying the only thing it knows how to say, namely, that the wheels are turning at a certain rate. The mistake, if a mistake is being made here at all, occurs in us, in what we *infer* must be true if what the speedometer says is true.

What, then, does a measuring instrument actually represent? Or, to put it more suggestively, what does the instrument really believe? Does the altimeter have altitude beliefs or merely pressure beliefs? Does the speedometer have vehicle-speed beliefs or merely wheel-rotation beliefs? Until we are in a position to answer these questions, we cannot say *how*, or even *whether*, it is possible to 'fool' the instrument. We cannot say whether, in situations like those described above, the instruments are misrepresenting anything, whether it is even possible to make them 'believe' something false.

It is time to stop describing instruments in such inappropriate ways. Although I think it sensible to speak of instruments representing the quantities they are designed to measure, I do not, of course, think they *say* or *believe* things. We cannot, literally, *fool* an instrument. They don't make *mistakes*. I allowed myself to speak this way in order to reveal my overall strategy. So before moving on to a discussion of creatures to which it does make sense to attribute genuine cognitive states (like belief and knowledge), let me describe an intermediate case. Some may find it more realistic, and hence more convincing, than examples involving speedometers and altimeters.

A frog in its natural habitat will flick with its tongue at small, moving dark spots. The neural mechanisms responsible for this response have, for fairly obvious reasons, been called 'bug detectors'. In the frog's natural habitat, all (or most) small, moving dark spots *are* bugs, a staple item in the frog's diet. Psychologists (with presumably better intentions than I had with the altimeter) have removed frogs from their natural habitat, projected small, moving dark *shadows* on a surface in front of the frog, and observed the creature's response. Not unexpectedly, the frog 'zaps' the moving shadow.

What shall we say about this situation? Has the frog mistakenly identified the shadow as a bug? Is the frog misrepresenting its surroundings? Does the frog have a false belief, a belief to the effect that *this* (small moving dark spot) is a bug? Or shall we say that the frog (assuming for the moment that it *has* beliefs) does not have 'bug' beliefs at all? Instead what it has are 'small-moving-dark-spot' beliefs? Since the frog *usually* operates in circumstances (swamps, ponds, etc.) where small moving dark spots *are* bugs, natural selection has favored the development of a zapping reflex to whatever the frog perceives as a small dark spot. If we take this latter view, then although psychologists can starve a frog in this artificial environment, they can't fool it. The frog never makes a mistake because it never represents, or *takes*, things to be other than they are. It represents the shadow *as* a small, moving dark spot, and this representation is perfectly correct. The frog goes hungry in this situation, not because it mistakenly sees dark spots *as* edible bugs, but because what it correctly sees as moving spots are not, in fact, edible bugs.

If we adopt this latter strategy in describing what the frog believes, then it becomes very hard, if not impossible, to fool the animal. If the frog has beliefs at all, it approaches infallibility in these beliefs. And this infallibility is achieved in the same way it was (or could be) achieved with the altimeter and speedometer — *viz.*, by tailoring the content of the belief (representation) to *whatever* properties of the stimulus trigger the relevant response. If we are willing to be less ambitious in this way about what we describe the frog as believing, we can be correspondingly more ambitious in what we describe the frog as knowing.

But there is, surely, a truth of the matter. The frog either believes there is a bug in front of it or it doesn't. It isn't up to *us* to determine the content of the frog's beliefs in the way it may be up to us to say what an altimeter represents.[1] Before we create, by fiat, infallible frogs we had better look to those factors, whatever they are, that determine the content of a creature's beliefs. Only when we are clear about this can we proceed to questions about the reliability of these beliefs—to traditional epistemological questions. This, then, brings us to the question of how belief content is determined—to the question of learning.

2. Learning

Dolphins have an extremely sensitive sonar system that allows them to detect, and in some cases identify, objects in the water fifty feet away. They have, for example, been taught to identify cylinders at this distance. The identification occurs whether the cylinders in question are short and squat or long and narrow, solid or hollow, metal or wood, red, yellow or blue. Regardless of the object's value along these other dimensions, the dolphin can distinguish the cylinders from the non-cylinders.

If a child of four achieved this level of discrimination, especially if its distinctive response to cylinders was the utterance of the *word* 'cylinder' we would doubtless credit it (perhaps prematurely) with the concept of a cylinder and, hence, with the capacity for holding beliefs to the effect that something was a cylinder. There are those, however, who prefer to be less liberal with dolphins or, indeed, with any creature lacking a natural language. Since I do not think this issue is particularly relevant to the point I wish to make with this example, I will continue to speak of the dolphin as believing of the cylinders it picks out that they are cylinders.

Suppose, now, that when the dolphin is being taught to identify cylinders, the trainer uses *only* cylinders made of plastic. All the non-cylinders, the cubes, spheres, pyramids, etc., are made of some other material—wood, say. Since the dolphin reaches criterion (as the psychologists say) on plastic objects, responding positively to all and only plastic objects, can we say that the dolphin has learned to recognize *plastic objects*, that it now, when responding positively to X, has a belief to the effect that *X* is plastic? Does the dolphin now have some crude notion of *plasticity*?

Of course not. The reason we are prepared to credit the dolphin with the concept of a cylinder (and, hence, with beliefs to the effect that *this* is a cylinder and *that* is not) is not *just* because it distinguishes cylinders from other shaped objects (for it does, with equal success, distinguish plastic from non-plastic objects) but because of our conviction that it was the *cylindricality* of these objects to which the creature was responding (and not their *plasticity*). The animal's sensitive sonar is capable (or so we believe) of picking up information about the shape of distant objects, and it was trained to respond in some distinctive way to *this* piece of information. There is no reason to think it was picking up, or responding to, information about the

1. Some philosophers, I know, would deny this. I make the assumption, nonetheless, because (1) I believe it, and (2) it makes my argument that much more difficult and, therefore, that much more significant if correct.

chemical constitution of these objects—to the fact that they were plastic. We could test this, of course. Merely place a wooden cylinder in the pool and observe the animal's response. A positive response would indicate that it was the cylindricality, not the plasticity, to which the animal has developed a sensitivity. It was, as I prefer to put it (more about this later), information about the object's shape, not information about its chemical structure, that guided the animal's discriminatory behavior during learning. It is this fact that lies behind our unwillingness to credit the dolphin with the concept *plastic* and our willingness (or greater willingness) to credit it with the concept of cylindricality, even though (given the restricted learning conditions) it became as successful in distinguishing plastic from non-plastic objects as it did in distinguishing cylinders from non-cylinders. Even if (cosmic coincidence) all and only cylinders were made of plastic so that our trained dolphins could infallibly detect plastic objects (or detect them as infallibly as they detected cylinders), this would not have the slightest tendency to make us say that they had acquired the concept of plastic or could now have beliefs about the plasticity of objects. The level of sophistication to which we are willing to rise in describing the belief content of the dolphin *is no higher* than the kind of information about objects to which we believe it sensitive. The dolphin can have 'cylinder' but not 'plastic' beliefs because, as far as we know anyway, it has a sensory system that allows it to pick up information about the shape, but not the chemical structure, of objects at a distance.

It is important to understand what is happening when we make these judgments, what kinds of considerations shape our decisions about what level of conceptual sophistication to assign an animal (whether it be a frog, a dolphin, or a human child). The decision about what concept to assign a creature, and hence the decision about what sorts of beliefs we may attribute to it is guided by our assessment of the sort of information the animal utilizes during learning to articulate, develop and refine its discriminatory and classificatory repertoire. If we are talking about an instrument, something that doesn't learn, then its representational powers, what it represents things as being, is a function of the information to which the instrument is sensitive. Since altimeters are not sensitive to information about the gross national product, no matter what I happen to write on the face of the instrument, an altimeter cannot represent or misrepresent the gross national product. But since the instrument *is* sensitive to information about pressure and, some would say, in some situations at least, to information about altitude, it is capable of both representing and misrepresenting these magnitudes.

This principle (the principle, namely, that the representational powers of a system are limited by its informational pick-up and processing capabilities) underlies many of our judgments about the conditions in which someone can and cannot learn. Why can't you teach a normally endowed child her colors in the dark? Because information about the *color* of the objects is not therein made available for shaping the child's discriminatory and identificatory responses. Even if the child succeeds in picking out all the blue objects (in virtue of the fact, say, that all and only the blue ones are furry), she will not, by this procedure, learn the concept *blue*. She will not *believe* of the next furry blue object she finds that it is blue. The most she will believe is that it is furry. Even if we taught her to say 'blue' every time she encountered a blue object in the dark, we would not, thereby, have given the child a *color* concept. We would merely have given her an eccentric way of expressing her concept of furryness.

The moral of the story is this: to learn what an *X* is, to acquire the capacity to represent something *as an X* (believe it to be an *X*), it is not enough to be shown *X*'s and non-*X*'s and to successfully distinguish between them. Unless the information that the *X*'s *are X* is made available to the learner (or instrument), and it is *this* information that is *used* to discriminate and classify, the system will not be representing anything as an *X*. Even if some concept is acquired, and even if this concept *happens* to be coextensive with that of *X* (thus allowing the subject to successfully distinguish the *X*'s from the non-*X*'s), the concept acquired will not be that of an *X*. The subject will not be able to believe of *X*'s that they are *X*. For the concept acquired during learning is determined by the kind of information to which the learner becomes sensitive, and if no information about the *X*-ness of objects is made available during learning (despite the availability of *X*'s), no such concept can develop.

I have begun to talk more and more about information, so let me pause a moment to explain what I mean by this way of talking. I mean nothing very technical or abstract. In fact, I mean pretty much what (I think) we all mean in talking of some event, signal or structure carrying (or embodying) information about another state of affairs. A message (i.e., some event, stimulus or signal) carries information about *X* to the extent to which one could learn (come to know) something about *X* from the message. And, in particular, the message carries the information that *X* is a dingbat, say, if and only if one could learn (come to know) that *X was* a dingbat from the message. This does not mean that one *must* learn that *X* is a dingbat from a message that carries this information. One may not, after all, know the code. The message may be in Chinese. When I say that one *could* learn that *X* was a dingbat from the message I mean, simply, that the message has whatever reliable connection with dingbats is required to enable a suitably equipped, but otherwise ignorant receiver, to learn from it that *X* is a dingbat.[2]

I think it is this sense of the term 'information' that is operative in a wide variety of ordinary contexts, and it is for this reason that I feel safe in saying that I am using the term as it is commonly used. We say that a pamphlet contains information about how to probate a will because we believe that someone could learn something about how to probate a will by consulting the pamphlet. Information booths are called information booths because the clerks working there either know, or can quickly find out, about matters of interest to the average patron. One can *come to know* by making inquiries at such places. Similarly, when scientists tell us that the pupil of the eye is a source of information about another person's feelings and attitudes, that a thunder signature contains information about the lightning channel that produced it, that the dance of a honey bee contains information as to the whereabouts of the nectar, or that the light from a star contains information

---

2. I assume here some kind of reliability account of knowledge or justification.

about the chemical composition of that body, the scientists are clearly referring to information as something capable of yielding knowledge. And *what* information a signal carries is identified with what one could learn from it. This, I submit, is the very same sense of 'information' in which we speak of books, newspapers and authorities as containing, or having, information about a particular topic.

This is not intended to be a philosophically illuminating analysis of information. At least no epistemologist would find it of any special interest. Rather than telling us anything important about knowledge, it uses the concept of knowledge to tell us something about information. But this merely indicates that information is a member of that constellation of epistemic terms that can be interdefined in fairly trivial ways.[3] This, though, is unimportant for my present purposes. What is important is the epistemic character of the concept of information and its connection with knowledge. For if this connection is as I have expressed it, then the upshot of my argument so far can be expressed as follows: what *concept* a person acquires during learning, and hence what beliefs he is henceforth capable of holding, is restricted to the kind of information he is capable of picking up and processing. But, in virtue of the connection between information and knowledge, we now see that this is equivalent to saying that the beliefs a person is capable of holding as a result of learning are restricted to the sorts of things that that person (given his information processing resources) is capable of knowing.

The argument is rather simple so let me recapitulate. To learn what a dingbat is, and hence to acquire the conceptual resources necessary for believing that something is a dingbat, one must not only be exposed to dingbats, but to the *information* that they are dingbats. Not only must this information be made available, it must be *picked up* and *used* by the learner to guide his discriminatory and identificatory responses *if* he is to be credited with the relevant concept. Since this is so, the learner cannot come to believe something is a dingbat unless he has the cognitive (i.e., information processing) resources for knowing that something is a dingbat.[4] Only someone who *can* know (or *could* know—the learner may have *lost* his capacity for picking up the required information) that this is a dingbat can believe it to be a dingbat.

It should be emphasized that this is a thesis about the relationship between what is believed and what is, or can be, known, *not* a thesis about what, if anything, can be known or believed. The thesis is, in other words, quite independent of one's views about what, if anything, dolphins, frogs or people can know (or believe) to be the case. I have not said that frogs can (in their natural habitat) know when a bug flies by. Nor have I denied this (e.g., by saying that they could only know that there

3. Although they can be interdefined in fairly trivial ways, they needn't be. In *Knowledge and the Flow of Information* (Bradford/MIT, 1981), I give an independent (of knowledge) analysis of information thus making the concept available for the analysis of knowledge.

4. Obviously one can believe something is a dingbat when it is not a dingbat—hence, believe things that *cannot* be known (because not the case). I hope it is clear from the wording in the text that I am not denying this obvious fact. The thesis is, rather, that if one has the concept of a *dingbat* (hence, capable of holding beliefs to the effect that something is a dingbat) then that something is a dingbat is the *sort* of thing one can know.

was a small dark spot moving by). And for purposes of this paper, I don't particularly care what a dolphin can know, or believe, about a cylinder immersed in its pool fifty feet away. I have my own ideas about these matters, but they are not relevant to the thesis I am presently defending. What I am arguing is that *whatever* view you take about what a creature can believe, you thereby commit yourself to a certain level of sophistication in the creature's capacity for picking up and processing information; if it can't pick up information about bugs, then it cannot hold beliefs about bugs (just as the altimeter that can't pick up information about the gross national product cannot represent this quantity). So *if* the frog does believe that there is a bug in front of it, then it is the sort of creature capable of picking up, processing, and responding to information about bugs and, specifically, the information that there are bugs in front of it. It is this *conditional* thesis for which I have been arguing. When we combine this conditional with what has been said about information, we reach the conclusion that anything the frog believes is the sort of thing it is (was[5]) capable of knowing.

3. Language and belief

With appropriate modifications, the same can be said about our own conceptual situation: the conditions that must obtain for the acquisition of simple concepts are the same conditions that make possible the *knowledge* that these concepts apply. In our own case, though, the possibilities for confusion about this matter are much greater. For we not only believe things, but we say things, and we sometimes say things we don't believe. That is, unlike the altimeter, frog and dolphin, we have dual representational systems and they are not always synchronized. It is, therefore, easy enough to attribute to the one the representational resources of the other—thus blurring the intimate relationship between belief and (the capacity for) knowledge.

Let me illustrate the problem in a simple-minded way. We will turn to a more interesting case in a moment. If I teach a child her colors and have her say 'circular' whenever a blue object is presented, what will this show (assuming the child learns her lesson) about what the child believes or about what kinds of mistakes she is capable of making? Clearly, when the child looks at a blue cube and says 'circular' she will be misrepresenting, linguistically misrepresenting, the properties of what she is talking about.[6] This, though, isn't very interesting. It certainly isn't a

---

5. The temporal qualifier should always be understood. A creature may have acquired a concept *at a time* when he possessed a fully functional sensory system, one capable of picking up and processing information of a certain kind. Once the concept is acquired, though, the creature may have *lost* this information processing capacity (for example, have gone blind), hence, losing the capacity to know what he can still believe.

6. I earlier (*circa* second draft) thought that what the child *said* when it said 'This is circular' was false. I thought this because it seemed to me that what the child was saying (with these words) was that the object was circular. Jon Barwise convinced me that this was not so. What the child is saying when it uses these words is that the object is blue. Hence, what the child is saying is true.

symptom of any *cognitive* or *conceptual* misrepresentation. The child *says*, 'This is circular' but she *believes* it is blue. Through an unfortunate piece of education, she does not use the correct word to express what she believes. What *she* means by 'circular' is *blue*. What we have done with this child is similar to what we earlier suggested doing with the altimeter: printing 'gross national product in dollars' on its face. In doing this we can make the instrument 'say' that the gross national product is increasing, but this is not really what the instrument is representing (or, more likely, misrepresenting). We have merely given it a way of 'saying' things it does not, indeed *cannot*, believe. And so it is with the child. The child's (linguistic) responses have a meaning that exceeds her (internal) powers of representation.

Something like this happens when children first learn to talk. The toddler who delights his mother by saying 'Mommy' whenever she appears disappoints her when he says the *same* thing to his Aunt Mildred. When the child is corrected ('No, Jimmy, I'm Mommy, that's Aunt Mildred'), what is this a correction of? A false belief? But does Jimmy really believe that this other woman is his mother? Probably not. It seems more likely that the child simply believes that Aunt Mildred is a woman, or a person, precisely what he believed of his mother when he called her 'Mommy', and that he is using the word 'Mommy' to express this less determinate notion. Correction here is not the weeding out of false beliefs, but the development of a more discriminating set of concepts and the correlative ability to express these more determinate concepts in linguistically appropriate ways.

Since, for most of us, the acquisition of our natural language goes hand-in-hand with the acquisition of the concepts to which this language gives expression, the ability to represent something verbally is developed in close association with the ability to represent something in the internal language of thought. Some philosophers prefer to say that these two abilities are not really distinct. That may or may not be so. I don't wish to take sides on this issue here. What is important for present purposes is the understanding that during learning our linguistic responses to stimuli have a meaning independent of whatever representational capacity the learner himself may have developed. Since this is so, the verbal mistakes that occur in classifying and identifying objects need not reflect a mismatch between the world and the respondent's inner representation of the world. This only mismatch may be between the world and the respondent's external (verbal) representation of that world.

This point is, I think, easy enough to accept when we are dealing with obvious examples like those described above. There are, however, profound implications for epistemology. Perhaps the best way to exhibit these implications is by another, less obvious, example.

Hilary Putnam has described a place, Twin Earth, in which there are two substances H_2O and XYZ, chemically different but both having the superficial properties of water.[7] By 'superficial' I mean the properties we (Earthlings) rely

7. 'The Meaning of "Meaning"' in *Language, Mind and Knowledge, Minnesota Studies in the Philosophy of Science*, 7, Minneapolis: University of Minnesota Press (1975); reprinted in *Mind, Language and Reality—Philosophical Papers*, Vol. 2, Cambridge, England (1975).

on (outside the laboratory) to identify something as water: taste, smell, feel, capacity for quenching thirst, etc. Some of the lakes and rivers on Twin Earth are filled with H_2O, others are filled with XYZ (here I depart from Putnam's example). It rains H_2O in some parts of the country, XYZ in other parts. Twin Earthlings called both substances 'water' since the liquids are (apart from elaborate chemical analysis, an analysis which they haven't yet perfected) indistinguishable.

Consider, now, a Twin Earthling (call him Tommy) being taught what water (or what the Twin Earthlings call 'water') is on a part of Twin Earth in which there is both H_2O and XYZ. As it turns out, quite by accident, Tommy learns what water is by being exposed only to H_2O (it only happened to rain H_2O on the days he was outside, no XYZ ever happened to come out of his faucets at home, etc.). After learning what water is to the complete satisfaction of his parents, friends, and teachers, Tommy is miraculously transported to Earth where there is to be found *only* H_2O (XYZ cannot exist in the earth's atmosphere). Since there are no other differences between Twin Earth and Earth, Tommy blends in without trouble. Everything Tommy says about water (using the word 'water') will correspond to what his Earthling friends say and believe about water (also using the word 'water').

As you may have expected, the question, once again, is not what Tommy says, but what Tommy believes. Tommy, I submit, does not have the same concept as his Earthling associates. Therefore, what Tommy *believes* when he says 'This is water' is not what his Earthling friends believe when they say 'This is water'. What Tommy means by 'water' is *either* H_2O *or* XYZ. This, of course, is how we (knowing all the facts of the case) would describe it, not Tommy. If asked, Tommy will say that he means *water*, by 'water' and he surely does mean this. But the point is that more things qualify as water for Tommy than for the Earthlings. If we should reverse the scenario and imagine an Earthling miraculously transported back to Twin Earth with Tommy, Tommy's belief of a puddle of XYZ that it was water (i.e., an instance of the concept he expresses with the word 'water') would be true while his Earthling friend's belief would be false. Since this is so, they must be expressing different beliefs with the words 'This is water'.

Putnam takes this result as showing that meanings are not in the head. Tommy and his Earthling friends can be identical in all relevant respects; yet, they have different concepts, different beliefs, different meanings. My intuitions (about this example) agree with Putnam's, but the moral I want to draw from this story goes beyond, and in some ways contrary to[8], the moral Putnam draws from it. I think this example neatly illustrates a principle expressed earlier, the principle, namely, that a system's representational capabilities are determined by its information

8. 'Contrary to' because the conclusion I draw from this example (as embellished) is that the extension of a concept (like 'water') is *not* determined by causal factors. The same things (for example, H_2O) *caused* Tommy to use the word 'water' during learning as caused his Earthling associates to use this word during learning. What determines the extension (and, hence, the concept) are not facts about causal relations, but facts about the kind of information available during learning. Information and causation are related, but only indirectly.

handling resources. Or, to give a more restricted (not to mention cruder) expression of the principle, an individual can believe (and, in this sense, represent) only what it has the information handling resources for knowing.

The difference between Tommy and his Earthling friends is to be found in the difference in the kind of information to which they were made responsive during the learning period when they acquired their respective concepts. Given the situation on Twin Earth, Tommy, though repeatedly exposed to H_2O (and never XYZ) was never exposed to the *information* that the liquid he saw was H_2O. All he ever received, processed, and responded to was a piece of disjunctive information, the information, namely, that the liquid was *either* H_2O *or* XYZ. This is all the information Tommy got because, on Twin Earth, this is all that one could learn about the character of the liquid from ordinary sensory transactions with it. Since it was this piece of information that was used to shape Tommy's discriminatory and identificatory responses, *this* is the concept he acquired and *this* is the kind of belief he subsequently has about the liquids he describes as water.

Since XYZ cannot be found on Earth (and this is no mere accident but a law of nature), Earthlings acquire a different concept because their discriminatory responses are shaped by a different piece of information: the information that the liquid is H_2O.[9] Since the lawful regularities prevailing in these two worlds are different, the kind of information to be found in physically indistinguishable signals is also different. Hence, the concepts developed in response to these physically indistinguishable signals are also different. This is why Tommy and his Earthling friends, although they *say* the same thing, although they were exposed to exactly *the same* liquids during learning (viz., H_2O), and although they developed their ideas in exactly the same way, have quite different beliefs about the liquid they see and describe.

The important point to notice about this example is how the concepts one develops, and, hence, the sorts of beliefs one is thereby capable of holding, neatly reflect one's epistemological strengths and limitations. There is, as it were, an epistemological pre-established harmony. We (Earthlings) have a more determinate concept than Tommy, a concept that if he possessed it on Twin Earth, he would be incapable of knowing (by ordinary sensory means) whether it ever, in fact, applied to the liquid running out of his faucet. Given the widespread prevalence of XYZ, Tommy would make frequent mistakes. He would, in other words, have a real epistemological problem *if he had our concept of water*.[10] But he doesn't have our

---

9. I here assume that it is a law on Earth (but not, of course, on Twin Earth) that anything exhibiting the normal sensible properties of water *is* H_2O. If this is too strong, then I assume that on Earth (but not, of course, on Twin Earth) one can come to know that something is H_2O by looking, tasting, smelling, etc. It is this fact that supports my claim (in the text) that on Earth (but not on Twin Earth) the ordinary sensory stimulation associated with our perception of water carries the information that it *is* water (that is, H_2O).

10. As I understand the Causal Theory (of natural kind terms) Tommy would (according to this theory) have our concept of water since, by hypothesis, H_2O figured *causally* (just as it did for Earthlings) in his acquisition of this concept. This, I think, shows what is wrong with a causal theory.

concept of water and, given that he learns in roughly the way we learn what water is, there is no way for him to get it. The concept he does acquire (a concept the extension of which I am expressing as 'either H_2O or XYZ') is a concept that he is cognitively prepared to apply to his surroundings. He *can know* that the liquid coming out of his faucet is what *he* means by 'water'.

To put the point in its most general form: if someone lives in a place where it is impossible to distinguish A-type things from B-type things, hence impossible to know that this particular thing is an A (or a B), then it is likewise impossible, under ordinary learning conditions, to develop a way of representing something as an A (or as a B). The most that will be developed is a way of representing something as A-or-B. And in this case we needn't worry about mistaking an A for a B (or *vice versa*) since we can never *take* anything as an A or as a B.

4. Conclusions and qualifications

I have been arguing for a perfectly general thesis and I am afraid that it cannot be defended in its most general form. There are exceptions that I have suppressed for expository purposes. So, before trying to state the upshot of this argument, let me briefly describe the qualification that is essential.

My thesis is meant to apply to simple or primitive concepts (representational structures), concepts that are not themselves composed of simpler conceptual elements (representational structures). In arguing that the possession of the concept X requires the possessor to have the resources for picking up, processing and responding to the information that something is X, the argument works only for simple, ostensively learned concepts. I do not wish to argue that we cannot *manufacture* out of a corpus of simple concepts, and the appropriate syntactical machinery, complex concepts for the application of which we lack the requisite information processing capabilities. That is, there are obviously beliefs involving complex concepts (e.g., the belief that X is a miracle, that Y is a random sequence, or that there are no unicorns) that we lack the cognitive resources for knowing to be true. And it certainly seems that with linguistically sophisticated creatures such as ourselves, these complex concepts will be a commonplace. But there can be no complex concepts without simple concepts, and it is to these latter primitive representational structures that the thesis of this paper is meant to apply.

The upshot, then, of this paper is that no matter how we choose to describe the conceptual sophistication of an agent, whether it be a frog, a dolphin, a computer or a human being, we are committed to that agent's having the cognitive resources for *knowing* how things stand with respect to the situation being represented—at least with regard to the agent's primitive concepts. This, I think, completely turns the tables on the skeptic. The traditional arguments that we cannot know what we purport to know because we lack the appropriate cognitive endowments, because the information on which we rely is always equivocal or ambiguous in some fundamental respect, is an argument which, if successful in relation to simple concepts, shows, not that we cannot know what we believe, but that we do not believe what we think we believe.[11] If the information we receive about X's is always too impoverished to specify an X *as an* X then admittedly, we have an epistemological problem about how we can ever know that there are X's. But we also have a problem about how we can ever believe that there are X's.

11. If the reader thinks it *could not* show this (*viz.*, that we do not believe what we think we believe), so much the worse for the view that we could entertain (simple) beliefs that we could not know to be true.

Chapter 29

A coherence theory of truth and knowledge

Donald Davidson

I N this paper I defend what may as well be called a coherence theory of truth and knowledge. The theory I defend is not in competition with a correspondence theory, but depends for its defence on an argument that purports to show that coherence yields correspondence.

The importance of the theme is obvious. If coherence is a test of truth, there is a direct connection with epistemology, for we have reason to believe many of our beliefs cohere with many others, and in that case we have reason to believe many of our beliefs are true. When the beliefs are true, then the primary conditions for knowledge would seem to be satisfied.

Someone might try to defend a coherence theory of truth without defending a coherence theory of knowledge, perhaps on the ground that the holder of a coherent set of beliefs might lack a reason to believe his beliefs coherent. This is not likely, but it may be that someone, though he has true beliefs, and good reasons for holding them, does not appreciate the relevance of reason to belief. Such a one may best be viewed as having knowledge he does not know he has: he thinks he is a sceptic. In a word, he is a philosopher.

Setting aside aberrant cases, what brings truth and knowledge together is meaning. If meanings are given by objective truth conditions there is a question how we can know that the conditions are satisfied, for this would appear to require a confrontation between what we believe and reality; and the idea of such a confrontation is absurd. But if coherence is a test of truth, then coherence is a test for judging that objective truth conditions are satisfied, and we no longer need to explain meaning on the basis of possible confrontation. My slogan is: correspondence without confrontation. Given a correct epistemology, we can be realists in all departments. We can accept objective truth conditions as the key to meaning, a realist view of truth, and we can insist that knowledge is of an objective world independent of our thought or language.

Since there is not, as far as I know, a theory that deserves to be called 'the' coherence theory, let me characterize the sort of view I want to defend. It is obvious that not every consistent set of interpreted sentences contains only true sentences, since one such set might contain just the consistent sentence S and another just

Donald Davidson, 'A Coherence Theory of Truth and Knowledge' in A. R. Malachowski (ed.) *Reading Rorty. Critical Responses to Philosophy and the Mirror of Nature (and Beyond)* (Oxford, Blackwell Publishers, 1990), pp. 120–38 reprinted by permission of the publisher and author.

the negation of *S*. And adding more sentences, while maintaining consistency, will not help. We can imagine endless state-descriptions—maximal consistent descriptions—which do not describe our world.

My coherence theory concerns beliefs, or sentences held true by someone who understands them. I do not want to say, at this point, that every possible coherent set of beliefs is true (or contains mostly true beliefs). I shy away from this because it is so unclear what is possible. At one extreme, it might be held that the range of possible maximal sets of beliefs is as wide as the range of possible maximal sets of sentences, and then there would be no point to insisting that a defensible coherence theory concerns beliefs and not propositions or sentences. But there are other ways of conceiving what it is possible to believe which would justify saying not only that all actual coherent belief systems are largely correct but that all possible ones are also. The difference between the two notions of what it is possible to believe depends on what we suppose about the nature of belief, its interpretation, its causes, its holders and its patterns. Beliefs for me are states of people with intentions, desires, sense organs; they are states that are caused by, and cause, events inside and outside the bodies of the entertainers. But even given all these constraints, there are many things people do believe, and many more that they could. For all such cases, the coherence theory applies.

Of course some beliefs are false. Much of the point of the concept of belief is the potential gap it introduces between what is held to be true and what is true. So mere coherence, no matter how strongly coherence is plausibly defined, can not guarantee that what is believed is so. All that a coherence theory can maintain is that most of the beliefs in a coherent total set of beliefs are true.

This way of stating the position can at best be taken as a hint, since there is probably no useful way to count beliefs, and so no clear meaning to the idea that most of a person's beliefs are true. A somewhat better way to put the point is to say there is a presumption in favour of the truth of a belief that coheres with a significant mass of belief. Every belief in a coherent total set of beliefs is justified in the light of this presumption, much as every intentional action taken by a rational agent (one whose choices, beliefs and desires cohere in the sense of Bayesian decision theory) is justified. So to repeat, if knowledge is justified true belief, then it would seem that all the true beliefs of a consistent believer constitute knowledge. This conclusion, though too vague and hasty to be right, contains an important core of truth, as I shall argue. Meanwhile I merely note the many problems asking for treatment: what exactly does coherence demand? How much of inductive practice should be included, how much of the true theory (if there is one) of evidential support must be in there? Since no person has a completely consistent body of convictions, coherence with *which* beliefs creates a presumption of truth? Some of these problems will be put in better perspective as I go along.

It should be clear that I do not hope to define truth in terms of coherence and belief. Truth is beautifully transparent compared to belief and coherence, and I take it as primitive. Truth, as applied to utterances of sentences, shows the disquotational feature enshrined in Tarski's Convention T, and that is enough to fix its domain of application. Relative to a language or a speaker, of course, so there is more to truth than Convention T; there is whatever carries over from language to language or speaker to speaker. What Convention T, and the trite sentences it declares true, like ' "Grass is green", spoken by an English speaker, is true if and only if grass is green', reveal is that the truth of an utterance depends on just two things: what the words as spoken mean, and how the world is arranged. There is no further relativism to a conceptual scheme, a way of viewing things, a perspective. Two interpreters, as unlike in culture, language and point of view as you please, can disagree over whether an utterance is true, but only if they differ on how things are in the world they share, or what the utterance means.

I think we can draw two conclusions from these simple reflections. First, truth is correspondence with the way things are. (There is no straightforward and non-misleading way to state this; to get things right, a detour is necessary through the concept of satisfaction in terms of which truth is characterized.[1]) So if a coherence theory of truth is acceptable, it must be consistent with a correspondence theory. Second, a theory of knowledge that allows that we can know the truth must be a non-relativized, non-internal form of realism. So if a coherence theory of know-ledge is acceptable, it must be consistent with such a form of realism. My form of realism seems to be neither Hilary Putnam's internal realism nor his metaphysical realism.[2] It is not internal realism because internal realism makes truth relative to a scheme, and this is an idea I do not think is intelligible.[3] A major reason, in fact, for accepting a coherence theory is the unintelligibility of the dualism of a conceptual scheme and a 'world' waiting to be coped with. But my realism is certainly not Putnam's metaphysical realism, for *it* is characterized by being 'radically non-epistemic', which implies that all our best researched and established thoughts and theories may be false. I think the independence of belief and truth requires only that *each* of our beliefs may be false. But of course a coherence theory cannot allow that all of them can be wrong.

But why not? Perhaps it is obvious that the coherence of a belief with a substantial body of belief enhances its chance of being true, provided there is reason to suppose the body of belief is true, or largely so. But how can coherence alone supply grounds for belief? Perhaps the best we can do to justify one belief is to appeal to other beliefs. But then the outcome would seem to be that we must accept philosophical scepticism, no matter how unshaken in practice our beliefs remain.

This is scepticism in one of its traditional garbs. It asks: why couldn't all my beliefs hang together and yet be comprehensively false about the actual world? Mere recognition of the fact that it is absurd or worse to try to *confront* our beliefs, one by one, or as a whole, with what they are about does not answer the question nor show the question unintelligible. In short, even a mild coherence theory like mine must provide a sceptic with a reason for supposing coherent beliefs are true. The partisan of a coherence theory can't allow assurance to come from outside the system of

1. See my 'True to the Facts', *The Journal of Philosophy*, Vol. 66 (1969), pp. 216–34.
2. Hilary Putnam, *Meaning and the Moral Sciences* (Routledge & Kegan Paul, London, 1978), p. 125.
3. See my 'On the Very Idea of a Conceptual Scheme', in *Proceedings and Addresses of the American Philosophical Association* (1974), pp. 5–20.

belief, while nothing inside can produce support except as it can be shown to rest, finally or at once, on something independently trustworthy.

It is natural to distinguish coherence theories from others by reference to the question whether or not justification can or must come to an end. But this does not define the positions, it merely suggests a form the argument may take. For there are coherence theorists who hold that some beliefs can serve as the basis for the rest, while it would be possible to maintain that coherence is not enough, although giving reasons never comes to an end. What distinguishes a coherence theory is simply the claim that nothing can count as a reason for holding a belief except another belief. Its partisan rejects as unintelligible the request for a ground or source of justification of another ilk. As Rorty has put it, 'nothing counts as justification unless by reference to what we already accept, and there is no way to get outside our beliefs and our language so as to find some test other than coherence.'[4] About this I am, as you see, in agreement with Rorty. Where we differ, if we do, is on whether there remains a question how, given that we cannot 'get outside our beliefs and our language so as to find some test other than coherence', we nevertheless can have knowledge of, and talk about, an objective public world which is not of our own making. I think this question does remain, while I suspect that Rorty doesn't think so. If this is his view, then he must think I am making a mistake in trying to answer the question. Nevertheless, here goes.

It will promote matters at this point to review very hastily some of the reasons for abandoning the search for a basis for knowledge outside the scope of our beliefs. By 'basis' here I mean specifically an epistemological basis, a source of justification.

The attempts worth taking seriously attempt to ground belief in one way or another on the testimony of the senses: sensation, perception, the given, experience, sense data, the passing show. All such theories must explain at least these two things: what, exactly, is the relation between sensation and belief that allows the first to justify the second? and, why should we believe our sensations are reliable, that is, why should we trust our senses?

The simplest idea is to identify certain beliefs with sensations. Thus Hume seems not to have distinguished between perceiving a green spot and perceiving that a spot is green. (An ambiguity in the word 'idea' was a great help here.) Other philosophers noted Hume's confusion, but tried to attain the same results by reducing the gap between perception and judgement to zero by attempting to formulate judgements that do not go beyond stating that the perception or sensation or presentation exists (whatever that may mean). Such theories do not justify beliefs on the basis of sensations, but try to justify certain beliefs by claiming that they have exactly the same epistemic content as a sensation. There are two difficulties with such a view: first, if the basic beliefs do not exceed in content the corresponding sensation they cannot support any inference to an objective world; and second, there are no such beliefs.

A more plausible line is to claim that we cannot be wrong about how things

4. Richard Rorty, *Philosophy and the Mirror of Nature* (Princeton University Press, Princeton, 1979), p. 178.

appear to us to be. If we believe we have a sensation, we do; this is held to be an analytic truth, or a fact about how language is used.

It is difficult to explain this supposed connection between sensations and some beliefs in a way that does not invite scepticism about other minds, and in the absence of an adequate explanation, there should be a doubt about the implications of the connection for justification. But in any case, it is unclear how, on this line, sensations justify the belief in those sensations. The point is rather that such beliefs require no justification, for the existence of the belief entails the existence of the sensation, and so the existence of the belief entails its own truth. Unless something further is added, we are back to another form of coherence theory.

Emphasis on sensation or perception in matters epistemological springs from the obvious thought: sensations are what connect the world and our beliefs, and they are candidates for justifiers because we often are aware of them. The trouble we have been running into is that the justification seems to depend on the awareness, which is just another belief.

Let us try a bolder tack. Suppose we say that sensations themselves, verbalized or not, justify certain beliefs that go beyond what is given in sensation. So, under certain conditions, having the sensation of seeing a green light flashing may justify the belief that a green light is flashing. The problem is to see how the sensation justifies the belief. Of course, if someone has the sensation of seeing a green light flashing, it is likely, under certain circumstances, that a green light is flashing. *We* can say this, since we know of his sensation, but *he* can't say it, since we are supposing he is justified without having to depend on believing he has the sensation. Suppose he believed he didn't have the sensation. Would the sensation still justify him in the belief in an objective flashing green light?

The relation between a sensation and a belief cannot be logical, since sensations are not beliefs or other propositional attitudes. What then is the relation? The answer is, I think, obvious: the relation is causal. Sensations cause some beliefs and in *this* sense are the basis or ground of those beliefs. But a causal explanation of a belief does not show how or why the belief is justified.

The difficulty of transmuting a cause into a reason plagues the anti-coherentist again if he tries to answer our second question: what justifies the belief that our senses do not systematically deceive us? For even if sensations justify belief in sensation, we do not yet see how they justify belief in external events and objects.

Quine tells us that science tells us that 'our only source of information about the external world is through the impact of light rays and molecules upon our sensory surfaces.'[5] What worries me is how to read the words 'source' and 'information'. Certainly it is true that events and objects in the external world cause us to believe things about the external world, and much, if not all, of the causality takes a route through the sense organs. The notion of information, however, applies in a non-metaphorical way only to the engendered beliefs. So 'source' has to be read simply

---

5. W. V. Quine, 'The Nature of Natural Knowledge', in *Mind and Language*, ed. S. Guttenplan (Clarendon Press, Oxford, 1975), p. 68.

as 'cause' and 'information' as 'true belief' or 'knowledge'. Justification of beliefs caused by our senses is not yet in sight.[6]

The approach to the problem of justification we have been tracing must be wrong. We have been trying to see it this way: a person has all his beliefs about the world—that is, all his beliefs. How can he tell if they are true, or apt to be true? Only, we have been assuming, by connecting his beliefs to the world, confronting certain of his beliefs with the deliverances of the senses one by one, or perhaps confronting the totality of his beliefs with the tribunal of experience. No such confrontation makes sense, for of course we can't get outside our skins to find out what is causing the internal happenings of which we are aware. Introducing intermediate steps or entities into the causal chain, like sensations or observations, serves only to make the epistemological problem more obvious. For if the intermediaries are merely causes, they don't justify the beliefs they cause, while if they deliver information, they may be lying. The moral is obvious. Since we can't swear intermediaries to truthfulness, we should allow no intermediaries between our beliefs and their objects in the world. Of course there are causal intermediaries. What we must guard against are epistemic intermediaries.

There are common views of language that encourage bad epistemology. This is no accident, of course, since theories of meaning are connected with epistemology through attempts to answer the question how one determines that a sentence is true. If knowing the meaning of a sentence (knowing how to give a correct interpretation of it) involves, or is, knowing how it could be recognized to be true, then the theory of meaning raises the same question we have been struggling with, for giving the meaning of a sentence will demand that we specify what would justify asserting it. Here the coherentist will hold that there is no use looking for a source of justification outside of other sentences held true, while the foundationalist will seek to anchor at least some words or sentences to non-verbal rocks. This view is held, I think, both by Quine and by Michael Dummett.

Dummett and Quine differ, to be sure. In particular, they disagree about holism, the claim that the truth of our sentences must be tested together rather than one by one. And they disagree also, and consequently, about whether there is a useful distinction between analytic and synthetic sentences, and about whether a satisfac-

---

6. Many other passages in Quine suggest that Quine hopes to assimilate sensory causes to evidence. In *Word and Object* (MIT Press, Cambridge, Mass., 1960), p. 22, he writes that 'surface irritations . . . exhaust our clues to an external world.' In *Ontological Relativity* (Columbia University Press, New York, 1969), p. 75 [in this volume pp. 269–70], we find that 'The stimulation of his sensory receptors is all the evidence anybody has had to go on, ultimately, in arriving at his picture of the world.' On the same page: 'Two cardinal tenets of empiricism remain unassailable . . . . One is that whatever evidence there is for science is sensory evidence. The other . . . is that all inculcation of meanings of words, must rest ultimately on sensory evidence.' In *The Roots of Reference* (Open Court Publishing, 1974), pp. 37–8, Quine says 'observations' are basic 'both in the support of theory and in the learning of language', and then goes on, 'What are observations? They are visual, auditory, tactual, olfactory. They are sensory, evidently, and thus subjective. . . . Should we say then that the observation is not the sensation. . . . ? No . . .' Quine goes on to abandon talk of observations for talk of observation sentences. But of course observation sentences, unlike observations, cannot play the role of evidence unless we have reason to believe they are true.

tory theory of meaning can allow the sort of indeterminacy Quine argues for. (On all these points, I am Quine's faithful student.)

But what concerns me here is that Quine and Dummett agree on a basic principle, which is that whatever there is to meaning must be traced back somehow to experience, the given, or patterns of sensory stimulation, something intermediate between belief and the usual objects our beliefs are about. Once we take this step, we open the door to scepticism, for we must then allow that a very great many—perhaps most—of the sentences we hold to be true may in fact be false. It is ironical. Trying to make meaning accessible has made truth inaccessible. When meaning goes epistemological in this way, truth and meaning are necessarily divorced. One can, of course, arrange a shotgun wedding by redefining truth as what we are justified in asserting. But this does not marry the original mates.

Take Quine's proposal that whatever there is to the meaning (information value) of an observation sentence is determined by the patterns of sensory stimulation that would cause a speaker to assent to or dissent from the sentence. This is a marvellously ingenious way of capturing what is appealing about verificationist theories without having to talk of meanings, sense-data, or sensations; for the first time it made plausible the idea that one could, and should, do what I call the theory of meaning without need of what Quine calls meanings. But Quine's proposal, like other forms of verificationism, makes for scepticism. For clearly a person's sensory stimulations could be just as they are and yet the world outside very different. (Remember the brain in the vat.)

Quine's way of doing without meanings is subtle and complicated. He ties the meanings of some sentences directly to patterns of stimulation (which also constitute the evidence, Quine thinks, for assenting to the sentence), but the meanings of further sentences are determined by how they are conditioned to the original, or observation sentences. The facts of such conditioning do not permit a sharp division between sentences held true by virtue of meaning and sentences held true on the basis of observation. Quine made this point by showing that if one way of interpreting a speaker's utterances was satisfactory, so were many others. This doctrine of the indeterminacy of translation, as Quine called it, should be viewed as neither mysterious nor threatening. It is no more mysterious than the fact that temperature can be measured in Centigrade or Fahrenheit (or any linear transformation of those numbers). And it is not threatening because the very procedure that demonstrates the degree of indeterminacy at the same time demonstrates that what is determinate is all we need.

In my view, erasing the line between the analytic and synthetic saved philosophy of language as a serious subject by showing how it could be pursued without what there cannot be: determinate meanings. I now suggest also giving up the distinction between observation sentences and the rest. For the distinction between sentences belief in whose truth is justified by sensations and sentences belief in whose truth is justified only by appeal to other sentences held true is as anathema to the coherentist as the distinction between beliefs justified by sensations and beliefs justified only by appeal to further beliefs. Accordingly, I suggest we give up the idea that meaning or knowledge is grounded on something that counts as an ultimate source of evidence. No doubt meaning and knowledge depend on experience, and experience ultimately on sensation. But this is the 'depend' of causality, not of evidence or justification.

I have now stated my problem as well as I can. The search for an empirical foundation for meaning or knowledge leads to scepticism, while a coherence theory seems at a loss to provide any reason for a believer to believe that his beliefs, if coherent, are true. We are caught between a false answer to the sceptic, and no answer.

The dilemma is not a true one. What is needed to answer the sceptic is to show that someone with a (more or less) coherent set of beliefs has a reason to suppose his beliefs are not mistaken in the main. What we have shown is that it is absurd to look for a justifying ground for the totality of beliefs, something outside this totality which we can use to test or compare with our beliefs. The answer to our problem must then be to find a *reason* for supposing most of our beliefs are true that is not a form of *evidence*.

My argument has two parts. First I urge that a correct understanding of the speech, beliefs, desires, intentions and other propositional attitudes of a person leads to the conclusion that most of a person's beliefs must be true, and so there is a legitimate presumption that any one of them, if it coheres with most of the rest, is true. Then I go on to claim that anyone with thoughts, and so in particular anyone who wonders whether he has any reason to suppose he is generally right about the nature of his environment, must know what a belief is, and how in general beliefs are to be detected and interpreted. These being perfectly general facts we cannot fail to use when we communicate with others, or when we try to communicate with others, or even when we merely think we are communicating with others, there is a pretty strong sense in which we can be said to know that there is a presumption in favour of the overall truthfulness of anyone's beliefs, including our own. So it is bootless for someone to ask for some *further* reassurance; that can only add to his stock of beliefs. All that is needed is that he recognize that belief is in its nature veridical.

Belief can be seen to be veridical by considering what determines the existence and contents of a belief. Belief, like the other so-called propositional attitudes, is supervenient on facts of various sorts, behavioural, neurophysiological, biological and physical. The reason for pointing this out is not to encourage definitional or nomological reduction of psychological phenomena to something more basic, and certainly not to suggest epistemological priorities. The point is rather understanding. We gain one kind of insight into the nature of the propositional attitudes when we relate them systematically to one another and to phenomena on other levels. Since the propositional attitudes are deeply interlocked, we cannot learn the nature of one by first winning understanding of another. As interpreters, we work our way into the whole system, depending much on the pattern of interrelationships.

Take for example the interdependence of belief and meaning. What a sentence means depends partly on the external circumstances that cause it to win some degree of conviction; and partly on the relations, grammatical, logical or less, that the sentence has to other sentences held true with varying degrees of conviction.

Since these relations are themselves translated directly into beliefs, it is easy to see how meaning depends on belief. Belief, however, depends equally on meaning, for the only access to the fine structure and individuation of beliefs is through the sentences speakers and interpreters of speakers use to express and describe beliefs. If we want to illuminate the nature of meaning and belief, therefore, we need to start with something that assumes neither. Quine's suggestion, which I shall essentially follow, is to take *prompted assent* as basic, the causal relation between assenting to a sentence and the cause of such assent. This is a fair place to start the project of identifying beliefs and meanings, since a speaker's assent to a sentence depends both on what he means by the sentence and on what he believes about the world. Yet it is possible to know that a speaker assents to a sentence without knowing either what the sentence, as spoken by him, means, or what belief is expressed by it. Equally obvious is the fact that once an interpretation has been given for a sentence assented to, a belief has been attributed. If correct theories of interpretation are not unique (do not lead to uniquely correct interpretations), the same will go for attributions of belief, of course, as tied to acquiescence in particular sentences.

A speaker who wishes his words to be understood cannot systematically deceive his would-be interpreters about when he assents to sentences—that is, holds them true. As a matter of principle, then, meaning, and by its connection with meaning, belief also, are open to public determination. I shall take advantage of this fact in what follows and adopt the stance of a radical interpreter when asking about the nature of belief. What a fully informed interpreter could learn about what a speaker means is all there is to learn; the same goes for what the speaker believes.[7]

The interpreter's problem is that what he assumed to know—the causes of assents to sentences of a speaker—is, as we have seen, the product of two things he is assumed not to know, meaning and belief. If he knew the meanings he would know the beliefs, and if he knew the beliefs expressed by sentences assented to, he would know the meanings. But how can he learn both at once, since each depends on the other?

The general lines of the solution, like the problem itself, are owed to Quine. I will, however, introduce some changes into Quine's solution, as I have into the statement of the problem. The changes are directly relevant to the issue of epistemological scepticism.

I see the aim of radical interpretation (which is much, but not entirely, like Quine's radical translation) as being to produce a Tarski-style characterization of truth for the speaker's language, and a theory of his beliefs. (The second follows from the first plus the presupposed knowledge of sentences held true.) This adds little to Quine's programme of translation, since translation of the speaker's language into one's own plus a theory of truth for one's own language add up to a theory of truth for the speaker. But the shift to the semantic notion of truth from the syntactic notion of translation puts the formal restrictions of a theory of truth

---

7. I now think it is essential, in doing radical interpretation, to include the desires of the speaker from the start, so that the springs of action and intention, namely both belief and desire, are related to meaning. But in the present essay it is not necessary to introduce this further factor.

in the foreground, and emphasizes one aspect of the close relation between truth and meaning.

The principle of charity plays a crucial role in Quine's method, and an even more crucial role in my variant. In either case, the principle directs the interpreter to translate or interpret so as to read some of his own standards of truth into the pattern of sentences held true by the speaker. The point of the principle is to make the speaker intelligible, since too great deviations from consistency and correctness leave no common ground on which to judge either conformity or difference. From a formal point of view, the principle of charity helps solve the problem of the interaction of meaning and belief by restraining the degrees of freedom allowed belief while determining how to interpret words.

We have no choice, Quine has urged, but to read our own logic into the thoughts of a speaker; Quine says this for the sentential calculus, and I would add the same for first-order quantification theory. This leads directly to the identification of the logical constants, as well as to assigning a logical form to all sentences.

Something like charity operates in the interpretation of those sentences whose causes of assent come and go with time and place: when the interpreter finds a sentence of the speaker the speaker assents to regularly under conditions he recognizes, he takes those conditions to be the truth conditions of the speaker's sentence. This is only roughly right, as we shall see in a moment. Sentences and predicates less directly geared to easily detected goings-on can, in Quine's cannon, be interpreted at will, given only the constraints of interconnections with sentences conditioned directly to the world. Here I would extend the principle of charity to favour interpretations that as far as possible preserve truth: I think it makes for mutual understanding, and hence for better interpretation, to interpret what the speaker accepts as true when we can. In this matter, I have less choice than Quine, because I do not see how to draw the line between observation sentences and theoretical sentences at the start. There are several reasons for this, but the one most relevant to the present topic is that this distinction is ultimately based on an epistemological consideration of a sort I have renounced: observation sentences are directly based on something like sensation—patterns of sensory stimulation—and this is an idea I have been urging leads to scepticism. Without the direct tie to sensation or stimulation, the distinction between observation sentences and others can't be drawn on epistemologically significant grounds. The distinction between sentences whose causes to assent come and go with observable circumstances and those a speaker clings to through change remains however, and offers the possibility of interpreting the words and sentences beyond the logical.

The details are not here to the point. What should be clear is that if the account I have given of how belief and meaning are related and understood by an interpreter is correct, then most of the sentences a speaker holds to be true—especially the ones he holds to most stubbornly, the ones most central to the system of his beliefs—most of these sentences *are* true, at least in the opinion of the interpreter. For the only, and therefore unimpeachable, method available to the interpreter automatically puts the speaker's beliefs in accord with the standards of logic of the interpreter, and hence credits the speaker with plain truths of logic. Needless to say there are degrees of logical and other consistency, and perfect consistency is not to be expected. What needs emphasis is only the methodological necessity for finding consistency enough.

Nor, from the interpreter's point of view, is there any way he can discover the speaker to be largely wrong about the world. For he interprets sentences held true (which is not to be distinguished from attributing beliefs) according to the events and objects in the outside world that cause the sentence to be held true.

What I take to be the important aspect of this approach is apt to be missed because the approach reverses our natural way of thinking of communication derived from situations in which understanding has already been secured. Once understanding has been secured we are able, often, to learn what a person believes quite independently of what caused him to believe it. This may lead us to the crucial, indeed fatal, conclusion that we can in general fix what someone means independently of what he believes and independently of what caused the belief. But if I am right, we can't in general first identify beliefs and meanings and then ask what caused them. The causality plays an indispensable role in determining the content of what we say and believe. This is a fact we can be led to recognize by taking up, as we have, the interpreter's point of view.

It is an artifact of the interpreter's correct interpretation of a person's speech and attitudes that there is a large degree of truth and consistency in the thought and speech of an agent. But this is truth and consistency by the interpreter's standards. Why couldn't it happen that speaker and interpreter understand one another on the basis of shared but erroneous beliefs? This can, and no doubt often does, happen. But it cannot be the rule. For imagine for a moment an interpreter who is omniscient about the world, and about what does and would cause a speaker to assent to any sentence in his (potentially unlimited) repertoire. The omniscient interpreter, using the same method as the fallible interpreter, finds the fallible speaker largely consistent and correct. By his own standards, of course, but since these are objectively correct, the fallible speaker is seen to be largely correct and consistent by objective standards. We may also, if we want, let the omniscient interpreter turn his attention to the fallible interpreter of the fallible speaker. It turns out that the fallible interpreter can be wrong about some things, but not in general; and so he cannot share universal error with the agent he is interpreting. Once we agree to the general method of interpretation I have sketched, it becomes impossible correctly to hold that anyone could be mostly wrong about how things are.

There is, as I noted above, a key difference between the method of radical inter- pretation I am now recommending, and Quine's method of radical translation. The difference lies in the nature of the choice of causes that govern interpretation. Quine makes interpretation depend on patterns of sensory stimulation, while I make it depend on the external events and objects the sentence is interpreted as being about. Thus Quine's notion of meaning is tied to sensory criteria, something he thinks that can be treated also as evidence. This leads Quine to give epistemic significance to the distinction between observation sentences and others, since observation sentences are supposed, by their direct conditioning to the senses, to have a kind of extra-linguistic justification. This is the view against which I argued in the first part of my paper, urging that sensory stimulations are indeed part of the causal chain that leads to belief, but cannot, without confusion, be considered to be evidence, or a source of justification, for the stimulated beliefs.

What stands in the way of global scepticism of the senses is in my view the fact that we must, in the plainest and methodologically most basic cases, take the objects of a belief to be the causes of that belief. And what we, as interpreters, must take them to be is what they in fact are. Communication begins where causes converge: your utterance means what mine does if belief in its truth is systematically caused by the same events and objects.[8]

The difficulties in the way of this view are obvious, but I think they can be overcome. The method applies directly, at best, only to occasion sentences—the sentences assent to which is caused systematically by common changes in the world. Further sentences are interpreted by their conditioning to occasion sentences, and the appearance in them of words that appear also in occasion sentences. Among occasion sentences, some will vary in the credence they command not only in the face of environmental change, but also in the face of change of credence awarded related sentences. Criteria can be developed on this basis to distinguish degrees of observationality on internal grounds, without appeal to the concept of a basis for belief outside the circle of beliefs.

Related to these problems, and easier still to grasp, is the problem of error. For even in the simplest cases it is clear that the same cause (a rabbit scampers by) may engender different beliefs in speaker and observer, and so encourage assent to sentences which cannot bear the same interpretation. It is no doubt this fact that made Quine turn from rabbits to patterns of stimulation as the key to interpretation. Just as a matter of statistics, I'm not sure how much better one approach is than the other. Is the relative frequency with which identical patterns of stimulation will touch off assent to 'Gavagai' and 'Rabbit' greater than the relative frequency with which a rabbit touches off the same two responses in speaker and interpreter? Not an easy question to test in a convincing way. But let the imagined results speak for Quine's method. Then I must say, what I must say in any case, the problem of error cannot be met sentence by sentence, even at the simplest level. The best we can do is cope with error holistically, that is, we interpret so as to make an agent as intelligible as possible, given his actions, his utterances and his place in the world. About some things we will find him wrong, as the necessary cost of finding him elsewhere right. As a rough approximation, finding him right means identifying the causes with the objects of his beliefs, giving special weight to the simplest cases, and countenancing error where it can be best explained.

Suppose I am right that an interpreter must so interpret as to make a speaker or agent largely correct about the world. How does this help the person himself who wonders what reason he has to think his beliefs are mostly true? How can he learn

8. It is clear that the causal theory of meaning has little in common with the causal theories of reference of Kripke and Putnam. Those theories look to causal relations between names and objects of which speakers may well be ignorant. The chance of systematic error is thus increased. My causal theory does the reverse by connecting the cause of a belief with its object.

about the causal relations between the real world and his beliefs that lead the interpreter to interpret him as being on the right track?

The answer is contained in the question. In order to doubt or wonder about the provenance of his beliefs an agent must know what belief is. This brings with it the concept of objective truth, for the notion of a belief is the notion of a state that may or may not jibe with reality. But beliefs are also identified, directly and indirectly, by their causes. What an omniscient interpreter knows a fallible interpreter gets right enough if he understands a speaker, and this is just the complicated causal truth that makes us the believers we are, and fixes the contents of our beliefs. The agent has only to reflect on what a belief is to appreciate that most of his basic beliefs are true, and among his beliefs, those most securely held and that cohere with the main body of his beliefs are the most apt to be true. The question, how do I know my beliefs are generally true? thus answers itself, simply because beliefs are by nature generally true. Rephrased or expanded, the question becomes, how can I tell whether my beliefs, which are by their nature generally true, are generally true?

All beliefs are justified in this sense: they are supported by numerous other beliefs (otherwise they wouldn't be the beliefs they are), and have a presumption in favour of their truth. The presumption increases the larger and more significant the body of beliefs with which a belief coheres, and there being no such thing as an isolated belief, there is no belief without a presumption in its favour. In this respect, interpreter and interpreted differ. From the interpreter's point of view, methodology enforces a general presumption of truth for the body of beliefs as a whole, but the interpreter does not need to presume each particular belief of someone else is true. The general presumption applied to others does not make them globally right, as I have emphasized, but provides the background against which to accuse them of error. But from each person's own vantage point, there must be a graded presumption in favour of each of his own beliefs.

We cannot, alas, draw the picturesque and pleasant conclusion that all true beliefs constitute knowledge. For though all of a believer's beliefs are to some extent justified to him, some may not be justified enough, or in the right way, to constitute knowledge. The general presumption in favour of the truth of belief serves to rescue us from a standard form of scepticism by showing why it is impossible for all our beliefs to be false together. This leaves almost untouched the task of specifying the conditions of knowledge. I have not been concerned with the canons of evidential support (if such there be), but to show that all that counts as evidence or justification for a belief must come from the same totality of belief to which it belongs.

Afterthoughts, 1987

The paper printed here was written for a colloquium organized by Richard Rorty for a Hegel Congress at Stuttgart in 1981. W. V. Quine and Hilary Putnam were the other participants in the colloquium. Our contributions were published in Kant *oder Hegel?*[9] After Stuttgart the four of us had a more leisurely exchange on the same topics at the University of Heidelberg. When the Pacific Division of the American Philosophical Association met in March of 1983, Rorty read a paper titled 'Pragmatism, Davidson, and Truth'. It was in part a comment on 'A Coherence Theory of Truth and Knowledge'. I replied. Rorty subsequently published his paper with revisions in *Truth and Interpretation: Perspectives on the Philosophy of Donald Davidson.*[10] This note continues the conversation.

A few ageing *philosophes*, which may include Quine, Putnam and Dummett, and certainly includes me, are still puzzling over the nature of truth and its connections or lack of connections with meaning and epistemology. Rorty thinks we should stop worrying; he believes philosophy has seen through or outgrown the puzzles and should turn to less heavy and more interesting matters. He is particularly impatient with me for not conceding that the old game is up because he finds in my work useful support for his enlightened stance; underneath my 'out-dated rhetoric' he detects the outlines of a largely correct attitude.

In his paper, both early and late, Rorty urges two things: that my view of truth amounts to a rejection of both coherence and correspondence theories and should properly be classed as belonging to the pragmatist tradition, and that I should not pretend that I am answering the sceptic when I am really telling him to get lost. I pretty much concur with him on both points.

In our 1983 discussion I agreed to stop calling my position either a coherence or a correspondence theory if he would give up the pragmatist theory of truth. He has done his part; he now explicitly rejects both James and Peirce on truth. I am glad to hold to my side of the bargain. If it had not already been published, I would now change the title of 'A Coherence Theory', and I would not describe the project as showing how 'coherence yields correspondence'. On internal evidence alone, as Rorty points out, my view cannot be called a correspondence theory. As long ago as 1969 I argued that nothing can usefully and intelligibly be said to correspond to a sentence;[11] and I repeated this in 'A Coherence Theory'. I thought then that the fact that in characterizing truth for a language it is necessary to put words into relation with objects was enough to give some grip for the idea of correspondence; but this now seems to me a mistake. The mistake is in a way only a misnomer, but terminological infelicities have a way of breeding conceptual confusion, and so it is here. Correspondence theories have always been conceived as providing an *explanation* or *analysis* of truth, and this a Tarski-style theory of truth certainly does not do. I would also now reject the point generally made against correspondence theories that there is no way we could ever tell whether our sentences or beliefs correspond to reality. This criticism is at best misleading, since no one has ever explained in what such a correspondence could consist; and, worse, it is predicated on the false assumption that truth is transparently epistemic.

9. Dieter Henrich (ed.), *Kant oder Hegel?* (Kett-Cotta, 1983).
10. Ernest LePore (ed.), *Truth and Interpretation: Perspectives on the Philosophy of Donald Davidson* (Blackwell, Oxford, 1986).
11. Donald Davidson, 'True to the Facts', reprinted in *Inquiries into Truth and Interpretation* (Oxford University Press, Oxford, 1984).

I also regret having called my view a 'coherence theory'. My emphasis on coherence was probably just a way of making a negative point, that 'all that counts as evidence or justification for a belief must come from the same totality of belief to which it belongs.' Of course this negative claim has typically led those philosophers who held it to conclude that reality and truth are constructs of thought; but it does not lead me to this conclusion, and for this reason if no other I ought not to have called my view a coherence theory. There is also a less weighty reason for not stressing coherence. Coherence is nothing but consistency. It is certainly in favour of a set of beliefs that they be consistent, but there is no chance that a person's beliefs will not tend to be self-consistent, since beliefs are individuated in part by their logical properties; what is not largely consistent with many other beliefs cannot be identified as a belief. The main thrust of 'A Coherence Theory' has little to do with consistency; the important thesis for which I argue is that belief is intrinsically veridical. This is the ground on which I maintain that while truth is not an epistemic concept, neither is it wholly severed from belief (as it is in different ways by both correspondence and coherence theories).

My emphasis on coherence was misplaced; calling my view a 'theory' was a plain blunder. In his paper Rorty stressed a minimalist attitude towards truth that he correctly thought we shared. It could be put this way: truth is as clear and basic a concept as we have. Tarski has given us an idea of how to *apply* the general concept (or try to apply it) to particular languages on the assumption that we already understand it; but of course he didn't show how to define it in general (he proved, rather, that this couldn't be done). Any further attempt to explain, define, analyse or explicate the concept will be empty or wrong: correspondence theories, coherence theories, pragmatist theories, theories that identify truth with warranted assertability (perhaps under 'ideal' or 'optimum' conditions), theories that ask truth to explain the success of science or serve as the ultimate outcome of science or the conversations of some elite, all such theories either add nothing to our understanding of truth or have obvious counter-examples. Why on earth should we expect to be able to reduce truth to something clearer or more fundamental? After all, the only concept Plato succeeded in defining was mud (dirt and water). Putnam's comparison of various attempts to characterize truth with the attempts to define 'good' in naturalistic terms seems to me, as it does to Rorty, apt. It also seems to apply to Putnam's identification of truth with idealized warranted assertability.[12] (*Realism and Reason*, Cambridge, 1983, p. xvii.)

A theory of truth for a speaker, or group of speakers, while not a definition of the general concept of truth, does give a firm sense of what the concept is good for; it allows us to say, in a compact and clear way, what someone who understands that speaker, or those speakers, knows. Such a theory also invites the question how an interpreter could confirm its truth—a question which without the theory could not be articulated. The answer will, as I try to show in 'A Coherence Theory', bring out essential relations among the concepts of meaning, truth and belief. If I am right, each of these concepts requires the others, but none is subordinate to, much less

12. Hilary Putnam, *Realism and Reason* (Cambridge University Press, Cambridge, 1983), p. xviii.

definable in terms of, the others. Truth emerges not as wholly detached from belief (as a correspondence theory would make it) nor as dependent on human methods and powers of discovery (as epistemic theories of truth would make it). What saves truth from being 'radically non-epistemic' (in Putnam's words) is not that truth is epistemic but that belief, through its ties with meaning, is intrinsically veridical.

Finally, how about Rorty's admonition to stop trying to answer the sceptic, and tell him to get lost? A short response would be that the sceptic has been told this again and again over the millennia and never seems to listen; like the philosopher he is, he wants an argument. To spell this out a bit: there is perhaps the suggestion in Rorty's 'Pragmatism, Davidson, and Truth' that a 'naturalistic' approach to the problems of meaning and the propositional attitudes will automatically leave the sceptic no room for manoeuvre. This thought, whether or not it is Rorty's, is wrong. Quine's naturalized epistemology, because it is based on the empiricist premise that what we mean and what we think is conceptually (and not merely causally) founded on the testimony of the senses, is open to standard sceptical attack. I was much concerned in 'A Coherence Theory' to argue for an alternative approach to meaning and knowledge, and to show that if this alternative were right, scepticism could not get off the ground. I agree with Rorty to this extent; I did not set out to 'refute' the sceptic, but to give a sketch of what I think to be a correct account of the foundations of linguistic communication and its implications for truth, belief and knowledge. If one grants the correctness of this account, one *can* tell the sceptic to get lost.

Where Rorty and I differ, if we do, is in the importance we attach to the arguments that lead to the sceptic's undoing, and in the interest we find in the consequences for knowledge, belief, truth and meaning. Rorty wants to dwell on where the arguments have led: to a position which allows us to dismiss the sceptic's doubts, and so to abandon the attempt to provide a general justification for knowledge claims—a justification that is neither possible nor needed. Rorty sees the history of Western philosophy as a confused and victorless battle between unintelligible scepticism and lame attempts to answer it. Epistemology from Descartes to Quine seems to me just one complex, and by no means unilluminating, chapter in the philosophical enterprise. If that chapter is coming to a close, it will be through recourse to modes of analysis and adherence to standards of clarity that have always distinguished the best philosophy, and will, with luck and enterprise, continue to do so.

Part V

Sources of Knowledge

Introduction

KNOWLEDGE can be subdivided according to the sources from which it arises. The basic sources of knowledge and justification are perception (including proprioception, i.e., awareness of the condition and activities of one's own body), introspection, testimony, memory, reason, and inference. This classification is a little arbitrary. Some epistemologists regard introspection not as an independent source of knowledge but as a form of perception. Memory is sometimes considered not as a source of knowledge but merely as a retention of knowledge already obtained in some other way. Inference is obviously not an independent source of knowledge since the premises or facts from which one infers a conclusion must come from elsewhere. And some philosophers would dispute the power of pure reason as a source of *a priori* knowledge. Despite these faults, though, we have chosen to classify the readings in this part according to these more or less standard categories.

Perception

There are many different views about the nature of perception, but the primary division is between *direct* (sometimes called 'naive') and *indirect* (sometimes called 'representative') realism.

Though conceding that there is a world of mind-independent objects that cause us to have experiences, representative realists argue that we do not directly perceive these external objects. What we directly perceive are the effects these objects have on us—an internal image, sense-datum, idea, or impression, i.e., a more or less (depending on circumstances) accurate representation of the external reality that helps produce it. Just as images appearing on a television screen represent their remote causes, the sensory images (visual, auditory, etc.) that occur in the mind—the sense-data of which we are directly aware—represent their external physical causes. Normal perception of external objects, then, turns out to be a type of indirect perception. Representative realists differ among themselves about the question of how much (if at all) the sense-data of which we are directly aware resemble external objects. Some take the external cause to have some of the properties (the so-called 'primary properties') of the datum (e.g., extension) and not others (the so-called 'secondary properties' e.g., colour).

Direct realism is closer to common sense in refusing to restrict perceptual awareness to an inner world of subjective experiences (sense-data). What we are directly aware of in sense perception are ordinary objects—trees, rocks, automobiles, and other people—things that (unlike sense-data) continue to exist when we are no longer aware of them. Our perception may sometimes be indirect—as when we see a person in a mirror or on television—but most of the times we see the things directly, without a physical (or mental) intermediary.

It is commonly supposed that direct realists have an easier answer than do indirect realists to sceptical questions about how we can know that there is an external reality and, if there is, what it is like. This is not necessarily so. Direct *awareness* of P does not automatically give one direct knowledge of P. One may not know that it is P one is aware of. One can perceive—as directly as one may please (i.e., no mirrors or reflections)—a spy, a thief, or a grandmother, without knowing that what one is (directly) aware of is a spy, a thief, or a grandmother. So, too, one may be directly aware of trees and rocks without knowing they are trees and rocks—objects that exist independently of one's perception of them. Philosophical and psychological theories about the *objects* of perception—about what objects we are, in perception, directly aware of—are not necessarily theories about what *facts* we can know. One can be a direct realist about perceptual objects (by maintaining that we are directly aware of physical objects) and a complete skeptic about the facts we know (by denying we know anything about these objects).

Unlike the above two forms of realism, *phenomenalism* (sometimes called 'idealism') denies an objective physical reality altogether. Everything that exists depends for its existence (like sense-data) on someone's awareness of it. In other words, nothing exists except sensations and the minds which experience them. The rest (what we normally take to be an independently existing physical world) is a mental construction or fiction.

There are two well-known arguments for representationalism and against (common sense) direct realism—the time-lag argument and the argument from illusion.

The time-lag argument appeals to the fact that perceiving a physical object is a causal process that takes time. This temporal lag is most dramatic in the case of distant objects (e.g., stars), but it exists for every physical object. Consequently, at the moment we see a physical object, the object could no longer exist. It could have ceased to exist during the time light was being transmitted to the eye. Yet, even if the object ceases to exist before we become aware of anything, we are aware of *something*. This something of which we are aware, since it cannot be the physical object itself, must be a sense-datum.

The argument from illusion can be given many forms, but there is one version that is particularly persuasive. Suppose someone hallucinates a kumquat. Her experience may be indistinguishable from the experience she has when she actually sees a kumquat. Yet, when hallucinating, she is not aware of a kumquat. What she is aware of is a mental image of a kumquat—call it a kumquat-image. Since the experience of a kumquat-image is, subjectively speaking, exactly like seeing a kumquat, it is plausible to suppose that seeing a kumquat is really seeing a kumquat-image. The only difference is that when one actually sees a kumquat, the experience is caused by a real kumquat. So even in the veridical perception of a kumquat, what one is directly aware of is a kumquat-image.

Direct realists have responses to both arguments. How plausible they are is an open question. A direct realist can insist that the time-lag argument only shows that we cannot see into the past, that we cannot see objects as they *were* a short (or, in the case of stars, a long) time ago. The argument from illusion is tougher. Direct realists must say that although the experiences are subjectively the same, what we are aware of in regular perception is different from what we are aware of in hallucination and dreams. In ordinary perception we are aware of physical objects. In hallucination and dreams, if we are aware of anything—and some direct realists would deny that we are (it only *seems* as though we are)—we are aware of mental entities.

Grice's (Chapter 30) causal theory of perception is a form of representative realism.

The core idea of the causal theory of perception is that to perceive an object is to have a sense-datum suitably caused by that object. To have a veridical perceptual experience, it is not enough that the world be the way one takes it to be; the world must cause one to take it that way.

Grice defends the causal theory of perception against two objections. The first objection states that the causal theory makes physical objects unobservable. Grice argues that just because we are not directly aware of physical objects does not mean that we cannot infer their probable presence. The second objection runs as follows: If the difference between perceiving and hallucinating lies in the suitable causal relations between the perceptual states and the world, then scepticism becomes unavoidable, for internally (veridical) perceptions are indistinguishable from hallucinations. Grice responds to this objection by providing a list of examples of suitable causal relations, and by saying that all perceptual states caused in relevantly similar ways to those examples are to count as cases of (veridical) perception.

Strawson (Chapter 31) argues for a version of direct realism and contrasts it with Ayer's phenomenalism and Mackie's representationalism. Towards the end of the essay, Strawson maintains, contrary to common opinion, that direct realism can be reconciled with representationalism. The standpoint of physical science favours representationalism, while the standpoint of common sense supports direct realism.

Introspection

Introspection is the attention the mind gives to itself and to its own operations. We engage in introspection to find out what we think, feel, or want. Introspection normally results in the self-ascription of some psychological property: I'm bored, unhappy, in love, excited, and so on. Descartes felt that beliefs grounded in attentive introspection were infallible (you could not be mistaken about what you thought and felt) and omniscient (one always knew which psychological states one was in). At least since Sigmund Freud, this doctrine about the transparency of the mind to itself is no longer widely accepted. However, despite the fact that introspective beliefs are subject to misinterpretation, self-deception, errors, and inattention, they possess an epistemic authority. Sincere first-person present-tense claims about thoughts and feelings seem to have an epistemic authority no second or third person claim can have. This intuition is called 'first-person authority' or 'privileged self-knowledge'.

There are two kinds of explanations for first-person authority of introspective beliefs. On one view, called 'detectivism', we are able to tell our thoughts because we are equipped with a cognitive mechanism or process by which we can detect their presence and nature. It is thanks to this mechanism that each of us is in a privileged position to talk about her mental states. According to another view, called 'constitutionism' we should not think of our mental states as separate from our judgements about them. My taking myself to be in a particular state of mind plays a constitutive role in determining the state of mind that I am in. First-person authority is due to the fact that what we think is often determined by what we take ourselves to think.

The selected articles discuss the doctrine of first-person authority against the background of *semantic externalism*. As was explained in the introduction to Part IV, semantic externalism is the view that the contents of many of our thoughts are determined at least in part by the states of the outside world. Putnam (Chapter 27), Dretske (Chapter 28) and Davidson (Chapter 29) use semantic externalism to show that sceptical hypotheses (e.g., that we might be brains in a vat) are incoherent for they assume that the world and our thoughts about it can logically and systematically come apart. Semantic externalism ties our mental content down to our actual environment so there is no possibility of massive error. Now, however, the sceptic could accept the externalist argument and simply redirect her sceptical attack: instead of doubting that we can know anything about the external world (e.g., that we are not brains in a vat), she now questions our ability to know what we believe about the external world (the content of our beliefs)—that we *think* we are not brains in a vat. Given semantic externalism, determining the content of a given mental state requires information beyond what is available to simple introspection or reflection. It seems that we must first acquire knowledge of the relevant environmental factors since what we think (according to semantic externalism) depends to some extent on the environment. If this reasoning is correct, it follows that semantic externalism only solves external-world scepticism at the cost of replacing it by a new and equally (or even more) puzzling sceptical problem, *content scepticism*: scepticism about what it is we actually think about the world.

There are three possible ways to respond to the challenge of content scepticism. First, content scepticism can be used to argue against the thesis of privileged self-knowledge. Wittgenstein, for example, is said to have held the view that we do not have knowledge, let alone privileged knowledge, of our mental states. Most people agree that this solution is too counterintuitive to be acceptable. Second, one can use the implausibility content scepticism to argue against semantic externalism. That is, if semantic externalism implies that we do not know what we think, then semantic externalism must be false since we certainly do know what we think. The advocates of this strategy are called 'incompatibilists'. Thirdly, one can argue that semantic externalism neither generates scepticism nor undermines privileged self-knowledge. Advocates of this strategy are called 'compatibilists'. Boghossian (Chapter 33) represents incompatibilism, while Burge (Chapter 32) and (with reservations) Bernecker (Chapter 34) are compatibilists.

Memory and testimony

Whether memory is a genuine source of knowledge is a controversial issue. Some philosophers maintain that memory only retains or preserves knowledge but does not produce new knowledge. Other philosophers insist that there are cases where a person first comes to know by remembering. What passes into the mind (before memory works on it to yield knowledge) is merely a datum or a belief, not knowledge. There are also cases where one can use memory images to discover what one did not know before. A favourite example is learning how many windows there were in the house you grew up in by imagining (with the aid of memory) walking through the house counting the windows in each room. One did not know before how many windows there were, now, with the aid of memory, one does.

Obviously, memory comes in all shapes and colours. Perhaps the most basic distinction between types of memory is the distinction between remembering *how* to do something (ride a bike or swim) and remembering *that* such-and-such is the case. Remembering that P is commonly called 'factual memory'. Factual memory can store either impersonal facts (that Vesuvius erupted in the year AD 79) or personal facts—things you experienced or did yourself. Personal factual memory can either be inferential (constructive) or non-inferential (reconstructive). Suppose this morning my secretary told me that my best friend called while I was out of the office. If what I later remember is that Bert called me, it is an instance of inferential knowledge for I have inferred 'Bert called' from 'my best friend called'. Furthermore, psychologists suggest that within non-inferential personal factual memories there is a kind of memory which deserves special attention and which they label 'episodic memory'. In episodic memory, one does not only remember that one had a particular experience but also remembers having it in a more direct, personal, way that involves associated imagery. Sometimes, for example, people remember things that happened to them when they were young (e.g., that they broke their leg when they were 5 years old) but they do not actually remember the event itself. They do not remember breaking it. Their factual memory that they broke it is the result, perhaps, of what their parents told them about the event.

Remembering can be analysed into three components: (i) a current cognitive attitude of the subject towards the remembered fact, (ii) a past experience of the subject relating to the remembered fact, and (iii) the right sort of connection between the past experience and the subsequent recall. According to Martin and Deutscher (Chapter 35), the connection between (i) and (ii) is interpreted as a causal connection: S remembers that P only if S's believing that P at an earlier time is a cause of her believing that P at the later time. Martin and Deutscher discuss in great detail the kind of causality involved in memory. They show that memory causality is rather weak, for it does not imply that the past experience is necessary for the subsequent recall.

Testimony is the source of an enormously large portion of our most important beliefs. *Prima facie*, one might think that testimony is not a distinct source of knowledge. It is, rather, merely a species of inferential knowledge. On this view, when one learns (from a friend or teacher, say) some fact, one always reasons (if only half consciously) in something like the following way: She said that P; she is a fairly reliable fellow and she should know about P; so P is probably true. We may sometimes reason in this way, but it is questionable whether we *always* reason in that way or whether such reasoning is even necessary. Thomas Reid pointed out that testimonial beliefs are typically basic or non-inferential. Normally, we just believe what people tell us, and we believe it in a way that is very much like the way we believe our eyes and ears when they 'tell' us what is happening around us.

The aim of Coady's (Chapter 36) paper is to promote Reid's view of testimony and to demonstrate the untenability of what he calls the 'reductionist' view of testimony. David Hume was a reductionist about testimony. He held that if testimony is to be vindicated as a source of knowledge it could only be by showing that the inference from 'She said that P' to 'P is (probably) true' is justified. On Hume's view, testimony reduces to perception, memory and inference. It is not an *independent* source of knowledge. Coady argues that if reductionism is correct, knowledge by testimony would be very rare. For only in the rarest instances do we reason at all in forming a belief based on what someone has told us. From Coady's alternative perspective, testimony is seen as a source of knowledge of broadly equal status to perception and memory.

Induction

Through inductive reasoning we can not only acquire new beliefs, but also justified beliefs and knowledge. It is employed in almost every branch of human inquiry. Inductive reasoning usually begins with observations about particular matters of fact (e.g., this raven is black, that raven is black) and derives a universal generalization (e.g., 'All ravens are black') or a prediction about as yet unexamined instances (e.g., 'The next raven I see will be black'). Such reasoning obviously runs risks. There is no guarantee that the conclusion will be true. Unless all ravens are examined, it is always possible that one might come across a raven that is not black. It is not essential that induction be about the future. The conclusion of an inductive argument can be about past or present (but as yet unexamined) cases.

Induction is one kind of inferential reasoning; deduction is another. In a valid deduction, the conclusion follows necessarily from the premisses, so that it is logically impossible for the premisses to be true and the conclusion to be false. In a valid induction, however, the evidence does not entail the conclusion. Inductive arguments can, at best, make their conclusion *probable*. The probablity of an inductively justified belief ranges from 0 to 1 with 0.5 representing the same likelihood of truth as of falsehood. Even high probability may not be enough to justify one in believing (and acting on) a conclusion. It depends on how much is at stake in being wrong. One might be justified in thinking Dogtrot will win the next race if all one plans to bet is a few dollars. Dogtrot has, after all, won most of his races. But if one's life savings are at stake, one may need better evidence.

It was David Hume who posed the traditional problem of induction. Hume's concern was to justify inductive reasoning. He observed that the premisses of inductive reasoning do not logically entail the conclusion. If we reply by saying that the premisses, although they do not logically imply the conclusion, none the less make it probable, we have the problem of trying to justify this additional premiss in the reasoning. How do we know (or why are we justified in believing), Hume will ask, that our conclusion is made more probable by our premisses. If we try to justify this fact, we are forced to fall back on either deductive or inductive reasoning, and the entire chain of reasoning starts to look circular. We are trying to justify induction by relying on induction. Hume's point is that it is impossible to non-circularly justify the belief that nature is uniform, a principle that seems to lie at the heart of all inductive reasoning.

Philosophers have tried to meet Hume's sceptical challenge in a wide variety of ways. Russell (Chapter 37) attempts to give an *a priori* justification of inductive methods. In the first part of his essay, Russell explains the Humean problem of induction. He then asserts that induction can only be justified by appeal to an *a priori* principle which he calls the 'principle of induction'. The success of Russell's approach depends, in part, on general epistemological theses about the possibility and nature of *a priori* knowledge (cf. Chapters 40–41).

Reichenbach (Chapter 38) accepts David Hume's point about the impossibility of justifying the belief that nature is uniform. Nevertheless, he attempts to *vindicate* induction. To vindicate a method involves showing that the method serves some purpose for which it is designed. Thus, Reichenbach argues that—even acknowledging Hume's scepticism—induction is better suited to the goal of predicting the future than other methods that might be adopted (e.g., crystal gazing, wild guessing).

Goodman (Chapter 39) introduced what he called the 'new riddle of induction' (Hume's problem is the 'old' riddle). The traditional view of induction took it to be like deduction in applying equally to all properties, but Goodman showed that there are restrictions to the use of inductive reasoning. Suppose that many emeralds have been examined before time *t* and have been found to be green. By time *t*, these observations support the hypothesis that the next emerald examined, after time *t*, will be green as well. Then Goodman introduces a new predicate 'grue', to show that things are not that simple. Something is grue if it is examined before time *t* and green, or not examined before time *t* and blue. Given this predicate, all the evidence that future emeralds will be green is equally evidence that they will be blue. Be that as it may, we are inclined to suppose that the green emeralds support the green-hypothesis but the grue emeralds don't support the grue-hypothesis. But what are reasons for preferring one over the other? Goodman formulates the problem in terms of the notion of *projectibility*: what makes 'green' but not 'grue' a projectible predicate? The new riddle of induction seems to demonstrate that sound inductive inferences are arbitrary because they depend on the actual language people use to formulate predictions.

The new riddle of induction has become a popular topic in analytic epistemology and philosophy of science. There are now about twenty different solutions to the problem. Goodman's own solution to the problem is that projectibility of a predicate (which predicates one *should* use in formulating inductive generalizations) has to do with its history. A projectible generalization is one whose predicates are well-entrenched, where this means that they have been used frequently in past generalizations.

A priori knowledge

One central debate, involving the sources of knowledge, concerns the importance of sense experience in our acquisition of knowledge. Some epistemologists have held that, while most beliefs are justified by appeal to one's experience of the world, there are some beliefs that are justified in a way that does not depend on appeal to perception. They are justified by reason or pure thought alone. Beliefs justified in the latter way are said to be justified *a priori* (latin for 'before') while beliefs justified in the former way are said to be justified empirically or *a posteriori* (latin for 'after'). *A priori* knowledge is before (or prior to) experience in a logical sense, though not necessarily before experience in time.

The contemporary discussion of *a priori* knowledge has been largely shaped by Immanuel Kant. Kant believed that one mark of the *a priori* was that of *necessity*: if P was knowable *a priori*, then P must be necessarily true (true in all possible worlds). A contingent proposition is one that is true in some possible worlds, false in others). Some necessary propositions are what Kant called *analytic* (or what we might think of as definitional) truths—e.g., all bachelors are married or triangles have three sides. A synthetic proposition is one which is not analytic, one whose truth does not derive from the meaning of the terms appearing in it—e.g., all bachelors weigh less than 800 pounds. One of the main concerns of Kant's *Critique of Pure Reason* was to show how there can be *a priori* knowledge not only of analytic propositions but also of synthetic propositions.

Contrary to Kant, Kripke (Chapter 40) argues that some contingently true propositions are knowable *a priori* and that some necessarily true propositions are knowable *a posteriori*. Kripke's example of a contingent truth which can be known *a priori* is 'the standard metre-stick in Paris is one metre long'. Since the standard metre-stick in Paris is used to fix the reference of the term 'one metre' we can know *a priori* that this stick is one metre long. However, the proposition is contingent since there are possible worlds in which the standard metre-stick is subjected to heat and therefore changes its length. Kripke's examples of a necessary truth which can only be known *a posteriori* are true identity statements involving proper names, such as 'Hesperus is Phosphorus'. This statement is necessarily true because there is no world in which the thing we refer to with the name 'Hesperus' (viz., Planet Venus) is not identical to the thing we refer to with the name 'Phosphorus' (viz., Planet Venus). Yet, though this proposition is necessary, we can only know it to be true by empirical means—by determining that the heavenly body appearing in the evening sky (the definition of 'Hesperus') is one and the same as the heavenly body appearing in the morning sky (definition of 'Phosphorus').

Kitcher (Chapter 41) proposes a reliabilist theory of *a priori* knowledge. Reliabilism holds that epistemic justification need not involve the possession by the believer of anything like a reason for thinking that the belief is true. A belief is justified if it is produced in a reliable way, whether or not the believer has any reason to think that this is so (cf. Chapters 7–9). According to Kitcher's reliabilist conception of the *a priori*, a belief that P is justified *a priori* if it can be justified by any (sufficiently rich) experience. Given any experience, our belief-forming mechanism would have produced true belief in P. Kitcher agrees with Kripke's attack on Kant's contention, that whatever proposition is knowable *a priori* is also necessarily true and conversely.

Further reading

Perception

Alston, W. P., *The Reliability of Sense Perception*, Ithaca, Cornell University Press, 1993.

Armstrong, D. M., *Perception and the Physical World*, London, Routledge & Kegan Paul, 1961.

Chisholm, R. M., *Perceiving. A Philosophical Study*, Ithaca, Cornell University Press, 1961.

Cornman, J., *Perception, Common Sense, and Science*, New Haven, Yale University Press, 1975.

Dancy, J., ed., *Perceptual Knowledge*, Oxford, Oxford University Press, 1988.

Dretske, F. I., *Seeing and Knowing*, Chicago, University of Chicago Press, 1969.

Dretske, F. I., *Knowledge and the Flow of Information*, Cambridge/MA, MIT Press, 1981, Ch. 6.

Føllesdal, D., 'Husserl's Theory of Perception', *Ajatus. Yearbook of the Philosophical Society of Finland* 36 (1976), pp. 95–105.

Fumerton, R. A., *Metaphysical and Epistemological Problems of Perception*, Lincoln, University of Nebraska Press, 1985.

Heil, J., *Perception and Cognition*, Berkeley, University of California Press, 1983.

Jackson, F., *Perception*, Cambridge, Cambridge University Press, 1977.

Pitcher, G. A., *Theory of Perception*, Princeton, Princeton University Press, 1971.

Price, H. H., *Perception*, London, Methuen, 1932.

Rock, I., *An Introduction to Perception*, New York, Macmillan, 1975.

Swartz, R. J., ed., *Perceiving, Sensing, and Knowing*, Garden City, Doubleday, 1965.

Strawson, P. F., *Freedom and Resentment and Other Essays*, London, Methuen, 1974, Ch. 4.

Tye, M., 'The Adverbial Approach to Visual Experience', *Philosophical Review* 93 (1984), pp. 195–225.

In addition consult the 'Further reading' section at the end of Part 2I.

Introspection

Brueckner, A., 'Trying to Get Outside Your Own Skin', *Philosophical Topics* 23 (1995), pp. 79–111.

Cassam, Q., ed., *Self-Knowledge*, Oxford, Oxford University Press, 1994.

Dretske, F. I., *Naturalizing the Mind*, Cambridge/MA, MIT Press, 1995, Ch. 2.

Falvey, K. and Owens, J., 'Externalism, Self-Knowledge, and Skepticism', *Philosophical Review* 103 (1994), pp. 107–37.

Gallois, A., *The World Without, the Mind Within. An Essay on First-Person Authority*, Cambridge, Cambridge University Press, 1996.

Ludlow, P. and Martin, N., eds, *Externalism and Self-Knowledge*, Stanford, CSLI Publications, 1998.

Lyons, W., *The Disappearance of Introspection*, Cambridge/MA, MIT Press, 1986.

Perry, J., *The Problem of the Essential Indexical and Other Essays*, New York, Oxford University Press, 1993.

Shoemaker, S., *Self-Knowledge and Self-Identity*, Ithaca, Cornell University Press, 1963.

Shoemaker, S., *The First-Person Perspective and Other Essays*, Cambridge, Cambridge University Press, 1996.

Wright, C., Smith, B. C. and Macdonald, C., eds., *Knowing Our Own Minds*, Oxford, Clarendon Press, 1998.

Memory

Audi, R., *Epistemology*, London, Routledge, 1998, Ch. 2.

Audi, R., 'Memorial Justification', *Philosophical Topics* 23 (1995), pp. 31–45.

Ayer, A. J., *The Problems of Knowledge*, Harmondsworth, Penguin Books, 1956, Ch. 4.

Brandt, R. B., 'The Epistemological Status of Memory Beliefs', *Philosophical Review* 64 (1955), pp. 78–95.

Ginet, C., *Knowledge, Perception, and Memory*, Dordrecht, Reidel, 1975, Ch. 7.

Ginet, C., 'Memory Knowledge', in G. H. R. Parkinson, ed., *The Handbook of Western Philosophy*, New York, Macmillan, 1988, pp. 159–78.

Lehrer, K. and Richard J., 'Remembering Without Knowing', *Grazer Philosophische Studien* 1 (1975), pp. 121–6.

Locke, D., *Memory*, London, Macmillan, 1971.

Malcolm, N., *Memory and Mind*, Ithaca, Cornell University Press, 1977.

Pollock, J. L., *Knowledge and Justification*, Princeton, Princeton University Press, 1974, Ch. 7.

Russell, B., *The Analysis of Mind*, London, Macmillan, 1921, Ch. 9.

Testimony

Audi, R., *Epistemology*, London, Routledge, 1998, Ch. 5.

Coady, C. A. J., *Testimony*, Oxford, Clarendon Press, 1992.

Fricker, E., 'The Epistemology of Testimony', *Proceedings of the Aristotelian Society*, Suppl. 61 (1987), pp. 57–83.

Hardwig, J., 'The Role of Trust in Knowledge', *Journal of Philosophy* 88 (1991), pp. 693–708.

Hume, D., *An Enquiry Concerning Human Understanding* (1777), ed. by L. A. Selby-Bigge, 3rd edition by P. H. Nidditch, Oxford, Clarendon Press, 1975, Section 10.

Reid, T., *An Inquiry into the Human Mind on the Principles of Common Sense* (1764), in his *Inquiries and Essays*, ed. by R.E. Beanblossom and K. Lehrer, Indianapolis, Hackett, 1983, Part 6, Section 24.

Schmitt, F. F., ed., *Socializing Epistemology. The Social Dimension of Knowledge*, Lanham/MD, Rowman & Littlefield, 1994.

Sosa, E., *Knowledge in Perspective. Selected Essays in Epistemology*, Cambridge, Cambridge University Press, 1991, Ch. 12.

Synthese 73 (1987), special issue on 'Social Epistemology'.

Welbourne, M., *The Community of Knowledge*, Aberdeen, Aberdeen University Press, 1986.

Induction

Carnap, R., *The Logical Foundations of Probability*, Chicago, University of Chicago Press, 1950.

Elgin, C. Z., ed., *Nelson Goodman's New Riddle of Induction*, New York, Garland, 1997.

Hempel, C. G., *Philosophy of Natural Science*, Englewood Cliffs/NJ, Prentice-Hall, 1966.

Hume, D., *An Enquiry Concerning Human Understanding* (1777), ed. by L. A. Selby-Bigge, 3rd edition by P. H. Nidditch, Oxford, Clarendon Press, 1975, Section 4, Part 2.

Jeffrey, R., *The Logic of Decision*, 2nd edition, Chicago, Chicago University Press, 1983.

Kyburg, H. E., Jr., *Probability and Inductive Logic*, New York, Macmillan, 1970.

Levi, I., *The Enterprise of Knowledge. An Essay on Knowledge, Credal Probability, and Chance*, Cambridge/MA, MIT Press, 1980.

Popper, K. R., *Objective Knowledge. An Evolutionary Approach*, Oxford, Clarendon Press, 1972, Ch. 1.

Reichenbach, H., *Theory of Probability*, Berkeley, University of California Press, 1949, Ch. 11.

Rescher, N., *Induction*, Oxford, Basil Blackwell, 1980.

Salmon, W. C., *The Foundations of Scientific Theory*, Pittsburgh, Pittsburgh University Press, 1967.

Skyrms, B., *Choice and Chance*, 3rd edition, Belmont/CA, Wadsworth, 1986.

Stalker, D., ed., *Grue! The New Riddle of Induction*, Chicago, Open Court, 1994.

Strawson, P. F., *Introduction to Logical Theory*, London, Methuen, 1952, Ch. 9.

Swinburne, R., ed., *The Justification of Induction*, Oxford, Oxford University Press, 1974.

Will, F. L., *Induction and Justification*, Ithaca, Cornell University Press, 1974.

A priori knowledge

BonJour, L., *In Defense of Pure Reason*, Cambridge, Cambridge University Press, 1998.

Carruthers, P., *Human Knowledge and Human Nature*, Oxford, Oxford University Press, 1992.

Grice, H. P. and Strawson, P. F., 'In Defense of a Dogma', *Philosophical Review* 65 (1956), pp. 141–58.

Hanson, P. and Hunter, B., eds., *Return of the A Priori*, Calgary, University of Calgary Press, 1992.

Kant, I., *Critique of Pure Reason* (1781/87), trans. N.K. Smith, London, Macmillan, 1964.

Kitcher, P., *The Nature of Mathematical Knowledge*, New York, Oxford University Press, 1983.

Lewis, C. I., 'A Pragmatic Conception of the A Priori', *Journal of Philosophy* 20 (1923), pp. 169–77.

Locke, J., *An Essay Concerning Human Understanding* (1690), ed. by P. H. Nidditch, Oxford, Oxford University Press, 1975.

Moser, P. K., ed., *A Priori Knowledge*, Oxford, Oxford University Press, 1987.

Pap, A., *Semantic and Necessary Truth*, New Haven, Yale University Press, 1958.

Philosophical Studies 92, No. 1–2 (1998), special issue on 'A Priori Knowledge'.

Plantinga, A., *The Nature of Necessity*, Oxford, Clarendon Press, 1974.

Putnam, H., *Realism and Reason. Philosophical Papers* 3, Cambridge, Cambridge University Press, 1983, Chs. 5–7.

Quine, W. V. and Ullian, J. S., *The Web of Belief*, 2nd edition, New York, Random House, 1978.

Stich, S., ed., *Innate Ideas*, Berkeley, University of California Press, 1975.

$$80 \quad (.20) = 16$$
$$92.3 \ (.25) = 23.075$$
$$92.3 \ (.25 \ = 23.075$$
$$92.3 \ (.25 \ = 23.075$$
$$4.0$$

Chapter 30

The causal theory of perception

H. P. Grice

I

THE Causal Theory of Perception (CTP) has for some time received comparatively little attention, mainly, I suspect, because it has been generally assumed
that the theory either asserts or involves as a consequence the proposition that
material objects are unobservable, and that the unacceptability of this proposition
is sufficient to dispose of the theory. I am inclined to regard this attitude to the CTP
as unfair or at least unduly unsympathetic and I shall attempt to outline a thesis
which might not improperly be considered to be a version of the CTP, and which is,
if not true, at least not too obviously false.

What is to count as holding a causal theory of perception? (1) I shall take it as
being insufficient merely to believe that the perception of a material object is always
to be causally explained by reference to conditions the specification of at least one
of which involves a mention of the object perceived; that, for example, the perception is the terminus of a causal sequence involving at an earlier stage some event or
process in the history of the perceived object. Such a belief does not seem to be
philosophical in character; its object has the appearance of being a very general
contingent proposition; though it is worth remarking that if the version of the CTP
with which I shall be primarily concerned is correct, it (or something like it) will
turn out to be a necessary rather than a contingent truth. (2) It may be held that the
elucidation of the notion of perceiving a material object will include some reference
to the role of the material object perceived in the causal ancestry of the perception
or of the sense-impression or sense-datum involved in the perception. This contention is central to what I regard as a standard version of the CTP. (3) It might be held
that it is the task of the philosopher of perception not to elucidate or characterize

H. P. Grice, 'The Causal Theory of Perception' in *Proceedings of the Aristotelian Society*, Suppl. Vol. 35
(1961), pp. 121–52 reprinted by permission of the author.

the ordinary notion of perceiving a material object, but to provide a rational reconstruction of it, to replace it by some concept more appropriate to an ideal or scientific language: it might further be suggested that such a redefinition might be formulated in terms of the effect of the presence of an object upon the observer's sense-organ and nervous system or upon his behaviour or 'behaviour-tendencies' or in terms of both of these effects. A view of this kind may perhaps deserve to be called a causal theory of perception; but I shall not be concerned with theories on these lines. (4) I shall distinguish from the adoption of a CTP the attempt to provide for a wider or narrower range of propositions ascribing properties to material objects a certain sort of causal analysis: the kind of analysis which I have in mind is that which, on *one* possible interpretation, Locke could be taken as suggesting for ascriptions of, for example, colour and temperature; he might be understood to be holding that such propositions assert that an object would, in certain standard conditions, cause an observer to have certain sorts of ideas or sense-impressions.

In Professor Price's *Perception*,[1] there appears a preliminary formulation of the CTP which would bring it under the second of the headings distinguished in the previous paragraph. The CTP is specified as maintaining (1) that in the case of all sense-data (not merely visual and tactual) 'belonging to' simply means *being caused* by, so that 'M is present to my senses' will be equivalent to 'M causes a sense-datum with which I am acquainted'; (2) that perceptual consciousness is fundamentally an inference from effect to cause. Since it is, I think, fair to say that the expression 'present to my senses' was introduced by Price as a special term to distinguish one of the possible senses of the verb 'perceive',[2] the first clause of the quotation above may be taken as propounding the thesis that 'I am perceiving M' (in one sense of that expression) is to be regarded as equivalent to 'I am having (or sensing) a sense-datum which is caused by M.' (The second clause I shall for the time being ignore.) I shall proceed to consider the feature which this version of the CTP shares with other non-causal theories of perception, namely, the claim that perceiving a material object involves having or sensing a sense-datum; for unless this claim can be made out, the special features of the CTP become otiose.

II

The primary difficulty facing the contention that perceiving involves having or sensing a sense-datum is that of giving a satisfactory explanation of the meaning of the technical term 'sense-datum'. One familiar method of attempting this task is that of trying to prove, by means of some form of the Argument from Illusion, the existence of objects of a special sort for which the term 'sense-datum' is offered as a class-name. Another method (that adopted in a famous passage by Moore) is that of giving directions which are designed to enable one to pick out items of the kind to which the term 'sense-datum' is to be applied. The general character of the

1. London, 1932, p. 66.
2. Cf. ibid. pp. 21–5.

objections to each of these procedures is also familiar, and I shall, for present purposes, assume that neither procedure is satisfactory.

Various philosophers have suggested that though attempts to indicate, or demonstrate the existence of, special objects to be called sense-data have all failed, nevertheless the expression 'sense-datum' can (and should) be introduced as a technical term; its use would be explicitly defined by reference to such supposedly standard locutions as 'So-and-so looks Φ (e.g. blue) to me', 'It looks (feels) to me as if there were a Φ so-and-so', 'I seem to see something Φ', and so on. Now it is not to my present purpose to consider how in detail such an explicit definition of the notion of a sense-datum might be formulated. I should, however, remark that this programme may be by no means so easy to carry through as the casual way in which it is sometimes proposed might suggest; various expressions are candidates for the key role in this enterprise, for example, 'looks' ('feels' etc.), 'seems', 'appears', and the more or less subtle differences between them would have to be investigated; and furthermore even if one has decided on a preferred candidate, not all of its uses would be suitable; if, for example, we decide to employ the expressions 'looks' etc., are we to accept the legitimacy of the sentence 'It looks indigestible to me' as providing us with a sense-datum sentence 'I am having an indigestible visual sense-datum'?

[...]

III

[...] I shall, however, for present purposes, assume that some range of uses of locutions of the form 'It looks (feels, etc.) to X as if' has the best chance of being found suitable. I shall furthermore assume that the safest procedure for the Causal Theorist will be to restrict the actual occurrences of the term 'sense-datum' to such classificatory labels as 'sense-datum statement' or 'sense-datum sentence'; to license the introduction of a 'sense-datum terminology' to be used for the re-expression of sentences incorporating the preferred locutions seems to me both unnecessary and dangerous. I shall myself, on behalf of the CTP, often for brevity's sake talk of sense-data or sense-impressions; but I shall hope that a more rigorous, if more cumbrous, mode of expression will always be readily available. I hope that it will now be allowed that, interpreted on the lines which I have suggested, the thesis that perceiving involves having a sense-datum (involves its being the case that some sense-datum statement or other about the percipient is true) has at least a fair chance of proving acceptable.

I turn now to the special features of the CTP. The first clause of the formulation quoted above[3] from Price's *Perception* may be interpreted as representing it to be a necessary and sufficient condition of its being the case that X perceives M that X's sense-impression should be causally dependent on some state of affairs involving M. Let us first enquire whether the suggested condition is necessary. Suppose that it looks to X as if there is a clock on the shelf; what more is required for it to be true to say that X sees a clock on the shelf? There must, one might say, actually be a clock on the shelf which is in X's field of view, before X's eyes. But this does not seem to

3. See above.

be enough. For it is logically conceivable that there should be some method by which an expert could make it look to X as if there were a clock on the shelf on occasions when the shelf was empty: there might be some apparatus by which X's cortex could be suitably stimulated, or some technique analogous to post-hypnotic suggestion. If such treatment were applied to X on an occasion when there actually was a clock on the shelf, and if X's impressions were found to continue unchanged when the clock was removed or its position altered, then I think we should be inclined to say that X did not see the clock which was before his eyes, just because we should regard the clock as playing no part in the origination of his impression. Or, to leave the realm of fantasy, it might be that it looked to me as if there were a certain sort of pillar in a certain direction at a certain distance, and there might actually be such a pillar in that place; but if, unknown to me, there were a mirror interposed between myself and the pillar, which reflected a numerically different though similar pillar, it would certainly be incorrect to say that I saw the first pillar, and correct to say that I saw the second; and it is extremely tempting to explain this linguistic fact by saying that the first pillar was, and the second was not, causally irrelevant to the way things looked to me.

There seems then a good case for allowing that the suggested condition is necessary; but as it stands it can hardly be sufficient. For in any particular perceptual situation there will be objects other than that which would ordinarily be regarded as being perceived, of which some state or mode of functioning is causally relevant to the occurrence of a particular sense-impression: this might be true of such objects as the percipient's eyes or the sun. So some restriction will have to be added to the analysis of perceiving which is under consideration. Price suggested that use should be made of a distinction between 'standing' and 'differential' conditions:[4] as the state of the sun and of the percipient's eyes, for example, are standing conditions in that (roughly speaking) if they were suitably altered, all the visual impressions of the percipient would be in some respect different from what they would otherwise have been; whereas the state of the perceived object is a differential condition in that a change in it would affect only some of the percipient's visual impressions, perhaps only the particular impression the causal origin of which is in question. The suggestion then is that the CTP should hold that an object is perceived if and only if some condition involving it is a differential condition of some sense-impression of the percipient. I doubt, however, whether the imposition of this restriction is adequate. Suppose that on a dark night I see, at one and the same time, a number of objects each of which is illuminated by a different torch; if one torch is tampered with, the effect on my visual impressions will be restricted, not general; the objects illuminated by the other torches will continue to look the same to me. Yet we do not want to be compelled to say that each torch is perceived in such a situation; concealed torches may illuminate. But this is the position into which the proposed revision of the CTP would force us.

I am inclined to think that a more promising direction for the CTP to take is to formulate the required restriction in terms of the way in which a perceived object

4. *Perception*, 70.

contributes towards the occurrence of the sense-impression. A conceivable course would be to introduce into the specification of the restriction some part of the specialist's account, for example to make a reference to the transmission of light-waves to the retina; but the objection to this procedure is obvious; if we are attempting to characterize the ordinary notion of perceiving, we should not explicitly introduce material of which someone who is perfectly capable of employing the ordinary notion might be ignorant. I suggest that the best procedure for the Causal Theorist is to indicate the mode of causal connection by examples; to say that, for an object to be perceived by X, it is sufficient that it should be causally involved in the generation of some sense-impression by X in the kind of way in which, for example, when I look at my hand in a good light, my hand is causally responsible for its looking at me as if there were a hand before me, or in which . . . (and so on), *whatever that kind of way may be*; and to be enlightened on that question one must have recourse to the specialist. I see nothing absurd in the idea that a non-specialist concept should contain, so to speak, a blank space to be filled in by the specialist; that this is so, for example, in the case of the concept of seeing is perhaps indicated by the consideration that if we were in doubt about the correctness of speaking of a certain creature with peculiar sense-organs as *seeing* objects, we might well wish to hear from a specialist a comparative account of the human eye and the relevant sense-organs of the creature in question. We do not, of course, ordinarily need the specialist's contribution; for we may be in a position to say that the same kind of mechanism is involved in a plurality of cases without being in a position to say what that mechanism is.[5]

At this point an objection must be mentioned with which I shall deal only briefly. The CTP as I have so expounded it, it may be said, requires that it should be linguistically correct to speak of the causes of sense-impressions which are involved in perfectly normal perceptual situations. But this is a mistake; it is quite unnatural to talk about the cause, say, of its looking to X as if there were a cat before him unless the situation is or is thought to be in some way abnormal or delusive; this being so, when a cause can, without speaking unnaturally, be assigned to an impression, it will always be something other than the presence of the perceived object. There is no natural use for such a sentence as 'The presence of a cat caused it to look at X as if there were a cat before him'; yet it is absolutely essential to the CTP that there should be.

In reply to this objection I will make three points. (1) If we are to deal sympathetically with the CTP we must not restrict the Causal Theorist to the verb 'cause'; we must allow him to make use of other members of the family of causal verbs or verb-phrases if he wishes. This family includes such expressions as 'accounts for', 'explains', 'is part of the explanation of', 'is partly responsible for', and it seems quite possible that some alternative formulation of the theory would escape this objection. (2) If I regard myself as being in a position to say 'There is a cat', or 'I see

---

5. It might be thought that we need a further restriction, limiting the permissible degree of divergence between the way things appear to X and the way they actually are. But objects can be said to be seen even when they are looked at through rough thick glass or distorting spectacles, in spite of the fact that they may then be unrecognizable.

a cat', I naturally refrain from making the weaker statement 'It looks to me as if there were a cat before me', and so, *a fortiori*, I refrain from talking about the cause of its looking to me thus. But to have made the weaker statement would have been to have said something linguistically correct and true, even if misleading; is there then any reason against supposing that it could have been linguistically correct and true, even if pointless or misleading, to have ascribed to a particular cause the state of affairs reported in the weaker statement? (3) X is standing in a street up which an elephant is approaching; he thinks his eyes must be deceiving him. Knowing this, I could quite naturally say to X, 'The fact that it looks to you as if there is an elephant approaching is accounted for by the fact that an elephant is approaching, not by your having become deranged.' To say the same thing to one's neighbour at the circus would surely be to say something which is true, though it might be regarded as provocative.

I have extracted from the first clause of the initial formulation of the CTP an outline of a causal analysis of perceiving which is, I hope, at least not obviously unacceptable. I have of course considered the suggested analysis only in relation to seeing; a more careful discussion would have to pay attention to non-visual perception; and even within the field of visual perception the suggested analysis might well be unsuitable for some uses of the word 'see', which would require a stronger condition than that proposed by the theory.

IV

Is the CTP, as so far expounded, open to the charge that it represents material objects as being in principle unobservable, and in consequence leads to scepticism about the material world? I have some difficulty in understanding the precise nature of the accusation, in that it is by no means obvious what, in this context, is meant by 'unobservable'.

1. It would be not unnatural to take 'unobservable' to mean 'incapable of being perceived'. Now it may be the case that one could, without being guilty of inconsistency, combine the acceptance of the causal analysis of perceiving with the view that material objects cannot in principle be perceived, if one were prepared to maintain that it is in principle impossible for material objects to cause sense-impressions but that this impossibility has escaped the notice of common sense. This position, even if internally consistent, would seem to be open to grave objection. But even if the proposition that material objects cannot be perceived is consistent with the causal analysis of perceiving, it certainly does not appear to be a consequence of the latter; and the exposition of the CTP has so far been confined to the propounding of a causal analysis of perceiving.

2. The critic might be equating 'unobservable' with 'not directly observable'; and to say that material objects are not directly observable might in turn be interpreted as saying that statements about material objects lack that immunity from factual mistake which is (or is supposed to be) possessed by at least some sense-datum statements. But if 'unobservable' is thus interpreted, it seems to be *true* that

material objects are unobservable, and the recognition of this truth could hardly be regarded as a matter for reproach.

3. 'Observation' may be contrasted with 'inference' as a source of knowledge and so the critic's claim may be that the CTP asserts or implies that the existence of particular material objects can only be a matter of inference. But in the first place, it is not established that the acceptance of the causal analysis of perceiving commits one to the view that the existence of particular material objects is necessarily a matter of inference (though this view is explicitly asserted by the second clause of Price's initial formulation of the CTP); and secondly, many of the critics have been phenomenalists, who would themselves be prepared to allow that the existence of particular material objects is, in some sense, a matter of inference. And if the complaint is that the CTP does not represent the inference as being of the right kind, then it looks as if the critic might in effect be complaining that the Causal Theorist is not a Phenomenalist. Apart from the fact that the criticism under discussion could now be made only by someone who not only accepted Phenomenalism but also regarded it as the only means of deliverance from scepticism, it is by no means clear that to accept a causal analysis of perceiving is to debar oneself from accepting Phenomenalism; there seems to be no patent absurdity in the idea that one could, as a first stage, offer a causal analysis of '*X* perceives *M*', and then re-express the result in phenomenalist terms. If the CTP is to be (as it is often regarded as being) a rival to Phenomenalism, the opposition may well have to spring from the second clause of the initial formulation of the theory.

There is a further possibility of interpretation, related to the previous one. If someone has seen a speck on the horizon which is in fact a battleship, we should in some contexts be willing to say that he has seen a battleship; but we should not, I think, be willing to say that he has observed a battleship unless he has recognized what he has seen as a battleship. The criticism levelled at the CTP may then be that it asserts or entails the impossibility in principle of *knowing*, or even of being reasonably assured, that one is perceiving a particular material object, even if one is in fact perceiving it. At this point we must direct our attention to the second clause of the initial formulation of the CTP, which asserted that 'perceptual consciousness is fundamentally an inference from effect to cause'. I shall assume (I hope not unreasonably) that the essence of the view here being advanced is that anyone who claims to perceive a particular material object *M* may legitimately be asked to justify his claim; and that the only way to meet this demand, in the most fundamental type of case, is to produce an acceptable argument to the effect that the existence of *M* is required, or is probably required, in order that the claimant's current sense-impressions should be adequately accounted for. A detailed exposition of the CTP may supplement this clause by supplying general principles which, by assuring us of correspondences between causes and effects, are supposed to make possible the production of satisfactory arguments of the required kind.

It is clear that, if the Causal Theorist proceeds on the lines which I have just indicated, he cannot possibly be accused of having *asserted* that material objects are unobservable in the sense under consideration; for he has gone to some trouble in an attempt to show how we may be reasonably assured of the existence of particular material objects. But it may be argued that (in which is perhaps a somewhat special sense of 'consequence') it is an unwanted consequence of the CTP that material objects are unobservable: for if we accept the contentions of the CTP (1) that perceiving is to be analysed in causal terms, (2) that knowledge about perceived objects depends on causal inference, and (3) that the required causal inferences will be unsound unless suitable general principles of correspondence can be provided, then we shall have to admit that knowledge about perceived objects is unobtainable: for the general principles offered, apart from being dubious both in respect of truth and in respect of status, fail to yield the conclusions for which they are designed; and more successful substitutes are not available. If this is how the criticism of the CTP is to be understood, then I shall not challenge it, though I must confess to being in some doubt whether this is what actual critics have really meant. My comment on the criticism is now that it is unsympathetic in a way that is philosophically important.

There seem to me to be two possible ways of looking at the CTP. One is to suppose an initial situation in which it is recognized that, while appearance is ultimately the only guide to reality, what appears to be the case cannot be assumed to correspond with what is the case. The problem is conceived to be that of exhibiting a legitimate method of arguing from appearance to reality. The CTP is then regarded as a complex construction designed to solve this problem; and if one part of the structure collapses, the remainder ceases to be of much interest. The second way of looking at the CTP is to think of the causal analysis of perceiving as something to be judged primarily on its intrinsic merits and not merely as a part of a solution to a prior epistemological problem, and to recognize that some version of it is quite likely to be correct; the remainder of the CTP is then regarded as consisting (1) of steps which appear to be forced upon one if one accepts the causal analysis of perceiving, and which lead to a sceptical difficulty, and (2) a not very successful attempt to meet this difficulty. This way of looking at the CTP recognizes the possibility that we are confronted with a case in which the natural dialectic elicits distressing consequences (or rather apparent consequences) from true propositions. To adopt the first attitude to the exclusion of the second is both to put on one side what may well be an acceptable bit of philosophical analysis and to neglect what might be an opportunity for deriving philosophical profit from the exposure of operations of the natural dialectic. This, I suggest, is what the critics have tended to do; though, no doubt, they might plead historical justification, in that the first way of looking at the CTP may have been that of actual Causal Theorists.

It remains for me to show that the CTP can be looked upon in the second way by exhibiting a line of argument, sceptical in character, which incorporates appropriately the elements of the CTP. I offer the following example. In the fundamental type of case, a bona fide claim to perceive a particular material object M is based on sense-datum statements; it is only in virtue of the occurrence of certain sense-impressions that the claimant would regard himself as entitled to assert the existence of M. Since the causal analysis of perceiving is to be accepted, the claim to perceive M involves the claim that the presence of M causally explains the occurrence of the appropriate sense-impressions. The combination of these considerations yields the conclusion that the claimant accepts the existence of *M on the grounds that* it is required for the causal explanation of certain sense-impressions; that is, the existence of *M* is a matter of causal inference from the occurrence of the sense-impressions. Now a model case of causal inference would be an inference from smoke to fire; the acceptability of such an inference involves the possibility of establishing a correlation between occurrences of smoke and occurrences of fire, and this is only possible because there is a way of establishing the occurrence of a fire otherwise than by a causal inference. But there is supposed to be no way of establishing the existence of particular material objects except by a causal inference from sense-impressions; so such inferences cannot be rationally justified. The specification of principles of correspondence is of course an attempt to avert this consequence by rejecting the smoke–fire model. (If this model is rejected, recourse may be had to an assimilation of material objects to such entities as electrons, the acceptability of which is regarded as being (roughly) a matter of their utility for the purposes of explanation and prediction; but this assimilation is repugnant for the reason that material objects, after having been first contrasted, as a paradigm case of uninvented entities, with the theoretical constructs or *entia rationis* of the scientist, are then treated as being themselves *entia rationis*.)

One possible reaction to this argument is, of course, 'So much the worse for the causal analysis of perceiving'; but, as an alternative, the argument itself may be challenged, and I shall conclude by mentioning, without attempting to evaluate, some ways in which this might be done. (1) It may be argued that it is quite incorrect to describe many of my perceptual beliefs (for example, that there is now a table in front of me) as 'inferences' of any kind, if this is to be taken to imply that it would be incumbent upon me, on demand, to justify by an argument (perhaps after acquiring further data) the contention that what appears to me to be the case actually is the case. When, in normal circumstances, it looks to me as if there were a table before me, I am entitled to say flatly that there is a table before me, and to reject any demand that I should justify my claim until specific grounds for doubting it have been indicated. It is essential to the sceptic to assume that any perceptual claim may, without preliminaries, be put on trial and that innocence, not guilt, has to be proved; but this assumption is mistaken. (2) The allegedly 'fundamental' case (which is supposed to underlie other kinds of case), in which a perceptual claim is to be establishable purely on the basis of some set of sense-datum statements, is a myth; any justification of a particular perceptual claim will rely on the truth of one or more further propositions about the material world (for example, about the percipient's body). To insist that the 'fundamental' case be selected for consideration is, in effect, to assume at the start that it is conceptually legitimate for me to treat as open to question all my beliefs about the material world at once; and the sceptic is not entitled to start with this assumption. (3) It might be questioned whether, given that I accept the existence of *M* on the evidence of certain sense-impressions, and given also that I think that *M* is causally responsible for those sense-impressions it follows that I accept the existence of *M on the grounds that* its existence is required in order to account for the sense-impressions. (4) The use made of the smoke—fire model in the sceptical argument might be criticized on two different grounds. First, if the first point in this paragraph is well made, there are cases in which the existence of a perceived object is not the conclusion of a causal inference, namely those in which it cannot correctly be described as a matter of inference at all. Secondly, the model should never have been introduced; for whereas the proposition that fires tend to cause smoke is supposedly purely contingent, this is not in general true of propositions to the effect that the presence of a material object possessing property P tends to (or will in standard circumstances) make it look to particular persons as if there were an object possessing P. It is then an objectionable feature of the sceptical argument that it first treats non-contingent connections as if they were contingent, and then complains that such connections cannot be established in the manner appropriate to contingent connections. The non-contingent character of the proposition that the presence of a red (or round) object tends to make it look to particular people as if there were something red (or round) before them does not, of course, in itself preclude the particular fact that it looks to me as if there were something red before me from being explained by the presence of a particular red object; it is a non-contingent matter that corrosive substances tend to destroy surfaces to which they are applied; but it is quite legitimate to account for a particular case of surface-damage by saying that it was caused by some corrosive substance. In each case the effect might have come about in some other way.

V

I conclude that it is not out of the question that the following version of the CTP should be acceptable: (1) It is true that X perceives M if, and only if, some present-tense sense-datum statement is true of X which reports a state of affairs for which M, in a way to be indicated by example, is causally responsible, and (2) a claim on the part of X to perceive M, if it needs to be justified at all, is justified by showing that the existence of M is required if the circumstances reported by certain true sense-datum statements, some of which may be about persons other than X, are to be causally accounted for. Whether this twofold thesis deserves to be called a Theory of Perception I shall not presume to judge; I have already suggested that the first clause neither obviously entails nor obviously conflicts with Phenomenalism; I suspect that the same may be true of the second clause. I am conscious that my version, however close to the letter, is very far from the spirit of the original theory; but to defend the spirit as well as the letter would be beyond my powers.

Chapter 31

Perception and its objects

Peter F. Strawson

I

A YER has always given the problem of perception a central place in his thinking. Reasonably so; for a philosopher's views on this question are a key both to his theory of knowledge in general and to his metaphysics. The movement of Ayer's own thought has been from phenomenalism to what he describes in his latest treatment of the topic as 'a sophisticated form of realism'.[1] The epithet is doubly apt. No adequate account of the matter can be simple; and Ayer's account, while distinguished by his accustomed lucidity and economy of style, is notably and subtly responsive to all the complexities inherent in the subject itself and to all the pressures of more or less persuasive argument which have marked the course of its treatment by philosophers. Yet the form of realism he defends has another kind of sophistication about which it is possible to have reservations and doubts; and, though I am conscious of being far from clear on the matter myself, I shall try to make some of my own doubts and reservations as clear as I can. I shall take as my text Chapters 4 and 5 of *The Central Questions of Philosophy*; and I shall also consider a different kind of realism—that advocated by J. L. Mackie in his book on Locke.[2] There are points of contact as well as of contrast between Ayer's and Mackie's views. A comparison between them will help to bring out the nature of my reservations about both.

According to Ayer, the starting-point of serious thought on the matter of perception consists in the fact that our normal perceptual judgements always 'go beyond' the sensible experience which gives rise to them; for those judgements carry implications which would not be carried by any 'strict account' of that experience.[3] Ayer sees ordinary perceptual judgements as reflecting or embodying what he calls the common-sense view of the physical world, which is, among other things, a realist view; and he sees that view itself as having the character of 'a theory with respect to the immediate data of perception'.[4] He devotes some space to an account of how the theory might be seen as capable of being developed by an individual observer

Peter F. Strawson, 'Perception and its Objects' in G. F. Macdonald (ed.) *Perception and Identity. Essays Presented to A. J. Ayer* (London, Macmillan, 1979), pp. 41–60 reprinted by permission of the publisher and author.

1. A. J. Ayer, *The Central Questions of Philosophy* (London, 1973) chs. 4 and 5, pp. 68–111.
2. J. L. Mackie, *Problems from Locke* (Oxford, 1976) chs. 1 and 2, pp. 7–71.
3. Ayer, *Central Questions*, pp. 81, 89.
4. Ibid. p. 88.

on the basis of the data available to him; though he disavows any intention of giving an actual history of the theory's development. The purpose of the account is, rather, to bring out those features of sensible experience which make it possible to employ the theory successfully and which, indeed, justify acceptance of it. For it is, he holds, by and large an acceptable theory, even though the discoveries of physical science may require us to modify it in certain respects.

Evidently no infant is delivered into the world already equipped with what Ayer calls the common-sense view of it. That view has to be acquired; and it is open to the psychologist of infant learning to produce at least a speculative account of the stages of its acquisition. Ayer insists, as I have remarked, that his own account of a possible line of development or construction of the common-sense view is not intended as a speculative contribution to the theory of infant learning. It is intended, rather, as an analysis of the nature of mature or adult perceptual experience, an analysis designed to show just how certain features of mature sensible experience vindicate or sustain the common-sense view which his embodied or reflected in mature perceptual judgements. Clearly the two aims here distinguished—the genetic-psychological and the analytic-philosophical—are very different indeed, and it will be of great importance not to confuse them. In particular it will be important to run no risk of characterizing mature sensible experience in terms adequate at best only for the characterization of some stage of infantile experience. It is not clear that Ayer entirely avoids this danger.

What is clear is that if we accept Ayer's starting-point, if we agree that our ordinary perceptual judgements carry implications not carried by a 'strict account' of the sensible experience which gives rise to them, then we must make absolutely sure that our account of that experience, in the form it takes in our mature life, is indeed strict—in the sense of strictly correct. Only so can we have any prospect of making a correct estimate of the further doctrines that the common-sense view of the world has the status of a *theory* with respect to a type of sensible experience which provides *data* for the theory; that this experience supplies the *evidence* on which the theory is based;[5] that the common-sense view can be regarded as *inferred* or at least inferrable from this evidence; and that our ordinary perceptual judgements have the character of *interpretations*,[6] in the light of theory, of what sensible experience actually presents us with.

But can we—and should we accept Ayer's starting-point? I think that, suitably interpreted, we both can, and should, accept it. Two things will be required of a strict account of our sensible experience or of any particular episode or slice of sensible experience: first, as I have just remarked, that it should in no way distort or misrepresent the character of that experience as we actually enjoy it, that is, that it should be a true or faithful account; secondly, that its truth, in any particular case, should be independent of the truth of the associated perceptual judgement, that is, that it should remain true even if the associated perceptual judgement is false. It is the second requirement on which Ayer lays stress when he remarks that those

5. Ibid. p. 89.
6. Ibid. p. 81.

judgements carry implications which would not be carried by any strict account of sensible experience; or, less happily in my opinion, that in making such judgements we take a step beyond what our sensible experience actually presents us with. But it is the first requirement to which I now wish to give some attention.

Suppose a non-philosophical observer gazing idly through a window. To him we address the request, 'Give us a description of your current visual experience', or 'How is it with you, visually, at the moment?' Uncautioned as to exactly what we want, he might reply in some such terms as these: 'I see the red light of the setting sun filtering through the black and thickly clustered branches of the elms; I see the dappled deer grazing in groups on the vivid green grass . . .' and so on. So we explain to him. We explain that we want him to amend his account so that, without any sacrifice of fidelity to the experience as actually enjoyed, it nevertheless sheds all that heavy load of commitment to propositions about the world which was carried by the description he gave. We want an account which confines itself strictly within the limits of the subjective episode, an account which would remain true even if he had seen nothing of what he claimed to see, even if he had been subject to total illusion.

Our observer is quick on the uptake. He does not start talking about lights and colours, patches and patterns. For he sees that to do so would be to falsify the character of the experience he actually enjoyed. He says, instead, 'I understand. I've got to cut out of my report all commitment to propositions about independently existing objects. Well, the simplest way to do this, while remaining faithful to the character of the experience as actually enjoyed, is to put my previous report in inverted commas or oratio obliqua and describe my visual experience as such as it would have been natural to describe in these terms, had I not received this additional instruction. Thus; "I had a visual experience such as it would have been natural to describe by saying that I saw, etc. . . . [or, to describe in these words, 'I saw . . . etc.'] were it not for the obligation to exclude commitment to propositions about independently existing objects." In this way [continues the observer] I *use* the perceptual claim—the claim it was natural to make in the circumstances—in order to characterize my experience, without actually making the claim. I render the perceptual judgement internal to the characterization of the experience without actually asserting the content of the judgement. And this is really the best possible way of characterizing the experience. There are perhaps alternative locutions which might serve the purpose, so long as they are understood as being to the same effect—on the whole, the more artificial the better, since their artificiality will help to make it clearer just to what effect they are intended to be. Thus we might have: "It sensibly seemed to me just as if I were seeing such-and-such a scene" or "My visual experience can be characterized by saying that I saw what I saw, supposing I saw anything, *as* a scene of the following character . . ."'

If my observer is right in this—and I think he is—then certain general conclusions follow. Our perceptual judgements, as Ayer remarks, embody or reflect a certain view of the world, as containing objects, variously propertied, located in a common space and continuing in their existence independently of our interrupted and relatively fleeting perceptions of them. Our making of such judgements implies our possession and application of concepts of such objects. But now it appears that we cannot give a veridical characterization even of the sensible experience which these judgements, as Ayer expresses it, 'go beyond', without reference to those judgements themselves; that our sensible experience itself is thoroughly permeated with those concepts of objects which figure in such judgements. This does not mean, that is, it does not follow directly from this feature of sensible experience, that the general view of the world which those judgements reflect must be true. That would be too short a way with scepticism. But it does follow, I think, that our sensible experience could not have the character it does have unless—at least before philosophical reflection sets in—we unquestioningly *took* that general view of the world to be true. The concepts of the objective which we see to be indispensable to the veridical characterization of sensible experience simply would not be in this way indispensable unless those whose experience it was initially and unreflectively took such concepts to have application in the world.

This has a further consequence: the consequence that it is quite inappropriate to represent the general, realist view of the world which is reflected in our ordinary perceptual judgements as having the status of a *theory* with respect to sensible experience; that it is inappropriate to represent that experience as supplying the *data* for such a theory or the *evidence* on which it is based or from which it is *inferred* or *inferrable*; that it is inappropriate to speak of our ordinary perceptual judgements as having the character of an *interpretation*, in the light of theory, of the content of our sensible experience. The reason for this is simple. In order for some belief or set of beliefs to be correctly described as a theory in respect of certain data, it must be possible to describe the data on the basis of which the theory is held in terms which do not presuppose the acceptance of the theory on the part of those for whom the data *are* data. But this is just the condition we have seen not to be satisfied in the case where the so-called data are the contents of sensible experience and the so-called theory is a general realist view of the world. The 'data' are laden with the 'theory'. Sensible experience is permeated by concepts unreflective acceptance of the general applicability of which is a condition of its being so permeated, a condition of that experience being what it is; and these concepts are of realistically conceived objects.

I must make it quite clear what I am saying and what I am not saying here. I am talking of the ordinary non-philosophical man. I am talking of us all before we felt, if ever we did feel, any inclination to respond to the solicitations of a general scepticism, to regard it as raising a problem. I am saying that it follows from the character of sensible experience as we all actually enjoy it that a common-sense realist view of the world does not in general have the status of a theory in respect of that experience; while Ayer, as I understand him, holds that it does. But I am not denying that to one who has seen, or thinks he has seen, that sensible experience might have the character it does have and *yet* a realist view of the world be false, to *him* the idea may well present itself that the best way of accounting for sensible experience as having that character is to accept the common realist view of the world or some variant of it. *He* might be said to adopt, as a theory, the doctrine that the common realist view of the world is, at least in some basic essentials, true. But this will be a philosopher's theory, designed to deal with a philosopher's problem. (I shall not here discuss its merits as such.) What I am concerned to dispute is the doctrine that a realist view of the world has, for any man, the status of a theory in relation to his sensible experience, a theory in the light of which he interprets that experience in making his perceptual judgements.

To put the point summarily, whereas Ayer says we take a step beyond our sensible experience in making our perceptual judgements, I say rather that we take a step back (in general) from our perceptual judgements in framing accounts of our sensible experience; for we have (in general) to include a reference to the former in framing a veridical description of the latter.

It may seem, on a superficial reading, that Ayer had anticipated and answered this objection. He introduces, as necessary for the characterization of our sensible experience, certain concepts of types of pattern, the names for which are borrowed from the names of ordinary physical objects. Thus he speaks of visual leaf patterns, chair patterns, cat patterns, and so on.[7] At the same time, he is careful, if I read him rightly, to guard against the impression that the use of this terminology commits him to the view that the employment of the corresponding physical-object concepts themselves is necessary to the characterization of our sensible experience.[8] The terminology is appropriate (he holds) simply because those features of sensible experience to which the terminology is applied are the features which govern our identifications of the physical objects we think we see. They are the features, 'implicitly noticed',[9] which provide the main clues on which our everyday judgements of perception are based.

This is ingenious, but I do not think it will do. This we can see more clearly if we use an invented, rather than a derived, terminology for these supposed features and then draw up a table of explicit correlations between the invented names and the physical-object names. Each artificial feature name is set against the name of a type of physical object: our perceptual identifications of seen objects as of that type are held to be governed by implicit noticings of that feature. The nature and significance of the feature names is now quite clearly explained and we have to ask ourselves whether it is these rather than the associated physical-object terms that we ought to use if we are to give a quite strict and faithful account of our sensible experience. I think it is clear that this is not so; that the idea of our ordinary perceptual judgements as being invariably based upon, or invariably issuing from, awareness of such features is a myth. The situation is rather, as I have already argued, that the employment of our ordinary, full-blooded concepts of physical objects is indispensable to a strict, and strictly veridical, account of our sensible experience.

Once again, I must make it clear what I am, and what I am not, saying. I have been speaking of the typical or standard case of mature sensible and perceptual experience. I have no interest at all in denying the thesis that there also occur cases of sensible experience such that the employment of full-blooded concepts of

7. Ayer, *Central Questions*, p. 91.
8. Ibid. p. 96.
9. Ibid. p. 91.

physical objects would not be indispensable, and may be inappropriate, to giving a strict account of the experience. Such cases are of different types, and there is one in particular which is of interest in the present connection. An observer, gazing through his window, may perhaps, by an effort of will, bring himself to see, or even will-lessly find himself seeing, what he knows to be the branches of the trees no longer *as* branches at all, but as an intricate pattern of dark lines of complex directions and shapes and various sizes against a background of varying shades of grey. The frame of mind in which we enjoy, if we ever do enjoy, this kind of experience is a rare and sophisticated, not a standard or normal, frame of mind. Perhaps the fact, if it is a fact, that we can bring ourselves into this frame of mind when we choose may be held to give a sense to the idea of our 'implicitly noticing' such patterns even when we are not in this frame of mind. If so, it is a sense very far removed from that which Ayer's thesis requires. For that thesis requires not simply the possibility, but the actual occurrence, in all cases of perception, of sensible experience of this kind. One line of retreat may seem to lie open at this point: a retreat to the position of saying that the occurrence of such experiences may be *inferred* even though we do not, in the hurry of life, generally notice or recall their occurrence. But such a retreat would be the final irony. The items in question would have changed their status radically: instead of data for a common-sense theory of the world, they would appear as consequences of a sophisticated theory of the mind.

This concludes the first stage of my argument. I have argued that mature sensible experience (in general) presents itself as, in Kantian phrase, an *immediate* consciousness of the existence of things outside us. (*Immediate*, of course, does not mean *infallible*.) Hence, the common realist conception of the world does not have the character of a 'theory' in relation to the 'data of sense'. I have not claimed that this fact is of itself sufficient to 'refute' scepticism or to provide a philosophical 'demonstration' of the truth of some form of realism; though I think it does provide the right starting-point for reflection upon these enterprises. But that is another story and I shall not try to tell it here. My point so far is that the ordinary human commitment to a conceptual scheme of a realist character is not properly described, even in a stretched sense of the words, as a theoretical commitment. It is, rather, something given with the given.

II

But we are philosophers as well as men; and so must examine more closely the nature of the realist scheme to which we are pre-theoretically committed and then consider whether we are not rationally constrained, as Locke and Mackie would maintain we are, to modify it quite radically in the light of our knowledge of physics and physiology. Should we not also, as philosophers, consider the question of whether we can rationally maintain any form of realism at all? Perhaps we should; but, as already remarked, that is a question I shall not consider here. My main object, in the present section, is to get a clear view of the main features of our pre-theoretical scheme before considering whether it is defensible, as it stands, or not, I go in a somewhat roundabout way to work.

I have spoken of our pre-theoretical scheme as realist in character. Philosophers who treat of these questions commonly distinguish different forms of realism. So do both Ayer and Mackie. They both mention, at one extreme, a form of realism which Mackie calls 'naïve' and even 'very naïve', but which might more appropriately be called 'confused realism'. A sufferer from confused realism fails to draw any distinction between sensible experiences (or 'perceptions') and independently existing things (or 'objects perceived') but is said (by Mackie expounding Hume) to credit the former with persistent unobserved existence.[10] It should be remarked that, if this is an accurate way of describing the naïve realist's conception of the matter, he must be very confused indeed, since the expression 'unobserved' already implies the distinction which he is said to fail to make. Speaking in his own person, Mackie gives no positive account of the naïve realist's view of things, but simply says that there is, historically, in the thought of each of us, a phase in which we fail to make the distinction in question.[11] It may indeed be so. The point is one to be referred to the experts on infantile development. But in any case the matter is not here of any consequence. For we are concerned with mature perceptual experience and with the character of the scheme to which those who enjoy such experience are pre-theoretically committed. And it seems to me as certain as anything can be that, as an integral part of that scheme, we distinguish, naturally and unreflectively, between our seeings and hearings and feelings—our perceivings—of objects and the objects we see and hear and feel; and hence quite consistently accept both the interruptedness of the former and the continuance in existence, unobserved, of the latter.

At the opposite extreme from naïve realism stands what may be called scientific or Lockian realism. This form of realism credits physical objects only with those of their properties which are mentioned in physical theory and physical explanation, including the causal explanation of our enjoyment of the kind of perceptual experience we in fact enjoy. It has the consequence that we do not, and indeed cannot, perceive objects as they really are. It might be said that this consequence does not hold in an unqualified form. For we perceive (or seem to perceive) objects as having shape, size, and position; and they really do have shape, size, and position and more or less such shape, size, and position as we seem to perceive them as having. But this reply misconstrues the intended force of the alleged consequence. We cannot in sense perception—the point is an old one—become aware of the shape, size and position of physical objects except by way of awareness of boundaries defined in some sensory mode—for example, by visual and tactile qualities such as scientific realism denies to the objects themselves; and no change in, or addition to, our sensory equipment could alter this fact. To perceive physical objects as, according to scientific realism, they really are would be to perceive them as lacking any such qualities. But this notion is self-contradictory. So it is a necessary consequence of

10. Mackie, *Problems*, p. 67.
11. Ibid. p. 68.

this form of realism that we do not perceive objects as they really are indeed, in the sense of the pre-theoretical notion of perceiving—that is, of immediate awareness of things outside us—we do not, on the scientific-realist view, perceive physical objects at all. We are, rather, the victims of a systematic illusion which obstinately clings to us even if we embrace scientific realism. For we continue to enjoy experience *as of* physical objects in space, objects of which the spatial characteristics and relations are defined by the sensible qualities we perceive them as having; but there are no such physical objects as these. The only true physical objects are items systematically correlated with and causally responsible for that experience; and the only sense in which we *can* be said to perceive them is just that they cause us to enjoy that experience.

These remarks are intended only as a *description* of scientific realism. I do not claim that they show it to be untenable. I shall return to the topic later.

In between the 'naïve' and the 'scientific' varieties, Ayer and Mackie each recognize another form of realism, which they each ascribe to 'common sense'. But there is a difference between Ayer's version of common-sense realism and Mackie's. For Mackie's version, unlike Ayer's, shares one crucial feature with scientific realism.

The theory of perception associated with scientific or Lockian realism is commonly and reasonably described as a representative theory. Each of us seems to himself to be perceptually aware of objects of a certain kind: objects in space outside us with visual and tactile qualities. There are in fact, on this view, no such objects; but these object appearances can in a broad sense be said to be representative of those actual objects in space outside us which are systematically correlated with the appearances and causally responsible for them. The interesting feature of Mackie's version of common-sense realism is that the theory of perception associated with it is no less a representative theory than that associated with Lockian realism. The difference is simply that common sense, according to Mackie, views object appearances as more faithful representatives of actual physical objects than the Lockian allows: in that common sense, gratuitously by scientific standards, credits actual objects in space outside us with visual and tactile as well as primary qualities. As Mackie puts it, common sense allows 'colours-as-we-see-them to be *resemblances* of qualities actually in the things'.[12] On both views, sensible experience has its own, sensible objects; but the common-sense view, according to Mackie, allows a kind of resemblance between sensible and physical objects which the scientific view does not.

I hope it is already clear that this version of common-sense realism is quite different from what I have called our pre-theoretical scheme. What we ordinarily take ourselves to be aware of in perception are not resemblances of physical things themselves. This does not mean, as already remarked, that we have any difficulty in distinguishing between our experiences of seeing, hearing and feeling objects and the objects themselves. That distinction is as firmly a part of our pre-theoretical scheme as is our taking ourselves, in general, to be immediately aware of those objects. Nor does it mean that we take ourselves to be immune from illusion,

12. Ibid. p. 64.

hallucination, or mistake. We can, and do, perfectly adequately describe such cases without what is, from the point of view of the pre-theoretical scheme, the quite gratuitous introduction of sensible objects interposed between us and the actual physical objects they are supposed to represent.

The odd thing about Mackie's presentation is that at one point he shows himself to be perfectly well aware of this feature of the real realism of common sense; for he writes, 'What we seem to see, feel, hear and so on . . . *are seen as real things without us*—that is, outside us. We just see things as being simply there, of such-and-such sorts, in such-and-such relations. . . .'[13] He goes on, of course, to say that 'our seeing them so is logically distinct from their being so', that we might be, and indeed are, wrong. But he would scarcely dispute that what is thus *seen as* real and outside us is also *seen as* coloured, as possessing visual qualities; that what is *felt as* a real thing outside us is also felt as hard or soft, smooth or rough-surfaced—as possessing tactile qualities. The real realism of common sense, then, does indeed credit physical things with visual and tactile properties; but it does so not in the spirit of a notion of representative perception, but in the spirit of a notion of direct or immediate perception.

Mackie's version of common-sense realism is, then, I maintain, a distortion of the actual pre-theoretical realism of common sense, a distortion which wrongly assimilates it, in a fundamental respect, to the Lockian realism he espouses. I do not find any comparable distortion in Ayer's version. He aptly describes the physical objects we seem to ourselves, and take ourselves, to perceive as 'visuo-tactual continuants'. The scheme as he presents it allows for the distinction between these items and the experiences of perceiving them and for the causal dependence of the latter on the former; and does so, as far as I can see, without introducing the alien features I have discerned in Mackie's account. It is perhaps debatable whether Ayer can consistently maintain the scheme's freedom from such alien elements while continuing to represent it as having the status of a 'theory' in relation to the 'data' of sensible experience. But, having already set out my objections to that doctrine, I shall not pursue the point.

Something more must be said, however, about the position, in the common-sense scheme, of the causal relation between physical object and the experience of perceiving it. Although Ayer admits the relation to a place in the scheme, he seems to regard it as a somewhat sophisticated addition to the latter, a latecomer, as it were, for which room has to be made in an already settled arrangement.[14] This seems to me wrong. The idea of the presence of the thing as accounting for, or being responsible for, our perceptual awareness of it is implicit in the pre-theoretical scheme from the very start. For we think of perception as a way, indeed the basic way, of informing ourselves about the world of independently existing things: we assume, that is to say, the general reliability of our perceptual experiences; and that assumption is the same as the assumption of a general causal dependence of our perceptual experiences on the independently existing things we

13. Mackie, *Problems*, p. 61.
14. Ayer, *Central Questions*, pp. 87–8.

take them to be of. The thought of my fleeting perception as a *perception* of a continuously and independently existing thing implicitly contains the thought that if the thing had not been there, I should not even have *seemed* to perceive it. It really should be obvious that with the distinction between independently existing objects and perceptual awareness of objects we already have the general notion of causal dependence of the latter on the former, even if this is not a matter to which we give much reflective attention in our pre-theoretical days.

Two things seem to have impeded recognition of this point. One is the fact that the correctness of the description of a perceptual experience as the perception of a certain physical thing *logically* requires the existence of that thing; and the *logical* is thought to exclude the *causal* connection, since only logically distinct existences can be causally related. This is not a serious difficulty. The situation has many parallels. Gibbon would not be the historian of the decline and fall of the Roman Empire unless there had occurred some actual sequence of events more or less corresponding to his narrative. But it is not enough, for him to merit that description, that such a sequence of events should have occurred and he should have written the sentences he did write. For him to qualify as the *historian* of these events, there must be a causal chain connecting them with the writing of the sentences. Similarly, the memory of an event's occurrence does not count as such unless it has its causal origin in that event. And the recently much canvassed 'causal theory of reference' merely calls attention to another instance of the causal link which obtains between thought and independently (and anteriorly) existing thing when the former is rightly said to have the latter as its object.

The second impediment is slightly more subtle. We are philosophically accustomed—it is a Humean legacy—to thinking of the simplest and most obvious kind of causal relation as holding between types of item such that items of both types are observable or experienceable and such that observation or experience of either term of the relation is distinct from observation or experience of the other: that is, the causally related items are not only distinct existences, but also the objects of distinct observations or experiences. We may then come to think of these conditions as constituting a requirement on all primitive belief in causal relations, a requirement which could be modified or abandoned only in the interests of theory. Since we obviously cannot distinguish the observation of a physical object from the experience of observing it—for they are the same thing—we shall then be led to conclude that the idea of the causal dependence of perceptual experience on the perceived object cannot be even an implicit part of our pre-theoretical scheme, but must be at best an essentially theoretical addition to it.

But the difficulty is spurious. By directing our attention to causal relations between *objects* of perception, we have simply been led to overlook the special character of perception itself. Of course, the requirement holds for causal relations between distinct objects of perception; but not for the relation between perception and its object. When x is a physical object and y is a perception of x, then x is *observed* and y is *enjoyed*. And in taking the enjoyment of y to be a perception of x, we *are* implicitly taking it to be caused by x.

This concludes the second phase of my argument. I have tried to bring out some main features of the real realism of common sense and of the associated notion of perception. From the standpoint of common-sense realism we take ourselves to be immediately aware of real, enduring physical things in space, things endowed with visual and tactile properties; and we take it for granted that these enduring things are causally responsible for our interrupted perceptions of them. The immediacy which common sense attributes to perceptual awareness is in no way inconsistent either with the distinction between perceptual experience and thing perceived or with the causal dependence of the former on the latter or the existence of other causally necessary conditions of its occurrence. Neither is it consistent with the occurrence of perceptual mistake or illusion—a point, like so many others of importance, which is explicitly made by Kant.[15] Both Ayer and Mackie, explicitly or implicitly, acknowledge that the common-sense scheme includes this assumption of immediacy—Mackie in a passage I have quoted, Ayer in his description of the common-sense scheme. Unfortunately, Mackie's acknowledgement of the fact is belied by his describing common-sense realism as representative in character and Ayer's acknowledgement of it is put in doubt by his describing the common-sense scheme as having the status of a theory in relation to sensible experience.

III

It is one thing to describe the scheme of common sense; it is another to subject it to critical examination. This is the third and most difficult part of my task. The main question to be considered, as already indicated, is whether we are rationally bound to abandon, or radically to modify, the scheme in the light of scientific knowledge.

Before addressing ourselves directly to this question, it is worth stressing—indeed, it is essential to stress—the grip that common-sense non-representative realism has on our ordinary thinking. It is a view of the world which so thoroughly permeates our consciousness that even those who are intellectually convinced of its falsity remain subject to its power. Mackie admits as much, saying that, even when we are trying to entertain a Lockian or scientific realism, 'our language and our natural ways of thinking keep pulling us back' to a more primitive view.[16] Consider the character of those ordinary concepts of objects on the employment of which our lives, our transactions with each other and the world, depend: our concepts of cabbages, roads, tweed coats, horses, the lips and hair of the beloved. In using these terms we certainly intend to be talking of independent existences and we certainly intend to be talking of immediately perceptible things, bearers of phenomenal (visuo-tactile) properties. If scientific or Lockian realism is correct, we cannot be doing both at once; it is confusion or illusion to suppose we can. If the things we talk of really have phenomenal properties, then they cannot, on this view, be

15. Kant, 'The Refutation of Idealism', in *Critique of Pure Reason*, B274–9.
16. Mackie, *Problems*, p. 68.

physical things continuously existing in physical space. Nothing perceptible—I here drop the qualification 'immediately', for my use of it should now be clear—is a physically real, independent existence. No two persons can ever, in this sense, perceive the same item: nothing at all is publicly perceptible.

But how deep the confusion or the illusion must go! How radically it infects our concepts! Surely we mean by a cabbage a kind of thing of which most of the specimens we have encountered have a characteristic range of colours and visual shapes and felt textures; and not something unobservable, mentally represented by a complex of sensible experiences which it causes. The common consciousness is not to be fobbed off with the concession that, after all, the physical thing has—in a way—a shape. The way in which scientific realism concedes a shape is altogether the wrong way for the common consciousness. The lover who admires the curve of his mistress's lips or the lover of architecture who admires the lines of a building takes himself to be admiring features of those very objects themselves; but it is the visual shape, the visually defined shape, that he admires. Mackie suggests that there is a genuine *resemblance* between subjective representation and objective reality as far as shape is concerned;[17] but this suggestion is quite unacceptable. It makes no sense to speak of a phenomenal property as *resembling* a non-phenomenal, abstract property such as physical shape is conceived to be by scientific realism. The property of looking square or round can no more resemble the property, so conceived, of being physically square or round that the property of looking intelligent or looking ill can resemble the property of being intelligent or being ill. If it seems to make sense to speak of a resemblance between phenomenal properties and physical properties, so conceived, it is only because we give ourselves pictures—phenomenal pictures—of the latter. The resemblance is with the picture, not the pictured.

So, then, the common consciousness lives, or has the illusion of living, in a phenomenally propertied world of perceptible things in space. We might call it the lived world. It is also the public world, accessible to observation by all: the world in which one man, following another's pointing finger, can see the very thing that the other sees. (Even in our philosophical moments we habitually contrast the colours and visual shapes of things, as being publicly observable, with the subjective contents of consciousness, private to each of us, though not thereby unknowable to others.)

Such a reminder of the depth and reality of our habitual commitment to the common-sense scheme does not, by itself, amount to a demonstration of that scheme's immunity from philosophical criticism. The scientific realist, though no Kantian, may be ready, by way of making his maximum concession, with a reply modelled on Kant's combination of empirical realism with transcendental idealism. He may distinguish between the uncritical standpoint of ordinary living and the critical standpoint of philosophy informed by science. We are humanly, or naturally—he may say—constrained to 'see the world' in one way (that is, to think of it as we seem to perceive it) and rationally, or critically, constrained to think of it in quite another. The first way (being itself a causal product of physical reality) has

17. Ibid., chs. 1 and 2, *passim.*

a kind of validity at its own level; but it is, critically and rationally speaking, an inferior level. The second way really is a correction of the first.

The authentically Kantian combination is open to objection in many ways; but, by reason of its very extravagance, it escapes one specific form of difficulty to which the scientific realist's soberer variant remains exposed. Kant uncompromisingly declares that space is in us; that it is 'solely from the human standpoint that we can speak of space, of extended things etc.',[18] that things as they are in themselves are not spatial at all. This will not do for the scientific realist. The phenomenally propertied items which we take ourselves to perceive and the apparent relations between which yield (or contribute vitally to yielding) our notion of space, are indeed declared to have no independent reality; but, when they are banished from the realm of the real, they are supposed to leave behind them—as occupants, so to speak, of the evacuated territory—those spatially related items which, though necessarily unobservable, nevertheless constitute the whole of physical reality. Ayer refers in several places to this consequence; and questions its coherence.[19] He writes, for example, 'I doubt whether the notion of a spatial system of which none of the elements can be observed is even intelligible.'

It is not clear that this difficulty is insuperable. The scientific realist will claim to be able to abstract the notion of a position in physical space from the phenomenal integuments with which it is originally and deceptively associated; and it is hard to think of a conclusive reason for denying him this power. He will say that the places where the phenomenally propertied things we seem to perceive seem to be are, often enough, places at which the correlated physically real items really are. Such a claim may make us uneasy; but it is not obvious nonsense.

Still, to say that a difficulty is not clearly insuperable is not to say that it is clearly not insuperable. It would be better to avoid it if we can. We cannot avoid it if we embrace unadulterated scientific realism and incidentally announce ourselves thereby as the sufferers from persistent illusion, however natural. We can avoid it, perhaps, if we can succeed in combining elements of the scientific story with our common-sense scheme without down-grading the latter. This is the course that Ayer recommends,[20] and, I suspect, the course that most of us semi-reflectively follow. The question is whether it is a consistent or coherent course. And at bottom this question is one of identity. Can we coherently identify the phenomenally pro-pertied, immediately perceptible things which common sense supposes to occupy physical space with the configurations of unobservable ultimate particulars by which an unqualified scientific realism purports to replace them?

I approach the question indirectly, by considering once again Mackie's version of common-sense realism. According to this version, it will be remembered, physical things, though not directly perceived, really possess visual and tactile qualities which resemble those we seem to perceive them as possessing; so that if, *per impossibile*, the veil of perception were drawn aside and we saw things in their true

18. Kant, 'Refutation of Idealism', in *Critique*, B42.
19. Ayer, *Central Questions*, pp. 84, 86–7, 110.
20. Ibid. pp. 110–11.

colours, these would turn out to be colours indeed and, on the whole, just the colours with which we were naïvely inclined to credit them. Mackie does not represent this view as absurd or incoherent. He just thinks that it is, as a matter of fact, false. Things *could* really be coloured; but, since there is no scientific reason for supposing they are, it is gratuitous to make any such supposition.

Mackie is surely too lenient to his version of common-sense realism. That version effects a complete logical divorce between a thing's being red and its being red-looking. Although it is a part of the theory that a thing which is, in itself, red has the power to cause us to seem to see a red thing, the logical divorce between these two properties is absolute. And, as far as I can see, that divorce really produces nonsense. The ascription of colours to things becomes not merely gratuitous, but senseless. Whatever may be the case with shape and position, colours are visibilia or they are nothing. I have already pointed out that this version of common-sense realism is not the real realism of common sense: *that* realism effects no logical divorce between being red and being red-looking; for it is a perceptually direct and not a perceptually representative realism. The things seen as coloured are the things themselves. There is no 'veil past which we cannot see'; for there is no veil.

But this does not mean that a thing which is red, that is, red-looking, has to look red all the time and in all circumstances and to all observers. There is an irreducible relativity, a relativity to what in the broadest sense may be called the perceptual point of view, built in to our ascriptions of particular visual properties to things. The mountains are red-looking at this distance in this light; blue-looking at that distance at that light; and, when we are clambering up them, perhaps neither. Such-and-such a surface looks pink and smooth from a distance; mottled and grainy when closely examined; different again, perhaps, under the microscope.

We absorb this relativity easily enough for ordinary purposes in our ordinary talk, tacitly taking some range of perceptual conditions, some perceptual point of view (in the broad sense) as standard or normal, and introducing an explicit acknowledgement of relativity only in cases which deviate from the standard. 'It looks purple in this light,' we say, 'but take it to the door and you will see that it's really green.' But sometimes we do something else. We shift the standard. Magnified, the fabric appears as printed with tiny blue and yellow dots. So those are the colours it really is. Does this ascription contradict 'it's really green'? No; for the standard has shifted. Looking at photographs, in journals of popular science, of patches of human skin, vastly magnified, we say, 'How fantastically uneven and ridgy it really is.' We study a sample of blood through a microscope and say, 'It's mostly colourless.' But skin can still be smooth and blood be red; for in another context we shift our standard back. Such shifts do not convict us of volatility or condemn us to internal conflict. The appearance of both volatility and conflict vanishes when we acknowledge the relativity of our 'reallys'.

My examples are banal. But perhaps they suggest a way of resolving the apparent conflict between scientific and common-sense realism. We can shift our point of view within the general framework of perception, whether aided or unaided by artificial means; and the different sensible-quality ascriptions we then make to the same object are not seen as conflicting once their relativity is recognized. Can we not see the adoption of the viewpoint of scientific realism as simply a more radical shift—shift to a viewpoint from which no characteristics are to be ascribed to things except those which figure in the physical theories of science and in 'the explanation of what goes on in the physical world in the processes which lead to our having the sensations and perceptions that we have'?[21] We can say that this is how things really are so long as the relativity of this 'really' is recognized as well; and, when it is recognized, the scientific account will no more conflict with the ascription to things of visual and tactile qualities than the assertion that blood is really a mainly colourless fluid conflicts with the assertion that it is bright red in colour. Of course, the scientific point of view is not, in one sense, a point of *view* at all. It is an intellectual, not a perceptual, standpoint. We could not occupy it at all, did we not first occupy the other. But we can perfectly well occupy both at once, so long as we realize what we are doing.

This method of reconciling scientific and common-sense realism requires us to recognize a certain relativity in our conception of the real properties of physical objects. Relative to the human perceptual standpoint the grosser physical objects are visuo-tactile continuants (and within that standpoint the phenomenal proper-ties they possess are relative to particular perceptual viewpoints, taken as standard). Relative to the scientific standpoint, they have no properties but those which figure in the physical theories of science. Such a relativistic conception will not please the absolute-minded. Ayer recommends a different procedure. He suggests that we should conceive of perceptible objects (that is, objects perceptible in the sense of the common-sense scheme) as being literally composed of the ultimate particles of physical theory, the latter being imperceptible, not in principle, but only empiric-ally, as a consequence of their being so minute.[22] I doubt, however, whether this proposal, which Ayer rightly describes as an attempt to *blend* the two schemes, can be regarded as satisfactory. If the impossibility of perceiving the ultimate com-ponents is to be viewed as merely empirical, we can sensibly ask what the con-ceptual consequences would be of supposing that impossibility not to exist. The answer is clear. Even if there were something which we counted as perceiving the ultimate particles, this would still not, from the point of view of scientific realism, count as perceiving them as they really are. And nothing could so count; for no phenomenal properties we seemed to perceive them as having would figure in the physical explanation of the causal mechanisms of our success. But, so long as we stay at this point of view, what goes for the parts goes for any wholes they compose. However gross those wholes, they remain, from this point of view, imperceptible in the sense of common sense.

Ayer attempts to form one viewpoint out of two discrepant viewpoints: to form a single, unified description of physical reality by blending features of two discrepant descriptions, each valid from its own viewpoint. He can seem to succeed only by doing violence to one of the two viewpoints, the scientific. I acknowledge the discrepancy of the two descriptions, but claim that, once we recognize the relativity

21. Mackie, *Problems*, p. 18.
22. Ayer, *Central Questions*, p. 110.

in our conception of the real, they need not be seen as in contradiction with each other. Those very things which from one standpoint we conceive as phenomenally propertied we conceive from another as constituted in a way which can only be described in what are, from the phenomenal point of view, abstract terms. 'This smooth, green, leather table-top', we say, 'is, considered scientifically, nothing but a congeries of electric charges widely separated and in rapid motion.' Thus we combine the two standpoints in a single sentence. The standpoint of common-sense realism, not explicitly signalled as such, is reflected in the sentence's grammatical subject phrase, of which the words are employed in no esoteric sense. The standpoint of physical science, explicitly signalled as such, is reflected in the predicate. Once relativity of description to standpoint is recognized, the sentence is seen to contain no contradiction; and, if it contains no contradiction, the problem of identification is solved.

I recognize that this position is unlikely to satisfy the determined scientific realist. If he is only moderately determined, he may be partially satisfied, and may content himself with saying that the scientific viewpoint is *superior* to that of common sense. He will then simply be expressing a preference, which he will not expect the artist, for example, to share. But, if he is a hard-liner, he will insist that the common-sense view is wholly undermined by science; that it is shown to be false; that the visual and tactile properties we ascribe to things are nowhere but in our minds; that we do not live in a world of perceptible objects, as understood by common sense, at all. He must then accept the consequence that each of us is a sufferer from a persistent and inescapable illusion and that it is fortunate that this is so, since, if it were not, we should be unable to pursue the scientific enterprise itself. Without the illusion of perceiving objects as bearers of sensible qualities, we should not have the illusion of perceiving them as space-occupiers at all; and without that we should have no concept of space and no power to pursue our researches into the nature of its occupants. Science is, not only the offspring of common sense; it remains its dependant. For this reason, and for others touched on earlier, the scientific realist must, however ruefully, admit that the ascription to objects of sensible qualities, the standard of correctness of such ascription being (what we take to be) intersubjective agreement, is something quite securely rooted in our conceptual scheme. If this means, as he must maintain it does, that our thought is condemned to incoherence, then we can only conclude that incoherence is something we can perfectly well live with and could not perfectly well live without.

Chapter 32

Individualism and self-knowledge*

Tyler Burge

THE problem I want to discuss derives from the juxtaposition of a restricted Cartesian conception of knowledge of one's own thoughts and a nonindividualistic conception of the individuation of thoughts. Both conceptions are complex and controversial. But I shall not explain them in detail, much less defend them. I shall explicate them just enough to make the shape of the problem vivid. Then I shall say something about solving the problem.

Descartes held that we know some of our propositional mental events in a direct, authoritative, and not merely empirical manner. I believe that this view is correct. Of course, much of our self-knowledge is similar to the knowledge of others' mental events. It depends on observation of our own behavior and reliance on others' perceptions of us. And there is much that we do not know, or even misconstrue, about our own minds. Descartes tended to underrate these points. He tended to overrate the power of authoritative self-knowledge and its potential for yielding metaphysical conclusions. Characterizing the phenomenon that interested Descartes is a substantial task. I shall not take on this task here. I think, however, that Descartes was right to be impressed with the directness and certainty of some of our self-knowledge. This is the point I shall rely on.

Descartes's paradigm for this sort of knowledge was the cogito. The paradigm includes not only this famous thought, but fuller versions of it—not merely 'I am now thinking', but 'I think (with this very thought) that writing requires concentration' and 'I judge (or doubt) that water is more common than mercury'. This

Tyler Burge, 'Individualism and Self-Knowledge' in the *Journal of Philosophy*, 85 (1988), pp. 649–63 reprinted by permission of Columbia University, New York.

* To be presented in an APA symposium on Individuation and Self-Knowledge, December 30, 1988. Donald Davidson will comment; see *Journal of Philosophy*, 85 (1988), pp. 664–5. Substantially this paper was the Nelson Lecture, University of Michigan, February 1986. I benefited from the occasion.

paradigm goes further toward illuminating knowledge of our propositional attitudes than has generally been thought. But I note it here only to emphasize that Descartes's views about the specialness of some self-knowledge are not merely abstract philosophical doctrine. It is certainly plausible that these sorts of judgments or thoughts constitute knowledge, that they are not products of ordinary empirical investigation, and that they are peculiarly direct and authoritative. Indeed, these sorts of judgments are self-verifying in an obvious way: making these judgments itself makes them true. For mnemonic purposes, I shall call such judgments *basic self-knowledge*.

Let us turn from knowledge of one's thoughts to individuation of one's thoughts. My view on this matter is that many thoughts are individuated nonindividualistically: individuating many of a person or animal's mental kinds—certainly including thoughts about physical objects and properties—is necessarily dependent on relations that the person bears to the physical, or in some cases social, environment. This view is founded on a series of thought experiments, which I shall assume are familiar.[1] Their common strategy is to hold constant the history of the person's bodily motion, surface stimulations, and internal chemistry. Then, by varying the environment with which the person interacts while still holding constant the molecular effects on the person's body, one can show that some of the person's thoughts vary. The details of the thought experiments make it clear that the variation of thoughts is indicative of underlying principles for individuating mental kinds. The upshot is that which thoughts one has—indeed, which thoughts one can have—is dependent on relations one bears to one's environment.

Our problem is that of understanding how we can know some of our mental events in a direct, nonempirical manner, when those events depend for their identities on our relations to the environment. A person need not investigate the environment to know what his thoughts are. A person does have to investigate the environment to know what the environment is like. Does this not indicate that the mental events are what they are independently of the environment?

By laying aside certain contrary elements in Descartes's views, one can reconstruct a tempting inference to an affirmative answer from his conception of self knowledge.

In reflecting on the demon thought experiment, one might think that, since we can know our thoughts authoritatively, while doubting whether there is any physical world at all, the natures of our thoughts—our thought kinds—must be independent of any relation to a physical world. A parallel inference is presupposed in Descartes's discussion of the real distinction between mind and body. In *Meditations* VI, he argues that the mind can exist independently of any physical entity. He does so by claiming that he has a 'clear and distinct idea' of himself as

1. Cf. my 'Individualism and the Mental,' *Midwest Studies in Philosophy*, 4 (1979): pp. 73–121; 'Other Bodies,' in *Thought and Object*, A. Woodfield, ed. (New York: Oxford, 1982); 'Individualism and Psychology,' *The Philosophical Review*, 95, 1 (1986): pp. 3–45; 'Cartesian Error and the Objectivity of Perception,' in *Subject, Thought, and Context*, P. Pettit and J. McDowell, eds. (New York: Oxford, 1986); 'Intellectual Norms and Foundations of Mind,' *Journal of Philosophy*, 83 (1986): pp. 697–720.

only a thinking and unextended thing, and a 'clear and distinct idea' of body as only an extended and unthinking thing. He claims that it follows that the mind that makes him what he is can exist independently of any physical body. The argument also occurs in *Principles* I, LX:

... because each one of us is conscious [through clear and distinct ideas] that he thinks, and that in thinking he can shut off from himself all other substance, either thinking or extended, we may conclude that each of us ... is really distinct from every other thinking substance and from every corporeal substance.[2]

Descartes also believed that he had 'clear and distinct ideas' of his thoughts. One might argue by analogy that, since one can 'shut off' these thoughts from all corporeal substance, they are independent for their natures from physical bodies in the environment, and presumably from other thinkers. This line of argument implies that knowledge of one's own thoughts guarantees the truth of individualism.[3]

The root mistake here has been familiar since Arnauld's reply. It is that there is no reason to think that Descartes's intuitions or self-knowledge give him sufficient clarity about the nature of mental events to justify him in claiming that their natures are independent of relations to physical objects. Usually, this point has been made against Descartes's claim to have shown that mental events are independent of a person's body. But it applies equally to the view that mental kinds are independent of the physical environment. One can know what one's mental events are and yet not know relevant general facts about the conditions for individuating those events. It is simply not true that the cogito gives us knowledge of the individuation conditions of our thoughts which enables us to 'shut off' their individuation conditions from the physical environment. Our thought experiments, which have directly to do with conditions for individuation, refute the independence claim.[4]

It is one thing to point out gaps in inferences from self-knowledge to individualism. It is another to rid oneself of the feeling that there is a puzzle here. Why is our having nonempirical knowledge of our thoughts not impugned by the fact that such thoughts are individuated through relations to an environment that we know only empirically?

Let us assume that our thoughts about the environment are what they are because of the nature of entities to which those thoughts are causally linked. According to our thought experiments, a person with the same individualistic physical history could have different thoughts if the environment were appropriately different. One senses that such a person could not, by introspection, tell the

2. *The Philosophical Works of Descartes*, Vol. I, E. S. Haldane and G. R. T. Ross trans. (New York: Dover, 1955), pp. 243–4.
3. Cf. *ibid.*, p. 190.
4. I have discussed this and other features of the inference in 'Cartesian Error and the Objectivity of Perception.' See also my 'Perceptual Individualism and Authoritative Self-Knowledge,' in *Contents of Thought*, R. Grimm and D. Merrill, eds. (Tucson: Arizona University Press, 1988). I now think that Descartes's views have more anti-individualistic elements than I realized in writing those articles. I hope to discuss these matters elsewhere.

difference between the actual situation (having one set of thoughts) and the counterfactual situation (having another).

This intuition must be articulated carefully. What do we mean by 'introspection'? In each situation, the person knows what his thoughts are; and in each situation the thoughts are different. If 'introspection' were explicated in terms of self-knowledge, there would be an introspectible difference.

Certainly, if one were stealthily shifted back and forth between actual situations that modeled the counterfactual situations, one would not notice some feature in the world or in one's consciousness which would tell one whether one was in the 'home' or the 'foreign' situation. But this remark does not capture the idea that the two lives would feel the same. The thoughts would not switch as one is switched from one actual situation to another twin actual situation. The thoughts would switch only if one remained long enough in the other situation to establish environmental relations necessary for new thoughts. So quick switching would not be a case in which thoughts switched but the introspection remained the same.

But slow switching could be such a case. Suppose that one underwent a series of switches between actual earth and actual twin earth so that one remained in each situation long enough to acquire concepts and perceptions appropriate to that situation. Suppose occasions where one is definitely thinking one thought, and other occasions where one is definitely thinking its twin.[5] Suppose also that the switches are carried out so that one is not aware that a switch is occurring. The continuity of one's life is not obviously disrupted. So, for example, one goes to sleep one night at home and wakes up in twin home in twin bed—and so on. (Your standard California fantasy.) Now suppose that, after decades of such switches, one is told about them and asked to identify when the switches take place. The idea is that one could not, by making comparisons, pick out the twin periods from the 'home' periods.

I grant these ideas. The person would have no signs of the differences in his thoughts, no difference in the way things 'feel.' The root idea is that at least some aspects of one's mental life are fixed by the chemical composition of one's body. One might call these aspects *pure phenomenological feels.* If one were uncomfortable with this notion, one could explicate or replace it in terms of an abstraction from the person's inability to discriminate between different mental events under the stated switching situations.

The upshot of all this is that the person would have different thoughts under the switches, but the person would not be able to compare the situations and note when and where the differences occurred. This point easily, though I think mistakenly, suggests the further point that such a person could not know what thoughts he had unless he undertook an empirical investigation of the environment which would bring out the environmental differences. But this is absurd. It is

5. Of course, there can arise difficult questions about whether one is still employing thoughts from the departed situation or taking over the thoughts appropriate to the new situation. I think that general principles govern such transitions, but such principles need not sharply settle all borderline cases. Insofar as one finds problems associated with actual switches distracting, one could carry out the objection I am articulating in terms of counterfactual situations.

absurd to think that, to know which thoughts we think, we must investigate the empirical environment in such a way as to distinguish our actual environment from various twin environments.

In basic self-knowledge, a person does individuate his thoughts in the sense that he knows the thought tokens as the thought tokens, and types, that they are. We know which thoughts we think. When I currently and consciously think that water is a liquid, I typically know that I think that water is a liquid. So much is clear.

How can one individuate one's thoughts when one has not, by empirical methods, discriminated the empirical conditions that determine those thoughts from empirical conditions that would determine other thoughts?

It is uncontroversial that the conditions for thinking a certain thought must be presupposed in the thinking. Among the conditions that determine the contents of first-order empirical thoughts are some that can be known only by empirical means. To think of something as water, for example, one must be in some causal relation to water—or at least in some causal relation to other particular substances that enable one to theorize accurately about water. In the normal cases, one sees and touches water. Such relations illustrate the sort of conditions that make possible thinking of something as water. To know that such conditions obtain, one must rely on empirical methods. To know that water exists, or that what one is touching is water, one cannot circumvent empirical procedures. But to *think* that water is a liquid, one need not *know* the complex conditions that must obtain if one is to think that thought. Such conditions need only be presupposed.

Now let us turn to knowledge of one's thoughts. Knowing what one is thinking when one has thoughts about physical entities presupposes some of the same conditions that determine the contents of the empirical thoughts one knows one is thinking. This is a result of the second-order character of the thoughts. A knowledgeable judgment that one is thinking that water is a liquid must be grounded in an ability to think that water is a liquid.

When one knows that one is thinking that p, one is not taking one's thought (or thinking) that p merely as an object. One is thinking that p in the very event of thinking knowledgeably that one is thinking it. It is thought and thought about in the same mental act. So any conditions that are necessary to thinking that will be equally necessary to the relevant knowledge that one is thinking that p. Here again, to think the thought, one need not know the enabling conditions. It is enough that they actually be satisfied.

Both empirical thoughts and thinking that one is thinking such thoughts presuppose conditions that determine their contents. In both cases, some of these conditions can be known to be satisfied only by empirical means. Why do these points not entail that one cannot know that one is thinking that such and such unless one makes an empirical investigation that shows that the conditions for thinking such and such are satisfied? The answer is complex, but it can be seen as a series of variations on the point that one must start somewhere.

It is helpful in understanding self-knowledge to consider parallel issues regarding perceptual knowledge. It is a fundamental mistake to think that perceptual knowledge of physical entities requires, as a precondition, knowledge of the conditions that make such knowledge possible. Our epistemic right to our perceptual judgments does not rest on some prior justified belief that certain enabling conditions are satisfied. In saying that a person knows, by looking, that there is food there, we are not required to assume that the person knows the causal conditions that make his perception possible. We certainly do not, in general, require that the person has first checked that the light coming from the food is not bent through mirrors, or that there is no counterfeit food in the vicinity. We also do not require that the person be able to recognize the difference between food and every imaginable counterfeit that could have been substituted.

In fact, it is part of our common conception of the objectivity of perception that there is no general guarantee that the perceiver's beliefs, dispositions, and perceptions could in every context suffice to discriminate the perceived object from every possible counterfeit. The possibility of unforeseeable misperceptions and illusions is fundamental to objectivity. So the very nature of objective perception insures that the perceiver need not have a perfect, prior mastery over the conditions for his perceptual success.

This point is obvious as applied to common practice. But it is the business of philosophy and the pleasure of skepticism to question common practice. My discussion of knowledge and individualism has proceeded on the unargued assumption that skepticism is mistaken. Granted this assumption, the point that perceptual knowledge does not require knowledge of its enabling conditions is obvious.

I shall not overburden this essay with an attempt to disarm skepticism. But it is worth noting that nearly all currently defended responses to skepticism, other than transcendental ones, agree in denying that perceptual knowledge must be justified by separately insuring that the enabling conditions hold and the skeptic's defeating conditions do not hold.[6] And since transcendental responses provide at most general guarantees against skepticism, the only tenable responses, which I know of, that attempt to justify particular perceptual knowledge claims in the face of skepticism take this route. I think that it is the right route.

I have maintained that perceptual knowledge of physical objects does not

---

6. This remark applies to reliabilist theories, Moorean theories that insist on the directness of perception, Quinean theories that attempt to show that the skeptic's doubt is covertly a bad empirical doubt, and Carnapian theories that attempt to show that the skeptic's question is somehow irrelevant to actual empirical claims. The words 'first' and 'separately' are crucial in my formulations. As against some reliabilist views that try to block skepticism by denying closure principles, I think that we can know that no demon is fooling us. But we know this by inferring it from our perceptual knowledge.

Several philosophers have thought that anti-individualism, combined with the view that we are authoritative about what thoughts we think, provides a 'transcendental' response to skepticism. Cf. Hilary Putnam, *Reason, Truth, and History* (New York: Cambridge, 1981) [Ch. 27 in this volume]. Putnam's argument is criticized by Anthony L. Brueckner, 'Brains in a Vat,' *Journal of Philosophy*, 83 (1986): pp. 148–67. I agree with Brueckner that Putnam's arguments do not do much to undermine skepticism. But Brueckner seems to hold that, if anti-individualism and the authority of self-knowledge are accepted, one would have an antiskeptical argument. He suggests that the assumption of anti-individualism undercuts the assumption of authoritative self-knowledge. I do not accept this suggestion. I believe, however, that there is no easy argument against skepticism from anti-individualism and authoritative self knowledge. This is a complicated matter best reserved for other occasions.

presuppose that one has first checked to insure that the background enabling conditions are fulfilled. The same point applies to knowledge of one's own mental events, particularly knowledge of the sort that interested Descartes. Such knowledge consists in a reflexive judgment which involves thinking a first-order thought that the judgment itself is about. The reflexive judgment simply inherits the content of the first-order thought.

Consider the thought, 'I hereby judge that water is a liquid'. What one needs in order to think this thought knowledgeably is to be able to think the first-order, empirical thought (that water is a liquid) and to ascribe it to oneself, simultaneously. Knowing one's thoughts no more requires separate investigation of the conditions that make the judgment possible than knowing what one perceives.

One knows one's thought to be what it is simply by thinking it while exercising second-order, self-ascriptive powers. One has no 'criterion,' or test, or procedure for identifying the thought, and one need not exercise comparisons between it and other thoughts in order to know it as the thought one is thinking. Getting the 'right' one is simply a matter of thinking the thought in the relevant reflexive way. The fact that we cannot use phenomenological signs or empirical investigation to discriminate our thoughts from other thoughts that we might have been thinking if we had been in a different environment in no way undermines our ability to know what our thoughts are. We 'individuate' our thoughts, or discriminate them from others, by thinking those and not the others, self-ascriptively. Crudely put, our knowledge of our own thoughts is immediate, not discursive. Our epistemic right rests on this immediacy, as does our epistemic right to perceptual beliefs. For its justification, basic self-knowledge in no way needs supplementation from discursive investigations or comparisons.[7]

So far I have stressed analogies between basic self-knowledge and perceptual belief. But there are fundamental differences. A requirement that, to know what thoughts we are thinking, we must be able first to discriminate our thoughts from twin thoughts is, in my view, even less plausible than the analogous position with regard to perceptual knowledge.

Why? In developing an answer to this question, I want to dwell on some fundamental ways in which perceptual knowledge of physical entities differs from the sort of self-knowledge that we have been featuring. We commonly regard perceptual knowledge as *objective*. For our purposes, there are two relevant notions of objectivity. One has to do with the relation between our perceptions and the physical entities that are their objects. We commonly think that there is no necessary relation between any one person's abilities, actions, thoughts, and perceptions up to and including the time of a particular perception, on one hand, and the natures of those entities which that person perceptually interacts with at that time, on the other. On any given occasion, our perceptions could have been misperceptions. The individual physical item that one perceptually interacts with at any given time is fundamentally independent from any one person's perceptions—and conceptions.

---

7. I shall not develop the issue of one's epistemic right to one's authoritative self-ascriptions here. It is an extremely complex issue, which deserves separate attention.

The nature of the physical entity could have been different even while one's perceptual states, and other mental states, remained the same.

This fact underlies a normative point about perception. We are subject to certain sorts of possible errors about empirical objects—misperceptions and hallucinations that are 'brute.' Brute errors do not result from any sort of carelessness, malfunction, or irrationality on our part. A person can be perceptually wrong without there being anything wrong with him. Brute errors depend on the independence of physical objects' natures from how we conceive or perceive them, and on the contingency of our causal relations to them. The possibility of such errors follows from the fact that no matter what one's cognitive state is like (so, no matter how rational or well-functioning one is) one's perceptual states could in individual instances fail to be veridical—if physical circumstances were sufficiently unfortunate.

There is a second sense in which perceptual knowledge is objective. This sense bears on the relation between one person's perceptions of an object and other persons' perceptions of the same object. The idea is that perceptual knowledge, like all other empirical knowledge, is impersonal. Any observer could have been equally well placed to make an observation. Others could have made an observation with the same type of presentation of the scene, if they had been in the same position at the relevant time. And this possible observation could have had the same justificatory status as the original observation. Even though empirical commitments must be made by persons, nothing relevant to the justification of any empirical commitment regarding the physical world has anything essentially to do with any particular person's making the commitment.

The paradigmatic cases of self-knowledge differ from perceptual knowledge in both of these respects. To take the first: in the case of cogito-like judgments, the object, or subject matter, of one's thoughts is not contingently related to the thoughts one thinks about it. The thoughts are self-referential and self-verifying. An error based on a gap between one's thoughts and the subject matter is simply not possible in these cases. When I judge: I am thinking that writing requires concentration, the cognitive content that I am making a judgment about is self-referentially fixed by the judgment itself; and the judgment is self-verifying. There is a range of cases of self-knowledge which extend out from this paradigm. I think that, in all cases of authoritative knowledge, brute mistakes are impossible. All errors in matters where people have special authority about themselves are errors which indicate something wrong with the thinker. Dealing with the whole range requires subtlety. But the point as applied to what I take to be the basic cases is straightforward. No errors at all are possible in strict cogito judgments; they are self-verifying.[8]

8. Mistakes about the *res* in *de re* judgments are not counterexamples to the claim that basic cogito-like judgments are self-verifying (hence infallible). Suppose I judge: I am thinking that my aunt is charming; and suppose that the person that I am judging to be charming is not my aunt (I have some particular person in mind). It is true that I am making a mistake about the identity of the person thought about; I have no particular authority about that, or even about her existence. But I am not making a mistake about what I am thinking about that person; there is no mistake about the intentional act and intentional content of the act. Authority concerns those aspects of the thought which have intentional (aboutness) properties. For me, those are the only aspects of the content of a thought.

The paradigmatic cases of self-knowledge also differ from perceptual knowledge in that they are essentially personal. The special epistemic status of these cases depends on the judgments' being made simultaneously from and about one's first-person point of view. The point of view and time of the judgment must be the same as that of the thought being judged to occur. When I judge: I am thinking that writing requires concentration, the time of the judgment and that of the thought being judged about are the same; and the identity of the first-person pronouns signals an identity of point of view between the judge and the thought being judged about. In all cases of authoritative self-knowledge, even in those cases which are not 'basic' in our sense, it is clear that their first-person character is fundamental to their epistemic status.

These differences between perceptual knowledge and authoritative self-knowledge ground my claim that it is even less plausible than it is in the case of perceptual knowledge to think that basic self-knowledge requires, as a precondition, knowledge of the conditions that make such knowledge possible.

Let us think about the difference as regards objectivity in the relation to an object. In the case of perceptual knowledge, one's perception can be mistaken because some counterfeit has been substituted. It is this possibility which tempts one into the (mistaken) view that, to have perceptual knowledge, one must first know something that rules out the possibility of a counterfeit. But in the cases of the cogito-like self-verifying judgments there is no possibility of counterfeits. No abnormal background condition could substitute some other object in such a way as to create a gap between what we think and what we think about. Basic self-knowledge is self-referential in a way that insures that the object of reference just is the thought being thought. If background conditions are different enough so that there is another object of reference in one's self-referential thinking, they are also different enough so that there is another thought. The person would remain in the same reflexive position with respect to this thought, and would again know, in the authoritative way, what he is thinking.

For example, imagine a case of slow switching between actual home and actual twin-home situations. In the former situation, the person may think 'I am thinking that twater is a liquid.' In the latter situation, the person may think 'I am thinking that water is a liquid.' In both cases, the person is right and as fully justified as ever. The fact that the person does not know that a switch has occurred is irrelevant to the truth and justified character of these judgments. Of course, the person may learn about the switches and ask 'Was I thinking yesterday about water or twater?'—and not know the answer. Here knowing the answer may sometimes indeed depend on knowing empirical background conditions. But such sophisticated questions about memory require a more complex story. If a person, aware of the fact that switching has occurred, were to ask 'Am I now thinking about water or twater?', the answer is obviously 'both.' Both concepts are used. Given that the thought is fixed and that the person is thinking it self-consciously, no new knowledge about the thought could undermine the self-ascription—or therefore its justification or authority.

In basic self-knowledge, one simultaneously thinks through a first-order thought (that water is a liquid) and thinks about it as one's own. The content of the first-order (contained) thought is fixed by nonindividualistic background conditions. And by its reflexive, self-referential character, the content of the second-order judgment is logically locked (self-referentially) onto the first-order content which it both contains and takes as its subject matter. Since counterfeit contents logically cannot undermine such self-knowledge, there should be no temptation to think that, in order to have such knowledge, one needs to master its enabling conditions.

The view I constructed on Descartes runs contrary. On that view, since basic self-knowledge is more certain than perceptual knowledge, it is more imperative that one be master of all its enabling conditions. One temptation toward this sort of reasoning may derive from construing self-knowledge as a perfected perceptual knowledge. If one thinks of one's relation to the subject matter of basic self-knowledge on an analogy to one's relation to objects of empirical investigation, then the view that one's thoughts (the subject matter) are dependent for their natures on relations to the environment will make it appear that one's knowledge of one's thoughts cannot be any more direct or certain than one's knowledge of the environment. If one begins by thinking of one's thoughts as objects like physical objects, except that one cannot misperceive or have illusions about them, then to explicate authoritative self-knowledge, one makes one of two moves. Either one adds further capacities for ruling out the possible sources of misperception or illusion in empirical perception, or one postulates objects of knowledge whose very nature is such that they cannot be misconstrued or misconceived. In the first instance, one grants oneself an omniscient faculty for discerning background conditions whose independence from us, in the case of perceptual knowledge, is the source of error. In the second instance, one imagines objects of thought (propositions that can be thought only if they are completely understood, or ideas whose *esse* is their *percipi*) whose natures are such that one cannot make any mistakes about them—objects of thought which one can 'see' from all sides at once. In either case, one takes oneself to have ultimate insight into the natures of one's thoughts.

This line of reasoning is deeply misconceived. One need only make it explicit to sense its implausibility. The source of our strong epistemic right, our justification, in our basic self-knowledge is not that we know a lot about each thought we know we have. It is not that we can explicate its nature and its enabling conditions. It is that we are in the position of thinking those thoughts in the second-order, self-verifying way. Justification lies not in the having of supplemental background knowledge, but in the character and function of the self-evaluating judgments.

Let us turn to the point that self-knowledge is personal. The view that anti-individualism is incompatible with authoritative self-knowledge is easily engendered by forgetting the essentially first-person character of self-knowledge. We switch back and forth between thinking our thoughts and thinking about ourselves from the point of view of another person who knows more about our environment than we do. This is a key to Descartes's skeptical thought experiments. And it would not be surprising if he tended to think about self-knowledge in such a way as to give it a sort of omniscience from the third-person point of view—in order to protect the first-person point of view from the fallibilities to which impersonal or third-person judgments (especially empirical judgments) are prone. Since we are not omniscient about empirical matters, it is natural to reduce the scope of the relevant third-person perspective so that the character of one's thoughts is independent of an environment about which we cannot be omniscient. Individualism ensues.

To illustrate the train of thought in a more concrete way: we think that we are thinking that water is a liquid. But then, switching to a third-person perspective, we imagine a situation in which the world is not as we currently think it is—a situation say, in which there is no water for us to interact with. We take up a perspective on ourselves from the outside. Having done this, we are easily but illegitimately seduced into the worry that our original first-person judgment is poorly justified unless it can somehow encompass the third-person perspective, or unless the third-person perspective on empirical matters is irrelevant to the character of the first-person judgment. In this fallen state, we are left with little else but a distorted conception of self-knowledge and a return to individualism.[9]

As one thinks a thought reflexively, it is an object of reference and knowledge, but simultaneously a constituent of one's point of view. The essential role that the first-person singular plays in the epistemic status of authoritative self-knowledge differentiates this knowledge not only from empirical knowledge, but so from most a priori knowledge, the justification of which does not depend on the first-person point of view in the same way.

The tendency to blur distinctions between a priori knowledge (or equally, knowledge involved in explication of one's concepts) and authoritative self-knowledge is, I think, an instance of Descartes's central mistake: exaggerating the implications of authoritative self-knowledge for impersonal knowledge of necessary truths. One clearly does not have first-person authority about whether one of one's thoughts is to be explicated or individuated in such and such a way. Nor is there any apparent

9. My knowledge that I am thinking that mercury is an element depends on an ability to think—not explicate—the thought that mercury is an element. Compare my knowledge that my words 'mercury is an element' are true if and only if mercury is an element. This knowledge depends on understanding the words 'mercury is an element' well enough to say with them, or think with them, that mercury is an element. It is this ability which distinguishes this knowledge from mere knowledge that the disquotation principle as applied to 'mercury is an element' is true (mere knowledge that the sentence '"mercury is an element" is true if and only if mercury is an element' is true). I know that my word 'mercury' applies to mercury (if to anything), not by being able to provide an explication that distinguishes mercury from every conceivable twin mercury, but by being a competent user of the word, whose meaning and reference are grounded in this environment rather than in some environment where the meaning of the word form would be different. The fact that one may not be able to explicate the difference between mercury and every possible twin mercury should not lead one to assimilate one's use of 'mercury' to knowledge of purely formal relationships (e.g., knowledge that all instances of the disquotation principle are true).

One other comparison: I know that I am here (compare: on earth) rather than somewhere else (compare: twin earth). My knowledge amounts to more than knowing I am wherever I am. I have normal ability to perceive and think about my surroundings. I have this knowledge because I perceive my surroundings and not other conceivable surroundings, and I have it even though other places that I could not distinguish by perception or description from here are conceivable. For a variety of reasons, one should not assimilate terms like 'water' to indexicals like 'here'. Cf. 'Other Bodies.' But these analogies may be helpful here.

reason to assume that, in general, one must be able to explicate one's thoughts correctly in order to know that one is thinking them.

Thus, I can know that I have arthritis, and know I think I have arthritis, even though I do not have a proper criterion for what arthritis is. It is a truism that to think one's thoughts, and thus to think cogito-like thoughts, one must understand what one is thinking well enough to think it. But it does not follow that such understanding carries with it an ability to explicate correctly one's thoughts or concepts via other thoughts and concepts; nor does it carry an immunity to failures of explication. So one can know what one's thoughts are even while one understands one's thoughts only partially, in the sense that one gives incomplete or mistaken explications of one's thoughts or concepts. One should not assimilate 'knowing what one's thoughts are' in the sense of basic self-knowledge to 'knowing what one's thoughts are' in the sense of being able to explicate them correctly—being able to delineate their constitutive relations to other thoughts.[10]

For its justification, basic self-knowledge requires only that one think one's thoughts in the self-referential, self-ascriptive manner. It neither requires nor by itself yields a general account of the mental kinds that it specifies. Conceptual explication—knowledge of how one's thought kinds relate to other thought kinds—typically requires more objectification: reasoning from empirical observation or reflection on general principles. It requires a conceptual mastery of the conditions underlying one's thoughts and a conceptual mastery of the rules one is following. These masteries are clearly beyond anything required to think thoughts in the second-order, self-ascriptive way. Explicative knowledge is neither self-verifying nor so closely tied to particular mental events or particular persons' points of view.[11]

Despite, or better because of, its directness and certainty, basic self-knowledge is limited in its metaphysical implications. It is nonetheless epistemically self-reliant. By itself it yields little of metaphysical interest; but its epistemic credentials do not rest on knowledge of general principles, or on investigation of the world.

10. Davidson's views about self-knowledge have some crucial points in common with mine. But he may be making this mistake when he writes that, if one concedes the possibility of partial understanding as I do, one must concede that anti-individualism undermines the authority of self-knowledge. Cf. his 'Knowing One's Own Mind,' *Proceedings and Addresses of the American Philosophical Association*, 60 (1987): p. 448. Cf. also 'First Person Authority,' *Dialectica*, 38 (1984): pp. 101–11. It is unclear to me why Davidson says this. I have discussed the distinction between the sort of understanding necessary to think and the sort of understanding necessary to explicate one's thoughts, in 'Individualism and the Mental'; 'Intellectual Norms and Foundations of Mind'; 'Frege on Sense and Linguistic Meaning,' in *The Analytic Tradition*, D. Bell and N. Cooper, eds (New York: Blackwell 1990); and 'Wherein is Language Social?' in *Reflections on Chomsky*, Alexander George, ed. (New York: Blackwell, 1991).

11. As I indicated earlier, basic self-knowledge is at most an illuminating paradigm for understanding a significant range of phenomena that count as self-knowledge. Thus, the whole discussion has been carried out under a major simplifying assumption. A full discussion of authoritative self-knowledge must explicate our special authority, or epistemic right, even in numerous cases where our judgments are not self-verifying or immune to error. I think, however, that reflection on the way that errors can occur in such cases gives not the slightest encouragement to the view that anti-individualism (as regards either the physical or social environments) is a threat to the authority of our knowledge of the contents of our thoughts.

Chapter 33

Content and self-knowledge

Paul A. Boghossian

Introduction

1. THIS paper argues that, given a certain apparently inevitable thesis about content, we could not know our own minds. The thesis is that the content of a thought is determined by its relational properties.

The problem can be stated roughly, but intuitively, like this. We sometimes know our thoughts directly, without the benefit of inference from other beliefs. (Indeed, given a plausible internalism about justification, this claim is not merely true but necessary.) This implies that we know our thoughts either on the basis of some form of inner observation, or on the basis of nothing. But there is a difficulty either way. On the one hand, given that the content properties of thoughts are individuated in terms of their relational properties, we could not know what we think merely by looking inwards. What we would need to see, if we are to know by mere looking, is not there to be seen. And, on the other, there appear to be serious objections to the suggestion that we may know our thoughts on the basis of nothing.[1]

The paper proceeds as follows. Part I explains why we could not know our thoughts on the basis of reasoning or inference. Part 2 explains why we could not know them on the basis of looking. And Part 2I explains why we could not know them on the basis of nothing.

I consider the skeptical claim about self-knowledge to have the status of a paradox: apparently acceptable premises lead to an unacceptable conclusion. For I do not seriously envisage that we do not know our own minds. Our capacity for

Paul A. Boghossian, 'Content and Self-Knowledge' in C. S. Hill (ed.), *Philosophical Topics* 17.1: *Philosophy of Mind* (Fayetteville, AR., University of Arkansas Press, 1989), pp. 5–26 reprinted by permission of the author.

1. How a contingent proposition might be known on the basis of nothing will be explained in part 2I. A word also about 'inner observation': It makes no difference to the argument of this paper if you think of inner observation as amounting to traditional introspection, or if you think of it as amounting to the operation of some Armstrong-style 'brain-scanner'. What *is* crucial to inner observation models of self-knowledge is the claim that beliefs about one's own thoughts are justified by the deliverances of some internal monitoring capacity, much like beliefs about the external environment are justified by the deliverances of an external monitoring capacity (perception).

    For 'brain-scanners' see D. Armstrong, *A Materialist Theory of the Mind* (London: Routledge & Kegan Paul, 1968). For a useful survey of various conceptions of introspection see William Lyons, *The Disappearance of Introspection* (Cambridge: MIT Press, 1986).

self-knowledge is not an optional component of our ordinary self-conception, a thesis we may be able to discard while preserving all that really matters. It is a fundamental part of that conception, presupposed by some of the very concepts that constitute it (consider intentional action). So long as we are not able to see our way clear to abandoning that conception—and I am assuming that we have not yet been shown how to do so—there can be no question of accepting the skeptical claim.[2]

The point of advancing it, then, is not to promote skepticism but understanding: I hope that by getting clear on the conditions under which self-knowledge is not possible, we shall better understand the conditions under which it is. I have to confess, however, that at the present time I am unable to see what those conditions might be.

A couple of preliminary remarks before we proceed. First, I propose to be reasonably serious in the use of the term 'knowledge': by 'self-knowledge' I shall mean not just a *true* belief about one's own thoughts, but a *justified* one. (I do not, however, propose to be so serious as to worry about the complexities induced by Gettier-style counterexamples.) Second, I want to keep the discussion as free as possible of problematic auxiliary assumptions about the nature of thought. In particular, I do not want to assume a 'language of thought' model of thinking. I hope one of these days to write a paper entitled 'The Language of Thought Hypothesis in the Philosophy of Mind.' It would argue that, contrary to what many people seem to believe, a language of thought model has profound and unexpected implications for the way we think about most mental phenomena. Issues about self-knowledge, in particular, are transformed by its assumption. The reason should be evident: a language of thought model implies that there are *type-type* correlations between certain purely formal and intrinsic properties of thoughts and their semantic properties. This is a heady assumption that stands to profoundly affect the account we are able to give of our capacity to know the semantic properties of thoughts. Too heady, I think, to be assumed uncritically and, hence, too heady for the purposes of this paper.

I. The character of self-knowledge

Inference and self-knowledge 2. Many extravagant claims have been made about our capacity to know our own minds. Descartes, who was responsible for the worst excesses, taught many subsequent generations of philosophers that self-knowledge was both infallible and exhaustive. In contrast with our knowledge of other people's minds, Descartes held, our access to our own contemporaneous mental states and events could issue neither in false belief nor in ignorance.

These famous Cartesian claims are not, of course, wholly without substance; for a certain restricted class of mental events—namely, sensations—they may even be true. For it does seem constitutive of, say, an occurrence of pain, that it register with

2. For arguments in support of the indispensability of the ordinary conception, see my 'The Status of Content,' in *The Philosophical Review* 99 (1990), pp. 157–84.

us precisely as an occurrence of pain. And so, it seems not conceivable, in respect of facts about pain, that we should be either ignorant of their existence or mistaken about their character, just as the Cartesian doctrine requires.

But the corresponding theses about contentful or representational states carry little contemporary conviction. That we harbor a multitude of thoughts of whose existence we are unaware is a presupposition not only of Freudian theory, but of much of present-day cognitive science. And phenomena that are intelligible only if infallibility is false—self-deception, for instance—seem pervasive.

3. A Cartesian account, then, of the distinction between first-person and third-person knowledge of mind must be rejected. But we should be wary, in correcting for Cartesian excess, of recoiling too far in the opposite direction. For there remains, even after we have discarded the problematic Cartesian claims, a profound asymmetry between the way in which I know my own thoughts and the way in which I may know the thoughts of others. The difference turns not on the epistemic status of the respective beliefs, but on the manner in which they are arrived at, or justified. In the case of others, I have no choice but to *infer* what they think from observations about what they do or say. In my own case, by contrast, inference is neither required nor relevant. Normally, I know what I think—what I believe, desire, hope or expect—without appeal to supplementary evidence. Even where such evidence is available, I do not consult it. I know what I think directly. I do not defend my self-attributions; nor does it normally make sense to ask me to do so.[3]

Ryle attempted to deny all this.[4] He tried to defend the view that there is no asymmetry between first-person and third-person access to mental states. In both cases, he maintained, the process is essentially the same: ordinary inspection of ordinary behavior gives rise to the discovery of patterns in that behavior, which in turn leads to the imputation of the appropriate propositional attitudes.

The claim carries no conviction whatever. The trouble is not merely that it runs counter to all the relevant appearances, offering an implausible explanation for the knowledge we have of our thoughts. The trouble is that, for much of what we do know about our own thoughts, it can offer no explanation at all. Consider an act of entertaining a particular proposition. You think: Even lousy composers sometimes write great arias. And you know, immediately on thinking it, that that is what you thought. What explanation can the Rylean offer of this? The difficulty is not merely that, contrary to appearance and the canons of epistemic practice, he has to construe the knowledge as inferential. The difficulty is that he has to construe it as involving inference from premises about behavior that you could not possibly possess. Your knowledge of that occurrent thought could not have been inferred from any premises about your behavior because that thought could not yet have come to have any traction on your behavior. So it's not merely that, on the Rylean view, you would have to know inferentially what you appear to know non-inferentially. It's that you would not know at all what you seem to know unproblematically.

3. Many philosophers have pointed this out. See, for example, D. Davidson, 'Knowing One's Own Mind,' *Proceedings of the American Philosophical Association* (1986): pp. 441–2.
4. See Gilbert Ryle, *The Concept of Mind* (London: Hutchinson, 1949).

Any inferential conception is likely to succumb to this sort of objection. Since the epistemic norms governing ascriptions of self-knowledge do not require possession of supplementary evidence, for any item of evidence insisted on by an inference-based account—whether it involve behavior or the environment or even the causal properties of thoughts—it should be possible to describe a situation in which you know your thoughts but you do not know the item in question.

Internalism and inferential self-knowledge 4. It is, actually, surprisingly little noticed that on an *internalist* conception of justification—a conception to which many philosophers remain profoundly sympathetic—knowledge of one's own mental states *has* to be non-inferential. On this view, the alternative is not merely implausible; it is incoherent. I shall explain.

The intuition that fuels internalism in the theory of justification is the thought that someone cannot count as justified in holding a certain belief if, judged from the standpoint of his own subjective conception of the situation, he may appear epistemologically irresponsible or irrational in accepting that belief. The intuition is effectively triggered by various examples in which, although a person's belief satisfies basic externalist demands—the belief is formed by a reliable belief-forming mechanism and so on—the person does not count as epistemically justified because, as far as he is concerned, he has no reason for accepting the belief and may, indeed, have reasons for rejecting it.

Consider Sam.[5] Sam believes himself to have the power of clairvoyance, though he has no reason for the belief and some evidence—in the form of apparently cogent scientific results—against it. One day he comes to believe, for no apparent reason, that the President is in New York City. He maintains this belief, appealing to his alleged clairvoyant power, even though he is at the same time aware of a massive amount of apparently cogent evidence, consisting of news reports, allegedly live television pictures, and so on, indicating that the President is at that time in Washington, D.C. Now the President is in fact in New York City, the evidence to the contrary being part of an official hoax. Moreover, Sam does in fact have completely reliable clairvoyant power under the conditions then satisfied, and his belief about the President did result from the operation of that power.

Is Sam justified in his belief about the President? Basic reliabilist demands are met; but the intuition persists that the belief cannot be epistemically justified because, judged from the standpoint of Sam himself, it is epistemically thoroughly irrational.

Examples such as this are at the heart of internalist dissatisfaction with externalist conceptions of justification; they motivate the requirement that, if a belief depends upon evidence, 'the knower [must] grasp the connection between the evidence and what it is evidence for,' if his belief is to be justified.[6]

---

5. The example is adapted from L. BonJour, *The Structure of Empirical Knowledge* (Cambridge: Harvard University Press, 1985), pp. 38–40 [in this volume pp. 185–7].

6. D. J. O'Connor and B. Carr, *Introduction to the Theory of Knowledge* (Minneapolis: University of Minnesota Press, 1982), p. 75. Of course, there are responses available to the externalist. I am not going to consider them here because I am not here trying to *argue* for internalism; I am just describing it. Again, for detailed discussion see BonJour, *op. cit.*

Suppose, then, that the proposition that p depends on the proposition that q. According to internalism, if I am to be justified in believing that p, I must believe that p as a result both of my recognition that I believe that q, and that a belief that q justifies a belief that p. Spelling this out in explicit detail, we have:

1. I believe that p.
2. I believe that q.
3. The proposition that q justifies the proposition that p.
4. I know that I believe that q.
5. I know that a belief that q justifies a belief that p.
6. I believe that p as a result of the knowledge expressed in 4 and 5.

5. Now, there is, of course, a *standard* problem in holding that all knowledge of empirical propositions is inferential, that all beliefs can be justified only by reference to other beliefs. This is the problem of the regress of justification: If the belief that p is to count as justified, then the belief that q on which its justification depends must itself be justified. But if *all* beliefs can be justified only by reference to other beliefs, then the belief that q must itself be justified by reference to other beliefs. And this threatens to lapse into a vicious regress.

Any theory of justification must confront this problem. The available non-skeptical options—Foundationalism and Coherentism—are well known and need not be rehearsed here.

The point I wish to make, however, is that there is a *special* problem sustaining a thoroughly inferential conception of *self-knowledge*, one that is independent of the *standard* problem of the regress of justification.

6. In order to bring it out, waive the standard problem: let us not require that if the non-intrinsically credible proposition that p is to be justifiably believed, then it has to rest on a belief that q that is itself justified; let us simply require that the belief that p be justified *relative* to the belief that q, in accordance with standard internalist requirements.

Where the subject matter of concern is knowledge of one's own beliefs, the belief that p will be a belief to the effect that I have a certain belief, say, that I believe that r. Since we are supposing that all self-knowledge is inferential, there must be a belief on which this belief rests. Let that be the belief that s. Now, what would have to be true if I am to be justified in believing that I believe that r?

Taking into account the fact that the belief in question is a belief concerning my own beliefs, the conditions that would have to be satisfied, if I am to be justified in believing that I believe that r, are these:

1′. I believe that I believe that r.
2′. I believe that s.
3′. The proposition that s justifies the proposition that I believe that r.
4′. I know that I believe that s.
5′. I know that a belief that s justifies the belief that I believe that r.
6′. I believe that I believe that r as a result of the knowledge expressed in 4′ and 5′.

The problem is transparent. In order to be justified in believing that I have a certain belief, I must already know that I have some other belief (4'): In order to know that I believe that r, I must antecedently know that I believe that s. But how was knowledge of *this* belief acquired? On the assumption that all self-knowledge is inferential, it could have been acquired only by inference from yet other known beliefs. And now we are off on a vicious regress.[7]

The problem with sustaining a thoroughly inferential conception of *self-knowledge* should have been evident from the start. For the ordinary notion of being justified in believing a non-intrinsically credible empirical proposition *presupposes* self-knowledge. For it presupposes that one has grasped the fact that one's belief in that proposition bears some appropriate epistemic relation to one's other beliefs. In ordinary epistemological discussions this does not emerge as a problem because those discussions tend to focus exclusively on the justification of belief concerning the external world; they tend, understandably, to take knowledge of the beliefs themselves for granted. When such knowledge is not taken for granted, however, it emerges very clearly that not *all* knowledge of one's beliefs can be inferential. On pain of a vicious regress, it must be possible to know the content of some mental states non-inferentially.[8]

7. The intuitive epistemic facts indicate that knowledge of one's mental states is direct. And an internalist conception of justification implies that it has to be. There are two ways to accommodate this claim.

We may conclude, on the one hand, that self-knowledge is not inferential because it is based on some form of inner observation; or, on the other, that it is not inferential because it is based on nothing—at any rate, on nothing empirical.

How might a contingent fact be known on the basis of nothing empirical? We shall consider that question in part 2I. Before that, however, I want to turn to asking whether we could know our thoughts on the basis of inner observation.

---

7. The regress does not particularly depend on the fact that the relation between the beliefs consists in *inference*. There are possible coherentist views according to which mediated justification consists not in inference but in 'membership' in an appropriate system of beliefs. All such views, applied to self-knowledge, are subject to the regress outlined in the text, given internalist assumptions. (I am indebted here to Crispin Wright.)

8. I am inclined to believe that (at least part of) what is going on in the famous passage that concludes Wittgenstein's discussion of rule-following in his *Philosophical Investigations* is an argument to this effect. The passage reads:

It can be seen that there is a misunderstanding here from the mere fact that in the course of our argument we give one interpretation after another; as if each one contented us at least for a moment, until we thought of yet another standing behind it. What this shows is that there is a way of grasping a rule that is *not an interpretation* . . . (PI: 201)

The textual evidence strongly indicates that Wittgenstein uses the term 'interpretation' to mean 'hypothesis as the meaning of.' Read this way, the passage says that the moral of the rule following 'paradox' is that there must be a way of grasping the content of a mental event without having to form hypotheses as to its content.

This is not the occasion to say what else might be going on in that passage or to defend this reading in greater detail.

II. Content and knowledge of content

8. The suggestion that I know about my thoughts by being introspectively aware of them seems, from a phenomenological standpoint anyway, overwhelmingly plausible. It is not simply that I have reliable beliefs about my thoughts. I catch some of my thoughts in the act of being thought. I think: If she says that one more time, I'm leaving. And I am aware, immediately on thinking it, that that is what I thought. Can 'inner awareness' provide the right explanation for how I know my thoughts?

There are many aspects to this question. An exhaustive treatment would distinguish carefully between occurrent events—fleeting thoughts, sudden fancies—and standing states—fixed beliefs, stable desires—and would worry about the epistemological ramifications of that distinction. It would also distinguish between the distinct attitudes that one may sustain toward a given content—judging, believing, desiring, entertaining—and explore any corresponding epistemic differences. Here, however, I shall not be concerned with these important nuances. For my worry is that, given certain currently prevailing orthodoxies about content, it is impossible to see how *any* contentful state could be known on the basis of inner observation.

The difficulty stems from the contemporary commitment to a relationist conception of content: the view that the content properties of mental states and events are determined by, or supervenient upon, their *relational* properties. Intuitively, the difficulty seems clear: how could anyone be in a position to know his thoughts merely by observing them, if facts about their content are determined by their relational properties? Articulating the intuitive problem in explicit detail is the task of the present part.

Anti-individualism and self-knowledge 9. The commitment to relationism is evident, of course, in *wide* or *anti-individualistic* conceptions of thought content. According to such views, many of a person's thought contents are necessarily dependent on relations that that person bears to the physical or, in some cases, social environment. The view is supported by a series of now-famous thought experiments. Their strategy is to show that two individuals who are molecule-for-molecule duplicates of each other, may nevertheless think different thoughts if their environments differ from each other in certain specified ways. Thus, Putnam has argued that *part* of what makes it true that some of my thoughts involve the concept *water*, is that it is typically *in re* H_2O that I token those thoughts; a duplicate of mine, who grew up in an indistinguishably similar environment except that in it the liquid that filled the lakes and swimming pools consisted of XYZ and not H_2O, would not have the concept *water* but some other concept, *twater*. Similarly, Tyler Burge has argued that part of what makes it true that some of my thoughts involve the concept *arthritis* is that I live in, and defer to, a community in which the concept of arthritis is used in a certain way; a duplicate of mine, who grew up in an indistinguishably similar community except that in it the use of the concept was extended so as to cover all rheumatoid ailments, would not have the concept *arthritis* but some other concept, *tharthritis*.

10. Now, doesn't it follow from such anti-individualistic views that we cannot know our thoughts in a direct, purely observational manner? The following line of reasoning might seem to lead rather swiftly to that conclusion. To know my water thoughts, I would have to know that they involve the concept *water* and not the concept *twater*. But I could not know whether my thought involves the concept *water* or the concept *twater* without investigating my environment. For what I would need to know is whether it was typically *in re* H_2O or typically *in re* XYZ that I token my thoughts; and I certainly would have to investigate my environment in order to know that. I could hardly know such facts by mere introspection. It would seem to follow, therefore, that I could not know the contents of my thought purely observationally: I would have to *infer* what I think from facts about my environment.

This line of reasoning is no doubt too swift. As it stands it appears to be making problematic assumptions about the conditions required for knowledge.[9] Consider perceptual knowledge. Someone may know, by looking, that he has a dime in his hand. But it is controversial, to put it mildly, whether he needs to know all the conditions that make such knowledge possible. He need not have checked, for example, that there is no counterfeit money in the vicinity, nor does he need to be able to tell the difference between a genuine dime and every imaginable counterfeit that could have been substituted. The ordinary concept of knowledge appears to call for no more than the exclusion of 'relevant' alternative hypotheses (however exactly that is to be understood); and mere logical possibility does not confer such relevance.

Similar remarks apply to the case of self-knowledge. And so, since under normal circumstances the *twater* hypothesis is not a relevant alternative, we ought not to assume, as the swift argument evidently does, that we could not know our actual thought contents unless we are able to discriminate between them and their various twin counterparts.

11. The swift argument, however, suggests a slower and more convincing argument for the same conclusion. For it seems fairly easy to describe scenarios in which the twin hypotheses *are* relevant alternatives, but in which they are, nevertheless, not discriminable non-inferentially from their actual counterparts.

Imagine that twin-earth actually exists and that, without being aware of it, S undergoes a series of switches between earth and twin-earth. Most anti-individualists agree that, if a person were to remain in each situation long enough, that person would eventually acquire the concepts appropriate to that situation.[10] There are two ways to imagine the final outcome. On the one hand, we may imagine that after a series of such switches, S ends up with *both* earthian and twin-earthian concepts: thoughts involving both *arthritis* and *tharthritis* are available to him. Or, alternatively, we may imagine that with every such slow switch a wholesale displacement of S's resident concepts takes place, so that at any given

9. This point is made in Tyler Burge, 'Individualism and Self-Knowledge,' *Journal of Philosophy*, 85 (Nov. 1988): pp. 654–5 [in this volume pp. 472–3].
10. Burge and Davidson are explicit about this.

time either the earthian or the twin-earthian concepts are available to him, but not both.

The story is usually told, I believe, in the second of these two ways; though so far as I can tell, it is perfectly coherent—and a lot more interesting—to tell it the other way. Still, in the interests of keeping matters as simple as possible, I shall follow tradition and imagine only the second version.[11] I invite you to consider, then, a thinker S, who, quite unawares, has been shuttled back and forth between earth and twin-earth, each time staying long enough to acquire the concepts appropriate to his current situation, and at the expense of the concepts appropriate to his previous situation.

What does S know? By assumption, he is not aware that the switches have taken place and nothing about his qualitative mental life or his perceived environment tips him off. Indeed, S may not even be aware of the existence of twin-earth or of the dependence of content on environment. As far as S is concerned, he has always lived on earth. If someone were to ask him, just after one set of twin-earthian concepts has been displaced by a set of earthian ones, whether he has recently thought thoughts involving an arthritis-like concept distinct from *arthritis*, S would presumably say 'no.' And yet, of course, according to the anti-individualist story, he has. His knowledge of his own past thoughts seems very poor, but not presumably because he simply can't *remember* them. Could it be because he never knew them?

Let us in fact confront that question directly. Does S know what he is thinking while he is thinking it? Suppose he is on twin-earth and thinks a thought that he would express with the words 'I have arthritis.' Could he know what he thought? The point to bear in mind is that the hypothesis that he thought *I have arthritis* is now a relevant alternative. He, of course, is not aware of that, but that doesn't change matters. Epistemic relevance is not a subjective concept. Someone may not be aware that there is a lot of counterfeit money in his vicinity; but if there is, the hypothesis that the dime-looking object in his hand is counterfeit needs to be excluded before he can be said to know that it is a dime. Similarly, S has to be able to exclude the possibility that his thought involved the concept *arthritis* rather than the concept *tharthritis*, before he can be said to know what his thought is. But this means that he has to *reason* his way to a conclusion about his thought; and reason to it, moreover, from evidence about his external environment which, by

11. The first version of the slow switching story involves questions that admit of no easy answer. Suppose both earthian and twin-earthian thoughts are simultaneously available to you. And suppose you think a thought that you would express with the words 'I have arthritis.' How is it determined whether this particular thought token involves the concept *arthritis* or the concept *tharthritis*? (This is not a question about how you would *know* whether it involved the one or the other; it's a question about what *makes it true* that it involves the one and not the other.) There seems to be no simple answer. It certainly does not seem right to say, for reasons that underlie the intuition that quick switching wouldn't suffice for change of content, that it is simply a function of the environment in which the thought is tokened. Nor are there other obvious dimensions of difference to appeal to: *ex hypothesi*, thoughts with the different contents would have exactly the same functional roles, the same linguistic expression and the same associated qualitative episodes (if any).

assumption, he does not possess. How, then, can he know his thought at all?—much less know it directly?[12]

Individualist content and self-knowledge 12. Ever since Putnam first invented twin-earth, philosophers have expressed concern about the compatibility of wide individuation with the direct character of self-knowledge.[13] In the previous section I have tried to show that these concerns are in order, that there is indeed a problem reconciling the thesis with the intuitive facts. As I shall try now to explain, however, the problem about self-knowledge was there all along and the recent emphasis on *widely* individuated content betrays a misunderstanding: even if no external factors were involved in fixing mental content, on any currently acceptable account of the internal determinants, the difficulty about self-knowledge would still remain.

The point is that according to currently prevailing orthodoxy, even the internal (or narrow) determinants of a mental event's content are relational properties of that *event* (although they are, of course, intrinsic properties of the *thinker* in whom the events occur.)

An example of a properly non-relationist conception of content is provided by the imagistic theory of the British Empiricists. According to this theory, thinking the thought that p involves entertaining an image that represents that p. And the facts in virtue of which an image represents a particular state of affairs are said to depend exclusively on the intrinsic properties of the image. Neither tenet is considered plausible today. Thinkings are not imagings; and, in any case, the representational properties of images are not determined by their intrinsic properties.

Indeed, according to temporary conviction, there is *no* property intrinsic to a mental event—certainly no *naturalistic* intrinsic property—that could serve as the complete determinant of that event's representational content. In effect, the only idea around about what narrow properties of an event might fix its content is the suggestion that it is some subset of the event's *causal* properties. The central functionalist idea here is that the content of a mental event is determined by that event's causal role in reasoning and deliberation and, in general, in the way the event interacts with other events so as to mediate between sensory inputs and behavioral outputs. On the assumption, then, that no external factors are involved in content individuation, the facts in virtue of which a thought is a thought about *water*, as opposed to a thought about *gin*, have to do with the thought's causal properties: thoughts with causal role R are thoughts about water, whereas thoughts with causal role R′ are thoughts about gin.

---

12. It is no objection to this argument to point out that, on *this* way of telling the switching story, S cannot even frame the hypothesis he is called upon to exclude. Someone may not have the concept of counterfeit money, but if there is a lot of counterfeit money in his vicinity, then he must be able to exclude the hypothesis that the coin in his hand is counterfeit before he can be said to know that it is a dime. The fact that he cannot so much as frame the relevant hypothesis does not absolve him of this requirement. In any case, any residual worries on this score can be averted, if necessary, by telling the switching story in the alternative way outlined in the text.

13. See, for example, Andrew Woodfield's remarks in the 'Introduction' to his collection *Thought and Object* (Oxford: Clarendon Press, 1982), p. viii. See also: Anthony Brueckner, 'Brains in a Vat,' *Journal of Philosophy*, 83 (1986): pp. 148–67.

Consider now a particular episode of thinking *water is wet*. How, on the dominant functionalist picture, might I know that that is what I thought? To know that I just had a *water* thought, as opposed to a *gin* thought (which, unlike a *twater* thought counts as a relevant alternative even in the absence of special circumstances) I would have to know, it seems, that my thought has the causal role constitutive of a *water* thought, as opposed to one constitutive of a *gin* thought. But it doesn't seem possible to know a thought's causal role directly. The point derives from Hume's observation that it is not possible to ascertain an item's causal properties non-inferentially, by mere inspection of its intrinsic properties; discovering them requires observation of the item's behavior over time.

But, again, this would appear to imply that I would have to *reason* my way to a thought's content; and reason to it, moreover, from facts about its causal role that I do not necessarily possess. How, then, could I know my thoughts at all?—much less know them directly?

Knowledge of relations 13. It might be suggested that the appearance of a difficulty here is being generated by appeal to a false principle: namely, that in order to know a mental event one must know how things stand with respect to the conditions that individuate that event.[14]

The cogency of the argument would certainly be at risk if such a principle were being assumed. For it is clearly not in general true that to know whether an object x has a property P one has to know how things stand with respect to the facts on which P supervenes. For example, the roundness of this coin in my hand supervenes on a mass of facts concerning the arrangement of molecules at its boundary; but I do not need to know those facts in order to know that the coin is round.

It is fortunate for my argument, therefore, that it assumes no such principle. What it does assume is different and considerably more plausible. Namely this: That you cannot tell by mere inspection of an object that it has a given *relational* or *extrinsic* property. This principle is backed up by appeal to the following two claims, both of which strike me as uncontestable. That you cannot know that an object has a given relational property merely by knowing about its *intrinsic* properties. And that mere inspection of an object gives you at most knowledge of its intrinsic properties.

Uncontestable or not, it may yet seem that there are exceptions to the principle that an extrinsic property can never be detected by mere inspection.

Consider monetary value. Being a dime is not an intrinsic property of an object: for something to be a dime it must bear a number of complicated relations to its economic and social environment. And yet, we seem often able to tell that something is a dime purely observationally, by mere inspection of its intrinsic properties. Counterexample.

Not quite. The reason an extrinsic property seems, in this case, ascertainable by

14. See Tyler Burge, *op. cit.*, p. 651 [in this volume p. 470]. See also his 'Cartesian Error and the Objectivity of Perception,' in *Contents of Thought*, R. Grimm and D. Merrill, eds. (Tucson: University of Arizona Press, 1988).

mere inspection, is due to the fact that possession of that property is correlated with possession of an intrinsic property that is ascertainable by mere inspection. The reason that the coin's dimehood seems detectable by mere inspection derives from the fact that its having the value in question is neatly encoded in several of its purely intrinsic properties: in the phrase 'ten cents' that is inscribed on it, and in several other of its size, shape, and design characteristics.

To see clearly that it is only because of this feature that we are able to 'inspect' the coin's value properties, consider a monetary system in which *all* coins, regardless of value, share their intrinsic properties: they are all minted of precisely the same metal, are all precisely of the same shape, size, and design. As far as their intrinsic properties are concerned, nothing serves to distinguish between coins of different value. Nevertheless, the coins are not all of equal value; and, let us suppose, what determines a coin's value is the mint it was minted at: coins minted at 'five cent' mints are worth five cents, those at 'ten cent' mints, ten cents, and so on. It should be obvious that the value of *these* coins is not ascertainable by mere inspection; one would have to know something about their historical properties.

If this is right, it shows that our normal ability to 'inspect' monetary value cannot help explain our ability to know our thought contents directly. First, because the feature that helps explain our knowledge in the former case—the correlation between the coin's monetary value and possession of certain intrinsic properties—does not obtain in the latter: facts about a thought token's content are not correlated with any of that token's purely intrinsic properties.[15] And second, because even if this were not true, that would still not explain how we might know our thoughts directly. For the process by which we know the coin's value is not really inspection, it's inference: you have to deduce that the coin is worth ten cents from your knowledge of its intrinsic properties plus your knowledge of how those intrinsic properties are correlated with possession of monetary value. And our knowledge of thought is not like that.

III. Is self-knowledge a cognitive achievement?

14. Many philosophers would agree, I think, with the conclusion of the previous part: that if we had to know our thoughts on the basis of inner observation, then we couldn't know our thoughts. It has certainly become very popular to claim that an observational model of self-knowledge is mistaken. Thus Burge:

If one thinks of one's relation to the subject matter of basic self-knowledge on an analogy to one's relation to objects of empirical investigation, then the view that one's thoughts (the subject matter) are dependent for their natures on relations to the environment will make it appear that one's knowledge of one's thoughts cannot be any more direct or certain than one's knowledge of the environment. . . . This line of reasoning is deeply misconceived.[16]

---

15. This would be false if a language of thought hypothesis were true.
16. Tyler Burge, 'Individualism and Self-Knowledge,' p. 660 [in this volume p. 477].

Donald Davidson has sounded a similar theme:

I can tell by examining my skin what my private or 'narrow' condition is, but nothing I can learn in this restricted realm will tell me that I am sunburned. The difference between referring to and thinking of water and referring to and thinking of twater is like the difference between being sunburned and one's skin being in exactly the same condition through another cause. The semantic difference lies in the outside world, beyond the reach of subjective or sublunar knowledge. So the argument might run.

This analogy, between the limited view of the skin doctor and the tunnel vision of the mind's eye, is fundamentally flawed.[17]

But it is not as if, in opposing an observational model of self-knowledge, these philosophers are suggesting that knowledge of thought is inferential. The claim is, rather, that the correct way to explain the direct and authoritative character of self-knowledge is to think of it as based on nothing—at any rate, on nothing empirical.

Cognitively insubstantial judgments Ordinarily, to know some contingent proposition you need either to make some observation, or to perform some inference based on some observation. In this sense, we may say that ordinary empirical knowledge is always a *cognitive achievement* and its epistemology always *substantial.* How could a judgment about a contingent matter of fact count as knowledge and yet not be a cognitive achievement? Or, to put the question another way, how could a contingent proposition be known directly, and yet not through observation?

Consider the judgment *I am here now.* Any token of this contingent judgment would be true and justified. But, in contrast with ordinary empirical judgments, the thinker is not required to possess any evidence for his judgment; he needs only to think it. The judgment is true and justified as soon as thought. The thinker counts as knowing something thanks not to the possession of any empirical evidence on his part, but simply courtesy of the concepts involved.

Consider another example. Suppose that the Kantian thesis, that experience of the world as containing substances is a precondition for experiencing it at all, is correct. It would follow, on such a view, (and ignoring for present purposes the distinction between experiencing and knowing), that knowledge that the (experienced) world contains substances is knowledge that is cognitively insubstantial. To know the fact in question a thinker is not required to possess any particular item of empirical evidence; he needs merely to experience. The truth of, and warrant for, the belief are secured, not by evidence, but by the satisfaction of certain very general conditions on experience. The thinker counts as knowing something thanks not to the possession of any evidence on his part, but simply courtesy of those general facts.

A third example. According to some philosophers, certain self-regarding judgments are essentially self-verifying. Antecedent to the judgment that I am jealous,

17. D. Davidson, 'Knowing One's Own Mind,' *Proceedings of the American Philosophical Association* (1986): p. 453.

for example, there may be no fact of the matter about whether I am; but thinking it makes it so.[18] The judgment that I am jealous, when made, is, therefore, both true and justified. But, again, no evidence is required for the judgment. To know the fact in question, I am not required to possess any particular item of empirical evidence; I need merely to make the judgment. I count as knowing something thanks not to the possession of any evidence on my part, but simply courtesy of the self-verifying nature of the judgment involved.

These examples illustrate three different kinds of contingent judgment which one may be justified in making even in the absence of any empirical evidence. The warrant for such judgments derives from other sources: from the meanings of the concepts involved, or from the satisfaction of certain general conditions, or from the judgment-dependent character of the phenomena being judged. Whatever the source, no observation, or inference based on observational premises, is required or relevant. These judgments, when known, constitute knowledge that is based on nothing empirical. In my terms, they are not cognitive achievements and are subject, therefore, to an insubstantial epistemology.[19]

The relevance of such judgments ought to be clear. So long as knowledge of thought is construed as dependent on evidence, it seems impossible to understand how we could know our thoughts. That is what the argument of the previous two parts amounts to. If, however, self-regarding judgments could be understood along cognitively insubstantial lines—as the sorts of judgment which, for one reason or another, might be known without empirical evidence—then we might be able to explain how we know our thoughts, consistent with the admission that we do not know them on the basis of observation, or of inference based on observation. Could self-knowledge be, in this way, cognitively insubstantial?

Cognitively insubstantial self-knowledge 15. It is hard to see how it could be. Knowledge that is not a cognitive achievement would be expected to exhibit certain characteristics—characteristics that are notably absent from self-knowledge. For instance, and unlike ordinary empirical knowledge, you would not expect cognitively insubstantial knowledge to be subject to direction: how much you know about your thoughts should not depend on how much *attention* you are paying to them, if you do not know your thoughts on the basis of evidence. And yet it does seem that, within bounds anyway, self-knowledge can be directed: one can decide

18. Jealousy is being used here merely for illustrative purposes. For reasons that are touched upon briefly below (see note 23), I actually rather doubt that judgments about jealousy are self-verifying in the sense bruited in the text.

19. Wittgenstein remarked, famously, that:
> It cannot be said of me at all (except perhaps as a joke) that *I know* I am in pain. What is it supposed to mean—except perhaps that I *am* in pain? (PI 246)

The remark has struck most philosophers as extremely implausible. A truth it may harbor, however, is that if (as seems right) it is constitutive of being in pain that one know that one is, then knowing that one is cannot count as a cognitive achievement: one doesn't count as being in pain unless one knows it. As against Wittgenstein, I am not sure that this point is best captured by denying that judgments about pain constitute 'knowledge'.

how much attention to direct to one's thoughts or images, just as one can decide how much attention to pay to objects in one's visual field.[20]

Or consider the fact that some adults are better than others at reporting on their inner states; and that most adults are better than children. How is this to be explained if self-knowledge is not to be thought of as an information-sensitive capacity that may be subject to cultivation or neglect?

The most important consideration, however, against an insubstantial construal of self-knowledge derives not so much from these observations but from a claim they presuppose: namely, that self-knowledge is both fallible and incomplete. In both the domain of the mental and that of the physical, events may occur of which one remains ignorant; and, in both domains, even when one becomes aware of an event's existence, one may yet misconstrue its character, believing it to have a property it does not in fact possess. How is this to be explained? I know of no convincing alternative to the following style of explanation: the difference between getting it right and failing to do so (either through ignorance or through error) is the difference between being in an epistemically favorable position with respect to the subject matter in question—being in a position to garner the relevant evidence—and not. To put this point another way, it is only if we understand self-knowledge to be a cognitive achievement that we have any prospect of explaining its admitted shortcomings.

There is an irony in this, if it's true. Since Descartes, self-knowledge has been thought to present special philosophical problems precisely because it was held to be immune to cognitive deficit. The assumption was that we knew—or anyway had some idea—how to explain *imperfect* cognitive mechanisms; what seemed to elude explanation was a cognitive faculty that never erred. This line of thought seems to be exactly backwards. If Descartes' hyperbolic claims were right—if self-knowledge really were immune to error and ignorance—the temptation to explain it in an epistemologically deflationary way would be overwhelming. As it is, however, the Cartesian claims are incorrect and the epistemology of self-knowledge, thereby, substantial.

16. Strange to discover, then, that deflationary accounts of self-knowledge appear to be gaining widespread acceptance.[21] I have already mentioned some general reasons for being suspicious of such accounts. In the remainder of this paper I propose to look at Burge's provocative proposal in detail, outlining the specific ways in which, as I see it, it fails as an account of self-knowledge.

---

20. This observation is made in D. H. Mellor. 'Conscious Belief,' *Proceedings of the Aristotelian Society* (1978).

21. See Tyler Burge, 'Individualism and Self-Knowledge'; Donald Davidson, 'Knowing One's Own Mind'; and John Heil, 'Privileged Access' in *Mind* 97 (1988): 238–51.

An interesting proposal, that seems to me to fall somewhere in between a substantial and an insubstantial conception as defined here, is outlined by Crispin Wright in his 'Wittgenstein's Rule-Following Considerations and the Central Project of Theoretical Linguistics,' in *Reflections on Chomsky*, A. George, ed. (Oxford: Blackwell, 1989), pp. 233–64. The proposal deserves extensive separate treatment. For a brief discussion see my 'The Rule-Following Considerations' in *Mind* 98 (1989), pp. 507–49.

Burge: self-knowledge and self-verification 17. According to Burge, it is a fundamental error to think that self-knowledge is a species of cognitive achievement. As he puts it, it is a mistake to think that, in order to know a thought, one must know a lot about it. Rather,

[t]he source of our strong epistemic right, our justification, in our basic self-knowledge is not that we know a lot about each thought we have... It is that we are in the position of thinking those thoughts in the second-order, self-verifying way.[22]

How is this to be understood?

Consider the following judgment about what I am thinking:

I judge: I am thinking that writing requires concentration.

In such a judgment, Burge points out, the subject matter of the judgment is not merely contingently related to the thoughts one thinks about it. The judgment is self-referential and self-verifying. The second-order judgment to the effect that I'm thinking that writing requires concentration could not exist unless I were to think, through that very thought, that writing requires concentration. The thought I am making a judgment about is self-referentially fixed by the judgment itself; and the judgment is thereby self-verifying. At least in this sort of case, then, it appears that one need know nothing about a thought in order to know that one has thought it; one need only think the thought as part of a second-order thought that asserts its occurrence. Since such thoughts are, as Burge correctly points out, logically self-verifying, they are guaranteed to be true as soon as thought. Hence, they would appear to constitute authoritative and non-inferential knowledge of thought, the relational character of the properties that determine thought content notwithstanding.

Burge calls this sort of self-verifying, self-regarding judgment *basic self-knowledge*. Let us start with the following question: how much of direct self-knowledge is basic self-knowledge? How well does Burge's paradigm explain the general phenomenon?

18. We may begin by noting that it does not at all explain our knowledge of our *standing* mental states. Judgments concerning such states, for example,

I judge: I *believe* that writing requires concentration

or

I judge: I *desire* that writing require concentration

are not self-verifying. I need not actually believe that writing requires concentration in order to think the first thought, nor actually desire that it require concentration to think the second. These self-regarding judgments do not conform to Burge's paradigm. This would appear to be a serious problem. After all, we do know about our beliefs and desires in a direct and authoritative manner, and Burge's proposal seems not to have the resources to explain how.

How does his proposal fare in connection with *occurrent* events? In this domain, too, its applicability seems rather limited. Self-regarding judgments about what I

22. Burge, *op. cit.*, p. 660 [in this volume p. 477].

occurrently desire or fear, for example, are manifestly not self-verifying, in that I need not actually desire or fear any particular thing in order to judge that I do. Thus, it may be that

I judge: I fear that writing requires concentration

without actually fearing that it does. The judgment is not self-verifying.

The best possible case for Burge's purposes will involve a self-regarding judgment about a mere thinking or entertaining of a proposition—a judgment of the form

I judge: I think that writing requires concentration.

And even here, the judgment will only prove self-verifying if the time at which the judgment is made is *absolutely coincident* with the time at which the thought being judged about is thought. In other words, the second-order judgment will be self-verifying only if it literally incorporates the very thought about which it is a judgment. It is only under this very special condition that the thinking of the proposition in question is presupposed by the very act of making a judgment about it; and, hence, only under this very special condition that the judgment is self-verifying.[23] If, for example, the judgment concerned an act of entertaining a proposition that preceded the act of making judgment by even the smallest interval of time, as in

I judge: I just now thought that writing requires concentration

then, since it need not be true that I had that thought *then* in order to make this judgment *now*, such a judgment would not be self-verifying and, hence, would constitute a species of self-knowledge that is not subject to Burge's deflationary paradigm.

But is it not precisely knowledge of this form—knowledge of what one has thought immediately after one has thought it—that we think of as central to our capacity for self-knowledge? We are struck by our ability to know, non-inferentially and authoritatively, that a certain mental event has occurred, immediately on its having occurred. We think: Writing requires concentration. And then we know, directly and unproblematically, that that is what we thought. A first-order thought occurs. And we are then able, without the benefit of inference, to form a correct judgment about what thought that was. The second-order judgment in these central cases is not self-verifying. Such cases are not instances of 'basic self-knowledge' in Burge's sense. How does his proposal help explain how they are possible? The fact that, *had* the thought been part of a second-order judgment, then that judgment would have been self-verifying, does not help explain how we are able to know what thought it was, given that it *wasn't* part of

---

23. This explains why second-order judgments about sudden wants or momentary frights cannot be self-verifying: these events are not mental performatives in the required sense. They cannot be brought about by the mere thinking of a second-order judgment; hence, they cannot be incorporated into a second-order judgment in the way required for self-verification.

such a judgment. First-order thoughts that are not part of second-order thoughts are directly knowable. Arguably, acts of knowing such thoughts are paradigm case's of self-knowledge. And Burge's proposal seems incapable of explaining how they are possible.

19. Still, even if Burge's proposal does not explain the central cases, does it not supply us with at least *one* case in which a thought is known directly despite the relational nature of its individuation conditions? And isn't that enough to dislodge our intuition that relationism is irreconcilable with directness?

If Burge's self-verifying judgments were instances of genuine knowledge, then they would indeed dislodge the problematic intuition. But I am not convinced that they are.

Consider again the case of the person who undergoes a series of slow switches between earth and twin-earth. Burge observes:

In the former situation, the person may think 'I am thinking that water is a liquid.' In the latter situation, the person may think 'I am thinking that twater is a liquid.' In both cases the person is right and as fully justified as ever. The fact that the person does not know that a switch has occurred is irrelevant to the truth and justified character of these judgments. Of course, the person may learn about the switches and ask 'Was I thinking yesterday about water or twater?'—and yet not know the answer. Here knowing the answer may sometimes depend on knowing empirical background conditions. But such sophisticated questions about memory require a more complex story.[24]

These remarks strike me as puzzling. They amount to saying that, although S will not know tomorrow what he is thinking right now, he does know right now what he is thinking right now. For any given moment in the present, say t1, S is in a position to think a self-verifying judgment about what he is thinking at t1. By Burge's criteria, therefore, he counts as having direct and authoritative knowledge at t1 of what he is thinking at that time. But it is quite clear that tomorrow he won't know what he thought at t1. No self-verifying judgment concerning his thought at t1 will be available to him then. Nor, it is perfectly clear, can he know by any other non-inferential means. To know what he thought at t1 he must discover what environment he was in at that time and how long he had been there. But there is a mystery here. For the following would appear to be a platitude about memory and knowledge: if S knows that p at t1, and if at (some later time) t2, S remembers everything S knew at t1, then S knows that p at t2. Now, let us ask: *why* does S not know today whether yesterday's thought was a *water* thought or a *twater* thought? The platitude insists that there are only two possible explanations: either S has forgotten or he *never* knew. But surely memory failure is not to the point. In discussing the epistemology of relationally individuated content, we ought to be able to exclude memory failure by stipulation. It is not as if thoughts with widely individuated contents might be easily known but difficult to remember. The only explanation, I venture to suggest, for why S will not know tomorrow what he is said to know today, is not that he has forgotten but that he never knew. Burge's

---

24. *op. cit.*, p. 659 [in this volume p. 476].

self-verifying judgments do not constitute genuine knowledge. What other reason is there for why our slowly transported thinker will not know tomorrow what he is said to know directly and authoritatively today?[25]

In sum, Burge's self-verifying judgments seem to me neither to explain the central cases, nor to provide particularly compelling examples of special cases in which a relationally individuated thought is known non-inferentially.

Conclusion 20. In this paper, I have attempted to map out the available theoretical options concerning self-knowledge. And I have argued that none of the options work. It seems to me that we have a serious problem explaining our ability to know our thoughts, a problem that has perhaps not been sufficiently appreciated. As I said in the introduction, however, the point of the exercise is not to promote skepticism, but understanding. I am confident that one of the options will work; but I think we need to think a lot harder before we are in a position to say which one.[26]

25. Obviously, this barely scratches the surface of the various issues that crop up here. A proper discussion would include, among other things, an account of what Burge's self-verifying judgments *do* constitute, if not a species of knowledge. Limitations of space prevent me from taking matters further in this paper.

26. For valuable comments on an earlier draft, or for helpful discussion of the issues, I am very grateful to David Velleman, Stephen Yablo, Barry Loewer, Jerry Fodor, Jennifer Church, and Crispin Wright.

Chapter 34

Externalism and the attitudinal component of self-knowledge

Sven Bernecker

EXTERNALISM about mental content is the view that the contents of many of our thoughts are determined at least in part by conditions which do not supervene on our nervous system. Many philosophers have thought that externalism undermines the natural and intuitively compelling idea that we possess authoritative and privileged knowledge of our thought contents. Since mental content is determined by affairs outside the brain, it seems that we must first acquire knowledge of the relevant environmental features to then be able to know the contents of our thoughts. If this reasoning is correct, externalism becomes dubious, since it is difficult to deny the intuition that we frequently have authoritative first person knowledge of thought content. Typically, our thought contents are capable of being known by us antecedently to our acquiring knowledge of the existence of any particular external object, and apart from special cases, we possess authority about our own mental states.

A number of externalists have tried to accommodate privileged self-knowledge and to neutralize scepticism about one's ability to authoritatively know one's own mind. The leading externalist theory of self-knowledge has been first worked out by T. Burge in 'Individualism and Self-Knowledge' and by J. Heil in 'Privileged Access.' Because Burge's presentation of the compatibilist argument is more detailed than Heil's, I will concentrate on his paper and refer to this compatibilist line as 'Burgean compatibilism'. Burgean compatibilism is not only the most promising but also the most widely accepted externalist theory of privileged self-knowledge. Among its advocates are A. Brueckner (1992), D. Davidson (1988, 1991), E. LePore & B. Loewer (1986), H. W. Noonan (1993), S. Shoemaker (1994), R. Stalnaker (1990), and C. Wright (1991).

In this paper I want to present a new incompatibilist challenge to Burgean compatibilism. I show that, though compatibilism explains knowing it is P I believe, it doesn't explain how I can have privileged knowledge that the state I occupy is a state of believing rather than, say, a state of doubting, or a state of expecting etc. But if I don't authoritatively know *that*, I cannot be said to possess privileged self-knowledge, for self-knowledge consists in the identification of the attitude as well as the content. Moreover, given externalism, self-knowledge of attitudinal component is vulnerable to a certain kind of error and so doesn't have the same kind of

Sven Bernecker, 'Externalism and the Attitudinal Component of Self-Knowledge' in *Noûs* 30 (1996), pp. 262–75 reprinted by permission of Blackwell Publications Inc.

privilege as self-knowledge of current content. The suggestion is that empirical investigation might be needed to know the attitudinal component of one's occurrent thought, because of external determination of the concept whereby this component is identified. I argue that Burgean compatibilism cannot be extended to provide a solution to this new incompatibilist challenge, and that there is no indication that there is some other externalist account to be had of the privilege of self-knowledge of attitudinal components. Thus, externalism is not consistent with the thesis that we possess privileged self-knowledge about the mode in which a thought content is realized.

1. Burgean compatibilism

Burge restricts his discussion of self-knowledge to so-called 'cogito-like judgments' or 'Cartesian thoughts'. These are judgments about one's conscious and occurrent first-order intentional states referring to physical objects. Examples of such judgments are 'I think (with this very thought) that writing requires concentration' and 'I judge, herewith, that there are physical entities'. The special authority of self-knowledge, he thinks, consists in its not being founded on inferences from sensory experiences or any other cognitive factors such as memory and background knowledge. My knowing the states of my mind doesn't depend on any additional information I have about myself or my environment. That self-knowledge is epistemically direct is to say it is contextually self-verifying: A Cartesian thought is made true by the mere thinking of it and is therefore immune to brute error.[1] Burge relies on nothing but the most general externalist view, notwithstanding the different kinds of externalism such as social externalism (Burge), causal-essentialist externalism (Putnam), and causal-informational externalism (Dretske). The compatibilist argument consists of three steps.

(1) The ability to think empirical thoughts depends on the obtaining of certain conditions some of which concern physical or social affairs. For my utterance 'water is wet' to express the proposition that water is wet, I (or others in my community) need to have been in causal contact with water (causal-essentialist externalism) or the experts in my community have to define 'water' as H_2O (social externalism). If none of the external enabling conditions are fulfilled because, say, I live and grew up on Putnam's Twin Earth, I could not think that water is wet. In order to *know* a proposition such as that water is wet I need to know that the external conditions obtain and to discover that I must investigate my empirical environment. However, I don't need to know that these external conditions obtain to be able to think the thought in question.

(2) Having privileged self-knowledge about a particular thought presupposes the ability to think that thought. I could not know or, for that matter, believe that I am thinking that water is wet if I lacked the capacity to think the thought that water

---

1. For Burge's views regarding the epistemic privilege of self-knowledge see Burge 1988, 1993, and 1996.

is wet. And I would in fact lack the ability to think this thought if certain external conditions had not obtained. Thus, the conditions for *knowing* my thought content are partly the same as the conditions for *thinking* the thought. The conditions for thinking a certain thought are also required for knowing (or believing) that one is thinking this thought.

(3) Not only can I think a thought without knowing that its external conditions obtain, I can also have knowledge of my thought content without knowing that the content-determining external conditions for thinking the thought obtain. Self-knowledge doesn't require the investigation of one's environment, because the content of the first-order thought is automatically contained in the content of the second-order thought and the contents of both thoughts are determined by the same causal relations of which one may be ignorant. Consider the first-order thought 'water is wet' and the self-referential thought 'I believe that water is wet'. The content of the that-clause (in the latter thought) is inherited from the first-order thought since the intentional content mentioned in the that-clause is not merely an object of reference or cognition; it is part of the higher-order cognition itself. Since the that-clause of Cartesian thoughts can never be gotten wrong, it follows that cogito-like judgments are contextually self-verifying or infallible. Cogito-like judgments are non-empirical and invulnerable to brute error.

In conclusion, knowledge of a Cartesian thought doesn't require knowledge of relational facts although it is those facts that determine the content of the thought contained in the Cartesian thought. To know that I am thinking that water is wet, I don't need to first acquire knowledge of either how experts in my community use 'water' (social externalism) or of the kind of substance I was in contact with when I learned 'water' (causal-essentialist externalism). The fact that I am able to think the thought that water is wet shows that the relevant external conditions are fulfilled. And since the ability to think this thought is a necessary condition for knowing that I am thinking this thought, my being able to know 'I am thinking that water is wet' shows that the external conditions do in fact obtain. Burge's crucial insight is that, in the case of Cartesian thoughts, the content of the first-order thought is automatically included or contained in the content of the second-order thought. For this reason I also refer to Burgean compatibilism as the 'inclusion theory of self-knowledge'.

2. Content and attitude

Earlier incompatibilist challenges to Burgean compatibilism focused on its commitment to epistemological reliabilism. Reliabilism claims that in order to have knowledge a believer need only, as a matter of fact, stand in some appropriate (probably causal) relation to facts. He need not know or (on some versions of the view even) believe that he does. Similarly, for a subject to have self-knowledge, he doesn't, in addition to having non-accidentally true beliefs about his first-order states, need to be able to justify these self-referential beliefs. Without the assumption of epistemological reliabilism, Burge's reasoning might explain why Cartesian thoughts are necessarily true; but it would fall short of accounting for self-*knowledge*.[2] I propose to set aside this debate and introduce a different line of criticism.

It is common practice to differentiate between the *content* and the *attitude* (character or force) of a thought. The propositional content of 'I believe that water is wet' is expressed by 'water is wet'. The attitude that is taken towards this content is that of believing. Other examples of attitudes are affirming, denying, wanting, fearing etc. Mental states represent the union of an attitude and a content. This conception of what is involved in the formation of mental states is popular at least since Descartes (1955, Vol. I, p. 159). Since mental states have an intentional as well as an attitudinal component, one can only be said to know one's state if one knows both what one takes to be its content and its attitude. Knowing that one believes that water is wet involves knowing that the first-order state is about what one expresses by 'water is wet' as well as knowing that the content is framed in the attitude of believing. Hence, self-knowledge consists in a *twofold* classification. Knowing that one is in mental state P means knowing that P includes a certain kind of attitude, H, and content, Q. Only when one recognizes P's H'hood and its Q'hood does one possess self-knowledge about P.

One can obviously regret something without having the concept 'to regret' and expect something without possessing the concept 'to expect'.[3] The same is true, I take it, for all kinds of propositional attitudes. However, knowing (or believing) that one regrets P requires having available the concept of regret. Knowing my first-order mental states therefore depends on me possessing the concepts of the attitudes the states are framed in. Possessing a concept is different from being able to define it. Self-knowledge certainly doesn't presuppose that one can enumerate all the necessary application conditions of the cognitive verbs one uses to refer to one's attitude types. However, the possession of attitude concepts involves some kind of 'cognitive achievement'. The concept 'to believe' illustrates this.

When I judge 'I believe that water is wet' I assert something about the propositional content of my belief, not about the veridicality of (what I take to be) the belief. I claim something about how things appear to me, not about how things are. The truth-maker of 'water is wet' is the world, the truth-maker of 'I believe that water is wet' is me. The epistemic difference between first- and second-order judgments has to do with the concept 'to believe'. The belief concept entails the distinction between reality and appearance. I can only know about my beliefs if I am, in principle, able to distinguish how things appear from how they are. Not having available this distinction means not being able to acquire self-knowledge about beliefs *as beliefs*. Children before the age of three are said to lack the concept of

---

2. Among those critical of reliabilism regarding introspective knowledge are Boghossian 1989; Brueckner 1990; Ludlow 1995.

3. For a differing opinion see Davidson 1985. He argues that in order to have a belief, it is necessary to have the concept of belief. Limitations of space prevent me from discussing this thesis.

belief since they take their thoughts as directly and correctly mirroring the world.[4] If this is so, they are unable to possess introspective knowledge of their beliefs as beliefs.

By not mentioning attitude concepts and the role they play for self-knowledge, the Burgean compatibilist conceals that the inclusion of content crucially depends on having available attitude concepts. Burge writes: 'One knows one's thought to be what it is simply by thinking it while exercising second-order, self-ascriptive powers' (1988, p. 656). To complete the inclusion theory he would have to mention that in addition to exercising self-ascriptive powers, one needs to have available various attitude concepts. Now, Burge could acknowledge this point and still hold on to his original formulation. For he restricts his compatibilist argument to pure cogito-like judgments which don't refer to any particular types of propositional attitudes such as belief and desire. In the remainder of the paper I will therefore focus on advocates of Burgean compatibilism who apply the inclusion theory also to standing states, such as beliefs.[5]

3. Privileged knowledge about one's modes of thinking

Self-knowledge doesn't only presuppose having available attitude concepts but also being able to identify one's attitudes. Burgean compatibilism demonstrates convincingly that higher-order beliefs about occurrent thought contents are formed in a truth-reliable way, but it has nothing to say on the issue of privileged access to the attitudinal components of one's thoughts. The reason is that a state's attitude isn't part of its content and it is only the content that is automatically included in the self-referential cognition. The question therefore arises whether and how externalism can explain privileged self-knowledge about the modes of one's thinking.

Self-knowledge is different from knowing the content of one's mental state and knowing that the state must have some attitude or other. Assuming that the transparency of the mind is not merely an otiose and decadent luxury, a device for self-absorbed wallowing, but that it has evolutionary value, knowledge of contents independent of attitudes is of no interest. If I know that I am in an intentional state with the content 'hungry bear to my left' but I don't know whether I believe this or doubt it, introspection doesn't enable me to control my behavior more effectively

4. Gopnik argues that children lack a representational model of the mind. Three-year-olds 'think of belief [. . .] as a matter of direct relation between the mind and objects in the world, not a relation mediated by representations or propositions. They think we simply believe X, tout court, just as, even in the adult view, we may simply see or want x, tout court, rather than seeing, wanting, or believing *that x*' (Gopnik 1993, p. 6; Perner 1991, pp. 82 and 189). Unfortunately, it is not entirely clear whether the young child exercises an erroneous conception of belief or whether it lacks the concept of belief altogether.

5. Cf. Falvey & Owens 1994, p. 118; Shoemaker 1994, p. 260 n; Wright 1991, p. 141 n.

than if I didn't have introspective capacities. What is true of regular introspective knowledge seems to carry over to privileged self-knowledge. If privileged access serves any evolutionary purpose it probably does so only if it also warrants authoritative knowledge of attitudes. Thus, should it turn out that, given externalism, self-knowledge of attitudinal components requires empirical investigation, Burgean compatibilism will lose much of its appeal. For although Burge is only committed to the compatibility of externalism with privileged knowledge of first-order *content* (and explicitly disavows the goal of giving a complete account of self-knowledge in all its varieties) most compatibilists, since unaware of the issue of attitude-identification, presume that the inclusion theory solves all compatibilist problems.

Consider a thought experiment that illustrates the logical independence of content-identification from attitude-identification. Imagine a thermometer connected to a tank filled with gasoline. The thermometer supplies information about the tank by representing the gasoline's temperature. Given causal-informational externalism, the thermometer's state *means* that the temperature of the gasoline is, say, 30° C.[6] On this view, meaning is reliable causal covariance. Something has content by virtue of being a reliable indicator of some state of the environment. Let's assume that the thermometer is such a reliable indicator. The position of the mercury thus means or signifies that the gasoline's temperature is 30° C. The thermometer expresses content but it doesn't *believe* that the temperature inside the tank is 30° C since thermometers don't have minds. Now, thermometers obviously cannot look inside or reflect on their representational states. However, one can imagine two representational devices, one containing information about the other. Suppose there is a sensor attached to the thermometer. If and only if the temperature is 30° C, the sensor is activated which sets off an alarm. Provided the system works properly, the state the alarm is in (on or off) carries information about the mercury's state (30° C or not 30° C). The alarm's state contains content about the thermometer's state which represents the temperature inside the tank. This is a case of second-order representation or content inclusion.[7] What this example shows is that content inclusion is not a sufficient condition for self-knowledge. Representational systems lacking propositional attitudes are nevertheless able to have reflexive content. The Burgean explanation of privileged self-knowledge by way of content being included in other content thus falls short of being a complete account of privileged self-knowledge of occurrent thought. For on the basis of this theory genuine self-knowledge cannot be distinguished from content inclusion in systems incapable of having attitudes. Instances of content inclusion

6. Cf. Dretske 1981, Ch. 3; Fodor 1990, Ch. 3 and 4. My example is modeled after a more developed thought experiment in Dretske 1994.
7. I bracket the following problem: From a representationalist point of view, introspective knowledge is not just a second-order representation of a first-order representation, but a representation of it *as a representation* (Dretske 1995, p. 61). The alarm's state represents the mercury's position, but it doesn't represent it as a representation of the gasoline's temperature.

only qualify as self-knowledge if the representational system has propositional attitudes.[8]

Given the logical independence of content- and attitude-identification, it is not surprising that there are cases where one is right about one's content but misconstrues one's attitudes or vice versa. Imagine you are waiting in the lobby of a cinema. The film has already started but your friend has not yet arrived. Your friend is normally on time. You think that you are *believing* that you have a rendezvous at this cinema. After ten minutes your belief dissolves into mere *hope* and while, for some time, you still think and sincerely say that you believe it, you are wrong about yourself. So as not to have to admit having made a mistake you deceive yourself by unconsciously misconstruing the attitude of your first-order thought. Another common source of misidentification of attitude types, besides self-deception, is lack of attention (cf. Wilson 1985). Moreover, there is a third source of error: One can misrepresent one's attitudes, because one possesses incomplete understanding of the concepts used to describe one's mental condition. It is this kind of error I will concentrate on, for it bears on externalism. In the remainder of the paper I will explore the relation between externalism and privileged self-knowledge of the modality of thought. Since limitations of space prevent me from considering this question for all kinds of externalism, I will focus on social externalism.

In a nutshell, social externalism claims that the contents of an individual mind are partly constituted by facts about the social environment. More precisely, concepts are constituted by their usage by the society and its experts. This is even the case if an individual is ignorant about how society uses a term. Bert is such an ignorant individual (Burge 1979). Bert thinks that arthritis is a disease that can strike the thigh as well as the joints. Burge insists that Bert's concept of arthritis is the same as the doctor's and specialist's. So, when Bert thinks or utters things about arthritis such as 'arthritis is painful' he is thinking or talking about the same thing as the doctor when he utters the same sentence. Society's use of a term partly determines the concepts of individuals in the society, even of such medically ignorant individuals as Bert.

Burge asserts that the application of the arthritis-example is very wide. Instead of 'arthritis', he writes, 'we could have used an artifact term, an ordinary natural kind word, a color adjective, a social role term, a term for a historical style, an abstract noun, an action verb, a physical movement verb, or any of various other sorts of words' (Burge 1979, p. 79). All that is required to get an arthritis-like example under way is that 'it is intuitively possible to attribute a mental state or event whose content involves a notion that the subject incompletely understands' (ibid.). Partial understanding in the required sense is common with respect to 'brisket', 'contract',

---

8. Reading 'Individualism and the Mental' one might come to attribute the following position to Burge: Information bearing states are differentiated from propositional states. The nature of propositional states is dependent on a language community, wherefore only humans qualify as bearers of meaning. Thermometers don't participate in communities and thus don't contain propositional states. In conversation, however, Burge maintained that meaning and content are not *necessarily* social phenomena. Given this view, Burge might have no problems attributing content to a thermometer.

'recession', 'sonata', 'deer', 'elm', 'pre-amplifier', 'carburetor', 'gothic', 'fermentation' (Burge 1979, p. 84) to only mention a few. The advantage of Burge's social externalism over other forms of externalism, such as Putnam's, is precisely that it isn't restricted to natural kind words but is applicable to most word classes. Apart from some sensation words and certain logical constants, social externalism is said to cover all words.

Nothing of what Burge has written conflicts with the idea that attitude concepts such as 'to believe', 'to doubt', 'to expect', etc. are partly determined by facts about how society uses these concepts. But if what is true of arthritis also applies to attitude concepts, one can imagine an arthritis-like example involving cognitive verbs. Suppose Bert has a brother, Oscar. While Bert is confused about 'arthritis', Oscar deviates from the language community with respect to 'to believe'. Oscar has an unusually coarse-grained concept of belief. It is in fact so general that he takes 'to believe', 'to suppose', 'to decide', and 'to consider' to be synonymous terms. In Oscar's language community, however, 'to believe' means the mental act of placing trust or confidence in a person or thing, 'to suppose' means to assume something without reference to its being true or false, 'to consider' means to believe after deliberation, and 'to decide' means to pronounce a judgment. Now, despite Oscar's confusion, social externalism seem committed to saying that the meaning of his concept 'belief' doesn't differ from what his language community means by it.

One day Oscar entertains the self-referential thought that he expresses by 'I am believing that arthritis is painful'. Given the inclusion theory, Oscar knows what his first-order thought is about, i.e. he knows its propositional content. However, let's suppose that, contrary to Oscar's contention, he doesn't *believe* but *supposes* that arthritis is painful. In other words, the mental condition Oscar describes as 'believing' other members of his language community would refer to as 'supposing'. Hence, Oscar's judgment 'I am believing that arthritis is painful' is (partly) false. Given his odd idiolect, Oscar is unable to realize this mistake simply by reflection. The reason is that he is unable to discriminate among believing, supposing, deciding, and considering. Even if he were told that his self-attribution is false, Oscar wouldn't be in a position to correct it just on the basis of information available to introspection. For all he knows the mental state he occupies could be an instance of supposing, deciding, or considering. To know that he *believes P*, Oscar would have to know that the mental state he is in has the kind of features that are constitutive of 'belief', as his fellow language users employ the term. But he cannot know *that*, without investigating his social environment. It follows that Oscar is unable to authoritatively know the attitudinal component of his thought. And since attitude-identification is a necessary aspect of self-knowledge, Oscar is unable to possess privileged self-knowledge about his mental condition.

This is the central argument. Let me explain the force of the argument in greater detail before I consider possible objections.

The Oscar-example shows that, through incomplete understanding, one can be vulnerable to error in judgments about one's attitudes. Now, the mere possibility of error doesn't necessarily undermine privileged self-knowledge. The reason is that very few compatibilists assert that self-knowledge is strictly infallible. Burge (and many others) claim that cogito-like judgments are only immune to *brute* error. He writes: 'Brute errors do not result from any sort of carelessness, malfunction, or irrationality on our part' (1988, p. 657). On this rather loose definition of what it means to be a brute mistake, Oscar's error could be considered both brute and unimportant. If he doesn't make the mistake all the time, it looks more like a defect of his cognitive system and doesn't qualify as a brute error. If, however, he *consistently* misidentified propositional attitudes, one could argue that it is in fact a brute mistake and that he lacks privileged access to this aspect of his mental life. However, the force of Oscar-like examples doesn't depend on the mistake being brute.

One might think that Oscar lacks privileged self-knowledge regarding his modes of thinking because his mistaken self-attribution is unremediable by introspection. The idea is that if by monitoring his mental condition, Oscar cannot discover that he doesn't *believe* but instead *supposes* that arthritis is painful, then his introspective knowledge of attitudes cannot be authoritative. This however doesn't necessarily follow.[9] Just because Oscar has to engage in empirical investigations to discover possible mistakes, doesn't mean that he lacks non-empirical (i.e. privileged)[10] self-knowledge. The possibility of introspectively unspottable errors, by itself, would only undermine non-empirical knowledge, if one proceeded on the following assumption taken from epistemological internalism: Non-empirical knowledge that P requires knowing non-empirically that one is justified in believing P. On this view, Oscar cannot have non-empirical knowledge of his attitudes. Even if he (for whatever reasons) correctly identified his mental mode as a belief, to know that it is a belief, he would have to know non-empirically that he is justified in thinking that it is a belief state he occupies; but he cannot know *that*, without engaging in social studies. The internalist reading of the Oscar-example can be dismissed since the inclusion theory of self-knowledge can only get off the ground if one assumes reliabilism. As was explained above, reliabilism is the idea that knowing P doesn't require knowing (or believing) that one knows P. Given reliabilism, it is unproblematic to assume that non-empirical self-knowledge is vulnerable to error discoverable only empirically.

The reason Oscar lacks privileged self-knowledge of his attitudes is that he cannot even distinguish among different attitudes. When he thinks 'I am believing that arthritis is painful', for all he knows he could suppose, decide, or consider that P. If he actually *believes* that arthritis is painful, his self-referential judgment comes out true, but it doesn't thereby qualify as knowledge—not even on a reliabilist conception of knowledge. For reliabilism maintains that what distinguishes knowledge from accidentally true belief is that the former results from a reliable belief-formation process. One doesn't need to have reasons for supposing that a belief is reliably produced, but it must be produced reliably to qualify as a piece of

9. I owe this point to Tyler Burge.
10. I take non-empirical self-knowledge to be a minimal notion of privileged access. What I call non-empirical knowledge, McKinsey (1991, p. 9) calls 'a priori knowledge.' Alston (1971) provides a good exposition of the spectrum of views on the epistemic status of self-knowledge. Different versions of the privileged access thesis are infallibility, omniscience, indubitability, incorrigibility, and self-warrant.

knowledge. But Oscar certainly isn't a reliable indicator of the kind of attitude he occupies. When his self-referential judgment 'I believe that arthritis is painful' is true, it is accidentally so. There is no mechanism that correlates (certain) changes in his attitudes with changes in his self-referential judgments. Oscar doesn't 'track the facts'. Another way of making this point is to say that Oscar cannot eliminate even relevant alternatives to what he claims to know, viz. that he *supposes P*. Thus, not even on an externalist conception of knowledge can Oscar be said to possess privileged self-knowledge about (some of) his attitudes.

Of course, Oscar is a rather special case. Just because *he* lacks privileged self-knowledge of attitudes if he cannot, on the basis of introspection, neutralize the hypothesis that he misrepresents his state of supposing as a belief state doesn't mean that *all of us*, in order to have privileged self-knowledge of our attitudes, need to be capable of discriminating, via introspection, states of believing from states of supposing. What is a relevant alternative for Oscar isn't therefore also a relevant alternative in the case of anybody else. Burgean compatibilists can therefore assert that in normal cases, where knowledge isn't defeated by unusual factors, self-knowledge of attitudinal components might *in some sense* be privileged. Whatever the account of the epistemic specialness of introspective knowledge of attitude might be, it has to differ from Burgean compatibilism. In the following section I will argue that there is no indication of there being any externalist account of the privilege of self-knowledge of attitudinal components.

4. Possible responses

How might advocates of Burgean compatibilism react to the suggestion that their position is unable to account for privileged self-knowledge of the attitudinal component of a first-order state? There seem to be two possible responses, none of which, however, is convincing.

(1) The Burgean compatibilist can try to mitigate the force of the sceptical argument by distinguishing between simple and complex attitudes. The idea is that, given externalism, I don't have privileged access to the *particular* type of attitude I am in, but I do know authoritatively that it is *some kind* of attitude. I am able to know that the state I occupy is some form of thinking, where 'thinking' is used as a cluster concept of attitude types. This is, for example, how Descartes used 'to think' in the famous cogito ergo sum argument. For Descartes 'cogitatio' or 'pensee' is any sort of conscious state or activity whatsoever; it can as well be a sensation or an act of will, a judgment or belief or intellectual questioning (Williams 1978, pp. 78/9). The role that thinking plays according to Descartes, Price attributes to 'entertaining'. Price describes the attitude of entertaining in this way:

The entertaining of propositions is the most familiar of all intellectual phenomena. It enters into every form of thinking and into many of our conative and emotional attitudes as well. Indeed, one might be inclined to say that it is the basic intellectual phenomenon; so fundamental that it admits of no explanation or analysis, but on the contrary all other forms of thinking have to be explained in terms of it (Price 1969, p. 192).

According to Chisholm (1981, p. 29) 'to consider' is the ur-attitude that underlies all others—the determinable of which complex attitudes are determinates. Descartes' thinking, Price's entertaining, and Chisholm's considering are attempts to get at the basis of attitudes, namely intentionality. The ur-attitude is pure directedness. Complex attitudes also involve concepts or dispositions. 'To expect', for example, requires the concept of future and 'to be certain' involves a certain doxastic commitment.

Given the distinction between simple and complex attitudes, an inclusion theorist might claim that we have a certain kind of authority about our simple attitudes, which doesn't extend to complex attitudes. Granting this move, we are still not told *how* one is supposed to know authoritatively of one's occurrent attitudes. The question is not whether or not we possess privileged self-knowledge of attitudinal components but whether externalism can account for it. Now, some compatibilists might try to neutralize epistemic scepticism about modes of thinking by claiming that simple attitude concepts are innate.[11] On this view, we come hard-wired with a set of simple attitude concepts and with the ability to use them correctly in describing our mental states. The consequence of this view is, of course, that mistakes of the kind Oscar is subject to are psychologically impossible. But even if simple attitude concepts were hard-wired in us, one could still run an Oscar-like example on complex attitude concepts. Thus, even if compatibilists could come up with a convincing story about privileged access to simple attitudes the question would remain how we are able to know non-empirically about our complex attitudes.

(2) The Burgean compatibilist might attempt to evade epistemic scepticism about modes of thinking by denying that attitude concepts can be clearly defined. On this view, attitude words are essentially vague just as ejaculations ('Oh', 'Ow', 'Yikes', etc.) are sometimes thought to be vague. With respect to these vocabularies there are ideolects but no unified usage. If attitude concepts are vague by their very nature, the idea of someone deviating from society's use of a term doesn't make any sense. Prima facie, this rejoinder has some intuitive force. In fact, most of us have some problem to state how our language community delineates 'to believe', 'to consider', 'to decide', 'to suppose', etc. Consequently, it might seem implausible to describe Oscar as *misidentifying* his mental state. Talk about misidentification only makes sense when there is a standard from which one can deviate. In the case of judgments involving 'to believe', 'to consider', 'to decide', and 'to suppose', the Burgean compatibilist might conclude, the categories 'true' and 'false' have no application.

Now, granted a considerable vagueness of cognitive verbs, there still remain plenty of cases where the idea of misidentification of intentional attitudes *does* make sense. Even if the vagueness of some attitude words doesn't allow us to clearly differentiate between 'to suppose' and 'to consider' or 'to decide' and 'to believe', we normally have no problems telling the difference between being sorry and hoping, regretting and remembering, doubting and proving etc. As long as there are some attitude words that can be defined relative to some other attitude words, one

11. This point was suggested to me by Tyler Burge.

can construe Oscar-like examples where an individual's usage of cognitive verbs, through incomplete understanding, deviates from the language community.

The discussion has been restricted to social externalism. It should be clear, however, that non-social externalism isn't more suitable to account for introspective knowledge of propositional attitudes. All versions of externalism have in common that intensions don't determine extensions. From this it follows that to possess a concept such as 'believing' one doesn't have to know any of the necessary application conditions of the concept. Since the conditions that determine a concept are said to be relational or external, it is hard to see how, by introspection alone, we can know what they are and whether they are fulfilled. Thus, any kind of externalism seems to conflict with the thesis of privileged self-knowledge of the attitudinal components of one's thoughts.

In sum, if attitude concepts are partly constituted by relational facts, the inclusion theory cannot succeed in explaining privileged access to the modality of one's thought. On the understanding (i) that the inclusion theory is the leading compatibilist theory, and (ii) that no version of externalism other than social externalism can account for privileged access to the modes of one's thinking, we can conclude: Externalism seems to be inconsistent with the thesis that we possess privileged access to the attitudes in which our thought contents are framed. And since knowing one's mental state requires knowing its content *and* its attitude, it follows that externalism is not fully consistent with privileged self-knowledge.[12]

12. For valuable comments on earlier drafts, or for helpful discussion of the issues, I am grateful to Peter Baumann, Dieter Henrich, Ariela Lazar, John Perry, Ken Taylor, and an anonymous referee. Special thanks to Tyler Burge and Fred Dretske.

References

Alston, W. 1971: 'Varieties of Privileged Access.' *American Philosophical Quarterly*, 8, pp. 223–41.

Boghossian, P. 1989: 'Content and Self-Knowledge.' *Philosophical Topics*, 17, pp. 5–26 [Ch. 33 in this volume].

Brueckner, A. 1990: 'Scepticism about Knowledge of Content.' *Mind*, 99, pp. 447–51.

Brueckner, A. 1992: 'What an Anti-Individualist Knows A Priori.' *Analysis*, 52, pp. 111–18.

Burge, T. 1979: 'Individualism and the Mental.' *Midwest Studies in Philosophy*, 4, pp. 73–121.

Burge, T. 1988: 'Individualism and Self-Knowledge.' *Journal of Philosophy*, 85, pp. 649–63 [Ch. 32 in this volume].

Burge, T. 1993: 'Content Preservation.' *Philosophical Review*, 102, pp. 457–88.

Burge, T. 1996: 'Our Entitlement to Self-Knowledge.' *Proceedings of the Aristotelian Society* 117, pp. 91–116.

Chisholm, R. M. 1981: *The First Person*. Minneapolis: University of Minnesota Press.

Davidson, D. 1985: 'Rational Animal' in E. LePore & B. McLaughlin, eds., *Actions and Events*, Oxford: Basil Blackwell, pp. 473–80.

Davidson, D. 1988: 'Reply to Burge.' *Journal of Philosophy*, 85, pp. 664–5.

Davidson, D. 1991: 'Epistemology Externalized.' *Dialectica*, 45, pp. 191–202.

Descartes, R. 1955: *Philosophical Works of Descartes*. E. S. Haldane & G. R. T. Ross, eds., New York: Dover.

Dretske, F. 1981: *Knowledge and the Flow of Information*. Cambridge: MIT Press

Dretske, F. 1994: 'Introspection.' *Proceedings of the Aristotelian Society*, 94, pp. 1–16.

Dretske, F. 1995: *Naturalizing the Mind*. Cambridge: MIT Press.

Falvey, K., Owens, J. 1994: 'Externalism, Self-Knowledge, and Skepticism.' *Philosophical Review*, 103, pp. 107–37.

Fodor, J. 1990: *A Theory of Content*. Cambridge: MIT Press.

Gopnik, A. 1993: 'How We Know Our Minds: The Illusion of First-Person Knowledge of Intentionality.' *Behavioral and Brain Sciences*, 16, pp. 1–14.

Heil, J. 1988: 'Privileged Access.' *Mind*, 97, pp. 238–51.

LePore, E., and Loewer, B. 1986: 'Solipsistic Semantics.' *Midwest Studies in Philosophy*, 10, pp. 595–614.

Ludlow, P. 1995: 'Externalism, Self-Knowledge, and the Prevalence of Slow Switching.' *Analysis*, 55, pp. 45–9.

McKinsey, M. 1991: 'Anti-Individualism and Privileged Access.' *Analysis*, 51, pp. 9–16.

Noonan, H. W. 1993: 'Object-Dependent Thoughts: A Case of Superficial Necessity but Deep Contingency?' in J. Heil and A. Mele, eds., *Mental Causation*, Oxford: Clarendon Press, pp. 283–308.

Perner, J. 1991: *Understanding the Representational Mind*. Cambridge: MIT Press.

Price, H. H. 1969: *Belief*. London: George Allen & Unwin.

Shoemaker, S. 1994: 'Self-Knowledge and "Inner Sense"' *Philosophy and Phenomenological Research*, 54, pp. 249–314.

Stalnaker, R. 1990: 'Narrow Content' in C. A. Anderson & J. Owens, eds., *Propositional Attitudes*, Stanford: CSLI Publications, pp. 131–45.

Williams, B. 1978: *Descartes*. London: Penguin Books.

Wilson, T. 1985: 'Strangers to Ourselves: The Origins and Accuracy of Beliefs about One's Own Mental States' in J. H. Harvey and G. Weary, eds., *Attribution*, Orlando: Academic Press, pp. 9–36.

Wright, C. 1991: 'Wittgenstein's Later Philosophy of Mind: Sensation, Privacy and Intention' in K. Puhl, ed., *Meaning Scepticism*, Berlin: Walter de Gruyter, pp. 126–47.

Memory and Testimony

Chapter 35

Remembering

C. B. Martin and Max Deutscher

1. Introductory distinctions

W<small>E</small> intend to define what it is to remember. Our account covers direct memory of events, remembering information, and remembering how to do things. There are differences between these three sorts of memory. Someone may remember how to swim and yet not remember those occasions on which he learned to swim. A man in the twentieth century may say truly that he remembers that Julius Caesar invaded Britain. What is impossible is that he remembers Caesar invading Britain. There are differences between 'He remembers going swimming,' 'He remembers that he went swimming,' and 'He remembers how to swim.'

Remembering how To say that someone remembers how to swim is at least to say that he has learned how. He may have taught himself or learned from another. It is also to say that, as a result of his learning to swim, he still has the skill needed to swim. He need not be able to swim; he may be paralyzed and unable to employ his skill. An account of the causal connection involved would not be the same as the one which we will give for remembering, but we shall not discuss this here. Some people insist that if a person can, for instance, give a fair account of how to swim, then he may be said to remember how to swim, though he has no skill at all at swimming. Perhaps it is better to speak here of remembering how a stroke goes, than of remembering how to do it. The difference between remembering and remembering *how* to do something cannot show itself better than in the case where some swimming *is* an example of remembering and not, as is usual, an example of remembering *how*.

Suppose that someone has never dog-paddled. He is not good at visualization and has never learned any words which would describe swimming. His method of representing the one time at which he saw a man dog-paddle is his actually doing the dog-paddle stroke. We can imagine him trying to remember the curious action that the man went through in the water. He cannot describe it, and cannot form any picture of it. He cannot bring it back. He gets into the water, experimenting a little, until suddenly he gets it right and exclaims, 'Aha, that's it!' To anyone who complains that the man would have no test for whether the stroke was remembered, unless he could visualize or describe the process, we point out that exactly the same difficulty attaches to answering the question 'What test does a person have for his visual imagery or description being correct?'

Two types of remembering that A person can remember that something happened even though it was before he was born, or was within his lifetime though not within his experience. In the same sense a person may be said to remember *that* he spent the first year of his life in a certain town, even though in this case what he remembers is within his experience. There is, however, a distinction between two radically different types of remembering that p. In the first type one sufficient reason why a man may be said *only* to remember that X happened is that he did not experience X happening. Another sufficient reason would be that his representation of the event is not (in a way which we shall describe in Sections 6 and 7) due to his experience of it. In such a case, he will have previously worked it out or heard about it quite independently of his own original perception of it. When speaking of this first type of case, we shall say that someone remembers that$_1$ something.

In the second type of case, the reason a man might be said only to remember that something happened is merely that there is a lack of detail in his *direct* memory. Thus the second type is quite unlike remembering that$_1$, where his source of information is not his own past experience of what he recounts. Here we shall speak of his remembering that$_2$ something. If someone is asked whether he remembers what he did last Friday at lunchtime, he may be able to say that he went down the street. Yet he may feel scarcely in a position to say that he remembers actually going down the street. What he needs in order to be able to say that he does remember going down the street is at least more detailed remembering that$_2$ certain things happened when he went down the street. As we shall go on to argue, this addition of detail must be due to the original perception. However, no amount of detailed remembering that various things happened on the walk is relevant to the question whether he remembers the walk unless his remembering that they occurred is of the second type. A precisely analogous point could be made in connection with the construction 'remembering what happened,' or 'remembering what something was like,' and we shall use the numbers 1 and 2 as subscripts in the same way. This second use of remembering that (or *what*) allows us to describe cases of remembering where we can bring back very little detail, although it is not restricted only to such cases. A considerable amount of remembering that$_2$ is *involved in* remembering an incident.

To say that someone remembers some fact such as Caesar's invasion of Britain is to say more than that he represents it correctly (we shall discuss 'representing' later). It is to say also that it or a representation of it has come within his experience or that he has worked it out. It is to say still more than this, too, since someone's learning a fact at some past time may have nothing to do with his now representing it. He may have no retention of his school lessons, and have just worked it out from various things he has read recently. Although in remembering a fact he learned at school a man does not *ipso facto* remember the learning of it, his present account must be given because of this previous learning. It is interesting that he might not have accepted what he was taught, experienced, or worked out on the past occasion, but later may remember that it was the case. For instance, he may have been in a mood which made him irrationally reject what he was taught. Later, with no new information, he may simply remember it.

We claim that a person can be said to remember something happening or, in general, remember something directly, only if he has observed or experienced it. This is not to be confused with the false doctrine that we always remember *only* what happened to ourselves.[1] Of course someone can remember his brother being married although it didn't happen to him. Still, unless he saw it, heard it, or otherwise perceived it happening, it is false to say he remembers his brother being married.

If someone remembers that$_1$ p, then some source of information, other than his own perception that p, is part of the cause of his now recounting what he learned. If someone was told something false, then naturally he cannot be said to remember that it was the case. This is in no way a failure of memory on his part (see Section 3 for an analogous and fuller discussion of this type of problem); he legitimately can be said to remember what he was told, whether it is true or false.

Normally one does not trouble to make a distinction between remembering what one was told a day ago and what one was told a year ago, when the very same fact is involved. Yet there is a basis for such a distinction, if we wished to draw one, and, furthermore there could be a reason to insist on making this distinction— namely, where consideration is given to the *responsibility* of the acceptance. For example, a year ago someone was told something by a reliable authority and also, a week ago, accepted the same fact from someone he had no reason to trust. In that case, the question whether he remembered what he was told a year ago rather than, or as well as, what he was told a week ago, would affect the answer to the question 'Does he now accept irresponsibly what he was told a week ago?' If the distinction were drawn as just suggested, then if a person is to remember what he was told *at a certain time*, his being told at that time must stand in the causal relation (which we shall specify in Sections 5, 6, and 7) to his representation of what he was told. A point must be made about what is demanded of the representation involved in remembering what one was told. It is not necessary either to represent one's being told, nor the fact which one was told, because it might not *be* a fact. Remembering that$_2$ is remembering directly, and so our discussion of the causal connection in Sections 5, 6, and 7 will automatically cover this concept also.

1. Cf. A. Flew, 'Locke and Personal Identity,' *Philosophy*, 26 (1951), p. 56.

Reliving the past and the role of imagery Although it is a mistake to insist that a person must have mental images of what he remembers, imagery is of importance for a number of reasons. For one thing, some people to whom imagery is very vivid and impressive *insist* that they do not 'really' remember something unless they can see it again in the mind's eye, or hear it again with the mind's ear. Furthermore, many things we remember might have been extremely difficult to describe in the first place. For instance, if someone cannot form a mental image of the sound of a *cor anglais*, or the look of affected concern on a person's face, or the taste of an avocado pear, then he may well be completely at a loss to recall such things in any other way.

Thus, it is easy to think that the notion of reliving the past, as something more than just remembering it, is coextensive with getting vivid imagery of it, supposing that the other conditions for memory are fulfilled. This, however, is not accurate. Two people engaged in animated discussion of something they were both involved in may be said to be reliving the incident, although they are not having mental images of the incident. Something of their past involvement with the events they remember comes out in their present feelings and in the way they describe the incident. Yet, although reliving something is not merely remembering it, reliving *need* not involve the sort of return of the past emotions and feelings which we have just described. It would seem at least that either imagery or the return of the old emotions about the incident must occur, each by itself being enough to allow us to speak of reliving as something more than merely remembering.

It may be said that two old soldiers are reliving the past when they are discussing and joking about some terrible events which they lived through. These old men may be having neither mental imagery of the events, nor may the original horror be, as it were, felt again. In such a case, we are more inclined to say that they would be merely reminiscing.

One last minor distinction should be made before we begin the main discussion. In our analysis we claim that to remember is at least to do something. Yet one can say of a person asleep, 'His memory is quite remarkable. He remembers the details of every car he has ever owned.' The difference between such a sense and the one we discuss is not the difference between two sorts of memory. It merely reflects the difference between remembering and the ability to remember. Since understanding of such a general ability is immediately dependent upon understanding of actual occurrences of remembering, we concentrate our attention on an analysis of the latter. Our discussion will deal primarily with cases of remembering. From time to time, however, we will point out how some of our remarks apply to cases of remembering *that* certain things happened.

2. The proposed analysis

If someone remembers something, whether it be 'public,' such as a car accident, or 'private,' such as an itch, then the following criteria must be fulfilled:

1. Within certain limits of accuracy he represents that past thing.

2. If the thing was 'public,' then he observed what he now represents.[2] If the thing was 'private,' then it was his.

3. His past experience of the thing was operative in producing a state or successive states in him finally operative in producing his representation.

These three statements express the condition which we consider to be separately necessary and jointly sufficient, if an event is to be an instance of remembering. The main body of the paper will be taken up with elucidation and argument for the necessity and sufficiency of these conditions. It will be found that two more clauses must be added to criterion 3, and these will be introduced and explained as the need for them arises. Obviously an explanation of the first criterion is needed, and in due course we also discuss 'limits of accuracy,' 'representation,' 'prompting,' and 'operative.'

3. Belief and remembering

There is some reason to say that the list of conditions is not sufficient. Locke in his *Essay Concerning Human Understanding* (Bk. II, ch. 10, sec. 2) and Russell in *The Analysis of Mind* (London, 1921 ch. 9) claim that if a person remembers something, then he must believe that it happened. Also Furlong in his recent book, *A Study in Memory* (London, 1951 pp. 73, 75, 93) and Harrod in an article, 'Memory' (*Mind*, 51 (1942), p. 53) require that a person believe that an event occurred before he can be said to remember it. These philosophers hold the position as something obvious, not as something to be stated and argued for. Hume, too, seems to require belief as a criterion. Russell and Harrod rely on belief as one of the necessities of a logical distinction between imagination and memory. B. Benjamin ('Remembering,' *Mind*, 65 [1956], pp. 321, 322) is one of the few who has challenged the view that one must believe if one remembers. More recently, J. T. Saunders ('Does All Memory Imply Factual Memory,' *Analysis*, 25 Suppl. (1965), p. 109) in criticism of Professor Norman Malcolm has claimed that memory is possible without belief.

If philosophers are in the egocentric predicament and an introspective mood when they try to define memory, then they will feel that they must find the difference between real and delusory remembering within their own experience. In that case they are very likely to assume that it is not possible for someone to remember something unless he believes it happened. With Hume, they may wonder which of their apparent memory images are real representations of the past, but they will not pick on an image as a memory unless at least they *believe* that it is a 'copy' or representation of a past event. This fact does not show that the philosophers we criticize are wrong, but it is an adequate explanation of their assumption.

It may seem obvious that a person does not remember something unless he

2. See Sec. 4, 2nd paragraph.

believes that it occurred. The 'obvious' leads to trouble, however. For one thing, surely people say, 'I don't know whether I am remembering this or imagining it,' suggesting that they could be remembering something, though they neither believe nor disbelieve that it happened. It may seem even more obvious that, even if belief is not necessary in remembering, absence of disbelief certainly is. But consider the following case.

Suppose that someone asks a painter to paint an imaginary scene. The painter agrees to do this and, taking himself to be painting some purely imaginary scene, paints a detailed picture of a farmyard, including a certain colored and shaped house, various people with detailed features, particular items of clothing, and so on. His parents then recognize the picture as a very accurate representation of a scene which the painter saw just once in his childhood. The figures and colors are as the painter saw them only once on the farm which he now depicts. We may add more and more evidence to force the conclusion that the painter did his work by no mere accident. Although the painter sincerely believes that his work is purely imaginary, and represents no real scene, the amazed observers have all the evidence needed to establish that in fact he is remembering a scene from childhood. What other explanation could there be for his painting being so like what he has seen?

Let us approach the matter from another direction. It is quite common in ordinary life to describe some past event, and then to be uncertain whether the description was from memory, or was founded on something one was told after the event. If it were impossible to remember while believing one is not remembering, one would be saved the embarrassment of thinking that one is originating a tune or an argument when one is not. Now, we can prove that if one may remember X, but not believe that one is remembering X, then it is possible that one should remember X and not believe that X happened.

Suppose that:

1. A remembers X, and A holds no belief that he remembers X.

We can easily suppose that, in addition, A is prepared to believe that the past event occurred only if either he believes that he remembers it, or believes that he has been told that it occurred, or has worked it out from something he has been told. (For brevity, let us say that in both the last two alternatives he believes that he has been 'told.')

That is to say:

2. A holds the belief that X occurred only if either he believes that he remembers X, or believes that he was told that X occurred.

Now, A tells some story about his past, and in fact this story is true, although he does not know it. He wonders whether he is remembering the story but, thinking it most implausible, he rejects this possibility. On the same ground, he rejects the idea that he has been told such a story.

This we may set down as:

3. *A* neither believes that he remembers *X*, nor believes that he has been told that *X* occurred.

From 3 and 2 we deduce that *A* does not hold the belief that *X* occurred. In conjunction with 1 this allows us to deduce that *A* does not believe that *X* occurred, but that he does remember that it did. Given that the three premises may express contingent truths, and are mutually consistent, we cannot deny that it can be true that *A* remembers something, but does not believe that it happened. It is impossible to deny that each premise may express a contingent truth. The set as it stands is formally consistent, and makes no assumption about the analysis of remembering. It can be proved inconsistent only by someone who simply presupposes that 1 entails that *A* believes that *X* occurred.

We suggested that introspection as a means of discovering the nature of remembering was likely to make the idea appear inescapable that to remember is at least to believe. On the other hand, if we adopt an uncritical linguistic approach to the matter, we are equally likely to be misled, since to say 'I remember *X* but believe that *X* did not happen' is bound to be incoherent. We must be wary about such first-person present-tense expressions of belief as 'I have boots on, but I believe that I do not.' This is equally incoherent, but the incoherence does not prove that, if I have boots on, I cannot believe that I do not have them on.

The incoherence of any utterance of the sentence in question is an important matter which merits considerable discussion, but in the context of this paper the following remarks must suffice.[3] It is generally accepted that '*A* remembers an event *X*' entails 'The event *X* occurred.' Hence the incoherence of the remark 'I remember *X*, but *X* never took place' needs no special explanation; it is the incoherence of sheer contradiction. Therefore, when a person asserts that he remembers *X*, what he says can be true only if *X* did occur. From this we can proceed to explain why 'I remember *X*, but I *believe* that *X* did not occur' is incoherent. When a man says that he has a belief, there are two avenues for argument with him—that is, that he does not have the belief which he says he has or, alternatively, that he is mistaken in holding the belief which he holds. In holding a belief a person must be either correct or mistaken. The incoherence of 'I remember going for a walk, but I do not believe that I went for a walk' is quite straightforward. Only if *X* did happen can a person be right when he asserts 'I remember *X*.' Only if *X* did not occur, however, can he be correct in his belief that *X* did not occur. Therefore it is impossible for a person to be right both in his claim to remember *X* and in his belief that *X* did not occur. Whatever the facts are he must be wrong. Since what the person *says* could be true, though he must be mistaken, this is not the same as a contradiction, although it is very like one. Thus we can explain why 'I remember going for a walk, but I believe that I did not go for a walk' is incoherent without assuming that to remember is at least to believe.

3. For further remarks on this topic, see Max Deutscher, 'A Note on Saying and Disbelieving,' *Analysis* (1965), pp. 53–7.

Since we do not include belief in our analysis of memory, we avoid puzzles of the sort which Miss Anscombe produces in her article, 'The Reality of the Past' (in *Philosophical Analysis*, M. Black, ed., Englewood Cliffs 1963). She puts forward the case of someone who at a certain time sees a wax dummy which he takes to be a man. Later on he says without lying that he remembers seeing a man at that time. What he says must be false. Yet, as she says, it is not his memory which is at fault. Von Leyden in a recent book, *Remembering* (New York, 1961), describes a similar case (p. 60) in an effort to deal with this very puzzling matter and is led to think that one can remember no physical thing, but only one's own experiences. Now, since we do not require that a person should believe that X happened when he remembers X, we do not require that he believe correctly. We argue that the man in Miss Anscombe's case may remember seeing the wax dummy, although he believes that he saw a man.

All the same, a problem arises for us from such a case. Is our first criterion correct? Does the person represent correctly what he remembers? It might be thought not. We have agreed that when the person says that he saw a man, his memory is not at fault, though he actually saw a wax dummy and not a man. But though his memory is not at fault, he cannot be said to remember seeing a man for the simple reason that there was not a man at that time to be remembered. Our criterion requires only that he represent correctly what he *does* remember. What could the person be said to remember here? It would depend on details of the case which are not mentioned by either Miss Anscombe or Von Leyden. Depending on how the person did see it, it might be said that he remembered seeing how the wax dummy looked—namely, like a man—supposing that what he later recounted was that he *saw* a man. Furthermore, it could be said that he remembers the shape of the nose of what he saw, the set of the eyes, the stance, and so on.

Yet is there not still a difficulty for criterion 1? What he may say is "I remember the shape of the man's nose. It was crooked and rather short". He is not correctly representing what he saw, since what he saw was a wax dummy's nose and so, according to the first criterion, he is not remembering. This, however, would be a misunderstanding. What the man does remember is the shape of the nose of what was in fact a wax dummy. Just as we can say that, so we can also say that he does correctly represent the shape of the nose of what was in fact a wax dummy. That he can correctly represent the shape of the nose is in no way vitiated by the fact that he is wrong about the stuff the nose was made of, or the nature of the nose's owner.

4. Concluding introductory remarks

Someone might think that our treatment of Miss Anscombe's case permits us to speak of a person remembering more than he has ever seen. (This would conflict with our second criterion.) It might be argued: 'If A sees B who is covered in a sheet, and later remembers the incident, then, although he might not believe it, *what he remembers* is B covered in a white sheet. All that A saw, however, was a white sheet.'

But this is just an equivocation on the 'what' in 'what he remembers' and in 'what he saw.' Just as we may say that what he remembers, although he does not believe it, is a man covered in a white sheet, so we may say that what he saw, although he does not believe it, was a man covered in a white sheet. Or we may wish to speak 'strictly' in both cases, and say that all he saw and all that he remembers is a white sheet. So long as one does not work with a double standard, there is no trouble for the criterion.

We can offer no argument for the sufficiency of our list of criteria other than the failure, after examination of cases, to find the need for a longer list. We move on to argue for the necessity of the conditions which we have named. Criterion 1 states: *Within certain limits of accuracy he represents that past thing.* Failure to fulfill this criterion is the most typical failure to remember. Somebody may have observed an event, but unless he is recounting it to himself, telling others or in some other way representing it, then, roughly speaking, he is not remembering that event. Even if it is true, as some psychoanalysts claim, that under suitable conditions we are able to remember anything which we have experienced, nobody actually remembers anything until he comes to the point of representing in some way what he has observed or experienced. We *intend* the vagueness of the phrase 'represents the past.' Already in connection with memory without belief, we have described an example in which painting was a case of remembering. At the beginning of the article we suggested that even to swim might be a form of representation.

What we have said about the types of representation is insufficient, and this is a claim rather than an admission, since we want to bring to notice that no philosophical writing on memory has so much as recognized the problem. On anyone's account of memory, it is not enough that someone should have observed or experienced something in the past. He must do something in the present. 'What sort of thing must he do in the present, in order to be said to remember?' is a difficult and very general question. It is similar to the question 'What sort of thing must a person do in order to be right or wrong about something?' and requires a full treatment by itself.

5. The causal criterion

In his article, 'The Empiricist Theory of Memory' (*Mind*, 63 (1954), p. 474) R. F. Holland maintains that the following conditions are adequate to determine that someone is remembering something.

(*a*) What he is recounting did in fact happen, exist, and so forth.
(*b*) He is not being currently informed about what happened, existed, and so forth.
(*c*) He observed what he now recounts.

It must be obvious that (*b*) is not a necessary condition for remembering, since someone might be remembering as well as being informed about the events which he remembers.

It must be equally clear that Holland has given an inadequate analysis. One has only to reflect on the case of a man who can tell you what happened to him when he was three months old but can do so only because his mother told him. As well as Holland's, Ryle's account of memory (*The Concept of Mind* (New York, 1949), pp. 272–279) does not leave enough room for real doubt about whether someone is remembering an event rather than remembering what he has been told about it, or making it up, or imagining. We have already argued that it is not necessary that a person believe what he remembers or believe that he remembers. Even if such conditions were necessary they would not, in conjunction with the first two criteria, be sufficient for remembering.

In the argument which follows for the necessity of the third criterion, we begin with clause (a) of it. Later we shall show why clauses (b) and (c) must be added.

Clause (a). To remember an event, a person must not only represent and have experienced it, but also his experience of it must have been operative in producing a state or successive states in him finally operative in producing his representation.

For brevity we consider only the memory of 'public' events, but the same considerations would apply to the memory of 'private' episodes and the memory of processes, physical objects, relations, dreams, and recollections themselves. First support for the principle arises from a consideration of the following case.

A man whom we shall call Kent is in a car accident and sees particular details of it, because of his special position. Later on, Kent is involved in another accident in which he gets a severe blow on the head as a result of which he forgets a certain section of his own history, including the first accident. He can no longer fulfill the first criterion for memory of the first accident. Some time after this second accident, a popular and rather irresponsible hypnotist gives a show. He hypnotizes a large number of people, and suggests to them that they will believe that they had been in a car accident at a certain time and place. The hypnotist has never heard a thing about Kent nor the details of Kent's accident, and it is by sheer coincidence that the time, place, and details which he provides are just as they were in Kent's first accident. Kent is one of the group which is hypnotized. The suggestion works and so, after the act is over, Kent satisfies criterion 1 again. He believes firmly that he has been in an accident. The accident as he believes it to be is just like the first one in which he was really involved. All along he had satisfied criterion 2, of course. Thus, while it is clear that he satisfies the first two criteria, it is very doubtful that he remembers.

If Kent's loss of memory had been due to psychological causes, then it would have been easy to suppose that in the case as described hypnosis had actually brought his memory back. Kent does not repeat anything else about the period of his life which had been blotted out, however; he just repeats what the others in the group repeat. Kent is certainly 'describing correctly' the first accident, as they all are, but his recounting of the first accident is not due, even in part, to his observing it. Like the others, he says what he does only because of the hypnotist's suggestion. It is for this reason that he cannot be said to be remembering the accident, despite the fact that he correctly recounts what he saw. Therefore the first two criteria are inadequate. If a person's account of what he saw is not due even in part to his seeing it, it cannot be said that he remembers what he saw. If a person *remembers* what he saw, his recounting it must be due in part to seeing it. Anyone who rejects this causal interpretation must himself explain its force. At the end of this article we shall argue against Malcolm's attempt to do so.

Ryle, in *The Concept of Mind* (p. 278), and Benjamin (*op. cit.*, pp. 323, 324), have expressly denied that any causal criterion is part of the definition of memory. Writers such as Harrod, Furlong, and Holland have ignored it. Let us make it quite clear that we do not claim that any causal connection is a logical connection. All we claim is that there is a causal connection between A's past observation of X and his present representation of it, and a logical connection between 'A's past observation of X is causally related to his present representation of it' and 'A remembers X'.

Malcolm (*Knowledge and Certainty*, (Englewood Cliffs, 1963), p. 237, par. 2) feels that someone who gave a causal account of memory would have to say that a statement of the actual causal mechanism involved would be entailed by 'A remembers X.' He says that 'our use of the language of memory carries no implication about our inner physiology.' We can agree with him, for what we claim in our causal account is that our use of 'language of memory' carries implications only that there is *some* continuous causal process or other. Nor, to use Benjamin's phrase, do we require that the actual causal connection which does exist is 'known by the vast majority of people.' Benjamin suggests that it is curious that people should be sure that some process has gone on without knowing just what process it is. It seems to us not in the least curious to claim this. It is just what many people do when they say that dialing a number makes the phone ring at the other end. They think that there is some process linking their action with the effect, but they have little or no idea what it is.

We offer the following subsidiary arguments for the general version of the causal criterion. Consider the example of the painter which we gave earlier. The onlookers were compelled to the conclusion that the painter was remembering something he saw in childhood. It would have been unreasonable for them to think that he would have done what he did if it had not been for some particular past observation. Criteria 1 and 2 were fulfilled, but this did not by itself establish that it was a case of memory. What finally established it as such was this: the only reasonable explanation of the fact that the painter put details, colors, people, and so on into his picture, just as he saw them only once in his childhood, is that he was remembering that scene from his childhood. (We talk of the 'only reasonable explanation' in the case described, of course. We do not suggest that in no case would there be an alternative explanation.) If to remember an event, however, were merely to represent it and to have observed it, then it would be absurd to pretend to *explain* the fact that someone gave a description which fitted something he had seen, by asserting that he must be remembering it.

To clinch this line of argument, we bring forward one of many similar cases from real life. A person has an apparent recollection of something from early childhood, and wonders whether he really remembers it. His parents may tell him that what he describes did happen, and that he witnessed it, but the discussion of whether he remembers it still goes on. They wonder whether his witnessing of the event has any connection with his now giving the story or whether his description can be completely explained by what he heard later. Whether he has been told about it in the meanwhile, how young he was at the time, and whether he has seen things very similar at many other times are all relevant to deciding whether he actually remembers the event. These facts are the same as those which are used to decide whether or not he would have given the story if he had *not* witnessed the event in his childhood. To decide that he would not have done so is to decide that his past witnessing is causally necessary for his present account. (We shall see that a cause need not be a necessary condition. Naturally, in such cases it is difficult to verify that someone does remember what he recounts.)

Yet another supplementary argument can be developed from the following considerations. Benjamin (*op. cit.*, p. 324) claims that there are no strict rules to decide whether a certain amount of correct description of a witnessed event is enough. Harrod (*op. cit.*, pp. 54, 56) says that there are no strict rules to decide between imagination, dreams, and so forth, and genuine memory. Neither of them saw quite how loose the rules are, if there are no criteria for memory other than those recognized in their analyses.

The person who recounts an event from early childhood may be perfectly accurate in giving details of the event. Yet, as we have seen, he may well not be remembering it, but only remembering that certain things happened to him then. Suppose that someone sees a scene with just one very unusual feature. Later on he is asked to describe what he saw at that time. All he gets right is that one unusual feature. Here we have good reason to say that he remembers the one feature, even when all the rest of his description is mistaken. The feature in the scene was unusual, so it was not likely that he would have put it in if he had not seen it. It is useful to see that a similar point also holds with respect to the first type of *remembering that*. If someone had been asked to remember a telephone number (to adapt a case from Benjamin's article) and had been correct about only one digit of the number, there would be no reason to think that he remembered even that one digit. Suppose, though, that he is able to say that the last number is 7, and that is all he can say. We might then be prepared to allow that he does remember what he says, since it is comparatively unlikely that he should have been correct by chance.

It seems that our 'rules' for how much a person must get right in order to be said to remember are completely confused, unless we use more criteria than are used by those philosophers we are criticizing. Even clause (a) of the causal criterion makes a considerable degree of order out of this chaos. For instance, Harrod's difficulties about distinguishing imagination and dreams from genuine memory are resolved. Sometimes what we take to be imagination may be memory, but usually it is not. In those cases where we take ourselves to imagine something, and our 'imagining' it is caused (in the way which we shall explain) by some previous experience or observation of it, then we are remembering whether or not we take ourselves to be. Unless Malcolm in his book *Dreaming* (London 1962) is right, dreams also may sometimes be memories. What we show is that one cannot expect to be able always to distinguish between these things for oneself.

6. Necessary and operative conditions

When philosophers speak of a necessary condition, they usually mean a generally necessary condition. Thus when they say that C is necessary for E, they are talking of types of events, not of events. To say that C is generally necessary for E is to say that there is no way of bringing about an event of type E, without an event of type C. For the most part, however, people speak of particular events as necessary for other particular events. It is not generally necessary for the production of flame that someone strike a match. Nevertheless, on a particular occasion, someone's striking a match can be necessary for the lighting of his cigarette at that time if there was then no other way of lighting the cigarette.

The above distinction may be made even if a particular event C is necessary for E, only when some description C' would hold of C, and some description E' would hold of E, such that 'If E' then C'' is a universal law. So, when we consider necessary causal conditions in examining occurrences of remembering, we are interested in the idea of occurrent conditions which are causally necessary for others. When we discuss the question whether, in remembering, the past experience must be causally necessary for the subsequent representation of it, we shall not be interested in the question whether the past experience is of a *type* which is *generally necessary* for a type of event of which the subsequent representation is an instance.

It might be thought that since we defend the causal criterion we are committed to saying that the past experience is causally *necessary* for the subsequent representation, since the past experience is clearly never *sufficient* for it. There are, however, causal conditions which are neither necessary nor sufficient.

For example, if a person is about to recount something and someone butts in and tells him about it anyway, then his having observed it himself is not necessary for his recounting it at that time. Yet that does not mean that he does not remember the past event, when he goes on to tell someone about it after being interrupted. Only if he had not recounted what he does, had he not experienced what he did, would his past experience be causally necessary for his present account. Had he not experienced what he did, he still would have recounted the same story, since he would have accepted his trustworthy friend's story. It seems scarcely believable, though, that he should not be remembering the event after his friend has butted in, and be remembering only what his friend told him.

There is another type of case in which someone could be said to remember something, though his having observed it is not causally *necessary* for his now recounting it. Suppose that he happened to glance around and notice a monkey turning a somersault. Someone else was watching then and would have told him that the monkey had turned a somersault, had the person not seen it doing so. Supposing that all the man can say later is that the monkey turned a somersault (second type of remembering that), it would then be false to say that his having seen it for himself was a causally *necessary* condition of his being able to say later that the monkey had turned a somersault. (Of course, his having experienced what he recounts is always a *logically* necessary condition of his later remembering it.)

In both of the types of cases described it is improbable that the person should have recounted what he did at exactly the same time, had he not seen for himself what he later recounted. It may be thought that at some level of accuracy a time discrepancy would be discoverable. Whether true or not, however, this is scarcely relevant. Within those same limits of accuracy which we use to decide at what moment particular events of the type under discussion have occurred, we may be able to say that the person would have recounted what he did at the same time, but from other causes.

In order to speak of a causal condition which may be necessary or sufficient but need be neither, we introduce the term 'operative.' A condition may be operative in producing another, even though the result would have been obtained at the same time by another method, had the operative condition not been present.

In order to discuss fully the need for this term, we would have to consider cases in which it seems that there may be two conditions, fulfilling exactly the same causal role, present simultaneously. Certainly neither could be described as necessary. Yet it can be very embarrassing to have to say that both, *or* either, are operative. A discussion of this tantalizing issue must be ruled out of court here.

Even the inclusion of clause (a)—*to remember an event, a person must not only represent and have experienced it, but also his experience of it must have been operative in producing a state or successive states in him finally operative in producing his representation*—in the list of criteria for remembering allows the admission of unwanted cases. It will be found that clause (b), which we shall introduce, excludes these.

To tell another story about the accident-prone Kent, let us say that he has told his friend Gray what he saw of an accident in which he was involved. Kent has a second accident in which he gets a blow on the head which destroys all memory of a period in his past, including the time at which the first accident occurred. When Gray finds that Kent can no longer remember the first accident, he tells him those details which Kent had told Gray in the period between the first and second accidents. After a little while Kent forgets that anyone has told him about the first accident, but still remembers what he was told by Gray. It is clear that he does not remember the accident itself. Think how Gray would feel about Kent's claims to remember the first accident again. He would know that Kent had been quite unable to say anything about it after the second accident, and that when he, Gray, had told him the story, there had been no signs of recognition on Kent's part. Kent had quite a period of his past blotted out, and he can tell nothing about that period except what Gray told him. So we have no reason to say that Gray's retelling Kent about the first accident actually revived Kent's memory. Kent witnessed the first accident, can now recount what he saw of it, but does not remember it. But if criteria 1 and 2 and clause (a) were sufficient, we should have to say that he did remember the first accident. In the case as just described, the causal chain between Kent's witnessing of the first accident and his correct retelling of it at the later date (after Gray had told him) is this: Kent's observation of the first accident resulted in his telling Gray the account of the accident as he witnessed it. Gray's hearing of Kent's story resulted in Gray's telling Kent about the first accident as Kent witnessed it. Kent's hearing Gray tell him about the accident resulted in Kent's retelling, at a later date, the account of the first accident.

This is to say that in the case as described, Kent's observation of the first accident was operative in producing his subsequent account of the event. Despite this, Kent does not remember, and therefore some additional clause must be introduced. The condition that the past observation be an operative condition for the present retelling is correct so far as it goes, but it is too weak. Strengthening the criterion so that the past observation must be a causally sufficient condition for the present retelling would be far too strong. Innumerable other factors and events are always necessary for representation of a past observation to occur. If all there was to say about causal conditions was that they were either simply operative or sufficient, either in general or in particular circumstances, this difficulty would be insuperable.

The most simple rule which would dismiss the troublesome case just described, and which fits the facts in our world, is that the causal chain between the past observation and the present representation of it should continue without interruption within the body of the person concerned. In the troublesome case the causal chain goes from Kent to Gray and back to Kent again. This criterion rules out conceivable cases of memory, however. We do not want to say that we can conceive only of humans remembering. Surely it is imaginable that we might find creatures who could represent the past as efficiently as we do, in the various ways we do, but who differ from us in the following respects. They carry a metal box around with them and, if they are separated from it, then they can remember nothing, no matter how recent. They are not born with the boxes. The boxes are made in a factory, and given them at birth, after which the creatures gradually develop the ability to remember. They do not ask the box questions about the past, but when they are connected with the box they remember as we do. This case shows that the suggested criterion is not strictly necessary.

We can also show that the proposed additional criterion does not rule out other spurious cases of memory, and in that sense is not strong enough. Suppose that a student could not remember$_2$ what he read in a chemistry book for an examination, and inscribed what he read into his palm with a hot needle. In the examination he writes down the correct formulae by feeling the marks on his palm. Here the causal chain does not extend beyond the body of the person and yet he does not remember$_2$ what he read in the chemistry book, but only what he inscribed on his palm. (We owe the idea for this case to Professor J. L. Mackie.) The alterations we do propose to the causal criterion deal correctly with these cases.

Although the rule we just tried, and the next we shall try, are both straw men, it is important to see that they do not work, and to understand why. Let us try out the addition to the causal criterion:

A subsequent *strict or complete prompting* concerning the thing remembered is not causally necessary for his representation of the thing at the later date.

'Complete prompting' is a technical term, and is explained in the following way.

A prompting is *complete* if the person cannot correctly give back any more in his representation of what happened in his past than was supplied by the prompting.

Let us speak of someone being *prompted* whenever he observes what he has seen before, or observes a representation of it, whether or not a person intentionally or unintentionally prompts him. A person is prompted if he just happens to read an account of something he once did, or if he happens to read a fictional story which by chance matches something in his own past, or if he sees some event very like another which he previously saw, or sees an object in much the same state as he saw it previously.

There is one important difference between being prompted verbally and being prompted by an observation of something resembling what one has observed before. If someone sees something which he has seen before, then even if he can give *no* detail of what he saw before which he did not gain from being prompted, his prompted representation *contains* the idea that he did see something like this before. No matter how much detail is supplied by observation of a replica of what has been previously observed, there is always, in such cases, the *additional* 'detail' of recognition. Only if he is being prompted verbally can he, in a *very* strict sense, be 'fully' prompted. When he is thus verbally prompted, so that he is even told that he has experienced before what he is being informed about, we shall say that he is *strictly prompted.*

It is important to realize that he need not, when verbally prompted, represent what he does as having happened in the past. If he is not told that it was in the past, and does not say so when he recounts what he has been prompted to say, then he has been fully but not strictly prompted. But if he is told that it happened some time in the past, and he can add nothing to that, then he has been strictly prompted.

The connection between strict prompting and linguistic prompting is this: only linguistic prompting can be strict prompting, but it can be complete without being strict. The proposed rule copes with the second accident case, since Kent could tell the story of the first accident only after Gray had told him *everything* about it again, and Kent could tell nothing of the accident which he was not told by Gray. The rule also allows that the people with the boxes do remember. Furthermore, it accords with the common-sense thought that someone who remembers something does not have to see it again, or something like it, or hear a full description of it, in order to tell about it.

7. A distinction between operative in the circumstances, and operative for the circumstances

Despite the apparent success of this modification described above, it is far too stringent as a general rule. What we need is a criterion which makes sense of the possibility that after a person is fully or even strictly prompted, he may or may not be remembering. If we can find such a criterion, then it will in fact allow us to say that a person who must be strictly prompted may or may not be remembering when he recounts what he has been prompted about. The cases which we shall describe to show this will, in fact, lead us to the correct rule. Very often a person must be prompted before he can remember, and this fact seems to be ruled out by the suggested extra criterion, although many cases of prompting would be accommodated since it is required only that *complete or strict* prompting should not be causally necessary. Nevertheless, the rule will not do for the following kind of reasons. Suppose that a person tries to remember what type of pancake he had at a place where fifty different sorts of pancakes are served, and cannot. After he is told, or it is suggested, that he had a banana pancake, he says, 'Ah, yes, now I remember.' But he can give no detail at all. He could be deceiving us and he could be deceiving himself, but such possibilities serve to emphasize that he might be correct, and deceiving nobody. He might be remembering that$_2$ he had a banana pancake, and not merely remembering that$_1$ he had a banana pancake, although he has been strictly prompted. Take another case. Someone cannot remember what he did the previous afternoon. He is told quite a long story about driving through certain towns, eating such-and-such foods at a picnic, and so on. Then he says, 'Now it all comes back.' He then recounts the whole story. Suppose that he had already been told the story in such a full way that there was nothing which he could reasonably add. It is more convincing if he can add important details, but the mere fact that he can repeat such a long story would normally show that he does genuinely remember many of the things he did on that afternoon. It would be highly unlikely that he could have retold such a story detail for detail, if he had not actually been on the picnic himself. (Of course, if he is a person with highly accurate short-term retention, then his ability to give the story word for word will not allay our suspicions that he remembers nothing but the story we have just given him.)

Even when a person has had to be strictly prompted it may be very unlikely that he would have followed this prompting with his own duplicate account if it had not been for his observation of whatever is in question. In such a case we normally have strong evidence to suppose that he remembers the event and not the prompting. Even in such a simple case as the one where someone 'remembers' only that$_2$ he had banana pancakes after he has had to be told that he had banana pancakes, we could find evidence for or against genuine remembering. If someone is given a list of fifteen pancakes including the one he is trying to remember, and picks the right one, we accept this as evidence for memory rather than for chance.

There *will* be cases of *strict* prompting where we will have no idea whether or not that prompting would have been followed by the correct account without observation of what the account is about. In such cases we will not be able to decide whether the person is remembering, but this is no objection to our theory, but the very reverse. One of the faults of analyses of memory which have recently been given is that they leave insufficient room for the real doubts which can arise concerning whether or not someone is remembering something. It is a common fact that there *can* be doubt whether a person who gives a true account of his own past is remembering. For instance, as pointed out earlier, we may fail to have enough evidence to decide whether someone who gives a true account of an incident from his childhood is remembering it or is merely repeating what he has been told by his parents.

We are now using clause (b) of criterion 3, which is:

In those cases where prompting is operative for the representation, his past experience of the thing represented is operative in producing the state (or the successive set of states) in him which is finally operative in producing the representation, *in* the circumstances in which he is prompted.

The past experience must not be operative only *for* the man's being prompted.

This may appear forbidding. What we must make clear is the difference between:

E (experience) being operative *for* the circumstance P (prompting) which helps to bring about R (representation)

and

E (experience) being operative *in* the circumstance P (prompting) which helps to bring about R (representation).

If A is operative for B and B is operative for C, then we shall say that A is operative *for* the circumstance B which is operative for C. If A is operative for B and B is operative for C, however, and as well as this A is operative for a factor B' other than B which acts with B to bring about C, then we shall say that A is operative for C *in* (as well as *for*) the circumstance B, which is operative for C. Clearly, A may be both operative for the circumstances B which help to bring about C, and operative in those circumstances.

Clause (b) deals with the troublesome version of the accident case in the following way. Kent was involved in the original accident and as a result told Gray about it. Because he had been told about it, Gray related the story back to Kent, after Kent had lost his memory in the second accident. Thus, Kent's original observation of the accident was a factor in bringing about his final account of it. His observation of the accident, however, is not operative in producing (through a successive set of states) his account of the accident *in* the circumstance of his being prompted. For that reason we do not say that he remembers the accident. We might put the matter another way. We could say that his past observation was not operative in bringing about his representation of the accident, *upon* prompting. Again, we might put it thus: his past experience is not operative in bringing about his representation of the accident, *given that* he is prompted.

8. The idea of a memory trace

Even when someone represents something from his own past and his past experience is part of the cause of his representing it *in* the circumstance of being prompted, still he may not be remembering anything. Suppose that someone sees something and as a result becomes suggestible to all sorts of 'promptings' whether true or false, concerning what he has done and observed. For brevity we shall say that this past experience has produced in him a 'suggestible' state. He is strictly prompted about something he really did see, and due to the suggestible state produced in him by that past observation he accepts the prompting. According to all the criteria which we have so far set down, he is remembering what he has seen. Yet surely in the case just described it does not follow that he is remembering anything beyond the story with which he was prompted.

Once this point is accepted, it might be thought obvious that it follows from the description of the case that he is *not* remembering anything beyond the story with which he was prompted. It might be thought that if someone has some memory of something, then he must be able to select correct from incorrect promptings. If there exists in him a suggestible state, then he accepts a true or false prompting equally readily. Presented with both he may not be able to choose, and he will be as liable to accept the false one as he is to accept the true one. If he is in this condition then, although he may be correctly representing something because he has seen it, it does not follow that he is remembering it. We shall see, however, that it does not follow that he is *not* remembering it.

This latest difficulty has been raised by means of a case in which the person's representation involves his holding a belief about the past. In fact, a precisely analogous problem arises in those cases in which his representing something does not involve belief, as in the case of the painter in Section 3. It is logically possible that someone should see something and as a result gain the power of highly accurate short-term retention. Then he might relate a story with which he had been prompted, due to this power produced in him by his own past observation of the matter which he relates. Thus he would satisfy all the criteria which we have enunciated so far. Yet it does not follow that he remembers anything beyond the story with which he has been prompted. Evidence for the supposition that he was remembering only the story and not the past event would be supplied if it were found that the truth of the promptings put to him about his own past had nothing to do with whether he related these stories upon being prompted with them. We must be careful to say that it does not follow in such a case that he is remembering; we must not say that it follows that he is *not* remembering. (The solution which we will give to the problem raised by the 'suggestible' state will also solve this problem.)

It is easy to see why it would be a mistake to say that a person *could* not be remembering, if the past experience recounted had produced a suggestible state in him. Sometimes he might remember the matter perfectly well if left alone. His past experience might have left him with a fair memory of what he experienced, but also it might have produced in him a suggestible state due to which he accepts any credible prompting. Thus it is possible that when he needs full prompting, it may revive his memory, even though, due to the suggestible state in him, he would have accepted a false prompting with equal readiness.

This may appear to make our problem insoluble. If we do not rule out his being in a suggestible state when we define remembering, we seem bound to admit inadmissible cases. Yet if we *do* rule that he must not be in a suggestible state, we rule out admissible cases.

The following rule might be thought to do the trick:

If the prompting elicits his representation, from a 'memory state' (rather than a 'suggestible state') then, if a false prompting at that time would have elicited a false representation of the event, the state to which this false prompting would be due must be something other than that state which led him to give a true representation upon being correctly prompted.

A difficulty arises with this common-sense method of coping with the difficulty, however. Call the memory state, taken together with the suggestible state, state M'. We can then say that M' is the basis of someone's representing his past upon being prompted about it, although the basis of his giving a false representation upon being falsely prompted would have been the very same state M'. Thus the proposed rule fails in its purpose, since the person may be remembering when his representation of the past, upon being prompted, is due to M'. According to the proposed rule he would *not* be remembering it. It is pointless to attempt to defend the rule thus:

Don't be silly! If the memory part of the M' state is responsible for his representation of the past, and the suggestible state is not operative for his representation, then he remembers, otherwise not.

The defense is pointless, since the rule simply fails to give an effective statement of the difference between the memory part of M' and the suggestible part of M'.

It is natural to attempt a counterfactual account of the memory state, thus:

The memory state for X is that state in the person, produced by his past experience of X, which leads him to accept or select a true prompting, and which is such that if no other state existed which would lead him to accept true or false promptings about X, then he would accept or select only true promptings about X.

This rule does at least avoid the difficulty raised in terms of the state M'. M' is not the memory state, since it is not true that if no other state relevant to the acceptance of promptings existed in him, he would select true from false promptings. This is because M' is a combination of the memory and the suggestible states. The rule suffers, however, from a far more radical defect than the previous one, which was merely inadequate. Who is to say what the man would do if no other state relevant to his accepting promptings, true or false, existed in him? It is not improbable that he would be a zombie.

The problem can be solved by recourse to the idea of a memory trace. This idea is an indispensable part of our idea of memory. Once we accept the causal model for memory we must also accept the existence of some sort of trace, or structural analogue of what was experienced. Even if someone could overcome the many difficulties of various kinds surrounding the idea of action at a distance, it could not be true to say that someone was remembering an event if his past experience of that event caused him, over a temporal gap, to recount it. There is an inevitable recourse to metaphors about the storage of our past experience involved in our idioms and thought about memory. Furthermore, if our past experience could act directly on us now, there would no longer be any reason to suppose that we could remember only what we had experienced ourselves. So long as we hold some sort of 'storage' or 'trace' account of memory, it follows that we can remember only what we have experienced, for it is in our experience of events that they 'enter' the storehouse. If we did not hold such an account, why should we not suppose that events which occurred years before we were born could cause us to recount their occurrence?

Some philosophers are inclined to think that to hold the notion of a causal connection to be part of the idea of memory is to hold the notion of actual causal connection to be part of the idea of memory. (See the section to follow on Professor Norman Malcolm.) Similarly, no doubt, they would think that our latest move commits us still more deeply to the idea that the common notion of memory contains the ideas which are found only in specialized areas of knowledge such as neurophysiology. But this is not so. People can understand the general requirements for a memory trace though they have little or no idea of the specific nature of such a trace. They may rely on as simple an explanation as that of a print of a coin in wax, or they may, like Wittgenstein, use examples such as the structural analogy between music and the groove in a gramophone record. For any increase in pitch of the music, there is an increase in the number of wriggles per unit length in the groove. For any increase in loudness of the music, there is an increase in deflection of the groove, and so on. Only a 'perfect' structural analogue would have a system of differences which mirrored, one to one, the differences in the original. Perhaps there is no sense to the idea of mirroring all the features of a thing, for there may be no sense in the notion of all the features of anything. But it is enough for our purposes that we can make sense of the idea of an analogue which contains at least as many features as there are details which a given person can relate about something he has experienced.

We can now deal directly with the problem of distinguishing between the suggestible and the memory state. It must be clear on the one hand that someone *may* not be remembering, if a past experience of an event has put him into a suggestible state in which he is prone to accept promptings whether true or false, for this suggestible state may not be a structural analogue of what was observed of the past event. At the same time, our past experience of the event may have produced a memory trace in us as well as a suggestible state. (This has the consequence that if we are put into both states and we need to be fully prompted, it is impossible to verify that we are remembering upon being prompted, without appealing to the sort of detailed physiological knowledge which is at the moment possessed by no one. It also might seem possible that the memory trace should itself be a suggestible state. This suggestion is full of difficulties, however, and we do not intend to pursue it.) Thus clause (c) of criterion 3 completes our analysis of remembering:

The state or set of states produced by the past experience must constitute a structural analogue of the thing remembered, to the extent to which he can accurately represent the thing.

9. Malcolm on remembering

Since the substance of this article was written, Professor Norman Malcolm has published a valuable contribution to the subject of memory in three chapters of his book, *Knowledge and Certainty* (Englewood Cliffs, 1963). Our account differs from his in various ways.

Malcolm claims that a person *B* remembers that *p* if and only if *B* knows that *p*, because he knew that *p*. This definition has three elements: the present knowledge that *p*, the previous knowledge that *p*, and the relationship between the present and previous knowledge expressed by saying that *B* knows that *p because* he previously knew that *p*. The elements are separately necessary and jointly sufficient conditions of factual memory. We shall consider these three conditions in turn.

Previous knowledge Suppose that someone sees something, but thinks that he is suffering a hallucination. The person sees something, but since he does not accept that he is seeing it, he fails to gain the knowledge that it is there in front of him. Some time later he learns that there had been nothing at all the matter with him at the time, and that he had really seen what he thought he had hallucinated. He is able to give a detailed and faithful account of what he saw. It is incorrect to insist that he cannot be remembering what he saw simply because at the time he had not believed his eyes. The question whether he remembers having distrusted his senses is quite distinct from the question whether he remembers seeing what he did. Naturally this case is different from the one described by Malcolm as a possible difficulty for his analysis (p. 223). In the case we suggest, the person is given no new information about what he saw. When he discovers that he had not been hallucinated previously, surely he will say, 'Well, of course, in that case, I remember *seeing. . . .*' This cannot be considered as one of Malcolm's 'elliptical' uses of 'remembers.'

Malcolm thinks that someone can know that he has a particular sensation only if he has a language in which to express this fact. It would take us too far afield to discuss this, but in conjunction with his requirement of previous knowledge for remembering, it leads Malcolm, in the following passage, to accept as an 'interesting consequence' what we consider to be a *reductio ad absurdum.*

I do not believe that there is any sense in which a dog or infant can be said to know that it has some sensation. I accept the consequence that a dog cannot be said to remember that he had a painful ear, and also the more interesting consequence that a human being cannot be said to remember that he had one, if he had it at a time before he knew enough language to be able to tell anyone that he had it. This point is connected with what Wittgenstein says about William James's Ballard (*Philosophical Investigations*, sec. 342).

We wonder what Malcolm would say about an adult deaf-mute.

Present knowledge We have argued that present belief is not a necessary condition for remembering (Section 3). It is clear that those arguments apply also to Malcolm's claim that present knowledge is a necessary condition.

The 'because' relationship Malcolm presents arguments against a causal interpretation of the 'because' in 'He now knows that p "because" he previously knew that p.' If these arguments are correct, then any causal analysis of remembering is mistaken.

Malcolm professes not to understand what is meant by causal dependence in connection with what would be meant by remembering. He says:

> What *could* fill the gap? I have mentioned three candidates: a persisting physiological state or process; continuous thinking about what is remembered; continuous unconscious thinking about what is remembered. We see that for different reasons none of these candidates can be included in the truth conditions for statements of the form 'A remembers that p.' I believe we do not have the conception of anything else that might fill the gap. In a sense, therefore, we do not know what it means to speak of a *gap* here (p. 238).

It seems that Malcolm has put forward the following invalid argument. 'P' does not entail 'Q.' 'P' does not entail 'R.' 'P' does not entail 'S.' Therefore 'P' does not entail 'Q or R or S.'

Whether or not Malcolm is right and his three alternatives are in fact the only conceivable ones, he has given no valid argument to show that 'B remembers that p' does not entail existence of some continuous causal process.

Our own view is that the relations between 'Some causal process exists' and 'This particular process exists' is not the same as the relation between a disjunction of statements that particular processes exist and any one of those statements. He feels that it is a mere piece of imagery to require that *some* (unknown) continuous causal connection should exist. He says, 'This feeling of the mysteriousness of memory, unless we assume a persisting state or process between the previous and the present knowledge, provides one *metaphysical* aspect of the topic of memory' (pp. 237, 238). This is very strange. The ordinary idea of a slot machine logically involves the idea of a device in which some mechanism or other is set in operation by the coin, which in some way delivers the appropriate goods. Is this idea a 'mere piece of imagery'? Although most ordinary people do not know how a slot machine works, they would not be prepared to call something a slot machine if it were opened up and found to have no works. To parody Malcolm: 'This feeling of the mysteriousness of a coin-in-the-slot machine, unless we assume a persisting state or process between the insertion of a coin and the appearance of cigarettes, provides one *metaphysical* aspect of the topic of coin-in-the-slot machines.'

There is evidence that Malcolm thinks that a singular causal statement, 'X causes Y' must entail a statement of the form 'In like circumstances, whenever X, then Y (pp. 232, 236; cf. Section 6 of this article). This makes him think that a causal account of memory is impossible. (As a matter of fact, he himself accepts as 'genuinely causal' (p. 237) a case in which it is no easier to formulate a law than in the cases which he dismisses. This slip of his suggests that the notion of *cause* which he actually uses is more liberal than the one he states.) He nowhere argues that there *is* no law relating past knowledge and present knowledge, in 'like' circumstances, in cases of remembering. (Given the unspecified phrase 'in like circumstances,' it is surely in no way obvious that there is no law relating his knowing a thing of a certain sort at one time with his knowing that thing at a later, *in like circumstances*.) Nor does he canvass any fresh arguments to resolve the well-known dispute whether causal statements can *ever* be analyzed in terms of regularities. Malcolm's account, '*B* now knows that *p*, *because* he knew that *p*', is:

A person *B* remembers that *p* from a time, *t*, if and only if *B* knows that *p*, and *B* knew that *p* at *t*, and if *B* had not known at *t* that *p* he would not now know that *p*.

This account is at once too strong and too weak. It is too strong for reasons given in Section VI (pp. 178–179). A person who remembers something might have another independent source of information. This point has recently been made by Stanley Munsat ('A Note on Factual Memory,' *Philosophical Studies*, 16 (1965), p. 33). The account is too weak for reasons similar to those given in section 6. For consider a case in which a person knows that *p* at time *t*, writes it in his diary, forgets it completely, and relearns that *p* from what he wrote in his diary. If he had no other source of information, then he would not now know that *p*, if he had not known that *p* at time *t*. Yet it does not follow that he remembers that *p* from time *t*. Often he will only remember that *p* from the time at which he subsequently reads his diary.

10. Conclusion

In conclusion we must guard against a certain misconstruction of our analysis of memory. It is this:

Take any case in which *A* observes an event *E*, *P* is a prompting, and *R* is *A*'s representation of *E*; *P* is part of the cause of *R*. In such a case, when *A* gives *R* he is not only remembering *E* but, according to the causal analysis of remembering given, he must be said to be remembering *P* as well as *E* since any representation of *E* is *ipso facto* a representation of any representation of *E*. Thus in remembering an event a person willy-nilly remembers any prompting which is part of the cause of his now giving the representation of his observation of the past event. But this is absurd and so the analysis is in some way incorrect.

Such an objection is based on a misunderstanding. Consider the case of a bird watcher who saw a yellow-tufted titmouse. He had never seen one before and so he described it in his diary. Suppose that years later his reading of his diary is part of the cause of a subsequent description he gives of what he originally saw. Such a supposition does not in the least imply that his reading of the diary is part of the cause of his representation of reading the diary, for the simple reason that he does *not* represent his reading the diary. There is a difference between his remembering the occasion of first seeing a yellow-tufted titmouse and his remembering reading what he put in his diary. Someone may remember with great clarity the occasion of seeing the bird, and yet not remember reading what he put in his diary. Or he may remember with great precision reading what he put in his diary, and yet not remember seeing the bird.

Summary As well as the usual distinctions made between remembering how to do something, remembering that something occurred, and remembering an occurrence or object, there is a distinction to be drawn between two different uses of 'remembers that.' Despite these various distinctions, the uses of 'remembers' resemble each other in their requirements of past perception, of correctness about what was perceived or learned, and of a causal connection between past perception and a subsequent representation of what was perceived or gained by perception. The exception is that in remembering how to do something, the requirement in the present may be that what was learned is done again, rather than represented. A careful examination of all that is required of the causal connection brings to the surface the complex and partly theoretical nature of our commonplace notion of remembering.

The analysis of remembering which we have given may be used to answer some skeptical questions about memory, and it has importance for other problems about knowledge, but an investigation of these implications is altogether another enterprise.

Chapter 36

Testimony and observation

C. A. J. Coady

IN answer to the question 'Why do you believe that?' or 'How do you know that?' it is proper to make such replies as 'I saw it' or 'It follows from this' or 'It usually happens like that' or 'Jones told me so.' There may be more than these four kinds of reply possible (e.g., 'It's a matter of insight,' 'I remember it,' 'I intuited it') and there may be more than one way of interpreting or taking any of them. Nonetheless there are *at least* these four kinds of reply possible and there are at least four standard ways of interpreting them which give rise to four prima facie categories of evidence: observation, deductive inference, inductive inference, and testimony. The first three have had a great deal of attention paid to them in philosophy but the fourth has been relatively neglected.[1] I hope to do something toward repairing that neglect; a neglect which certainly cannot have arisen from the insignificance of the role played by testimony in the forming of beliefs in the community since as Hume notes: '. . . there is no species of reasoning more common, more useful, and even necessary to human life, than that which is derived from the testimony of men and the reports of eye-witnesses and spectators.'[2]

Hume is, indeed, one of the few philosophers I have read who has offered anything like a sustained account of testimony and if any view has a claim to the title of 'the received view' it is his. In what follows I shall examine and criticize Hume's position in the hope of throwing light on more general issues concerning the nature and status of testimony. Hume's account of the matter is offered in his essay on Miracles which is Sect. 10 of *An Enquiry Concerning Human Understanding*. Essentially his theory constitutes a reduction of testimony as a form of evidence or support to the status of a species (one might almost say, a mutation) of inductive

C. A. J. Coady, 'Testimony and Observation' in *American Philosophical Quarterly* 10 (1973), pp. 149–55 reprinted by permission of the publisher.

1. A notable non-neglector is Professor H. H. Price who has discussed the issue in his recent book, *Belief* (London and New York, 1969). His chapter on this ('The Evidence of Testimony') has a quite different orientation to my discussion although he shows himself to be well aware of some of those defects in the traditional approach to which I shall be directing attention. Sydney Shoemaker also touches upon some of the issues discussed here in ch. 6 of his book *Self-Knowledge and Self-Identity* (Ithaca, 1963). Although Shoemaker is not primarily concerned with testimony he does, as I do, reject the idea that the validity of testimony could be established by observation. His arguments, however, are very different from mine and reflect his basic concern with certain problems of self-knowledge and memory. They also reflect certain Wittgensteinian assumptions about memory, language, and philosophy which I do not wish either to discuss or employ in what follows.

2. Sect. 88, David Hume, *An Enquiry Concerning Human Understanding* (Oxford, 1957). All quotations hereafter from this work are taken from L. A. Selby-Bigge's Second Edition of the *Enquiries* published by Clarendon Press, Oxford. Bracketed page references in my text are to that edition.

inference. And, again, insofar as inductive inference is reduced by Hume to a species of observation and consequences attendant upon observations then in a like fashion testimony meets the same fate. So we find him saying immediately after the piece quoted above:

This species of reasoning, perhaps, one may deny to be founded on the relation of cause and effect. I shall not dispute about a word. It will be sufficient to observe that our assurance in any argument of this kind is derived from no other principle than our observation of the veracity of human testimony, and of the usual conformity of facts to the reports of witnesses. It being a general maxim, that no objects have any discoverable connexion together, and that all the inferences, which we can draw from one to another, are founded merely on our experience of their constant and regular conjunction; it is evident that we ought not to make an exception to this maxim in favour of human testimony, whose connexion with any event seems, in itself, as little necessary as any other. (p. 111.)

And elsewhere in the same essay he says:

The reason why we place any credit in witnesses and historians, is not derived from any *connexion*, which we perceive *a priori*, between testimony and reality, but because we are accustomed to find a conformity between them. (p. 113.)

This is the view that I want to contest and, as it is convenient to have a label, I shall call it the Reductionist Thesis and shall employ the abbreviation R.T. to refer to it. My criticism begins by calling attention to a fatal ambiguity in the use of terms like 'experience' and 'observation' in the Humean statement of R.T. We are told by Hume that we only trust in testimony because experience has shown it to be reliable but where experience means individual observation and the expectations it gives rise to, this seems plainly false and, on the other hand, where it means common experience (i.e., the reliance upon the observations of others) it is surely question-begging. To take the second horn of the dilemma first—let us call it R.T.[2]—we find Hume speaking of '*our* observation of the veracity of human testimony' and '*our* experience of their constant and regular conjunction.' And it is clear enough that Hume often means to refer by such phrases to the common experience of mankind and not to the mere solitary observations of David Hume. Our reliance upon testimony as an institution, so to speak, is supposed to be based on the same kind of footing as our reliance upon laws of nature (Hume thinks of this as an important premiss in his critique of miracles) and he speaks of the 'firm and unalterable experience' which has established these laws. It is an important part of his argument that a miracle must be a violation of the laws of nature and so he says:

It is no miracle that a man, seemingly in good health, should die on a sudden: because such a kind of death, though more unusual than any other, has yet been frequently observed to happen. But it is a miracle that a dead man should come to life; because that has *never* been observed in any age or country. There must therefore be a uniform experience against every miraculous event, otherwise the event would not merit that appellation. (p. 115.)

We may ignore, for our purposes here, the validity of this highly debatable account of a law of nature and the blatant question-begging of his '*never* been observed in any age or country' and yet gather from this extract the need Hume has to mean by 'experience,' 'observation,' and the like, the common experience of mankind. Clearly his argument does not turn on the fact, for instance that *he* has 'frequently observed' the sudden death of a man 'seemingly in good health'—it is quite likely that Hume (like most of us) never had occasion to observe personally anything of the kind. And the point is surely clinched by his reference to 'uniform experience' and his use of the phrase 'observed in any age or country.'

Evidently then, R.T., as actually argued by Hume, is involved in vicious circularity since the experience upon which our reliance upon testimony as a form of evidence is supposed to rest is itself reliant upon testimony which cannot itself be reduced in the same way. The idea of taking seriously someone else's observations, someone else's experience, already requires us to take their testimony (in this case, reports of what they observe) equally seriously. It is ludicrous to talk of their observations being the major part of our justification in taking their reports seriously when we have to take their reports seriously in order to know what their observations are.

Hume's conflation of personal and communal observation can be further illustrated by a passage from the *Treatise of Human Nature* (Bk. I, Pt. IV, Sect. 2). Discussing our reasons for believing in the continued, independent existence of material things, he says:

I receive a letter, which, upon opening it, I perceive by the handwriting and subscription to have come from a friend, who says he is two hundred leagues distant. It is evident I can never account for this phenomenon, conformable to my experience in other instances, without spreading out in my mind the whole sea and continent between us, and supposing the effects and continued existence of posts and ferries, according to my memory and observation. (p. 196, Selby-Bigge edition.)

Here we have Hume using 'my' observation when he is clearly not entitled to do so since there is probably no single person who has personally observed the complete path of even *one* letter from the moment it leaves the sender's hand to the moment it reaches its destination. Hume might have observed postmen, posts, ferries, etc., but his beliefs about what they do (his belief in the postal system) is dependent upon a complicated web of testimony, a highlight among which would no doubt be what he was told by his teachers or parents. And yet, 'my memory and observation.' How easy it is to appropriate at a very fundamental level what is known by report and what is known by personal observation. Similarly, that babies are born of women in a certain way is known to all of us and it is a fact of observation but very few of us have ever observed it for ourselves.

So much for the second part of the dilemma but what of the first part—let us call it R.T.[1] Surely we can, on Hume's behalf, retract his incautious commitment to common experience and state the R.T. in terms of personal observations alone. My claim was that so stated R.T.[1] is plainly false but this has yet to be shown. R.T.[1] would run something like this:

We rely upon testimony as a species of evidence *because* each of us observes for himself a constant and regular conjunction between what people report and the way the world is. More particularly, we each observe for ourselves a constant conjunction between kinds of report and kinds of situation so that we have good inductive grounds for expecting this conjunction to continue in the future.

My justification for bringing in the idea of a kind of report correlating with a kind of situation is Hume himself:

And as the evidence, derived from witnesses and human testimony, is founded on past experience, so it varies with the experience, and is regarded either as a *proof* or a *probability* according as the conjunction between any particular kind of report and any kind of object has been found to be constant or variable. (p. 112.)

Now I characterized this sort of position as 'plainly false' because it seems absurd to suggest that, individually, we have done anything like the amount of fieldwork that R.T.[1] requires. As mentioned earlier, most of us have never seen a baby born nor have we examined the circulation of the blood nor the actual geography of the world nor any fair sample of the laws of the land nor have we made the observations that lie behind our knowledge that the lights in the sky are heavenly bodies immensely distant nor a vast number of other observations that R.T.[1] would seem to require. Some people have of course made them *for us* but we are precluded from taking any solace from this fact under the present interpretation of R.T. So it was this general situation that made me speak of R.T.[1] as plainly false.

But the matter is perhaps more complex than such a characterization would indicate as can be seen by considering a possible rejoinder by the defenders of R.T.[1]. This rejoinder might run as follows: 'You are ignoring the very important provision, made by Hume, that the conjunction in individual experience is between kinds of report and kinds of object. This cuts down the amount of observing that has to be done and makes the project a manageable one for an individual.' I think I may reasonably plead 'not guilty' to this accusation inasmuch as I intended the list above (of conjunctions never checked personally by most of us) to be more than a recital of particular conjunctions that R.T.[1] requires us to have personally checked. The list was supposed to be typical in the sense that it indicated *areas* in which we rightly accept testimony without ever having engaged in the sort of checking of reports against personal observation that R.T.[1] demands.

But quite apart from this, there seem to me to be serious difficulties in the very idea of finding constant conjunctions between (in Hume's words) 'any particular kind of report and any kind of object.' Hume wants these conjunctions to be something like the kinds of conjunctions he thinks are required to establish causal laws and even laws of nature. In such matters the decisive constant conjunctions are between one kind of object and another kind of object. But whatever we think about the idea of a kind of object, the notion of a kind of report surely requires some explanation in this context. Unfortunately Hume does nothing to provide such an explanation and since the matter is also of interest in its own right I shall risk a digression to consider some possible interpretations and their implications before turning to a different, and perhaps more decisive, difficulty for the type of approach represented by R.T.[1].

It seems to me that 'kind of report' may be meant to refer either to the kind of speaker who gives the report or to the kind of content the report contains. If it is the former that is intended (and some of Hume's remarks *seem* to indicate this) then presumably the kind of speaker will not be determined by such considerations as color of skin or nationality or hair-style or height, rather, the relevant kind will have something to do with authority or expertise or credentials to say. So the R.T.[1] would go something like: We rely upon testimony because we have each personally observed a correlation between expert (or authoritative) reports and the kinds of situations reported in a large number of cases.

But the major difficulty for this interpretation is that a man's being an expert or an authority on some matter cannot be a matter of mere inspection in the way that his being white or tall is. That some man is an expert on, say, geography or South East Asian politics, is either known on the testimony of others (by far the most usual case) or it has to be established by observing some high correlation between his reports and the relevant situations in the world. If the former then we are no further advanced upon the R.T. program of justification since the same problem of establishing expertise must arise again and again. But if the latter, then the notion of an authority or an expert no longer provides us with any specification of *a kind of report*. That is to say, we cannot use the idea of *a kind of report* as equivalent to *report of a kind of speaker* and then proceed to validate testimony along the lines of R.T.[1] because the kind of correlation situation *the existence of which we would supposedly be investigating* would have to be known by us to exist already before we could set up the terms of the investigation.[3]

This indicates that the business of establishing constant conjunctions between kinds of report and kinds of situation must begin with the interpretation of 'kinds of report' as 'reports of kinds of situation.' And certainly this seems to be a natural way of interpreting Hume's intentions at this point. An initial problem for this interpretation concerns the degree of generality that should attach to the content of a report before it qualifies as a kind of report. That is to say, some sort of decision would presumably be required as to whether or not the report 'There is a sick lion in Taronga Park Zoo' belonged to the kind medical report or geographical report or empirical report or existence report. Perhaps it could be said to belong to all of them or to some and not to others but whatever was said it would be of consider-able importance to the establishing of conjunctions, since a decision here is a decision about the actual identity of the conjunctions and hence, in consequence, about the degree of correlation likely to be established. For instance, if the report were treated as belonging to the kind 'existence report' then it might be that Jones had personally established quite a large number of conjunctions between existence reports and the relevant existence situations without this being any real reason for accepting the report in question. (Compare with: 'There is a Martian in my study' which is equally well supported by Jones's personal experience of existence reports.) On the other hand, if it were treated as a medical report then Jones may have had very little personal experience of correlations between medical reports

3. It may appear that part of this difficulty could be met by recourse to the qualification 'report of a so-called expert' but this is mere appearance since we require some assurance that we are checking the reports of those who are not merely self-styled experts but widely acknowledged as such and this sort of assurance could only be had by reliance upon testimony.

and medical facts yet this would hardly be a real reason for not accepting the report. In addition, Jones would, on Hume's hypothesis, now have a strong reason for accepting the report if he classifies it one way and no reason for accepting it if he classifies it another way. Since either classification is logically permissible then it seems to be purely a matter of whim whether Jones has or has not good reason for accepting the report. Clearly some sort of non-arbitrary restriction on the scope of 'report of a kind of situation' is required to make this notion of any real value in the elaboration of R.T.[1]. Here, however, I shall pursue no further the interpretation of 'kind of report' and the difficulties involved in specifying clearly the sort of correlations required by R.T.[1] because, on the perhaps dubious assumption that the difficulties are soluble, I want to raise what seems to me to be a more fundamental problem.

This difficulty consists in the fact that the whole enterprise of R.T.[1] in its present form requires that we understand what testimony is independently of knowing that it is, in general, a reliable form of evidence about the way the world is. This is, of course, the point of Hume's saying:

The reason why we place any credit in witnesses and historians, is not derived from any *connexion*, which we perceive *a priori*, between testimony and reality, but because we are accustomed to find a conformity between them. (p. 113.)

It is a clear implication from this that we might have discovered (though in fact we did not) that there was no conformity at all between testimony and reality. Hume's position requires the possibility that we clearly isolate the reports that people make about the world for comparison by personal observation with the actual state of the world and find a high, low, or no correlation between them. But it is by no means clear that we can understand this suggestion. To take the most extreme discovery: imagine a world in which an extensive survey yields no correlation between reports and (individually observed) facts. In such a colossally topsy-turvy world what evidence would there possibly be for the existence of reports at all? Imagine a community of Martians who are in the mess that R.T.[1] allows as a possibility. Let us suppose for the moment that they have a language which we can translate (there are difficulties in this supposition as we shall see shortly) with names for distinguishable things in their environment and suitable predicative equipment. We find, however, to our astonishment, that whenever they construct sentences addressed to each other in the absence (from their vicinity) of the things designated by the names but when they are, as we should think, in a position to *report* then they seem to say what we (more synoptically placed) can observe to be false. But in such a situation there would be no reason to believe that they even had the practice of reporting. There would be no behavior or setting for what we know as reporting. There would, for instance, be no reliance upon the utterances of others; just this curious fantasy practice rather like the fantasy games of children ('Mummy, there's a burglar in the house') but generalized to the stage where we can discern no point in the activity at all, even a parasitic point. The supposition that reports could be divorced from reality in this way is like the supposition that orders might never be obeyed. If there were Martians who uttered certain sounds in a tone of voice like the tone we use in ordering we might initially conjecture that they were issuing orders in making these sounds but this conjecture would just be refuted if it were found that these sounds never had any effect that might be described as obedience upon any audience.

But actually the situation with reporting and testifying is even worse than this because the supposed Martian community seem to be in trouble even about the content of the utterances that are alleged to be non-correlated reports. The question of the meaning or content of what they say in their alleged reports is of great importance because the task of looking for a correlation or conjunction of the Humean type is dependent upon knowing what state of affairs is supposed to correlate with the utterance. The principle of correlation has to be given by the meaning of the utterances because, after all, *any* utterance is correlated with or conjoined to *any* situation according to *some* principle of matching. So, even if we allow, for the sake of argument, that we can understand what it is for the Martians to engage in reporting, we cannot accept the coherence of the no-correlation story unless we can understand what Martian reports actually say. But it is precisely here that serious difficulties arise and to see how they arise we must look more closely at the supposed Martian situation.

Although I have not tried to define testimony (and there are problems facing any such attempt) it should be clear that, on any plausible definition, a very high proportion of the statements made by a community over a sample period will have to be testimony statements. These utterances will contrast with such speech episodes as soliloquies, musings, and conjectures. In the Martian community a common vocabulary is employed across different speech acts so that, as with us, the same form of words may be used for either conjecture or testimony (e.g., 'He pushed her in') although there may also be speech-act indicators available of an Austinian or Searlean form ('I testify that . . .' 'I conjecture that . . .'). Suppose then that we encounter a Martian who uses the utterance 'Kar do gnos u grin' in the presence of a tree in a garden. Perhaps he waves a languid hand at the tree as he does so. We speculate that this utterance means, can be translated as, 'There is a tree in the garden' and, in particular, that 'gnos' means 'tree.'[4] We then find, however, that the Martian frequently uses 'gnos' in remarks in situations not involving the presence of a tree in his observational vicinity. Some few of these remarks we assess as mere conjectures (and I shall ignore the problems raised by the question of how this assessment is made) but the majority we decide to be testimony. So we find the Martian saying things of the form: 'Kar do gnos u grin,' 'Kar do gnos u bilt,' 'Kar do gnos u tonk' and we guess that these mean 'There is a tree in the garden,' 'There is a tree in the study,' 'There is a tree in the field,' or whatever. But then we find that there never is a tree in the garden or in the study or in the field and that in fact this Martian never uses 'gnos' to make a true statement when he is talking (non-conjecturely) to others about, as it seems, absent trees. Furthermore, *no* Martian

---

4. There is perhaps a problem in working out what he is up to and hence a puzzle as to how we are even entitled to speculate that his utterance means *this* but suppose that there is enough about his behavior to permit us to conclude that he is soliloquizing in the fashion of one who is struck by the existence of that particular tree in that particular garden.

ever uses 'gnos' to make a true report about absent trees though they make, as we surmise, constant attempts to do so. Furthermore, no Martian ever contradicts or corrects another Martian about absent trees on the basis of his own observation or the 'testimony' of others *since* by hypothesis no testimony ever matches the facts. Surely in this sort of set-up we would have to conclude that 'gnos' did not mean 'tree' or that it did not mean it unambiguously or possibly that the Martians have a device for negation which we have not yet uncovered (so that 'Kar do gnos u grin' really means 'There isn't a tree in the garden') or perhaps that the Martians are totally incomprehensible to us. Indeed this last conclusion would be considerably fortified by the fact that the linguistic chaos described above is generated on behalf of not just one sound 'gnos' that the Martians utter but by every sound which is supposed to be a word and upon the reference of which the truth or falsity of an alleged report could turn!

It might be complained at this point that I have not described the Martian community in sufficient detail and I readily concede that my account of their circumstances is somewhat sketchy. Possibly an attempt could be made to fill out such details as whether their non-veridical testimony has the form of a massive mistake or a massive deception but any such attempt would, I believe, only add support to my conclusion that their supposed situation is eventually unintelligible to us. I am content if enough has been said of their plight to raise serious doubts about the task of identifying the contents of Martian-type reports and hence of establishing Humean correlations in such a world. The general point here is that although making true reports with words is not the same thing as using the words correctly, nonetheless the ability to make true reports with words *is* connected with using the words correctly and this ability is something that can only be exhibited (even to the persons themselves) in the consistent making of true reports.

There is a further point to be made about the connection of testimony with meaning. If we take it that teaching someone the meaning of words involves the giving of reports and testimony then the present form of R.T.[1] is in even hotter water than before since the suggestion that no reports in fact conform to reality involves the claim that our imagined Martians never report to the Martian children the actual use of their words. Here the idea that the Martians have a public language gets no grip at all.[5] I do not intend exploring this difficulty any further, however, since I am not clear whether Hume would regard such remarks as ' "Cat" means one of these' or ' "Cat" is the word for a four-legged etc.' as pieces of testimony. I think it quite likely that he would insofar as he would probably regard them as reports upon the empirical fact that such terms are used in a certain way in a certain community. I do not want to prejudge the question of whether they are such reports but if they are or if the proponent of R.T. believes that they are then he has no way at all of setting up the possibility upon which his theory rests.

5. The problem arises dramatically in the teaching situation but it might be objected that it is a merely contingent fact that languages are acquired by teaching. I am not altogether clear about the import here of the phrase 'a merely contingent fact' but in any event essentially the same difficulty arises in the correction situation. It is surely unimaginable that a community could operate a common language without the resources for correcting the inevitable divergences from correct use.

Let us summarize our progress to date. From Hume's account of testimony I extracted a reductionist thesis which had two forms. I argued that the second form, R.T.², which justified testimony in terms of common experience was circular and that the first form, R.T.¹, which justified testimony in terms of individual observation was simply false since our reliance upon testimony rightly goes beyond anything that could be justified by personal observations. I then considered the rejoinder that R.T.¹ might be more plausible if great weight were put upon the observation of constant conjunction between kinds of report and kinds of object and I argued that much was unclear about what was to count as a kind of report, and hence what was to count as a correlation, for the purposes of R.T.¹. In any case R.T.¹ surely requires that any such investigation into conjunctions of reports with states of affairs might conclude that there were no such correlations between the two. The supposition that such a situation obtained was pursued for the purpose of reductio ad absurdum and I argued that in such a situation, (a) there could be no such things as reports, (b) even if there were reports, there could be no way of establishing Humean correlations or non-correlations since there could be no way of determining the contents of the alleged reports in order to correlate them, and (c) the idea of a public language seems undermined.

Am I then saying, in opposition to Hume, that there *is* an a priori connection between testimony and reality? An answer to this question would have to rely on a comprehensive theory of knowledge which could determine the conditions under which an a priori connection holds between some x and reality and hence not only whether there is such a connection between testimony and reality but also whether such a connection holds, say, between perception and reality. I cannot provide such a theory here but I do not understand the idea that testimony could exist in a community and yet it be possible to discover empirically that it had no 'connection with reality?' Hence, I suspect that the problem of justifying testimony is a pseudo-problem and that the evidence of testimony constitutes a fundamental category of evidence which is not reducible to, or justifiable in terms of, such other basic categories as observation or deductive inference. This opinion I have not proved but if my argument so far is correct then there is no sense to the idea of justifying testimony by observation, at least where this involves anything like a search for Humean correlations.[6]

Now, of course, none of this sloganizing means that there is no such thing as mistaken or lying testimony and it is, I think, the fact that there are conditions and circumstances under which we disregard the reports of witnesses which Hume sees as providing support for R.T. independently of his methodological doctrine that there can be no necessary connection between any one object (or kind of object) and any other object (or kind of object).

6. I have not of course proved that our reliance on testimony may not be 'justified' in some other manner. Russell, for one, has attempted (in *Human Knowledge Its Scope and Limits* [New York, 1948]) to justify testimony by recourse to a principle of analogy and Price (*op. cit.*) by recourse to a methodological rule. I hope it is clear from what has been said in this paper, however, that such attempts face very serious difficulties, some of which are simple extensions of the difficulties faced by Hume.

Were not the memory tenacious to a certain degree, had not men commonly an inclination to truth and a principle of probity; were they not sensible to shame, when detected in a falsehood: Were not these, I say, discovered by *experience* to be qualities, inherent in human nature, we should never repose the least confidence in human testimony. A man delirious, or noted for falsehood and villainy, has no manner of authority with us. (p. 112.)

Hume's argument is not fully explicit here but he seems to be claiming that since we sometimes discover by observation and experience that some testimony is *unreliable* (i.e., 'A man delirious or noted for falsehood or villainy has no manner of authority with us') then we must discover the general *reliability* of testimony by the same method. But this surely has only to be stated to be seen to be invalid for the fact that observation can sometimes uncover false testimony does nothing toward showing that the general reliability of testimony depends upon observation in the way R.T. requires.

Furthermore, the fact that observation will sometimes lead us to reject some piece of testimony needs to be set against two other facts, namely—

(a) That other testimony sometimes leads us to reject some piece of testimony without personal observation entering into the matter. Consider, for instance, Hume's *very* example of the man noted for delirium or falsehood or villainy.

(b) That testimony sometimes leads us to reject some piece of observation. There are many different sorts of cases here. In philosophical discussions about perception one is apt to hear quite a lot about people who 'see' a table in front of them in optimum observational conditions but become convinced that there is no table there because everyone around them says there isn't. Less fancifully, this case springs from those in which the testimony of others assures us that we are or are not hallucinated. Furthermore, there are often situations where we accept correction of our ordinary mis-observations from reports of others:—'Look at that herd of cows,' 'They're not cows they're rock formations.' Or we observe a scuffle between three men and the upshot is that one of them is stabbed. There were four of us observing it and I hold that the man stabbed himself but the others maintain stoutly that one of the other two, namely Smith, delivered the blow. I capitulate. Surely this could be the reasonable thing to do in some circumstances. Indeed, it would seem equally as valid, on Hume's line of argument, to claim that since testimony sometimes leads us to abandon an observation then we rely upon observation in general only because we have established its reliability on the basis of testimony. But I think Hume would hardly be happy with *this* employment of his mode of argument.

Induction

Chapter 37

On induction

Bertrand Russell

I N almost all our previous discussions we have been concerned in the attempt to get clear as to our data in the way of knowledge of existence. What things are there in the universe whose existence is known to us owing to our being acquainted with them? So far, our answer has been that we are acquainted with our sense-data, and, probably, with ourselves. These we know to exist. And past sense-data which are remembered are known to have existed in the past. This knowledge supplies our data.

But if we are to be able to draw inferences from these data—if we are to know of the existence of matter, of other people, of the past before our individual memory begins, or of the future, we must know general principles of some kind by means of which such inferences can be drawn. It must be known to us that the existence of some one sort of thing, A, is a sign of the existence of some other sort of thing, B, either at the same time as A or at some earlier or later time, as, for example, thunder is a sign of the earlier existence of lightning. If this were not known to us, we could never extend our knowledge beyond the sphere of our private experience; and this sphere, as we have seen, is exceedingly limited. The question we have now to consider is whether such an extension is possible, and if so, how it is effected.

Let us take as an illustration a matter about which none of us, in fact, feel the slightest doubt. We are all convinced that the sun will rise tomorrow. Why? Is this belief a mere blind outcome of past experience, or can it be justified as a reasonable belief? It is not easy to find a test by which to judge whether a belief of this kind is reasonable or not, but we can at least ascertain what sort of general beliefs would suffice, if true, to justify the judgement that the sun will rise tomorrow, and the many other similar judgements upon which our actions are based.

It is obvious that if we are asked why we believe that the sun will rise tomorrow, we shall naturally answer, 'Because it always has risen every day'. We have a firm

Bertrand Russell, 'On Induction' in *The Problems in Philosophy* (London, William and Norgate, 1912), pp. 93–108 reprinted by permission of The Bertrand Russell Peace Foundation Limited, Nottingham.

belief that it will rise in the future, because it has risen in the past. If we are challenged as to why we believe that it will continue to rise as heretofore, we may appeal to the laws of motion: the earth, we shall say, is a freely rotating body, and such bodies do not cease to rotate unless something interferes from outside, and there is nothing outside to interfere with the earth between now and tomorrow. Of course it might be doubted whether we are quite certain that there is nothing outside to interfere, but this is not the interesting doubt. The interesting doubt is as to whether the laws of motion will remain in operation until tomorrow. If this doubt is raised, we find ourselves in the same position as when the doubt about the sunrise was first raised.

The *only* reason for believing that the laws of motion will remain in operation is that they have operated hitherto, so far as our knowledge of the past enables us to judge. It is true that we have a greater body of evidence from the past in favour of the laws of motion than we have in favour of the sunrise, because the sunrise is merely a particular case of fulfilment of the laws of motion, and there are countless other particular cases. But the real question is: Do *any* number of cases of a law being fulfilled in the past afford evidence that it will be fulfilled in the future? If not, it becomes plain that we have no ground whatever for expecting the sun to rise tomorrow, or for expecting the bread we shall eat at our next meal not to poison us, or for any of the other scarcely conscious expectations that control our daily lives. It is to be observed that all such expectations are only *probable*; thus we have not to seek for a proof that they *must* be fulfilled, but only for some reason in favour of the view that they are *likely* to be fulfilled.

Now in dealing with this question we must, to begin with, make an important distinction, without which we should soon become involved in hopeless confusions. Experience has shown us that, hitherto, the frequent repetition of some uniform succession or coexistence has been a *cause* of our expecting the same succession or coexistence on the next occasion. Food that has a certain appearance generally has a certain taste, and it is a severe shock to our expectations when the familiar appearance is found to be associated with an unusual taste. Things which we see become associated, by habit, with certain tactile sensations which we expect if we touch them; one of the horrors of a ghost (in many ghost-stories) is that it fails to give us any sensations of touch. Uneducated people who go abroad for the first time are so surprised as to be incredulous when they find their native language not understood.

And this kind of association is not confined to men; in animals also it is very strong. A horse which has been often driven along a certain road resists the attempt to drive him in a different direction. Domestic animals expect food when they see the person who usually feeds them. We know that all these rather crude expectations of uniformity are liable to be misleading. The man who has fed the chicken every day throughout its life at last wrings its neck instead, showing that more refined views as to the uniformity of nature would have been useful to the chicken.

But in spite of the misleadingness of such expectations, they nevertheless exist. The mere fact that something has happened a certain number of times causes animals and men to expect that it will happen again. Thus our instincts certainly cause us to believe that the sun will rise tomorrow, but we may be in no better a position than the chicken which unexpectedly has its neck wrung. We have therefore to distinguish the fact that past uniformities *cause* expectations as to the future, from the question whether there is any reasonable ground for giving weight to such expectations after the question of their validity has been raised.

The problem we have to discuss is whether there is any reason for believing in what is called 'the uniformity of nature'. The belief in the uniformity of nature is the belief that everything that has happened or will happen is an instance of some general law to which there are *no* exceptions. The crude expectations which we have been considering are all subject to exceptions, and therefore liable to disappoint those who entertain them. But science habitually assumes, at least as a working hypothesis, that general rules which have exceptions can be replaced by general rules which have no exceptions. 'Unsupported bodies in air fall' is a general rule to which balloons and aeroplanes are exceptions. But the laws of motion and the law of gravitation, which account for the fact that most bodies fall, also account for the fact that balloons and aeroplanes can rise; thus the laws of motion and the law of gravitation are not subject to these exceptions.

The belief that the sun will rise tomorrow might be falsified if the earth came suddenly into contact with a large body which destroyed its rotation; but the laws of motion and the law of gravitation would not be infringed by such an event. The business of science is to find uniformities, such as the laws of motion and the law of gravitation, to which, so far as our experience extends, there are no exceptions. In this search science has been remarkably successful, and it may be conceded that such uniformities have held hitherto. This brings us back to the question: Have we any reason, assuming that they have always held in the past, to suppose that they will hold in the future?

It has been argued that we have reason to know that the future will resemble the past, because what was the future has constantly become the past, and has always been found to resemble the past, so that we really have experience of the future, namely of times which were formerly future, which we may call past futures. But such an argument really begs the very question at issue. We have experience of past futures, but not of future futures, and the question is: Will future futures resemble past futures? This question is not to be answered by an argument, which starts from past futures alone. We have therefore still to seek for some principle which shall enable us to know that the future will follow the same laws as the past.

The reference to the future in this question is not essential. The same question arises when we apply the laws that work in our experience to past things of which we have no experience—as, for example, in geology, or in theories as to the origin of the Solar System. The question we really have to ask is: 'When two things have been found to be often associated, and no instance is known of the one occurring without the other, does the occurrence of one of the two, in a fresh instance, give any good ground for expecting the other?' On our answer to this question must depend the validity of the whole of our expectations as to the future, the whole of the results obtained by induction, and in fact practically all the beliefs upon which our daily life is based.

It must be conceded, to begin with, that the fact that two things have been found often together and never apart does not, by itself, suffice to *prove* demonstratively that they will be found together in the next case we examine. The most we can hope is that the oftener things are found together, the more probable it becomes that they will be found together another time, and that, if they have been found together often enough, the probability will amount *almost* to certainty. It can never quite reach certainty, because we know that in spite of frequent repetitions there sometimes is a failure at the last, as in the case of the chicken whose neck is wrung. Thus probability is all we ought to seek.

It might be urged, as against the view we are advocating, that we know all natural phenomena to be subject to the reign of law, and that sometimes, on the basis of observation, we can see that only one law can possibly fit the facts of the case. Now to this view there are two answers. The first is that, even if *some* law which has no exceptions applies to our case, we can never, in practice, be sure that we have discovered that law and not one to which there are exceptions. The second is that the reign of law would seem to be itself only probable, and that our belief that it will hold in the future, or in unexamined cases in the past, is itself based upon the very principle we are examining.

The principle we are examining may be called the *principle of induction*, and its two parts may be stated as follows:

(*a*) When a thing of a certain sort A has been found to be associated with a thing of a certain other sort B, and has never been found dissociated from a thing of the sort B, the greater the number of cases in which A and B have been associated, the greater is the probability that they will be associated in a fresh case in which one of them is known to be present;

(*b*) Under the same circumstances, a sufficient number of cases of association will make the probability of a fresh association nearly a certainty, and will make it approach certainty without limit.

As just stated, the principle applies only to the verification of our expectation in a single fresh instance. But we want also to know that there is a probability in favour of the general law that things of the sort A are *always* associated with things of the sort B, provided a sufficient number of cases of association are known, and no cases of failure of association are known. The probability of the general law is obviously less than the probability of the particular case, since if the general law is true, the particular case must also be true, whereas the particular case may be true without the general law being true. Nevertheless the probability of the general law is increased by repetitions, just as the probability of the particular case is. We may therefore repeat the two parts of our principle as regards the general law, thus:

(*a*) The greater the number of cases in which a thing of the sort A has been found associated with a thing of the sort B, the more probable it is (if no cases of failure of association are known) that A is always associated with B;

(*b*) Under the same circumstances, a sufficient number of cases of the association of A with B will make it nearly certain that A is always associated with B, and will make this general law approach certainty without limit. .

It should be noted that probability is always relative to certain data. In our case, the data are merely the known cases of coexistence of A and B. There may be other data, which *might* be taken into account, which would gravely alter the probability. For example, a man who had seen a great many white swans might argue, by our principle, that on the data it was *probable* that all swans were white, and this might be a perfectly sound argument. The argument is not disproved by the fact that some swans are black, because a thing may very well happen in spite of the fact that some data render it improbable. In the case of the swans, a man might know that colour is a very variable characteristic in many species of animals, and that, therefore, an induction as to colour is peculiarly liable to error. But this knowledge would be a fresh datum, by no means proving that the probability relatively to our previous data had been wrongly estimated. The fact, therefore, that things often fail to fulfil our expectations is no evidence that our expectations will not *probably* be fulfilled in a given case or a given class of cases. Thus our inductive principle is at any rate not capable of being *disproved* by an appeal to experience.

The inductive principle, however, is equally incapable of being *proved* by an appeal to experience. Experience might conceivably confirm the inductive principle as regards the cases that have been already examined; but as regards unexamined cases, it is the inductive principle alone that can justify any inference from what has been examined to what has not been examined. All arguments which, on the basis of experience, argue as to the future or the unexperienced parts of the past or present, assume the inductive principle; hence we can never use experience to prove the inductive principle without begging the question. Thus we must either accept the inductive principle on the ground of its intrinsic evidence, or forgo all justification of our expectations about the future. If the principle is unsound, we have no reason to expect the sun to rise tomorrow, to expect bread to be more nourishing than a stone, or to expect that if we throw ourselves off the roof we shall fall. When we see what looks like our best friend approaching us, we shall have no reason to suppose that his body is not inhabited by the mind of our worst enemy or of some total stranger. All our conduct is based upon associations which have worked in the past, and which we therefore regard as likely to work in the future; and this likelihood is dependent for its validity upon the inductive principle.

The general principles of science, such as the belief in the reign of law, and the belief that every event must have a cause, are as completely dependent upon the inductive principle as are the beliefs of daily life. All such general principles are believed because mankind have found innumerable instances of their truth and no instances of their falsehood. But this affords no evidence for their truth in the future, unless the inductive principle is assumed.

Thus all knowledge which, on a basis of experience tells us something about what is not experienced, is based upon a belief which experience can neither confirm nor confute, yet which, at least in its more concrete applications, appears to be as firmly rooted in us as many of the facts of experience. The existence and justification of such beliefs—for the inductive principles [...] is not the only example—raises some of the most difficult and most debated problems of philosophy.

Chapter 38

The pragmatic justification of induction

Hans Reichenbach

T HE nontautological character of induction has been known a long time; Bacon had already emphasized that it is just this character to which the importance of induction is due. If inductive inference can teach us something new, in opposition to deductive inference, this is because it is not a tautology. This useful quality has, however, become the center of the epistemological difficulties of induction. It was David Hume who first attacked the principle from this side; he pointed out that the apparent constraint of the inductive inference, although submitted to by everybody, could not be justified. We believe in induction; we even cannot get rid of the belief when we know the impossibility of a logical demonstration of the validity of inductive inference; but as logicians we must admit that this belief is a deception—such is the result of Hume's criticism. We may summarize his objections in two statements:

1. We have no logical demonstration for the validity of inductive inference.

2. There is no demonstration a posteriori for the inductive inference; any such demonstration would presuppose the very principle which it is to demonstrate.

These two pillars of Hume's criticism of the principle of induction have stood unshaken for two centuries, and I think they will stand as long as there is a scientific philosophy.

[...]

Inductive inference cannot be dispensed with because we need it for the purpose of action. To deem the inductive assumption unworthy of the assent of a philosopher, to keep a distinguished reserve, and to meet with a condescending smile the attempts of other people to bridge the gap between experience and prediction is cheap self-deceit; at the very moment when the apostles of such a higher philosophy leave the field of theoretical discussion and pass to the simplest actions of daily life, they follow the inductive principle as surely as does every earth-bound mind. In any action there are various means to the realization of our aim; we have to make a choice, and we decide in accordance with the inductive principle. Although there is no means which will produce with certainty the desired effect, we do not leave the choice to chance but prefer the means indicated by the principle of

Hans Reichenbach, 'The Pragmatic Justification of Induction' in *Experience and Prediction. An Analysis of the Foundation and the Structure of Knowledge* (Chicago, University of Chicago Press, 1938), pp. 341–2, 346–51, 355–7 reprinted by permission of Maria Reichenbach.

induction. If we sit at the wheel of a car and want to turn the car to the right, why do we turn the wheel to the right? There is no certainty that the car will follow the wheel; there are indeed cars which do not always so behave. Such cases are fortunately exceptions. But if we should not regard the inductive prescription and consider the effect of a turn of the wheel as entirely unknown to us, we might turn it to the left as well. I do not say this to suggest such an attempt; the effects of skeptical philosophy applied in motor traffic would be rather unpleasant. But I should say a philosopher who is to put aside his principles any time he steers a motorcar is a bad philosopher.

It is no justification of inductive belief to show that it is a habit. It *is* a habit; but the question is whether it is a good habit, where 'good' is to mean 'useful for the purpose of actions directed to future events.' If a person tells me that Socrates is a man, and that all men are mortal, I have the habit of believing that Socrates is mortal. I know, however, that this is a good habit. If anyone had the habit of believing in such a case that Socrates is not mortal, we could demonstrate to him that this was a bad habit. The analogous question must be raised for inductive inference. If we should not be able to demonstrate that it is a good habit, we should either cease using it or admit frankly that our philosophy is a failure.

Science proceeds by induction and not by tautological transformations of reports. Bacon is right about Aristotle; but the *novum organon* needs a justification as good as that of the *organon*. Hume's criticism was the heaviest blow against empiricism; if we do not want to dupe our consciousness of this by means of the narcotic drug of aprioristic rationalism, or the soporific of skepticism, we must find a defense for the inductive inference which holds as well as does the formalistic justification of deductive logic.

[. . .]

We shall now begin to give the justification of induction which Hume thought impossible. In the pursuit of this inquiry, let us ask first what has been proved, strictly speaking, by Hume's objections.

Hume started with the assumption that a justification of inductive inference is only given if we can show that inductive inference must lead to success. In other words, Hume believed that any justified application of the inductive inference presupposes a demonstration that the conclusion is true. It is this assumption on which Hume's criticism is based. His two objections directly concern only the question of the truth of the conclusion; they prove that the truth of the conclusion cannot be demonstrated. The two objections, therefore, are valid only in so far as the Humean assumption is valid. It is this question to which we must turn: Is it necessary, for the justification of inductive inference, to show that its conclusion is true?

A rather simple analysis shows us that this assumption does not hold. Of course, if we were able to prove the truth of the conclusion, inductive inference would be justified; but the converse does not hold: a justification of the inductive inference does not imply a proof of the truth of the conclusion. The proof of the truth of the conclusion is only a sufficient condition for the justification of induction, not a necessary condition.

The inductive inference is a procedure which is to furnish us the best assumption concerning the future. If we do not know the truth about the future, there may be nonetheless a best assumption about it, i.e., a best assumption relative to what we know. We must ask whether such a characterization may be given for the principle of induction. If this turns out to be possible, the principle of induction will be justified.

An example will show the logical structure of our reasoning. A man may be suffering from a grave disease; the physician tells us: 'I do not know whether an operation will save the man, but if there *is* any remedy, it is an operation.' In such a case, the operation would be justified. Of course, it would be better to know that the operation will save the man; but, if we do not know this, the knowledge formulated in the statement of the physician is a sufficient justification. If we cannot realize the sufficient conditions of success, we shall at least realize the necessary conditions. If we were able to show that the inductive inference is a necessary condition of success, it would be justified; such a proof would satisfy any demands which may be raised about the justification of induction.

Now obviously there is a great difference between our example and induction. The reasoning of the physician presupposes inductions; his knowledge about an operation as the only possible means of saving a life is based on inductive generalizations, just as are all other statements of empirical character. But we wanted only to illustrate the logical structure of our reasoning. If we want to regard such a reasoning as a justification of the principle of induction, the character of induction as a necessary condition of success must be demonstrated in a way which does not presuppose induction. Such a proof, however, can be given.

If we want to construct this proof, we must begin with a determination of the aim of induction. It is usually said that we perform inductions with the aim of foreseeing the future. This determination is vague; let us replace it by a formulation more precise in character:

The aim of induction is to find series of events whose frequency of occurrence converges toward a limit.

We choose this formulation because we found that we need probabilities and that a probability is to be defined as the limit of a frequency; thus our determination of the aim of induction is given in such a way that it enables us to apply probability methods. If we compare this determination of the aim of induction with determinations usually given, it turns out to be not a confinement to a narrower aim but an expansion. What we usually call 'foreseeing the future' is included in our formulation as a special case; the case of knowing with certainty for every event A the event B following it would correspond in our formulation to a case where the limit of the frequency is of the numerical value 1. Hume thought of this case only. Thus our inquiry differs from that of Hume in so far as it conceives the aim of induction in a generalized form. But we do not omit any possible applications if we determine the principle of induction as the means of obtaining the limit of a frequency. If we have limits of frequency, we have all we want, including the case considered by Hume; we have then the laws of nature in their most general form, including both statistical and so-called causal laws—the latter being nothing but a special case of statistical laws, corresponding to the numerical value 1 of the limit of the frequency. We are entitled, therefore, to consider the determination of the limit of a frequency as the aim of the inductive inference.

Now it is obvious that we have no guaranty that this aim is at all attainable. The world may be so disorderly that it is impossible for us to construct series with a limit. Let us introduce the term 'predictable' for a world which is sufficiently ordered to enable us to construct series with a limit. We must admit, then, that we do not know whether the world is predictable.

[...]

These considerations lead, however, to a more precise formulation of the logical structure of the inductive inference. We must say that, if there is any method which leads to the limit of the frequency, the inductive principle will do the same; if there is a limit of the frequency, the inductive principle is a sufficient condition to find it. If we omit now the premise that there is a limit of the frequency, we cannot say that the inductive principle is the necessary condition of finding it because there are other methods using a correction c_n. There is a set of equivalent conditions such that the choice of one of the members of the set is necessary if we want to find the limit; and, if there is a limit, each of the members of the set is an appropriate method for finding it. We may say, therefore, that the *applicability* of the inductive principle is a necessary condition of the existence of a limit of the frequency.

The decision in favor of the inductive principle among the members of the set of equivalent means may be substantiated by pointing out its quality of embodying the smallest risk; after all, this decision is not of a great relevance, as all these methods must lead to the same value of the limit if they are sufficiently continued. It must not be forgotten, however, that the method of clairvoyance is not, without further ado, a member of the set because we do not know whether the correction c_n occurring here is submitted to the condition of convergence to zero. This must be proved first, and it can only be proved by using the inductive principle, viz., a method known to be a member of the set: this is why clairvoyance, in spite of all occult pretensions, is to be submitted to the control of scientific methods, i.e., by the principle of induction.

It is in the analysis expounded that we see the solution of Hume's problem.[1] Hume demanded too much when he wanted for a justification of the inductive inference a proof that its conclusion is true. What his objections demonstrate is only that such a proof cannot be given. We do not perform, however, an inductive inference with the pretension of obtaining a true statement. What we obtain is a wager; and it is the best wager we can lay because it corresponds to a procedure the applicability of which is the necessary condition of the possibility of predictions. To fulfil the conditions sufficient for the attainment of true predictions does not lie in our power; let us be glad that we are able to fulfil at least the conditions necessary for the realization of this intrinsic aim of science.

1. This theory of induction was first published by the author in 'Die logischen Grundlagen des Wahrscheinlichkeitsbegriffs' in *Erkenntnis*, 3 (1933), pp. 401–25, esp. 421–5. A more detailed exposition was given in the author's *Wahrscheinlichkeitslehre*, § 80 [English translation: *Theory of Probability*, Berkeley 1949, University of California Press].

Chapter 39

The new riddle of induction

Nelson Goodman

CONFIRMATION of a hypothesis by an instance depends rather heavily upon features of the hypothesis other than its syntactical form. That a given piece of copper conducts electricity increases the credibility of statements asserting that other pieces of copper conduct electricity, and thus confirms the hypothesis that all copper conducts electricity. But the fact that a given man now in this room is a third son does not increase the credibility of statements asserting that other men now in this room are third sons, and so does not confirm the hypothesis that all men now in this room are third sons. Yet in both cases our hypothesis is a generalization of the evidence statement. The difference is that in the former case the hypothesis is a *lawlike* statement; while in the latter case, the hypothesis is a merely contingent or accidental generality. Only a statement that is *lawlike*—regardless of its truth or falsity or its scientific importance—is capable of receiving confirmation from an instance of it; accidental statements are not. Plainly, then, we must look for a way of distinguishing lawlike from accidental statements.

So long as what seems to be needed is merely a way of excluding a few odd and unwanted cases that are inadvertently admitted by our definition of confirmation, the problem may not seem very hard or very pressing. We fully expect that minor defects will be found in our definition and that the necessary refinements will have to be worked out patiently one after another. But some further examples will show that our present difficulty is of a much graver kind.

Suppose that all emeralds examined before a certain time t are green.[1] At time t, then, our observations support the hypothesis that all emeralds are green; and this is in accord with our definition of confirmation. Our evidence statements assert that emerald a is green, that emerald b is green, and so on; and each confirms the general hypothesis that all emeralds are green. So far, so good.

Now let me introduce another predicate less familiar than 'green'. It is the predicate 'grue' and it applies to all things examined before t just in case they are green but to other things just in case they are blue. Then at time t we have, for each evidence statement asserting that a given emerald is green, a parallel evidence statement asserting that that emerald is grue. And the statements that emerald a is grue, that emerald b is grue, and so on, will each confirm the general hypothesis that all emeralds are grue. Thus according to our definition, the prediction that all

Nelson Goodman, 'The New Riddle of Induction' in *Facts, Fiction and Forecast* (4th ed.) (Cambridge, MA, Harvard University Press, 1983), pp. 72–83 reprinted by permission of Nelson Goodman.

1. Although the example used is different, the argument to follow is substantially the same as that set forth in my note 'A Query on Confirmation', *Journal of Philosophy* 43 (1946), pp. 383–5.

emeralds subsequently examined will be green and the prediction that all will be grue are alike confirmed by evidence statements describing the same observations. But if an emerald subsequently examined is grue, it is blue and hence not green. Thus although we are well aware which of the two incompatible predictions is genuinely confirmed, they are equally well confirmed according to our present definition. Moreover, it is clear that if we simply choose an appropriate predicate, then on the basis of these same observations we shall have equal confirmation, by our definition, for any prediction whatever about other emeralds—or indeed about anything else.[2] As in our earlier example, only the predictions subsumed under lawlike hypotheses are genuinely confirmed; but we have no criterion as yet for determining lawlikeness. And now we see that without some such criterion, our definition not merely includes a few unwanted cases, but is so completely ineffectual that it virtually excludes nothing. We are left once again with the intolerable result that anything confirms anything. This difficulty cannot be set aside as an annoying detail to be taken care of in due course. It has to be met before our definition will work at all.

Nevertheless, the difficulty is often slighted because on the surface there seem to be easy ways of dealing with it. Sometimes, for example, the problem is thought to be much like the paradox of the ravens. We are here again, it is pointed out, making tacit and illegitimate use of information outside the stated evidence: the information, for example, that different samples of one material are usually alike in conductivity, and the information that different men in a lecture audience are usually not alike in the number of their older brothers. But while it is true that such information is being smuggled in, this does not by itself settle the matter as it settles the matter of the ravens. There the point was that when the smuggled information is forthrightly declared, its effect upon the confirmation of the hypothesis in question is immediately and properly registered by the definition we are using. On the other hand, if to our initial evidence we add statements concerning the conductivity of pieces of other materials or concerning the number of older brothers of members of other lecture audiences, this will not in the least affect the confirmation, according to our definition, of the hypothesis concerning copper or of that concerning this lecture audience. Since our definition is insensitive to the bearing upon hypotheses of evidence so related to them, even when the evidence is fully declared, the difficulty about accidental hypotheses cannot be explained away on the ground that such evidence is being surreptitiously taken into account.

A more promising suggestion is to explain the matter in terms of the effect of this other evidence not directly upon the hypothesis in question but *indirectly* through other hypotheses that *are* confirmed, according to our definition, by such evidence.

---

2. For instance, we shall have equal confirmation, by our present definition, for the prediction that roses subsequently examined will be blue. Let 'emerose' apply just to emeralds examined before time *t*, and to roses examined later. Then all emeroses so far examined are grue, and this confirms the hypothesis that all emeroses are grue and hence the prediction that roses subsequently examined will be blue. The problem raised by such antecedents has been little noticed, but is no easier to meet than that raised by similarly perverse consequents. [. . .]

Our information about other materials does by our definition confirm such hypotheses as that all pieces of iron conduct electricity, that no pieces of rubber do, and so on; and these hypotheses, the explanation runs, impart to the hypothesis that all pieces of copper conduct electricity (and also to hypothesis that none do) the character of lawlikeness—that is, amenability to confirmation by direct positive instances when found. On the other hand, our information about other lecture audiences *dis*confirms many hypotheses to the effect that all the men in one audience are third sons, or that none are; and this strips any character of lawlikeness from the hypothesis that all (or the hypothesis that none) of the men in *this* audience are third sons. But clearly if this course is to be followed, the circumstances under which hypotheses are thus related to one another will have to be precisely articulated.

The problem, then, is to define the relevant way in which such hypotheses must be alike. Evidence for the hypothesis that all iron conducts electricity enhances the lawlikeness of the hypothesis that all zirconium conducts electricity, but does not similarly affect the hypothesis that all the objects on my desk conduct electricity. Wherein lies the difference? The first two hypotheses fall under the broader hypothesis—call it 'H'—that every class of things of the same material is uniform in conductivity; the first and third fall only under some such hypothesis as—call it 'K'—that every class of things that are either all of the same material or all on a desk is uniform in conductivity. Clearly the important difference here is that evidence for a statement affirming that one of the classes covered by H has the property in question increases the credibility of any statement affirming that another such class has this property; while nothing of the sort holds true with respect to K. But this is only to say that H is lawlike and K is not. We are faced anew with the very problem we are trying to solve: the problem of distinguishing between lawlike and accidental hypotheses.

The most popular way of attacking the problem takes its cue from the fact that accidental hypotheses seem typically to involve some spatial or temporal restriction, or reference to some particular individual. They seem to concern the people in some particular room, or the objects on some particular person's desk; while lawlike hypotheses characteristically concern all ravens or all pieces of copper whatsoever. Complete generality is thus very often supposed to be a sufficient condition of lawlikeness; but to define this complete generality is by no means easy. Merely to require that the hypothesis contain no term naming, describing, or indicating a particular thing or location will obviously not be enough. The troublesome hypothesis that all emeralds are grue contains no such term; and where such a term does occur, as in hypotheses about men in *this room*, it can be suppressed in favor of some predicate (short or long, new or old) that contains no such term but applies only to exactly the same things. One might think, then, of excluding not only hypotheses that actually contain terms for specific individuals but also all hypotheses that are equivalent to others that do contain such terms. But, as we have just seen, to exclude only hypotheses of which *all* equivalents contain such terms is to exclude nothing. On the other hand, to exclude all hypotheses that have *some* equivalent containing such a term is to exclude everything; for even the hypothesis

All grass is green

has an equivalent

All grass in London or elsewhere is green.

The next step, therefore, has been to consider ruling out predicates of certain kinds. A syntactically universal hypothesis is lawlike, the proposal runs, if its predicates are 'purely qualitative' or 'non-positional'.[3] This will obviously accomplish nothing, if a purely qualitative predicate is then conceived either as one that is equivalent to some expression free of terms for specific individuals, or as one that is equivalent to no expression that contains such a term; for this only raises again the difficulties just pointed out. The claim appears to be rather that at least in the case of a simple enough predicate we can readily determine by direct inspection of its meaning whether or not it is purely qualitative. But even aside from obscurities in the notion of 'the meaning' of a predicate, this claim seems to me wrong. I simply do not know how to tell whether a predicate is qualitative or positional, except perhaps by completely begging the question at issue and asking whether the predicate is 'well-behaved'—that is, whether simple syntactically universal hypotheses applying it are lawlike.

This statement will not go unprotested. 'Consider', it will be argued, 'the predicates "blue" and "green" and the predicate "grue" introduced earlier, and also the predicate "bleen" that applies to emeralds examined before time t just in case they are blue and to other emeralds just in case they are green. Surely it is clear', the argument runs, 'that the first two are purely qualitative and the second two are not; for the meaning of each of the latter two plainly involves reference to a specific temporal position.' To this I reply that indeed I do recognize the first two as well-behaved predicates admissible in lawlike hypotheses, and the second two as ill-behaved predicates. But the argument that the former but not the latter are purely qualitative seems to me quite unsound. True enough if we start with 'blue' and 'green', then 'grue' and 'bleen' will be explained in terms of 'blue' and 'green' and a temporal term. But equally truly, if we start with 'grue' and 'bleen', then 'blue' and 'green' will be explained in terms of 'grue' and 'bleen' and a temporal term; 'green', for example, applies to emeralds examined before time t just in case they are grue, and to other emeralds just in case they are bleen. Thus qualitativeness is an entirely relative matter and does not by itself establish any dichotomy of predicates. This relativity seems to be completely overlooked by those who contend that the qualitative character of a predicate is a criterion for its good behavior.

Of course, one may ask why we need worry about such unfamiliar predicates as 'grue' or about accidental hypotheses in general, since we are unlikely to use them

3. Carnap took this course in his paper 'On the Application of Inductive Logic', *Philosophy and Phenomenological Research*, 8 (1947), pp. 133–47, which is in part a reply to my 'A Query on Confirmation', op. cit. The discussion was continued in my note 'On Infirmities of Confirmation Theory', *Philosophy and Phenomenological Research*, 8 (1947), pp. 149–51; and in Carnap's 'Reply to Nelson Goodman', same journal, same volume, pp. 461–2.

in making predictions. If our definition works for such hypotheses as are normally employed, isn't that all we need? In a sense, yes; but only in the sense that we need no definition, no theory of induction, and no philosophy of knowledge at all. We get along well enough without them in daily life and in scientific research. But if we seek a theory at all, we cannot excuse gross anomalies resulting from a proposed theory by pleading that we can avoid them in practice. The odd cases we have been considering are clinically pure cases that, though seldom encountered in practice, nevertheless display to best advantage the symptoms of a widespread and destructive malady.

We have so far neither any answer nor any promising clue to an answer to the question what distinguishes lawlike or confirmable hypotheses from accidental or non-confirmable ones; and what may at first have seemed a minor technical difficulty has taken on the stature of a major obstacle to the development of a satisfactory theory of confirmation. It is this problem that I call the new riddle of induction.

[...]

At the beginning of this lecture, I expressed the opinion that the problem of induction is still unsolved, but that the difficulties that face us today are not the old ones; and I have tried to outline the changes that have taken place. The problem of justifying induction has been displaced by the problem of defining confirmation, and our work upon this has left us with the residual problem of distinguishing between confirmable and non-confirmable hypotheses. One might say roughly that the first question was 'Why does a positive instance of a hypothesis give any grounds for predicting further instances?'; that the newer question was 'What is a positive instance of a hypothesis?'; and that the crucial remaining question is 'What hypotheses are confirmed by their positive instances?'

The vast amount of effort expended on the problem of induction in modern times has thus altered our afflictions but hardly relieved them. The original difficulty about induction arose from the recognition that anything may follow upon anything. Then, in attempting to define confirmation in terms of the converse of the consequence relation, we found ourselves with the distressingly similar difficulty that our definition would make any statement confirm any other. And now, after modifying our definition drastically, we still get the old devastating result that any statement will confirm any statement. Until we find a way of exercising some control over the hypotheses to be admitted, our definition makes no distinction whatsoever between valid and invalid inductive inferences.

The real inadequacy of Hume's account lay not in his descriptive approach but in the imprecision of his description. Regularities in experience, according to him, give rise to habits of expectation; and thus it is predictions conforming to past regularities that are normal or valid. But Hume overlooks the fact that some regularities do and some do not establish such habits; that predictions based on some regularities are valid while predictions based on other regularities are not. Every word you have heard me say has occurred prior to the final sentence of this lecture; but that does not, I hope, create any expectation that every word you will hear me say will be prior to that sentence. Again, consider our case of emeralds. All those examined before time t are green; and this leads us to expect, and confirms the prediction, that the next one will be green. But also, all those examined are grue; and this does not lead us to expect, and does not confirm the prediction, that the next one will be grue. Regularity in greenness confirms the prediction of further cases; regularity in grueness does not. To say that valid predictions are those based on past regularities, without being able to say *which* regularities, is thus quite pointless. Regularities are where you find them, and you can find them anywhere. As we have seen, Hume's failure to recognize and deal with this problem has been shared even by his most recent successors.

As a result, what we have in current confirmation theory is a definition that is adequate for certain cases that so far can be described only as those for which it is adequate. The theory works where it works. A hypothesis is confirmed by statements related to it in the prescribed way provided it is so confirmed. This is a good deal like having a theory that tells us that the area of a plane figure is one-half the base times the altitude, without telling us for what figures this holds. We must somehow find a way of distinguishing lawlike hypotheses, to which our definition of confirmation applies, from accidental hypotheses, to which it does not.

[Here] I have been [dealing] solely [with] the problem of induction, but what has been said applies equally to the more general problem of projection. As pointed out earlier, the problem of prediction from past to future cases is but a narrower version of the problem of projecting from any set of cases to others. We saw that a whole cluster of troublesome problems concerning dispositions and possibility can be reduced to this problem of projection. That is why the new riddle of induction, which is more broadly the problem of distinguishing between projectible and non-projectible hypotheses, is as important as it is exasperating.

Our failures teach us, I think, that lawlike or projectible hypotheses cannot be distinguished on any merely syntactical grounds or even on the ground that these hypotheses are somehow purely general in meaning.

A Priori Knowledge

Chapter 40

A priori knowledge, necessity, and contingency

Saul A. Kripke

Pʜɪʟᴏsᴏᴘʜᴇʀs have talked (and, of course, there has been considerable controversy in recent years over the meaningfulness of these notions) about various categories of truth, which are called 'a priori', 'analytic', 'necessary'—and sometimes even 'certain' is thrown into this batch. The terms are often used as if *whether* there are things answering to these concepts is an interesting question, but we might as well regard them all as meaning the same thing. Now, everyone remembers Kant (a bit) as making a distinction between 'a priori' and 'analytic'. So maybe this distinction is still made. In contemporary discussion very few people, if any, distinguish between the concepts of statements being a priori and their being necessary. At any rate I shall *not* use the terms 'a priori' and 'necessary' interchangeably here.

Consider what the traditional characterizations of such terms as 'a priori' and 'necessary' are. First the notion of a prioricity is a concept of epistemology. I guess the traditional characterization from Kant goes something like: a priori truths are those which can be known independently of any experience. This introduces another problem before we get off the ground, because there's another modality in the characterization of 'a priori', namely, it is supposed to be something which *can* be known independently of any experience. That means that in some sense it's *possible* (whether we do or do not in fact know it independently of any experience) to know this independently of any experience. And possible for whom? For God? For the Martians? Or just for people with minds like ours? To make this all clear might involve a host of problems all of its own about what sort of possibility is in question here. It might be best therefore, instead of using the phrase 'a priori truth',

Saul A. Kripke, 'A Priori Knowledge, Necessity and Contingency' in *Naming and Necessity* (Cambridge, MA., Harvard University Press, 1980), pp. 34–9, 48–50, 53–8, 99–105, 108–9 reprinted by permission of Saul A. Kripke.

to the extent that one uses it at all, to stick to the question of whether a particular person or knower knows something a priori or believes it true on the basis of a priori evidence.

I won't go further too much into the problems that might arise with the notion of a prioricity here. I will say that some philosophers somehow change the modality in this characterization from *can* to *must*. They think that if something belongs to the realm of a priori knowledge, it couldn't possibly be known empirically. This is just a mistake. Something may belong in the realm of such statements that *can* be known a priori but still may be known by particular people on the basis of experience. To give a really common-sense example: anyone who has worked with a computing machine knows that the computing machine may give an answer to whether such and such a number is prime. No one has calculated or proved that the number is prime; but the machine has given the answer: this number is prime. We, then, if we believe that the number is prime, believe it on the basis of our knowledge of the laws of physics, the construction of the machine, and so on. We therefore do not believe this on the basis of purely a priori evidence. We believe it (if anything is a posteriori at all) on the basis of a posteriori evidence. Nevertheless, maybe this could be known a priori by someone who made the requisite calculations. So 'can be known a priori' doesn't mean '*must* be known a priori'.

The second concept which is in question is that of necessity. Sometimes this is used in an epistemological way and might then just mean a priori. And of course, sometimes it is used in a physical way when people distinguish between physical and logical necessity. But what I am concerned with here is a notion which is not a notion of epistemology but of metaphysics, in some (I hope) non-pejorative sense. We ask whether something might have been true, or might have been false. Well, if something is false, it's obviously not necessarily true. If it is true, might it have been otherwise? Is it possible that, in this respect, the world should have been different from the way it is? If the answer is 'no', then this fact about the world is a necessary one. If the answer is 'yes', then this fact about the world is a contingent one. This in and of itself has nothing to do with anyone's knowledge of anything. It's certainly a philosophical thesis, and not a matter of obvious definitional equivalence, either that everything a priori is necessary or that everything necessary is a priori. Both concepts may be vague. That may be another problem. But at any rate they are dealing with two different domains, two different areas, the epistemologic and the metaphysical. Consider, say, Fermat's last theorem—or the Goldbach conjecture. The Goldbach conjecture says that an even number greater than 2 must be the sum of two prime numbers. If this is true, it is presumably necessary, and, if it is false, presumably necessarily false. We are taking the classical view of mathematics here and assume that in mathematical reality it is either true or false.

If the Goldbach conjecture is false, then there is an even number, n, greater than 2, such that for no primes p_1 and p_2, both $< n$, does $n = p_1 + p_2$. This fact about n, if true, is verifiable by direct computation, and thus is necessary if the results of arithmetical computations are necessary. On the other hand, if the conjecture is true, then every even number exceeding 2 is the sum of two primes. Could it then be the case that, although in fact every such even number is the sum of two primes, there might have been such an even number which was not the sum of two primes? What would that mean? Such a number would have to be one of 4, 6, 8, 10, . . .; and, by hypothesis, since we are assuming Goldbach's conjecture to be true, each of these can be shown, again by direct computation, to be the sum of two primes. Goldbach's conjecture, then, cannot be contingently true or false; whatever truth-value it has belongs to it by necessity.

But what we can say, of course, is that right now, as far as we know, the question can come out either way. So, in the absence of a mathematical proof deciding this question, none of us has any a priori knowledge about this question in either direction. We don't know whether Goldbach's conjecture is true or false. So right now we certainly don't know anything a priori about it.

Perhaps it will be alleged that we *can* in principle know a priori whether it is true. Well, maybe we can. Of course an infinite mind which can search through all the numbers can or could. But I don't know whether a finite mind can or could. Maybe there just is no mathematical proof whatsoever which decides the conjecture. At any rate this might or might not be the case. Maybe there is a mathematical proof deciding this question; maybe every mathematical question is decidable by an intuitive proof or disproof. Hilbert thought so; others have thought not; still others have thought the question unintelligible unless the notion of intuitive proof is replaced by that of formal proof in a single system. Certainly no one formal system decides all mathematical questions, as we know from Gödel. At any rate, and this is the important thing, the question is not trivial; even though someone said that it's necessary, if true at all, that every even number is the sum of two primes, it doesn't follow that anyone knows anything a priori about it. It doesn't even seem to me to follow without some further philosophical argument (it is an interesting philo-sophical question) that anyone *could* know anything a priori about it. The 'could', as I said, involves some other modality. We mean that even if no one, perhaps even in the future, knows or will know a priori whether Goldbach's conjecture is right, in principle there is a way, which *could* have been used, of answering the question a priori. This assertion is not trivial.

The terms 'necessary' and 'a priori', then, as applied to statements, are *not* obvi-ous synonyms. There may be a philosophical argument connecting them, perhaps even identifying them; but an argument is required, not simply the observation that the two terms are clearly interchangeable. (I will argue below that in fact they are not even coextensive—that necessary a posteriori truths, and probably contingent a priori truths, both exist.)

I think people have thought that these two things must mean the same for these reasons:

First, if something not only happens to be true in the actual world but is also true in all possible worlds, then, of course, just by running through all the possible worlds in our heads, we ought to be able with enough effort to see, if a statement is necessary, that it is necessary, and thus know it a priori. But really this is not so obviously feasible at all.

Second, I guess it's thought that, conversely, if something is known a priori it must be necessary, because it was known without looking at the world. If it depended on some contingent feature of the actual world, how could you know it without looking? Maybe the actual world is one of the possible worlds in which it would have been false. This depends on the thesis that there can't be a way of knowing about the actual world without looking that wouldn't be a way of knowing the same thing about every possible world. This involves problems of epistemology and the nature of knowledge; and of course it is very vague as stated. But it is not really *trivial* either. More important than any particular example of something which is alleged to be necessary and not a priori or a priori and not necessary, is to see that the notions are different, that it's not trivial to argue on the basis of something's being something which maybe we can only know a posteriori, that it's not a necessary truth. It's not trivial, just because something is known in some sense a priori, that what is known is a necessary truth.

Another term used in philosophy is 'analytic'. Here it won't be too important to get any clearer about this in this talk. The common examples of analytic statements, nowadays, are like 'bachelors are unmarried'. Kant (someone just pointed out to me) gives as an example 'gold is a yellow metal', which seems to me an extraordinary one, because it's something I think that can turn out to be false. At any rate, let's just make it a matter of stipulation that an analytic statement is, in some sense, true by virtue of its meaning and true in all possible worlds by virtue of its meaning. Then something which is analytically true will be both necessary and a priori. (That's sort of stipulative.)

Another category I mentioned was that of certainty. Whatever certainty is, it's clearly not obviously the case that everything which is necessary is certain. Certainty is another epistemological notion. Something can be known, or at least rationally believed, a priori, without being quite certain. You've read a proof in the math book; and, though you think it's correct, maybe you've made a mistake. You often do make mistakes of this kind. You've made a computation, perhaps with an error.

[...]

Let's use some terms quasi-technically. Let's call something a *rigid designator* if in every possible world it designates the same object, a *non-rigid* or *accidental designator* if that is not the case. Of course we don't require that the objects exist in all possible worlds. Certainly Nixon might not have existed if his parents had not gotten married, in the normal course of things. When we think of a property as essential to an object we usually mean that it is true of that object in any case where it would have existed. A rigid designator of a necessary existent can be called *strongly rigid*.

One of the intuitive theses I will maintain in these talks is that *names* are rigid designators. Certainly they seem to satisfy the intuitive test: although someone other than the US President in 1970 might have been the US President in 1970 (e.g. Humphrey might have), no one other than Nixon might have been Nixon. In the same way, a designator rigidly designates a certain object if it designates that object wherever the object exists; if, in addition, the object is a necessary existent, the designator can be called *strongly rigid*. For example, 'the President of the US in 1970' designates a certain man, Nixon; but someone else (e.g. Humphrey) might have been the President in 1970, and Nixon might not have; so this designator is not rigid.

In these lectures I will argue, intuitively, that proper names are rigid designators, for although the man (Nixon) might not have been the President, it is not the case that he might not have been Nixon (though he might not have been *called* 'Nixon'). Those who have argued that to make sense of the notion of rigid designator, we must antecedently make sense of 'criteria of transworld identity' have precisely reversed the cart and the horse; it is *because* we can refer (rigidly) to Nixon, and stipulate that we are speaking of what might have happened to *him* (under certain circumstances), that 'transworld identifications' are unproblematic in such cases.[1]

The tendency to demand purely qualitative descriptions of counterfactual situations has many sources. One, perhaps, is the confusion of the epistemological and the metaphysical, between a prioricity and necessity. If someone identifies necessity with a prioricity, and thinks that objects are named by means of uniquely identifying properties, he may think that it is the properties used to identify the object which, being known about it a priori, must be used to identify it in all possible worlds, to find out which object is Nixon. As against this, I repeat: (1) Generally, things aren't 'found out' about a counterfactual situation, they are stipulated; (2) possible worlds need not be given purely qualitatively, as if we were looking at them through a telescope. And we will see shortly that the properties an object has in every counterfactual world have nothing to do with properties used to identify it in the actual world.

[...]

Above I said that the Frege–Russell view that names are introduced by description could be taken either as a theory of the meaning of names (Frege and Russell seemed to take it this way) or merely as a theory of their reference. Let me give an example, not involving what would usually be called a 'proper name', to illustrate this. Suppose someone stipulates that 100 degrees centigrade is to be the temperature at which water boils at sea level. This isn't completely precise because the pressure may vary at sea level. Of course, historically, a more precise definition was given later. But let's suppose that this were the definition. Another sort of example in the literature is that one metre is to be the length of *S* where *S* is a certain stick or bar in Paris. (Usually people who like to talk about these definitions then try to make 'the length of' into an 'operational' concept. But it's not important.)

Wittgenstein says something very puzzling about this. He says: 'There is one thing of which one can say neither that it is one metre long nor that it is not one metre long, and that is the standard metre in Paris. But this is, of course, not to ascribe any extraordinary property to it, but only to mark its peculiar role in the

---

1. Of course I don't imply that language contains a name for every object. Demonstratives can be used as rigid designators, and free variables can be used as rigid designators of unspecified objects. Of course when we specify a counterfactual situation, we do not describe the whole possible world, but only the portion which interests us.

language game of measuring with a metre rule.'[2] This seems to be a very 'extra-ordinary property', actually, for any stick to have. I think he must be wrong. If the stick is a stick, for example, 39.37 inches long (I assume we have some different standard for inches), why isn't it one metre long? Anyway, let's suppose that he is wrong and that the stick is one metre long. Part of the problem which is bothering Wittgenstein is, of course, that this stick serves as a standard of length and so we can't attribute length to it. Be this as it may (well, it may not be), is the statement 'Stick S is one metre long', a necessary truth? Of course its length might vary in time. We could make the definition more precise by stipulating that one metre is to be the length of S at a fixed time t_0. Is it then a necessary truth that stick S is one metre long at time t_0? Someone who thinks that everything one knows a priori is necessary might think: 'This is the *definition* of a metre. By definition, stick S is one metre long at t_0. That's a necessary truth.' But there seems to me to be no reason so to conclude, even for a man who uses the stated definition of 'one metre'. For he's using this definition not to *give the meaning* of what he called the 'metre', but to *fix the reference*. (For such an abstract thing as a unit of length, the notion of reference may be unclear. But let's suppose it's clear enough for the present purposes.) He uses it to fix a reference. There is a certain length which he wants to mark out. He marks it out by an accidental property, namely that there is a stick of that length. Someone else might mark out the same reference by another accidental property. But in any case, even though he uses this to fix the reference of his standard of length, a metre, he can still say, 'if heat had been applied to this stick S at t_0, then at t_0 stick S would not have been one metre long'.

   Well, why can he do this? Part of the reason may lie in some people's minds in the philosophy of science, which I don't want to go into here. But a simple answer to the question is this: Even if this is the *only* standard of length that he uses,[3] there is an intuitive difference between the phrase 'one metre' and the phrase 'the length of S at t_0'. The first phrase is meant to designate rigidly a certain length in all possible worlds, which in the actual world happens to be the length of the stick S at t_0. On the other hand 'the length of S at t_0' does not designate anything rigidly. In some counterfactual situations the stick might have been longer and in some shorter, if various stresses and strains had been applied to it. So we can say of this stick, the same way as we would of any other of the same substance and length, that if heat of a given quantity had been applied to it, it would have expanded to such and such a length. Such a counterfactual statement, being true of other sticks with identical physical properties, will also be true of this stick. There is no conflict between that counterfactual statement and the definition of 'one metre' as 'the length of S at t_0', because the 'definition', properly interpreted, does *not* say that the phrase 'one metre' is to be *synonymous* (even when talking about counterfactual situations) with the phrase 'the length of S at t_0', but rather that we have *determined the reference* of the phrase 'one metre' by stipulating that 'one metre' is to be a *rigid*

2. *Philosophical Investigations*, §50.
3. Philosophers of science may see the key to the problem in a view that 'one metre' is a 'cluster concept'. I am asking the reader hypothetically to suppose that the 'definition' given is the *only* standard used to determine the metric system. I think the problem would still arise.

designator of the length which is in fact the length of S at t_0. So this does *not* make it a necessary truth that S is one metre long at t_0. In fact, under certain circumstances, S would not have been one metre long. The reason is that one designator ('one metre') is rigid and the other designator ('the length of S at t_0') is not.

What then, is the *epistemological* status of the statement 'Stick S is one metre long at t_0', for someone who has fixed the metric system by reference to stick S? It would seem that he knows it a priori. For if he used stick S to fix the reference of the term 'one metre', then as a result of this kind of 'definition' (which is not an abbreviative or synonymous definition), he knows automatically, without further investigation, that S is one metre long.[4] On the other hand, even if S is used as the standard of a metre, the *metaphysical* status of 'S is one metre long' will be that of a contingent statement, provided that 'one metre' is regarded as a rigid designator: under appropriate stresses and strains, heatings or coolings, S would have had a length other than one metre even at t_0. (Such statements as 'Water boils at 100 degrees centigrade, at sea level' can have a similar status.) So in this sense, there are contingent a priori truths. More important for present purposes, though, than accepting this example as an instance of the contingent a priori, is its illustration of the distinction between 'definitions' which fix a reference and those which give a synonym.

In the case of names one might make this distinction too. Suppose the reference of a name is given by a description or a cluster of descriptions. If the name *means the same* as that description or cluster of descriptions, it will not be a rigid designator. It will not necessarily designate the same object in all possible worlds, since other objects might have had the given properties in other possible worlds, unless (of course) we happened to use essential properties in our description. So suppose we say, 'Aristotle is the greatest man who studied with Plato'. If we used that as a *definition*, the name 'Aristotle' is to mean 'the greatest man who studied with Plato'. Then of course in some other possible world that man might not have studied with Plato and some other man would have been Aristotle. If, on the other hand, we merely use the description to *fix the referent* then that man will be the referent of 'Aristotle' in all possible worlds. The only use of the description will have been to pick out to which man we mean to refer. But then, when we say counterfactually 'suppose Aristotle had never gone into philosophy at all', we need not mean 'suppose a man who studied with Plato, and taught Alexander the Great, and wrote this and that, and so on, had never gone into philosophy at all', which might seem like a contradiction. We need only mean, 'suppose that *that man* had never gone into philosophy at all'.

It seems plausible to suppose that, in some cases, the reference of a name is indeed fixed *via* a description in the same way that the metric system was fixed. When the mythical agent first saw Hesperus, he may well have fixed his reference by saying, 'I shall use "Hesperus" as a name of the heavenly body appearing in yonder position in the sky.' He then fixed the reference of 'Hesperus' by its apparent

---

4. Since the truth he knows is contingent, I choose *not* to call it 'analytic', stipulatively requiring analytic truths to be both necessary and a priori.

celestial position. Does it follow that it is part of the *meaning* of the name that Hesperus has such and such position at the time in question? Surely not: if Hesperus had been hit earlier by a comet, it might have been visible at a different position at that time. In such a counterfactual situation we would say that Hesperus would not have occupied that position, but not that Hesperus would not have been Hesperus. The reason is that 'Hesperus' rigidly designates certain heavenly body and 'the body in yonder position' does not—a different body, or no body might have been in that position, but no other body might have been Hesperus (though another body, not Hesperus; might have been *called* 'Hesperus'). Indeed, as I have said, I will hold that names are always rigid designators.

[. . .]

I guess the main thing I'll talk about now is identity statements between names. But I hold the following about the general case. First, that characteristic theoretical identifications like 'Heat is the motion of molecules', are not contingent truths but necessary truths, and here of course I don't mean just physically necessary, but necessary in the highest degree—whatever that means. (Physical necessity *might* turn out to be necessity in the highest degree. But that's a question which I don't wish to prejudge. At least for this sort of example, it might be that when something's physically necessary, it always is necessary *tout court*.) Second, that the way in which these have turned out to be necessary truths does not seem to me to be a way in which the mind–brain identities could turn out to be either necessary or contingently true. So this analogy has to go. It's hard to see what to put in its place. It's hard to see therefore how to avoid concluding that the two are actually different.

Let me go back to the more mundane case about proper names. This is already mysterious enough. There's a dispute about this between Quine and Ruth Barcan Marcus.[5] Marcus says that identities between names are necessary. If someone thinks that Cicero is Tully, and really uses 'Cicero' and 'Tully' as names, he is thereby committed to holding that his belief is a necessary truth. She uses the term 'mere tag'. Quine replies as follows, 'We may tag the planet Venus, some fine evening, with the proper name "Hesperus". We may tag the same planet again, some day before sunrise, with the proper name "Phosphorus". When we discover that we have tagged the same planet twice our discovery is empirical. And not because the proper names were descriptions.'[6] First, as Quine says when we discovered that we tagged the same planet twice, our discovery was empirical. Another example I think Quine gives in another book is that the same mountain seen from Nepal and from Tibet, or something like that, is from one angle called 'Mt. Everest' (you've heard of that); from another it's supposed to be called 'Gaurisanker'. It can actually be an empirical discovery that Gaurisanker is Everest. (Quine says that the example is actually false. He got the example from Erwin Schrödinger. You wouldn't think the inventor of wave mechanics got things that wrong. I don't know where the mistake is supposed to come from. One could certainly imagine this

5. Ruth Barcan Marcus, 'Modalities and Intensional Languages' (comments by W. V. Quine, plus discussion), *Boston Studies in the Philosophy of Science*, vol. 1, (Dordrecht: Reidel, 1963), pp. 77–116.
6. p. 101.

situation as having been the case; and it's another good illustration of the sort of thing that Quine has in mind.)

What about it? I wanted to find a good quote on the other side from Marcus in this book but I am having trouble locating one. Being present at that discussion, I remember[7] that she advocated the view that if you really have names, a good dictionary should be able to tell you whether they have the same reference. So someone should be able, by looking in the dictionary, to say that Hesperus and Phosphorus are the same. Now this does not seem to be true. It does seem, to many people, to be a consequence of the view that identities between names are necessary. Therefore the view that identity statements between names are necessary has usually been rejected. Russell's conclusion was somewhat different. He did think there should never be any empirical question whether two names have the same reference. This isn't satisfied for ordinary names, but it is satisfied when you're naming your own sense datum, or something like that. You say, 'Here, this, and that (designating the same sense datum by both demonstratives).' So you can tell without empirical investigation that you're naming the same thing twice; the conditions are satisfied. Since this won't apply to ordinary cases of naming, ordinary 'names' cannot be genuine names.

What should we think about this? First, it's true that someone can use the name 'Cicero' to refer to Cicero and the name 'Tully' to refer to Cicero also, and not know that Cicero is Tully. So it seems that we do not necessarily know a priori that an identity statement between names is true. It doesn't follow from this that the statement so expressed is a contingent one if true. This is what I've emphasized in my first lecture. There is a very strong feeling that leads one to think that, if you can't know something by a priori ratiocination, then it's got to be contingent: it might have turned out otherwise; but nevertheless I think this feeling is wrong.

Let's suppose we refer to the same heavenly body twice, as 'Hesperus' and 'Phosphorus'. We say: Hesperus is that star over there in the evening; Phosphorus is that star over there in the morning. Actually, Hesperus is Phosphorus. Are there really circumstances under which Hesperus wouldn't have been Phosphorus? Supposing that Hesperus is Phosphorus, let's try to describe a possible situation in which it would not have been. Well, it's easy. Someone goes by and he calls two *different* stars 'Hesperus' and 'Phosphorus'. It may even be under the same conditions as prevailed when we introduced the names 'Hesperus' and 'Phosphorus'. But are those circumstances in which Hesperus is not Phosphorus or would not have been Phosphorus? It seems to me that they are not.

Now, of course I'm committed to saying that they're not, by saying that such terms as 'Hesperus' and 'Phosphorus', when used as names, are rigid designators. They refer in every possible world to the planet Venus. Therefore, in that possible world too, the planet Venus is the planet Venus and it doesn't matter what any other person has said in this other possible world. How should *we* describe this situation? He can't have pointed to Venus twice, and in the one case called it 'Hesperus' and in the other 'Phosphorus', as we did. If he did so, then 'Hesperus is Phosphorus'

7. p. 115.

would have been true in that situation too. He pointed maybe neither time to the planet Venus—at least one time he didn't point to the planet Venus, let's say when he pointed to the body he called 'Phosphorus'. Then in that case we can certainly say that the name 'Phosphorus' might not have referred to Phosphorus. We can even say that in the very position when viewed in the morning that we found Phosphorus, it might have been the case that Phosphorus was not there—that something else was there, and that even, under certain circumstances it would have been *called* 'Phosphorus'. But that still is not a case in which Phosphorus was not Hesperus. There might be a possible world in which, a possible counterfactual situation in which, 'Hesperus' and 'Phosphorus' weren't names of the things they in fact are names of. Someone, if he did determine their reference by identifying descriptions, might even have used the very identifying descriptions we used. But still that's not a case in which Hesperus wasn't Phosphorus. For there couldn't have been such a case, given that Hesperus is Phosphorus.

Now this seems very strange because in advance, we are inclined to say, the answer to the question whether Hesperus is Phosphorus might have turned out either way. So aren't there really two possible worlds—one in which Hesperus was Phosphorus, the other in which Hesperus wasn't Phosphorus—in advance of our discovering that these were the same? First, there's one sense in which things might turn out either way, in which it's clear that that doesn't imply that the way it finally turns out isn't necessary. For example, the four-colour theorem might turn out to be true and might turn out to be false. It might turn out either way. It still doesn't mean that the way it turns out is not necessary. Obviously, the 'might' here is purely 'epistemic'—it merely expresses our present state of ignorance, or uncertainty.

But it seems that in the Hesperus–Phosphorus case, something even stronger is true. The evidence I have before I know that Hesperus is Phosphorus is that I see a certain star or a certain heavenly body in the evening and call it 'Hesperus', and in the morning and call it 'Phosphorus'. I know these things. There certainly is a possible world in which a man should have seen a certain star at a certain position in the evening and called it 'Hesperus' and a certain star in the morning and called it 'Phosphorus'; and should have concluded—should have found out by empirical investigations—that he names two different stars, or two different heavenly bodies. At least one of these stars or heavenly bodies was not Phosphorus, otherwise it couldn't have come out that way. But that's true. And so it's true that given the evidence that someone has antecedent to his empirical investigation, he can be placed in a sense in exactly the same situation, that is a qualitatively identical epistemic situation, and call two heavenly bodies 'Hesperus' and 'Phosphorus', without their being identical. So in that sense we can say that it might have turned out either way. Not that it might have turned out either way as to Hesperus's being Phosphorus. Though for all we knew in advance, Hesperus wasn't Phosphorus, that couldn't have turned out any other way, in a sense. But being put in a situation where we have exactly the same evidence, qualitatively speaking, it could have turned out that Hesperus was not Phosphorus; that is, in a counterfactual world in which 'Hesperus' and 'Phosphorus' were not used in the way that we use them, as names of this planet, but as names of some other objects, one could have had qualitatively identical evidence and concluded that 'Hesperus' and 'Phosphorus' named two different objects.[8] But we, using the names as we do right now, can say in advance, that if Hesperus and Phosphorus are one and the same, then in no other possible world can they be different. We use 'Hesperus' as the name of a certain body and 'Phosphorus' as the name of a certain body. We use them as names of those bodies in all possible worlds. If, in fact, they are the *same* body, then in any other possible world we have to use them as a name of that object. And so in any other possible world it will be true that Hesperus is Phosphorus. So two things are true: first, that we do not know a priori that Hesperus is Phosphorus, and are in no position to find out the answer except empirically. Second, this is so because we could have evidence qualitatively indistinguishable from the evidence we have and determine the reference of the two names by the positions of two planets in the sky, without the planets being the same.

Of course, it is only a contingent truth (not true in every other possible world) that the star seen over there in the evening is the star seen over there in the morning, because there are possible worlds in which Phosphorus was not visible in the morning. But that contingent truth shouldn't be identified with the statement that Hesperus is Phosphorus. It could only be so identified if you thought that it was a necessary truth that Hesperus is visible over there in the evening or that Phosphorus is visible over there in the morning. But neither of those are necessary truths even if that's the way we pick out the planet. These are the contingent marks by which we identify a certain planet and give it a name.

[...]

We have concluded that an identity statement between names, when true at all, is necessarily true, even though one may not know it a priori. Suppose we identify Hesperus as a certain star seen in the evening and Phosphorus as a certain star, or a certain heavenly body, seen in the morning; then there may be possible worlds in which two different planets would have been seen in just those positions in the evening and morning. However, at least one of them, and maybe both, would not have been Hesperus, and then that would not have been a situation in which Hesperus was not Phosphorus. It might have been a situation in which the planet seen in this position in the evening was not the planet seen in this position in the morning; but that is not a situation in which Hesperus was not Phosphorus. It might also, if people gave the names 'Hesperus' and 'Phosphorus' to these planets, be a situation in which some planet other than Hesperus was called 'Hesperus'. But even so, it would not be a situation in which Hesperus itself was not Phosphorus.[9]

Some of the problems which bother people in these situations as I have said,

8. There is a more elaborate discussion of this point in the third lecture, in *Naming and Necessity*, where its relation to a certain sort of counterpart theory is also mentioned.

9. Recall that we describe the situation in our language, not the language that the people in that situation would have used. Hence we must use the terms 'Hesperus' and 'Phosphorus' with the same reference as in the actual world. The fact that people in that situation might or might not have used these names for different planets is irrelevant. So is the fact that they might have done so using the very same descriptions as we did to fix their references.

come from an identification, or as I would put it, a confusion, between what we can know a priori in advance and what is necessary. Certain statements—and the identity statement is a paradigm of such a statement on my view—if true at all must be necessarily true. One does know a priori, by philosophical analysis, that if such an identity statement is true it is necessarily true.

Chapter 41

A priori knowledge*

Philip Kitcher

I

'A PRIORI' has been a popular term with philosophers at least since Kant distinguished between a priori and a posteriori knowledge. Yet, despite the frequency with which it has been used in twentieth century philosophy, there has been little discussion of the concept of apriority.[1] Some writers seem to take it for granted that there are propositions, such as the truths of logic and mathematics, which are a priori; others deny that there are any a priori propositions. In the absence of a clear characterization of the a priori/a posteriori distinction, it is by no means obvious what is being asserted or what is being denied.

'A priori' is an epistemological predicate. What is *primarily* a priori is an item of knowledge.[2] Of course, we can introduce a derivative use of 'a priori' as a predicate of propositions:[3] a priori propositions are those which we could know a priori. Somebody might protest that current practice is to define the notion of an a priori proposition outright, by taking the class of a priori propositions to consist of the truths of logic and mathematics (for example). But when philosophers allege that truths of logic and mathematics are a priori, they do not intend merely to recapitu-

Philip Kitcher, 'A Priori Knowledge' in *The Philosophical Review* 89 (1980) pp. 3–23. Copyright 1980 Cornell University, reprinted by permission of the publisher and the author.

* I am grateful to several members of the Department of Philosophy at the University of Michigan for their helpful comments on a previous version of this paper, and especially to Alvin Goldman and Jaegwon Kim for their constructive suggestions. I would also like to thank Paul Benacerraf, who first interested me in the problem of characterizing a priori knowledge, and prevented many errors in early analyses. Above all, I am indebted to Patricia Kitcher and George Sher, who have helped me to clarify my ideas on this topic. Patricia Kitcher's advice on issues in the philosophy of mind relevant to §V was particularly valuable.

1. There are some exceptions. Passing attention to the problem of defining apriority is given in John Pollock, *Knowledge and Justification* (Princeton 1974) Chapter 10; R. G. Swinburne 'Analyticity, Necessity and Apriority,' (*Mind*, 84, 1975, pp. 225–43) especially pp. 238–41; Edward Erwin 'Are the Notions "A Priori Truth" and "Necessary Truth" Extensionally Equivalent?' (*Canadian Journal of Philosophy*, 3, 1974, pp. 591–602), especially pp. 593–7. The inadequacy of much traditional thinking about apriority is forcefully presented in Saul Kripke's papers 'Identity and Necessity' (in Milton K. Munitz (ed.), *Identity and Individuation*, New York, 1971, pp 135–64), especially pp. 149–51, and 'Naming and Necessity' (in D. Davidson and G. Harman (eds.), *Semantics of Natural Language*, D. Reidel, 1972, pp. 253–355, 763–9), especially pp. 260–4.

2. See Kripke, loc. cit.

3. For ease of reference, I take propositions to be the objects of belief and knowledge, and to be what declarative sentences express. I trust that my conclusions would survive any successful elimination of propositions in favor of some alternative approach to the objects of belief and knowledge.

late the definition of a priori propositions. Their aim is to advance a thesis about the epistemological status of logic and mathematics.

To understand the nature of such epistemological claims, we should return to Kant, who provided the most explicit characterization of a priori knowledge: 'we shall understand by a priori knowledge, not knowledge which is independent of this or that experience, but knowledge absolutely independent of all experience.'[4] While acknowledging that Kant's formulation sums up the classical notion of apriority, several recent writers who have discussed the topic have despaired of making sense of it.[5] I shall try to show that Kant's definition can be clarified, and that the concept of a priori knowledge can be embedded in a naturalistic epistemology.

II

Two questions naturally arise. What are we to understand by 'experience'? And what is to be made of the idea of independence from experience? Apparently, there are easy answers. Count as a person's experience the stream of her sensory encounters with the world, where this includes both 'outer experience', that is, sensory states caused by stimuli external to the body, and 'inner experience,' that is, those sensory states brought about by internal stimuli. Now we might propose that someone's knowledge is independent of her experience just in case she could have had that knowledge whatever experience she had had. To this obvious suggestion there is an equally obvious objection. The apriorist is not ipso facto a believer in innate knowledge: indeed, Kant emphasized the difference between the two types of knowledge. So we cannot accept an analysis which implies that a priori knowledge could have been obtained given minimal experiences.[6]

Many philosophers (Kant included) contend both that analytic truths can be known a priori and that some analytic truths involve concepts which could only be acquired if we were to have particular kinds of experience. If we are to defend their doctrines from immediate rejection, we must allow a minimal role to experience, even in a priori knowledge. Experience may be needed to provide some concepts. So we might modify our proposal: knowledge is independent of experience if any experience which would enable us to acquire the concepts involved would enable us to have the knowledge.

It is worth noting explicitly that we are concerned here with the *total* experience of the knower. Suppose that you acquire some knowledge empirically. Later you deduce some consequences of this empirical knowledge. We should reject the suggestion that your knowledge of those consequences is independent of experience because, at the time you perform the deduction, you are engaging in a process of

4. *Critique of Pure Reason* (B2–3).
5. See Pollock, loc. cit., Swinburne, loc. cit., Erwin, loc. cit.
6. Someone might be tempted to propose, conversely, that all innate knowledge is a priori (cf. Swinburne op. cit. p. 239). In 'The Nativist's Dilemma,' (*Philosophical Quarterly*, 28, 1978, pp. 1–16), I have argued that there may well be no innate knowledge and that, if there were any such knowledge, it would not have to be a priori.

reasoning which is independent of the sensations you are then having.[7] As Kant recognized,[8] your knowledge, in cases like this, is dependent on your total experience: different total sequences of sensations would not have given you the premises for your deductions.

Let us put together the points which have been made so far. A person's experience at a particular time will be identified with his sensory state at the time. (Such states are best regarded physicalistically in terms of stimulation of sensory receptors, but we should recognize that there are both 'outer' and 'inner' receptors.) The total sequence of experiences X has had up to time t is *X's life at t*. A life will be said to be *sufficient for X for p* just in case X could have had that life and gained sufficient understanding to believe that p. (I postpone, for the moment, questions about the nature of the modality involved here.) Our discussion above suggests the use of these notions in the analysis of a priori knowledge: X knows a priori that p if and only if X knows that p and, given any life sufficient for X for p, X could have had that life and still have known that p. Making temporal references explicit: at time t X knows a priori that p just in case, at time t, X knows that p and, given any life sufficient for X for p, X could have had that life at t and still have known, at t, that p. In subsequent discussions I shall usually leave the temporal references implicit.

Unfortunately, the proposed analysis will not do. A clearheaded apriorist should admit that people can have empirical knowledge of propositions which can be known a priori. However, on the account I have given, if somebody knows that p and if it is possible for her to know a priori that p, then, apparently, given any sufficiently rich life she could know that p, so that she would meet the conditions for a priori knowledge that p. (This presupposes that modalities 'collapse,' but I don't think the problem can be solved simply by denying the presupposition.) Hence it seems that my account will not allow for empirical knowledge of propositions that can be known a priori.

We need to amend the analysis. We must differentiate situations in which a person knows something empirically which could have been known a priori from situations of actual a priori knowledge. The remedy is obvious. What sets apart corresponding situations of the two types is a difference in the ways in which what is known is known. An analysis of a priori knowledge must probe the notion of knowledge more deeply than we have done so far.

III

We do not need a general analysis of knowledge, but we do need the *form* of such an analysis. I shall adopt an approach which extracts what is common to much recent work on knowledge, an approach which may appropriately be called 'the

---

7. Pollock (op. cit. p. 301) claims that we can only resist the suggestion that this knowledge is independent of experience by complicating the notion of experience. For the reason given in the text, such desperate measures seem to me to be unnecessary.
8. See the example of the man who undermines the foundations of his house, (*Critique of Pure Reason*, B3).

psychologistic account of knowledge.'[9] The root idea is that the question of whether a person's true belief counts as knowledge depends on whether the presence of that true belief can be explained in an appropriate fashion. The difference between an item of knowledge and mere true belief turns on the factors which produced the belief; thus the issue revolves around the way in which a particular mental state was generated. It is important to emphasize that, at different times, a person may have states of belief with the same content, and these states may be produced by different processes. The claim that a process produces a belief is to be understood as the assertion that the presence of the current state of belief is to be explained through a description of that process. Hence the account is not committed to supposing that the original formation of a belief is relevant to the epistemological status of later states of belief in the same proposition.[10]

The question of what conditions must be met if a belief is to be explained in an appropriate fashion is central to epistemology, but it need not concern us here. My thesis is that the distinction between knowledge and true belief depends on the characteristics of the process which generates the belief, and this thesis is independent of specific proposals about what characteristics are crucial. Introducing a useful term, let us say that some processes *warrant* the beliefs they produce, and that these processes are *warrants* for such beliefs. The general view of knowledge I have adopted can be recast as the thesis that X knows that p just in case X correctly believes that p and X's belief was produced by a process which is a warrant for it. Leaving the task of specifying the conditions on warrants to general epistemology, my aim is to distinguish a priori knowledge from a posteriori knowledge. We discovered above that the distinction requires us to consider the ways in which what is known is known. Hence I propose to reformulate the problem: let us say that X knows a priori that p just in case X has a true belief that p and that belief was produced by a process which is an *a priori warrant* for it. Now the crucial notion is that of an a priori warrant, and our task becomes that of specifying the conditions which distinguish a priori warrants from other warrants.

At this stage, some examples may help us to see how to draw the distinction. Perception is an obvious type of process which philosophers have supposed *not* to engender a priori knowledge. Putative a priori warrants are more controversial. I shall use Kant's notion of pure intuition as an example. This is not to endorse the

---

9. Prominent exponents of this approach are Alvin Goldman, Gilbert Harman and David Armstrong. See: Alvin Goldman. 'A Causal Theory of Knowing' (*Journal of Philosophy*, 64, 1967, pp. 357–72) [Ch. 4 in this volume], 'Innate Knowledge' (in Stephen P. Stich (ed.) *Innate Ideas* [Berkeley, 1975] pp. 111–20), 'Discrimination and Perceptual Knowledge' (*Journal of Philosophy*, 72, 1976, pp. 771–91), 'What is Justified Belief?' (in George S. Pappas (ed.) *Justification and Knowledge*, [Dordrecht, 1979]); Gilbert Harman, *Thought* (Princeton, 1973); David Armstrong, *Belief, Truth and Knowledge* (Cambridge, 1973).

10. Psychologistic epistemologies are often accused of confusing the context of discovery with the context of justification. For a recent formulation of this type of objection, see Keith Lehrer, *Knowledge* (Oxford, 1974), pp. 123ff. I have tried to show that psychologistic epistemology is not committed to mistakes with which it is frequently associated in 'Frege's Epistemology,' (*Philosophical Review*, 88, 1979, pp. 235–62). I shall consider the possibility of an apsychologistic approach to apriority in §VII below.

claim that processes of pure intuition are a priori warrants, but only to see what features of such processes have prompted Kant (and others) to differentiate them from perceptual processes.

On Kant's theory, processes of pure intuition are supposed to yield a priori mathematical knowledge. Let us focus on a simple geometrical example. We are supposed to gain a priori knowledge of the elementary properties of triangles by using our grasp on the concept of triangle to construct a mental picture of a triangle and by inspecting this picture with the mind's eye.[11] What are the characteristics of this kind of process which make Kant want to say that it produces knowledge which is independent of experience? I believe that Kant's account implies that three conditions should be met. The same type of process must be *available* independently of experience. It must produce *warranted* belief independently of experience. And it must produce *true* belief independently of experience. Let us consider these conditions in turn.

According to the Kantian story, if our life were to enable us to acquire the appropriate concepts (the concept of a triangle and the other geometrical concepts involved) then the appropriate kind of pure intuition would be available to us. We could represent a triangle to ourselves, inspect it, and so reach the same beliefs. But, if the process is to generate *knowledge* independently of experience, Kant must require more of it. Given any sufficiently rich life, if we were to undergo the same type of process and gain the same beliefs, then those beliefs would be warranted by the process. Let us dramatize the point by imagining that experience is unkind. Suppose that we are presented with experiments which are cunningly contrived so as to make it appear that some of our basic geometrical beliefs are false. Kant's theory of geometrical knowledge presupposes that if, in the circumstances envisaged, a process of pure intuition were to produce geometrical belief then it would produce warranted belief, despite the background of misleading experience.

So far I have considered how a Kantian process of pure intuition might produce warranted belief independently of experience. But to generate *knowledge* independently of experience, a priori warrants must produce warranted *true* belief in counterfactual situations where experiences are different. This point does not emerge clearly in the Kantian case because the propositions which are alleged to be known a priori are taken to be necessary, so that the question of whether it would be possible to have an a priori warrant for a false belief does not arise. Plainly, we could ensure that a priori warrants produce warranted *true* belief independently of experience by declaring that a priori warrants only warrant necessary truths. But this proposal is unnecessarily strong. Our goal is to construe a priori knowledge as knowledge which is independent of experience, and this can be achieved, without closing the case against the contingent a priori, by supposing that, in a counterfactual situation in which an a priori warrant produces belief that p then p. On this account, a priori warrants are ultra-reliable; they never lead us astray.[12]

11. More details about Kant's theory of pure intuition can be found in my paper 'Kant and the Foundations of Mathematics' (*Philosophical Review*, 84, 1975, pp. 23–50), especially pp. 28–33.

12. For further discussion of this requirement and the possibility of the contingent a priori, see §V below.

Summarizing the conditions that have been uncovered, I propose the following analysis of a priori knowledge.

(1) X knows a priori that p if and only if X knows that p and X's belief that p was produced by a process which is an a priori warrant for it.

(2) α is an a priori warrant for X's belief that p if and only if α is a process such that, given any life e, sufficient for X for p, then

(a) some process of the same type could produce in X a belief that p

(b) if a process of the same type were to produce in X a belief that p then it would warrant X in believing that p

(c) if a process of the same type were to produce in X a belief that p then p.

It should be clear that this analysis yields the desired result that, if a person knows a priori that p then she could know that p whatever (sufficiently rich) experience she had had. But it goes beyond the proposal of §2 in spelling out the idea that the knowledge be obtainable in the same way. Hence we can distinguish cases of empirical knowledge of propositions which could be known a priori from cases of actual a priori knowledge.

IV

In this section, I want to be more explicit about the notion of 'types of processes' which I have employed, and about the modal and conditional notions which figure in my analysis. To specify a process which produces a belief is to pick out some terminal segment of the causal ancestry of the belief. I think that, without loss of generality, we can restrict our attention to those segments which consist solely of states and events internal to the believer.[13] Tracing the causal ancestry of a belief beyond the believer would identify processes which would not be available independently of experience, so that they would violate our conditions on a priori warrants.

Given that we need only consider psychological processes, the next question which arises is how we divide processes into types. It may seem that the problem can be sidestepped: can't we simply propose that to defend the apriority of an item of knowledge is to claim that that knowledge was produced by a psychological process and that *that very process* would be available and would produce warranted true belief in counterfactual situations where experience is different? I think it is easy to see how to use this proposal to rewrite (2) in a way which avoids reference to 'types of processes.' I have not adopted this approach because I think that it shortcuts important questions about what makes a process the same in different counterfactual situations.

Our talk of processes which produce belief was originally introduced to articulate the idea that some items of knowledge are obtained in the same way while others are obtained in different ways. To return to our example, knowing a theorem

13. For different reasons, Goldman proposes that an analysis of the general notion of warrant (or, in his terms, justification) can focus on psychological processes. See section 2 of 'What is Justified Belief?'

on the basis of hearing a lecture and knowing the same theorem by following a proof count, intuitively, as different ways of knowing the theorem. Our intuitions about this example, and others, involve a number of different principles of classification, with different principles appearing in different cases. We seem to divide belief-forming processes into types by considering content of beliefs, inferential connections, causal connections, use of perceptual mechanisms and so forth. I suggest that these principles of classification probably do not give rise to one definite taxonomy, but that, by using them singly, or in combination, we obtain a number of different taxonomies which we can and do employ. Moreover, within each taxonomy, we can specify types of processes more or less narrowly.[14] Faced with such variety, what characterization should we pick?

There is probably no privileged way of dividing processes into types. This is not to say that our standard principles of classification will allow *anything* to count as a type. Somebody who proposed that the process of listening to a lecture (or the terminal segment of it which consists of psychological states and events) belongs to a type which consists of itself and instances of following a proof, would flout *all* our principles for dividing processes into types. Hence, while we may have many admissible notions of types of belief-forming processes, corresponding to different principles of classification, some collections of processes contravene all such principles, and these cannot be admitted as genuine types.[15]

My analysis can be read as issuing a challenge to the apriorist. If someone wishes to claim that a particular belief is an item of a priori knowledge then he must specify a segment of the causal ancestry of the belief, consisting of states and events internal to the believer, and type-identity conditions which conform to some principle (or set of principles) of classification which are standardly employed in our divisions of belief-forming processes (of which the principles I have indicated above furnish the most obvious examples). If he succeeds in doing this so that the requirements in (2) are met, his claim is sustained; if he cannot, then his claim is defeated.

The final issue which requires discussion in this section is that of explaining the modal and conditional notions I have used. There are all kinds of possibility, and claims about what is possible bear an implicit relativization to a set of facts which are held constant.[16] When we say, in (2), that, given any sufficiently rich life, X could have had a belief which was the product of a particular type of process, should we conceive of this as merely logical possibility or are there some features of the actual

14. Consider, for example, a Kantian process of pure intuition which begins with the construction of a triangle. Should we say that a process of the same type must begin with the construction of a triangle of the same size and shape, a triangle of the same shape, any triangle, or something even more general? Obviously there are many natural classifications here, and I think the best strategy is to suppose that an apriorist is entitled to pick any of them.

15. Strictly, the sets which do not constitute types are those which violate correct taxonomies. In making present decisions about types, we assume that our current principles of classification are correct. If it should turn out that those principles require revision then our judgments about types will have to be revised accordingly.

16. For a lucid and entertaining presentation of the point, see David Lewis, 'The Paradoxes of Time Travel,' (*American Philosophical Quarterly*, 13, 1976, pp. 145–52), pp. 149–51.

world which are tacitly regarded as fixed? I suggest that we are not just envisaging any logically possible world. We imagine a world in which X has similar mental powers to those he has in the actual world. By hypothesis, X's experience is different. Yet the capacities for thinking, reasoning, and acquiring knowledge which X possesses as a member of *homo sapiens* are to remain unaffected: we want to say that X, *with the kinds of cognitive capacities distinctive of humans*, could have undergone processes of the appropriate type, even if his experiences had been different.[17]

Humans might have had more faculties for acquiring knowledge than they actually have. For example, we might have had some strange ability to 'see' what happens on the other side of the Earth. When we consider the status of a particular type of process as an a priori warrant, the existence of worlds in which such extra faculties come into play is entirely irrelevant. Our investigation focusses on the question of whether a particular type of process would be available to a person with the kinds of faculties people actually have, not on whether such processes would be available to creatures whose capacities for acquiring knowledge are augmented or diminished. Conditions (2(b)) and (2(c)) are to be read in similar fashion. Rewriting (2(b)) to make the form of the conditional explicit, we obtain: for any life e sufficient for X for p and for any world in which X has e, in which he believes that p, in which his belief is the product of a process of the appropriate kind, and *in which X has the cognitive capacities distinctive of humans*, X is warranted in believing that p. Similarly, (2(c)) becomes: for any life e sufficient for X for p and for any world in which X has e, in which he believes that p, in which his belief is the product of a process of the appropriate kind, *and in which X has the cognitive capacities distinctive of humans*, p. Finally, the notion of a life's being sufficient for X for p also bears an implicit reference to X's native powers. To say that a particular life enables X to form certain concepts is to maintain that, given the genetic programming with which X is endowed, that life allows for the formation of the concepts.

The account I have offered can be presented more graphically in the following way. Consider a human as a cognitive device, endowed initially with a particular kind of structure. Sensory experience is fed into the device and, as a result, the device forms certain concepts. For any proposition p, the class of experiences which are sufficiently rich for p consists of those experiences which would enable the device, with the kind of structure it actually has, to acquire the concepts to believe that p. To decide whether or not a particular item of knowledge that p is an item of a priori knowledge we consider whether the type of process which produced the belief that p is a process which would have been available to the device, with the kind of structure it actually has, if different sufficiently rich experiences had been fed into it, whether, under such circumstances, processes of the type would warrant belief that p, and would produce true belief that p.

Seen in this way, claims about apriority are implicitly indexical, in that they

---

17. Of course, X might have been more intelligent, that is, he might have had better versions of the faculties he has. We allow for this type of change. But we are not interested in worlds where X has extra faculties.

inherit the indexical features of 'actual.'[18] If this is not recognized, use of 'a priori' in modal contexts can engender confusion. The truth value of 'Possibly, X knows a priori that p' can be determined in one of two ways: we may consider the proposition expressed by the sentence at our world, and inquire whether there is a world at which that proposition is true; or we may ask whether there is a world at which the sentence expresses a true proposition. Because of the covert indexicality of 'a priori,' these lines of investigation may yield different answers. I suspect that failure to appreciate this point has caused trouble in assessing theses about the limits of the a priori. However, I shall not pursue the point here.[19]

V

At this point, I want to address worries that my analysis is too liberal, because it allows some of our knowledge of ourselves and our states to count as a priori. Given its Kantian psychologistic underpinnings, the theory appears to favor claims that some of our self-knowledge is a priori. However, two points should be kept in mind. Firstly, the analysis I have proposed can only be applied to cases in which we know enough about the ways in which our beliefs are warranted to decide whether or not the conditions of (2) are met. In some cases, our lack of a detailed account of how our beliefs are generated may mean that no firm decision about the apriority of an item of knowledge can be reached. Secondly, there may be cases, including cases of self-knowledge, in which we have no clear pre-analytic intuitions about whether a piece of knowledge is a priori.

Nevertheless, there are some clear cases. Obviously, any theory which implied that I can know a priori that I am seeing red (when, in fact, I am) would be suspect. But, when we apply my analysis, the unwanted conclusion does not follow. For, if the process which leads me to believe that I am seeing red (when I am) can be triggered in the absence of red, then (2(c)) would be violated. If the process cannot be triggered in the absence of red, then, given some sufficiently rich experiences, the process will not be available, so that (2(a)) will be violated. In general, knowledge of any voluntary mental state—such as pains, itches or hallucinations—will work in the same way. Either the process which leads from the occurrence of pain to the belief that I am in pain can be triggered in the absence of pain, or not: if it can, (2(c)) would be violated, if it cannot, then (2(a)) would be violated.

This line of argument can be sidestepped when we turn to cases in which we have the power, independently of experience, to put ourselves into the appropriate states.

18. The idea that 'actual' is indexical is defended by David Lewis in 'Anselm and Actuality,' (*Noûs*, 4, 1970, pp. 175–88). In 'The Only Necessity is Verbal Necessity,' (*Journal of Philosophy*, 74, 1977, pp. 71–85), Bas van Fraassen puts Lewis' ideas about 'actual' in a general context. The machinery which van Fraassen presents in that paper can be used to elaborate the ideas of the present paragraph.

19. Jaegwon Kim has pointed out to me that, besides the 'species-relative' notion of apriority presented in the text, there might be an absolute notion. Perhaps there is a class of propositions which would be knowable a priori by any being whom we would count as a rational being. Absolute a priori knowledge would thus be that a priori knowledge which is available to all possible knowers.

For, in such cases, one can propose that the processes which give us knowledge of the states cannot be triggered in the absence of the states themselves *and* that the processes are always available because we can always put ourselves into the states.[20] On this basis, we might try to conclude that we have a priori knowledge that we are imagining red (when we are) or thinking of Ann Arbor (when we are). However, the fact that such cases do not fall victim to the argument of the last paragraph does not mean that we are compelled to view them as cases of a priori knowledge. In the first place, the thesis that the processes through which we come to know our imaginative feats and our voluntary thoughts cannot be triggered in the absence of the states themselves requires evaluation—and, lacking detailed knowledge of those processes, we cannot arrive at a firm judgment here. Secondly, the processes in question will be required to meet (2(b)) if they are to be certified as a priori warrants. This means that, whatever experience hurls at us, beliefs produced by such processes will be warranted. We can cast doubt on this idea by imagining that our experience consists of a lengthy, and apparently reliable, training in neuro-physiology, concluding with a presentation to ourselves of our own neurophysio-logical organization which appears to show that our detection of our imaginative states (say) is slightly defective, that we always make mistakes about the contents of our imaginings. If this type of story can be developed, then (2(b)) will be violated, and the knowledge in question will not count as a priori. But, even if it cannot be coherently extended, and even if my analysis does judge our knowledge of states of imagination (and other 'voluntary' states) to be a priori, it is not clear to me that this consequence is counterintuitive.

In fact, I think that one can make a powerful case for supposing that *some* self-knowledge is a priori. At most, if not all, of our waking moments, each of us knows of herself that she exists.[21] Although traditional ideas to the effect that self-knowledge is produced by some 'non-optical inner look' are clearly inadequate, I think it is plausible to maintain that there are processes which do warrant us in believing that we exist—processes of reflective thought, for example—and which belong to a general type whose members would be available to us independently of experience.[22] Trivially, when any such process produces in a person a belief that she exists that belief is true. All that remains, therefore, is to ask if the processes of the

20. In characterizing pain as an involuntary state one paragraph back I may seem to have under-estimated our powers of self-torture. But even a masochist could be defeated by unkind experience: as he goes to pinch himself his skin is anesthetized.

21. I shall ignore the tricky issue of trying to say exactly what is known when we know this and kindred things. For interesting explorations of this area, see Hector-Neri Castañeda, 'Indicators and Quasi-indicators' (*American Philosophical Quarterly*, 4, 1967, pp. 85–100), 'On the Logic of Attributions of Self-Knowledge to Others,' (*Journal of Philosophy*, 65, 1968, pp. 439–56); John Perry, 'Frege on Demonstratives,' (*Philosophical Review*, 86, 1977, pp. 474–97), 'The Problem of the Essential Index-ical,' (*Noûs*, 13, 1979, pp. 3–21). The issue of how to represent the content of items of self-knowledge may force revision of the position taken in footnote 3 above: it may not be possible to identify objects of belief with meanings of sentences. Although such revision would complicate my analysis, I don't think it would necessitate any fundamental modifications.

22. This presupposes that our knowledge of our existence does not result from some special kind of 'inner sensation.' For, if it did, different lives would deprive us of the warrant.

type in question inevitably warrant belief in our own existence, or whether they would fail to do so, given a suitably exotic background experience. It is difficult to settle this issue conclusively without a thorough survey of the ways in which reflective belief in one's existence can be challenged by experience, but perhaps there are Cartesian grounds for holding that, so long as the belief is the product of reflective thought, the believer is warranted, no matter how wild his experience may have been. If this is correct, then at least some of our self-knowledge will be a priori. However, in cases like this, attributions of apriority seem even less vulnerable to the criticism that they are obviously incorrect.

At this point we must consider a doctrinaire objection. If the conclusion of the last paragraph is upheld then we can know some contingent propositions a priori.[23] Frequently, however, it is maintained that only necessary truths can be known a priori. Behind this contention stands a popular argument.[24] Assume that a person knows a priori that p. His knowledge is independent of his experience. Hence he can know that p without any information about the kind of world he inhabits. So, necessarily p.

This hazy line of reasoning rests on an intuition which is captured in the analysis given above. The intuition is that a priori warrants must be ultra-reliable: if a person is entitled to ignore empirical information about the type of world she inhabits then that must be because she has at her disposal a method of arriving at belief which guarantees *true* belief. (This intuition can be defended by pointing out that if a method which could produce false belief were allowed to override experience, then we might be blocked from obtaining knowledge which we might otherwise have gained.) In my analysis, the intuition appears as (2(c)).[25]

However, when we try to clarify the popular argument we see that it contains an invalid step. Presenting it as a *reductio*, we obtain the following line of reasoning. Assume that a person knows a priori that p but that it is not necessary that p. Because p is contingent there are worlds at which p is false. Suppose that the person had inhabited such a world and behaved as she does at the actual world. Then she would have had an a priori warrant for a false belief. This is debarred by (2(c)). So we must conclude that the initial supposition is erroneous: if someone really does know a priori that p then p is necessary.

23. Kripke (loc. cit.) has attempted to construct examples of contingent propositions which can be known a priori. I have not tried to decide here whether his examples are successful, since full treatment of this question would lead into issues about the analysis of the propositions in question which are well beyond the scope of the present paper. For a discussion of some of the difficulties involved in Kripke's examples, see Keith Donnellan 'The Contingent A Priori and Rigid Designators' (*Midwest Studies in Philosophy*, 2, 1977, pp. 12–27).

24. Kripke seems to take this to be the main argument against the contingent a priori. See 'Naming and Necessity,' p. 263.

25. As the discussion of this paragraph suggests, there is an intimate relation between my requirements (2(b)) and (2(c)). Indeed, one might argue that (2(b)) would not be met unless (2(c)) were also satisfied—on the grounds that one cannot allow a process to override experience unless it guarantees truth. The subsequent discussion will show that this type of reasoning is more complicated than appears. Hence, although I believe that the idea that a priori warrants function independently of experience does have implications for the reliability of these processes, I have chosen to add (2(c)) as a separate condition.

Spelled out in this way, the argument fails. We are not entitled to conclude from the premise that there are worlds at which p is false the thesis that there are worlds at which p is false *and* at which the person behaves as she does at the actual world. There are a number of propositions which, although they could be false, could not both be false and also believed by us. More generally, there are propositions which could not both be false and also believed by us in particular, definite ways. Obvious examples are propositions about ourselves and their logical consequences: such propositions as those expressed by tokens of the sentences 'I exist,' 'I have some beliefs,' 'There are thoughts,' and so forth. Hence the attempted *reductio* breaks down and allows for the possibility of a priori knowledge of some contingent propositions.

I conclude that my analysis is innocent of the charge of being too liberal in ascribing to us a priori knowledge of propositions about ourselves. Although it is plausible to hold that my account construes some of our self-knowledge as a priori, none of the self-knowledge it takes to be a priori is clearly empirical. Moreover, it shows how a popular argument against the contingent a priori is flawed, and how certain types of contingent propositions—most notably propositions about ourselves—escape that argument. Thus I suggest that the analysis illuminates an area of traditional dispute.

VI

I now want to consider two different objections to my analysis. My replies to these objections will show how the approach I have developed can be further refined and extended.

The first objection, like those considered above, charges that the analysis is too liberal. My account apparently allows for the possibility that a priori knowledge could be gained through perception. We can imagine that some propositions are true at any world of which we can have experience, and that, given sufficient experience to entertain those propositions, we could always come to know them on the basis of perception. Promising examples are the proposition that there are objects, the proposition that some objects have shapes, and other, similar propositions. In these cases, one can argue that we cannot experience worlds at which they are false and that any (sufficiently rich) experience would provide perceptual warrant for belief in the propositions, regardless of the specific content of our perceptions. If these points are correct (and I shall concede them both, for the sake of argument), then perceptual processes would qualify as a priori warrants. Given any sufficiently rich experience, some perceptual process would be available to us, would produce warranted belief and, *ex hypothesi*, would produce warranted *true* belief.

Let us call cases of the type envisaged cases of *universally empirical* knowledge. The objection to my account is that it incorrectly classifies universally empirical knowledge as a priori knowledge. My response is that the classical notion of apriority is too vague to decide such cases: rather, this type of knowledge only becomes apparent when the classical notion is articulated. One could defend the classification of universally empirical knowledge as a priori by pointing out that such knowledge requires no particular type of experience (beyond that needed to obtain the concepts, of course). One could oppose that classification by pointing out that, even though the content of the experience is immaterial, the knowledge is still gained by perceiving, so that it should count as a posteriori.

If the second response should seem attractive, it can easily be accommodated by recognizing a stronger and a weaker notion of apriority. The weaker notion is captured in (1) and (2). The stronger adds an extra requirement: no process which involves the operation of a perceptual mechanism is to count as an a priori warrant.

At this point, it is natural to protest that the new condition makes the prior analysis irrelevant. Why not define a priori knowledge outright as knowledge which is produced by processes which do not involve perceptual mechanisms? The answer is that the prior conditions are not redundant: knowledge which is produced by a process which does not involve perceptual mechanisms need not be independent of experience. For the process may fail to generate warranted belief against a backdrop of misleading experience. (Nor may it generate true belief in all relevant counterfactual situations.) So, for example, certain kinds of thought-experiments may generate items of knowledge given a particular type of experience, but may not be able to sustain that knowledge against misleading experiences. Hence, if we choose to exclude universally empirical knowledge from the realm of the a priori in the way suggested, we are building on the analysis given in (1) and (2), rather than replacing it.

A different kind of criticism of my analysis is to accuse it of revealing the emptiness of the classical notion of apriority. Someone may suggest that, in exposing the constraints on a priori knowledge, I have shown that there could be very little a priori knowledge. Although I believe that this suggestion is incorrect, it is worth pointing out that, even if it is granted, my approach allows for the development of weaker notions which may prove epistemologically useful.

Let me first note that we can introduce approximations to a priori knowledge. Suppose that A is any type of process all of whose instances culminate in belief that p. Define the *supporting class* of A to be that class of lives, e, such that, (a) given e, some process in A could occur (and so produce belief that p), (b) given e, any process in A which occurred would produce warranted true belief that p. (Intuitively, the supporting class consists of those lives which enable processes of the type in question to produce knowledge.) The *defeating class* of A is the complement of the supporting class of A within the class of lives which are sufficient for p. A priori warrants are those processes which belong to a type whose defeating class is null. But we can be more liberal, and allow approximations to a priori knowledge by considering the size and/or nature of the defeating class. We might, for example, permit the defeating class to contain those radically disruptive experiences beloved of sceptics. Or we can define a notion of *contextual* apriority by allowing the defeating class to include experiences which undermine 'framework principles.'[26]

26. This notion of contextual apriority has been used by Hilary Putnam. See, for example, his paper 'It Ain't Necessarily So,' (Chapter 15 of H. Putnam, *Mathematics, Matter and Method. Philosophical Papers, Volume I*, Cambridge, 1975) and 'There is At Least One A Priori Truth' (*Erkenntnis*, 13, 1978, pp. 153–70), especially p. 154.

Or we may employ a concept of *comparative* apriority by ordering defeating classes according to inclusion relations. Each of these notions can serve a useful function in delineating the structure of our knowledge.

VII

Finally, I want to address a systematic objection to my analysis. The approach I have taken is blatantly psychologistic. Some philosophers may regard these psychological complications as objectionable intrusions into epistemology. So I shall consider the possibility of rival apsychologistic approaches.

Is there an acceptable view of a priori knowledge which rivals the Kantian conception? The logical positivists hoped to understand a priori knowledge without dabbling in psychology. The simplest of their proposals was the suggestion that X knows a priori that p if and only if X believes that p and p is analytically true.[27]

Gilbert Harman has argued cogently that, in cases of factual belief, the nature of the reasons for which a person believes is relevant to the question of whether he has knowledge.[28] Similar considerations arise with respect to propositions which the positivists took to be a priori. Analytic propositions like synthetic propositions, can be believed for bad reasons, or for no reasons at all, and, when this occurs, we should deny that the believer knows the propositions in question. Assume, as the positivists did, that mathematics is analytic, and imagine a mathematician who comes to believe that some unobvious theorem is true. This belief is exhibited in her continued efforts to prove the theorem. Finally, she succeeds. We naturally describe her progress by saying that she has come to know something she only believed before. The positivistic proposal forces us to attribute knowledge from the beginning. Worse still, we can imagine that the mathematician has many colleagues who believe the theorem because of dreams, trances, fits of Pythagorean ecstasy, and so forth. Not only does the positivistic approach fail to separate the mathematician after she has found the proof from her younger self, but it also gives her the same status as her colleagues.

A natural modification suggests itself: distinguish among the class of analytic truths those which are elementary (basic laws of logic, immediate consequences of definitions, and, perhaps, a few others), and propose that elementary analytic truths can be known merely by being believed, while the rest are known, when they are known a priori, by inference from such truths. Even this restricted version of the original claim is vulnerable. If you believe the basic laws of logic because you have learned them from an eminent mathematician who has deluded himself into believing that the system of *Grundgesetze* is consistent and true, then you do not have a priori knowledge of those laws. Your belief in the laws of logic is undermined by evidence which you do not currently possess, namely the evidence which would

---

27. See A. J. Ayer, *Language, Truth and Logic,* (London 1936), Chapter 4, and M. Schlick, 'The Foundation of Knowledge' (in A. J. Ayer (ed.) *Logical Positivism* (New York, 1959) pp. 209–27) especially p. 224.
28. *Thought* Chapter 2; see also Goldman 'What is Justified Belief?' Section 1.

expose your teacher as a misguided fanatic. The moral is obvious: apsychologistic approaches to a priori knowledge fail because, for a priori knowledge as for factual knowledge, the reasons for which a person believes are relevant to the question of whether he knows.

Although horror of psychologizing prevented the positivists from offering a defensible account of a priori knowledge, I think that my analysis can be used to articulate most of the doctrines that they wished to defend. Indeed, I believe that many classical theses, arguments and debates can be illuminated by applying the analysis presented here. My aim has been to prepare the way for investigations of traditional claims and disputes by developing in some detail Kant's conception of a priori knowledge. 'A priori' has too often been a label which philosophers could attach to propositions they favored, without any clear criterion for doing so. I hope to have shown how a more systematic practice is possible.

Notes on the Contributors

William P. Alston, Emeritus Professor of Philosophy at Syracuse University, Department of Philosophy, Hall of Languages, Syracuse, NY 13244, USA.

David M. Armstrong, Emeritus Professor of Philosophy at the University of Sydney, Department of Traditional and Modern Philosophy, Main Quad, A14, NSW Australia 2006.

J. L. Austin (1911–1960) was Professor of Philosophy at Oxford Unversity.

A. J. Ayer (1910–1989) was Wykeham Professor of Logic at Oxford University and Fellow of Wolfson College, Oxford University.

Kent Bach, Professor of Philosophy at San Francisco State University, Department of Philosophy, 1600 Holloway Ave., San Francisco, CA 94132, USA.

Sven Bernecker, Assistant Professor of Philosophy at the University of Munich, Department of Philosophy, Geschwister-Scholl-Platz 1, 80539 Munich, Germany.

Paul A. Boghossian, Professor of Philosophy at the New York University, Department of Philosophy, 100 Washington Square East, New York, NY 10003, USA.

Laurence BonJour, Professor of Philosophy at the University of Washington, Department of Philosophy, Seattle, WA 98195–3350, USA.

Tyler Burge, Professor of Philosophy at the University of California at Los Angeles, Department of Philosophy, Los Angeles, CA 90095–1451, USA.

Roderick M. Chisholm (1916–1999) was Professor of Philosophy at Brown University.

C. A. J. Coady, Boyce Gibson Professor of Philosophy at the University of Melbourne, Department of Philosophy, Old Arts Building, Parkville, Victoria 3052, Australia.

Donald Davidson, Willis S. and Marion Slusser Professor of Philosophy at the University of California at Berkeley, Department of Philosophy, Berkeley, CA 94720, USA.

Max Deutscher, Emeritus Professor of Philosophy at Macquarie University, Department of Philosophy, Division of Society, Culture, Media and Philosophy, Sydney NSW 2109, Australia.

Fred Dretske, Emeritus Professor of Philosophy at Stanford University and Senior Research Fellow at Duke University, Department of Philosophy, Durham, NC 27708, USA.

Richard Feldman, Professor of Philosophy at the University of Rochester, Department of Philosophy, Rochester, NY 14627, USA.

Richard Foley, Professor of Philosophy at the State University of New Jersey at Rutgers, Department of Philosophy, Davison Hall, Douglass College, New Brunswick, NJ 08903, USA.

Edmund L Gettier, Professor of Philosophy at the University of Massachusetts at Amherst, Department of Philosophy, Amherst, MA 01003, USA.

Alvin I. Goldman, Regents Professor of Philosophy at the University of Arizona, Department of Philosophy, Tucson, AZ 85721–0027, USA.

Nelson Goodman (1906–1998) was Professor of Philosophy at Harvard University.

H. P. Grice (1913–1988) was Fellow at St. John's College, Oxford University and Professor of Philosophy at the University of California at Berkeley.

Jaegwon Kim, William Herbert Perry Faunce Professor of Philosophy at Brown University, Department of Philosophy, Providence, RI 02912, USA.

Philip Kitcher, Professor of Philosophy at Columbia University, Department of Philosophy, 1150 Amsterdam Ave., New York, NY 10027, USA.

Saul A. Kripke, Emeritus Professor at Princeton University, Department of Philosophy, Princeton, NJ 08544–1006, USA.

Keith Lehrer, Regents Professor of Philosophy at the University of Arizona, Department of Philosophy, Tucson, AZ 85721–0027, USA.

David Lewis, Professor of Philosophy at Princeton University, Department of Philosophy, Princeton, NJ 08544–1006, USA.

C. B. Martin, Professor of Philosophy at the University of Calgary, Department of Philosophy, Calgary, Alberta, Canada T2N 1N4.

Robert Nozick, Pellegrino Professor of Philosophy at Harvard University, Department of Philosophy, Cambridge, MA 02138, USA.

Thomas D. Paxson, Jr., Professor of Philosophy at Southern Illinois University at Edwardsville, Department of Philosophical Studies, Edwardsville, IL62026–1433, USA.

H. H. Price (1899–1984) was Wykeham Professor of Logic at Oxford University.

Hilary Putnam, Cogan University Professor of Philosophy at Harvard University, Department of Philosophy, Cambridge, MA02138, USA.

W. V. Quine, Emeritus Professor of Philosophy at Harvard University, Department of Philosophy, Cambridge, MA 02138, USA.

Hans Reichenbach (1891–1953) was Professor of Philosophy at the University of Berlin and at the University of California at Los Angeles.

Bertrand Russell (1872–1970) was Professor of Philosophy at Cambridge University.

Wilfrid Sellars (1912–1989) was Professor of Philosophy at the University of Pittsburgh.

Peter F. Strawson, Emeritus Professor of Philosophy at Oxford University and Honorary Fellow of St. John's, University, and Magdalen Colleges, Oxford University, Oxford OX 14AU, England.

Barry Stroud, Mills Professor of Philosophy at the University of California at Berkeley, Department of Philosophy, Berkeley, CA 94720, USA.

Peter Unger, Professor of Philosophy at the New York University, Department of Philosophy, 100 Washington Square East, New York, NY 10003, USA.

Index of Names

OXFORD

UNIVERSITY PRESS

Great Clarendon Street, Oxford OX2 6DP

Oxford University Press is a department of the University of Oxford.
It furthers the University's objective of excellence in research, scholarship,
and education by publishing worldwide in

Oxford New York

Auckland Bangkok Buenos Aires Cape Town Chennai
Dar es Salaam Delhi Hong Kong Istanbul Karachi Kolkata
Kuala Lumpur Madrid Melbourne Mexico City Mumbai Nairobi
São Paulo Shanghai Taipei Tokyo Toronto

Oxford is a registered trade mark of Oxford University Press
in the UK and in certain other countries

Published in the United States
by Oxford University Press Inc., New York

British Library Cataloguing in Publication Data

Data available

Library of Congress Cataloging in Publication Data

Data available

ISBN 0-19-875261-X

10 9 8 7 6 5 4

Typeset in Adobe Minion
by RefineCatch Limited, Bungay, Suffolk
Printed in Great Britain by
Ashford Colour Press
Gosport, Hants